The Judaic Tradition

TEXTS EDITED AND INTRODUCED BY NAHUM N. GLATZER

BEHRMAN HOUSE INC., PUBLISHERS

Published by Behrman House, Inc.

235 Watchung Ave., West Orange, N.J. 07052

Manufactured in the United States of America

Revised edition with a new introduction,
copyright © 1969 by Nahum N. Glatzer,
first published as a Beacon Paperback in 1969

Library of Congress catalog card number: 69-17798

Part One, copyright © 1961 by Nahum N. Glatzer, first
published under the title *The Rest Is Commentary*
by Beacon Press in 1961

Part Two, copyright © 1963 by Nahum N. Glatzer, first
published under the title *Faith and Knowledge*
by Beacon Press in 1963

Part Three, copyright © 1965 by Nahum N. Glatzer, first
published under the title *The Dynamics of Emancipation*
by Beacon Press in 1965

Other copyrighted materials are acknowledged at the
end of each Part of this book

Library of Congress Cataloging in Publication Data
Main entry under title:

The Judaic tradition.

Reprint. Originally published: Boston:
Beacon Press, [1969]
Includes bibliographies.
1. Judaism—History—Sources. 2. Judaism—
Collected works. 3. Jews—Social conditions.
I. Glatzer, Nahum Norbert, 1903–
BM40.J86   1982   296.1   82-12956
ISBN 0-87441-344-3

Contents

PART ONE: *The Rest Is Commentary*

Introduction to "The Rest Is Commentary"   3

I. *Wisdom — Divine and Human*   23

    In Praise of Wisdom / *Wisdom of Ben Sira*   23
    The Ideal Scribe / *Wisdom of Ben Sira*   31
    Manifestation of God in Nature / *Wisdom of Ben Sira*   32
    The High Priest, Simon, Son of Johanan / *Wisdom of Ben Sira*   34
    Wisdom and the Order of This World / *Wisdom of Solomon*   36

II. *For the Sake of Freedom of Religion*   43

    The Origin of the Maccabean Rebellion / *First Book of Maccabees*   44
    The Rededication of the Temple / *First Book of Maccabees*   52
    Simon's Beneficent Rule / *First Book of Maccabees*   54
    Martyrdom of the Seven Brothers and Their Mother / *Second Book of Maccabees*   58

III. *The Hope for a New Age*   62

    The Day of Judgment / *Book of Enoch*   62
    The Victory of the Righteous / *Book of Enoch*   64
    The Elect One / *Book of Enoch*   65
    A New Priesthood / *Testament of Levi*   66
    Thou Art Our King / *Psalms of Solomon*   68

IV. *Sectarian Brotherhoods*   73

    Rules of the Dead Sea, or Qumran, Brother-
    hood / *Manual of Discipline*   73

    From the Source of His Knowledge: A Psalm
    / *Manual of Discipline*   79

    Hymns of the Dead Sea Brotherhood /
    Thanksgiving Hymns   81

    The Order of the Essenes / *Philo: Every
    Good Man Is Free*   85

    The Sect of the Therapeutae / *Philo: On the
    Contemplative Life*   90

V. *Re-Reading a Biblical Work*   100

    Job the Saint / *Testament of Job*   100

VI. *Interpreting Jewish Faith to the World*   115

    Hellenist Exposition of Scripture / *Philo's
    Commentaries*   115

    The Emperor's Statue / *Philo: Legacy to
    Gaius*   123

    I Take Refuge / *Prayer of Asenath*   135

    Inspired Reason / *Fourth Book of Macca-
    bees*   136

    In Defense of Judaism / *Flavius Josephus:
    Against Apion*   138

VII. *After the Fall of Jerusalem*   154

    The Heroes of Masada / *Flavius Josephus:
    The Jewish War*   154

    The Vision of a New Era / *Fourth Book of
    Ezra*   159

    The Vision of the Disconsolate Woman /
    Fourth Book of Ezra   168

    The Consolation of Zion / *Apocalypse of
    Baruch*   173

    The Ten Martyrs / *Talmud and Midrash*   175

VIII. *From the Ordinances of the Talmudic Masters*   184

    The Order of Benedictions / *Mishnah
    Berakhot*   185

    The Seder Ceremony / *Mishnah Pesahim*   188

Contents

IX. *Beliefs and Opinions of the Talmudic Masters*   191

Hillel the Elder / *Talmud and Midrash*   191

The Ways of Good Life / *Talmud Tractate Berakhot*   199

Creation and Man / *Talmud and Midrash*   204

God-Man-World / *Talmud and Midrash*   208

Revelation and the Study of the Law / *Talmud and Midrash*   218

Israel: A Holy Community / *Talmud and Midrash*   230

Peace / *Talmud and Midrash*   233

Exile and Redemption / *Talmud and Midrash*   235

Reflections on the Book of Job / *Talmud and Midrash*   239

Prayers of the Masters / *Talmud Tractate Berakhot*   245

Reflections on Life / *Seder Eliyahu Rabba*   247

Notes to "The Rest Is Commentary"   253

Sources and Acknowledgments for "The Rest Is Commentary"   262

PART TWO: *Faith and Knowledge*

Introduction to "Faith and Knowledge"   269

Prelude   277

Knowledge and Faith / *Abraham ibn Ezra, Joseph Caspi, and Solomon ibn Gabirol*   277

I. *God*   279

The Oneness of God / *Moses Maimonides*   279

Knowledge of God / *Moses Maimonides*   282

In the Presence of God / *Solomon ibn Gabirol*   286

Lord Where Shall I Find Thee? / *Judah ha-Levi*   289

II. *The Love for God*   293
  "Thou Shalt Love . . ." / *Moses Maimonides,
   Bahya ibn Pakuda, the Zohar, Moses Hay-
   yim Luzzatto*   293
  Why Is My Loved One Wroth / *Moses ibn
   Ezra*   298
  The Universality of Love / *Judah Abrahanel
   (Leone Ebreo)*   299
  Saintliness / *Moses Hayyim Luzatto*   303

III. *The Faith of Israel*   305
  The Duties of the Heart / *Bahya ibn Pakuda* 305
  The Servant of God / *Judah ha-Levi*   308
  The Faith of Abraham / *Moses Maimonides*   313
  Devotion / *Moses Maimonides*   315
  The Seven Benedictions at the Marriage Serv-
   ice / *Prayer Book*   316

IV. *Man*   318
  Man — the Center of the Universe / *Saadia
   Gaon*   318
  On Creation / *Moses Maimonides*   321
  On Free Will / *Moses Maimonides*   323
  The Creation of Man / *Moses Nahmanides*   327
  Argument for the Immortal Soul / *Leone
   Modena*   329
  The Man and His Soul / *A Midrash*   332
  The Bridge of Time / *Yedayah ha-Bedersi*   336
  Healing / *Jacob ben Asher*   336
  The End of Man / *Prayer Book*   337

VI. *Knowledge*   343
  The Study of Torah / *Moses Maimonides*   343
  In Praise of Learning, Education, and the
   Good Life / *Judah ibn Tibbon*   347
  The Gift of the Law / *Obadiah ben Abraham* 353
  Proposed Jewish Academy in Mantua / *David
   Provenzal*   353
  The Inner Life of the Jews in Poland /
   Nathan Hannover   357

Contents

The House of Study in Padua / *An Eight-eenth-Century Document*   365

VI. *The Ways of Good Life*   372

A Poet's Ethical Counsel / *Solomon ibn Gabirol*   372

Simple Piety / *Judah the Pious*   377

A Brief Summary of Ethical Rules / *Yehiel ben Yekutiel*   379

Humility / *Moses Hayyim Luzzatto*   380

At Peace with the World / *Joel ben Abraham Shemariah*   382

The Middle Course / *Solomon Ganzfried*   384

VII. *The Community of Israel*   388

The God of Abraham and the God of Aristotle / *Judah ha-Levi*   388

The Event on Sinai / *Moses Maimonides*   391

The Proselyte / *Moses Maimonides*   395

Benediction / *When Facing Martyrdom*   396

Why Catastrophes Come / *Solomon Alami*   397

The Parable of the Precious Stones / *Solomon ibn Verga*   403

Equality / *Jacob ben Abba Mari Anatoli*   405

The Hebrews among the Nations / *Simone Luzzatto*   405

VIII. *The Sabbath*   411

Shield of Our Fathers / *Prayer Book*   411

The Sanctity of the Sabbath / The *Zohar*   411

The Sabbath Bride / *Israel ibn al-Nakawa*   414

The Sabbath and the Days of the Week / *Judah Loew ben Bezalel*   415

Sanctification / *Prayer Book*   416

IX. *The Ways of the Mystics*   419

Mystical Understanding of Jewish Concepts / The *Zohar*   419

The Practice of Mystical Meditation / *Abraham Abulafia*   424

The Search for Truth / *Solomon ibn Adret*   427
Life in Safed / *Solomon Shloemel ben Hay-
    yim Meinstrl*   428
The Life of Rabbi Isaac Luria / *Solomon
    Shloemel ben Hayyim Meinstrl*   434
In the Presence of the Divine / *Moses Cord-
    overo*   437

x. *The Ways of the Hasidim*   441
Israel ben Eliezer, the Baal Shem Tov /
    Hasidic Accounts   441
Communion with God and Men / *Abraham
    Kalisker*   446
The Teachings of Mendel of Kotzk / *Hasidic
    Accounts*   447
In Preparation for the Day of Atonement /
    A Hasidic Account   453
Death / *Hasidic Teachings*   456

xi. *The Land of Israel, Exile, and Redemption*   459
Jerusalem / *Benjamin of Tudela*   459
Mystic Drama of Jerusalem / The *Zohar*   463
Ten Kings / *A Midrash*   465
The Suffering of the Messiah / *A Midrash*   467
Creation and World's History / *Moses
    Nahmanides*   469
Messiah the Teacher   470
The Dance of the Righteous / *Judah Loew
    ben Bezalel*   473
Has the Messiah Come? / *Moses
    Nahmanides*   475
A Visit to Paradise / *Immanuel ben
    Solomon of Rome*   484
The Messianic Age / *Moses Maimonides*   488

Epilogue   492
The Holy One Is Within Thee / *Eleazar ben
    Judah*   492

Notes to "Faith and Knowledge"   493

Contents

Sources and Acknowledgments for "Faith and
   Knowledge   497

            PART THREE: *The Dynamics of Emancipation*

Introduction to "The Dynamics of Emancipation"   505

   I. *In the Perspective of Emancipation*   509
         A Definition of Judaism / *Moses Mendelssohn* 509
         The Jewish Community and the State / *Doc-*
            trinal Decisions of the Grand Sanhedrin   512
         Scholarship and Emancipation / *Leopold*
            Zunz   514
         The Hebrews and the Greeks / *Heinrich*
            Graetz   518
         Israel within the Organism of Humanity /
            Moses Hess   526
         Auto-Emancipation / *Leo Pinsker*   532
         Emancipation / *James Darmesteter*   535
         Emancipation and Judaism / *Samson*
            Raphael Hirsch   538
         A Spiritual Nation / *Simon Dubnov*   543
         What Are the Jews? / *Erich Kahler*   547
         Jacob-Israel and the World / *Yitzhak*
            Lamdan   552

  II. *Rethinking Jewish Faith*   554
         Judaism and Mankind / *Abraham Geiger*   554
         Faith / *Abraham Isaac Kook*   556
         The Voice of Jacob / *Richard Beer-Hofmann* 559
         A Minority Religion / *Leo Baeck*   561
         Thou Shalt / *Leo Baeck*   565
         God and Man / *Martin Buber*   567
         A New Learning / *Franz Rosenzweig*   573

 III. *Religious Movements in Modern Judaism*   580
         A Democratic Theocracy / *Samuel Belkin*   580
         The Need for Reform / *Samuel Hirsch*   584

Necessity of Change / *Appeal by Berlin Reformers, 1845*   587

Intelligent Religion / *Isaac Mayer Wise*   590

Conservative Judaism / *Alexander Kohut*   592

Creative Judaism / *Mordecai M. Kaplan*   594

Towards a Kingdom of Priests / *Louis Finkelstein*   606

IV. *The Dark Years*   608

Wear the Yellow Badge with Pride / *Robert Weltsch*   608

A Prayer Before Kol Nidre, Germany, 1935 / *Leo Baeck*   612

The Meaning of This Hour / *Abraham Joshua Heschel*   614

The Slain in the Valley of Death / *Judah L. Magnes*   619

If God Lets Me Live / *Anne Frank*   622

I Believe / *An Inscription*   623

On the Agenda: Death / *A Document of the Jewish Resistance*   623

Jewish Destiny as the DP's See It / *Samuel Gringauz*   631

Before the Monument in the Warsaw Ghetto / *Albert Einstein*   642

The Indictment of Adolf Eichmann / *Gideon Hausner*   643

A Plea for the Dead / *Elie Wiesel*   654

V. *Zionism and the Land of Israel*   659

On the Return to the Land of Israel / *Moses Montefiore*   659

The Universal Significance of Zion / *Henry Pereira Mendes*   661

The Jewish State / *Theodor Herzl*   662

Opening Address, First Zionist Congress / *Theodor Herzl*   672

The Ideal of Labor / *A. D. Gordon*   678

On Zionism, the Land of Israel, and the
    Arabs / *Albert Einstein*   682
The Zionist Declaration of Independence   686
The State of Israel, Opening Address at the
    Kneset / *Chaim Weizmann*   687
Statements on the Arab Refugee Problem /
    Martin Buber and David Ben-Gurion   692
Towards a New World / *David Ben-Gurion*   696
Israel / *Karl Shapiro*   704

VI. *The American Scene*   706
A Call to the Educated Jew / *Louis D.*
    Brandeis   706
A Letter to Henry Ford / *Louis Marshall*   713
The American Jew in Our Day / *Waldo*
    Frank   715
Re-Examination / *Ludwig Lewisohn*   723
Patterns of Survival / *Salo W. Baron*   733
The American Council for Judaism / *Elmer*
    Berger   738
Sufferance Is the Badge / *Abram L. Sachar*   741
Why I Choose to be a Jew / *Arthur A. Cohen*   744
The Issue Is Silence / *Joachim Prinz*   755

VII. *Allowing the Heart to Speak*   758
Reawakening of My Religious Feelings /
    Heinrich Heine   758
Job's Dungheap / *Bernard Lazare*   763
A Confession of My Faith / *Aimé Pallière*   767
The Road Home / *Nathan Birnbaum*   774
Lullaby for Miriam / *Richard Beer-Hofmann*   778
All in Vain / *Jakob Wassermann*   779
Before the Statue of Apollo / *Saul*
    Tchernichovsky   780
Credo / *Harry Friedenwald*   783
Of the Jewish Religion / *Albert Einstein*   784
What I Believe / *Sholem Asch*   786
His Father's Judaism / *Franz Kafka*   790

Why I Am a Jew / *Edmond Fleg*   795
The Air and Earth of Vitebsk / *Marc Chagall*   797
I Live in You, in Each of You / *Abraham
    Isaac Kook*   799
On Being a Jewish Person / *Franz
    Rosenzweig*   800

Notes to "The Dynamics of Emancipation"   802

*Sources and Acknowledgments for "The Dynamics of
    Emancipation"*   809

Suggestions for Further Reading   817

Index   825

Foreword

The Judaic Tradition is a classic, both as mirror and as milestone. This anthology of some 200 texts reflects the richness and dynamism of twenty-two centuries of Jewish life and thought; it also serves as testimony to the modern-traditional career of its creator, Nahum Glatzer. The three volumes of this work were published serially, then together as a collection, in the 1960's. That decade witnessed a dramatic upsurge in Jewish learning, both within the North American Jewish community and in secular universities throughout the United States and Canada. I am one of the many teachers who as students benefited greatly from *The Judaic Tradition*, so it is a great honor for me to introduce this important work to the next generation.

Nahum Norbert Glatzer was born on March 25, 1903, in Lemberg, Austria. From 1920 to 1922 he attended the Samson Breuer Yeshiva in Frankfort on the Main, but he ultimately decided to devote himself to a career of scholarship rather than the rabbinate. In Frankfort he met Franz Rosenzweig, founder of the Freies Juedisches Lehrhaus, were Glatzer served as lecturer from 1923 until 1929, when Rosenzweig's death caused suspension of the Lehrhaus's activities. In 1931 Glatzer earned a Ph.D. from the University of Frankfort, where in the following year he succeeded Martin Buber in the chair of Jewish Religious History and Ethics.

With the rise to power of the Nazis in 1933, Glatzer fled to Palestine and became a teacher of Bible at Bet Sefer Reali in Haifa. Four years later, since university teaching opportunities in Palestine were far fewer than the number of qualified scholars seeking them, he visited the United States and accepted faculty appointments at the Hebrew Theological College and the College of Jewish Studies in Chicago. Subsequently, Glatzer taught at a number of American colleges and universities and served as editor-in-chief of Schocken Books, until in 1950 he received the first major faculty position in Judaic studies at the recently founded Brandeis University. In 1973 Glatzer became Professor Emeritus at Brandeis; since that time he has served as University Professor at Boston University, as well as holding distinguished visiting positions at a number of other universities.

Glatzer's scholarship and teaching have been of such scope and vitality that it is impossible here even to list his publications, positions, and honors. By way of summary, at least three important themes deserve mention: Glatzer's continuation of the legacy of Franz Rosenzweig, his contribution as a pioneer of Judaic studies in America, and his presentation and interpretation of Jewish literature from ancient to modern.

Glatzer is careful to describe himself as a "follower" rather than a "disciple" of Rosenzweig, arguing that his work on the seminal European thinker "may not be definitive." Nonetheless, Glatzer has written extensively about Rosenzweig's life and thought, as well as about the extraordinary Frankfort Lehrhaus. It was Glatzer, for example, who in 1952 first told the remarkable story of Rosenzweig's "conversion" on the Day of Atonement, 1913, when Rosenzweig discarded his decision to become a Christian and set out instead to recover his Jewish identity. Equally dramatic is Glatzer's unique portrayal of Rosenzweig's spiritual courage in the face of pain and paralysis in the last years of his life. Biographical recollections and insights such as these preserve the living context of Rosenzweig's work in religious philosophy and education. The importance of Glatzer as Rosenzweig's English language tradent is cited in a 1966 symposium, *The Condition of Jewish Belief*, which concluded that Rosenzweig was "the single greatest influence on the religious thought of North American Jewry."

Rosenzweig, Glatzer has written, "wanted to reopen the silenced dialogue between the presently living generation and classical Judaism." This description applies equally well to Glatzer himself. When he arrived in the United States, only Hebrew colleges, rabbinical seminaries, and a handful of secular universities offered courses in Judaic studies; now some 400 colleges and universities offer Judaica courses, several dozen sponsor graduate training in various aspects of the field, and the professional Association for Jewish Studies (of which Glatzer was a founder in 1969) has some 1000 members. Glatzer himself has raised up many disciples during his four decades of teaching in the United States; they are to be found on the faculties of universities both in this country and in Israel. More than a dozen of these scholars contributed to a *festschrift* on the occasion of Glatzer's seventieth birthday; earlier, he was the first faculty member at Brandeis to be awarded an honorary doctorate, and the first Brandeis *Studies and Texts* Judaica volume was dedicated to his honor as well. The foreword to his *festschrift* includes this apt description: "He combines patient, meticulous scholarship with an abiding sensitivity to human and religious issues. . . . We . . . feel graced to have studied with him."

Indeed, thousands who have never met Glatzer nevertheless have studied "with" him, since his publications illumine an enormous range of Jewish sources throughout the ages. From the classical era his interests include Job, Hillel, Philo, Josephus, and Midrash; his modern concerns, besides Rosenzweig, include Leopold Zunz and the *Wissenschaft des Judentums* school, Franz Kafka, S. Y. Agnon, and Buber. To these diverse subjects Glatzer has applied several talents: careful research and creative scholarship, judicious editing, and thoughtful exegesis. His readership includes academicians and those who seek religious instruction, experts and popular audiences alike. All of them benefit from Glatzer's efforts to establish a "living relationship" between Judaism and the contemporary world.

The Judaic Tradition, like all of Glatzer's works, embraces its subject. The result is a presentation that makes clear both the varied contexts and the essential continuities of Jewish life and thought. Thus Glatzer is able to show what makes Judaism a tradition, that is, its relevance to particular Jewish community circumstances and needs and its coherence in linking the generations one to another.

Glatzer continually alerts the reader to relations between Jews and the larger environment in which they live. He probes the dialectic between particularism and universalism, whether in the Hellenistic world of antiquity, the Christian and Islamic settings of the Middle Ages, or the secularization of modernity. Always the Jews are a minority, yet everywhere they are significant, both for their adaptation and for their readiness to remain apart.

From the beginning, Glatzer demonstrates that the intellectual and emotional content of Judaism is inseparable from the perils and promise of Jewish history. His introductions and notes bring to life the sources here explicated—the crises Jews confronted in every age, and the hopes they held for the future. In this fashion, the most contemporary texts well illustrate the life setting in which *The Judaic Tradition* was composed. Elie Wiesel's "A Plea for the Dead" evokes the destruction of European Jewry, Ben Gurion's "Towards a New World" represents modern Zionism, and Joachim Prinz's "The Issue of Silence" speaks for the Jewish activism of the American diaspora center.

Text and commentary, always the media of the Judaic tradition, here unfold in artistic formulation. To them one need add only the instruction of Hillel: "Go, study."

David Altshuler
The Charles E. Smith Professor of Judaic
Studies, George Washington University,
Washington, D.C.

Preface

The present issue is a consolidated edition of three volumes that appeared separately in 1961, 1963, and 1965 as parts of *Beacon Texts in the Judaic Tradition*.

This source book attempts to present significant examples from the vast and manifold post-Biblical Jewish literature in the various parts of the world.

The first part, "The Rest Is Commentary," covers the period of Judaic antiquity, i.e., the period from the Second Temple (or Second Jewish Commonwealth) through the Talmudic age. The writings of the period include the so-called Biblical Apocrypha, the writings of the Dead Sea or Qumran sect, the philosopher Philo of Alexandria, the historian Flavius Josephus of Jerusalem and Rome, and the works of Talmud and Midrash. As much as possible comprehensive passages were chosen; only from Talmudic-Midrashic sources were brief, pithy sayings taken, as exemplary for at least one type of this literature. On the whole the sequence is chronological.

The second part, "Faith and Knowledge," deals with the major currents of thought and belief in medieval, and especially, but not exclusively, in European Judaism. Medieval Jewry built its literature upon the foundations of Judaic antiquity. Certain main themes of antiquity recur in the Middle Ages in new forms and with different emphases. However, not only the literary form and style have changed, but, despite the parallels, much of the substance. One pivotal theme remained outside the scope of presentation: the Halakha, i.e., the analysis, interpretation, and codification of Jewish law. No selection in translation can pretend to communicate an adequate impression of this branch of learning; here, silence seemed preferable.

The term Middle Ages is somewhat inexact; in the Jewish realm, the "age between" antiquity and the modern period stretches beyond the era generally called the medieval.

The third part, "The Dynamics of Emancipation," attempts to present the Jew in the modern age. The division of the material reflects the major events and concerns in modern—and especially English-speaking—Jewry: the phenomenon of political and cultural emancipation; the religious movements; the catastrophe of the thirties and forties of this century; the realization of the vision of an independent State of Israel; the place of the Jew in the United States. Appended is a series of expressions of personal beliefs, experiences, and opinions, which, it was felt, should not be subsumed under the overt and more official utterances.

The translations from the original (some selections rendered into English for the first time) have been revised in places; a few of the texts have been abridged; omissions are, as a rule, indicated by three dots in brackets.

In addition to the introductions to each of the three parts there are prefatory notes to the individual selections that offer the most essential historical and biographical background facts. The "Suggestions for Further Reading" have been updated by a supplement.

The content of this source book is designed to reflect a variety of views, opinions, and moods, with the student and general reader invited to participate in the discourse. The intent of the work is, therefore, to impart information and to stimulate thought, rather than to suggest a definite stand. Judiac tradition, a product of many centuries. has had room for many different minds and souls.

The original volumes were dedicated "to Fanny with brotherly affection," "to Richard and Joyce Stiebel in friendship," and "to Anne with love."

Nahum N. Glatzer

Brandeis University
November 1968

PART ONE

"The Rest Is Commentary"

Introduction

The era that commences about 500 B.C. and ends about A.D. 500 is the time in which Judaism originated and took shape. Ancient Biblical Israel, whose history came to an end with the destruction of the Jerusalem temple in 586 B.C. and the Babylonian captivity (586 to 538), underwent a thorough transformation before it became the religion, culture, world-view and destiny that we call Judaism.

An edict of Cyrus (538 B.C.), founder of the Persian Empire, made it possible for the Jewish exiles in Babylonia to return to Jerusalem and to rebuild the temple. Only a small group returned to Zion, and the land allotted to its members was small. It measured about one thousand square miles, and much of this territory was desert. But those who returned from exile were the first of a new people of Judaea, and the allotted land was the site of a new state, one which was to create a fateful chapter in the history of Western civilization.

Among the important men of the new Zion was the prophet Zechariah, who conceived what became the challenge both of Jerusalem and of the Jews dispersed in the various Near Eastern and Mediterranean centers: "Not by might, nor by power, but by my spirit, saith the Lord of hosts" (Zech. 4:6). In his vision Jerusalem, as yet an insignificant, much neglected city, became "the city of truth" (8:3) and of peace (8:12), the center of worship of a universal God (14:9). A short period later, the prophet Malachi saw monotheism spreading "from the rising of the sun even unto the going down of the same . . . and in every place offerings are presented unto my name" (1:11). Judaea was a more or less autonomous priestly state within the Persian Empire; but the priests, ever in peril of falling from their sacred mission into a temple bureaucracy, would do well, Malachi felt, to follow the example of Aaron, the first priest: "The law of truth was

in his mouth . . . he walked with Me in peace and uprightness. . . . For the priest's lips should keep knowledge . . .
for he is the messenger of the Lord" (2:6-7).

It was about a century after the Return that the Jewish
community was established on a solid foundation, politically,
culturally and economically. This was due largely to the work
of two Babylonian Jews: Nehemiah, who administered Judaea
as Persian governor, and Ezra the scribe. The latter, empowered by the Persian king, Artaxerxes, made the Torah of
Moses the basis of communal and private life. He is said to
have introduced the reading and interpretation of the Law
as the central element in the synagogue liturgy and in education. The Biblical books of Ezra and Nehemiah, based partly
on personal memoirs of the men concerned, include an account (chapter 8 of Nehemiah) of the great gathering of the
people of Jerusalem at which Ezra read the Law for the first
time, thus re-enacting on a more human, almost secular, stage,
the drama of the revelation on Sinai.

And when the seventh month was come, and the children of Israel were
in their cities, all the people gathered themselves together as one man into the
broad place that was before the water gate; and they spoke unto Ezra the
scribe to bring the book of the Law of Moses, which the Lord had commanded
to Israel.

And Ezra the priest brought the Law before the congregation, both
men and women, and all that could hear with understanding, upon the first
day of the seventh month.

And he read therein before the broad place that was before the water
gate from early morning until midday, in the presence of the men and the
women, and of those that could understand; and the ears of all the people were
attentive unto the book of the Law.

And Ezra the scribe stood upon a pulpit of wood, which they had made
for the purpose. . . .

And Ezra opened the book in the sight of all the people—for he was
above all the people—and when he opened it, all the people stood up. And
Ezra blessed the Lord, the great God. And all the people answered: "Amen,
Amen," with the lifting up of their hands; and they bowed their heads and
fell down before the Lord with their faces to the ground.

Also Jeshua, and Bani . . . caused the people to understand the Law;
and the people stood in their place. And they read in the book, in the Law of

God, distinctly; and they gave the sense, and caused them to understand the reading.

And Nehemiah . . . and Ezra, the priest, the scribe, and the Levites that taught the people, said unto all the people: "This day is holy unto the Lord your God; mourn not, nor weep." For all the people wept, when they heard the words of the Law.

Then he said unto them: "Go your way, eat the fat, and drink the sweet, and send portions unto him for whom nothing is prepared; for this day is holy unto our Lord; neither be ye grieved; for the joy of the Lord is your strength." . . .

And all the people went their way to eat, and to drink, and to send portions, and to make great mirth, because they had understood the words that were declared unto them.

Post-Exilic Judaism, therefore, was established upon the late-prophetic and Ezraic foundations. From the first source it drew its knowledge of God, its passion for justice, its vision of a new Zion; from the Ezraic, its will to translate prophetic ideals into the practice of daily life, its emphasis on learning, its dedication to the community. The cultivation of these virtues made for the spiritual unity of Israel under the various political constellations and fated difficulties. The synagogue, school and home were the centers of this culture, while the temple in Jerusalem remained its official symbol. True, the priest ministered to the elaborate ritual of the Jerusalem sanctuary and the high priest headed the Commonwealth; but the other functions of Judaism were open to all. Among the interpreters of the Law, bearers of tradition, teachers of wisdom and leaders of communities, we find priests and laymen, traditionalists and reformers, rich and poor, sons of Israel or descendants of heathens. What mattered here was knowledge, conduct, dedication. This application of the democratic principle to a religious civilization was the source of much vitality, color and creative tension, especially in the first half of the thousand years of history with which this book is concerned.

The reader will do well to keep in mind that the century of Malachi, Nehemiah and Ezra is also the age of Pericles and the century of the achievement of Greek drama by the poets Aeschylus, Euripides, Sophocles and Aristophanes; of histori-

ographers Herodotus and Thucydides and the creation of the
Acropolis; of the sculptor Phidias and those who, like Anaxagoras, advanced philosophical thought. Compared with this
profusion of beauty, the material culture of Judaea is negligible indeed. There all energies were devoted to the education
of man as an individual, as a member of society, as a partner in
the sacred community of worshipers.

The fourth century, the second of the Persian rule over
Yehud, as Judaea was called, left us no dated documents from
which we could reconstruct the history of the period. Then
in 333 B.C., Alexander the Great conquered the Persian Empire and with it Syria and Palestine, and Judaea appeared as a
still small but internally mature, highly developed commonwealth. Around the urban center in Jerusalem were clustered
numerous agricultural communities. Within their own groups,
and in whatever contact they had with the world around
them, the farmers followed the teachings of simple piety and
of brotherly love. Biblical laws concerning release of debts, the
sabbatical year, gifts due to those in need of them, the regulations against interest on loans, all sought to establish justice
in practical life, to eliminate unfair profit and to safeguard
peace. In truly fascinating researches of recent date, Professor
Y. F. Baer of Jerusalem[1] has identified these farmers with the
Early Pious Men (*Hasidim ha-Rishonim*) known to us only
from later literature (the Mishnah); in many details of the
laws followed by these communities, Baer found parallels to
the laws of Solon, the Athenian reformer, and to the regulations of the classical Greek Polis as we read them in Plato's
Laws. Thus in the society of the Early Hasidim we recognize
a synthesis of the traditions of ancient Israel and some of the
tenets of the independent Greek republics.

Alexander's conquests brought East and West together,
and laid the foundation for a unified world civilization to
which both East and West were to contribute. The grandiose
idea did not materialize, but it remained a powerful cultural
stimulus for centuries to come. On a lower level, Hellenic
fashions, ways of life and modes of thought and belief pene-

trated the East, commingled with and at times replaced ancient cultures and religious disciplines.

After Alexander's death (323 B.C.), his generals ("Successors") divided his realm among themselves. Palestine came under Egyptian (Ptolomaic) domination. In the third century, thousands of Jews migrated to Alexandria, Egypt, the newly established center of the world commerce which gradually succeeded Athens as the capital of Greek learning and Hellenist civilization. In due course the Jews in Alexandria formed a community organization and enjoyed autonomous jurisdiction. They spoke Greek and accepted Greek modes of life. The educated class was, in various degrees, versed in Greek writings; its own literary products demonstrate a synthesis of Hebrew and Greek wisdom. The Greek translation of the Five Books of Moses (the Septuagint, later to include translations of the entire Hebrew Bible) became the authoritative sacred scripture of the Alexandrian and all Greek-speaking Jews. The high religious and ethical principles, expounded and propagated in the commonly understood language, attracted many proselytes. On the other hand, a measure of exclusiveness on the part of the Jews and resistance to indiscriminate mingling gave rise to anti-Semitism, which, in turn, accounted for a good number of apologetic writings in which the Jews tried to present their religion.

In this atmosphere grew some of the works later included in the Biblical Apocrypha, such as the Wisdom of Solomon (see "Wisdom and the Order of this World") which combines Greek notions about God, world and man with the Hebrew praise of simple piety, and the Fourth Book of Maccabees (see "Inspired Reason") which, in enumerating the forms of wisdom (prudence, justice, manliness, temperance) shows Stoic influence. Jewish Hellenist thought at its maturest stage is represented by Philo of Alexandria (see "Hellenist Exposition of Scripture") in whose thought Scriptures and Plato blended in profound harmony. As Professor Harry A. Wolfson of Harvard has demonstrated,[2] it was this Philonian system that provided the intellectual basis for the religious philosophy of Christian antiquity and the Middle Ages.

Judaea presumably continued in the cultivation of the Ezraic heritage, but lack of original sources prevents us from tracing this development. We are better informed about another strain of culture that found a renewed expression in post-Ezraic Judaea: the tradition of "wisdom" as the trusted guide to the good life. Schools of wisdom trained young men in the art of prudent living and counseled personal self-perfection and striving for the ever distant goal of wisdom, because "when a man has finished, then does he but begin." The Biblical Apocrypha preserve the Wisdom of (Joshua, Jesus) Ben Sira, a good example of this type of literature (see "In Praise of Wisdom" and "Manifestation of God in Nature").

In Judaea too there is evidence of a strong Hellenist influence on the Jewish population. Hellenic cities neighbored on Jewish areas; in addition, there were mixed settlements of Jews and Greeks. In the market place and in general contacts of life, the Jew met the Greek soldier, trader, artisan. The more advanced Greek technical civilization, the liberalizing physical culture as acquired in the gymnasia and at athletic games impressed the sons of the well-to-do, while the scholars and thinkers came to appreciate Greek rationalism, humanism and methods of thought.

The meeting of East and West resulted in many and intricate changes in the political, social, religious and personal life in Judaea. The extreme positions are marked on the one hand by the radical Hellenizers, who repudiated the traditional religious mores and advocated assimilation to the ways of the pagans, and on the other by the loyalists (the later Pharisees), who adhered to and cultivated their belief in the eternity of the Bible, its laws, its sacred history and promise for the future of Israel. Professors Elias Bickerman of Columbia University[3] and W. F. Albright of Johns Hopkins University[4] have shown that these advocates of Torah had adopted some important aspects of liberal Hellenism. Systematic rules of scriptural interpretation, certain forms of legal thinking and the emphasis on organized education are matters that have their roots in Biblical Israel and Ezraic Judaism, but their decisive development and final shape is due to the climate of Hellenism. In a way, this acceptance of Greek influence is a continuation of the process which we noted in the communities of the Early Hasidim. This voluntary, organic and creative Hellenization within Judaism must be clearly distinguished from the imitative, arrogant, opportunistic Hellenist assimilation of the upper classes in Jerusalem.

In the first decades of the second century B.C., the antagonism between Judaism and Hellenism gave way to open conflict. The aristocratic, well-to-do Jews in Jerusalem, supported by the higher echelons of the temple priesthood, cultivated Greek modes of social and cultural life: Greek language, gymnasia, games, dress, habits of eating and entertainment. Its advocates hoped that such assimilation would relieve Judaea's isolation in the Hellenist world around it. Jerusalem was to be counted among the Hellenist cities of the Eastern Mediterranean region; it was to become a second Antioch, the king's residence.

The Hellenist transformation of Judaism was opposed by the simple people of Jerusalem, the farming communities outside the city, the Hasidim ("the pious"), the lower clergy —men and women who best realized the threat to the God-given moral and religious order of Israel.

In 198 B.C., Antiochus III brought Palestine under the sway of the Syrian (Seleucid) power. When Antiochus IV Epiphanes inherited the Seleucids' throne (175 B.C.), a critical stage of the Hellenization problem was reached. This politically unsuccessful king (Rome interfered with his Egyptian expedition) pursued a policy of forced Hellenization which was to serve his narrow political ambitions. But Antiochus "Epimanes" (the mad man), as his title was parodied at home made Hellenization identical with heathenization. In 167 B.C. he abolished the Torah as the Jewish constitution, had an altar to Zeus erected in the Jerusalem temple and had a hog offered as sacrifice. This act provoked loyal, non-Hellenist Jews to an over-all revolt. The insurrection, known as the Maccabean rebellion, turned both against the king and against the Jewish Hellenist party in Jerusalem (headed by the high priests, first Jason, then Menelaus), which supported the king's aims and which, in turn, received support from the king. Rebellion seemed to be the only means of preventing Jerusalem from becoming a pagan center and of regaining the freedom of religion. The rise of a small group of volunteer fighters against the Seleucid armies did not hold any promise of success. But the rebels were upheld by their belief that the outcome of this war must matter to the Lord of history. (See "The Origin of the Maccabean Rebellion," "The Rededication of the Temple" and "Simon's Beneficent Rule").

The community of the Hasidim that joined the small fighting force of Judah the Maccabee (the "hammerer") found the ideology of its action in the Biblical Book of Daniel. Its unknown author, witness to the events, interpreted his time and the function of the hasidic supporters of the rebellion in the context of the ancient prophetic view of Israel and within the scope of world history. In his apocalyptic vision ("revealing" events and their hidden meaning), past history appeared to be a sequence of heathen empires that were permitted to rule the world: Babylonian, Medic, Persian and Greek. The fourth of the kingdoms to quote from chapter 7, "shall devour the whole earth, and shall tread it down, and break it in pieces." The king "shall speak words against the Most High, and shall wear out the saints of the Most High; and he shall think to change the seasons and the law." But "his dominion shall be taken away, to be consumed and to be destroyed unto the end."

> I saw in the night visions,
> And, behold, there came with the clouds of heaven
> One like unto a son of man,
> And he came even to the Ancient of days [God],
> And he was brought near before Him.
> And there was given him dominion,
> And glory, and a kingdom,
> That all the peoples, nations, and languages

Should serve him;
His dominion is an everlasting dominion, which shall not pass away,
And his kingdom that which shall not be destroyed.

Thus "judgment was given for the saints of the Most High; and the time came, and the saints possessed the kingdom." "And the kingdom and the dominion, and the greatness of the kingdoms under the whole heaven, shall be given to the people of the saints of the Most High; their kingdom is an everlasting kingdom, and all dominions shall serve and obey them."

Thus, it was thought, the hour had come when the era of the "four kingdoms" would be superseded by the "Kingdom of God." The wickedness and the cruelty of the pagan world, symbolized in Daniel's vision by fierce beasts, was to be replaced by the realm symbolized by the image of man ("son of man"), and headed by Israel, the "people of the saints." Inspired by this view of the historic drama, the pious willingly fought, suffered—and waited.

The Maccabees (or, as they are also called, the Hasmoneans, i.e., from the family of Hasmon) won their fight. Independence of Judaea was achieved in 140 B.C. under Simon, a brother of Judah the Maccabee (see "Simon's Beneficent Rule"). Rulers, kings and high priests from the Hasmonean family headed the Jewish state and expanded its territory to its ancient Biblical frontiers. But these largely secular developments were not at all a realization of the hopes of the Book of Daniel. The power-minded, conquering Hasmonean kingdom was no "dominion of the saints of the Most High." The Hasidim withdrew as soon as religious liberty was achieved and left the field to those who knew that only political freedom would provide a basis for freedom of worship and for cultural growth. Daniel's visions, however, remained important for the future of religious and historical thought. They served as prototype and model for later apocalyptic writings (see "The Hope for a New Age" from the Book of Enoch, "The Vision of a New Era" and "The Vision of the Disconsolate Women" from the Fourth Book of Ezra and "The Consolation of Zion," from the Apocalypse of Baruch). Daniel's attempt to interpret history as world history, as a meaningful, interrelated progression of events, and the idea of the "Four Kingdoms" were the concepts that excited the historical and political imagination of ages to come, Jewish and Christian. Naturally, the fourth and last of the kingdoms to precede the new, hoped-for age (which in the Book of Daniel was referred to as Greece) was now interpreted to be the Roman Empire. The enigmatic numbers of days (1,290, or 1,335) to expire before the inception of the Messianic age (Dan. 12:11-12) occupied the speculative mind of Western mankind for centuries. Also, the tales of martyrdom and of steadfastness in the face of tyranny and oppression (see "Martyrdom of the Seven Brothers and their Mother" from the Second Book of Maccabees and "Inspired Reason" from the Fourth Book of Maccabees) served as an example of dedication and personal heroism in both Judaism and Christianity.

The Maccabean uprising, as we have seen, was in the main a reaction against the violent attempt to replace the Judaic by Hellenic institutions. A peaceful, friendly penetration of Hellenism would have effected an entirely different course of historic development. The Hellenist transformation of Judaism might have succeeded and might have forced a remnant of loyal Jews into a sectarian existence. It was, as Emil Schürer said, "just the extreme and radical character of this [Hellenist] attempt that saved Judaism,"[5] because the Judaism that emerged from the Hellenist crisis was stronger than before, a determined socioreligious entity, ever more clearly conscious of its place in the world. Instead of permitting an expansion in all possible directions to face the threat of superficiality of purpose and mediocrity of expression, Judaism now championed concentration on practically one field, the religious, and that in its broadest sense. Within this realm, Judaism could adapt freely from the Greeks. The scholarly vocabulary of the period contains some three thousand borrowed words, mostly Greek. The Hebrew term *Keneset ha-Gedolah* (Great Assembly) was replaced by the Hellenistic term *Sanhedrin*. Platonic and Stoic ideas merged with the ancient prophetic and Ezraic views and doctrines. While the conduct of daily life was regulated by a sober discipline of the Law, the mind was trained to face argument and opposition, to cultivate discrimination and understanding. Socratic dialectic became one of the intellectual forces that molded thinking in the schools of Judaea. Unmediated divine revelation was regarded as a revered fact of the past, but it was no longer considered as the source of new human knowledge. Tradition of the elders counted as a treasure of accumulated experience but no longer as the sole guide to action. Only logical and systematic reasoning was recognized as a valid authority for the understanding of the inherited Scriptures (record of the word of God and His way in history) and in the search for norms of the good life. Rational argument and logical analysis became the instrument of discourse as recorded in the Talmud, that monumental record of life, thought and legal deliberation of some five hundred years following the Maccabean period. The list of logical rules to be applied to the exposition, mainly of legal texts in the Bible (until this day this list is being recited by pious Jews in the daily morning prayer), goes back to Hellenistic rhetoric. The principle of rationality and order is as much Hebraic as it is Greek.

The most representative scholar in Jerusalem of the post-Maccabean and early talmudic era is Hillel the Elder (*ca.* 60 B.C. to *ca.* A.D. 10), founder of the "House (or School) of Hillel." (See "Hillel the Elder"). His interests as scholar, legislator and teacher range over practically all fields of Jewish law, civil and ritual. In this respect Hillel, despite his new directions and emphases (which do not concern us here), is a link in the unbroken chain of the tradition of Israel. His ethical teachings, though in the main rooted in the same tradition, show remarkable parallels with Stoic thought, especially with the tenets of Seneca, in part his contemporary. Hillel spoke of the soul as a guest in the human body, and Seneca of God who dwells as a guest in the body. Hillel's saying, "If I am not for myself, who is for me?" runs parallel to Seneca's, "It is your duty to try your best . . . there is no dependency upon others." Hillel's admonition against an attitude of "when I shall have leisure I shall study" reminds one of Seneca's "Do not excuse yourself with: I shall have leisure later and then I shall seek wisdom." Hillel's "Do not judge your fellow man until you have stood in his place" differs only a little from Seneca's "We should put ourselves in that place in which the man with whom we are angry is to be found," and both point in the direction of Epictetus' advice: "Give no judgment from another tribunal before you have yourself been judged at the tribunal of absolute justice." [6]

These continued contacts between Jewish and Hellenic thought suggest a general atmosphere of rationalism and humanism that motivated the thinking of the intelligentsia in both Hellenism and Judaism. Both believed that education should aim at the "wise man," not the businessman or the politician. *Paideia*, the Greek idea of perfection through education, classically enunciated by Professor Werner Jaeger,[7] finds a corresponding motif in Judaism. Here, the dedicated study of the Torah, a study of the divine word which renews the experience of revelation of Sinai (see "Revelation and the Study of the Law"), is to lead to the perfection of the individual and to moral action.

At this point the correspondence ends. That in the end Judaism did not merge with Hellenism, as the pre-Maccabean Jewish Hellenists desired, is due to the differences between the two cultures, differences basic and contrasting.

The philosophic doctrines of late antiquity, lofty as they were, were mindful only of the upper classes. In Plato's ideal state the masses of men are held in bondage. Aristotle considers some human beings to be slaves by nature; the Stoa saw in the multitude, but *typhloi*, blind fools. To be sure, there is in the Stoa an awareness of the equality of men and a feeling of compassion with suffering humanity. But the words were purer than the deeds. The ideal remained *apatheia*, indifference towards any disturbance of the quiet inner life of the wise, and *ataraxia*, equanimity of mind. Judaism, on the other hand, was less concerned with the definition of the ideal than it was with the application of the ideal to real life. Here the affirmation of the ideal and social legislation had to be supplemented by active personal responsibility for the needs of one's neighbor. Compassion and charity were not to be only expressions of humaneness but *imitatio dei*. And not only moral action, but all other aspects of life as directed by the Law, liturgic and civil, dietary and criminal, ceremonial and agricultural, were considered an acknowledgment and fulfillment of the divine will. The determination to defend also this aspect of religion contributed greatly to the separation of Israel in the ancient world.

In the period of the Hasmonean kingdom (142 to 63 B.C.), the various cultural trends in Judaea crystallized to form three distinct groups, known as the Sadducees, the Pharisees and the Dead Sea, or Qumran, Brotherhood (Essenes).

The Sadducees had their origin in the temple hierarchy (the name, Hebrew, Z*edukim*, is probably derived from Zadok, chief priest under King Solomon). This group comprised the conservative element of the population, the priestly aristocracy, prosperous merchants and landowners. Worldly in politics and general view of life, they preserved rigidly the ancient religious traditions, as contained in the Biblical documents, and opposed innovations in religious practice and progress in doctrine. They "disregard fate entirely and place God beyond the commission or the very sight of evil. Good and evil, they contend, are man's choice, and everyone is free to embrace one or the other according to his will. The soul's permanence after death and the punishments and rewards of Hades they reject" (Josephus).[8]

The middle class was represented by the Pharisees (Hebrew, *Perushim*, indicating separation from "the unclean" and dedication to the sacred). Their liberal interpretation of Torah was meant to form a bridge between the ancient word and the requirements of the present, and, at the same time, to expand and deepen the relevance of Torah. They cultivated the personal element in religion and the spiritual meaning of the ritual. The center of their public life was less the official sanctuary in Jerusalem than the synagogues and houses of study. As compared with the Sadducees, the Pharisees were progressive, ever ready to prevent religious views from becoming rigid doctrines and dogmas. The New Testament mentions in one breath Pharisees and hyocrites. Hypocrisy and intolerance undoubtedly existed among the Pharisees, but this hardly suggests what the movement was. Rather it is the humble and humane Hillel the Elder and his disciples who are a living demonstration of Pharisaism.

As the supporters of nonradical Hellenism or their descendants, merged with the Sadducees, so, we may assume, some of the descendants of the early Hasidim became a part of the Pharisaic movement, and within it continued to represent some of the hasidic ideals. The radical Jewish Hellenists disappeared in the mainstream of Eastern Mediterranean Hellenism. The uncompromising adherents of the hasidic ideology, and those of the Pharisees of a related persuasion, alienated by the conduct of public affairs at the Hasmonean court and by the secularization of the Jerusalem priesthood, went to the wilderness in the Dead Sea region. There they established the order of the Essenes, or joined already existing groups of pious hermits. The exact composition of this sectarian movement is not yet established. Its history is still a matter of conjecture, but the importance of the sect for the understanding of contemporaneous Judaism and for early Christianity is generally recognized. The oath of a newly admitted member of the brotherhood is an indication of its general tendency; the initiated one swore that

> he will exercise piety toward God;
> observe justice towards men;
> do no harm to any one . . . ;
> he will abhor the wicked and be helpful to the good;
> show fidelity to all men . . . ;
> he will be a lover of truth and reprove those who tell lies,
> he will keep his hands clear from theft
> and his soul from unlawful gains.[9]

This is what Josephus says in his detailed description of the Essenes. For Philo's presentation of this sect, see "The Essenes," taken from his essay Every Good Man Is Free. (See also "The Dead Sea, or Qumran, Brotherhood" from the Manual of Discipline, and "Hymns of the Dead Sea Brotherhood" from its collection of Thanksgiving Hymns.)

In the caves which for many centuries preserved parts of the library of the Dead Sea community have been found some portions of the apocryphal book the Testaments of the Twelve Patriarchs (see "A New Priesthood") and fragments of the apocalyptic Book of Enoch (see "The Judgment and the New Age"), works which illustrate the deep disappointment with their time and the passionate awaiting of a better day in the future for those who shall deserve a future. The loyal Jews in Jerusalem shared this hope with the sectarians in the wilderness.

A sect of Jewish hermits, the Therapeutae, existed also in Egypt, a description of which is offered by Philo (see "The Therapeutae").

Rome, with its gradual conquest of all countries in the Eastern Mediterranean region, first interfered in Judaea in 63 B.C., when Pompey entered Jerusalem. Herod the Great (37 to 4 B.C.), descendant of the Idumaeans (a people converted to Judaism by the Hasmonean ruler, John Hyrcanus), ruled in Judaea by the grace of Rome (see "Thou Art Our King" from the Psalms of Solomon). Judaea's dependence on Rome (see "The Emperor's Statue") strained the endurance of those who wished to preserve inner independence. It was probably during this period that an unknown, sensitive author reread the Book of Job and recast the story of the tragic tension between the inscrutable Creator and rebellious man into a song of love between a silently suffering creature and a gracious God, a late outpouring of the hasidic spirit (see "Testament of Job the Saint").

The Judaeo-Roman war of A.D. 66, which had resulted from the unbearable tension between Jerusalem and Rome, ended in A.D. 73 with the destruction of Jerusalem and the temple. The last fortress to hold out against the overwhelming Roman forces was Masada (see "The Heroes of Masada," described by Flavius Josephus). Judaea became a Roman province.

The catastrophe of the fall of Jerusalem evoked different reactions. The apocalyptic visionaries, spiritual descendants

of Daniel, tried to interpret the event in a cosmic context and
to keep alive the hope in a new Jerusalem (see "The Vision
of a New Era" and "The Vision of the Disconsolate Woman"
from the Fourth Book of Ezra, and "The Consolation of
Zion" from the Apocalypse of Baruch). The early Christian
community saw in the fall of Zion a confirmation of its beliefs in God's rejection of the people of Israel and His election
of a New Israel, the Church. The Pharisees, founders of rabbinic (or normative, or classical) Judaism, rallied around
Johanan ben Zakkai (called the youngest disciple of Hillel
the Elder), who taught that the central institutions of Jerusalem were to be replaced by an intensified cultivation of
learning and practice of *hesed*, loving-kindness. He emphasized the prophetic dictum: "I desire mercy (*hesed*), not
sacrifices."

The Dead Sea Brotherhood ceased to exist. The party
of the Sadducees disappeared from sight. The Jewish community of Alexandria suffered destruction. On the other hand,
the Jewish communities in Babylonia, established long ago,
were augmented by refugees of the war in Judaea and developed into major centers of Judaism and Jewish studies in the
centuries to come. Among the numerous Jewish communities
scattered throughout the Roman Empire, the one in Rome
should be mentioned. There lived Flavius Josephus, the
former Judaean general (defending Galilee) and later adviser to the Roman army besieging Jerusalem. In Rome, under
the patronage of the ruling house, Josephus wrote his *Jewish
War*, *Antiquities* and his outline of Judaic thought and institutions (see "In Defense of Judaism" from *Against Apion*).

The subjugated Jews in Judaea rose once more against
Rome (under Bar Kokhba, 132 to 135), and were again defeated. A period of martyrdom followed. The victims, lovingly
remembered (see "The Ten Martyrs"), became a prototype
of those who suffered persecution in the Middle Ages.

All intellectual and spiritual energies of the post-destruc-
tion period were concentrated on the interpretation and the
formulation of the laws (*Halakhah*, the rule to go by), and on
reflection upon past history, the lives of great men, on issues

of faith and wisdom, ethics and folklore (*Haggadah,* homiletics). Stress was laid on precision of expression, on brevity of report; stylistic beauty for beauty's sake, literary elegance, was no longer practiced. The originally oral character of transmission, the pointed discussion among scholars in the houses of study, the dialogue between master and disciple, the pithy comment on a Biblical passage—all these traits are evident in the voluminous records that emerged from this activity: the Mishnah, codification of the laws, completed about A.D. 200, the Palestinian and Babylonian Talmuds, interpretations of the Mishnah, completed at the end of the fourth and fifth centuries respectively, the Midrashim (plural of Midrash, exposition, scriptural exegesis), and collections of Haggadah material, compiled in the talmudic period and in the following centuries. (See "The Order of Benedictions" and "The Seder Ceremony" as samples from the Mishnah, "The Ways of Good Life" as a sample of Haggadah from one of the talmudic tractates, the following eight selections as samples of haggadic material culled from various talmudic-midrashic sources, and "Reflections on Life" from *Tanna debe Eliyahu,* a late haggadic compendium. Talmudic discussion of legal and ritual material is not included here.)

Information on what really mattered to the talmudic teachers is given in the one nonlegal treatise of the Mishnah, *Abot* (Fathers), which includes the chief sayings and religioethical maxims attributed to about sixty masters. The following condensation of this treatise may provide some background to our selections from the talmudic and midrashic writings.

Chief among the virtues is the study of the Law. Torah is one of the three things upon which the universe is based (the other two being the divine worship and loving-kindness). A person ought to attach himself to a master and to a companion for joint study; irregular hours of study are to be avoided. Those who grow up among the sages will cultivate silence; they will say little and do much. The study of Torah is to be combined with some worldly occupation (for such an arrangement will not leave time for idleness), but business tends to overly occupy a person's mind. Therefore, it is better to reduce such activity in order to concentrate one's efforts on Torah. The true way of learning is: Eat a morsel of bread with salt, drink water by measure, sleep upon the ground, live a life of trouble while you toil in the Law; then you will be happy in this world and in the world to come. He who fulfills the Torah in the midst of poverty shall in the end fulfill it in plenty; he who neglects it in plenty shall in the end neglect it in poverty. Knowledge cannot be inherited; man must "prepare himself" for this serious pursuit. The day is short and work is plentiful. It is not one's function to finish the work, yet he is not free to desist from it. He who takes upon himself the yoke of Torah frees himself from the yoke of government and the yoke of worldly troubles. When people sit together—a group of ten, or five, or three or two—and study Torah, or even if a man alone meditates on the Law, the divine presence abides there. An assembly which is for the sake of heaven will in the end be established. Equally, a controversy which is for the sake of heaven will in the end be established.

But learning has to result in action. He that studies in order to teach is granted the means to learn and to teach; he who learns in order to practice (what he learns) is granted the means to learn and to teach, to observe and to practice. Wisdom will endure if it is exceeded by proper action; he whose wisdom exceeds his deeds, his wisdom will not endure. No selfish motive may prompt a person in the pursuit of learning. The Torah may not be made a crown for the aggrandizement of the student nor a spade wherewith to dig. He who makes profit from the words of the Torah removes his life from the world.

As the disciple honors his master, so will the teacher have regard for his pupil. His honor will be dear to him as the honor of his associate, the honor of his associate as the reverence of his master, and the reverence of his master as the fear of God in heaven.

The learned man will go out and practice charity and good deeds toward his fellow man. He will be guided by a humble consideration of man's origin, his ultimate disintegration and the final day of judgment. He will emulate the Patriarch Abraham and cultivate good will, a humble spirit and soul. He will avoid jealousy, lust and ambition. He will never despise a human being or discriminate against anything, for there is no man who has not his hour, and there is no thing that has not its place. There are three crowns: the crown of Torah, the crown of priesthood and the crown of royalty; yet there is a higher crown still: the crown of a good name. Three things uphold this world: truth, judgment and peace. The realm of human action borders on the realm of the divine. He in whom the spirit of men takes delight, in him the spirit of God takes delight. It is a sign of God's love for man that He created him in His image; but it is a sign of even greater love that man was made to be aware of this fact. An unexplainable tension exists between divine providence and human choice. Everything is foreseen by God, yet the right of choice is given to man. God judges the world by grace, but human works are decisive. Man lives in a divine universe; whatever He has created in His world He created but for His glory.

In such a spirit did the "sages" and their disciples construct their lives and their view of the world.

In the centuries after the destruction of Jerusalem (the talmudic period), Judaism had further withdrawn from the stage of world history. The greatness of Rome ceased to be a problem. Concentrating on its spiritual heritage, Israel was satisfied with serving the Lord in its tiny synagogues and schools and with creating islands of sanctity in the world. But contacts with the world did not cease. The theory of Israel as a completely segregated community in exile can no longer be maintained as correct. But contacts rarely implied communion; the world had fallen apart into mutually exclusive entities in which tolerance was a rare virtue.

The diversity of writings, representative examples of which are offered in this volume, will gain a measure of coherence if we understand them as attempts on the part of the Jewish community to face the encounter with a variety of cultural and human situations and as responses to their challenges. While fixing its gaze on what is ultimately essential, Israel endeavored to translate it into the language of any given hour in history, thus cultivating the "rest" of the teaching "which is commentary."

I. Wisdom—Divine and Human

In Praise of Wisdom

FROM THE WISDOM OF BEN SIRA

A note on Ben Sira. The ancient Near East—and, for that matter, the ancient world—developed early a type of writing which deals with human life and its personal, social, political and religious problems. The source of this "wisdom" is neither divine revelation nor philosophical reason but the actual experience of life, both as handed down from the forefather and as personally encountered. The wise man (Hebrew, *Hakham*), as distinguished from the priest, prophet or philosopher, taught first and foremost that the good life was a life of righteousness before God and man. Then, love and regard for one's fellow man, self-respect, contentment, pursuit of knowledge and under-standing that the beginning and the end of wisdom is "the fear of the Lord" were emphasized.

Wisdom (or *Hokhmah*) literature is represented in the Hebrew Bible by the Proverbs (*Mishle*), Ecclesiastes (*Kohelet*), a number of Psalms and Job—the latter being a profound challenge of the self-sufficiency of human knowledge and wisdom, and of the theory that there is a connection between righteous living and happiness.

The Apocrypha preserve in this literary form the Wisdom of Ben Sira and the Wisdom of Solomon.

The Wisdom of Joshua (Jesus) Ben Sira (or Sirach), or Ecclesiasticus of the English Versions, was written in Jerusalem, between 200 and 180 B.C. About half a century later, the author's grandson translated the book from its original Hebrew into Greek for the benefit of the Jewish community in Egypt. This version became a part of the Greek Bible; similarly, a Syriac translation, incorporated into the Syriac Bible (*Peshitta*), is based on the Hebrew original. The original Hebrew text, quotations of which appear in the talmudic literature, went out of circulation in the later Middle Ages. Only in 1896 and shortly afterward were parts of the Hebrew text (eleventh to twelfth centuries) that go back to the original discovered in the *Genizah* (storeroom) of an old Cairo synagogue.

Ben Sira's work offers an invaluable picture of life in Jerusalem before the Maccabean uprising. The nation, according to him, was divided into two groups: (1) the wealthy, worldly and morally unrestrained; (2) the poor, humble and pious. However, the differences had not yet taken shape in the form of organized factions or doctrinal leadership, and the point had not yet been reached where coexistence became impossible.

The origin of wisdom

All wisdom cometh from the Lord,
  And is with Him forever.
The sand of the seas, and the drops of rain,
  And the days of eternity—who can number them?
The height of the heaven, and the breadth of the earth,
  And the deep—who can trace them out?
Before them all was Wisdom created,
  And prudent insight from everlasting.
The root of Wisdom, to whom hath it been revealed?
  And her subtle thoughts, who hath known them?
One there is, greatly to be feared,
  The Lord sitting upon His throne;
He himself created her, and saw, and numbered her,
  And poured her out upon all His works;
Upon all flesh in measure,
  But without measure doth He grant her to them that love
    Him.

The fear of the Lord is the true wisdom

The fear of the Lord is glory and exultation,
  And gladness, and a crown of rejoicing.
The fear of the Lord delighteth the heart,
  And giveth gladness, and joy, and length of days.
Whoso feareth the Lord, it shall go well with him at the last,

And in the day of his death he shall be blessed.
To fear the Lord is the beginning of Wisdom,
    And with the faithful was she created in the womb.
With faithful men is she, and she hath been established from
       eternity;
    And with their seed shall she continue.
To fear the Lord is the fullness of Wisdom,
    And she satiateth men with her fruits.
She filleth all her house with pleasant things,
    And her garners with her produce.
The crown of Wisdom is the fear of the Lord,
    And increaseth peace and life and health.
She is a strong staff and a glorious stay,
    And everlasting honor to them that hold her fast.
To fear the Lord is the root of Wisdom,
    And her branches are length of days.

If thou desire Wisdom, keep the commandments,
    And the Lord will give her freely unto thee.
For the fear of the Lord is wisdom and instruction,
    And faith and meekness are well-pleasing unto Him.
My son, disobey not the fear of the Lord,
    And approach it not with a double heart.
Be not a hypocrite in the sight of men,
    And take good heed to thy lips.
Exalt not thyself lest thou fall,
    And bring disgrace upon thyself,
And the Lord reveal thy hidden thoughts,
    And cast thee down in the midst of the assembly,
Because thou camest not unto the fear of the Lord,
    And thy heart was full of deceit.

On free will

Say not: "From God is my transgression,"
    For that which He hateth made He not.
Say not: "It is He that made me to stumble,"
    For there is no need of evil men.
Evil and abomination doth the Lord hate,

And He doth not let it come nigh to them that fear Him.
God created man from the beginning,
　And placed him in the hand of his inclination.[1]
If thou so desirest, thou canst keep the commandment,
　And it is wisdom to do His good pleasure.
Poured out before thee are fire and water,
　Stretch forth thine hand unto that which thou desirest.
Life and death are before man,
　That which he desireth shall be given to him.
Sufficient is the wisdom of the Lord,[2]
　He is mighty in power, and seeth all things.
And the eyes of God behold his works,
　He knoweth every deed of man.
He commanded no man to sin,
　Nor gave strength to men of lies.

A man's duties

Despise no man who is in bitterness of spirit,
　Remember that there is one who exalteth and humbleth.
Devise not evil against a brother,
　Nor do the like against a friend or a neighbor withal.
Take no delight in lies of any sort,
　For the outcome thereof will not be pleasant.
Prate not in the assembly of elders,
　And repeat not words in thy prayer.
Hate not laborious work,
　Nor husbandry, for it was ordained of God.
Number not thyself among sinful men,
　Remember that wrath will not tarry.
Humble thy pride greatly,
　For the expectation of man is decay.

Change not a friend for money,
　Nor a natural brother for gold of Ophir.
Reject not a wise wife;
　And a well-favored wife is above pearls.
Maltreat not a servant that serveth truly,
　Nor a hireling who giveth his life for thee.

A wise slave love as thyself,
  And withhold not from him his freedom.
Hast thou cattle, look to them thyself,
  And if they are profitable, keep them.
Hast thou sons, correct them,
  And give them wives in their youth.
Hast thou daughters, keep their bodies,
  And show them not a pleasant countenance.
Marry thy daughter, and sorrow will depart,
  But bestow her upon a man of understanding.
Hast thou a wife, forsake her not,
  But trust not thyself to one that hateth thee.
Honor thy father with thy whole heart,
  And forget not thy mother who bare thee.
Remember that of them thou wast begotten,
  And how canst thou recompense them for what they have
    done for thee?

Also to the poor stretch out thy hand,
  That the blessing may be perfected.
A gift hath grace in the sight of every man living,
  And also from the dead withhold not kindness.
Withdraw not thyself from them that weep,
  And mourn with them that mourn.
Forget not to visit the sick,
  For thou wilt be loved for that.
In all thy doings remember thy last end,
  Then wilt thou never do corruptly.

Of women

Be not jealous over the wife of thy bosom,
  Lest she learn malice against thee.
Give not thyself unto a woman,
  So as to let her trample down thy manhood.
Meet not a strange woman,
  Lest thou fall into her nets.
With a female singer have no converse,
  Lest thou be taken in her snares.

On a maiden fix not thy gaze,
   Lest thou be entrapped in penalties with her.
Give not thyself unto the harlot,
   Lest thou lose thine inheritance.
Look not round about thee in the streets of a city,
   And wander not about in the broad places thereof.
Hide thine eye from a lovely woman,
   And gaze not upon beauty which is not thine;
By the comeliness of a woman many have been ruined,
   And this way passion flameth like fire.
With a married woman sit not at table,
   And mingle not wine in her company;
Lest thou incline thine heart towards her,
   And in thy blood fallest into destruction.

I would rather dwell with a lion and a dragon,
   Than keep house with a wicked woman.
The wickedness of a woman maketh black her look,
   And darkeneth her countenance like that of a bear.
In the midst of his friends her husband sitteth,
   And involuntarily he sigheth bitterly.
There is but little malice like the malice of a woman,
   May the lot of the wicked fall upon her!
As a sandy ascent to the feet of the aged,
   So is a woman of tongue to a quiet man.
Fall not because of the beauty of woman,
   And be not ensnared for the sake of what she possesseth;
For hard slavery and a disgrace it is,
   If a wife support her husband.
A humbled heart and a sad countenance,
   And a heart-wound, is an evil wife.
Hands that hang down, and palsied knees,
      Thus shall it be with a wife that maketh not happy her
         husband.
From a woman did sin originate,
   And because of her we all must die.
Give not water an outlet,

Nor to a wicked woman power.
If she go not as thou would have her,
     Cut her off from thy flesh.

A good wife—blessed is her husband,
     The number of his days is doubled.
A worthy wife cherisheth her husband,
     And he fulfilleth the years of his life in peace.
A good wife is a good gift:
     She shall be given to him that feareth God, for his portion.
Whether rich or poor, his heart is cheerful,
     And his face is merry at all times.

The training of children

He that loveth his son will continue to lay strokes upon him,[3]
     That he may rejoice over him at the last.
He that disciplineth his son shall have satisfaction of him,
     And among his acquaintance glory in him.
He that teacheth his son maketh his enemy jealous,
     And in the presence of friends exulteth in him.
When his father dieth he dieth not altogether,[4]
     For he hath left one behind him like himself.
In his life he saw and rejoiced,
     And in death he hath not been grieved.
Against enemies he hath left behind an avenger,
     And to friends one that requiteth favor.
He that pampereth his son shall bind up his wounds,
     And his heart trembleth at every cry.

An unbroken horse becometh stubborn,
     And a son left at large becometh headstrong.
Cocker thy son and he will terrify thee;
     Play with him and he will grieve thee.
Laugh not with him, lest he vex thee,
     And make thee gnash thy teeth at the last.
Let him not have freedom in his youth,
     And overlook not his mischievous acts.
Bow down his neck in his youth,

And smite his loins sore while he is little—
Lest he become stubborn and rebel against thee,
    And thou experience anguish of soul on his account.
Discipline thy son, and make his yoke heavy,
    Lest in his folly he stumble.

The physician

Cultivate the physician in accordance with the need of him,
    For him also hath God ordained.[5]
It is from God that the physician getteth wisdom,
    And from the king he receiveth gifts.
The skill of the physician lifteth up his head,
    And he may stand before nobles.
God hath created medicines out of the earth,
    And let not a discerning man reject them.
Was not the water made sweet by the wood,[6]
    That He might make known to all men His power?
And He gave men discernment,
    That they might glory in His mighty works,
By means of them the physician assuageth pain,
    And likewise the apothecary prepareth a confection:
That His work may not cease,
    Nor health from the face of His earth.
My son, in sickness be not negligent;
    Pray unto God, for He can heal.
Turn from iniquity, and purify thy hands;
    And from all transgressions cleanse thy heart.[7]
Give a meal-offering with a memorial,
    And offer a fat sacrifice to the utmost of thy means.
And to the physician also give a place;
    Nor should he be far away, for of him there is need.
For there is a time when successful help is in his power;
    For he also maketh supplication to God,
To make his diagnosis successful,
    And the treatment, that it may promote recovery.
But he that sinneth before his Maker
    Let him fall into the hands of the physician.

The Ideal Scribe

FROM THE WISDOM OF BEN SIRA

He that applieth himself to the fear of God,
And setteth his mind upon the Law of the Most High,
He searcheth out the wisdom of all the ancients,
And is occupied with the prophets of old.
He heedeth the discourses of men of renown,
And entereth into the deep things of parables;
Searcheth out the hidden meaning of proverbs,
And is conversant with the dark sayings of parables;
He serveth among great men,
And appeareth before princes;
He traveleth through the lands of the peoples,[8]
Testeth good and evil among men;
He is careful to seek unto his Maker,
And before the Most High entreateth mercy;
He openeth his mouth in prayer,
And maketh supplication for his sins.

If it seem good to God Most High,
He shall be filled with the spirit of understanding.
He himself poureth forth wise sayings in double measure,
And giveth thanks unto the Lord in prayer.
He himself directeth counsel and knowledge,
And setteth his mind on their secrets.
He himself declareth wise instruction,
And glorieth in the law of the Lord.
His understanding many do praise,
And never shall his name be blotted out:
His memory shall not cease,
And his name shall live from generation to generation.
His wisdom doth the congregation tell forth,

And his praise the assembly publisheth.
If he live long, he shall be accounted happy more than a
    thousand;
And when he cometh to an end, his name sufficeth.

Manifestation of God in Nature

FROM THE WISDOM OF BEN SIRA

The beauty of the [heavenly] height is the pure firmament,
    And the firm heaven poureth out light.
The sun when it goeth forth maketh heat to shine—
    How awe-inspiring is the work of the Lord.
At noontide it bringeth the world to boiling heat,
    And before its scorching ray who can maintain himself?
Like a glowing furnace which keepeth the casting hot,
    So the sun's dart setteth the mountains ablaze:
A tongue of flame consumeth the inhabited world,
    And with its fire the eye is scorched.
For great is the Lord that made it,
    And His word maketh His mighty [servant] brilliant.
Moreover, the moon He made for its due season,
    To rule over periods and for an everlasting sign:
By the moon are determined the feasts and times prescribed,
    A light-giver waning with her course:
Month by month she reneweth herself—
    How wonderful is she in her changing!
The army-signal of the cloud-vessels on high,
    She paveth the firmament with her shining.

The beauty of heaven, and the glory, are the stars,
    And a gleaming ornament in the heights of God.
At the word of the Holy One they take their prescribed place,
    And they sleep not at their watches.
Behold the rainbow and bless its Maker,
    For it is majestic exceedingly in majesty:

It encompasseth the heavenly vault with its glory,
    And the hand of God hath spread it out in pride.
His might marketh out the lightning,
    And maketh brilliant the flashes of His judgment.
On that account He hath created a treasure house,
    And He maketh the clouds fly like birds.
By His mighty power He maketh strong the clouds,
    And the hailstones are broken.
His thunder's voice maketh His earth to be in anguish
    And by His strength He shaketh mountains.
The terror of Him stirreth up the south wind,
    The whirlwind of the north, hurricane, and tempest;
Like flocks of birds, He sheddeth abroad His snow,
    And like settling locusts is the fall thereof.
The beauty of the whiteness dazzleth the eyes,
    And the heart marveleth at the raining thereof.
The hoarfrost also He poureth out like salt,
    And maketh the crystals sparkle like sapphire.
The icy blast of the north wind He causeth to blow,
    And hardeneth the pond like a bottle.
Over every basin of water He spreadeth a crust,
    And the pond putteth on as it were a breastplate.
It burneth up the produce of the mountains as a drought,
    And the sprouting pasture as a flame.
A healing for all such is the distillation of the clouds,
    Even the dew, alighting to bring refreshment after heat.
By His counsel He hath stilled the deep,
    And hath planted the islands in the ocean.
They that go down to the sea tell of its extent,
    And when our ears hear it we are astonished.
Therein are marvels, the most wondrous of His works,
    All kinds of living things, and whales created.
By reason of Him their end prospereth,
    And at His word what He wills is done.

More like this we will not add,
    And the conclusion of the matter is: He is all.
We will sing praises, because we cannot fathom;

For greater is He than all His works.
Terrible is the Lord exceedingly,
  And wonderful are His mighty acts.
Ye that magnify the Lord, lift up your voice,
  As much as ye can, for there is still more!
Ye that exalt Him, renew your strength,
  And weary not, for ye cannot fathom Him!
Who hath seen Him, that he may tell thereof?
  And who shall magnify Him as he is?
The number of things mysterious is greater even than these,
  And I have seen but few of His works.
Everything hath the Lord made,
  And to the pious hath He given wisdom.

The High Priest, Simon, Son of Johanan

FROM THE WISDOM OF BEN SIRA

Great among his brethren and the glory of his people
  Was Simon, son of Johanan the priest.[9]
In whose time the House[10] was renovated,
  And in whose days the Temple was fortified;
In whose days the wall was built,
  Having turrets for protection like a king's palace;
In whose time a reservoir was dug,
  A water cistern like the sea in its abundance.
He took thought for his people to preserve them from robbers,
  And fortified his city against the enemy.
How glorious was he when he looked forth from the Tent,[11]
  And when he came out from the sanctuary!
Like a morning star from between the clouds,
  And like the full moon on the feast days;
Like the sun shining upon the Temple of the Most High,
  And like the rainbow becoming visible in the cloud;
Like a flower on the branches in the days of the first-fruits,[12]
  And as a lily by the water brooks,

As the sprout of Lebanon on summer days,
    And as the fire of incense in the censer;
Like a golden vessel beautifully wrought,
    Adorned with all manner of precious stones;
Like a luxuriant olive tree full of berries,
    And like an oleaster abounding in branches.
When he put on his glorious robes,
    And clothed himself in perfect splendor,
When he went up to the altar of majesty,
    And made glorious the court of the sanctuary;
When he took the portions from the hand of his brethren,
    While standing by the blocks of wood,
Around him the garland of his sons,
    Like young cedar trees in Lebanon;
And like willows by the brook did they surround him,
    All the sons of Aaron in their glory,
And the Lord's fire-offering in their hands,
    In the presence of the whole congregation of Israel.

Until he had finished the service of the altar
    And arranging the rows of wood of the Most High,
And stretched forth his hand to the cup,
    And poured out of the blood of the grape;
Yet, poured it out at the foot of the altar,
    A sweet-smelling savor to the Most High, the All-King.
Then the sons of Aaron sounded
    With the trumpets of beaten work;
Yea, they sounded and caused a mighty blast to be heard
    For a remembrance before the Most High.
Then all flesh hasted together
    And fell upon their faces to the earth,
To worship before the Most High,
    Before the Holy One of Israel.
And the sound of the song was heard,
    And over the multitude they made sweet melody;
And all the people of the land cried
    In prayer before the Merciful One,
Until he had finished the service of the altar,

And His ordinances had brought him nigh unto Him.
Then he descended, and lifted up his hands
    Upon the whole congregation of Israel,
And the blessing of the Lord was upon his lips,
    And he glorified himself with the name of the Lord.
And again they fell down, now to receive
    The pardon of God from him.

Now bless the God of all,
    Who doeth wondrously on earth,
Who exalteth man from the womb,
    And dealeth with him according to His will.
May He grant you wisdom of heart,
    And may there be peace among you.
May His mercy be established with Simon,
    And may He raise up for him the covenant of Phinehas;[13]
May one never be cut off from him;
    And as to his seed, may it be as the days of heaven.

Wisdom and the Order of This World

FROM THE WISDOM OF SOLOMON

A *note on the* Wisdom of Solomon. Wisdom is not merely a guide to a prudent and most efficient way of life, or an advocation of righteousness. Reminiscent of the position of the *Logos* in Stoic philosophy, Wisdom is held to be "the holy spirit from on high," "penetrating all things by reason of her pureness." It is "the breath of the power of God," the source of all truth. Such exaltation of the cosmic rôle of Wisdom, implied in earlier works of this category, is the hallmark of the Wisdom of Solomon.

There are various scholarly opinions on the authorship and date of the book. The soundest seems to be the view of Charles Cutler Torrey, who considers it to be a composite work, the first half (chapters 1 to 10) having been originally a Hebrew poetical composition, that the author of the second half, which is Greek rhetoric of the Alexandrian type, translated into Greek. The book as a whole presents a beautiful blend of Hebraic piety and elements of Greek philosophy. Its doctrine of the immortality of the soul is Platonic. To give the work greater authority it was, like Proverbs and Ecclesiastes, attributed to King Solomon, the wisest of men. The most probable date of its composition seems to be around 100 B.C.

Wisdom is a spirit that loveth man

Love righteousness, ye that be judges of the earth,
Thank ye of the Lord with a good mind,
And in singleness of heart seek ye him;
Because he is found of them that tempt him not,
And is manifested to them that do not distrust him.
For crooked thoughts separate from God;
And the [supreme] Power, when it is brought to the proof,
            putteth to confusion the foolish;
Because wisdom will not enter into a soul that deviseth evil,
Nor dwell in a body held in pledge by sin.
For the holy spirit of discipline will flee deceit,
And will start away from thoughts that are without
            understanding,
And will be scared away when unrighteousness approacheth.

For wisdom is a spirit that loveth man,
And she will not hold a blasphemer guiltless for his lips;
Because God is witness of his reins,
And is a true overseer of his heart,
And a hearer of his tongue:
Because the spirit of the Lord filleth the world,
And that which holdeth all things together[14] hath knowledge
            of every voice.
Therefore no man that uttereth unrighteous things shall be
            unseen;
Neither shall justice, when it punisheth, pass him by.
For the counsels of the ungodly shall be searched out;
And the report of his words shall come unto the Lord
For the punishment of his lawless deeds:
Because there is a zealous ear that listeneth to all things,
And the noise of murmurings is not hid.
Beware then of unprofitable murmuring,
And refrain your tongue from blasphemy;

Because no secret utterance shall go forth with impunity;
And a mouth that lieth destroyeth the soul.

Court not death in the error of your life;
Neither draw upon yourselves destruction by the works of your
        hands:[15]
Because God made not death;
Neither delighteth he when the living perish:
For he created all things that they might have being:
And the products of the world are healthsome,
And there is no poison of destruction in them:
Nor hath Hades royal dominion upon earth;
For righteousness is immortal.

God—lover of souls

To be greatly strong is Thine at all times;
And the might of Thine arm who shall withstand?
Because the whole world before Thee is as a grain in a balance,
And as a drop of dew that at morning cometh down upon the
        earth.
But Thou hast mercy on all men, because Thou hast power to
        do all things,
And Thou overlookest the sins of men to the end they may
        repent.[16]
For Thou lovest all things that are,
And abhorrest none of the things which Thou didst make;
For never wouldst Thou have formed anything if Thou didst
        hate it.
And how would anything have endured, except Thou hadst
        willed it?
Or that which was not called by Thee, how would it have
        been preserved?
But Thou sparest all things, because they are Thine,
O Sovereign Lord, Thou lover of souls;
For Thine incorruptible spirit is in all things.
Wherefore Thou dost chastise by little and little them that
        fall from the right way,

And, putting them in remembrance by the very things wherein
      they sin, dost Thou admonish them,
That escaping from their wickedness they may believe on
      Thee, O Lord.

Wisdom is a breath of the power of God

There is in wisdom a spirit: understanding, holy,
Alone in kind, manifold,
Subtile, freely moving,
Clear in utterance, unpolluted,
Distinct, that cannot be harmed,
Loving what is good, keen, unhindered,
Beneficent, loving toward man,
Steadfast, sure, free from care,
All-powerful, all-surveying,
And penetrating through all spirits
That are quick of understanding, pure, subtile.
For wisdom is more mobile than any motion;
Yea, she pervadeth and penetrateth all things by reason of her
      pureness.
For she is a breath of the power of God,
And a clear effluence of the glory of the Almighty;
Therefore can nothing defiled find entrance into her.
For she is a radiance from everlasting light
And an unspotted mirror of the working of God,
And an image of his goodness.
And she, though but one, hath power to do all things;
And remaining in herself, reneweth all things:
And from generation to generation passing into holy souls
She maketh them friends of God[17] and prophets.[18]
For nothing doth God love save him that dwelleth with
      wisdom.
For she is fairer than the sun,
And above all the constellations of the stars:
Being compared with light, she is found to be before it;
For the light of day succeedeth night,

But against wisdom evil doth not prevail;
But she reacheth from one end of the world to the other with
    full strength,
And ordereth all things well.

Solomon desired wisdom as a bride

Her I loved and sought out from my youth,[19]
And I sought to take her for my bride.
And I became enamored of her beauty.
She proclaimeth her noble birth in that it is given her to live
    with God,
And the Sovereign Lord of all loved her.
For she is initiated into the knowledge of God,
And she chooseth out for him his works.
But if riches are a desired possession in life,
What is richer than wisdom, which worketh all things?
And if understanding worketh,
Who more than wisdom is an artificer of the things that are?
And if a man loveth righteousness,
The fruits of wisdom's labor are virtues,
For she teacheth self-control and understanding, righteous-
    ness, and courage;[20]
And there is nothing in life for men more profitable than
    these.
And if a man longeth even for much experience,
She knoweth the things of old, and divineth the things to
    come:
She understandeth subtilties of speeches and interpretations
    of dark sayings:
She foreseeth signs and wonders, and the issues of seasons and
    times.
I determined therefore to take her unto me to live with me,
Knowing that she is one who would give me good thoughts
    for counsel,
And encourage me in cares and grief.
Because of her I shall have glory among multitudes,
And honor in the sight of elders, though I be young.
I shall be found of a quick discernment when I give judgment,

And in the presence of princes I shall be admired.
When I am silent, they shall wait for me;
And when I open my lips, they shall give heed unto me;
And if I continue speaking, they shall lay their hand upon
    their mouth.
Because of her I shall have immortality,
And leave behind an eternal memory to them that come after
    me.
I shall govern peoples,
And nations shall be subjected to me.
Dread princes shall fear me when they hear of me:
Among my people I shall show myself a good ruler, and in war
    courageous.
When I come into my house, I shall find rest with her;
For converse with her hath no bitterness,
And to live with her hath no pain, but gladness and joy.
When I considered these things in myself,
And took thought in my heart how that in kinship unto
    wisdom is immortality,
And in her friendship is good delight,
And in the labors of her hands is wealth that faileth not,
And in assiduous communing with her is understanding,
And great renown in having fellowship with her words,
I went about seeking how to take her unto myself.

Immortality

God created man for eternal life,
And made him an image of His own proper being;
But by the envy of Satan death entered into the world,[21]
And they that belong to his realm experience it.
But the souls of the righteous are in the hand of God,
And no torment shall touch them.
In the eyes of fools they seemed to die;
And their departure was accounted to be their hurt,
And their going from us to be their ruin:
But they are in peace.[22]
For though in the sight of men they be punished,
Their hope is full of immortality;

And having borne a little chastening, they shall receive great
      good;
Because God tested them, and found them worthy of Himself.
As gold on the furnace He proved them,
And as a whole burnt offering He accepted them.
And in the time of their visitation they shall shine forth,
And like sparks among stubble they shall run to and fro.
They shall judge nations, and have dominion over peoples;
And the Lord shall reign over them for evermore.
They that trust on Him shall understand truth,
And the faithful shall abide with Him in love;
Because grace and mercy are to His chosen,
And He will graciously visit His holy ones.

II. For the Sake of Freedom of Religion

A Note on the First and the Second Book of Maccabees. When in 168 B.C. King Antiochus IV Epiphanes of Syria, in pursuit of a forced Helleni-zation in his realm, decreed the abolition of the Mosaic law and commanded the introduction of the pagan cult in the Temple of Jerusalem, people were ready to rebel against both the Syrian overlord and the Jewish Hellenist party within, to fight for the freedom of religion and, later, for the political inde-pendence of Judaea. This rebellion, its progress and its outcome, are the theme of the First Book of Maccabees. It tells the story of the accession of Antiochus IV Epiphanes, the dramatic rise of the priest Mattathias of Modin and his five sons, the battles waged, primarily by the most heroic among the sons, Judah the Maccabee ("the Hammer"), the rededication of the Temple (commemo-rated in the *Hanukkah* ["dedication"] festival), the military pursuits of Judah's brother Jonathan and the actions of the last surviving brother, Simon (died 134 B.C.). It was Simon who brought the war to an end, secured independence, renewed a treaty of friendship with Sparta and Rome and established his family as the ruling house in Judaea.

The unknown author, a witness of the rebellion, wrote his book around 125 B.C.; the Hebrew original disappeared in the first Christian century; the extant Greek text is a translation from the Hebrew. The author, a skilled his-torian who took the historical writings of the Bible as his model, stands on the side of the Maccabean fighters. His aim is not propaganda but an objective, straightforward account of the events. His book is the most important source for this crucial period in history.

In contradistinction to the factual, down-to-earth history of the First Book of Maccabees, the Second is a passionate tale of the indomitable faith and spirit of resistance to tyranny that motivated the rebels. The book, whose content corresponds, roughly, to the first seven chapters of First Maccabees, is a condensation of a no longer extant history of the period in five books by a certain Jason of Cyrene. The unknown epitomist lived in Egypt, possibly in

Alexandria, and wrote in Greek towards the end of the second pre-Christian century. The book aimed at making Jews in the Diaspora aware of the heroism of their brethren in Jerusalem and at deepening their affection for the Temple. This purpose was served by the story of the steadfast old scribe, Eleazar, who chose death to transgression of the dietary laws, and the account of the martyrdom of the mother and her seven sons (our selection). In periods of religious persecution, Jews and Christians alike drew strength and comfort from the memory of these witnesses for the "faith," a term that gained prominence in Jewish thought of the era.

The Origin of the Maccabean Rebellion

FROM THE FIRST BOOK OF MACCABEES

The victory of Alexander the Great

And it came to pass after Alexander [356–323 B.C.], the son of Philip the Macedonian, who came from the land of Chittim [Greece], had smitten Darius [III, Codomannus], king of the Persians and Medes, that he reigned in his stead. He waged many wars, and won strongholds, and slew kings, and pressed forward to the ends of the earth, and took spoils from many peoples. But when the land was silenced before him, he became exalted, and his heart was lifted up. Then he gathered together a very mighty army, and ruled over lands and peoples and principalities; they became tributary unto him.

After these things he took to his bed, and perceived that he was about to die. Then he called his chief ministers, men who had been brought up with him from his youth, and divided his kingdom among them while he was yet alive. Alexander had reigned twelve years [336–323 B.C.] when he died. And his ministers ruled, each in his particular domain. After he was dead they all assumed the diadem, as did their sons after them for many years; they wrought much evil on the earth.

Antiochus Epiphanes and the Hellenists

A sinful shoot came forth from them, Antiochus Epiphanes, the son of Antiochus [III] the king [reigned 223–187 B.C.], who had been a hostage in Rome.[1] He became king in the one hundred and thirty-seventh year of the Greek kingdom.[2] In those days there came forth out of Israel lawless men[3] who persuaded many, saying: "Let us go and make a covenant with the nations around us; for since we separated ourselves from them many evils have come upon us."

The saying appeared good in their eyes; and certain of the people went eagerly to the king who gave them authority to introduce the customs of the heathen. They built a gymnasium in Jerusalem according to the manner of the heathen. They also submitted themselves to uncircumcision[4] and repudiated the holy covenant; yea, they joined themselves to the heathen and sold themselves to do evil.

Antiochus subdues Egypt

When, in the opinion of Antiochus, the kingdom was sufficiently established, he determined to exercise dominion also over the land of Egypt, in order that he might rule over two kingdoms. So he pushed forward into Egypt [171–170 B.C.] with an immense force, with chariots, elephants and horsemen, together with a great fleet. He waged war against Ptolemy [VI, Philometor], king of Egypt. Ptolemy turned back from before him and fled while many were wounded. They captured the fortified cities in Egypt; and he took the spoils from the land of Egypt.[5]

The desecration of the Temple

After he had smitten Egypt, Antiochus returned in the one hundred and forty-third year [170 B.C.], and went up against Israel and Jerusalem with a great army. In his arrogance he entered the Temple, and took the golden altar, the candlestick for the light and all its accessories, the table of the shewbread, the cups, the bowls and the golden censers, the veil, the crowns; and the golden adornment on the facade of the Temple he scaled off entirely. He took the silver, the gold, and the choice vessels; he also took the hidden treasures which he found. Having taken everything, he returned to his own land. He made a great slaughter and spoke most arrogantly.

And there was great mourning in Israel in every place;
Both the rulers and elders groaned;
Virgins and young men languished,
The beauty of the women faded away;
Every bridegroom took up lament,
She that sat in the bridal chamber mourned.
The land was moved for her inhabitants,
And all the house of Jacob was clothed with shame.

Jerusalem occupied by Apollonius

After two years, the king sent a chief collector of tribute[6] to the cities of Judah; and he came to Jerusalem with a great host. He spoke to them peaceful words in subtilty, so that they had confidence in him. Then he fell upon the city suddenly, and smote it with a grievous stroke, destroying much people in Israel. He took the spoils of the city, burned it with fire, and pulled down its houses and the walls surrounding it. They led captive the women and the children, and took possession of the cattle. They fortified the city of David with a great and strong wall with strong towers, so that it was made into a citadel[7] for them. They placed there a sinful nation, lawless men; and they strengthened themselves in it. They stored up arms and provisions, and after collecting together the spoils of Jerusalem, they laid them up there. It became a sore menace, for it was a place to lie in wait in against the sanctuary, an evil adversary to Israel continually.

They shed innocent blood on every side of the sanctuary,
And they defiled the sanctuary.
Because of them the inhabitants of Jerusalem fled,
She became a dwelling for strangers,
Being herself estranged to her offspring,

And her children forsook her.
Her sanctuary became desolate as a wilderness,
Her feasts were turned into mourning,
Her sabbaths into shame,
Her honor into contempt.
According as her glory had been so was now her dishonor
    increased,
And her high estate was turned to mourning.

Edict of Antiochus; religious persecution

Then the king wrote to his whole kingdom, that all
should be one people, and that every one should give up his
laws. All the nations acquiesced in accordance with the command of the king. Even many in Israel took delight in his
worship and began sacrificing to idols and profaned the
Sabbath.

Furthermore, the king sent letters by messengers to Jerusalem and to the cities of Judah to the effect that they should
practice customs foreign to the land, and that they should
cease the whole burnt offerings and sacrifices, and drink offerings in the sanctuary, that they should profane the Sabbaths
and feasts, and pollute the sanctuary and those who had been
sanctified; that they should build high places, and sacred
groves and shrines for idols, and that they should sacrifice
swine and other unclean animals; that they should leave their
sons uncircumcised, and defile themselves by every kind of
uncleanness and profanation, so that they might forget the
Law and change all the ordinances.[8] Whoever should not act
according to the word of the king, should die.

In this manner he wrote to all his kingdom, and appointed overseers over all the people and commanded the
cities of Judah to sacrifice, every one of them. Many of the
people joined them, all those who had forsaken the Law;
these did evil in the land, and caused Israel to hide in all
manner of hiding places.

On the twenty-fifth day of Kislev [December] in the one
hundred and forty-sixth year [168 B.C.] they set up upon the

altar an "abomination of desolation," [9] and in the cities of
Judah on every side they established altars; they offered sacrifice at the doors of the houses and in the streets. The books of
the Law which they found they rent in pieces and burned.
With whomsoever was found a book of the covenant, and if
he was found consenting unto the Law, such an one was, according to the king's sentence, condemned to death. Thus did
they in their might to the Israelites who were found month by
month in their cities.

On the twenty-fifth day of the month they sacrificed
upon the altar which was upon the altar of burnt-offering. According to the decree, they put to death the women who had
circumcised their children, hanging their babes round their
necks, and they put to death their families, together with
those who had circumcised them. Nevertheless many in Israel
stood firm and determined in their hearts that they would not
eat unclean things, and chose rather to die so that they might
not be defiled with meats, thereby profaning the holy covenant; and they did die. Exceeding great wrath came upon
Israel.

The uprising under Mattathias

In those days Mattathias, the son of John, the son of
Simeon, a priest of the sons of Joarib,[10] moved from Jerusalem
and dwelt at Modin.[11] He had five sons: John, who was surnamed Gaddi, Simon, who was called Thassi, Judah who was
called Maccabee, Eleazar, who was called Auaran, and Jonathan, who was called Apphus.

When Mattathias saw the blasphemous things that were
done in Judah and in Jerusalem, he said, "Woe is me, why
was I born to behold the ruin of my people and the ruin of the
holy city, and to sit still there while it was being given into
the hand of enemies, and the sanctuary into the hand of
strangers?"

Her house has become as a man dishonored;
Her glorious vessels are carried away captive;
Her infants have been slain in her streets,

Her young men with the sword of the enemy.
What nation hath the kingdom not taken possession of,
Of what nation hath it not seized the spoils?
Her adornment hath all been taken away,
Instead of a free woman she is become a slave.
And, behold, our holy things, and our beauty, and our glory
        have been laid waste,
The heathen have profaned them! To what purpose should we
        continue to live?

Mattathias and his sons rent their garments, covered themselves with sackcloth, and mourned greatly.

Then the king's officers who were enforcing the apostasy came to the city of Modin to make them sacrifice. Many from Israel went unto them; but Mattathias and his sons gathered themselves together. The king's officers said to Mattathias: "A leader art thou, illustrious and great in this city, and upheld by sons and brothers. Do thou, therefore, come first, and carry out the king's command, as all the nations have done, and all the people of Judah, and they that have remained in Jerusalem; then shalt thou and thy house be numbered among the friends of the king, and thou and thy sons shall be honored with silver and gold and many gifts."

Mattathias answered and said in a loud voice: "If all the nations within the king's dominions obey him by forsaking, every one of them, the worship of their fathers, and have chosen for themselves to follow his commands, yet will I and my sons and my brethren walk in the covenant of our fathers. Heaven forbid that we should forsake the Law and the ordinances; but the law of the king we will not obey by departing from our worship either to the right or to the left."

As he ceased speaking these words, a Jew came forward in the sight of all to sacrifice upon the altar in Modin, in accordance with the king's command. When Mattathias saw it, his zeal was kindled, and his heart quivered with wrath. His indignation burst forth for judgment so that he ran and slew him on the altar; at the same time he also killed the king's officer who had come to enforce the sacrificing, pulled down the altar. Thus he showed his zeal for the Law, as Phinehas had done in the case of Zimri the son of Salom.[12] Then Mattathias cried out with a loud voice in the city, saying, "Let everyone that is zealous for the Law and would maintain the covenant follow me!"

He and his sons fled unto the mountains, and left all that they possessed in the city.

At that time many who were seeking righteousness and judgment went down to the wilderness to abide there, they and their sons, their wives, and their cattle, for misfortunes fell hardly upon them. It was reported to the king's officers and to the troops that were in Jerusalem, the city of David, that men who had rejected the king's command had gone down to hiding places in the wilderness. Many ran after them, overtook them, encamped against them, and set the battle in array against them on the Sabbath day. They said to them: "Let it suffice now; come forth and do according to the command of the king, and ye shall live." But they answered, "We will not come forth, nor will we do according to the command of the king and thereby profane the Sabbath day." Thereupon they attacked them. But they answered them not nor did they cast a stone at them, nor block up their hiding places, saying, "Let us all die in our innocence; Heaven and earth bear us witness that ye destroy us wrongfully." They attacked them on the Sabbath, and they died, they, their wives, their children, and their cattle, about a thousand souls.

When Mattathias and his friends heard this, they mourned greatly for them. One said to another, "If we all do as our brethren have done, and do not fight against the heathen for our lives and our ordinances, they will soon destroy us from off the earth." They took counsel on that day, saying, "Whosoever attacketh us on the Sabbath day, let us fight against him, that we may not all die as our brethren died in their hiding places."

Then were there gathered unto them a company of the Hasidim,[13] mighty men of Israel, each one willingly offering themselves in defense of the Law. All they that fled from the evils joined them and reinforced them. They mustered a host and smote sinners in their anger, and lawless men in their wrath; and the rest fled to the heathens to save themselves. Mattathias and his friends went about, and pulled down the altars, and circumcised by force the children that were un-circumcised, as many as they found within the borders of Israel. They pursued after the sons of pride, and the work pros-pered in their hand. Thus they rescued the Law out of the hand of the heathen and the kings, neither suffered they the sinner to triumph.

His last words

When the days drew near that Mattathias should die, he said unto his sons:

Now have pride and arrogance gotten strong; this is a season of destruction and wrath of indignation. My children, be zealous for the Law, and give your lives for the covenant of your fathers. Call to mind the deeds of the fathers which they did in their generations, that ye may receive great glory and everlasting name.

Was not Abraham found faithful in temptation,[14] and it was reckoned unto him for righteousness? Joseph in the time of his distress,[15] kept the commandment and became lord of Egypt. Phinehas, our father,[16] for that he was zealous exceed-ingly, obtained the covenant of an everlasting priesthood. Joshua[17] for fulfilling the word became a judge in Israel. Caleb[18] for bearing witness in the congregation obtained land as an heritage. David[19] for being merciful inherited the throne of a kingdom for ever and ever. Elijah[20] for that he was ex-ceeding zealous for the Law was taken up into heaven. Hana-niah, Azariah and Mishael,[21] believing in God, were saved from the flame. Daniel,[22] for his innocence, was delivered from the mouth of the lions.

And thus consider ye from generation to generation: all who hope in Him shall want nothing. Be not afraid of the words of a sinful man, for his glory shall be dung and worms. Today he shall be lifted up, and to-morrow he shall in no wise be found, because he is returned unto his dust, and his thought will have perished. And ye, my children, be strong and show yourselves men on behalf of the Law, for therein shall ye obtain glory. Behold Simon your brother, I know that he is a man of counsel; give ear unto him always; he shall be a father unto you. Judah the Maccabee, he hath been strong and mighty from his youth; he shall be your leader and shall fight the battle of the people. And ye, take you unto you all those who observe the Law, and avenge the wrong of your people. Render a recompense to the heathen, and take heed to the commandments of the Law.

Then he blessed them and was gathered to his fathers. He died in the one hundred and forty-sixth year [168–167 B.C.], and his sons buried him in the sepulchres of his fathers at Modin; and all Israel made great lamentation for him.

The Rededication of the Temple

FROM THE FIRST BOOK OF MACCABEES

Judah and his brethren said: "Behold, our enemies are discomfited,[23] let us go up to cleanse the sanctuary and dedicate it."

All the army was gathered together, and they went up to mount Zion. They saw our sanctuary laid desolate and the altar profaned, the gates burned up, and shrubs growing in the courts as in a forest or upon one of the mountains, and the chambers of the priests pulled down; they rent their garments and made great lamentation, and put ashes on their heads, and fell on their faces to the ground, blew solemn blasts upon the trumpets, and cried unto heaven.

Judah appointed a certain number of men to fight against those in the citadel, until he should have cleansed the sanctuary. He chose blameless priests, such as had delight in the Law, and they cleansed the sanctuary, carrying out the stones that had defiled it into an unclean place. They took counsel concerning the altar of burnt offerings, which had been profaned, what they should do with it. A good idea occurred to them, namely, to pull it down, lest it should be a reproach unto them, because the heathen had defiled it; so they pulled down the altar, and laid down the stones in the Temple mount, in a convenient place, until a prophet should come and decide as to what should be done concerning them. They took whole stones according to the Law,[24] and built a new altar after the fashion of the former one; they built the sanctuary and the inner parts of the Temple, and hallowed the courts. They made the holy vessels new, and brought the candlestick, the altar of incense and the table into the Temple. They burned incense on the altar, and lighted the lamps that were on the candlestick in order to give light in the Temple. They set loaves of bread upon the table, hung up the veils, and finished all the works which they had undertaken.

They rose up early in the morning on the twenty-fifth day of the ninth month which is the month Kislev [December], in the one hundred and forty-ninth year [165 B.C.], and offered sacrifice according to the Law upon the new altar of burnt offerings which they had made. At the corresponding time and on the day on which the heathen had profaned it, on that day was it rededicated, with songs and harps and lutes and cymbals. All the people fell upon their faces and worshiped, and gave praise to Heaven, to Him who had prospered them. They celebrated the dedication of the altar for eight days,[25] brought burnt offerings with gladness, and offered a sacrifice of deliverance and praise.

They also decked the front of the Temple with crowns of gold and small shields, and rededicated the gates and the chambers of the priests, and furnished them with doors. Thus there was exceeding great gladness among the people, and the reproach of the heathen was turned away. Judah and his brethren and the whole congregation of Israel ordained that the days of the dedication of the altar should be kept in their seasons year by year for eight days, from the twenty-fifth of the month Kislev, with gladness and joy. At that season they built high walls and strong towers around mount Zion, lest the heathen should come and tread them down, as they had

done before. He set there a force to keep it, and they fortified
Beth Zur to keep it, that the people might have a stronghold
facing Idumaea.[26]

Simon's Beneficent Rule

FROM THE FIRST BOOK OF MACCABEES

The land of Judah had rest all the days of Simon;[27] he
sought the good of his nation; his authority and glory pleased
them all his days. In addition to all his other glory was this
that he took Joppa[28] for a harbor, and made it a place of entry
for the ships of the sea.

An ode in his honor

He enlarged the borders of his nation,
And ruled over the land.
He gathered together many that had been in captivity,
And he ruled over Gazara, and Beth Zur, and the citadel.
He took away uncleannesses therefrom,
And there was none that could resist him.
They tilled their land in peace,
The land gave her increase,
And the trees of the plains their fruit.
Old men sat in the streets,
All spoke together of the common weal,
And the young men put on glorious and warlike apparel.
For the cities he provided food,
And furnished them with defensive works,
Until his glorious name was proclaimed to the end of the
    earth.
He made peace in the land,
And Israel rejoiced with great joy.
Everyone sat under his vine and his fig tree,
There was none to make them afraid;
No one was left in the land to fight them

And the kings were discomfited in those days.
He strengthened all that were brought low of his people.
He sought out the Law,
And put away the lawless and wicked.
He glorified the sanctuary,
And multiplied the vessels of the Temple.

Renewal of the alliance with Rome

When it was heard in Rome that Jonathan[29] was dead, and even unto Sparta,[30] they were exceeding sorry. But as soon as they heard that his brother Simon was made high priest in his stead, and ruled the country and the cities therein, they wrote to him on tablets of brass, to renew with him the friendship and the confederacy which they had established with Judah and Jonathan his brethren; they were read before the congregation in Jerusalem.

Now this is the copy of the letter which the Spartans sent:

The rulers and the city of the Spartans, unto Simon the high priest, and unto the elders, the priests and the rest of the people of the Jews, our brethren, greeting. The ambassadors that were sent to our people made report to us of your glory and honor, and we were glad for their coming. We did register the things that were spoken by them in the public records, as follows: "Numenius, son of Antiochus, and Antipater, son of Jason, the Jews' ambassadors, came to us to renew the friendship with us." It pleased the people to receive the men honorably and to place the copy of their words among the public records, to the end that the people of the Spartans might have a memorial thereof. Moreover they wrote a copy of these things unto Simon the high priest.

After this Simon sent Numenius to Rome having a great shield of gold of a thousand pound weight,[31] to confirm the confederacy with them.

Elevation to high priesthood

When the people heard these things, they said: "What

thanks shall we give to Simon and his sons? For he, and his brethren and his father's house have made themselves strong, and have chased away in fight the enemies of Israel from them, and established liberty for it."

They wrote on tablets of brass, and set them upon a pillar on mount Zion. This is the copy of the writing:

On the eighteenth day of Elul [August-September], in the one hundred and seventy-second year [141 B.C.]—that is the third year of Simon the high priest, prince of the people of God—in a great congregation of priests and people and princes of the nation and elders of the country, the following was promulgated by us. Forasmuch as oftentimes there have been wars in the country, Simon the son of Mattathias, the son of the children of Joarib, and his brethren put themselves in jeopardy, and withstood the enemies of their nation, that their sanctuary and the Law might be upheld; thus they glorified their nation with great glory. Jonathan assembled their nation together, and became their high priest and was gathered to his people.

Then their enemies determined to invade their country and stretch forth their hands against their sanctuary. Then rose up Simon and fought for his nation, and spent much of his own substance, armed the valiant men of his nation and gave them wages. He fortified the cities of Judaea and Beth Zur on the borders of Judaea, where the arms of the enemies were formerly held, and set there a garrison of Jews. He fortified Joppa which is by the sea, and Gazara which is upon the borders of Ashdod, wherein the enemies formerly dwelt; he placed Jews there, and whatsoever things were needed for the sustenance of these he put in them.

When the people saw the faith of Simon and the glory which he sought to bring to his nation, they made him their leader and high priest,[32] because he had done all these things, and because of the justice and faith which he kept to his nation, and because he sought in every manner to exalt his people. In his days things prospered in his hands, so that the heathen were taken away out of their country, as well as those that were in the city of David, in Jerusalem, who had made themselves a citadel, out of which they used to issue and pollute all things around the sanctuary, doing great hurt unto its purity. He made Jews to dwell therein and fortified it for the safety of the country and of the city, and he made high the walls of Jerusalem.

King Demetrius [of Syria] confirmed him in the high priesthood in consequence of these things, and made him one of his Friends, and treated him with great honor. For he had heard that the Jews had been proclaimed by the Romans friends and confederates and brethren, and that they had met the ambassadors of Simon honorably. And the Jews and the priests were well pleased that Simon should be their leader and high priest for ever, until a faithful prophet should arise; and that he should be a captain over them, so that he would set them over their works, and over the country, the arms or the strongholds; that he should take charge of the sanctuary, and that he should be obeyed by all, and that all contracts in the country should be written in his name; that he should be clothed in purple and wear gold; that it should not be lawful for anyone among the people or among the priests to set at nought any of these things, or to gainsay the things spoken by him, or to gather an assembly in the country without him, or that any other should be clothed in purple or wear a buckle of gold; but that whoever should do otherwise, or set at nought any of these things, should be liable to punishment.

All the people consented to ordain for Simon that it should be done according to these words. Simon accepted and consented to fill the office of high priest, to be captain and governor of the Jews and of the priests and to preside over all matters.

They commanded to put this writing on tablets of brass and to set them up within the precinct of the sanctuary in a conspicuous place; copies of this they caused to be placed in the treasury, to the end that Simon and his sons[33] might have them.

Martyrdom of the Seven Brothers
and Their Mother

FROM THE SECOND BOOK OF MACCABEES

It also came to pass that seven brothers and their mother were arrested and shamefully lashed with whips and scourges, by the king's orders, that they might be forced to taste the forbidden swine's flesh. But one of them spoke up for the others and said: "Why question us? What wouldst thou learn from us? We are prepared to die rather than transgress the laws of our fathers."

The king in his exasperation ordered pans and cauldrons to be heated, and, when they were heated immediately, ordered the tongue of the speaker to be torn out, had him scalped and mutilated before the eyes of his brothers and mother, and then had him put on the fire, all maimed and crippled as he was, but still alive, and set to fry in the pan. As the vapor from the pan spread abroad, the sons and their mother exhorted one another to die nobly, uttering these words: "The Lord God beholdeth this, and truly will have compassion on us, even as Moses declared in his Song, which testifieth against them to their face, saying, 'And he will have compassion on His servants'" (Deut. 32:36).

When the first had died after this manner, they brought the second to the shameful torture, tearing off the skin of his head with the hair and asking him: "Wilt thou eat, before we punish thy body limb by limb?" But he answered in the language of his fathers and said to them, "No." So he too underwent the rest of the torture, as the first had done. But when he was at the last gasp, he said: "Thou cursed miscreant! Thou dost dispatch us from this life, but the King of the Universe shall raise us up, who have died for His laws, and revive us to life everlasting."

After him the third was made a mocking-stock. When he was told to put out his tongue, he did so at once, stretching forth his hands courageously, with the noble words: "These I had from heaven; for His name's sake I count them naught; from Him I hope to get them back again." So much so that the king himself and his company were astounded at the spirit of the youth, for he thought nothing of his sufferings.

When he too was dead, they tortured the fourth in the same shameful fashion. When he was near his end, he said: "It is better for those who perish at men's hands to cherish hope divine that they shall be raised up by God again; but thou—thou shalt have no resurrection to life."

Next they brought the fifth and handled him shamefully. But he looked at the king and said: "Holding authority among men, thou doest what thou wilt, poor mortal; but dream not that God hath forsaken our race. Go on, and thou shalt find how His sovereign power will torment thee and thy seed!"

After him they brought the sixth. When he was at the point of death he said: "Deceive not thyself in vain! We are suffering this on our own account, for sins against our own God. That is why these awful horrors have befallen us. But think not thou shalt go unpunished for daring to fight against God."

The mother, however, was a perfect wonder; she deserves to be held in glorious memory. Thanks to her hope in God, she bravely bore the sight of seven sons dying in a single day. Full of noble spirit and nerving her weak woman's heart with the courage of a man, she exhorted each of them in the language of their fathers, saying: "How you were ever conceived in my womb, I cannot tell! It was not I who gave you the breath of life or fashioned the elements of each! It was the Creator of the Universe who fashioneth men and deviseth the generation of all things, and He it is who in mercy will restore to you the breath of life even as you now count yourselves naught for his laws' sake."

Now Antiochus [Epiphanes] felt that he was being humiliated, but overlooking the taunt of her words, he made an appeal to the youngest brother, who still survived, and even promised on oath to make him rich and happy and a Friend and a trusted official of State, if he would give up his fathers' laws. As the young man paid no attention to him, he summoned his mother and exhorted her to counsel the lad to save himself. So, after he had exhorted her at length, she agreed to persuade her son.

She leaned over to him and, jeering at the cruel tyrant, spoke thus in her fathers' tongue: "My son, have pity on me. Nine months I carried thee in my womb, three years I suckled thee; I reared thee and brought thee up to this age of thy life. My child, I beseech thee, lift thine eyes to heaven and earth, look at all that is therein, and know that God did not make them out of the things that already existed. So is the race of men created. Fear not this butcher, but show thyself worthy of thy brothers; accept thy death, that by God's mercy I may receive thee again together with thy brothers."

Ere she had finished, the young man cried: "What are you waiting for? I will not obey the king's command, I will obey the command of the law given by Moses to our fathers. But thou, who hast devised all manner of evil against the Hebrews, thou shalt not escape the hands of God. We are suffering for our own sins, and though our living Lord is angry for a little, in order to rebuke and chasten us, He will again be reconciled to His own servants. But thou, thou impious wretch, vilest of all men, be not vainly uplifted with thy proud, uncertain hopes, raising thy hand against His servants; thou hast not yet escaped the judgment of the Almighty God who seeth all. These our brothers, after enduring a brief pain, have now drunk of everflowing life, in terms of God's covenant, but thou shalt receive by God's judgment the just penalty of thine arrogance. I, like my brothers, give up body and soul for our fathers' laws, calling on God to show favor to our nation soon, and to make thee acknowledge, in torment and affliction, that He alone is God, and to let the Almighty's wrath, justly fallen on the whole of our nation, end in me and in my brothers."

Then the king fell into a fury and had him handled

worse than the others, so exasperated was he at being mocked. Thus he also died pure, trusting absolutely in the Lord. Finally, after her sons, the mother also perished.

Let this suffice for the enforced sacrifices and the excesses of barbarity.

III. The Hope for a New Age

A note on the Book of Enoch. Enoch is the early Biblical personage who "walked with God, and he was not; for God took him" (Gen. 5:24). His name, therefore, lent itself well as a title for apocalyptic writings. Our Book of Enoch is preserved mainly in an Ethiopic version, made from the Greek translation of a Hebrew (or Aramaic) original. The book—written probably in or soon after the year 95 B.C.— is a composite structure. Its several sections represent revelations accorded to Enoch on his journeys through heavenly and earthly regions.

The book deals with the origin of sin, angels and demons, the judgment of the wicked, bliss of the righteous, resurrection and future life, the Messiah (having supernatural characteristics), and the new Jerusalem. One of the sections (chapters 85 to 90) is a vision of the history of the world up to the founding of the Messianic kingdom. Enoch's notions of the kingdom, the anointed one (Messiah), the son of man, the elect one, exerted an influence on the teachings of early Christianity.

The Day of Judgment

FROM THE BOOK OF ENOCH

In those days[1] when He hath brought a grievous fire upon you,
Whither will ye flee, and where will ye find deliverance?
And when He launches forth His word against you
Will you not be affrighted and fear?
And all the luminaries shall be affrighted with great fear,
And all the earth shall be affrighted and tremble and be
      alarmed.

And all the angels shall execute their commands[2]
And shall seek to hide themselves from the presence of the
      Great Glory,
And the children of earth shall tremble and quake;
And ye sinners shall be cursed for ever,
And ye shall have no peace.
Fear ye not, ye souls of the righteous,
And be hopeful ye that have died in righteousness.
And grieve not if your soul into Sheol[3] has descended in grief,
And that in your life your body fared not according to your
      goodness,
But wait for the day of the judgment of sinners
And for the day of cursing and chastisement.
And yet when ye die the sinners speak over you:[4]
"As we die, so die the righteous,
And what benefit do they reap for their deeds?
Behold, even as we, so do they die in grief and darkness,
And what have they more than we?
From henceforth we are equal.
And what will they receive and what will they see for ever?
Behold, they too have died,
And henceforth for ever shall they see no light."

     I tell you, ye sinners, ye are content to eat and drink, and
rob and sin, and strip men naked, and acquire wealth and see
the good days. Have ye seen the righteous how their end falls
out, that no manner of violence is found in them till their
death? [The sinners answer:] "Nevertheless they perished and
became as though they had not been, and their spirits descended into Sheol in tribulation."

     Now, therefore, I swear to you, the righteous, by the glory
of the Great and Honored and Mighty One in dominion, and
by His greatness I swear to you.
I know a mystery
And have read the heavenly tablets,
And have seen the holy books,
And have found written therein and inscribed regarding them:

That all goodness and joy and glory are prepared for them,
And written down for the spirits of those who have died in
        righteousness,
And that manifold good shall be given to you in recompense
        for your labors,
And that your lot is abundantly beyond the lot of the living.
And the spirits of you who have died in righteousness shall
        live and rejoice,
And their spirits shall not perish, nor their memorial from
        before the face of the Great One
Unto all the generations of the world: wherefore no longer
        fear their contumely.

The Victory of the Righteous

FROM THE BOOK OF ENOCH

In those days a change shall take place for the holy and elect,
And the light of days shall abide upon them,
And glory and honor shall turn to the holy,
On the day of affliction on which evil shall have been treas-
        ured up against the sinners.
And the righteous shall be victorious in the name of the Lord
        of Spirits:
And He will cause the others to witness this
That they may repent
And forgo the works of their hands.
They shall have no honor through the name of the Lord of
        Spirits,
Yet through His name shall they be saved,
And the Lord of Spirits will have compassion on them,
For His compassion is great.
And He is righteous also in His judgment,
And in the presence of His glory unrighteousness also shall
        not maintain itself:
At his judgment the unrepentant shall perish before Him.

And from henceforth I will have no mercy on them, saith the
Lord of Spirits.

In those days shall the earth also give back that which has
been entrusted to it,[5]
And Sheol also shall give back that which it has received,
And hell shall give back that which it owes.
For in those days the Elect One[6] shall arise,
And he shall choose the righteous and holy from among them:
For the day has drawn nigh that they should be saved.
And the Elect One shall in those days sit on My throne,
And his mouth shall pour forth all the secrets of wisdom and
counsel:
For the Lord of Spirits hath given them to him and hath
glorified him.
And in those days shall the mountains leap like rams,
And the hills also shall skip like lambs satisfied with milk,
And the faces of all the angels in heaven shall be lighted up
with joy.
And the earth shall rejoice,
And the righteous shall dwell upon it,
And the elect shall walk thereon.

The Elect One

FROM THE BOOK OF ENOCH

For wisdom is poured out like water,
And glory faileth not before him for evermore.
For he is mighty in all the secrets of righteousness,
And unrighteousness shall disappear as a shadow,
And have no continuance;
Because the Elect One standeth before the Lord of Spirits,
And his glory is for ever and ever,
And his might unto all generations.
And in him dwells the spirit of wisdom,
And the spirit which gives insight,

And the spirit of understanding and of might,
And the spirit of those who have fallen asleep in righteousness.
And he shall judge the secret things,
And none shall be able to utter a lying word before him;
For he is the Elect One before the Lord of Spirits according to
      His good pleasure.

A New Priesthood

FROM THE TESTAMENT OF LEVI

A note on the Testaments of the Twelve Patriarchs. The Biblical narratives of the blessings given by Jacob and Moses before their deaths, the former addressing his sons (chapter 49 of Genesis), the latter the tribes of Israel (chapter 33 of Deuteronomy), became in a later period a ready framework for ethical and religious teaching. The Testaments of the Twelve Patriarchs, dating from the first pre-Christian century or the first years of the present era, lets each of the twelve sons of Jacob, before his end came, review his life and impart instruction to his descendants. In these accounts Biblical stories blend with later midrashic legends. In their ethics the Testaments view man's love for God and for his fellow-man as complementary tenets ("Love the Lord through all your life, and one another with a true heart," Testament of Dan 5:3). This love is unconditional: "If a man sin against thee, cast forth the poison of hate and speak peaceably to him, and in thy soul hold no guile" (Testament of Gad 6:3). It is universal: in the last Temple "the twelve tribes shall be gathered together and all the Gentiles" (Testament of Benjamin 9:2). In the following passage the author envisages a new, Messianic priesthood, which will replace the priesthood that had failed its office.

     The work, written in Hebrew, is preserved in Greek translation and in versions, such as the Armenian, based on the Greek. Early church writers made additions to the text.

. . . Then[7] shall the Lord raise up a new priest.
And to him all the words of the Lord shall be revealed;
And he shall execute a righteous judgment upon the earth
      for a multitude of days.
And his star shall arise in heaven as of a king,
Lighting up the light of knowledge as the sun the day,

And he shall be magnified in the world.
He shall shine forth as the sun on the earth,
And shall remove all darkness from under heaven,
And there shall be peace in all the earth.
The heavens shall exult in his days.
And the earth shall be glad,
And the clouds shall rejoice;
And the knowledge of the Lord shall be poured forth upon
the earth, as the water of the seas;
And the angels of the glory of the presence of the Lord shall
be glad in him.
The heavens shall be opened,
From the temple of glory shall come upon him sanctification,
With the Father's voice as from Abraham to Isaac.
And the glory of the Most High shall be uttered over him,
And the spirit of understanding and sanctification shall rest
upon him.
For he shall give the majesty of the Lord to His sons in truth
for evermore;
And there shall none succeed him for all generations for ever.
And in his priesthood the heathens shall be multiplied in
knowledge upon the earth,
And enlightened through the grace of the Lord:
In his priesthood shall sin come to an end,
And the lawless shall cease to do evil,
And the just shall rest in him.
And he shall open the gates of the garden of Eden,[8]
And shall remove the threatening sword against man.
And he shall give to the saints to eat from the tree of life,
And the spirit of holiness shall be on them.
Beliar[9] shall be bound by him,
And he shall give power to His children to tread upon the evil
spirits.
And the Lord shall rejoice in His children,
And be well pleased in His beloved ones for ever.
Then shall Abraham and Isaac and Jacob exult,
And I will be glad,
And all the saints shall clothe themselves with joy.

Thou Art Our King

FROM THE PSALMS OF SOLOMON

A note on the Psalms of Solomon. After initial successes, the rule of
the Hasmonean kings proved to be a failure; the great hopes attached to
Jewish kingship had not materialized. Kings Alexander Jannaeus (103–76) and
Aristobulus II (67–63) had favored the worldly, aristocratic Sadducean party
and had forsaken the Pharisees, defenders of the heritage of Israel. The quarrel about the throne of Jerusalem between the brothers Hyrcanus II and
Aristobulus II brought about the invasion of the holy city by Pompey (63
B.C.). The unknown psalmist, writing in Judaea about the middle of the first
pre-Christian century, voices the sentiments of the pious in the land. His
fervent hope is for the coming of the true—Messianic—king "to purge
Jerusalem, making it holy as of old."

The original Hebrew form of the Psalms is lost; they have been preserved in Greek translation. An ancient Syrian version was made from
Greek. The most important of the eighteen psalms is the seventeenth, here
reproduced.

O Lord, Thou art our King for ever and ever,
For in Thee, O God, doth our soul glory.
How long are the days of man's life upon the earth?
As are his days, so is the hope set upon him.
But we hope in God, our deliverer;
For the might of our God is for ever with mercy,
And the kingdom of our God is for ever over the nations in
     judgment.

Thou, O Lord, didst choose David to be king over Israel,
And swaredst to him touching his seed that never should his
     kingdom fail before Thee.
But, for our sins, sinners[10] rose up against us;
They assailed us and thrust us out;
What Thou hadst not promised to them,[11] they took away
     with violence.
They in no wise glorified Thy honorable name;

They set a [worldly] monarchy in place of that which was
     their excellency;
They laid waste the throne of David in tumultuous arrogance.

But Thou, O God, didst cast them down, and remove their
     seed from the earth,
In that there rose up against them a man that was alien to our
     race.[12]
According to their sins didst Thou recompense them, O God;
So that it befell them according to their deeds.
God showed them no pity;
He sought out their seed and let not one of them go free.
Faithful is the Lord in all His judgments
Which He doeth upon the earth.

The lawless one[13] laid waste our land so that none inhabited it,
They destroyed young and old and their children together.
In the heat of his anger he sent them away even unto the
     west,[14]
And he exposed the rulers of the land unsparingly to derision.
Being an alien the enemy acted proudly,
And his heart was alien from our God.
And all . . . Jerusalem,
As also the nations . . .
And the children of the covenant in the midst of the mingled
     peoples . . .
There was not among them one that wrought in the midst of
     Jerusalem mercy and truth.
They that loved the assemblies of the pious[15] fled from them,
As sparrows that fly from their nest.
They wandered in deserts that their lives might be saved from
     harm,
And precious in the eyes of them that lived abroad was any
     that escaped alive from them.
Over the whole earth were they scattered by lawless men.
Therefore the heavens withheld the rain from dropping upon
     the earth,
Springs were stopped that sprang perennially out of the deeps,
     that ran down from lofty mountains.

For there was none among them that wrought righteousness
    and justice;
From the chief of them to the least of them all were sinful;
The king was a transgressor, and the judge disobedient, and
    the people sinful.

Behold, O Lord, and raise up unto them their king, the son of
    David,[16]
At the time in the which Thou seest, O God, that he may
    reign over Israel Thy servant.
And gird him with strength, that he may shatter unrighteous
    rulers,
And that he may purge Jerusalem from nations that trample
    her down to destruction.
Wisely, righteously he shall thrust out sinners from the in-
    heritance,
He shall destroy the pride of the sinner as a potter's vessel.
With a rod of iron he shall break in pieces all their substance,
He shall destroy the godless nations with the word of his
    mouth;
At his rebuke nations shall flee before him,
And he shall reprove sinners for the thoughts of their heart.

And he shall gather together a holy people, whom he shall
    lead in righteousness,
And he shall judge the tribes of the people that has been sanc-
    tified by the Lord his God.
And he shall not suffer unrighteousness to lodge any more in
    their midst,
Nor shall there dwell with them any man that knoweth wick-
    edness,
For he shall know them, that they are all sons of their God.
And he shall divide them according to their tribes upon the
    land,
And neither sojourner nor alien shall sojourn with them any
    more.
He shall judge peoples and nations in the wisdom of his right-
    eousness. Selah.

And he shall have the heathen nations to serve him under his
      yoke;
And he shall glorify the Lord in a place to be seen of all the
      earth;
And he shall purge Jerusalem, making it holy as of old:
So that nations shall come from the ends of the earth to see
      his glory,
Bringing as gifts her sons who had fainted,
And to see the glory of the Lord, wherewith God hath glori-
      fied her.
And he shall be a righteous king, taught of God, over them,
And there shall be no unrighteousness in his days in their
      midst,
For all shall be holy and their king the anointed of the Lord.
For he shall not put his trust in horse and rider and bow,
Nor shall he multiply for himself gold and silver for war,
Nor shall he gather confidence from a multitude for the day
      of battle.
The Lord Himself is his king, the hope of him that is mighty
      through his hope in God.

All nations shall be in fear before him,
For he will smite the earth with the word of his mouth for
      ever.
He will bless the people of the Lord with wisdom and glad-
      ness,
And he himself will be pure from sin, so that he may rule a
      great people.
He will rebuke rulers, and remove sinners by the might of his
      word;
And relying upon his God, throughout his days he will not
      stumble;
For God will make him mighty by means of His holy spirit,
And wise by means of the spirit of understanding, with
      strength and righteousness.
And the blessing of the Lord will be with him: he will be
      strong and stumble not;

His hope will be in the Lord: who then can prevail against
  him?
He will be mighty in his works, and strong in the fear of God,
He will be shepherding the flock of the Lord faithfully and
  righteously,
And will suffer none among them to stumble in their pasture.
He will lead them all aright,
And there will be no pride among them that any among them
  should be oppressed.
This will be the majesty of the king of Israel whom God
  knoweth;
He will raise him up over the house of Israel to correct him.
His words shall be more refined than costly gold, the choicest;
In the assemblies he will judge the peoples, the tribes of the
  sanctified.
His words shall be like the words of the holy ones in the midst
  of sanctified peoples.
Blessed be they that shall be in those days,
In that they shall see the good fortune of Israel which God
  shall bring to pass in the gathering together of the
  tribes.
May the Lord hasten His mercy upon Israel!
May He deliver us from the uncleanness of unholy enemies!
The Lord Himself is our king for ever and ever.

IV. Sectarian Brotherhoods

The Rules of the Dead Sea, or Qumran, Brotherhood

FROM THE MANUAL OF DISCIPLINE

A note on the Dead Sea Manual of Discipline. This document, which introduces us to some of the beliefs and practices of the Dead Sea Brotherhood, is so far the most significant historically of the scrolls which began to be discovered in 1947. Qumran, one of the chief seats of the sect, was situated at the northern end of the western shore of the Dead Sea. The sect, which is either identical with the brotherhood of the Essenes (known to us from the accounts of Philo, Josephus and Pliny the Elder) or closely related to it, flourished from the second half of the second pre-Christian century to the time of the Judaeo-Roman war in A.D. 68.

Among the reasons that led to the exodus of this "remnant" of the faithful from the centers of Judaea and to the formation of the desert brotherhood were: the protest against the worldly character of the Hasmonean kingdom and the priesthood; differences in calendar calculation; the determination to establish a true community of brethren, to lead a life dedicated to purity of body and soul, observance of the law, community of goods, continuous study, obedience to authority, and the preparation for the Day of Judgment which would bring the victory of the "sons of light" over the "sons of darkness." Rigid laws regulated the admittance of new members and the details of life in the community.

The manuscript of the Manual (known also as Rule of the Community) consists of eleven columns. The prose text of the order of the brotherhood is followed (on columns X-XI) by a closing hymn, a statement of the sect's religious beliefs and a fair example of its poetic style.

Social relations

Now this is the practice of the men of the Community

who dedicate themselves to turn from all evil and to hold firmly to all that He commanded according to His good pleasure: to separate themselves from the congregation of perverse men, to become a Community in Torah and in property, answering [their legal questions] according to the sons of Zadok,[1] the priests who keep the covenant, and according to the majority[2] of the men of the Community who hold firmly to the covenant.

According to their judgment the divinely guided decision is reached with regard to every matter, whether Torah, or property, or laws, to practice truth, unity and humility, righteousness, and justice, and loving devotion, and walking humbly in all their ways, in which none shall walk in the stubbornness of his heart to go astray after his own heart and his own eyes and his own impulsive desire; but EAM[3] is to circumcise in the Community the uncircumcision of desire and the stiff neck, to lay a foundation of truth for Israel (for the Community of eternal covenant), to atone for all those who dedicate themselves for holiness among Aaron and for a house of truth in Israel and for those who join them for Community, and for suit, and for judgment, so as to convict all transgressors of ordinances.

The oath of admission

Now these are to direct their ways according to all these ordinances:

When they are admitted into the Community: everyone who enters into the council of the Community, shall enter into the covenant of God in the sight of all the dedicated ones. Then he shall take a binding oath to return to the Torah of Moses according to all that he commanded, with wholeness of heart and wholeness of soul towards all that is revealed of it to [or, for] the Sons of Zadok, the priests who keep the covenant and who seek His good pleasure, and to [or, for] the majority of the men of their covenant who communally dedicate themselves to His truth and to walking in His good pleasure.

He shall further bind himself by a covenant to separate

himself from all perverse men who walk in the way of wickedness. For these are not reckoned in His covenant, for they have not sought or inquired after Him in His ordinances to know the unconscious sins into which they have strayed incurring guilt; while the conscious sins they have done wilfully, with the result that they raise up anger unto judgment and unto the exacting of vengeance through the curses of the covenant, bringing upon themselves the great judgments unto an eternal destruction without remnant.

Separation from the wicked

These may not enter into water to [be permitted to] touch the Purity of the holy men,[4] for they will not be cleansed unless they have turned from their wickedness, for uncleanness clings to all transgressors of His word. He [who enters the covenant must] further [swear that he will] not unite with a [perverse] man in his labor and in his property, lest he cause him to incur guilt of transgression; for he must keep far from him in every matter, for thus it is written: "Thou shalt keep far from every false matter" (Exod. 23:7).

And further, no man of the men of the community may answer [legal questions] according to their opinion in regard to any teaching or laws. Moreover, he may not eat anything of theirs, nor drink, nor take from their hand anything whatsoever except for a price, as it is written:

"Cease ye from man whose breath is in his nostrils,
For of what value is he to be reckoned?" Isa. 2:22).

For all who are not reckoned in His covenant are to be separated, both they and all they have; and the holy men may not rely upon any of the deeds of vanity. For vain are all who do not recognize His covenant; and all who despise His word He will destroy from the world, since all their deeds are uncleanness before Him and uncleanness is in all their property.

The examination of those entering the community

Now, when he [the neophyte] enters into the covenant to do according to all these ordinances, to be united to a holy congregation, they shall examine his spirit in the Community between a man and his fellow with respect to his understanding and his deeds in Torah, in accordance with the views of the sons of Aaron who are dedicated unitedly to establish His covenant and to administer all His ordinances which He commanded [them] to do, and in accordance with the views of the majority of Israel[5] who are dedicated to turn unitedly to His covenant.

Then one shall enroll them in order, each before his fellow, according to his understanding and his deeds, that they all may obey each his fellow, the lesser the greater; and they shall examine their spirit and their deeds, year by year to promote each according to his understanding and the perfection of his way, or to retard him according to his perversions, that each may reprove his fellow in truth and humility and loving devotion to each other.

Complaints and accusations

One shall not speak to his brother in anger, or in complaint, or with a [stiff] neck, or a wicked spirit; nor shall he hate him [in the uncircumcision] of his heart—though he shall reprove him on the very day so as not to incur guilt because of him. Indeed, a man shall not bring accusation against his fellow in the presence of the Many[6] who has not been subject to [previous] reproof before witnesses.

The common life

In these [regulations] let them walk in all their dwellings, everyone who is present, each with his fellow. The lesser shall obey the greater, in regard to goods and means. They shall eat communally, and bless communally, and take counsel communally; and in every place where there are ten men of the council of the Community, there shall not cease from among them a man who is priest. And let each one according to his assigned position sit before him; and in that order let them be asked for their counsel with regard to every matter.

And it shall be when they arrange the table to eat, or

[arrange] the wine to drink, the priest shall first stretch out his hand to invoke a benediction with the first of the bread and the wine. And in whatever place the ten are, there shall not cease to be a man who expounds the Torah day and night continually, [expounding] in turns each to his fellow. And let the Many keep awake in Community a third of all the nights of the year in order to read aloud from the Book and to expound laws and to bless in Community.

The Supreme Council

In the Council of the Community [there shall be] twelve laymen and three priests who are perfect in all that is revealed of the whole Torah, through practicing truth and righteousness and justice and loving devotion and walking humbly each with his fellow in order to maintain faithfulness in the land with a steadfast intent and with a broken spirit, and to expiate iniquity through practicing justice and [through] the anguish of the refining furnace, and to walk with all in the measure of truth and in the proper reckoning of the time.

The community during the eschatological period

When these things came to pass in Israel, the Council of the Community will have been established in truth:

As an eternal planting, a holy house for Israel,
A most holy institution of Aaron,
True witnesses with regard to judgment,[7]
And the chosen of divine acceptance to atone for the earth,
And to render to the wicked their desert.
That is the tried wall, the costly corner bulwark,
Whose foundations shall not be shaken asunder,
Nor be dislodged from their place!

A most holy abode belongs to Aaron in the knowledge of them all that they may be a covenant of religion and offer up an agreeable odor; and a house of perfection and truth is in Israel to establish a covenant with eternal ordinances. These will be acceptable to make atonement for the earth and to

decree the condemnation of wickedness that there may be
no more perversity.

The separate life and the going to the wilderness

When these [men] have become established in the institution of the Community for two years' time in perfection
of way, they shall separate themselves as holy [or, as a sanctu-
ary] within the council of the men of the Community; and
every matter which was hidden from Israel and is found by a
man who searches [studies], let him not hide it from these out
of fear of an apostate spirit.

Now when these things come to pass in Israel to the
Community, according to these rules, they will separate themselves from the midst of the habitation of perverse men to go
to the wilderness to clear there the way of God,[8] as it is
written:

In the wilderness clear the way of [the Lord];[9]

Level in the desert a highway for our God (Isa. 40:3):[10]
that [means] studying the Torah which He commanded
through Moses, so as to do according to all that was revealed
time after time and according to that which the prophets revealed through His Holy Spirit.

Temporary exclusion

As for anyone of the men of the Community, [in] the
covenant of the Community, who wilfully removes a word
from all that He commanded, he shall not touch the Purity of
the holy men; nor shall he have any knowledge of any of their
counsel, until his deeds are purified from every kind of perversity that he may walk in perfection of way. Then he shall be
admitted to the Council according to the judgment of the
Many; and afterward he shall be enrolled in his assigned position; and according to this law shall it be for every one who
joins the Community.

From the Source of His Knowledge: A Psalm

FROM THE MANUAL OF DISCIPLINE

With thanksgiving I will open my mouth,
the righteous acts of God shall my tongue recount always
and the faithlessness of men until their transgression is
     complete.
Empty words I will banish from my lips,
unclean things and perversions from the knowledge of my
     mind.
With wise counsel I will conceal knowledge,[11]
and with knowing prudence I will hedge about wisdom
with a firm limit, to preserve fidelity
and strong justice according to the righteousness of God.
I will exalt the decree with the measuring-line of times,
and will teach the practice of righteousness,
loyal love for the humble,
and strengthening of hands for the fearful of heart;
for the erring in spirit understanding;
to instruct the fainting with doctrine,
to answer humbly before the haughty of spirit,
and with a broken spirit to men of injustice,
who point the finger and speak wickedly
and are envious of wealth.

But as for me, my judgment belongs to God,
and in His hand is the blamelessness of my conduct
together with the uprightness of my heart;
and in His righteousness my transgression will be wiped out.
For from the source of His knowledge He has opened up my
     light;
my eye has gazed into His wonders
and the light of my heart penetrates the mystery that is to be.
That which is eternal is the staff of my right hand;
on a strong rock is the way I tread;

before nothing will it be shaken.
For the faithfulness of God is the rock I tread,
and His strength is the staff of my right hand.
From the source of His righteousness is my judgment.
A light is in my heart from His marvelous mysteries;
my eye has gazed on that which is eternal,
sound wisdom which is hidden from the man of knowledge,
and prudent discretion from the sons of man,
a source of righteousness and reservoir of strength
together with a spring of glory hidden from the company of
  flesh.
To those whom God has chosen He has given them for an
  eternal possession;
He has given them an inheritance in the lot of the holy ones
and with the sons of heaven has associated their company
for a council of unity and a company of a holy building,
for an eternal planting
through every period that is to be.

But I belong to wicked mankind,
to the company of erring flesh;
my iniquities, my transgression, my sin,
with the iniquity of my heart
belong to the company of worms and those who walk in
  darkness.

For the way of a man is not his own,
a man does not direct his own steps;
for judgment is God's
and from His hand is blamelessness of conduct.
By His knowledge everything comes to pass
and everything that is He establishes by His purpose;
and without Him nothing is done.

As for me, if I slip,
the steadfast love of God is my salvation forever;
and if I stumble in the iniquity of flesh,
my vindication in the righteousness of God will stand to
  eternity.

If He lets loose my distress,
from the pit He will deliver my soul;
He will direct my steps to the way.

In His mercy He has brought me near,
And in His righteousness He will cleanse me from the im-
        purity of man,
from the sin of the sons of man.
Thanks be to God for His righteousness,
to the Most High for His majesty!

Hymns of the Dead Sea Brotherhood

FROM THE THANKSGIVING HYMNS

Among the manuscripts found in the caves where the Dead Sea Brotherhood deposited its literary treasures are some thirty-five chapters and numerous
fragments of Hymns. In them the unknown poet gives utterance to his faith.
He thanks his Lord for protecting him from his adversaries, for "illumining
his face," and for having chosen him for the task of interpreting the knowledge
of "wondrous mysteries." Man sins, but God's steadfast love "redeems the
soul of the poor." E. L. Sukenik, one of the first interpreters of the Dead
Sea scrolls, and his son Yigael Yadin suggested that the writer of the Hymns
is none other than the leader of the Brotherhood, the "Teacher of Righteousness."

Streams in dry ground

I thank Thee, O Lord, because Thou hast put me
at a source of flowing streams in dry ground,
a spring of water in a land of drought,
channels watering a garden of delight,
a place of cedar and acacia,
together with pine for Thy glory,
trees of life in a fount of mystery,
hidden amid all trees that drink water.
They shall put forth a branch for an eternal planting,
taking root before they sprout.

They shall send out their roots to the stream;
its stump shall be exposed to the living water;
and it shall become an eternal source.
When there is a branch on it,
all the beasts of the forest will feed on it;
its stump will be trampled by all that pass by,
its branches by every winged bird;
and all the springs of water shall rise against it.
For in their planting they go astray,
and do not send out a root to the stream.
But he who causes a holy branch
to sprout for a planting of truth
is hiding his mystery, without its being thought of;
without its being known, he is sealing it up.
And Thou, O God, hast put a hedge about its fruit
in the mystery of mighty men of valor and holy spirits;
and a flame of fire turning every way.

They seek Thee with a double heart

I thank Thee, O Lord,
for Thou hast enlightened my face for Thy covenant. . . .
I shall seek Thee . . .
As the perfect dawn Thou shinest upon me.
But they . . . have made smooth their words
false phrases . . .
Distraught without understanding,
they have turned their deeds to folly,
    . . . for they have become loathsome to themselves.
When Thou dost work mightily in me, they do not regard me,
but drive me from my land like a bird from its nest,
and all my neighbors and friends are driven far from me;
they have regarded me as a broken vessel.

They are interpreters of lies and seers of deceit;
they devised baseness against me,
exchanging Thy law, which Thou didst cut into my heart,
for smooth things for Thy people.
They withheld the draught of knowledge from the thirsty,

and for their thirst made them drink vinegar;
so that God beheld their error,
going mad at their feasts,
being caught in their nets.

But Thou, O God, dost despise every purpose of Belial;[12]
it is Thy counsel that will stand,
and the purpose of Thy heart that is established forever.
But they are hapless, they plan devices of Belial;
they seek Thee with a double heart,
and are not established in Thy truth.
A root bearing poisonous and bitter fruit is in their plans,
and with the stubbornness of their hearts they go about.
They have sought Thee among idols,
and have set the stumbling block of their iniquity before their
        faces.
They have come to seek Thee
following the directions of false prophets, enticed by error.
Then, with strange lips
and an alien tongue they speak to Thy people,
making foolish by deceit all their works.
For they did not heed Thy instruction;
they did not listen to Thy word;
for they said of the vision of knowledge, "It is not right,"
and of the way of Thy heart, "It is not that."

But Thou, O God, wilt answer them,
judging them in Thy power
according to their idols and their many transgressions,
that they may be caught in their own plans,
in which they are estranged from Thy covenant.
Thou wilt cut off in judgment all men of deceit,
and seers of error will be found no more;
for there is no foolishness in all Thy works
or deceit in the devices of Thy heart.
Those who please Thee will stand before Thee forever;
those who walk in the way of Thy heart will be established
        to eternity.

As for me, while leaning upon Thee
I will rise and stand up against those who despise me,
and my hand will be against all who scorn me;
for they do not regard me,
though Thou didst work mightily in me
and didst appear to me in Thy strength to enlighten them;
Thou didst not plaster with shame
the faces of all those who consulted me,
who assembled for Thy covenant and heard me,
those who walk in the way of Thy heart
and present themselves to Thee in the company of the holy
          ones.
Thou wilt bring forth their judgment forever,
and truth with equity.
Thou wilt not mislead them by the hand of the hapless,
according to their plotting against them;
but wilt put the fear of them on Thy people,
a shattering for all the peoples of the lands,
to cut off in judgment all transgressors of Thy words.

Through me Thou hast enlightened the faces of many,
and hast made them strong until they were numberless;
for Thou hast given me knowledge of Thy wondrous mysteries,
and in Thy wondrous company Thou hast wrought powerfully
          with me;
Thou hast wrought wondrously in the presence of many,
for the sake of Thy glory
and to make known to all the living Thy mighty works.

Who that is flesh could do aught like this,
what thing formed of clay could do such wonders?
For man lives in iniquity from the womb,
and in faithless guilt to old age.
I know that righteousness does not belong to a man,
nor to a son of man blamelessness of conduct;
to the Most High God belong all works of righteousness.
A man's way is not established
except by the spirit which God created for him,
to make blameless a way for the sons of man,

that they may know all His works
in the might of His power and the greatness of His mercy
to all the sons of His good pleasure.

As for me, shaking and trembling have seized me,
and all my bones are broken;
my heart melts like wax before the fire,
and my knees go like water falling on a slope.
For I remember my guilty deeds,
together with the faithlessness of my fathers,
when the wicked rose against Thy covenant,
the hapless against Thy word.
Then I said, " For my transgression
I am left outside of Thy covenant."
But when I remembered the strength of Thy hand,
together with the abundance of Thy mercy,
I rose and stood up, and my spirit became strong,
standing firm before affliction;
for I leaned on Thy steadfast love
and Thy abundant mercy.

The Order of The Essenes

FROM PHILO: EVERY GOOD MAN IS FREE

In Philo of Alexandria (*ca.* 30 B.C.–A.D. 40) Hebraic (Biblical and early rabbinic) traditions and Greek critical philosophy, revelation and reason, meet and merge. In his ingeniously constructed integration of the two sources of truth, Philo, as H. A. Wolfson has demonstrated, laid the foundation for the entire realm of medieval European philosophy. The theology of Origen, Augustine and Thomas Aquinas is built upon Philo's reading of Plato in the light of Biblical faith.

In one of his minor works, *Every Good Man Is Free* (*Quod omnis probus liber sit*), written in his youth, Philo expounded the Stoic doctrine that the wise man alone is free, for true freedom and independence consist in "following God." Among the examples for his thesis, Philo cites the order of the Essenes and offers a description of their way of life.

For other accounts of the Essenes, see Flavius Josephus, *The Jewish War*, Book II, chapter 8, and the Manual of Discipline of the Dead Sea Brotherhood, which is identical with, or closely related to, the Essenes.

Introduction

Palestinian Syria, too, has not failed to produce high moral excellence. In this country live a considerable part of the very populous nation of the Jews, including as it is said, certain persons, more than four thousand in number, called the Essenes. Their name which is, I think, a variation, though the form of the Greek is inexact, of *hosiotes* (holiness), is given them, because they have shown themselves especially devout in the service of God, not by offering sacrifices of animals, but by resolving to sanctify the minds.

Ways of life

The first thing about these people is that they live in villages and avoid the cities because of the iniquities which have become inveterate among city dwellers, for they know that their company would have a deadly effect upon their own souls, like a disease brought by a pestilential atmosphere. Some of them labor on the land and others pursue such crafts as cooperate with peace and so benefit themselves and their neighbors. They do not hoard gold and silver or acquire great slices of land because they desire the revenues therefrom, but provide what is needed for the necessary requirements of life.

For while they stand almost alone in the whole of mankind in that they have become moneyless and landless by deliberate action rather than by lack of good fortune, they are esteemed exceedingly rich, because they judge frugality with contentment to be, as indeed it is, an abundance of wealth. As for darts, javelins, daggers, or the helmet, breastplate or shield, you could not find a single manufacturer of them, nor, in general, any person making weapons or engines or plying any industry concerned with war, nor, indeed, any of the peaceful kind, which easily lapse into vice, for they have not the vaguest idea of commerce either wholesale or retail or

marine, but pack the inducements to covetousness off in disgrace.

No slavery

Not a single slave is to be found among them, but all are
free, exchanging services with each other, and they denounce
the owners of slaves, not merely for their injustice in outraging
the law of equality, but also for their impiety in annulling the
statute of Nature, who mother-like has born and reared all
men alike, and created them genuine brothers, not in mere
name, but in very reality, though this kinship has been put to
confusion by the triumph of malignant covetousness, which
has wrought estrangement instead of affinity and enmity instead of friendship.

Teachings

As for philosophy they abandon the logical part to quib-
bling verbalists as unnecessary for the acquisition of virtue,
and the physical to visionary praters as beyond the grasp of
human nature, only retaining that part which treats philosophically of the existence of God and the creation of the
universe. But the ethical part they study very industriously,
taking for their trainers the laws of their fathers, which could
not possibly have been conceived by the human soul without
divine inspiration.

The Sabbath

In these they are instructed at all other times, but particularly on the seventh days. For that day has been set apart
to be kept holy and on it they abstain from all other work and
proceed to sacred spots which they call synagogues. There,
arranged in rows according to their ages, the younger below
the elder, they sit decorously as befits the occasion with attentive ears. Then one takes the books and reads aloud and
another of especial proficiency comes forward and expounds
what is not understood. For most of their philosophical study
takes the form of allegory, and in this they emulate the tradi-

tion of the past. They are trained in piety, holiness, justice, domestic and civic conduct, knowledge of what is truly good, or evil, or indifferent, and how to choose what they should and avoid the opposite, taking for their defining standards these three, love of God, love of virtue, love of men.

Love of God and man

Their love of God they show by a multitude of proofs, by religious purity[13] constant and unbroken throughout their lives, by abstinence from oaths, by veracity, by their belief that the Godhead is the cause of all good things and nothing bad; their love of virtue, by their freedom from the love of money or reputation or pleasure, by self-mastery and endurance, again by frugality, simple living, contentment, humility, respect for law, steadiness and all similar qualities; their love of men by benevolence and sense of equality, and their spirit of fellowship, which defies description, though a few words on it will not be out of place. First of all then no one's house is his own in the sense that it is not shared by all, for besides the fact that they dwell together in communities, the door is open to visitors from elsewhere who share their convictions.

Community of goods

Again they all have a single treasury and common disbursements; their clothes are held in common and also their food through their institutions of public meals. In no other community can we find the custom of sharing roof, life and board more firmly established in actual practice. And that is no more than one would expect. For all the wages which they earn in the day's work they do not keep as their private property, but throw them into the common stock and allow the benefit thus accruing to be shared by those who wish to use it. The sick are not neglected because they cannot provide anything, but have the cost of their treatment lying ready in the common stock, so that they can meet expenses out of the greater wealth in full security. To the elder men too is given the respect and care which real children give to their parents, and they receive from countless hands and minds a full and generous maintenance for their latter years.

Athletes of virtue

Such are the athletes of virtue produced by a philosophy free from the pedantry of Greek wordiness, a philosophy which sets its pupils to practise themselves in laudable actions, by which the liberty which can never be enslaved is firmly established. Here we have a proof. Many are the potentates who at various occasions have raised themselves to power over the country. They differed both in nature and the line of conduct which they followed. Some of them carried their zest for outdoing wild beasts in ferocity to the point of savagery. They left no form of cruelty untried. They slaughtered their subjects wholesale, or like cooks carved them piecemeal and limb by limb whilst still alive, and did not stay their hands till justice who surveys human affairs visited them with the same calamities. Others transformed this wild frenzy into another kind of viciousness. Their conduct showed intense bitterness, but they talked with calmness, though the mask of their milder language failed to conceal their rancorous disposition. They fawned like venomous hounds yet wrought evils irremediable and left behind them throughout the cities the unforgettable sufferings of their victims as monuments of their impiety and inhumanity. Yet none of these, neither the extremely ferocious nor the deep-dyed treacherous dissemblers, were able to lay a charge against this congregation of Essenes or holy ones here described. Unable to resist the high excellence of these people, they all treated them as self-governing and freemen by nature and extolled their communal meals and that ineffable sense of fellowship, which is the clearest evidence of a perfect and supremely happy life.

The Sect of the Therapeutae

FROM PHILO: ON THE CONTEMPLATIVE LIFE

Philo of Alexandria presented the Essenes as pursuing the "active life" within their brotherhoods. In his treatise On the Contemplative Life (*De vita contemplativa*) he describes a sect of Jewish hermits, men and women, settled on Lake Mareotis in the neighborhood of Alexandria, in Egypt, who follow a "life of contemplation," completely renouncing the world. Philo maintains that other such ascetic settlements existed "in many places in the inhabited world," but there is no evidence for this fact. The church historian Eusebius of Caesarea (third to fourth centuries) believed the Therapeutae to have been a society of early Christian monks. This assumption is historically erroneous; the sect adhered to the laws and institutions of Judaism. But the interest of the Church in this religious retreat helped to preserve Philo's treatise.

Introduction

[14]. . . By sight I do not mean the sight of the body but of the soul, the sight which alone gives a knowledge of truth and falsehood. But it is well that the Therapeutae, a people always taught from the first to use their sight, should desire the vision of the Existent and soar above the sun of our senses and never leave their place in this company which carries them on to perfect happiness. And those who set themselves to this service, not just following custom nor on the advice and admonition of others but carried away by a heaven-sent passion of love, remain rapt and possessed like bacchanals or Corybants until they see the object of their yearning.

Then such is their longing for the deathless and blessed life that thinking their mortal life already ended they abandon their property to their sons or daughters or to other kinsfolk, thus voluntarily advancing the time of their inheritance, while those who have no kinsfolk give them to comrades and friends. For it was right that those who have received ready to their hand the wealth that has eyes to see should surrender, the blind wealth to those who are still blind in mind. [. . .]

Community

So when they have divested themselves of their possessions and have no longer aught to ensnare them they flee
without a backward glance and leave their brothers, their
children, their wives, their parents, the wide circle of their
kinsfolk, the groups of friends around them, the fatherlands
in which they were born and reared, since strong is the attraction of familiarity and very great its power to ensnare. And
they do not migrate into another city like the unfortunate or
worthless slaves who demand to be sold by their owners and
so procure a change of masters but not freedom. For every
city, even the best governed, is full of turmoils and disturb-
ances innumerable which no one could endure who has ever
been even once under the guidance of wisdom. Instead of this
they pass their days outside the walls pursuing solitude in
gardens or lonely bits of country, not from any acquired habit
of misanthropical bitterness but because they know how unprofitable and mischievous are associations with persons of
dissimilar character.

This kind exists in many places in the inhabited world,
for perfect goodness must needs be shared both by Greeks and
the world outside Greece, but it abounds in Egypt in each of
the nomes as they are called and especially round Alexandria.
But the best of these votaries journey from every side to settle
in a certain very suitable place which they regard as their
fatherland. This place is situated above the Mareotic Lake on
a somewhat low-lying hill very happily placed both because
of its security and the pleasantly tempered air. The safety is
secured by the farm buildings and villages round about and
the pleasantness of the air by the continuous breezes which
arise both from the lake which debouches into the sea and
from the open sea hard by. For the sea breezes are light, the
lake breezes close and the two combining together produce a
most healthy condition of climate.

The houses of the society thus collected are exceedingly
simple, providing protection against two of the most pressing
dangers, the fiery heat of the sun and the icy cold of the air.

They are neither near together as in towns, since living at close quarters is troublesome and displeasing to people who are seeking to satisfy their desire for solitude, nor yet at a great distance because of the sense of fellowship which they cherish, and to render help to each other if robbers attack them.

Sanctuary

In each house there is a consecrated room which is called a sanctuary or closet and closeted in this they are initiated into the mysteries of the sanctified life. They take nothing into it, either drink or food or any other of the things necessary for the needs of the body, but laws and oracles delivered through the mouth of prophets, and psalms and anything else which fosters and perfects knowledge and piety. They keep the memory of God alive and never forget it, so that even in their dreams the picture is nothing else but the loveliness of divine excellences and powers. Indeed many when asleep and dreaming give utterance to the glorious verities of their holy philosophy.

Prayer and readings

Twice every day they pray, at dawn and at eventide; at sunrise they pray for a fine, bright day, fine and bright in the true sense of the heavenly daylight which they pray may fill their minds. At sunset they ask that the soul may be wholly relieved from the press of the senses and the objects of sense and sitting where she is consistory and council chamber to herself pursue the quest of truth. The interval between early morning and evening is spent entirely in spiritual exercise. They read the Holy Scriptures and seek wisdom from their ancestral philosophy by taking it as an allegory, since they think that the words of the literal text are symbols of something whose hidden nature is revealed by studying the underlying meaning.

They have also writings of men of old, the founders of their way of thinking, who left many memorials of the form used in allegorical interpretation and these they take as a kind of archetype and imitate the method in which this principle is carried out. And so they do not confine themselves to contemplation but also compose hymns and psalms to God in all sorts of metres and melodies which they write down with the rhythms necessarily made more solemn.

The Sabbath

For six days they seek wisdom by themselves in solitude in the closets mentioned above, never passing the outside door of the house or even getting a distant view of it. But every seventh day they meet together as for a general assembly and sit in order according to their age in the proper attitude, with their hands inside the robe, the right hand between the breast and the chin and the left withdrawn along the flank. Then the senior among them who also has the fullest knowledge of the doctrines which they profess comes forward and with visage and voice alike quiet and composed gives a well-reasoned and wise discourse. He does not make an exhibition of clever rhetoric like the orators or sophists of today but follows careful examination by careful expression of the exact meaning of the thoughts, and this does not lodge just outside the ears of the audience but passes through the hearing into the soul and there stays securely. All the others sit still and listen showing their approval merely by their looks or nods.

This common sanctuary in which they meet every seventh day is a double enclosure, one portion set apart for the use of the men, the other for the women. For women too regularly make part of the audience with the same ardor and the same sense of their calling. The wall between the two chambers rises up from the ground to three or four cubits built in the form of a breastwork, while the space above up to the roof is left open. This arrangement serves two purposes; the modesty becoming to the female sex is preserved, while the women sitting within earshot can easily follow what is said since there is nothing to obstruct the voice of the speaker.

Daily life

They lay self-control to be as it were the foundation of

their soul and on it build the other virtues. None of them would put food or drink to his lips before sunset since they hold that philosophy finds its right place in the light, the needs of the body in the darkness, and therefore they assign the day to the one and some small part of the night to the other. Some in whom the desire for studying wisdom is more deeply implanted even only after three days remember to take food. Others so luxuriate and delight in the banquet of truths which wisdom richly and lavishly supplies that they hold out for twice that time and only after six days do they bring themselves to taste such sustenance as is absolutely necessary.

They have become habituated to abstinence like the grasshoppers who are said to live on air[15] because, I suppose, their singing makes their lack of food a light matter. But to the seventh day as they consider it to be sacred and festal in the highest degree they have awarded special privileges as its due, and on it after providing for the soul refresh the body also, which they do as a matter of course with the cattle too by releasing them from their continuous labor. Still they eat nothing costly, only common bread with salt for a relish flavored further by the daintier with hyssop, and their drink is spring water. For as nature has set hunger and thirst as mistresses over mortal kind they propitiate them without using anything to curry favor but only such things as are actually needed and without which life cannot be maintained. Therefore they eat enough to keep from hunger and drink enough to keep from thirst but abhor surfeiting as a malignant enemy both to soul and body.

As for the two forms of shelter, clothes and housing, we have already said that the house is unembellished and a makeshift constructed for utility only. Their clothing likewise is the most inexpensive, enough to protect them against extreme cold and heat, a thick coat of shaggy skin in winter and in summer a vest or linen shirt. For they practise an all-round simplicity knowing that its opposite, vanity, is the source of falsehood as simplicity is of truth, and that both play the part of a fountainhead of other things, since from falsehood flow the manifold forms of evil and from truth abundant streams of goodness both human and divine. [. . .]

Festal meetings

I will [now] describe the festal meetings of those who have dedicated their own life and themselves to knowledge and the contemplation of the verities of nature, following the truly sacred instructions of the prophet Moses [. . .].

They assemble, white-robed and with faces in which cheerfulness is combined with the utmost seriousness, but before they recline, at a signal from a member of the Rota,[16] which is the name commonly given to those who perform these services, they take their stand in a regular line in an orderly way, their eyes and hands lifted up to heaven, eyes because they have been trained to fix their gaze on things worthy of contemplation, hands in token that they are clean from gain taking and not defiled through any cause of the profit-making kind. So standing they pray to God that their feasting may be acceptable and proceed as He would have it.

After the prayers the seniors recline according to the order of their admission, since by senior they do not understand the aged and grey headed who are regarded as still mere children if they have only in late years come to love this rule of life, but those who from their earliest years have grown to manhood and spent their prime in pursuing the contemplative branch of philosophy, which indeed is the noblest and most godlike part. The feast is shared by women also, most of them aged virgins, who have kept their chastity not under compulsion, like some of the Greek priestesses, but of their own free will in their ardent yearning for wisdom. Eager to have her for their life mate, they have spurned the pleasures of the body and desire no mortal offspring but those immortal children which only the soul that is dear to God can bring to the birth unaided[17] because the Father has sown in her spiritual rays enabling her to behold the verities of wisdom.

The order of reclining is so apportioned that the men sit by themselves on the right and the women by themselves on the left. Perhaps it may be thought that couches though not costly still of a softer kind would have been provided for people of good birth and high character and trained practice in philosophy. Actually they are plank beds of the common kinds of wood, covered with quite cheap strewings of native papyrus, raised slightly at the arms to give something to lean on.

For while they mitigate somewhat the harsh austerity of Sparta, they always and everywhere practice a frugal contentment worthy of the free, and oppose with might and main the love-lures of pleasure. They do not have slaves to wait upon them as they consider that the ownership of servants is entirely against nature. For nature has borne all men to be free, but the wrongful and covetous acts of some who pursued that source of evil, inequality, have imposed their yoke and invested the stronger with power over the weaker.

In this sacred banquet there is, as I have said, no slave, but the services are rendered by free men who perform their tasks as attendants not under compulsion nor yet waiting for orders, but with deliberate good will anticipating eagerly and zealously the demands that may be made. For it is not just any free men who are appointed for these offices but young members of the association chosen with all care for their special merit who as becomes their good character and nobility are pressing on to reach the summit of virtue. They give their services gladly and proudly like sons to their real fathers and mothers, judging them to be the parents of them all in common, in a closer affinity than that of blood, since to the right minded there is no closer tie than noble living. And they come in to do their office ungirt and with tunics hanging down, that in their appearance there may be no shadow of anything to suggest the slave.

In this banquet—I know that some will laugh at this, but only those whose actions call for tears and lamentation—no wine is brought during those days but only water of the brightest and clearest, cold for most of the guests but warm for such of the older men as live delicately. The table too is kept pure from the flesh of animals; the food laid on it is loaves of bread with salt as a seasoning, sometimes also flavored with hyssop as a relish for the daintier appetites. Abstinence from wine is enjoined by right reason as for the priest when sacrificing, so to these for their lifetime. For wine acts like a drug producing folly, and costly dishes stir up that most insatiable of animals,[18] desire.

Learned discourse

Such are the preliminaries. But when the guests have laid themselves down arranged in rows, as I have described, and the attendants have taken their stand with everything in order ready for their ministry, the President of the company, when a general silence is established—here it may be asked when is there no silence—well at this point there is silence even more than before so that no one ventures to make a sound or breathe with more force than usual—amid this silence, I say, he discusses some question arising in the Holy Scriptures or solves one that has been propounded by someone else.

In doing this he has no thought of making a display, for he has no ambition to get a reputation for clever oratory but desires to gain a closer insight into some particular matters and having gained it not to withhold it selfishly from those who if not so clear-sighted as he have at least a similar desire to learn. His instruction proceeds in a leisurely manner; he lingers over it and spins it out with repetitions, thus permanently imprinting the thoughts in the souls of the hearers, since if the speaker goes on descanting with breathless rapidity the mind of the hearers is unable to follow his language, loses ground and fails to arrive at apprehension of what is said. His audience listen with ears pricked up and eyes fixed on him always in exactly the same posture, signifying comprehension and understanding by nods and glances, praise of the speaker by the cheerful change of expression which steals over the face, difficulty by a gentler movement of the head and by pointing with a fingertip of the right hand. The young men standing by show no less attentiveness than the occupants of the couches.

The exposition of the sacred scriptures treats the inner meaning conveyed in allegory. For to these people the whole book of the law seems to resemble a living creature with the literal ordinances for its body and for its soul the invisible meaning laid up in its wording. It is in this meaning especially that the rational soul begins to contemplate the things akin to itself and looking through the words as through a mirror beholds the marvelous beauties of the concepts, unfolds and removes the symbolic coverings and brings forth the thoughts and sets them bare to the light of day for those who need but a little reminding to enable them to discern the inward and hidden through the outward and visible.

When then the President thinks he has discoursed enough and both sides feel sure that they have attained their object, the speaker in the effectiveness with which his discourse has carried out his aims, the audience in the substance of what they have heard, universal applause arises showing a general pleasure in the prospect of what is still to follow. Then the President rises and sings a hymn composed as an address to God, either a new one of his own composition or an old one by poets of an earlier day who have left behind them hymns in many measures and melodies, hexameters and iambics, lyrics suitable for processions or in libations and at the altars, or for the chorus whilst standing or dancing, with careful metrical arrangements to fit the various evolutions. After him all the others take their turns as they are arranged and in the proper order while all the rest listen in complete silence except when they have to chant the closing lines or refrains, for then they all lift up their voices, men and women alike.

When everyone has finished his hymns the young men bring in the tables mentioned a little above on which is set the truly purified meal of leavened bread seasoned with salt mixed with hyssop [. . .].

Sacred vigil

After the supper they hold the sacred vigil which is conducted in the following way. They rise up all together and standing in the middle of the refectory form themselves first into two choirs, one of men and one of women, the leader and precentor chosen for each being the most honored amongst them and also the most musical. Then they sing hymns to God composed of many measures and set to many melodies, sometimes chanting together, sometimes taking up the harmony antiphonally, hands and feet keeping time in accompaniment, and rapt with enthusiasm reproduce sometimes the lyrics of the procession, sometimes of the halt and of the wheeling and counterwheeling of a choric dance.

Then when each choir has separately done its own part in the feast, having drunk as in the Bacchic rites of the strong wine of God's love they mix and both together become a single choir, a copy of the choir set up of old beside the Red Sea[19] in honor of the wonders there wrought. [. . .] It is on this model above all that the choir of the Therapeutae of either sex, note in response to note and voice to voice, the treble of the women blending with the bass of the men, create an harmonious concent, music in the truest sense. Lovely are the thoughts, lovely the words and worthy of reverence the choristers, and the end and aim of thoughts, words and choristers alike is piety. Thus they continue till dawn, drunk with this drunkenness in which there is no shame, then not with heavy heads or drowsy eyes but more alert and wakeful than when they came to the banquet, they stand with their faces and whole body turned to the east and when they see the sun rising they stretch their hands up to heaven and pray for bright days and knowledge of the truth and the power of keen sighted thinking. And after the prayers they depart each to his private sanctuary once more to ply the trade and till the field of their wonted philosophy.

So much then for the Therapeutae, who have taken to their hearts the contemplation of nature and what it has to teach, and have lived, in the soul alone, citizens of heaven and the world, presented to the Father and Maker of all by their faithful sponsor Virtue, who has procured for them God's friendship and added a gift going hand in hand with it, true excellence of life, a boon better than all good fortune and rising to the very summit of felicity.

V. Re-Reading a Biblical Work

Job the Saint

THE TESTAMENT OF JOB

Following the pattern of Biblical and apocryphal "testaments" (see the introductory note to the Testaments of the Twelve Patriarchs), this midrashic work recasts and reinterprets the story of Job in the form of parting words which the sufferer addresses to the children born to him after his restoration. It bears the title: "Testament of Job, the blameless, the sainted, the conqueror in many contests."

The Hebrew original of the work, composed in the last pre-Christian century, is lost. Two Greek versions made from the Hebrew, each represented by one manuscript, became known in the nineteenth century. In 1897 Kaufmann Kohler published an English translation and introduction to this fascinating document.

The Biblical Book of Job presents a Job whose experience of evil causes him to question God's interest in His creation. Justice, central in prophetic religion, seems to have been renounced by God Himself, who absurdly "destroyeth the innocent and the wicked" (Job 9:22). "The earth is given into the hand of the wicked" (9:24), God is remote, and man, "knowing" this true state of reality, is isolated from both God and world. Job's anguished cry "Answer Thou me" (13:22) is heeded and the voice of the remote, silent God is heard "out of the whirlwind" (chapters 38 to 40). The Creator allows man to behold the vast panorama of the universe. One thing alone is missing in this majestic picture of heaven and earth: man. Now Job realizes ("knows") his insignificance. But it is God who has revealed this knowledge to man.

In recasting the drama of Job, the unknown author of the Testament did not need to work toward what is the culmination of the story in the Biblical Book of Job: God's appearance and answer to the rebellious sufferer. In the Testament, Job never doubts divine justice. His agony affects the faith of the world around him, but he himself remains firm in his trust. He has lost everything, except the knowledge of the divine presence. The Biblical Job fears the distant, silent, God; Job of the Testament can love him: "I shall from love of God endure until the end." Thus Satan, who in the Biblical Job is but the initiator of the tension between Job and God, remains in the Testament a fighting antagonist throughout the drama, and his spirit imbues Elihu, the youngest of Job's "friends." Against the mighty but perishable realm of the Evil One, Job represents the eternal kingdom of God. K. Kohler seems justified in assigning the composition of the Testament to the community of the early Hasidim. It is indeed a hasidic interpretation of the Job problem, a reading that does not admit the communion between God and man to be disturbed by the sad and sorry state of this world.

On the day he [Job] became sick and knew that he would have to leave his bodily abode, he called his seven sons and his three daughters together and spoke to them as follows:

Form a circle around me, children, and hear, and I shall relate to you what the Lord did for me and all that happened to me. For I am Job your father. Know ye then my children, that you are the generation of a chosen one [Abraham] and take heed of your noble birth.

For I am of the sons of Esau. My brother is Nahor, and your mother is Dinah. By her have I become your father. For my first wife died with my other ten children in bitter death. Hear now, children, and I will reveal unto you what happened to me.

I was a very rich man living in the East in the land Ausitis [Utz], and before the Lord had named me Job, I was called Jobab.

The beginning of my trial was thus. Near my house there was the idol of one worshipped by the people; and I saw constantly burnt offerings brought to him as a god.

Then I pondered and said to myself: "Is this he who made heaven and earth, the sea and us all? How will I know the truth?"

In that night as I lay asleep, a voice came and called: "Jobab! Jobab! rise up, and I will tell thee who is the one whom thou wishest to know. This, however, to whom the people bring burnt offerings and libations, is not God, but this is the power and work of the Seducer [Satan] by which he beguiles the people."

When I heard this, I fell upon the earth and I prostrated myself saying: "O my Lord who speakest for the salvation of my soul, I pray thee, if this is the idol of Satan, I pray thee, let me go hence and destroy it and purify this spot. For there is none that can forbid me doing this, as I am the king of this land, so that those that live in it will no longer be led astray."

The voice that spoke out of the flame answered to me: "Thou canst purify this spot. But behold, I announce to thee what the Lord ordered me to tell thee. For I am the archangel of God." And I said: "Whatever shall be told to his servant, I shall hear." And the archangel said to me: "Thus speaketh the Lord: If thou undertakest to destroy, and takest away the image of Satan, he will set himself with wrath to wage war against thee, and he will display against thee all his malice. He will bring upon thee many and severe plagues, and take from thee all that thou hast. He will take away thine children, and will inflict many evils upon thee. Then thou must wrestle like an athlete and sustain pain, sure of thy reward, and overcome trials and afflictions.

"But when thou endurest, I shall make thy name renowned throughout all generations of the earth until to the end of the world. I shall restore thee to all that thou hadst had, and the double part of what thou shalt lose will be given to thee in order that thou mayest know that God does not consider the person but giveth to each who deserveth the good. And also to thee shall it be given, and thou shalt put on a crown of amarant. And at the resurrection thou shalt awaken for eternal life. Then shalt thou know that the Lord is just, and true and mighty."

Whereupon, my children, I replied: "I shall from love of God endure until death all that will come upon me, and I shall not shrink back." Then the angel put his seal upon me and left me.

After this I rose up in the night and took fifty slaves and went to the temple of the idol and destroyed it to the ground.

I went back to my house and gave orders that the door should be firmly locked; saying to my doorkeepers: "If somebody shall ask for me, bring no report to me, but tell him: He investigates urgent affairs; he is inside."

Then Satan disguised himself as a beggar and knocked heavily at the door, saying to the doorkeeper:

"Report to Job and say that I desire to meet him."

[Having failed to get Job into his hand, Satan secured from God the power to take away Job's wealth with which he supported "the poor that came from all the lands." "The four doors of my house were opened" and the poor "could take whatever they needed." After the feasts held by his children, Job offered sacrifices and gifts to the poor, in case the children have sinned "in a haughty spirit"; he said: "May my children never think evil towards God in their hearts."]

While I lived in this manner, the Seducer could not bear to see the good I did, and he demanded the warfare of God against me. And he came upon me cruelly. First he burnt up the large number of sheep, then the camels, then he burnt up the cattle and all my herds; or they were captured not only by enemies but also by such as had received benefits from me. And the shepherds came and announced that to me. But when I heard it, I gave praise to God and did not blaspheme.

When the Seducer learned of my fortitude, he plotted new things against me. He disguised himself as King of Persia and besieged my city, and after he had led off all that were therein, he spoke to them in malice, saying in boastful language: "This man Job who has obtained all the goods of the earth and left nothing for others, he has destroyed and torn down the temple of god. Therefore shall I repay to him what he has done to the house of the great god. Now come with me and we shall pillage all that is left in his house."

The [men of the city] answered and said to him: "He has seven sons and three daughters. Take heed lest they flee into other lands and they may become our tyrants and then come over us with force and kill us." And he said: "Be not at all afraid. His flocks and his wealth have I destroyed by fire, and the rest have I captured, and behold his children shall I kill." Having spoken thus, he went and threw the house upon my children and killed them.

My fellow-citizens, seeing that what was said by him had become true, came and pursued me and robbed me of all that was in my house. I saw with mine own eyes the pillage of my house, and men without culture and without honor sat at my table and on my couches, and I could not remonstrate against them. For I was exhausted like a woman with her loins let loose from multitude of pains, remembering chiefly that this warfare had been predicted to me by the Lord through His angel. I became like one who, when seeing the rough sea and the adverse winds, while the lading of the vessel in mid-ocean is too heavy, casts the burden into the sea, saying: "I wish to destroy all this only in order to come safely into the city so that I may take as profit the rescued ship and the best of my things." Thus did I manage my own affairs.

But there came another messenger and announced to me the ruin of my own children, and I was shaken with terror. And I tore my clothes and said: "The Lord hath given, the Lord hath taken. As it hath deemed best to the Lord, thus it hath come to be. May the name of the Lord be blessed."

When Satan saw that he could not put me to despair, he went and asked my body of the Lord in order to inflict plague on me, for the Evil One could not bear my patience. Then the Lord delivered me into his hands to use my body as he wanted, but He gave him no power over my soul.

Satan came to me as I was sitting on my throne still mourning over my children. He resembled a great hurricane and turned over my throne and threw me upon the ground; I continued lying on the floor for three hours. Then he smote me with a hard plague from the top of my head to the toes of my feet. Thereupon I left the city in great terror and woe and sat down upon a dunghill, my body being worm-eaten. [. . .]

Thus I endured for seven years, sitting on a dunghill outside of the city while being plague-stricken. I saw with mine own eyes my longed-for children [carried by angels to heaven]. My humbled wife who had been brought to her bridal chamber in such great luxuriousness and with spearmen as bodyguards, I saw do a water-carrier's work like a slave in the house of a common man in order to win some bread and bring it to me.

[When she was no longer permitted to bring him food, Satan sold her three loaves of bread for the hair of her head. The Seducer "troubled her heart greatly" and she lost her faith.]

Then my wife came near me, and crying aloud and weeping she said "Job! Job! how long wilt thou sit upon the dunghill outside of the city, pondering yet for a while and expecting to obtain your hoped-for salvation!" I have been wandering from place to place, roaming about as a hired servant, behold thy memory has already died away from earth. My sons and the daughters that I carried on my bosom and the labors and pains that I sustained have been for nothing? And thou sittest in the malodorous state of soreness and worms, passing the nights in the cold air. I have undergone all trials and troubles and pains, day and night until I succeeded in bringing bread to thee. [. . .] Who would then not be astonished saying: "Is this Sitis, the wife of Job, who had fourteen curtains to cover her inner sitting room, and doors within doors so that he was greatly honored who would be brought near her, and now behold, she barters off her hair for bread!

"Who had camels laden with goods, and they were brought into remote lands to the poor, and now she sells her hair for bread!

"Behold her who had seven tables immovably set in her house at which each poor man and each stranger ate, and now she sells her hair for bread.

"Behold her who had the basin wherewith to wash her feet made of gold and silver, and now she walks upon the ground and sells her hair for bread!

"Behold her who had her garments made of byssus interwoven with gold, and now she exchanges her hair for bread!

"Behold her who had couches of gold and of silver, and now she sells her hair for bread!"

In short then, Job, after the many things that have been said to me, I now say in one word to thee: "Since the feebleness of my heart has crushed my bones, rise then and take these loaves of bread and enjoy them, and then speak some word against the Lord and die! For I too, would exchange the torpor of death for the sustenance of my body."

But I replied to her: "Behold I have been for these seven years plague-stricken, and I have stood the worms of my body, and I was not weighed down in my soul by all these pains. And as to the word which thou sayest: 'Speak some word against God and die!,' together with thee I will sustain the evil which thou seest, and let us endure the ruin of all that we have. Yet thou desirest that we should say some word against God and that He should be exchanged for the great Pluto.

"Why dost thou not remember those great goods which we possessed? If these goods come from the lands of the Lord, should not we also endure evils and be high-minded in everything until the Lord will have mercy again and show pity to us? Dost thou not see the Seducer stand behind thee and confound thy thoughts in order that thou shouldst beguile me?"

Then he turned to Satan and said: "Why dost thou not come openly to me? Stop hiding thyself, thou wretched one. Does the lion show his strength in the weasel cage? Or does the bird fly in the basket? I now tell thee: Go away and wage thy war against me."

Satan went off from behind my wife, placed himself before me crying and he said: "Behold, Job, I yield and give way to thee who art but flesh while I am a spirit. Thou art plague-stricken, but I am in great trouble. For I am like a wrestler contesting with a wrestler who has, in a singlehanded combat, torn down his antagonist and covered him with dust and broken every limb of his, whereas the other one who lies beneath, having displayed his bravery, gives forth sounds of triumph testifying to his own superior excellence. Thus thou, O Job, art beneath and stricken with plague and pain, and yet thou hast carried the victory in the wrestling match with me, and behold, I yield to thee." Then he left me abashed. Now my children, do you also show a firm heart in all the evil that happens to you, for greater than all things is firmness of heart.

At this time the kings heard what had happened to me and they rose and came to me, each from his land to visit me and to comfort me. When they came near me, they cried with a loud voice and each tore his clothes. After they had prostrated themselves, touching the earth with their heads, they sat down next to me for seven days and seven nights, and none spoke a word. They were four in numbers: Eliphaz, the king of Teman, and Baldad, and Sophar, and Elihu. And when they had taken their seat, they conversed about what had happened to me.

Now when for the first time they had come to me and I had shown them my precious stones, they were astonished and said: "If of us three kings all our possessions would be brought together into one, it would not come up to the precious stones of Jobab's kingdom. For thou art of greater nobility, than all the people of the East." When therefore, they now came to the land of Ausitis to visit me, they asked in the city: "Where is Jobab, the ruler of this whole land?" And they told them concerning me: "He sitteth upon the dunghill outside of the city; for he has not entered the city for seven years." [. . .]

The kings drew nigh and Eliphaz began and said: "Art thou, indeed, Job, our fellow-king? Art thou the one who owned the great glory? Art thou he who once shone like the sun of day upon the whole earth? Art thou he who once resembled the moon and the stars effulgent throughout the night?" I answered him and said: "I am," and thereupon all wept and lamented, and they sang a royal song of lamentation, their whole army joining them in a chorus.

And again Eliphaz said to me: "Art thou he who had ordered seven thousand sheep to be given for the clothing of the poor? Whither, then hath gone the glory of thy throne?

"Art thou he who had ordered three thousand cattle to

do the ploughing of the field for the poor? Whither, then hath thy glory gone!" [. . .]

And when Eliphaz had for a long time cried and lamented, while all the others joined him, so that the commotion was very great, I said to them: "Be silent and I will show you my throne, and the glory of its splendor: My glory will be everlasting. The whole world shall perish, and its glory shall vanish, and all those who hold fast to it, will remain beneath, but my throne is in the upper world, and its glory and splendor will be to the right of the Savior in the heavens. My throne exists in the life of the "holy ones" and its glory in the imperishable world. For rivers will be dried up and their arrogance shall go down to the depth of the abyss, but the streams of the land in which my throne is erected, shall not dry up, but shall remain unbroken in strength.

"The kings perish and the rulers vanish, and their glory and pride is as the shadow in a looking glass, but my kingdom lasts forever and ever, and its glory and beauty is in the chariot of my Father."

When I spoke thus to them, Eliphaz became angry and said to the other friends: "For what purpose is it that we have come here with our hosts to comfort him? Behold, he upbraids us. Therefore let us return to our countries. This man sits here in misery wormeaten amidst an unbearable state of putrefaction, and yet he challenges us saying: 'Kingdoms shall perish and their rulers, but my Kingdom, says he, shall last forever.'" Eliphaz, then, rose in great commotion, and, turning away from them in great fury, said: "I go hence. We have indeed come to comfort him, but he declares war to us in view of our armies."

But then Baldad seized him by the hand and said: "Not thus ought one to speak to an afflicted man, and especially to one stricken down with so many plagues. Behold, we, being in good health, dared not approach him on account of the offensive odor, except with the help of plenty of fragrant aroma. But thou, Eliphaz, art forgetful of all this. Let me speak plainly. Let us be magnanimous and learn what is the cause.

Must he in remembering his former days of happiness not become mad in his mind? Who should not be altogether perplexed seeing himself thus lapse into misfortune and plagues? But let me step near him that I may find by what cause is he thus?"

And Baldad rose and approached me saying: "Art thou Job?" and he said: "Is thy heart still in good keeping?" And I said: "I did not hold fast to the earthly things, since the earth with all that inhabit it is unstable. But my heart holds fast to the heaven, because there is no trouble in heaven."

Then Baldad rejoined and said: "We know that the earth is unstable, for it changes according to season. At times it is in a state of peace, and at times it is in a state of war. But of the heaven we hear that it is perfectly steady. But art thou truly in a state of calmness? Therefore let me ask and speak, and when thou answerest me to my first word, I shall have a second question to ask, and if again thou answerest in well-set words, it will be manifest that thy heart has not been unbalanced."

And he said: "Upon what dost thou set thy hope?" And I said: "Upon the living God." And he said to me: "Who deprived thee of all thou didst possess? And who inflicted thee with these plagues?" And I said: "God." And he said: "If thou still placest thy hope upon God, how can He do wrong in judgment, having brought upon thee these plagues and misfortunes, and having taken from thee all thy possessions? And since He has taken these, it is clear that He has given thee nothing. No king will disgrace his soldier who has served him well as body-guard?" I answered saying: "Who understands the depths of the Lord and of His wisdom to be able to accuse God of injustice?" [. . .]

Then Sophar rejoined and said: "We do not inquire after our own affairs, but we desire to know whether thou art in a sound state, and behold, we see that thy reason has not been shaken. What now dost thou wish that we should do for thee? Behold, we have come here and brought the physicians of three kings, and if thou wishest, thou mayest be cured by them." But I answered and said: "My cure and my restoration cometh from God, the Maker of physicians."

And when I spoke thus to them, behold, there my wife Sitis came running, dressed in rags, from the service of the master by whom she was employed as slave; though she had been forbidden to leave, lest the kings, on seeing her, might take her as captive. When she came, she threw herself prostrate to their feet, crying and saying: "Remember, Eliphaz and ye other friends, what I was once with you, and how I have changed, how I am now dressed to meet you." Then the kings broke forth in great weeping and, being in double perplexity, they kept silent. But Eliphaz took his purple mantle and cast it about her to wrap herself up with it.

But she asked him saying: "I ask as favor of you, my Lords, that you order your soldiers that they should dig among the ruins of our house which fell upon my children, so that their bones could be brought in a perfect state to the tombs. For we have, owing to our misfortune, no power at all, and so we may at least see their bones. For have I like a brute the motherly feeling of wild beasts that my ten children should have perished on one day and not to one of them could I give a decent burial?"

Then the kings gave order that the ruins of my house should be dug up. But I prohibited it, saying: "Do not go to the trouble in vain; for my children will not be found, for they are in the keeping of their Maker and Ruler."

The kings answered and said: "Who will gainsay that he is out of his mind and raves? For while we desire to bring the bones of his children back, he forbids us to do so saying: 'They have been taken and placed in the keeping of their Maker.' Therefore prove unto us the truth." But I said to them: "Raise me that I may stand up." They lifted me, holding up my arms from both sides. I stood upright, pronounced first the praise of God, and after the prayer I said to them: "Look with your eyes to the East." And they looked and saw my children with crowns near the glory of the King, the Ruler of heaven.

When my wife Sitis saw this, she fell to the ground and prostrated herself before God, saying: "Now I know that my memory remains with the Lord." After she had spoken this, and the evening came, she went to the city, back to the master whom she served as slave, and lay herself down at the manger of the cattle and died there from exhaustion.

When her despotic master searched for her and did not find her, he came to the fold of his herds, and there he saw her stretched out upon the manger dead, while all the animals around were crying about her. And all who saw her wept and lamented, and the cry extended throughout the whole city. Then the people brought her down and wrapt her up and buried her by the house which had fallen upon her children. The poor of the city made a great mourning for her and said: "Behold this Sitis whose like in nobility and in glory is not found in any woman. Alas! she was not found worthy of a proper tomb!" The dirge for her you will find in the record.

But Eliphaz and those that were with him were astonished at these things, and they sat down with me and replying to me, spoke in boastful words concerning me for twenty-seven days. They repeated it again and again that I suffered deservedly thus for having committed many sins, and that there was no hope left for me; I retorted to these men in zest of contention myself. And they rose in anger, ready to part in wrathful spirit.

But Elihu conjured them to stay yet a little while until he would have shown them what it was. "For," said he, "so many days did you pass, allowing Job to boast that he is just. But I shall no longer suffer it. For from the beginning did I continue crying over him, remembering his former happiness. But now he speaks boastfully and in overbearing pride, he says that he has his throne in the heavens. Therefore, hear me, and I will tell you what is the cause of his destiny." Then, imbued with the spirit of Satan, Elihu spoke hard words which are written down in the records left of Elihu. After he had ended, God appeared to me in a storm and in clouds, and spoke, blaming

Elihu and showing me that he who had spoken was not a man,
but a wild beast.

[When the three friends finally realized their error, God
pardoned them "through His servant Job." However, "He did
not deign to pardon Elihu" for "he has loved the beauty of the
serpent." A hymn by Eliphaz concludes the story of the
friends.]

> Righteous is the Lord, and His judgments are true,
> With Him there is no preference of person,
> for He judgeth all alike.
> Behold, the Lord cometh!
> Behold, the holy ones have been prepared!
> The crowns and the prizes of the victors precede them!
> Let the saints rejoice, and let their hearts exult in gladness;
> for they shall receive the glory which is in store for them.
> Our sins are forgiven,
> our injustice has been cleansed,
> but Elihu hath no remembrance among the living.

After Eliphaz had finished the hymn, we rose and went
back to the city, each to the house where they lived. [Here is
the part missing which told of Job's restoration.]

And the people made a feast for me in gratitude and delight of God, and all my friends came back to me. [. . .]

Then the Lord blessed all that was left to me, and after
a few days I became rich again in merchandise, in flocks and
all things which I had lost, and I received all in double number
again. Then I also took as wife your mother and became the
father of you ten in place of the ten children that had died.

And now, my children, let me admonish you: "Behold I
die. You will take my place. Do not forsake the Lord. Be
charitable towards the poor; do not disregard the feeble. Take
not unto yourselves wives from strangers.

"Behold, my children, I shall divide among you what I
possess, so that each may have control over his own and have
full power to do good with his share." After he had spoken
thus, he brought all his goods and divided them among his
seven sons, but he gave nothing of his goods to his daughters.

Then they said to their father: "Our lord and father! Are we not also thy children? Why, then, dost thou not also give us a share of thy possessions?" Then said Job to his daughters: "Do not become angry my daughters. I have not forgotten you. Behold, I have preserved for you a possession better than that which your brothers have taken." [Job gave them three-stringed magic girdles by means of which his own leprosy was cured. As soon as his daughters put these girdles around their bodies they were transfigured and, in the voices of angels, sang hymns echoing the mysteries of heaven].

And Job lay down from sickness on his couch, yet without pain and suffering, because his pain did not take strong hold of him on account of the charm of the girdle which he had wound around himself. After three days Job saw the holy angels come for his soul. Instantly he rose, took the cithara and gave it to his daughter Day [Yemima]. And to Kassia [Perfume] he gave a censer with perfume and to Amalthea's Horn [Keren Happukh] he gave a timbrel in order that they might bless the holy angels who came for his soul. They took these, and sang, and played on the psaltery and praised and glorified God in the holy dialect.

After this came He who sitteth upon the great chariot and kissed Job, while his three daughters looked on, but the others saw it not. He took the soul of Job and soared upward, taking the soul by the arm and carrying her upon the chariot, and He went towards the East. His body, however, was brought to the grave, while the three daughters marched ahead, having put on their girdles and singing hymns in praise of God.

Then held Nahor his brother and his seven sons, with the rest of the people and the poor, the orphans and the feeble ones, a great mourning over him saying: "Woe unto us, for today has been taken from us the strength of the feeble, the light of the blind, the father of the orphans. The receiver of strangers has been taken off, the leader of the erring, the cover of the naked, the shield of the widows. Who would not mourn for the man of God!"

And as they were mourning in this and in that form, they would not suffer him to be put into the grave. After three days, however, he was finally put into the grave like one in sweet slumber, and he received the name of the good who will remain renowned throughout all generations of the world.

He left seven sons and three daughters, and there were no daughters found on earth, as fair as the daughters of Job. The name of Job was formerly Jobab, and he was called Job by the Lord. He had lived before his plague eighty five years, and after the plague he took the double share of all; hence also his years he doubled, which is one hundred and seventy years. Thus he lived altogether two hundred and fifty-five years. And he saw sons of his sons unto the fourth generation. It is written that he will rise up with those whom the Lord will reawaken. To our Lord be glory. Amen.

VI. Interpreting Jewish Faith to the World

Hellenist Exposition of Scripture

FROM PHILO'S COMMENTARIES

A note on Philo. From the Stoics, Philo (see introductory note to "The Order of the Essenes") learned the method of allegory (a term derived from Greek rhetoric) by which a text, the literal meaning of which no longer satisfies, is interpreted to imply a deeper, or more universal, philosophical or religious meaning. The text then no longer concerns itself with concrete, temporal, historically limited inquiries but with abstract, eternal, universally valid issues. By using this method, which Philo brought to systematic perfection, he rediscovered in Scripture ideas of Platonic philosophy. The Bible, as he interpreted it, tells not the story of three patriarchs, historic ancestors of a historic nation, but of three men who symbolically represent three types of man's relationship to God; Abraham is the symbol of man who knows God through learning, Isaac through inspiration, Jacob through ascetic life. These three types unite in the "most pure mind" and "lover of virtue," symbolized by Moses.

The Stoics, who inherited allegory from pre-Platonic philosophers, used this method in an effort to harmonize the Greek myths—which were no longer believed—with their own philosophy. Philo employed allegory in order to teach the Bible as being the authentic document of the correspondence of Hebraic and Greek wisdom.

The following selections, taken from his commentaries (written in Greek), are examples of Philo's thinking and his method of Biblical interpretation.

On hiding from the presence of God

"And Adam and his wife hid themselves from the pres-

ence of the Lord God amongst the trees of the garden"
(Gen. 3:8). Here Scripture acquaints us with the principle
that the wicked are homeless.[1] For if virtue constitutes the
true city of the wise, then he who cannot participate in virtue
is an exile from that city. And the wicked cannot participate
in virtue, and so they are exiled, they are fugitives. But he who
flees from virtue, at once hides himself from God.

For if the wise are visible to God—since they are his
friends—the wicked are apparently all hidden and concealed
from him, since they are enemies of right reason. Scripture
testifies that the wicked man has no home and no habitation,
in the allusion to Esau in his "hairy mantle" (Gen. 25:25) and
guise of sinfulness, for it is said: "Esau was a cunning hunter,
a man of the field" (Gen. 25:27). For wickedness bound on
the hunt for passions, and foolishly hastening in pursuit of
boorishness,[2] cannot live in the city of virtue. Jacob, on the
other hand, who is full of wisdom, is a citizen of virtue and
dwells in virtue, for of him it is said: "And Jacob was a quiet
man, dwelling in tents" (Gen. 25:27). And this is also the
reason why it is said: "And it came to pass, because the mid-
wives feared God, that they made themselves houses" (Exod.
1:21).[3] For such souls as seek out the hidden secrets of God
—and that means "bringing the male children to the birth"
(Exod. 1:17)—build up the works of virtue in which they
choose to dwell. Thus it is shown in what sense the wicked
are without a home and without a habitation, since they are
exiled from the precincts of virtue, while the good have received wisdom as their house and as their city.

Now we shall investigate in what sense it can be said of a
person that he is hiding from God. It is impossible to understand these words we have before us in Scripture, unless we
give them an allegorical interpretation. For God fills and penetrates everything; he has left nothing empty and void of his
presence. How then could anyone be in a place where God is
not? Another passage testifies to this: "The Lord, He is God
in heaven above, and upon the earth beneath; there is none
else" (Deut. 4:39). And further on: "Behold, I will stand before thee" (Exod. 17:6). For before anything was created,

there was God, and he is found everywhere, so that no one can hide from him. Why should this fill us with wonder? We could not escape from the elements of all things created, even if we had cause to wish to hide from them. Just try to flee from water and air, from the sky or from the whole of the world! We are, of necessity, caught in their compass, for no one can flee from the world. But if we cannot hide from parts of the world, and from the world itself, how then could we hide from the presence of God? Never! So what is meant by the expression "hid themselves"? The wicked believe that God is in a certain place, that he does not encompass, but that he is encompassed. And so they think they can hide, because the Creator of all life is not in that part of the world which they have selected for their hiding place.

Thus we have shown in what way the wicked are fugitives and hide from God. Now we shall see where they hide. "Amongst the trees of the garden" (Gen. 3:8) is what we read, that is, in the center of the mind, which is, so to speak, in the middle of the garden, that is, of the whole soul. He who flees from God, flees into himself. For there are two kinds of mind, the mind of the universe, and that is God, and the mind of individual man. And the one flees from his own mind to the mind of the universe—for whoever leaves his own mind, avows therewith that the works of the mortal mind are as nothing, and ascribes everything to God. But the other flees from God, and declares that not God is the cause of anything at all, but that he himself is the cause of all that comes to pass. Thus there are many who believe that all the things in the world go their own course by themselves, without a guide, and that it is the spirit of man that has invented the arts, crafts, laws, customs, state institutions, and the rights of the individual and the community, both in regard to men and to beasts, that are without reason. But you, O my soul, see the difference between these two points of view. For the one leaves the perishable mortal mind, which has been created, and chooses for its true aid the primordial and immortal mind of the universe. But the other, which sets aside God, foolishly courts as its ally the human mind, which is not even able to help itself.

Revelation in the Sinai desert

Having related in the preceding treatises the lives of
those whom Moses judged to be men of wisdom, who are set
before us in the Sacred Books as founders of our nation and in
themselves unwritten laws, I shall now proceed in due course
to give full descriptions of the written laws. And if some allegorical interpretation should appear to underlie them, I shall
not fail to state it. For knowledge loves to learn and advance
to full understanding and its way is to seek the hidden meaning rather than the obvious.

To the question why he [Moses] promulgated his laws in
the depths of the desert instead of in cities we may answer in
the first place that most cities are full of countless evils, both
acts of impiety towards God and wrongdoing between man
and man. For everything is debased, the genuine overpowered
by the spurious, the true by the specious, which is intrinsically
false but creates impressions whose plausibility serves but to
delude. So too in cities there arises that most insidious of
foes, Pride [or, vanity], admired and worshipped by some who
add dignity to vain ideas by means of gold crowns and purple
robes and a great establishment of servants and cars, on which
these so-called blissful and happy people ride aloft, drawn
sometimes by mules and horses, sometimes by men, who bear
the heavy burden on their shoulders, yet suffer in soul rather
than in body under the weight of extravagant arrogance.

Pride is also the creator of many other evils, boastfulness,
haughtiness, inequality, and these are the sources of wars, both
civil and foreign, suffering no place to remain in peace whether
public or private, whether on sea or on land. Yet why dwell on
offences between man and man? Pride also brings divine
things into utter contempt, even though they are supposed to
receive the highest honors. But what honor can there be if
truth be not there as well, truth honorable both in name and
function, just as falsehood is naturally dishonorable? This
contempt for things divine is manifest to those of keener
vision. For men have employed sculpture and painting to
fashion innumerable forms which they have enclosed in

shrines and temples and after building altars have assigned celestial and divine honors to idols of stone and wood and suchlike images, all of them lifeless things. Such persons are happily compared in the sacred Scriptures to the children of a harlot; for as they in their ignorance of their one natural father ascribe their paternity to all their mother's lovers, so too throughout the cities those who do not know the true, the really existent God have deified hosts of others who are falsely so called. Then as some honor one, some another god, diversity of opinion as to which was best waxed strong and engendered disputes in every other matter also. This was the primary consideration which made him prefer to legislate away from cities.

He [Moses] had also a second object in mind. He who is about to receive the holy laws must first cleanse his soul and purge away the deep-set stains which it has contracted through contact with the motley promiscuous horde of men in cities. And to this he cannot attain except by dwelling apart, nor that at once, but only long afterwards, and not till the marks which his old transgressions have imprinted on him have gradually grown faint, melted away and disappeared. In this way, too, good physicians preserve their sick folk: they think it unadvisable to give them food or drink until they have removed the causes of their maladies. While these still remain, nourishment is useless, indeed harmful, and acts as fuel to the distemper. Naturally therefore he first led them away from the highly mischievous associations of cities into the desert, to clear the sins out of their souls, and then began to set the nourishment before their minds—and what should this nourishment be but laws and words of God?

He had a third reason as follows: Just as men when setting out on a long voyage do not begin to provide sails and rudders and tillers when they have embarked and left the harbor, but equip themselves with enough of the gear needed for the voyage while they are still staying on shore, so Moses did not think it good that they should just take their portions and settle in cities and then go in quest of laws to regulate their civic life, but rather should first provide themselves with the rules for that life and gain practice in all that would surely enable the communities to steer their course in safety, and then settle down to follow from their use, in harmony and fellowship of spirit and rendering to every man his due.

Some, too, give a fourth reason which is not out of keeping with the truth but agrees very closely with it. As it was necessary to establish a belief in their minds that the laws were not the inventions of a man but quite clearly the oracles of God, he led the nation a great distance away from cities into the depths of a desert, barren not only of cultivated fruits but also of water fit for drinking, in order that, if after lacking the necessaries of life and expecting to perish from hunger and thirst they suddenly found abundance of sustenance self-produced—when heaven rained the food called manna[4] and the shower of quails from the air to add relish to their food—when the bitter water grew sweet and fit for drinking and springs gushed out of the steep rock—they should no longer wonder whether the laws were actually the pronouncements of God, since they had been given the clearest evidence of the truth in the supplies which they had so unexpectedly received in their destitution. For He who gave abundance of the means of life also bestowed the wherewithal of a good life; for mere life they needed food and drink which they found without making provision; for the good life they needed laws and ordinances which would bring improvement to their souls.

We may properly ask why, when all these many thousands were collected in one spot, He thought good in proclaiming His ten oracles to address each not as to several persons but as to one, [e.g.] "Thou shalt not commit adultery," "Thou shalt not kill," "Thou shalt not steal," and so too with the rest. One answer which must be given is that He wishes to teach the readers of the sacred Scriptures a most excellent lesson, namely that each single person, when he is law-abiding and obedient to God, is equal in worth to a whole nation, even the most populous, or rather to all nations, and if we may go still farther, even to the whole world. And therefore elsewhere, when He praises a certain just man, He says, "I am thy God," though He was also the God of the world. And thus we see that all the rank and file who are posted in the same line and give a like satisfaction to their commander, have an equal share of approbation and honor.

A second reason is that a speaker who harangues a multitude in general does not necessarily talk to any one person, whereas if he addresses his commands or prohibitions as though to each individual separately, the practical instructions given in the course of his speech are at once held to apply to the whole body in common also. If the exhortations are received as a personal message, the hearer is more ready to obey, but if collectively with others, he is deaf to them, since he takes the multitude as a cover for disobedience.

A third reason is that He wills that no king or despot swollen with arrogance and contempt should despise an insignificant private person but should study in the school of the divine laws and abate his supercilious airs, and through the reasonableness or rather the assured truth of their arguments unlearn his self-conceit. For if the Uncreated, the Incorruptible, the Eternal, Who needs nothing and is the maker of all, the Benefactor and King of kings and God of gods could not brook to despise even the humblest, but deigned to banquet him on holy oracles and statutes, as though he should be the sole guest, as though for him alone the feast was prepared to give good cheer to a soul instructed in the holy secrets and accepted for admission to the greatest mysteries, what right have I, the mortal, to bear myself proud-necked, puffed-up and loud-voiced, towards my fellows, who, though their fortunes be unequal, have equal rights of kinship because they can claim to be children of the one common mother of mankind, nature? So then, though I be invested with the sovereignty of earth and sea, I will make myself affable and easy of access to the poorest, to the meanest, to the lonely who have none close at hand to help them, to orphans who have lost both parents, to wives on whom widowhood has fallen, to old men either childless from the first or bereaved by the early death of those whom they begot. For as I am a man, I shall not deem it right to adopt the lofty grandeur of the pompous stage, but make nature my home and not overstep her limits. I will inure my mind to have the feelings of a human being, not only because the lot both of the prosperous and the unfortunate may change to the reverse we know not when, but also because it is right that even if good fortune remains securely established, a man should not forget what he is. Such was the reason, as it seems to me, why he willed to word the series of his oracles in the singular form, and delivers them as though to one alone.

The Sabbath

On this day we are commanded to abstain from all work, not because the law inculcates slackness; on the contrary it always inures men to endure hardship and incites them to labor, and spurns those who would idle their time away, and accordingly is plain in its directions to work the full six days. Its object is rather to give men relaxation from continuous and unending toil and by refreshing their bodies with a regularly calculated system of remissions, to send them out renewed to their old activities. For a breathing space enables not merely ordinary people but athletes also to collect their strength and with a stronger force behind them to undertake promptly and patiently each of the tasks set before them.

Further, when He forbids bodily labor on the seventh day, He permits the exercise of the higher activities, namely, those employed in the study of the principles of virtue's lore. For the law bids us take the time for studying philosophy and thereby improve the soul and the dominant mind. So each seventh day there stand wide open in every city thousands of schools of good sense, temperance, courage, justice and the other virtues in which the scholars sit in order quietly with ears alert and with full attention, so much do they thirst for the draught which the teacher's words supply, while one of special experience rises and sets forth what is the best and sure to be profitable and will make the whole of life grow to something better.

But among the vast number of particular truths and

principles there studied, there stand out practically high above the others two main heads: one of duty to God as shewn by piety and holiness, one of duty to men as shewn by humanity and justice, each of them splitting up into multiform branches, all highly laudable. These things shew clearly that Moses does not allow any of those who used his sacred instruction to remain inactive at any season. But since we consist of body and soul, he assigned to the body its proper tasks and similarly to the soul what falls to its share, and his earnest desire was, that the two should be waiting to relieve each other. Thus while the body is working, the soul enjoys a respite, but when the body takes its rest, the soul resumes its work, and thus the best forms of life, the theoretical and the practical, take their turn in replacing each other. The practical life has six as its number allotted for ministering to the body. The theoretical has seven for knowledge and perfection of the mind.

The Emperor's Statue

FROM PHILO: LEGACY TO GAIUS

The tranquil government of Augustus and Tiberius was followed by the rule of the mentally unbalanced Gaius Caligula (37–41). To please the self-deifying emperor and also to harm the large Jewish community in Alexandria, the Roman prefect, Flaccus, ordered the erection of the emperor's statues in the synagogues. The Jews resisted this idolatry, and a pogrom—the first in history—ensued. In the year 40 the Alexandrian Jews sent a deputation, headed by Philo, to Rome. The Greeks, too, sent a delegation, led by the Jew-baiter Apion. At the same time the emperor ordered his image set up in the Temple in Jerusalem, instructing the legate of Syria, Petronius, to effect the command. Agrippa I, grandson of King Herod, whom Caligula had appointed king over a part of the land of Israel, decided to write a letter to the emperor, his childhood friend, to plead for the revocation of the order so offensive to Jewish monotheist thinking. This epistle, reproduced on the following pages, is recorded by Philo, who also wrote a vivid account of the (unsuccessful) embassy to Caligula (*Legacy to Gaius*). The death of Caligula

(41) made his order obsolete. His successor Claudius restored peace in Jerusalem and in Alexandria.

Having taken tablets, Agrippa wrote to Gaius in the following manner:

O master, fear and shame have taken from me all courage to come into your presence to address you; since fear teaches me to dread your threats; and shame, out of respect for the greatness of your power and dignity, keeps me silent. But a letter will show my request, which I now here offer to you as my earnest petition.

In all men, O emperor! a love of their country is innate, and an eager fondness for their national customs and laws. Concerning these matters there is no need that I should give you information, since you have a heartfelt love of your own country, and a deep-seated respect for your national customs. [. . .]

I am, as you know, a Jew; Jerusalem is my country, in which there is erected the holy temple of the most high God. I have kings for my grandfathers and for my ancestors,[5] the greater part of whom have been called high priests, looking upon their royal power as inferior to their office as priests; thinking that the high priesthood is as much superior to the power of a king, as God is superior to man; for that the one is occupied in rendering service to God, and the other has only the care of governing them.

Accordingly, I, being one of this nation, and being attached to this country and to such a temple, address to you this petition on behalf of them all; on behalf of the nation, that it may not be looked upon by you in a light contrary to the true one; since it is a most pious and holy nation, and one from the beginning most loyally disposed to your family.

For in all the particulars in which men are enjoined by the laws, and in which they have it in their power to show their piety and loyalty, my nation is inferior to none whatever in Asia or in Europe, whether it be in respect of prayers, or of the supply of sacred offerings [. . .] by which means they show their loyalty and fidelity more surely than by their mouth and tongue, providing it by the designs of their honest hearts, not indeed saying that they are friends to Caesar, but being so in reality.

Concerning the holy city I must now say what is necessary. Jerusalem, as I have already stated, is my native city, and the metropolis, not only of the one country of Judaea, but also of many, by reason of the colonies which it has sent out from time to time into the bordering districts of Egypt, Phoenicia, Syria in general, and especially that part of it which is called Coele-Syria, and also with those more distant regions of Pamphylia, Cilicia, the greater part of Asia Minor as far as Bithynia and the furthermost corners of Pontus. And in the same manner into Europe, into Thessaly, Boeotia, Macedonia, Aetolia, Attica, Argos, Corinth and all the most fertile and wealthiest districts of Peloponnesus. Not only are the continents full of Jewish colonies, but also all the most celebrated islands are so too; such as Euboea and Cyprus and Crete.

I say nothing of the countries beyond the Euphrates, for all of them except a very small portion, and Babylon, and all the satrapies around, which have any advantages whatever of soil or climate, have Jews settled in them. So that if my native land is, as it reasonably may be, looked upon as entitled to a share in your favor, it is not one city only that would then be benefited by you, but ten thousand of them in every region of the habitable world, in Europe, in Asia, and in Africa, on the continent, in the islands, on the coasts and in the inland parts. It corresponds well to the greatness of your good fortune, that, by conferring benefits on one city, you should also benefit ten thousand others, so that your renown may be celebrated in every part of the habitable world, and many praises of you may be combined with thanksgiving. [. . .]

I indeed am perfectly aware that I belong to the class which is in subjection to a lord and master, and also that I am admitted to the honor of being one of your companions, being inferior to you in respect of my birthright and natural rank, and inferior to no one whomsoever, not to say the most eminent of all men, in good will and loyalty towards you, both because that is my natural disposition, and also in consequence of the number of benefits with which you have enriched me;[6] so that if I in consequence had felt confidence to implore you myself on behalf of my country, if not to grant to it the Roman constitution, at least to confer freedom and a remission of taxes on it, I should not have thought that I had any reason to fear your displeasure for preferring such a petition to you, and for requesting that most desirable of all things, your favor, which it can do you no harm to grant, and which is the most advantageous of all things for my country to receive.

For what can possibly be a more desirable blessing for a subject nation than the good will of its sovereign? It was at Jerusalem, O emperor! that your most desirable succession to the empire was first announced; the news of your advancement spread from the holy city all over the continent on each side, and was received with great gladness. On this account that city deserves to meet with favor at your hands; for, as in families the eldest children receive the highest honors as their birthright, because they were the first to give the name of father and mother to their parents, so, in like manner, since this is first of all the cities in the east to salute you as emperor, it ought to receive greater benefit from you than any other; or if not greater, at all events as great as any other city.

Having now advanced these pleas on the ground of justice, and made these petitions on behalf of my native country, I now come at last to my supplication on behalf of the Temple. O my lord and master, Gaius! this Temple has never, from the time of its original foundation until now, admitted any form made by hands, because it has been the abode of God. Now, pictures and images are only imitations of those gods who are perceptible to the outward senses; but it was not considered by our ancestors to be consistent with the reverence due to God to make any image or representation of the invisible God. [. . .]

On which account, no one, whether Greek or barbarian, satrap, or king, or implacable enemy; no sedition, no war, no capture, no destruction, no occurrence that has ever taken place, has ever threatened this Temple, with such innovation as to place in it any image, or statue, or any work of any kind made with hands; for, though enemies have displayed their hostility to the inhabitants of the country, still, either reverence or fear has possessed them sufficiently to prevent them from abrogating any of the laws which were established at the beginning, as tending to the honor of the Creator and Father of the universe; for they knew that it is these and similar actions which bring after them the irremediable calamities of heaven-sent afflictions. [. . .]

But why need I invoke the assistance of foreign witnesses when I have plenty with whom I can furnish you from among your own countrymen and friends? Marcus Agrippa,[7] your own grandfather on the mother's side, the moment that he arrived in Judaea, when Herod, my grandfather, was king of the country, thought fit to go up from the seacoast to the metropolis, which was inland. And when he had beheld the Temple, and the decorations of the priests, and the piety and holiness of the people of the country, he marveled, looking upon the whole matter as one of great solemnity and entitled to great respect, and thinking that he had beheld what was too magnificent to be described. And he could talk of nothing else to his companions but the magnificence of the Temple and every thing connected with it.

Therefore, every day that he remained in the city, by reason of his friendship for Herod, he went to that sacred place, being delighted with the spectacle of the building, and of the sacrifices, and all the ceremonies connected with the worship of God, and the regularity which was observed, and the dignity and honor paid to the high priest, and his grandeur when arrayed in his sacred vestments and when about to begin the sacrifices.[8] And after he had adorned the Temple with all the offerings in his power to contribute, and had conferred many benefits on the inhabitants, doing them many important services, and having said to Herod many friendly things, and having been replied to in corresponding terms, he was conducted back again to the seacoast, and to the harbor, and that not by one city only but by the whole country, having branches strewed in his road, and being greatly admired and respected for his piety.

What again did your other grandfather, the emperor Tiberius[9] do? Does not he appear to have adopted an exactly similar line of conduct? At all events, during the three and twenty years that he was emperor, he preserved the form of worship in the Temple as it had been handed down from the earliest times, without abrogating or altering the slightest particular of it.

Moreover, I have it in my power to relate one act of ambition on his part, though I suffered an infinite number of evils when he was alive; but nevertheless the truth is considered dear, and much to be honored by you. Pilate[10] was one of the emperor's lieutenants, having been appointed governor of Judaea. He, not more with the object of doing honor to Tiberius than with that of vexing the multitude, dedicated some gilt shields in the palace of Herod, in the holy city; which had no form nor any other forbidden thing represented on them except some necessary inscription which mentioned these two facts, the name of the person who had placed them there, and the person in whose honor they were so placed there. But when the multitude heard what had been done, and when the circumstance became notorious, then the people, putting forward the four sons of the king [Herod], who were in no respect inferior to the kings themselves, in fortune or in rank, and his other descendants, and those magistrates who were among them at the time, entreated him to alter and to rectify the innovation which he had committed in respect of the shields; and not to make any alteration in their national customs, which had hitherto been preserved without any interruption, without being in the least degree changed by any king or emperor.

But when he steadfastly refused this petition (for he was a man of a very inflexible disposition, and very merciless as well as very obstinate), they cried out: "Do not cause a sedition; do not make war upon us; do not destroy the peace which exists. The honor of the emperor is not identical with dishonor to the ancient laws; let it not be to you a pretence for heaping insult on our nation. Tiberius is not desirous that any of our laws or customs shall be destroyed. And if you yourself say that he is, show us either some command from him, or some letter, or something of the kind, that we, who have been sent to you as envoys, may cease to trouble you, and may address our supplications to your master."

But this last sentence exasperated him in the greatest possible degree, as he feared lest they might in reality go on an embassy to the emperor, and might impeach him with respect to other particulars of his government, in respect of his corruption, and his acts of insolence, and his rapine, and his habit of insulting people, and his cruelty, and his continual murders of people untried and uncondemned, and his never-ending, gratuitous and most grievous inhumanity. Therefore, being exceedingly angry, and being at all times a man of most ferocious passions, he was in great perplexity, neither venturing to take down what he had once set up, nor wishing to do any thing which could be acceptable to his subjects, and at the same time being sufficiently acquainted with the firmness of Tiberius on these points.

Those who were in power in our nation, seeing this, and perceiving that he was inclined to change his mind as to what he had done, but that he was not willing to be thought to do so, wrote a most supplicatory letter to Tiberius. And he, when he had read it, what did he say of Pilate, and what threats did he utter against him! But it is beside our purpose at present to relate to you how very angry he was, although he was not very liable to sudden anger; the facts speak for themselves. Immediately, without putting any thing off till the next day, he wrote a letter, reproaching and reviling him in the most bitter manner for his act of unprecedented audacity and wickedness, and commanding him immediately to take down the shields and to convey them away from the metropolis of Judaea to Caesarea,[11] [. . .] in order that they might be set up in the temple of Augustus. And accordingly, they were set up in that edifice. And in this way he provided for two matters: both for the honor due to the emperor, and for the preservation of the ancient customs of the city.[12]

Now the things set up on that occasion were shields, on which there was no representation of any living thing whatever engraved. But now the thing proposed to be erected is a colossal statue. Moreover, then the erection was in the dwelling house of the governor; but they say, that which is now contemplated is to be in the inmost part of the Temple, in the very holy of holies itself, into which, once in the year, the high priest enters, on the day called the great fast,[13] to offer incense, and on no other day, being then about in accordance with our national law also to offer up prayers for a fertile and ample supply of blessings, and for peace to all mankind. [. . .] Great are the precautions taken by our lawgiver with respect to the holy of holies, as he determined to preserve it alone inaccessible to and untouched by any human being.

How many deaths then do you not suppose that the people, who have been taught to regard this place with such holy reverence, would willingly endure rather than see a statue introduced into it? I verily believe that they would rather slay all their whole families, with their wives and children, and themselves last of all, in the ruins of their houses and families, and Tiberius knew this well. And what did your great-grandfather, the most excellent of all emperors that ever lived upon the earth, he who was the first to have the appellation of Augustus given him, on account of his virtue and good fortune; he who diffused peace in every direction over earth and sea, to the very furthest extremities of the world? Did not he, when he had heard a report of the peculiar characteristics of our Temple, and that there is in it no image or representation made by hands, no visible likeness of Him who is invisible, not attempt at any imitation of his nature, did not he, I say, marvel at and honor it? For as he was imbued with something more than a mere smattering of philosophy, inasmuch as he had deeply feasted on it, and continued to feast on it every day, he partly retraced in his recollection all the precepts of philosophy which his mind had previously learnt, and partly also he kept his learning alive by the conversation of the literary men who were always about him; for at his banquets and entertainments, the greatest part of the time was devoted to learned conversation, in order that not only his friends' bodies but their minds also might be nourished.

And though I might be able to establish this fact, and demonstrate to you the feelings of Augustus, your great-grandfather, by an abundance of proofs, I will be content with two. In the first place, he sent commandments to all the governors of the different provinces throughout Asia, because he heard that the sacred first fruits were neglected, enjoining them to permit the Jews alone to assemble together in the synagogues,[14] for that these assemblies were not revels, which from drunkenness and the intoxication proceeded to violence, so as to disturb the peaceful condition of the country, but were rather schools of temperance and justice, as the men who met in them were students of virtue, and contributed the first fruits every year, sending commissioners to convey the holy things to the Temple in Jerusalem.

In the next place, he commanded that no one should hinder the Jews, either on their way to the synagogues, or when bringing their contributions, or when proceeding in obedience to their national laws to Jerusalem, for these things were expressly enjoined, if not in so many words, at all events in effect. [. . .] He [also] commanded perfect sacrifices of whole burnt offerings to be offered up to the most high God every day, out of his own revenues, which are performed up to the present time, and the victims are two sheep and a bull, with which Caesar honored the altar of God, well knowing that there is in the Temple no image erected, either in open sight or in any secret part of it.[15] But that great ruler, who was inferior to no one in philosophy, considered within himself, that it is necessary in terrestrial things, that an especial holy place should be set apart for the invisible God, who will not permit any visible representation of himself to be made, by which to arrive at a participation in favorable hopes and the enjoyment of perfect blessings.

And your grandmother, Julia Augusta,[16] following the

example of so great a guide in the paths of piety, did also adorn the Temple with some golden vials and censers, and with a great number of other offerings, of the most costly and magnificent description; and what was her object in doing this, when there is no statue erected within the Temple? For the minds of women are, in some degree, weaker than those of men, and are not so well able to comprehend a thing which is appreciable only by the intellect, without any aid of objects addressed to the outward senses; but she, as she surpassed all her sex in other particulars, so also was she superior to them in this, by reason of the pure learning and wisdom which had been implanted in her, both by nature and by study; so that, having a masculine intellect, she was so sharp-sighted and profound, that she comprehended what is appreciable only by the intellect, even more than those things which are perceptible by the outward senses, and looked upon the latter as only shadows of the former.

Therefore, O master, having all these examples most nearly connected with yourself and your family, of our purposes and customs, derived from those from whom you are sprung, of whom you are born, and by whom you have been brought up, I implore you to preserve those principles which each of those persons whom I have mentioned did preserve; they who were themselves possessed of imperial power do, by their laws, exhort you, the emperor; they who were august, speak to you who are also Augustus; your grandfathers and ancestors speak to their descendant; numbers of authorities address one individual, all but saying, in express words: Do not you destroy those things in our councils which remain, and which have been preserved as permanent laws to this very day; for even if no mischief were to ensue from the abrogation of them, still, at all events, the result would be a feeling of uncertainty respecting the future, and such uncertainty is full of fear, even to the most sanguine and confident, if they are not despisers of divine things.

If I were to enumerate the benefits which I myself have received at your hands, the day would be too short for me; besides the fact that it is not proper for one who has undertaken to speak on one subject to branch off to a digression about some other matter. Even if I should be silent, the facts themselves speak and utter a distinct voice. You released me when I was bound in chains and iron.[17] Who is there who is ignorant of this? But do not, after having done so, O emperor, bind me in bonds of still greater bitterness: for the chains from which you released me surrounded a part of my body, but those which I am now anticipating are the chains of the soul, which are likely to oppress it wholly and in every part; you abated from me a fear of death, continually suspended over my head; you received me when I was almost dead through fear; you raised me up as it were from the dead. Continue your favor, O master, that your Agrippa may not be driven wholly to forsake life; for I shall appear (if you do not do so) to have been released from bondage, not for the purpose of being saved, but for that of being made to perish in a more conspicuous manner. [. . .]

I am willing to descend from this spendid position in which you have placed me; I do not deprecate a return to the condition in which I was a short time ago; I will give up everything; I look upon everything as of less importance than the one point of preserving the ancient customs and laws of my nation unaltered; for if they are violated, what could I say, either to my fellow countrymen or to any other men? It would follow of necessity that I must be looked upon as one of two things, either as a betrayer of my people, or as one who is no longer accounted a friend by you. And what could be a greater misery than either of these two things? For if I am still reckoned among the company of your friends, I shall then receive the imputation of treason against my own nation, if neither my country is preserved free from all misfortune, nor even the Temple left inviolate. [. . .]

Having written this letter and sealed it, he sent it to Gaius, and then shutting himself up he remained in his own house, full of agony, confusion, disorder and anxiety, as to what was the best way of approaching and addressing the emperor; for he and his people had incurred no slight danger, but they had reason to apprehend expulsion from their country, slavery and utter destruction, as impending not only over those who were dwelling in the holy land, but over all the Jews in every part of the world.

But the emperor, having taken the letter and read it, and having considered every suggestion which was contained in it, was very angry, because his intentions had not been executed; and yet, at the same time, he was moved by the appeals to his justice and by the supplications which were thus addressed to him, and in some respects he was pleased with Agrippa, and in some he blamed him.

He blamed him for his excessive desire to please his fellow countrymen, who were the only men who had resisted his orders and shown any unwillingness to submit to his deification; but he praised him for concealing and disguising none of his feelings, which conduct he said was a proof of a liberal and noble disposition. Therefore being somewhat appeased, at least as far as appearance went, he condescended to return a somewhat favorable answer, granting to Agrippa that highest and greatest of all favors, the consent that this erection of his statue should not take place; and he commanded letters to be written to Publius Petronius the governor of Syria, enjoining him not to allow any alterations or innovations to be made with respect to the temple of the Jews. Nevertheless, though he did grant him the favor, he did not grant it without any alloy, but he mingled with it a grievous terror; for he added to the letter the following:

"If any people in the bordering countries, with the exception of the metropolis itself, wishing to erect altars or temples, nay, images or statues, in honor of me and of my family are hindered from doing so, I charge you at once to punish those who attempt to hinder them, or else to bring them before the tribunal."

Now this was nothing else but a beginning of seditions and civil wars, and an indirect way of annulling the gift which he appeared to be granting. For some men, more out of a desire of mortifying the Jews than from any feelings of loyalty towards Gaius, were inclined to fill the whole country with erections of one kind or another. But they who beheld the violation of their national customs practised before their eyes were resolved above all things not to endure such an injury unresistingly. But Gaius, judging those who were thus excited to disobedience to be worthy of the most severe punishment possible, a second time ordered his statue to be erected in the Temple. However, by the providence and care of God, who beholds all things and governs all things in accordance with justice, not one of the neighboring nations made any movement at all; so that there was no occasion for these commands being carried into effect, and these inexorably appointed calamities all terminated in only a moderate degree of blame.

I Take Refuge

THE PRAYER OF ASENATH

A Hellenistic Midrash tells of the conversion of beautiful Asenath, daughter of Potiphar, Pharaoh's chief counselor, who fell in love with Biblical Joseph. She renounced her family's idols, gave to the poor her costly robes and jewelry, acknowledged the God of mercy and compassion and prayed. Having thus become a proselyte, Joseph married her and both received Pharaoh's blessing. The story has all the signs of Hellenistic propaganda for the Jewish faith. Rabbinic and patristic sources do not mention this Midrash, but the original Greek rendition has been preserved, as also have been a Syriac, Armenian and Slavonic translation. Asenath's prayer is here reproduced.

I take refuge with Thee, O Lord.
As the little child flees in fear to the father,
and the father takes it to his bosom,
so do Thou stretch forth Thy hands as a loving father
and save me from the enemy who pursues me as a lion,
from Satan, the father of the Egyptian gods,
who desires to devour me
because I have despised his children, the Egyptian gods.
Deliver me from his hands,
lest he cast me into the fire;

lest the monster of the deep eat me up,
and I perish forever.
Save me;
for my father and mother deny me
and I have no hope nor refuge but Thy mercy,
O Lover of men,
Helper of the broken-hearted.
There is no father so good and sweet as Thou, O Lord.
All the houses my father gives me as possessions are for a time
    and perishable;
but the houses of Thy possession, O Lord,
are indestructible and last forever.

Inspired Reason

FROM THE FOURTH BOOK OF MACCABEES

Basing his material on Second Maccabees, an author writing in Greek
at the beginning of the Christian era, composed a treatise, known as the
Fourth Book of Maccabees, in which he tried to demonstrate "the power of
inspired reason over the passions and over pain." He believed that adherence
to Torah would lead to attainment of the central virtues of Stoic philosophy.
The treatise is a good example of the symbiosis of Hellenist and Jewish
thought. Our selection is its concluding chapter.

O Israelites, children born of the seed of Abraham, obey
this Law, and be righteous in all ways, recognizing that Inspired Reason is lord over the passions, and over pains, not
only from within, but from without ourselves; by which means
those men, delivering up their bodies to the torture for righteousness' sake, not only won the admiration of mankind, but
were deemed worthy of a divine inheritance. And through
them the nation obtained peace and restoring the observance
of the Law in our country has captured the city from the
enemy.

Vengeance has pursued the tyrant Antiochus [Epiph-
anes] upon earth, and in death he suffers punishment. For

when he failed utterly to constrain the people of Jerusalem to live like heathens and abandon the customs of our fathers, he thereupon left Jerusalem and marched away against the Persians.

Now these are the words that the mother of the seven sons, the righteous woman, spoke to her children:

"I was a pure maiden, and I strayed not from my father's house, and I kept guard over the rib that was builded into Eve. No seducer of the desert, no deceiver in the field, corrupted me; nor did the false, beguiling Serpent sully the purity of my maidenhood; I lived with my husband all the days of my youth; but when these my sons were grown up, their father died.

"Happy was he; for he lived a life blessed with children, and he never knew the pain of their loss. Who, while he was yet with us, taught you the Law and the prophets. He read to us of Abel who was slain by Cain, and of Isaac who was offered as a burnt offering, and of Joseph in the prison. And he spake to us of Phinehas, the zealous priest, and he taught you the song of Hananiah, Azariah, and Mishael in the fire. And he glorified also Daniel in the den of lions, and blessed him; and he called to your minds the saying of Isaiah, 'Yea even though thou pass through the fire, the flame shall not hurt thee' (Isa. 43:2). He sang to us the words of David the psalmist, 'Many are the afflictions of the just' (Ps. 34:20). He quoted to us the proverb of Solomon, 'He is a tree of life to all them that do his will.' (Prov. 3:18). He confirmed the words of Ezekiel, 'Shall these dry bones live?' (Ezek. 37:3). For he forgot not the song that Moses taught, which teaches, 'I will slay and I will make alive. This is your life and the blessedness of your days.' " (Deut. 32:39; 30:20).

Ah, cruel was the day, and yet not cruel, when the cruel tyrant of the Greeks set the fire blazing for his barbarous braziers, and with his passions boiling brought to the catapult and back again to his tortures the seven sons of the daughter of Abraham, and blinded the eyeballs of their eyes, and cut out their tongues, and slew them with many kinds of torment. For which cause the judgment of God pursued, and shall pursue, the accursed wretch. But the sons of Abraham with their victorious mother are gathered together unto the place of their ancestors, having received pure and immortal souls from God, to whom be glory for ever and ever. Amen.

In Defense of Judaism

FROM FLAVIUS JOSEPHUS: AGAINST APION

After completing his major works, *The Jewish War* and *The Jewish Antiquities*, Flavius Josephus wrote (about A.D. 96) a short book, *Against Apion* (*Contra Apionem*). The title refers to a first-century grammarian and anti-Jewish author of Alexandria. The attacks by Apion and other pagan writers directed against Josephus' historiography and the Jewish religion in general caused Josephus to write this presentation of his religious beliefs and to state his position in the intellectual world around him. He reveals a detailed knowledge of Greek literature and an understanding of the contribution of the Greek philosophers to human thought, but criticizes the Greeks for neglecting the records of their history, for ignoring religion in their legislation, and for the immorality of their gods. In discussing ancient writers, Josephus quotes works now lost and surviving only in these quotations.

In his passionately eloquent exposition, Josephus pictures ancient Israel not as a state (the fall of which he described in his works) but as a religious society. Israel is a people with a political, historical past. Its true task, however, is to maintain an extraterritorial society dedicated to religious life and fellowship and cultivating a universally applicable faith.

Introduction

Now as Apollonius Molon,[18] Lysimachus[19] and some others, partly from ignorance, but chiefly from ill will, have written treatises about our lawgiver Moses and our laws, which are neither fair nor true, calumniating Moses as an imposter and deceiver, and asserting that our laws teach us wickedness and not virtue, I intend to state briefly, to the best of my ability, our constitution as a whole and its details. For I think it will then be plain that the laws we have are most excellently adapted for the advancement of piety, and for the interests of society, and for general philanthropy, as also for justice, for sustaining labors with fortitude, and for contempt of death. [. . .]

I would say this first, that those who were lovers of order and laws—one law for all—and who first introduced them, when men were living without law and order, may well have this testimony, that they were better than other men in mildness and natural virtue. And certainly such persons endeavor to have every thing they introduce believed to be very ancient, that they may not be thought to imitate others, but may rather seem themselves to have suggested an orderly way of life to others. Since, then, this is the case, the excellence of a legislator is seen in seeing what is best, and in persuading those who are to use the laws he ordains to have a good opinion of them, and the excellence of a people is seen in their abiding by the laws, and making no changes in them either in prosperity or adversity.

The work of Moses

Now, I say that our legislator is the most ancient of all the legislators who are anywhere recorded. For Lycurgus and Solon, and Zaleucus, the legislator of the Locrians, and all those legislators who are admired by the Greeks, seem to be of yesterday if compared with our legislator, indeed the very word "law" was not so much as known in old times among the Greeks.[20] Homer bears me out in this, for he never uses the word law in all his poems. Indeed there was in his time no such thing, but the multitude was governed by undefined opinions and by the orders of their kings. They continued also a long time after Homer in the use of these unwritten customs, although they frequently changed them to suit a particular emergency. But our legislator, who was of so much greater antiquity than the rest (as even those who speak against us upon all occasions admit), exhibited himself to the people as their best guide and counsellor; he included in his legislation the whole conduct of life, and persuaded his people to accept it, and brought it to pass that those who were acquainted with his laws did most carefully observe them.

[. . .] When [our legislator] had first persuaded himself that his actions and designs were governed by God's will, he thought it his duty to impress that notion above all things upon the multitude; for those who believe that God surveys their lives cannot bear the thought of sin. Such was our legislator, who was no imposter, or deceiver, as his revilers say unjustly, but such a one as they boast Minos [of Crete] to have been among the Greeks, and other legislators after him. For some of them maintained that they had their laws from God, and Minos referred the oracular origin of his laws to Apollo and his oracle at Delphi, whether they thought they were really so derived, or that they could so more easily persuade the people to obey them. And as to who made the best laws, and who had the truest of God, it is easy to determine this by comparing the laws themselves together, for it is time that we come to that point.

Theocracy

There are innumerable differences in detail in the customs and laws that prevail among all mankind; for some legislators have permitted their governments to be monarchies, others oligarchies, and others democracies. But our legislator had no regard to any of these things, but ordained our government to be what, by a strained expression, may be termed a theocracy, ascribing the sovereignty and authority to God. He persuaded all to look to Him as the author of all good things that were enjoyed either in common by all mankind, or by each individual privately, and of all that they themselves obtained by prayer in their greatest straits. He informed them also that it was impossible to escape God's observation, either in any of their outward actions, or in any of their inward thoughts. Moreover, he represented God as One, unbegotten,[21] and immutable through all eternity, surpassing all mortal conception in beauty, and though known to us by His power, yet unknown to us as to His essence. I do not now say that the wisest of the Greeks were taught these notions of God by principles that Moses supplied them with; but they have borne emphatic witness that these notions are good and agreeable to the nature and majesty of God.

Greek philosophy versus Jewish religion

For Pythagoras, Anaxagoras, Plato, the Stoics that succeeded them, and almost all other philosophers, seem to have had similar notions about the nature of God. But these men disclosed those true notions to the few, because the body of the people were prepossessed by other opinions, while our legislator, who made his actions square with his laws, not only prevailed upon his contemporaries to agree to his notions, but so firmly imprinted this faith in God upon all their posterity, that it could never be moved. And the reason why our lawgiver in his legislation far exceeded all other legislators in usefulness to all, is that he did not make religion a part of virtue, but had the insight to make the various virtues parts of religion; I mean justice, fortitude, self-control, and the mutual harmony in all things of the members of the community with one another.[22] All our actions and studies and words have a connection with piety towards God; for our lawgiver has left none of these things indefinite or undetermined.

There are two ways of arriving at any discipline or moral conduct of life; the one is by instruction in words, the other by exercises in practice. Now all other lawgivers separated these two ways in their codes, and choosing the one of those methods which best pleased them, neglected the other. Thus did the Lacedaemonians and Cretans teach by exercises in practice, and not by words; while the Athenians and almost all the other Greeks made laws about what was to be done or left undone, but neglected exercising people thereto in practice.

But our legislator very carefully joined these two methods of instruction together. He neither left these exercises in practice to go on without verbal instruction, nor did he permit the hearing of the Law to proceed without exercises in practice. Beginning immediately with the earliest infancy, and the partaking of every one's food, he left nothing of the very smallest consequence to be done at the pleasure and caprice of the persons themselves; he made fixed rules and laws what sorts of food they should abstain from, and what sorts they should make use of, as also what intercourse they should have with others; what diligence they should use in their occupations, and what times of rest should be interposed; that, by living under those laws as under a father and master, we might be guilty of no sin either from wilfulness or ignorance.

Knowledge and conduct of life

He did not suffer the pretext of ignorance to be valid. He showed the Law to be the best and most necessary of instructions, for he ordained the people to leave off all their other occupations, and assemble together to hear the Law and to be perfectly instructed in it, not once or twice or on several occasions, but every week; a thing which all other legislators seem to have neglected.

Indeed most of mankind are so far from living according to their own laws, that they hardly know them. Only when they have sinned do they learn from others that they have transgressed the law. Even those who are in the highest and most important offices confess they are not acquainted with their laws, and are obliged to take experts in those laws for their assessors in the administration of public affairs. But if anyone only were to ask anyone of our people about our laws, he could more easily tell them all than he could tell his own name. Because of our having learned them as soon as ever we became sensible of anything, we have them as it were engraven on our souls. Transgressors are but few; it is impossible, when any do offend to escape punishment by excuses.

And it is this very thing that principally creates such wonderful oneness of mind among us. For our having one and the same religious belief, and our having no difference from one another in our course of life and manners, brings about among us the most excellent accord in human character. Among us alone will no one hear any discourses about God that contradict one another, which are yet frequent among other nations (and this is true not only among ordinary persons, according to one's personal disposition, but some of the philosophers also have been bold enough to indulge in such speculations; some attempting to argue against the existence of God,[23] others taking away His providence over mankind).[24]

Nor will anyone perceive amongst us any difference in the conduct of our lives. The actions of all among us are common, and we have one doctrine about God, which chimes in with our law and affirms that He surveys all things. And as to the conduct of our lives, that we consider that all things ought to have piety for their end, anybody may hear even from our women and dependents [. . .].

Government

As we are ourselves persuaded that our Law was made in accordance with the will of God, it would be impious for us not to observe the same. For what is there in it that anybody would change, or what could one invent better, or what could one borrow from other people's laws more excellent? Would any have the entire framework of our constitution altered? And what could be a better or more righteous policy than ours which makes us esteem God the head of the universe, which commits to the priests generally the administration of the principal affairs, and entrusts the rule over the other priests to the supreme high priest? Nor did our legislator, at their first appointment, advance these priests to that dignity for their riches, or for any other fortuitous advantages, but he entrusted the managment of divine worship mainly to those who exceeded others in powers of persuasion and in self-control. These men had the strict care of the Law, and had the rest of the people's conduct committed to them: for the priests were ordained to be overseers of everything, and to be judges in doubtful cases, and to be the punishers of condemned persons.

What form of government then can be more saintly than this? What more worthy worship can be paid to God than we pay, where the entire body of the people are prepared for religion, where an extraordinary degree of care is required in the priests, and where the whole polity is so ordered as if it were some sacred ceremony? For what foreigners, when they solemnize such festivals, and call them mysteries and initiations, are not able to observe even for a few days, we observe with much pleasure and unshaken resolution during our whole lives.

What are the things then that we are commanded or forbidden? They are simple and well known.

God

The first command is concerning God; it affirms that God is almighty and perfect and blessed, self-sufficing and sufficient for all; He is the beginning, the middle and the end of all things. He is manifest in His works and benefits, and more manifest than any other being; but His form and magnitude is most obscure. All materials, let them be ever so costly, are unworthy to compose an image of Him, and all arts are inartistic to express the notion of Him. We cannot see anything like Him, nor is it agreeable to piety to conjecture about Him. We see His works, the light, the heaven, the earth, the sun and moon, the waters, the generations of animals and the growth of fruits. God did not make these things with hands nor with labor, nor did He need the assistance of any to co-operate with Him.[25] His will resolved they should be made and be good also, and they were made and became good immediately. All men ought to follow and worship Him in the exercise of virtue; for this way of worship of God is the most saintly.

There is also but one temple for one God (for like ever loveth like), common to all men, because God is common to all. His priests are continually occupied by His worship, led by him who is head of the line. His office is to offer sacrifices to God with his fellow-priests, to see that the laws are observed, to determine controversies, and to punish those convicted of wrong-doing. He that does not submit to him is subject to the same punishment as for impiety towards God Himself.

When we offer sacrifices to Him, we do not take this as an occasion for drunken self-indulgence (for such excesses are against the will of God) but for sobriety, orderliness, and readiness for our other occupations. At these sacrifices we ought first to pray for the welfare of all, and after that for our own (for we are made for fellowship with one another), and he who prefers the common good to his own private good is especially acceptable to God. And let our prayers and supplications be made to God, not so much that He would give us what is good, (for He has already given that of His own accord, and distributed it alike to all,) as that we may duly receive it, and having received it, keep it. The law has also appointed several purifications at our sacrifices, whereby we are cleansed after a funeral, after any nocturnal pollution, and after union with our wives, and after some other occasions [. . .].

The family

What are our marriage laws? The Law recognizes no connection of the sexes but the natural connection between a man and his wife, and that only for the procreation of children; it abhors sodomy, and death is the punishment for that crime. The law commands us also, when we marry, not to have regard to dowry, nor to take a woman by violence, nor to persuade her by deceit and guile, but to demand her in marriage of him who has power to give her away and is fit to do so because of his nearness of kin. For the legislator says that a woman is inferior to her husband in all things. Let her, therefore, be obedient to him; not that he should ill-treat her, but that she may be directed; for God has given the authority to the husband. A husband is to lie only with his wife, and to seduce another man's wife is a wicked thing, which, if any one ventures upon, death is inevitably his punishment, as it is also his who forces a virgin betrothed to another man.

The Law, moreover, enjoins us to bring up all our offspring, and forbids women to cause abortion of what is begotten, or to destroy the foetus in any other way, for she will be an infanticide who thus destroys life and diminishes the human race. If any one, therefore, commits adultery or seduction, he cannot be considered pure. Why, even after the regular union of man and wife, the Law enjoins that they shall both wash themselves [. . .].

Moreover the Law does not permit us to feast at the births of our children, and so make excuses for drinking to excess, but it ordains that the very beginning of life should be sober. It also commands us to bring our children up in learning, and to make them conversant with the laws and acquainted with the acts of their forefathers, that they may imitate them, and, being grounded in them, may neither transgress them nor have any excuse for ignorance of them.

Our Law also provides for the decent burial of the dead, but without any extravagant expense at their funerals or the erection of conspicuous monuments. It orders that the nearest relations should perform their obsequies. It also ordains that all who pass by when any one is buried should accompany the funeral and join in the lamentation. It also orders that the house and its inhabitants should be purified after the funeral is over [. . .].

The Law also ordains, that parents should be honored next after God himself, and orders the son who does not requite them for the benefits he has received from them, but comes short on any occasion, to be handed over to justice and stoned. It also says that young men should pay due respect to every elder, because God is the eldest of all beings. It does not give permission to conceal anything from our friends, for that is not friendship which will not trust them. It also forbids the revelation of their secrets, if subsequent enmity arise between them. If any judge take bribes, his punishment is death.[26] He that neglects one that begs for aid, when he is able to relieve him, is liable to be called to account. What one has not entrusted to another, cannot be required back again. No one is to touch another's goods. He that lends money must not receive interest. These, and many more of the like sort are the rules that unite us in the bonds of society with one another.

Aliens and humanity at large

It will also be worth our while to see what equity our legislator would have us exercise in our treatment of aliens. For it will then appear that he made the best provision he possibly could, that we should neither infringe our own polity, nor show a grudging spirit to those who would cultivate a friendship with us. Thus our legislator receives in a friendly manner all those who wish to come and live under our laws, esteeming relationship to lie not only in family ties but also in similarity of life and manners. But he does not allow those who come to us only to sojourn for a time to be admitted into communion with us.

There are, however, various things which our legislator ordered us as obligatory on us to impart to all men; as to give fire, water, and food, to all that require them, to show them the way, and not to let any corpse lie unburied. He also would have us treat those accounted our enemies with moderation. For he does not allow us to set their country on fire, nor does he permit us to cut down their fruit trees; he also forbids us to strip those that have been slain in war. He has also provided for such as are taken captive, that they may not be ill-treated, especially women. Indeed, he has taught us gentleness and humanity so effectually, that he has not neglected the care of brute beasts, permitting no other than the regular use of them, and forbidding any other. If any of them flee to our houses like suppliants, we are forbidden to slay them. Nor may we kill the dams with their young ones; and we are obliged, even in an enemy's country, to spare and not kill those animals that labor for mankind. Thus has our lawgiver contrived to teach us merciful conduct every way, using such laws to instruct us therein, while those who break these laws are to be punished without excuse.

Reward, punishment and obedience to the Law

Most offences with us are capital, as if any one is guilty of adultery, if any forces a virgin, if any one is so impudent as to attempt to commit sodomy with a male, or if the person solicited submits to be so used. The Law is also equally inexorable for slaves. If any one cheats another in measures or weights, or makes a knavish bargain and sale to cheat, another, or if any one steal what belongs to another, and takes what he never deposited, all these have punishments allotted them which are not on the same scale as with other nations, but more severe. And as to misbehavior to parents, or impiety to God, for the very intention the offender is put to death immediately.

For those, on the other hand, who act according to the

laws the reward is not silver nor gold, nor again a crown of wild olive or parsley, nor any such public mark of commendation. Each one, having his own conscience bearing him witness, believes (on the word of the legislator, confirmed by the sure testimony of God) that to those that observe laws, even though they should be obliged to die willingly for them, God has granted that they shall come into being again, and after their vicissitudes have a better life than they had before. I should have hesitated to write thus at this time, were it not well known to all from their actions, that many of our people have frequently bravely resolved to endure any suffering rather than speak one word against the law. [. . .]

I venture to say, that no one can tell of so many, nay, of more than one or two, that have abandoned our laws, or feared death, I do not mean that easiest of deaths which happens in battles, but that which comes with bodily tortures, and seems to be the hardest death of all. Indeed I think those that have conquered us have put us to such deaths, not from their hatred to us when they had got us in their power, but rather from their desire to see a wonderful sight, namely, that there are men in the world, who believe the only evil is being compelled to do or to speak any thing contrary to their laws!

Nor ought men to wonder at us, if we are more courageous in dying for our laws than all other men are. For other men do not easily submit to what seem the easiest of our practices, I mean such things as working with our hands, and simple diet, and being contented to eat and drink and lie with our wives by rule, as also in respect to luxury, and again in the constant observance of our days of rest. For those that can use their swords in war, and can put their enemies to flight when they attack them, cannot bear to submit to rules about their mode of everyday living; whereas our being accustomed willingly to submit to laws in these cases makes us readier to show our fortitude upon other occasions.

Criticism of Greek institutions

[. . .] It is the custom of our country to keep our own laws, and not to advance criticism of the laws of others; our legislator has expressly forbidden us to jeer or rail at gods recognized by others, out of respect to the very name of God. But as our antagonists think to run us down by a comparison of their religion and ours, it is not possible to keep silence, especially as what I shall now say to confute these men will not be an invention of mine, but has been already said by many of the highest reputation.

For who among those that have been admired among the Greeks for wisdom has not greatly censured not only the most famous poets, but also the most esteemed legislators, for spreading originally among the masses such notions concerning the gods as that they may be allowed to be as numerous as they themselves have a mind to declare, and that they are begotten by one another, and that in all kinds of ways. They also classify them in their places and ways of living, as one would classify various kinds of animals, placing some under the earth, others in the sea, the oldest of them all being bound in Tartarus. In the case of those gods to whom they have allotted heaven, they have set over them one who in name is their father, but in his actions a tyrant and despot; so that his wife and brother and daughter, whom he brought forth from his own head, made a conspiracy against him to seize upon him and confine him, as he had himself seized upon and confined his own father.

[. . .] Now what sensible person would not be provoked at such stories, to rebuke those that made them up, and to condemn the great silliness of those that believe them? They have even deified Terror and Fear, and even Madness and Fraud, and other of the vilest passions. And they have persuaded cities to offer sacrifices to the better sort of these gods. Thus they have been absolutely forced to esteem some gods as the givers of good things, and to call others averters of evil. These last they endeavor to move, as they would the vilest of men, by gifts and presents, expecting to receive some great mischief from them unless they bribe them as it were by such offerings.

[. . .] Nothing that I have said was unknown to those who were real philosophers among the Greeks, nor were they ignorant of the frigid pretensions of allegories. So they justly despised them and agreed with us in forming true and becoming notions of God. From this standpoint Plato would not admit into his republic any poet, and dismisses even Homer himself with panegyric, after placing a garland on his head and pouring ointment upon him, that he should not destroy right notions about God with his fables.[27] Plato also especially imitated our legislator in that he enjoined his citizens to pay to nothing more attention than to this, that every one of them should learn their laws accurately; as also that they should not have foreigners mixing with their own people at random, but that the republic should be pure, and consist only of those who obeyed the laws.

Apollonius Molon failed to consider this, when he accused us of not admitting those who have their own preconceptions about God, and having no fellowship with those who choose to observe a different way of living to ourselves. For this method is not peculiar to us, but common to all men, not to Greeks only, but also to men of the greatest reputation among the Greeks. The Lacedaemonians continually expelled foreigners and would not suffer their own citizens to travel abroad, suspecting that both these things would tend to the detriment of their laws. And perhaps there may be some reason to blame the rigid severity of the Lacedaemonians, for they gave no one the privilege of citizenship or indeed leave to live among them; whereas we, though we do not think fit to imitate the ways of others, yet willingly admit those that desire to share ours. And I think I may reckon this a proof both of our humanity and magnanimity.

But I shall say no more about the Lacedaemonians. And as to the Athenians, who glory in having made their city common to all men, Apollonius did not know what their behavior was either, for they punished without mercy those who did but speak one word about the gods contrary to their laws. On what other account was Socrates put to death? Certainly he neither betrayed their city to its enemies, nor was he guilty of any sacrilege; but it was because he swore by novel oaths, and affirmed either in earnest, or, as some say, only in jest, that a demon used to intimate to him what he should or should not do, that he was condemned to die by drinking hemlock. His accuser also complained that he corrupted the young men, because he induced them to despise the policy and laws of their city. Such was the punishment of Socrates, though a citizen of Athens.

And Anaxagoras of Clazomenae[28] was within a few votes of being condemned to death, because he said the sun, which the Athenians thought a god, was a red-hot mass of fire. They also made public proclamation, that they would give a talent to any one who would kill Diagoras of Melos,[29] because he was said to have laughed at their mysteries. Protagoras[30] also, who was thought to have written something about the gods that was not admitted by the Athenians, would have been arrested and put to death, if he had not fled quickly. Nor need we at all wonder that they thus treated such considerable men, seeing that they did not even spare women. For indeed they slew a certain priestess, because she was accused by somebody of initiating people into the worship of foreign gods; this was forbidden by their laws, and capital punishment was decreed to any who introduced a foreign god. But it is manifest that those who made such a law did not believe the gods of other nations to be really gods, else they would not have grudged themselves the advantage of having more gods than they already had. Such was the happy administration of the affairs of the Athenians.

The Scythians and the Persians

The Scythians also take a pleasure in killing men, and differ little from brute beasts, yet they think it reasonable to have their institutions upheld and they put to death Anacharsis,[31] a person greatly admired for his wisdom by the Greeks, because on his return home to them he appeared full of Greek customs. One may also find many to have been punished among the Persians on the very same account. But it is plain that Apollonius was greatly pleased with the laws of the Persians and admired them, doubtless because the Greeks had a taste of their courage and held similar opinions about the

gods! This similarity of opinion in religious matters was exhibited in their burning temples, and their courage in coming
and almost entirely enslaving the Greeks. And Apollonius imitated all the Persian practices, forcing other men's wives and
castrating their sons.

Judaism

Now with us it is a capital crime, if any one thus ill-treats
even a brute beast. And neither the fear of our conquerors, nor
the desire of imitating what other nations hold in esteem, has
been able to draw us away from our own laws. Nor have we
exercised our courage in undertaking wars to increase our
wealth, but only to continue in the observation of our laws.
For though we bear other losses with patience, yet when any
persons would compel us to violate our laws, we then choose
to go to war, even against tremendous odds, and bear the
greatest calamities to the last with much fortitude. [. . .]

It will be found that our laws have always inspired imitation and still more admiration in all other men. For the
earliest Greek philosophers, though to all appearance they
observed the laws of their own countries, yet in their actions
and philosophical notions followed our legislator, instructing
men to live simply and to have friendly communications with
one another. Moreover, multitudes have had a great inclination now for a long time to follow our religious observances;
there is not one city of the Greeks or barbarians, nor any nation, where our custom of resting on the seventh day has not
reached, and by whom our fasts and lighting of lamps and
many of our prohibitions in the matter of food are not observed. They also endeavor to imitate our mutual concord with
one another, the charitable distribution of our goods, our diligence in the crafts, and our fortitude in undergoing the dis-
tresses in behalf of our laws. And what is most wonderful, our
Law has no bait of pleasure to allure men to it, but only gains
ground on its own merits; and as God himself pervades all the
world, so has the Law passed through all the world. [. . .]
Even if we were unable ourselves to understand the excellence
of our laws, yet would the number of those who desire to

imitate them induce us to pride ourselves upon them. [. . .]

As to our laws themselves, more words are unnecessary. They can be seen for themselves, and evidently do not teach impiety, but the truest piety in the world; not calling men to misanthropy, but encouraging people to share what they have with one another freely; being enemies to injustice and eager for righteousness, anxious to banish idleness and extravagant living, teaching men to be content with what they have, and to work with determination; forbidding men to make war from a desire of greed, but making men bold in defending the laws; inexorable in punishing malefactors, admitting no sophistry of words, but ever established themselves by actions. Actions we adduce as surer proofs than what is written only.

And so I boldly say that we have become the teachers of other men in a great number of most excellent ideas. What is more excellent than inviolable piety? What is more just than obedience to the laws? What is more beneficial than mutual love and concord, neither to be divided by calamities, nor to become injurious and seditious in prosperity; to despise death when we are in war, and to apply ourselves in peace to crafts and agriculture; and to be persuaded that God surveys and directs everything everywhere? If these precepts had either been written before by others, or more exactly observed, we should have owed them thanks as their disciples, but if it is plain that we have made more use of them than any other men, and if we have proved that the original invention of them is our own, let the Apions and Molons and all others who delight in lies and abuse stand confuted.

VII. After the Fall of Jerusalem

The Heroes of Masada

FROM FLAVIUS JOSEPHUS: THE JEWISH WAR

When Rome conquered Judaea and Jerusalem fell (A.D. 70), there still remained three fortresses, strongly defended by the remnants of the Jewish rebels (*sicarii*). The last of them, Masada, defended by Eleazar, stubbornly resisted the concentrated Roman attack. The mighty fortress of Masada, overlooking the southwest shore of the Dead Sea, had been fortified by Jonathan, brother of Judah the Maccabee, and perfected under Herod the Great. The rock of Masada was high and steep. After overcoming serious strategic difficulties, the Romans built a solid bank for the operation of the battering ram. Eleazar, descendant of Judah the Galilean (leader of the Jewish rebels in the period of Herod), and his men had resolved "never to serve the Romans nor any master other than God, who alone is the true and just lord of mankind." Unable to offer further resistance, Eleazar bid his men to commit mass suicide and preserve their freedom, rather than "taste slavery." Some were ready to follow Eleazar, other, "of softer mold," were moved by pity for their wives and children and refused. Eleazar, therefore, renewed his proposal in a second speech, presented below.

The fall of Masada (April 73) ended the seven years' Judaeo-Roman war. The account of the defense of Masada and its fall is given by Flavius Josephus in the seventh book of his *The Jewish War*.

Thus spoke Eleazar:

Truly I was greatly mistaken in thinking that I was aiding brave men in their struggles for freedom—men determined to live with honor or to die. But you are, it seems, no better than the common herd in virtue or in courage, since you are afraid even of that death which will deliver you from the direst evils, though you ought neither to delay nor wait for a counsellor. For from of old and the first dawn of reason, have our nation's laws and divine revelation, confirmed by the deeds and noble spirit of our forefathers, continued to teach us that life, not death, is a misfortune to men.

For it is death that sets the soul at liberty, and permits it to depart to its proper and pure abode, where it will be free from every misery. But so long as it is imprisoned in a mortal body and infected with its pains, it is, to speak most truly, dead; for association with what is mortal befits not that which is divine. Great, it is true, is the power of the soul, even while imprisoned in the body, its sensible instrument, that invisibly, it moves and advances in its actions beyond the range of mortal nature. But it is not until, freed from that weight which hangs suspended from it and drags it down to earth, the soul has reassumed its proper sphere that it enjoys a blessed strength and a power wholly unrestricted, remaining, as does God himself, invisible to human eyes.

For certainly it is not seen when it is in the body. It enters unperceived and unseen still withdraws, its own nature one and uncorruptible, though a cause of change to the body. Because whatever the soul has touched lives and flourishes, whatever it is removed from withers and dies; so much is there in it of immortality.

[Here follows a reference to sleep, during which the soul "converses with God because of its relationship to Him," and a discourse on the Indian view of death as the release of the soul from the body. "Should we hold baser notions than the Indians?"]

But even had we from the first been educated in opposite principles and taught that to live is the supreme good and death a calamity, the occasion still is one that calls upon us to bear death cheerfully, since we die by the will of God and out of necessity. For long ago, so it seems, God issued against the entire Jewish nation a common decree—that we were to be deprived of life if we did not use it rightly. Do not ascribe the blame to yourselves, nor the credit to the Romans, that this war with them has involved us all in ruin. It is not their

might that has caused these things to pass, a more powerful
agent has intervened to give them the semblance of victory.

[Here follow examples of persecutions of Jews outside
Judaea and not occasioned by the Romans.]

Perhaps, however, it was because they were in a foreign
land and unable to offer any opposition to their enemies that
these were killed. But had not all those of us who waged war
against the Romans in our own country sufficient reason to
entertain hopes of certain victory? We had arms, walls, fortresses well nigh impregnable, and a spirit not to be shaken by
any perils in the cause of liberty. But these advantages helped
us only for a brief season, and only served to buoy us up with
hopes, proving in the end to be the source of greater misfortunes. For, as if provided not for the security of those who had
prepared them but for the more glorious triumph of our foes,
all has been taken, all has fallen into the hands of our enemies.
Those who perished in battle we cannot but count happy, for
they died defending, not betraying, liberty. But the multitudes
who have been subjected to the Romans—who would not pity
them? Who would not make haste to die, ere he suffered the
same fate as they? Some have expired upon the rack, some
under the torture of fire and from scourges. Some, half-
devoured by wild beasts, have, after affording derision and
merriment to their foes, been preserved alive to furnish these
beasts with a second repast. But those men are to be deemed
most miserable who, still living, often pray for death, yet cannot obtain it.

And where is now that great city, the metropolis of the
entire Jewish nation, protected by so many walls, secured by
so many forts and by the vastness of its towers, which could
hardly contain its implements of war and had so many myriads
of men to fight for it? What has become of that city of ours
which, so it was believed, God himself had founded? Uprooted
from its foundations, it has been swept away and its sole preserved memorial is the camp of its destroyers still planted
upon its ruins! Hapless old men are sitting among the ashes
of the Temple, and a few women, reserved by our enemies for
the basest of injuries.

Who of us, then, casting these things in his mind, shall bear to see the sun, even could he live unendangered? Who is so much his country's foe, so unmanly, so fond of life, not to regret that he is still alive? How I would that we had all been dead ere we had seen that holy city overthrown by hostile hands, our holy Temple so profanely uprooted! But since we were beguiled by a not ignoble hope that we might possibly be able to avenge her on her foes, and that hope is now forever vanished, leaving us alone in our distress, let us hasten to die honorably. Let us take pity on ourselves, our children, and our wives while it is still in our power to show them pity. For we were born to die, as were those whom we have begotten; and this even the fortunate cannot escape. But insult and servitude and the sight of our wives being led to infamy with their children, these, among men, are not natural or necessary evils; though those who do not prefer death, when death is in their power, must suffer even these because of their cowardice.

Elated with courage, we revolted against the Romans, and when bidden to assent to an offer of safety, would not listen to them. Who then, if they take us alive, does not anticipate their fury? Wretched will be the young, whose strong bodies can sustain many tortures, wretched, too, the old, whose age cannot endure afflictions! One man will see his wife dragged away by violence, another hear the voice of his child crying to a father whose hands are bound. But ours are still free and grasp the sword. While they are so free, let them do us honorable service. Let us die unenslaved by our foes, and, in a state of freedom, depart, together with our wives and children, from this life. That is what our laws command us to do, what our wives and children implore of us. God himself has brought this upon us, and the contrary is what the Romans, who fear lest any of us die before they capture us, desire. Instead of giving them their hoped-for pleasure in the possession of our persons, let us hasten, then to leave them in awe at our death and admiration at our fortitude.

While still anxious to inspire them with courage, Eleazar was cut short by his hearers, who, filled with uncontrollable ardor, were all in haste to commit the deed. [. . .] Natural passion and love were still alive in every breast, but the belief that what they had resolved to do was best for those dearest to them vanquished everything. They clasped and fondly embraced their wives and took their children in their arms, clinging to them and weeping as they kissed them for the last time. At the same time, and as if executing the deed with the hands of strangers, they carried out what they had resolved to do, deriving consolation in the exigency of slaying them from contemplation of the miseries they would endure if they fell into the hands of their enemies. Nor did anyone waver in the execution of this terrible task; all, in the end, perpetrated the deed upon their closest kin. Oh, wretched victims of necessity, to whom it seemed the lesser evil to slay with their own hands their wives and children!

Unable thereupon, to endure their anguish at the deed they had committed, and deeming it a wrong to the slain to survive them even for a moment, they hurriedly made a heap of all their effects, set it on fire, then chose by lot ten of their number to slay the rest. Stretched at the side of his fallen wife and children, with his arms about them, each then offered his throat to those who were to execute the rueful office. The latter, after slaying all without flinching, adopted [for their own death] the same lot-drawing procedure. The one to whose lot it fell to kill the other nine was, after so doing, to destroy himself on the bodies of his companions. None lacked the courage to equal the others in either execution or suffering. Eventually, the nine bared their throats. The last survivor examined all the bodies to see whether in so widespread a slaughter any perchance were left who still required his hand. On ascertaining that all were dead, he set fire to the palace, then drove his sword in one collected effort through his body, and fell by the side of his family.

They died believing that not a single soul among them was left alive to be subject to the Romans. But five children, an elderly woman, and still another woman, related to Eleazar and in sagacity and wisdom superior to most of her sex, escaped by hiding in the subterranean aqueducts when the rest were intent on slaughter. Including women and children, nine hundred and sixty perished on this occasion. [. . .]

The Romans, still expecting opposition, were in arms at daybreak. Having planked bridges from the mounds to the fortress, they advanced to the assault. When they saw no enemy but [only] fearful solitude on every side, flames within, and silence, they were at a loss to conjecture what had happened. In an effort to call forth some of those within, they shouted, as if at the discharge of a missile. On hearing the noise, the women emerged from their retreat and told the Romans what had occurred, one of them describing fully both what was said and how the deed was perpetrated. But the Romans, unable to credit so desperate an act, did not accept her account. In an attempt to quelch the flames, they quickly opened a passage through them, and reached the palace. Here they encountered the mounds of the slain. Instead of rejoicing at the death of their foes, they admired the courage of their resolve and the intrepid contempt of death so many had shown by such a deed as this.

The Vision of a New Era

FROM THE FOURTH BOOK OF EZRA

The fall of Jerusalem in the year A.D. 70 gave rise to the question: How could it come to be that ungodly Rome ("Babylon" in our text) triumphed over Zion, the city chosen by God and recipient of Messianic promises? Why had the Kingdom of God, envisaged as imminent by Daniel, failed to be established? The answer is revealed to the apocalyptic writer, hiding behind the name of the post-Exilic leader, Ezra. The catastrophe that befell Jerusalem is but a symbol of the state of the world at large, he postulates. The era which began with the fall of the first man is an era of evil and is to come to an end. The present rule of wickedness is a sign that the end is near. Thus the visionary's pessimism engulfs the whole historic existence of mankind. Daniel's vision is reinterpreted, with the "fourth kingdom" taken to refer to Rome. The divine plan calls for a new world. The Messiah, a transcendental figure, will appear and inaugurate a New Jerusalem. This new era of bliss on earth is not to endure; after four hundred years all humanity—including the Messiah—will die and the world will be "turned into the primeval silence seven days" (i.e., years). Only then will a universal resurrection take place and all men stand in judgment before the "splendor of the brightness of the Most High." And only in a "world to come" will the failure of Creation and of human history be rectified. Notwithstanding this failure, God says to the visionary, "Thou comest far short of being able to love my creation more than I."

The designation of this apocalypse as the "fourth" Ezra is to distinguish it from the Biblical Book of Ezra, the Book of Nehemiah, called in the Septuagint the "Second Ezra," and from the apocryphal book of Ezra. The Hebrew, or Aramaic, original is lost, and so is the Greek translation. Our knowledge of the book is based on the Syriac, Latin and other translations made from the Greek. Some of the ideas and terms of the book reappear in the New Testament Book of Revelation. The fourth of the seven visions of the book, the "Vision of the Disconsolate Women," which is among the selections here reproduced, finds its parallel in midrashic literature.

Introduction

In the thirtieth year after the downfall of the City,[1] I, Salathiel—who am also Ezra[2]—was in Babylon, and as I lay upon my bed I was disquieted . . . and my mind was preoccupied with my thoughts; because I saw Zion's desolation on the one hand matched with the abundant wealth of Babylon's[3] inhabitants on the other. And my spirit was stirred profoundly, and in my agitation I began to address the Most High.

Whence the evil?

And I said: O Lord my Lord, was it not Thou who in the beginning, when Thou didst form the earth—and that Thyself alone—didst speak and commandedst the dust, so that it gave Thee Adam,[4] a lifeless body? But yet it was both itself the formation of Thy hands and Thou breathedst into him the breath of life, so that he was made living before Thee. And Thou didst lead him into Paradise, which Thy right hand did plant before ever the earth came forward; and to him Thou commandedst one only commandment of Thine, but he transgressed it. Forthwith Thou appointedst death for him and for his generations, and from him were born nations and tribes, peoples and clans innumerable. And every nation walked after their own will, and behaved wickedly before Thee, and were ungodly—but Thou didst not hinder them.

Nevertheless again in due time Thou broughtest the Flood upon the earth and upon the inhabitants of the world, and destroyedst them. And their fate was one and the same; as death overtook Adam, so the Flood overwhelmed these. Nevertheless one of them Thou didst spare—Noah with his household and with him all the righteous his descendants.

And it came to pass that when the inhabitants upon the earth began to multiply, and there were born children also and peoples and nations many, that they began to practice ungodliness more than former generations. And it came to pass that when they practiced ungodliness before Thee, Thou didst choose Thee one from among them whose name was Abraham: him Thou didst love, and unto him only didst Thou reveal the end of the times secretly by night; and with him Thou didst make an everlasting covenant, and didst promise him that Thou wouldst never forsake his seed. And Thou gavest him Isaac, and to Isaac Thou gavest Jacob and Esau. And Thou didst set apart Jacob for Thyself, but Esau Thou didst hate; and Jacob became a great host. And it came to pass that when Thou leadest forth his seed out of Egypt, and didst bring them to the Mount Sinai,

Thou didst bow down the heavens,
didst make the earth quake
and convulsedst the world—
Thou didst cause the deeps to tremble
and didst alarm the spheres.
And Thy glory went through the four gates of fire, earthquake,
    wind, and cold,
To give the law to Jacob's seed
and the Commandment to the generation of Israel.

And yet Thou didst not take away from them the evil heart, that Thy Law might bring forth fruit in them. For the first Adam, clothing himself with the evil heart, transgressed and was overcome; and likewise also all who were born of him.[5] Thus the infirmity became inveterate; the Law indeed was in the heart of the people, but in conjunction with the evil germ; so what was good departed, and the evil remained.

So the times passed away and the years came to an end; and then Thou didst raise up for Thyself a servant whose name was David; and Thou commandedst him to build the City which is called after Thy name, and to offer Thee oblations therein of Thine own. And after this had been done many years, the inhabitants of the City committed sin, in all things doing even as Adam and all his generations had done: for they also had clothed themselves with the evil heart: and so Thou gavest Thy city over into the hands of Thine enemies.

Then I said in my heart: Are their deeds any better that inhabit Babylon? Has He for this rejected Zion? It came to pass when I came hither and saw ungodly deeds innumerable, and myself saw many sinners these thirty years, that my heart was perturbed. For I have seen
how Thou dost suffer the sinners
and dost spare the ungodly,
how Thou hast destroyed thy people
and preserved Thine enemies;
and hast not made known at all unto any how this course of Thine shall be abandoned. Have the deeds of Babylon been better than those of Zion? Has any other nation known Thee beside Israel? Or what tribes have so believed Thy covenants as those of Jacob?—whose reward nevertheless hath not appeared nor their labor borne fruit! For I have gone hither and thither through the nations and seen them in prosperity, although unmindful of Thy commandments.

Now, therefore, weigh Thou our iniquities, and those of the inhabitants of the world, in the balance and so shall be found which way the turn of the scale inclines. Or when was it that the inhabitants of the earth did not sin before Thee? Or what nation hath so kept Thy precepts? Individual men of note indeed Thou mayst find to have kept Thy precepts; but nations Thou shalt not find.

The divine reply

Thereupon the angel answered me who had been sent to

me, and whose name was Uriel;[6] and he said to me: Thy heart hath utterly failed thee regarding this world; and thinkest thou to comprehend the way of the Most High?

Then said I: Yes, my Lord.

And he answered me, and said: Three ways have I been sent to show thee, and three similitudes to set before thee: if thou canst declare me one of these I also will show thee the way thou desirest to see, and teach thee whence comes the evil heart.

And I said: Speak on, my Lord.

Then he said unto me:

Come, weigh me the weight of the fire;
Or measure me the measure of the wind,
Or recall me the day that is past.

Then answered I and said: Who of the earth-born could do so that thou shouldst ask me about such matters?

And he said to me: Had I asked thee
How many dwellings are in the heart of the sea?
Or how many springs in the source of the deep?
Or how many ways above the firmament?
Or where are the portals of Hades?
Or where the paths of Paradise?
Perchance thou wouldst have said to me:
Into the deep I have not descended,
nor as yet gone down into Hades;
Neither to heaven have I ever ascended,
nor entered Paradise.

But now I have only asked thee of the fire, the wind, and the day that is past—things without which thou canst not be; and yet thou hast vouchsafed me no answer about them!

He said moreover unto me: What belongs to thee—the things that have intermingled with thy growth—thou art incapable of understanding; how then should thy vessel[7] be able to comprehend the way of the Most High? For the way of the Most High has been formed without measure, how, then, should it be possible for a mortal in a corruptible world to understand the ways of the Incorruptible?

And when I heard these things I fell upon my face and said unto him: It would have been better that we had never been created than having come into the world to live in sins and suffer, and not to know why we suffer.[8]

And he answered me and said: Once upon a time the woods of the trees of the field went forth, and took counsel, and said: Come, let us go and make war against the sea, that it may retire before us, and we will make us more woods. In like manner also the waves of the sea took counsel, and said: Come, let us go up and wage war against the wood of the field, that there also we may win us more territory.

The counsel of the wood was in vain, for the fire came and consumed it; likewise, also, the counsel of the waves of the sea, for the sand stood up and stopped them. If thou, now, hadst been judge between them whom wouldst thou have justified or whom condemned? I answered and said: Both have taken a foolish counsel; for to the wood the land has been assigned, and to the sea a place to bear its waves.

Then he answered me and said: Thou hast judged aright; but why hast thou not given judgment in thine own case? For just as the earth has been assigned to the wood, and the place of the sea to bear its waves; even so the dwellers upon earth can understand only what is upon the earth, and they who are above the heavens that which is above the heavenly height.

The New Age

Then answered I and said: I beseech thee, O Lord, wherefore have I been endowed with an understanding to discern? For I meant not to ask about the ways above but of those things we daily experience;
Why is Israel to the heathen given over for reproach,
thy beloved people to godless tribes given up?
The Law of our fathers has been brought to destruction,
the written covenants exist no more;
We vanish from the world as locusts,
our life is as a breath.
We indeed are not worthy to obtain mercy; but what will He

do for His own name whereby we are called? It is about these things that I have asked.

Then he answered me and said: If thou survive thou shalt see, and if thou livest long thou shalt marvel; for the age is hastening to its end. Because it is unable to bear the things promised in their season to the righteous; for this age is full of sorrow and impotence.

For the evil concerning which thou askest me is sown, but the ingathering of it has not yet come. Unless, therefore, that which is sown be reaped, and unless the place where the evil is sown shall have passed away, the field where the good is sown cannot come. For a grain of evil seed was sown in the heart of Adam from the beginning, and how much fruit of ungodliness has it produced unto this time, and shall yet produce until the threshing-floor come!

Reckon up, now, in thine own mind: if a grain of evil seed has produced so much fruit of ungodliness, when once the ears of the good seed shall have been sown without number, how great a floor shall they be destined to fill?

Then I answered and said: How long and when shall these things be coming to pass? For our years are few and evil.

And he answered me and said: Thy haste may not exceed that of the Most High; for thou art hastening for thine own self, but the Exalted One on behalf of many.

Were not these questions of thine asked by the souls of the righteous in their chambers?[9] How long are we to remain here? When cometh the fruit upon the threshing-floor of our reward?

And to them the archangel Jeremiel[10] made reply, and said: Even when the number of those like yourself is fulfilled![11]
For he has weighed the age in the balance,
And with measure has measured the times,
And by number has numbered the seasons:
Neither will he move nor stir things,
till the measure appointed be fulfilled.[12]

Then I answered and said: O Lord my Lord, but behold

we are all full of ungodliness. Is it, perchance, on our account that the threshing-floor of the righteous is kept back—on account of the sins of the dwellers upon earth?

So he answered me and said: Go and ask the woman who is pregnant, when she has completed her nine months, if her womb can keep the birth any longer within her?

Then said I: No, Lord, it cannot. And he said to me: The netherworld and the chambers of souls are like the womb: for just as she who is in travail makes haste to escape the anguish of the travail; even so do these places hasten to deliver what has been entrusted to them from the beginning. Then to thee it shall be showed concerning those things that thou desirest to see.

The end will come soon

Then I answered and said: If I have found favor in thy sight, and if it be possible, and if I be sufficient, show me this also: whether there be more to come than is past, or whether the more part is already gone by us? For what is gone by I know, but what is to come I know not.

And he said to me: Stand to the right, and I will explain the meaning of a similitude unto thee.

So I stood, and saw, and lo! a blazing furnace passed by before me; and it happened that when the flame had gone by I looked and lo! the smoke remained still.

Thereupon there passed by before me a cloud full of water, and sent down much rain with a storm; and when the rainstorm was past the drops remained therein still.

Then said he unto me: Consider for thyself; for as the rain is more than the drops, and as the fire is greater than the smoke, so has the measure of what is past exceeded by far; but there are still left over—the drops and the smoke!

The signs which precede the end

Then I made supplication, and said: Thinkest thou that I shall live in those days?

He answered me, and said: As for the signs concerning which thou askest me, I may tell thee of them in part; but concerning thy life I have not been sent to speak to thee, nor have I any knowledge thereof.

Concerning the signs, however:

Behold, the days come when the inhabitants of earth shall be seized with great panic,
And the way of truth shall be hidden,
and the land be barren of faith.

And iniquity shall be increased above that which thou thyself now seest or that thou hast heard of long ago. And the land that thou seest now to bear rule shall be a pathless waste; and men shall see it forsaken: if the Most High grant thee to live, thou shalt see it after the third period in confusion.

Then shall the sun suddenly shine forth by night
and the moon by day:
And blood shall trickle forth from wood,
and the stone utter its voice:
The peoples shall be in commotion,
the outgoings of the stars shall change.

And one whom the dwellers upon earth do not look for shall wield sovereignty,[13] and the birds shall take to general flight,
and the sea shall cast forth its fish.
And one whom the many do not know will make his voice heard by night; and all shall hear his voice.
And the earth o'er wide regions shall open,
and fire burst forth for a long period:
The wild beasts shall desert their haunts;
and women bear monsters.
Salt water shall be found in the sweet;
friends shall attack one another suddenly.
Then shall intelligence hide itself,
and wisdom withdraw to its chamber—
by many shall be sought and not found.

And unrighteousness and incontinency shall be multiplied upon the earth. One land shall also ask another and say: Is Righteousness—that doeth the right—passed through thee? And it shall answer, No.

And it shall be
In that time men shall hope and not obtain,
shall labor and not prosper.

Such are the signs I am permitted to tell thee; but if thou wilt pray again, and weep as now, and fast seven days, thou shalt hear again greater things than these.

Conclusion

Then I awoke, and my body trembled greatly; my soul also was wearied even unto fainting. But the angel who came and spake with me took hold of me, strengthened me, and set me up upon my feet.

The Vision of the Disconsolate Woman

FROM THE FOURTH BOOK OF EZRA

And when I spake thus[14] in my heart I lifted up my eyes, and saw a woman upon the right; and lo! she was mourning and weeping with a loud voice, and was much grieved in mind, and her clothes were rent and there were ashes upon her head. Then I dismissed my thoughts in which I had been preoccupied, and turned to her and said: Wherefore weepst thou? And why art thou grieved in thy mind? And she said unto me: Suffer me, my lord, to indulge my sorrow and continue my grief, for I am embittered in soul and deeply afflicted.

And I said unto her: What has befallen thee? tell me.

She said unto me: I, thy servant, was barren, and bore no child, though I had a husband thirty years. Both hourly and daily during these thirty years I besought the Most High night and day.

And it came to pass after thirty years
God heard thy handmaid
and looked upon my affliction;
He considered my distress,
and gave me a son.

And I rejoiced in him greatly, I and my husband and all my fellow townsfolk, and we gave great glory unto the Mighty One. And I reared him with great travail. So when he was grown up, I came to take him a wife, and made a feast day.

And it came to pass when my son entered into his wedding chamber, he fell down and died. Then I removed the lights, and all my fellow townsfolk rose up to comfort me; but I remained quiet until the night of the next day. And it came to pass when they were all quiet and desisted from consoling, as I remained quiet, I rose up by night, and fled, and came to this field, as thou seest. And I purpose never again to return to the city, but here to stay and neither eat nor drink, but continually to mourn and to fast till I die.

Then I left the thoughts in which I was still occupied, and answered her in anger, and said: O thou above all other women most foolish! Seest thou not our mourning, and what has befallen us? How Zion, the mother of us all, is in great grief and deep affliction? It is right now to mourn, seeing that we all mourn, and to grieve, seeing that we are all grief-stricken; thou, however, art grief-stricken for one son. But ask the earth, and she shall tell thee, that it is she who ought to mourn the fall of so many that have sprung into being upon her. Yea, from the beginning all who have been born, and others who are to come—lo! they go almost all into perdition, and the multitude of them comes to destruction. Who, then, should mourn the more? Ought not she that has lost so great a multitude? or thou who grieved but for one? But if thou sayest to me: My lamentation is not like the earth's, for I have lost the fruit of my womb

which I bare with pains

and brought forth with sorrows—

but as regards the earth, it is according to the course of nature; the multitude present in it is gone as it came: then I say to thee: Just as thou hast borne offspring with sorrow, even so also the earth has borne her fruit, namely man, from the beginning unto him that made her.

Now, therefore, keep thy sorrow within,

and bear gallantly the misfortunes that have befallen thee.

For if thou wilt acknowledge God's decree to be just, thou
shalt receive thy son again in due time, and shalt be praised
among women. Therefore go into the city to thy husband.
And she said unto me: I will not do so: I will not enter the
city, but here will I die. So I proceeded to speak further unto
her, and said: No, woman! no, woman! do not do so;
but suffer thyself to be prevailed upon by reason of Zion's
        misfortunes,
be consoled by reason of Jerusalem's sorrow.
For thou seest how
our sanctuary is laid waste,
our altar thrown down;
our Temple destroyed,
our harp laid low;
our song is silenced,
our rejoicing ceased;
the light of our lamp is extinguished,
the ark of our covenant spoiled;
our holy things are defiled,
the name that is called upon us is profaned [. . .]
and what is more than all—
Zion's seal is now sealed up dishonored,
and given up into the hands of them that hate us.
Do thou, then, shake off thy great grief,
abandon thy much sorrow,
That the Mighty One may again forgive thee,
and the Most High give thee rest,
a respite from thy troubles!

     And it came to pass, while I was talking to her, lo!
her countenance on a sudden shone exceedingly,
and her aspect became brilliant as lightning,
so that I was too much afraid to approach her, and my heart
was terrified exceedingly: and while I was debating what this
might mean, she suddenly uttered a loud and fearful cry, so
that the earth shook at the noise. And when I looked, lo! the
woman was no longer visible to me, but there was a City
builded, and a place showed itself of large foundations. Then

I was afraid, and cried with a loud voice, and said: Where is Uriel, the angel who came unto me at the first? For he it is who has caused me to fall into this great bewilderment;
and so my prayer is made futile,
and my request disappointed!

And while I was speaking thus, lo! the angel came to me, who had come to me at the first; and when he saw that I lay on the ground as one dead, my understanding being confused, he grasped my right hand and strengthened me, and set me on my feet, and said to me:
What aileth thee?
Why art thou so disquieted?
Wherefore is thy understanding confused,
and the thoughts of thy heart?
And I said: Because thou hast forsaken me! Yet I did as thou commandedst, and went into the field, and lo! I have seen—and yet see—that which I am unable to express.

And he said unto me: Stand up like a man, and I will advise thee. Then said I: Speak on, my lord; only forsake me not, lest I die to no purpose.
For I have seen what I did not know and heard what I do not
    understand.
Or is my mind deceived,
And my soul in a dream?
Now, therefore, I beseech thee to show thy servant concerning
    this perplexity!
And he answered me, and said:
Hear me, and I will teach thee,
and tell thee concerning the things thou art afraid of;
for the Most High hath revealed many secrets unto thee.
For he hath seen thy righteous conduct,
how thou hast sorrowed continually for thy people,
and mourned greatly on account of Zion—
The matter, therefore, is as follows. The woman who appeared to thee a little while ago, whom thou sawest mourning and begannest to comfort: whereas now thou seest no likeness of a woman any more, but a builded City hath appeared unto

thee: and whereas she told thee of the misfortune of her son—this is the interpretation.

This woman, whom thou sawest, is Zion, whom thou now beholdest as a builded City. And whereas she said unto thee that she was barren thirty years: the reason is that there were three years[15] in the world before any offering was offered there [in Zion]. And it came to pass after three years that Solomon built the City, and offered offerings: then it was that the barren bare a son. And whereas she told thee that she reared him with travail: that was the divine dwelling in Jerusalem. And whereas she said unto thee: My son entering into his marriage-chamber died, and that misfortune befell her—this was the fall of Jerusalem that has come to pass. And lo! thou hast seen the heavenly pattern of her,[16] how she mourned her son, and thou didst begin to comfort her for what had befallen.

Now, the Most High seeing
that thou art grieved deeply
and art distressed wholeheartedly on account of her;
hath showed thee the brilliance of her glory,
and her majestic beauty.

Therefore I bade thee come into the field where no foundation of any building is, for in the place where the City of the Most High was about to be revealed no building-work of man could endure.

Therefore be not thou afraid, and let not thy heart be terrified; but go in and see the brightness and vastness of the building, as far as it is possible for thee with the sight of thine eyes to see!
Then shalt thou hear as much as the hearing of thine can hear.
For thou art blessed above many,
and art named before the Most High as but few!

And he departed from me. And I went forth and walked in the field greatly magnifying and praising the Most High on account of the marvelous acts which he performs in due season; and because he governs the times, and the things which come to pass in due time.

The Consolation of Zion

FROM THE APOCALYPSE OF BARUCH

This apocalypse is attributed to the prophet Jeremiah's disciple Baruch, who, after the destruction of Jerusalem, is bidden to "remain amid the desolation of Zion" and be shown the end of days. The historical background, time of composition of the work, and the major themes are, in broad outline, the same as the time, situation, and teachings of the Fourth Ezra. Different is Baruch's belief in free will as opposed to the Fourth Ezra's emphasis on the fateful sin of Adam. In contradistinction to Ezra's vision of the rule of God over the entire world, Baruch pictures the Messianic kingdom as an earthly one, without, however, losing sight of the universally human aspects of Jewish eschatology. In the end, this "world of corruption will vanish," and after a period of judgment, the Lord "will renew His creation," "gather the dispersed," and "renew Zion in glory." As Joseph Klausner has pointed out, some of Baruch's Messianic vision resembles the views in the early parts of the Talmud and Midrash.

Originally written in Hebrew, the book was translated into Greek. Both original and translation disappeared. Only a Syriac version, done from the Greek, survived.

To those among the Jews whom the destruction of Jerusalem and the Temple led to the depths of despair, apocalyptic writings such as Fourth Ezra and Baruch opened new vistas of a new creation, a supernatural order of things, a new Jerusalem, an eternal world.

And I, Baruch [. . .] came to my people, and I called my first-born son and my friends, and seven of the elders of the people, and I said unto them:

Behold, I go unto my fathers
According to the way of all the earth.

But withdraw ye not from the way of the law,
But guard and admonish the people which remain,
Lest they withdraw from the commandments of the Mighty
    One.

For ye see that He whom we serve is just,
And our Creator is no respecter of persons.

And see ye what hath befallen Zion,
And what hath happened to Jerusalem.

For the judgment of the Mighty One shall be made known,
And His ways, which, though past finding out, are right.

For if ye endure and persevere in His fear,
And do not forget His law,
The times shall change over you for good,
And ye shall see the consolation of Zion.

Because whatever is now is nothing,
But that which shall be is very great.
For everything that is corruptible shall pass away,
And everything that dies shall depart,
And all the present time shall be forgotten,
Nor shall there be any remembrance of the present time,
        which is defiled with evils.
For that which runs now runs unto vanity,
And that which prospers shall quickly fall and be humiliated.

For that which is to be shall be the object of desire,
And for that which comes afterwards shall we hope;
For it is a time that passes not away,
And the hour comes which abides for ever.

And the new world comes which does not turn to corruption
        those who depart to its blessedness,
And has no mercy on those who depart to torment,
And leads not to perdition those who live in it.

For these are they who shall inherit that time which has been
        spoken of,
And theirs is the inheritance of the promised time.

These are they who have acquired for themselves treasures of
        wisdom,
And with them are found stores of understanding,
And from mercy have they not withdrawn,

And the truth of the law have they preserved.

For to them shall be given the world to come,
But the dwelling of the rest who are many shall be in the fire.

Do ye therefore so far as ye are able instruct the people, for that labor is ours. For if ye teach them, ye will quicken them.

And my son and the elders of the people answered and said unto me: Has the Mighty One humiliated us to such a degree as to take thee from us quickly?

And truly we shall be in darkness,
And there shall be no light to the people who are left.
For where again shall we seek the law,
Or who will distinguish for us between death and life?

And I said unto them: The throne of the Mighty One I cannot resist;
Nevertheless, there shall not be wanting to Israel a wise man
Nor a son of the law to the race of Jacob.

But only prepare ye your hearts, that ye may obey the law,
And be subject to those who in fear are wise and understanding;
And prepare your souls that ye may not depart from them.

For if ye do these things,
Good tidings shall come unto you.

The Ten Martyrs

FROM THE TALMUD AND MIDRASH

Two generations after the fall of Jerusalem, Judaea again rose against Rome. The rebellion, led by Bar Kokhba (132–135), which ended in a Roman victory, was followed by a period of persecution. Talmudic tradition preserves the memory of ten chief scholars who suffered martyrdom rather than bow to the imperial decree that forbade the study of the Torah, ordination of dis-

ciples, and the observance of certain laws. In defying the empire of Rome,
the martyrs died for the "sanctification of the Name" and as exponents of the
Kingdom of God. It was Rabbi Akiba's death especially that served as an
example to later-day Jewish martyrs. The story of the Ten Martyrs became one
of the motifs in medieval Jewish liturgy. The dramatic account of martyrdom
is recited in the service of the Day of Atonement.

Simon ben Gamliel and Ishmael

It is written: "And a stranger shalt thou not wrong, neither
shalt thou oppress him. Ye shall not afflict any widow, or
fatherless child. If thou afflict them in any wise—for if they
cry at all unto Me, I will surely hear their cry" (Exod. 22:20-
22).

Rabbi Ishmael and Rabbi Simon were on the way to their
execution.

Rabbi Simon said to Rabbi Ishmael: Rabbi, my heart is
consumed, for I do not know why I am to be executed.

Rabbi Ishmael said to Rabbi Simon: Perhaps a man once
came to you to hear judgment, or to consult you about something, and you let him wait until you had emptied your
goblet, or fastened your sandals, or put on your cloak? The
Torah says: "If thou afflict them in any wise" (Exod. 22:22).
It counts the same whether you afflict them greatly or only a
little!

Then the other said to him: You have consoled me,
Rabbi!

A highborn Roman matron fastened her gaze upon
Ishmael, for he was a man of great beauty, and in this he was
like Joseph, the son of Jacob. She said to the executioners:
Tell him to raise his head, so that I can see him; I shall grant
him his life.

But he did not heed her request. When she repeated the
same thing a second and a third time, Ishmael answered:
Shall I forfeit my life in the world to come for an hour of
pleasures such as those!

When the godless woman heard this answer, she said to
the executioners: Flay him!

They went to work. They began at his chin and flayed the skin of the righteous from his face. When they came to his forehead, to the place where the phylacteries are fastened, Ishmael uttered a piercing scream that shook the earth, and cried: Lord of the universe, will you not have mercy upon me?

A voice from heaven answered him: If you accept the suffering to which you have been sentenced, it is well; if not, I shall let the world lapse back into chaos.

Then Ishmael willingly suffered martyrdom.

Akiba

"And thou shalt love the Lord thy God with all thy heart, and with all thy soul, and with all thy might" (Deut. 6:5).

Rabbi Akiba taught: "With all thy soul"—that means: You shall love God even in that hour in which he takes your soul from you.[17]

When Akiba was led off to be executed—it was the hour in which "Hear, O Israel" is recited—they gashed his flesh with iron combs, but he willingly took the punishment of heaven upon himself. When he avowed his faith, he drew out the last word, which testifies that God is One, and the breath of life left him while he was saying the word "One."

Then a voice sounded from heaven: Hail to you, Akiba, whose last breath was spent upon the word "One."

The angels said to God: Such is the Torah, and such is its reward? Is it not written: "To die by Thy hand, O Lord"— "thy hand" (Ps. 17:14), but not the hand of man?

Then He answered them: "Their portion is . . . life!" (*ibid.*).

And a voice rang out: Blessed be you, Akiba, you who have been elected to life in the world to come!

"Gather My saints, those that have made a covenant with Me by sacrifice" (Ps. 50:5). The "saints"—those are the righteous whom every age brings forth. "Those that have made a covenant" are, above all, the three in the fiery furnace— Hananiah, Mishael, and Azariah. And the "sacrifice" refers to Akiba and his friends, who were willing to let themselves be slaughtered for the sake of the Torah.

Judah ben Baba

The memory of the man whose name is Judah ben Baba is
held in high honor. Once the wicked empire of Rome had a
devastating law proclaimed, to the effect that ordination of
scholars would no longer be permitted. The master who laid
his hands upon his disciple and ordained him was to be executed, likewise the disciple who submitted to the laying on of
hands on the part of his master. A city in which such an act
took place was to be destroyed, and everything within the
bounds of the place in which it occurred, torn down.

What did Rabbi Judah ben Baba do? He went to a
place flanked on two sides by high mountains, and equally
distant from two great cities, between [. . .] Usha and
Shefaram. There he himself ordained five to teacherhood—
Meir, Judah, Simon, Jose, and Eleazar ben Shammua; and
some say that Nehemiah was also included.

When their enemies discovered them, Judah ben Baba
said to the five: My sons, flee!

They said: But master, what will become of you?

He replied: I shall lie here before them as if I were a
stone that none cares to move.

It is told that the enemy did not leave that place until
three hundred lances had pierced Rabbi Judah, and his body
was like a sieve.

Hananyah ben Teradyon

About Hananyah ben Teradyon they relate that he was in the
act of reading the Torah when the bailiffs came to fetch him.
When they found him deep in his book, they said: Have you
not been sentenced to be burned to death?

He answered them, saying: "The Rock, His work is perfect: for all His ways are justice" (Deut. 32:4).

Hananyah's wife asked him: What is to be my fate?

He answered her: Death by the sword.

Thereupon she said: "A God of faithfulness and without
iniquity, just and right is He" (*ibid.*).

Hananyah's daughter asked him: And what has been decreed for me?

His answer was: Your father has been condemned to burn to death, your mother to be slain; you, however, will be forced to sit in a house of harlots.

Then she cried out: "The Lord of hosts, great in counsel, and mighty in work"! (Jer. 32:18-19).

How holy were these three people, the master, his wife, and his daughter—in the very hour when they had to submit to the judgment of heaven, they thought of three verses in the Scriptures that deal with justice and the judgment of God!

They relate:

When Hananyah was led away to be burned to death, his daughter wept. He asked her: My daughter, why do you weep?

She answered him: I weep for the Torah that is to be burned with you.

He answered: The Torah is fire, and no fire can burn fire itself.

They seized him and wrapped him in the scroll of the Torah, heaped faggots around him and lit the pyre. But they took woolen cloths, soaked them in water, and laid them on his heart, so that he should not die too quickly.

His disciples said: Rabbi, what do you see?

He replied: I see the parchment consumed by fire, but the letters of the Scriptures are flying aloft.

They continued: Rabbi, open your mouth wide, that the fire may enter more swiftly.

He said: It is better that only He who gave the soul should take it, rather than that men do anything to hasten it on its way.

Then the executioner said to Rabbi Hananyah: If I quicken the flames and take the cooling cloth from your heart—will you bring me into eternal life?

The martyr answered: That I will do.

The Roman went on: Swear it.

And Rabbi Hananyah gave him his oath. At once the executioner quickened the flames, took the woolen cloths from the teacher's heart, and soon after, his soul left his body. But the executioner threw himself into the fire.

Then a voice sounded from heaven, and called: Hananyah ben Teradyon and the Roman executioner are both chosen for the life in the world to come!

Concerning this event, Rabbi Judah the Prince once said with tears: One man can win eternal life in an hour, while another needs many years.

Hutzpit, the interpreter

Then Hutzpit, the interpreter, was to be put to death. He was a very old man—a hundred and thirty years old—beautiful in face and form, and like one of God's angels. They told the emperor of his great age and of his beauty, and begged him to show mercy to this one man.

The emperor turned to the condemned and asked him: What is your age?

Hutzpit replied: One hundred and thirty years less one day, and I beg of you to give me this one day.

The emperor said: What difference does it make whether you die today or tomorrow?

The old man answered: There are two commandments that I should like to carry out one more time. I want to recite "Hear, O Israel" this evening and tomorrow morning, so that once more I may avow the almighty and awful God as my king.

The emperor said: You people who are bold in your manners and bold of spirit, how long will you continue to cling to your God who has not the power to help you?

When Rabbi Hutzpit heard these words, he wept bitterly and clutched his clothes to rend them, because of his anguish in hearing the name of the Lord blasphemed in this way. He addressed the emperor: Woe to you, O prince! What will you do on the Day of Judgment, when the Lord punishes Rome and your gods!

Then the emperor said: How long am I to dally words with this old man? And he bade them slay him with the sword, stone him, and hang him.

Yeshebab, the Scribe

Concerning Yeshebab, the scribe, they relate that he was ninety on the day he was to be executed.

His disciples asked him: What is to become of us?

Their teacher answered: Cleave to one another, love peace and justice; perhaps there is hope.

They say that the day on which this holy man was killed, was the second day of the week, the day on which he usually fasted.

His pupils asked him whether he did not wish to strengthen himself with food before he died.

He answered them: Should the servant not be content to be like his master? Should I not be content to resemble my master Judah ben Baba? He died fasting, and so I too shall do.

And the godless Roman bade them kill the devout man just as he was about to recite "Hear, O Israel." At the words, "And the Lord spoke unto Moses" (Num. 15:37) he gave up the ghost.

A voice was heard and it cried: Blessed be you, Rabbi Yeshebab, who never for an instant faltered from the law of Moses!

Hanina ben Hakhinai

The day on which Hanina ben Hakhinai was to be executed, was the day of preparation for the Sabbath.

He began to pronounce the benediction ushering in the holy day, and got as far as the words, "And God . . . hallowed it—" (Gen. 2:3) but he had not finished speaking when he was killed.

A voice issued from heaven and cried: Happy are you, Hanina, son of Hakhinai, who were yourself a holy man, and whose soul flew on high at the word "hallowed"!

Judah ben Dama

Then it was the turn of the teacher, Judah ben Dama, to suffer punishment. But the day on which he was to be executed was the day before the Feast of Tabernacles, and so the devout man said to the emperor: By your life, wait a little until I have blessed this holiday and praised God, who gave us the Torah.

The ruler said: So even now you still cling to the belief that there is a God who gave you the Torah?

The son of Dama said: Yes.

The emperor scoffed and said: And what reward does your faith promise you?

Judah replied in the words of the psalmist: "Oh, how abundant is Thy goodness, which Thou hast laid up for them that fear Thee" (Ps. 31:20).

The emperor said: There are no fools greater than you who believe in a life after death.

To this Rabbi Judah replied: There are no fools greater than you who deny the living God. Oh, how shamed and dishonored you will be when you see us, God's people, walking in the light of life, while you thirst in the deepest abyss!

When he heard these words, the emperor's anger flared up. He commanded the teacher to be tied by the hair to a horse's tail and dragged through the streets of Rome, and after this he was to be torn to pieces besides.

Eleazar ben Shammua

Eleazar ben Shammua was the last to suffer death. He was a hundred and five years old, and no one had ever heard of his occupying himself with useless matters, or quarreling with his friends, even though his views differed from theirs. Eleazar ben Shammua was of a gentle and humble spirit, and had spent eighty years of his life fasting. The day on which he was to be executed was the Day of Atonement.

His disciples asked him: Tell us what your eyes behold!

He answered: [. . .] My sons, I see the soul of every righteous man cleansing itself in the well of Shiloah, so that it may be purified for entering the school of heaven, where Akiba will teach. And the angels bring golden chairs for the righteous, who seat themselves upon them in purity.

After these words, the emperor bade them execute this devout man.

A voice was heard: Hail to you, Eleazar ben Shammua, you who have been pure, and whose soul has risen from the body in a state of purity!

The captive children

Once it happened that four hundred boys and girls were captured for shameful purposes.

They realized why they were wanted and said:

If we drown in the sea, shall we have the life of the world to come?

The eldest of them expounded:

"The Lord said . . . I will bring them back from the depths of the sea" (Ps. 68:23).

"I will bring them back"—those who drown in the sea.

As soon as the girls heard this, they all leaped into the sea.

The boys argued:

If these, whose nature it is to succumb, do so,

how much more ought we to do so, whose nature it is not to succumb.

They too leaped into the sea.

And it is of them that Scripture says:

"For Thy sake are we killed all the day; we are accounted as sheep for the slaughter" (Ps. 44:23).

VIII. From the Ordinances of the Talmudic Masters

A *note on the Mishnah*. The Mishnah is the record of the Oral Law, which was believed to have been revealed on Mount Sinai together with the Written Law as contained in Scripture. This Oral Law, adhered to by the Pharisees and rejected by the Sadducees (who accepted as valid the Written Law only), was taught and interpreted in the academies of Palestine from about the second pre-Christian century onwards. After several attempts made in various generations of scholars to transcribe these traditions, such codification was achieved by Judah the Prince in Tiberias in about A.D. 200.

The Mishnah ("Repetition," teaching by repetition), is divided into six "orders" and sixty-three tractates. It covers the laws pertaining to all aspects of life: agriculture and business; property and labor; family; Sabbath and holy seasons; sacrifice, offerings, and prayer; purity and uncleanness; the administration of justice. Both laws of practical application and those no longer of practical value (e.g., the Temple regulations) were preserved. If traditions varied between the schools, the variant views were recorded. No dogmatic definition was intended; *Halakhah*, law, was thought of as a living organism that called for the human mind to cultivate it.

The masters represented in the Mishnah are called *Tannaim* (plural of *Tanna*, teacher). The language of the Mishnah is Hebrew, which, however, incorporated many Aramaic, Greek, and some Latin elements; the style is terse, precise.

Very few complete manuscripts of the Mishnah have survived; the work was first printed in Naples, in 1492.

The following are selections from the Tractate Berakhot ("Benedictions") and the Tractate Pesahim ("Passover"). Underlying the first selection is the thought that the Jew is to pronounce a blessing on every occasion of life. The second is the earliest record of the Seder, the home celebration on the eve of Passover that has taken the place of the ancient ritual of the sacrifice of the Paschal lamb.

The Order of Benedictions

FROM MISHNAH BERAKHOT

What benediction do they say over fruits? Over the fruit of trees a man says, "[Blessed art Thou Lord our God, King of the Universe] who createst the fruit of the tree," except over wine, for over wine a man says ". . . who createst the fruit of the vine."

Over the fruits of the earth a man says, ". . . who createst the fruit of the ground," except over bread, for over bread a man says ". . . who bringest forth bread from the earth." And over vegetables a man says, ". . . who createst the fruit of the ground"; but Rabbi Judah says, ". . . who createst divers kinds of herbs."

If over the fruits of trees he said the benediction, "[Blessed art thou . . .] who createst the fruit of the ground," he has fulfilled his obligation; but if over the fruits of the earth he said, ". . . who createst the fruit of the tree," he has not fulfilled his obligation. If over them all he said, "[Blessed art thou . . .] by whose word all things exist," he has fulfilled his obligation.

Over aught that does not grow from the earth he should say, ["Blessed art thou . . .] by whose word all things exist." Over soured wine or unripe fallen fruits or over locusts he should say, ". . . by whose word all things exist." Over milk, cheese, or eggs he should say, ". . . by whose word all things exist." Rabbi Judah says: Over aught that is of the nature of a curse [like spoilt fruit or locust] no benediction should be said.

When a man has before him many kinds [of food], Rabbi Judah says: If there is among them one of the seven kinds, [i.e., wheat, barley, grapes, figs, pomegranates, olive oil and (date) honey] he must say the benediction over that one. But the Sages say: He may say the benediction over which of them he will.

If he said the benediction over the wine before the meal he need not say it over the wine after the meal. If he said the benediction over the savory before the meal he need not say it over the savory after the meal. If he said it over the bread he need not say it over the savory; but if he said it over the savory he is not exempt from saying it over the bread. The School of Shammai say: Or over aught that was cooked in the pot.

If men sit [apart] to eat, each should say the benediction for himself; if they reclined [around the table together] one should say the benediction for all. If wine is brought to them during the meal each should say the benediction for himself; but if after the meal, one should say the benediction for all, and he, too, should say the benediction over the burning spices even though they are brought in only after the meal is over.

If salted relish was first brought before him together with bread he should say the benediction over the salted relish and he need not say it over the bread, since the bread is but an accompaniment. This is the general rule: where there is a main food and aught that is but an accompaniment to it, the benediction should be said over the main food and it need not be said over the accompaniment.

If a man ate figs, grapes or pomegranates, he should say the three benedictions after them.[1] So Rabban Gamaliel. But the sages say: One benediction, the substance of the three. Rabbi Akiba says: Even if he ate but boiled vegetables for his meal he must say the three benedictions after them. If he drank water to quench his thirst he should say, "[Blessed art thou . . .] by whose word all things exist." Rabbi Tarfon says: [He should say,] ". . . who createst many living beings and their wants (for all the means thou hast created wherewith to sustain the life of each of them. Blessed be He who is the life of all worlds)."

If a man saw a place where miracles had been wrought for Israel he should say, "Blessed is he that wrought miracles for our fathers in this place." [If he saw] a place from which idolatry had been rooted out he should say, "Blessed is he that rooted out idolatry from our land."

[If he saw] shooting stars, earthquakes, lightnings, thunders and storms he should say, "Blessed is He whose power and might fill the world." [If he saw] mountains, hills, seas, rivers and deserts he should say, "Blessed is the author of creation." Rabbi Judah says: If a man saw the Great Sea[2] he should say, "Blessed is he that made the Great Sea," but only if he sees it at intervals of time. For rain and good tidings he should say, "Blessed is He, the good and the doer of good." For bad tidings he should say, "Blessed is He, the true Judge."

If a man built a house or bought new vessels he should say, "Blessed is He that hath given us life [and hath preserved us and enabled us to reach this season]." A man should say the benediction for misfortune regardless of [any consequent] good, and for good fortune regardless of [any consequent] evil. If a man cries out [to God] over what is past, his prayer is vain. Thus if his wife was with child and he said, "May it be Thy will that my wife shall bear a male," this prayer is vain. If he was returning from a journey and heard a sound of lamentation in the city and said, "May it be Thy will that they [which make lamentation] be not of my house," this prayer is vain.

He that enters into a town should pray twice: once on his coming in and once on his going forth. Ben Azzai says: Four times: twice on his coming in and twice on his going forth, offering thanks for what is past and making supplication for what is still to come.

Man is bound to bless [God] for the evil even as he blesses [God] for the good, for it is written, "And thou shalt love the Lord thy God with all thy heart and with all thy soul and with all thy might" (Deut. 6:5). "With all thy heart" means with both thine impulses, thy good impulse and thine evil impulse; "and with all thy soul" means even if He takes away thy soul; "and with all thy might"—with all thy wealth. Another explanation is: "With all thy might [*meodekha*]"—for whichever measure [*middah*] He measures out to thee, do thou give Him thanks [*modeh*] exceedingly [*bimeod meod*].

A man should not behave himself unseemly while opposite the Eastern Gate [of the Temple] since it faces toward
the Holy of Holies. He may not enter into the Temple Mount
with his staff or his sandal or his wallet, or with the dust upon
his feet, nor may he make of it a short bypath; still less may he
spit there.

At the close of every benediction in the Temple they
used to say "[Blessed be the God of Israel], for everlasting";
but after the heretics[3] had taught corruptly and said that there
is but one world, it was ordained that they should say, "From ·
everlasting to everlasting."

And it was ordained that a man should salute his fellow
with [the use of] the Name [of God]; for it is written, "And,
behold, Boaz came from Bethlehem, and said unto the reapers,
The Lord be with you. And they answered him, The Lord
bless thee" (Ruth 2:4). And it is written: "The Lord is with
thee, thou mighty man of valor" (Judg. 6:12). And it is written: "And despise not thy mother when she is old" (Prov.
23:22). And it is written: "It is time to work for the Lord:
they have made void the Law" (Ps. 119:126). Rabbi Nathan
explains: They have made void thy law because it was a time
to work for the Lord.[4]

The Seder Ceremony

FROM MISHNAH PESAHIM

On the eve of Passover, when the late afternoon approaches,[5] a man must eat naught until nightfall. Even the
poorest in Israel must not eat unless he sits down to table, and
they must not give them less than four cups of wine to drink
even if it is from the [Paupers'] Dish.[6]

After they have mixed him[7] his first cup, the School of
Shammai say: He says the benediction first over the [holy]
day and then the benediction over the wine. And the School of

Hillel say: He says the benediction first over the wine and then the benediction over the day.

When [food] is brought before him he eats it seasoned with lettuce, until he is come to the bread condiment [the bitter herbs]; they bring before him unleavened bread and lettuce, and the *haroseth*,[8] although *haroseth* is not a religious obligation. Rabbi Eliezer ben Rabbi Zadok says: It is a religious obligation. And in the Holy City they used to bring before him the complete Passover-offering.

They then mix him the second cup. And here the son asks his father (and if the son has not enough understanding his father instructs him [how to ask]): "Why is this night different from other nights? For on other nights we eat seasoned food once, but this night twice; on other nights we eat leavened or unleavened bread, but this night all is unleavened;[9] on other nights we eat flesh roast, stewed, or cooked, but this night all is roast."[10] And according to the understanding of the son his father instructs him. He begins with the disgrace[11] and ends with the glory; and he expounds from "A wandering Aramean was my father" (Deut. 26:5), until he finishes the whole section.

Rabban Gamaliel[12] used to say: Whosoever has not said [the verses[13] concerning] these three things at Passover has not fulfilled his obligation. And these are they: Passover, unleavened bread, and bitter herbs: "Passover"—because God passed over the houses of our fathers in Egypt; "unleavened bread"—because our fathers were redeemed from Egypt; "bitter herbs"—because the Egyptians embittered the lives of our fathers in Egypt.

In every generation a man must so regard himself as if he came forth himself out of Egypt, for it is written: "And thou shalt tell thy son in that day saying, It is because of that which the Lord did for me when I came forth out of Egypt" (Exod. 13:8). Therefore are we bound to give thanks, to praise, to glorify, to honor, to exalt, to extol, and to bless him who wrought all these wonders for our fathers and for us. He brought us out from bondage to freedom, from sorrow to gladness, and from mourning to a Festival day, and from darkness to great light, and from servitude to redemption; so let us say before him the Hallelujah.[14]

How far do they recite [the Hallel]? The School of Shammai say: To "A joyful mother of children"[15] and the School of Hillel say: To "A flintstone into a springing well."[16] And this is concluded with the [benediction recounting] Redemption.

Rabbi Tarfon says: "He that redeemed us and redeemed our fathers from Egypt and brought us to this night to eat therein unleavened bread and bitter herbs." But there is no concluding benediction.

Rabbi Akiba adds: "Therefore, O Lord our God and the God of our fathers, bring us in peace to the other set feasts and festivals which are coming to meet us, while we rejoice in the building-up of Thy city and are joyful in Thy worship; and may we eat there of the sacrifices and of the Passover-offerings whose blood has reached with acceptance the wall of Thy altar, and let us praise Thee for our redemption and for the ransoming of our soul. Blessed art Thou, O Lord, who hast redeemed Israel!"

After they have mixed for him the third cup he says the benediction over his meal. [Over] a fourth [cup] he completes the "Hallel" and says after it the benediction over song. If he is minded to drink [more] between these cups he may drink; only between the third and the fourth cups he may not drink.

After the Passover meal they should not disperse to join in revelry.[17] [. . .]

IX. Beliefs and Opinions of the Talmudic Masters

Hillel the Elder

FROM THE TALMUD AND MIDRASH

Jewish tradition credits Hillel with reconstructing the Torah, which Ezra the Scribe helped make the constitution of Judaea and which had been "forgotten" in the course of the rapid advance of the Hasmonean rule and the spread of Hellenism. Hillel's activity falls in the historic period marked by Herod's pro-Roman policy, the rivalries between the Pharisees and Sadducees, the deterioration of the official priesthood, the segregation of the Essene or Dead Sea sect in the Jordan region. It was a period of tensions, disappointments, and Messianic expectations, so vividly expressed in some of the apocryphal writings. Born around 60 B.C. in Babylonia, Hillel came to Jerusalem in about 40 B.C., studied in the schools of Shemaiah and Abtalion, and, roughly, between 30 B.C. and A.D. 10 taught in Jerusalem.

Hillel supplemented the body of teachings known from a scrupulously guarded tradition by a system of interpretation which allowed the student to derive the teachings from the written word of the Torah. This emphasis on "learning" made the Torah a living concern of an ever widening group of disciples and of the people at large. The commandments are many, Hillel taught, but they can be reduced to one: loving kindness. In *hesed*, loving concern, man emulates God. By a number of legislative measures, Hillel helped the poor and underprivileged classes. His ideal was the true and just community (as against the state), for which he found a model in the early hasidic groups (from which possibly the Essenes derived). He welcomed proselytes and accorded them equality of rights. His attitude of peacefulness, mercy, and forgiveness is in contrast to the stringency and harshness of his colleague, Shammai. Both Hillel and Shammai headed schools that bear their names; in most instances, however, the opinion of the School of Hillel prevailed. Hillel's work made possible the reconstruction of Judaism after the fall of Jerusalem His youngest disciple, Johanan ben Zakkai, assumed the leadership of the remnant.

The stories about Hillel and the sayings attributed to him are scattered in the vast literature of Talmud and Midrash.

The re-established Torah

In ancient days when the Torah was forgotten from Israel,
Ezra came up from Babylon[1] and re-established it.
Then it was again forgotten
until Hillel the Babylonian came up and re-established it.

Education

It was said of Hillel
that he had not neglected any of the words of the Wise but
      had learned them all;
he had studied all manners of speech,
even the utterance of mountains, hills and valleys,
the utterance of trees and plants,
the utterance of beasts and animals,
tales of spirits, popular stories and parables,
everything he had learned.

Disciples

"Raise many disciples."[2]
The School of Shammai says:
One ought teach only a student who is wise, humble, of a
      good family and rich.
The School of Hillel says:
One ought to teach every man;
for there were many transgressors in Israel who came close to
      the study of the Torah
and from them issued righteous men, pious and worthy.

On disseminating knowledge

When there are those who want to gather, you scatter [the
      seed of teaching];

when there are those who scatter, you gather.
[That is to say:]
If you see a generation to which the Torah is dear, you spread
        [its knowledge];
but if you see a generation to which the Torah is not dear, you
        gather it and keep it to yourself.

Peace

Be of the disciples of Aaron [the priest],
loving peace, pursuing peace.
Be one who loves his fellow-creatures
and draws them near to the Torah.

How did Hillel bring his fellow-man near to the Torah?
One day Hillel stood in the gate of Jerusalem and met people
        going out to work.
He asked: How much will you earn today?
One said, A denarius; the other said, Two denarii.
He asked them: What will you do with the money?
They gave answer: We will pay for the necessities of life.
Then he said to them:
Why don't you rather come with me and gain knowledge of
        the Torah,
that you may gain life in this world
and life in the world to come?
Thus Hillel was wont to do all his days and has brought many
        under the wings of heaven.[3]

The ignorant cannot be a hasid

The uneducated knows not fear of sin;
the ignorant cannot be a pious man.
The timid is not apt to learn,
the impatient is not fit to teach.
He whose whole time is absorbed in business will not attain
        wisdom.
In a place where [a man is needed and] there are no men,
        strive to be a man.

Torah

The more flesh, the more worms;
the more possessions, the more worry;
the more women, the more witchcraft;
the more maidservants, the more immorality;
the more menservants, the more thieving.
[But:]
The more Torah, the more life;
the more study and contemplation, the more wisdom;
the more counsel, the more discernment;
the more charity, the more peace.

Do not separate yourself from the community.
Trust not in yourself until the day of your death;
judge not your fellow-man until you have come to his place;
say not of a thing which cannot be understood that it will be
        understood in the end;
say not: When I have leisure I will study:
perchance you will never have leisure.

With people

Do not appear naked [among the dressed]
neither dressed [among the naked];
do not appear standing [among those who sit]
neither sitting [among those who stand];
do not appear laughing [among those who weep]
neither weeping [among those who laugh].
The rule is: Do not deviate from the usage of men.

Teachings

If I am not for myself—who is for me?
and being for mine own self—what am I?
and if not now—when?

A good name, once acquired, is your own possession;
he who has knowledge of the Torah has life in the world to
        come.

A name made famous is a name lost.
Knowledge that does not grow will shrink.
He who refuses to teach faces death.
He who uses the crown of learning for material gains vanishes.

Hillel saw a skull floating on the face of the water.
He said to it:
Because you have drowned others, they have drowned you;
but those that drowned you will, at the last, themselves be
       drowned.[4]

My humiliation is my exaltation;
my exaltation is my humiliation.

The human body

Once when Hillel was taking leave of his disciples, they said to him: Master, whither are you going?

He replied: To do a pious deed. They said: What may that be? He replied: To take a bath. They said: Is that a pious deed?

He replied: Yes; if in the theaters and circuses the images of the king must be kept clean by the man to whom they have been entrusted, how much more is it a duty of man to care for the body, since man has been created in the divine image and likeness.

[In a parallel situation, Hillel answered the disciples' question:]
I am going to do a kindness to the guest in the house.
When the disciples asked whether he had a guest every day,
       he answered:
Is not my poor soul a guest in the body? Today it is here,
       tomorrow it is gone.

Beautiful bride

What is being sung while one dances before the bride?
The School of Shammai says: The bride is described as she is.
The School of Hillel says: One [always] sings: Beautiful and
       graceful bride!

Based on this the sages say: A man's heart should always be
    outgoing in dealing with people.

Disaster

It once came to pass that Hillel the Elder was returning from
    a journey when he heard screams from the direction of
    the city.
He said: I am confident that this does not come from my
    house.
Concerning him, Scripture says:
"He shall not be afraid of evil tidings; his heart is steadfast,
    trusting in the Lord" (Ps. 112:7).

The poor man

There was a man of a wealthy family who had become poor.
Hillel provided him with a horse to ride upon and with a
    servant to run before him.
One day he could not find a servant, so he himself ran before
    him for three miles.

The wager

Two men made a wager with each other: he who would go
    and make Hillel angry would receive four hundred *zuz*.
One of them said: I will go and make him angry.
That day was Sabbath eve, and Hillel was washing his head.
The men went, passed by the door of his house, and cried:
Is Hillel here? Is Hillel here?
Hillel wrapped himself up and came out to meet him:
My son what do you wish?
—I have a question to ask.
He said to him: Ask my son, ask.
—Why are the heads of the Babylonians round?
Hillel answered: My son, you have asked an important ques-
    tion:—Because they have no skilled midwives.
The man went out, waited a while and returned.
[The scene is twice more repeated, the important questions
    being: Why are the eyes of the Palmyreans bleared?

Why are the feet of the Africans wide? Hillel answered
and the man promised to come with more problems.
Seeing that it was impossible to exhaust the master's
patience, he asked him:]
Are you the Hillel whom they call the prince of Israel?
Yes, answered Hillel.
The man said: If that is you, I wish, there may not be many
like you in Israel. Why, my son? asked Hillel. Because
I have lost four hundred *zuz* through you.
Said Hillel: Watch out; I may cause you to lose much money
but I will not easily lose my patience.

The entire Torah on one foot

A certain heathen came to Shammai and said to him:
Convert me provided that you teach me the entire Torah
while I stand on one foot.
Shammai drove him away with the builder's cubit which was
in his hand.
He went to Hillel who said to him:
What is hateful to you, do not do to your neighbor:[5]
that is the entire Torah;
the rest is commentary;
go and learn it.

Every day

It was told of Shammai the Elder: Whenever he found
a fine portion he said: This will be for the Sabbath. If later he
found a finer one, he put aside the second for the Sabbath
and ate the first; thus, whatever he ate, was meant for the
honor of the Sabbath.

But Hillel the Elder had a different way, for all his works
were for the sake of heaven; he used to say: "Blessed be the
Lord, day by day He beareth our burden" (Ps. 68:20).

Man

Our masters taught:
For two and half years the Schools of Schammai and Hillel
have maintained a dispute;

the former said: It would have been better if man had not
    been created;
the School of Hillel said: It is better for man to have been
    created than not to have been created.
They took a vote and came to this decision:
It would have been better had man not been created;
yet, since he had been created, let him pay close attention to
    his actions, those past and those before him.

The rival schools

The words of both schools are the words of the living God,
but the law follows the ruling of the School of Hillel
because the Hillelites were gentle and modest,
and studied both their own opinions and the opinions of the
    other school,
and humbly mentioned the words of the other school before
    theirs.
The preference accorded to the School of Hillel teaches you
that he who humbles himself the Lord raises up,
and he who exalts himself the Lord humbles;
greatness flees him who seeks greatness;
greatness may follow him who flees from greatness.
He who [impatiently] tries to force time, is thrown back by
    time;
he who [patiently] yields to time, finds time standing by him.

The heavenly voice

One day some wise men were assembled in the upper chamber
    of one Gurya's house in Jericho;
a heavenly voice was granted them that announced:
There is among you one man who would deserve that the
    Divine Presence rest upon him, but his generation is
    not worthy of it.
Thereupon all the eyes were fixed upon Hillel the Elder.
And when he died, they lamented over him:
"The pious man, the humble man, the disciple of Ezra [is no
    more]."

The Ways of Good Life

FROM THE TALMUD TRACTATE BERAKHOT

A note on the Talmud. The academies of Palestine and Babylonia took the Mishnah as the basic text to be studied, compared with other collections of traditions, and interpreted to apply to new conditions. The record of these deliberations is called Gemara ("Completion"), which together with the Mishnah constitutes the Talmud ("Study"). The relevant material from the Palestinian schools was compiled around A.D. 400, and is known as the Palestinian (or Jerusalem) Talmud. A century later the material of the schools in Babylonia was gathered and edited, to form the Babylonian Talmud. The latter, due to its greater richness, became the body of writings studied in the traditional houses of learning throughout the centuries.

While the Mishnah is a code of laws, the Talmud is a cyclopedia ranging over the entire realm of human life. Non-legal subjects, theology, history, ethics, life of the sages, legends, folklore (material referred to as Haggadah, or Agada, narrative, as distinguished from Halakhah, law) fill about one-third of the Babylonian Talmud (which contains some 2,500,000 words), and about 15 per cent of the Palestinian Talmud (which contains some 750,000 words.) The masters of the Talmud are called Amoraim (plural of Amora, speaker). The language varies between Aramaic (Western Aramaic in the Palestinian, Eastern Aramaic in the Babylonian Talmud) and Hebrew.

The most important manuscript of the Palestinian Talmud is in Leyden in the Netherlands. The best manuscript of the Babylonian Talmud is in Munich, written in 1343. The first complete printed edition appeared in Venice 1520 to 1523 f. The commentaries on the Talmud are a library in themselves.

The following is a selection of haggadic passages culled from one of the tractates, Berakhot ("Benedictions").

Every day

[Towards the end of his career, Moses said:]
"Keep silence and hear, O Israel; this day thou art become a
    people unto the Lord thy God" (Deut. 27:9).
But was the Torah given to Israel on that day?

Was not that day at the end of the forty years in the
      wilderness?
But—this is to teach you that every day the Torah is dear to
      those who study it,
as on the day it was given from Mount Sinai.

The gist of it

Which is the small section on which all the principles of the
      Torah depend?
—"In all thy ways know Him
And He will direct thy paths" (Prov. 3:6).

The gates of Torah

Learn with all your heart, and with all your soul,
to know My ways,
to watch at the gates of My Torah.
Keep My Torah in your heart,
may the fear of Me be before your eyes;
guard your mouth from all sin,
purify and sanctify yourself from faults and transgressions,
and I will be with you in every place.

My neighbor

The masters of Jabneh[6] were wont to say:
I am [God's] creature, and my fellow man is [God's] creature.
My work is in the city and his work is in the country.
I rise early to go to my work,
and he rises early to go to his work.
As he cannot excel in my work,
so do I not excel in his work.
And should you say, I do more, and he does less—
We have learned:[7]
"The one more, the other less—if only his heart is directed to
      heaven."

Brothers

Let man ever be subtle in the fear of God,

giving a soft answer that turneth away wrath.[8]
Let him increase the peace with his brothers, with his relatives,
     and with all men,
even with the heathen in the market place,
that he may be beloved above and desired below,
and well received by all his fellow creatures.

The final goal

The goal of wisdom is repentance and good works.
So that a man may not study the Torah and learn the
     Tradition
and then set foot on his father, or his mother,
or his master, or on him who is greater than he in wisdom and
     in rank.
Thus it is said:
"The fear of the Lord is the beginning of wisdom;
a good understanding have all they that do thereafter"
     (Ps. 111:10).

Chastisements of love

If a man sees chastisements coming upon him, let him search
     his conduct.
If he has searched his conduct and found nothing, let him
     attribute it to his idleness in Torah.
And if he has done this and found nothing,
surely they are chastisements of [God's] love [for man].
As it is said: "For whom the Lord loveth He correcteth"
     (Prov. 3:12).

Old men

Have care for an old man who has forgotten his learning under
     duress.
For it was said:
Both the whole tablets [of the Law] and the fragments of the
     tablets were placed in the Ark of the Covenant.

Animals first

It is forbidden for a man to eat before having fed his beast.

For it is said: "And I will give grass in the field for thy cattle"
and [only] afterwards: "And thou shalt eat and be satisfied"
        (Deut. 11:15).

Sinners

Some outlaws lived in the neighborhood of Rabbi Meir, and
        caused him much trouble.
Because of this he prayed that they might die.
Whereupon Beruriah, his wife, said to him:
What are you thinking of?
Is it because it is written: "Let sins cease out of the earth"
        (Ps. 104:35)?
but does it say "sinners"?
"Sins" is what is written!
And more than this:
Look at the end of the verse: "And let the wicked be no
        more."
When sin will cease there will be no more wicked.
Rather pray for them, that they may repent and be wicked
        no more.
Rabbi Meir prayed for them,
and they repented.

Far and near

In that place where the penitents stand, the perfectly right-
        eous cannot stand,
as it is written:
"Peace, peace, to him that is far off and to him that is near
        (Isa. 57:19)"—
first to him who was far off,
then to him who is near!

Let a man ever say:
All that the Compassionate One does is for good.

Let a man's words ever be few before the Holy One, blessed
        be he.
For it is said:

"Be not rash with thy mouth, and let not thy heart be hasty to
utter a word before God; for God is in heaven, and
thou upon earth; therefore let thy words be few"
(Eccles. 5:1).

Beauty

Rabbi Eliezer fell ill and Rabbi Johanan went in to visit him.
He saw Rabbi Eliezer lying in a dark [windowless] room.
Rabbi Johanan bared his arm and the room lit up.
He saw that Rabbi Eliezer was crying. He said to him: Why
are you crying?
Is it for the Torah in which you have not learned enough?
We have learned: The one more, the other less—if only his
heart is directed to heaven.[9]
If because of sustenance you lack—
not every man merits two tables.[10]
If because of [the lack of] children?
see, this is the bone of my tenth son.[11]
Rabbi Eliezer replied to him:
I am crying over this beauty of yours, which is to wither in the
dust.
He said to him:
You are right to cry over that.
And they wept together.

The blessing

When Rabbi Johanan ben Zakkai fell ill, his disciples went in
to visit him [. . .]. They spoke to him, saying: Master, give us your blessing.
He said to them: May it be His will that the fear of heaven be
upon you like the fear of those who are of flesh and
blood.
They asked: Only so much?
He answered them: Would that it were so much! For you
must know that when a man wants to commit a transgression, he says: I hope no man sees me!

When Rabbi Eliezer fell ill, his disciples came to visit him.

They said to him:

Master, teach us the ways of life, that by following them, we
     may become worthy of life in the world to come.

He said to them:

Take heed of the honor of your colleagues,

Keep your children from superficiality, but have them sit at
     the feet of scholars;

and when you pray know before Whom you stand;

thus you will be worthy of the life in the world to come.

In farewell

When the masters departed from the school of Rabbi Ammi—
     some say from the school of Rabbi Hanina—they said
     to him:

May you see your world in your life,

may your aim be fulfilled in the life of the world to come,

your hope throughout the generations.

Let your heart meditate in understanding,

your mouth utter wisdom,

your tongue be abundant in songs of jubilation.

May your eyelids look straight before you,

your eyes glow with the light of the Torah,

your face shine with the radiance of heaven,

your lips proclaim knowledge,

your reins rejoice in uprightness,

your feet hasten to hear the words of the Ancient of Days.[12]

Creation and Man

FROM THE TALMUD AND MIDRASH

The first chapter of Genesis inspired some of the leading talmudic sages
to engage in esoteric cosmology. The Mishnah discouraged the expounding of
the mysteries of "The Work of Creation" except to a single student. But open
to all was meditation upon the majesty of the Creator, the beauty and pur-

posefulness of the world, which is but one continuous creation, and upon man's rightful place in the universe.

In its time

"He has made everything beautiful in its time" (Eccles. 3:11)
—in its due time was the world created.
The world was not fit to be created before then.
The Holy One, blessed be he, kept creating worlds and desolating them, creating worlds and desolating them,
until he created these [worlds of heaven and earth].
Then he said: "These please me; those did not please me."

In the beginning

"In the beginning God created" (Gen. 1:1).
It is not written, "The Lord created":[13]
First there rose within His mind the plan
of creating the world with the attribute of justice;
then He saw that thus the world could not endure,
and He set first the attribute of mercy and added it to the at-
tribute of justice.
That is why [later] it is written:
"In the day that the Lord God made earth and heaven"
(Gen. 2:4).

Between heaven and earth

You find that the Holy One, blessed be he, created heaven
and earth with wisdom.
On the first day He created heaven and earth.
Five days were left: one day he created something on high, and
something below, the next.
He created the firmament on high on the second day; on the
third "Let the waters . . . be gathered together"
below.
On the fourth day "Let there be lights" on high; on the fifth
"Let the waters swarm" below.
Only the sixth day was left for something to be created on it.
The Holy One, blessed be he, said:
If I create something on high, the earth will be indignant,

if I create something below, heaven will be indignant.
What was it the Holy One, blessed be he, did?
He created man from that which is below, and the soul from
      that which is on high.

Origins

The first man, his dust was gathered together from all the
      world;
his body came from Babylon, his head from the land of Israel,
      and his limbs from the other countries.

In the past Adam was created from the earth and Eve was
      created from Adam; from then, "in our image, after
      our likeness" (Gen. 1:26):
Neither man without woman
nor woman without man,
nor the two of them without Divine Presence.[14]

The crown of creation

Man was created on the eve of Sabbath—and for what reason?
So that in case his heart grew proud, one might say to him:
Even the gnat was in creation before you were there!

Singularity[15]

Man was created single, to teach you
that whosoever wreck a single soul
Scripture considers to have wrecked a complete world,
and whosoever sustain a single soul
Scripture considers to have sustained a complete world.
Also: he was created single to keep peace among the human
      creatures:
that no man might say to his fellow,
my father was greater than your father.

For you[16]

In the hour when the Holy One, blessed be he, created the
      first man,

he took him and let him pass before all the trees of the garden
     of Eden,
and said to him:
See my works, how fine and excellent they are!
Now all that I have created for you have I created.
Think upon this, and do not corrupt and desolate my world;
for if you corrupt it, there is no one to set it right after you.

When iron was created, the trees began to tremble.
Said iron to them:
Why do you tremble? Let none of your wood enter me, and
     not one of you will be injured.

Grow!

There is no grass without its own guardian star in the
     firmament
which strikes it and says to it, Grow!

Evil desire

"And God saw everything that He had made, and behold, it
     was very good" (Gen. 1:31).
"Behold, it was very good"—that is the evil desire.[17]
But is the evil desire good?
Yet were it not for the evil desire,
men would not build homes, or take wives, or propagate, or
     engage in business.

. . . They said:
This being a time of Grace, let us pray for mercy for the evil
     desire.
They prayed and the evil desire was delivered to them.
The prophet [Zechariah] said to them:
Know, if you destroy this one, the world will come to an end.
They imprisoned it for three days:
then they sought a new-laid egg in all the land of Israel,
and not one could be found.

Coming and going

When a man comes into the world, his hands are clenched,

as though to say: All the entire world is mine; now I shall acquire it.
And when he goes out of the world, his hands are wide open,
as though to say: I have acquired nothing from this world.

Order

You will be called by your name,
you will be seated in your place,
you will be given what is yours.
No man touches what is meant for his fellow.
No kingdom touches its neighbor by so much as a hairs-
breadth.

Everything is foreseen
and everything is laid bare
yet everything is in accordance with the will of man.

God-Man-World

FROM THE TALMUD AND MIDRASH

This selection of teachings, culled from the talmudic and midrashic writings, should be read against the background of the apocalyptic writings. In contradistinction to the pessimism of the apocalyptic writers, their disappointment with this world, and ardent, yet passive, expectation of a new aeon to come, the talmudic masters courageously approached the issues of life, moving about in a world governed by divine mercy, and by so doing they overcame the tragedy of the fall of Jerusalem which, in the case of the apocalyptic, had turned into a catastrophe.

Justice

"Shall not the Judge of all the earth do justly?" (Gen. 18:25).
[Abraham said to God:]
If it is the world you seek, there can be no [stern] justice;
and if it is [stern] justice you seek, there can be no world.
Why do you grasp the rope by both ends,
seeking both the world and [stern] justice?

Let one of them go,
for if you do not relent a little, the world cannot endure.

Sustenance

"And the people shall go out and gather a day's portion every
day" (Exod. 16:4).[18]
He that created the day created the sustenance of the day.
A man who has something to eat today, and says, What shall
I eat tomorrow—lo, he is lacking in faith.

Have you ever seen beast or fowl that have a trade, yet they
sustain themselves without trouble, though they were
created only to serve me—
and I was created to serve my Maker; how much more ought
I to sustain myself without trouble—
but I have acted wickedly, and have spoiled my sustenance.

Ascent

The Torah leads to deliberation, deliberation leads to zeal,
zeal leads to cleanness, cleanness leads to continence,
continence leads to purity, purity leads to godliness,
godliness leads to humility, humility leads to the fear
of sin, the fear of sin leads to holiness, holiness leads
to the Holy Spirit, the Holy Spirit leads to resurrection;
but among all qualities, piety is the greatest.
Another opinion: Humility is the greatest among them all—
as it is written: "The spirit of the Lord God is upon
me; because the Lord hath anointed me to bring good
tidings unto the humble" (Isa. 61:1).

The imitation of God

"To walk in all His ways" (Deut. 11:22):
those are the ways of the Holy One, blessed be he.
As it is said: "The Lord . . . merciful and gracious, long-
suffering and abundant in goodness and truth; keeping
mercy unto the thousandth generation, forgiving iniquity and transgression and sin . . ." (Exod. 34:6).[19]

This means: As the Omnipresent is called merciful and
     gracious,
you too must be merciful and gracious, and give freely to all.
As the Holy One, blessed be he, is called righteous,
you too must be righteous.
As the Holy One, blessed be he, is called kindly,
you too must be kindly.

It is written: "After the Lord your God shall ye walk"
     (Deut. 13:5).
What does this mean? Is it possible for man to walk after the
     Presence of God? What it means is that we shall walk
     after the attributes of the Holy One, blessed be he.
As he clothes the naked—for it is written, "And the Lord God
     made for Adam and his wife garments of skins, and
     clothed them" (Gen. 3:21)—thus you also shall do:
     you shall clothe the naked.
The Holy One, blessed be he, visited the sick, as it is written:
     "And the Lord appeared unto him by the terebinth of
     Mamre" (Gen. 18:1)—thus you also shall do: you shall
     visit the sick.
The Holy One, blessed be he, comforted those who mourned,
     as it is written: "And it came to pass after the death of
     Abraham, that God blessed Isaac his son" (Gen.
     25:11). Do likewise: comfort those who mourn.
The Holy One, blessed be he, buried the dead, as it is written:
     "And He buried him [Moses] in the valley in the land
     of Moab" (Deut. 34:6). Do likewise: bury the dead.

The Torah: It begins with the showing of mercy and it ends
     with the showing of mercy.
It begins with the showing of mercy, as it is written:
     "And the Lord God made for Adam and for his wife
     garments of skins, and clothed them."
It ends with the showing of mercy, as it is written: "And He
     buried him in the valley in the Land of Moab."

Four answers

Wisdom was asked: The sinner, what is his destiny?

She replied: "Evil pursueth sinners" (Prov. 13:21).
Prophecy was asked: The sinner, what is his destiny?
She replied: "The soul that sinneth, it shall die" (Ezek. 18:4).
The Torah was asked: The sinner, what is his destiny?
She replied: Let him bring a guilt offering, and atonement
      shall be made for him;
as it is written: "And it shall be accepted for him to make
      atonement for him" (Lev. 1:4).
The Holy One, blessed be he, was asked:
The sinner, what is his destiny?
He replied:
Let him turn in repentance, and atonement shall be made for
      him; as it is written:
"Good and upright is the Lord; therefore doth He instruct
      sinners in the way" (Ps. 25:8).

Of their own free will

"The Lord loveth the righteous" (Ps. 146:8).

Says the Holy One, blessed be he: They love me, and I love them also. And why does the Holy One, blessed be he, love the righteous? Because their righteousness is not a matter of heritage or family.

You will find that the priests form a father's house and the Levites form a father's house, for it is said: "O house of Aaron, bless ye the Lord; O house of Levi, bless ye the Lord" (Ps. 135:19-20). A man may wish to become a priest and yet he cannot; he may wish to become a Levite and yet he cannot. And why? Because his father was no priest, or no Levite.

But if a man, Jew or gentile, wishes to be righteous, he can be this, because the righteous do not form a house. Therefore it is said: "Ye that fear the Lord, bless ye the Lord" (Ps. 135:20). It is not said, *house* of those that fear the Lord, but ye that fear the Lord, for they form no father's house.

Of their own free will, they have come forward and loved the Holy One, blessed be he. And that is why he loves them.

The heart

A man of flesh and blood, if he has a vessel,

so long as the vessel is whole, he is happy with it;
broken, he does not wish it.
But not so the Holy One, blessed be he.
So long as the vessel is whole, he does not wish to see it;
broken, he wishes it.
And what is the favorite vessel of the Holy One, blessed be
     he?
The heart of man.
If the Holy One, blessed be he, sees a proud heart, he does not
     wish it;
as it is said: "Every one that is proud in heart is an abomina-
     tion to the Lord" (Prov. 16:5).
—Broken, he says: This is mine;
as it is said: "The Lord is nigh unto them that are of a broken
     heart" (Ps. 34:19).

Of every man whose spirit is haughty, the Holy One, blessed
     be he, says:
He and I cannot dwell together in the world.

Destiny

Everyone that humbles himself the Holy One, blessed be he,
     lifts up;
and everyone that lifts himself up the Holy One, blessed be
     he, humbles.
Everyone that pursues greatness, greatness flees;
and everyone that flees greatness, greatness pursues.
Everyone that pushes his hour ahead, his hour pushes him
     back;
and everyone that stands back for his hour, his hour stands by
     him.

Rain

Hanan the Hidden was the son of the daughter of Honi the
     Circle-Drawer.[20]
When the world was in need of rain, the masters would send
     the school children to him,
and they would clutch the hem of his cloak and say to him:

Father, give us rain.

He said to Him:

Master of the Universe, do it for the sake of these who do not
know the difference between the Father who gives rain
and a father who does not give rain.

Mercy not sacrifice

Once Rabban Johanan ben Zakkai[21] went forth from Jerusalem; and Joshua [his disciple] walked behind him.

When he beheld the sanctuary in ruins, Joshua said: Woe to
us, that it has been destroyed! The place where Israel's
iniquities found atonement!

Then the other said to him: My son, do not let it grieve you!
We have atonement equal to that other. And what is
that?

Deeds of loving-kindness,

as it is written: "For I desire mercy, and not sacrifice" (Hos.
6:6).

Honor due to parents and to God

Great is the honoring of father and mother;

yes, the Holy One, blessed be he, even gave it precedence
over the honor due to Him.

It is written,

"Honor thy father and thy mother" (Exod. 20:12),

and it is written,

"Honor the Lord with thy substance" (Prov. 3:9).

Wherewith can you honor Him?

With that wherewith He has endowed you:

You set aside the gleaning, the forgotten sheaf at the corner
of the field;[22]

you set aside the heave offering, the first tithe, the second
tithe,

the tithe for the poor, and the loaf;

you see to the booth, and the branch of the palm tree, the
ram's horn, thy phylacteries and the fringes;[23]

you give food to the poor and the hungry, and you slake those
who thirst.

If you have substance, you are bound to do all of this,
if you have none, you are not bound to do this.
But when it comes to the honoring of father and mother,
it is the same whether you have something to give or have
          nothing to give:
"Honor thy father and thy mother"—
even if you have to go begging at doors.

Rabbi Joseph,
when he heard the sound of his mother's steps, said:
I shall rise before the Divine Presence that is coming.

Captivity

If a man is in captivity with his father and his master,
he comes before his master,
his master comes before his father.
His mother comes before them all.

The law and more

It happened to Rabbah bar Hanan that some porters broke a
          barrel of his wine.
He took away their cloaks.[24]
They went and told Rav [the judge].
He said to Rabbah: Give them back their cloaks.
Rabbah asked him: Is that the law?
He replied: Yes: "That thou mayest walk in the way of good
          men" (Prov. 2:20).
He gave them back their cloaks.
The porters said to Rav: We are poor men, and have worked
          all day, and are in need, and have nothing.
Rav said to Rabbah: Go and pay them.
He asked him: Is that the law?
He replied: Yes: "And keep the paths of the righteous"
          (*ibid.*).[25]

Let everyone enter

Rabbi Judah the Prince[26] opened his granary in the years of
          drought. He said:

Let those who have studied the Torah enter, and those who
 have studied the Mishnah, those who have studied the
 Gemara, those who have studied the Halakhah, and
 those who have studied the Haggadah—but let no ignoramus enter!

Jonathan ben Amram pressed forward and entered. He said:
 Master, feed me!

Rabbi Judah said to him: Have you studied the Torah, my
 son?

He said: No.

Have you studied the Mishnah?

He said: No.

If so, how can I feed you?

He said: Feed me as you would a dog or a crow.

Rabbi Judah fed him. After he had gone, Rabbi Judah sat
 regretting what he had done and said: Alas, for I have
 given my bread to an ignoramus.

Then Simon his son said to Rabbi Judah:

Perhaps that was Jonathan ben Amram, your disciple who has
 refused all his life to profit from the Torah.

They investigated, and found this to be so.

Then Rabbi Judah said: Let everyone enter.

The sufferings

The sufferings of Rabbi Judah the Prince came upon him with
 a certain event, and after a certain other event they
 went from him.

They came upon him with a certain event—how was that? A
 calf that was being led off to slaughter came and hid
 its head in the lap of Rabbi Judah's robe and wept.
 But he said: Go, that is what you were created for.

Then it was said: Because he did not have mercy, suffering
 shall come upon him.

After a certain other event they went from him: One day
 Rabbi Judah's serving maid was sweeping the house,
 and she wanted to sweep out and cast forth some young
 weasels. But he said: Let them be; it is written: "The
 Lord is good to all; and His tender mercies are over all

His works" (Ps. 145:9).

Then it was said: Because he has shown mercy, mercy shall
also be shown to him.

Jesters

Rav Beroka of Be Hozae was often in the market at Be Lapat.[27]

There he would meet [the Prophet] Elijah.[28] Once he said to
Elijah:

Is there anyone in this market who shall have the world to
come?

Elijah said to him: No.

They were standing there when two men came along.

Elijah said to him: These shall have the world to come.

Rav Beroka went to them and said: What is your occupation?

They said to him:

We are jesters, and make the sad to laugh.

When we see two men quarreling,

we strive hard to make peace between them.

The guardian of chastity

The masters saw in a dream how a donkey-driver prayed and
rain fell.

The masters sent for him, and he was brought before them.

They asked him: What is your trade?

He replied: I am a donkey-driver.

They asked him: What good thing have you done?

He replied:

Once I hired my donkey to a woman who was crying in the
street.

I asked her: What is the matter?

She replied:

My husband is in prison, and I must do whatever I must in
order to buy his freedom.

So I went and sold my donkey, and brought her the money;
and I said to her:

Here it is; free your husband, and do not sin!

Then the masters said to him:

You are worthy to pray, and to be answered.

Demands

The woman demands with her heart
and the man demands with his mouth.
This is a good quality in women.

Blood

Someone came before Raba and said:
The chief of my town has ordered me:
Go and kill so and so; if you do not, I will have you killed.
Raba said to him: Let him kill you, but you must not kill.
What do you think, your blood is redder than another man's?
Perhaps his blood is redder than yours.

Commendation

When Akabia ben Mahalalel was dying, his son said to him:
Father, commend me to some of your comrades.
Akabia said to him:
I will not commend you.
His son said to him: Is it because of some fault you have
found in me?
He said to him:
No. But your deeds will endear you, and your deeds will es-
trange you.

They that love Him

Our masters have taught:
They that are shamed, and do not shame others,
that hear their disgrace, and do not retort,
that act out of love, and rejoice in chastisements—
it is of them that Scripture says:
"But they that love Him be as the sun when he goeth forth in
his might" (Judg. 5:31).

Today

Rabbi Eliezer said:

Turn to God one day before your death.

His disciples asked him: Does a man know on which day he
　　　　will die?

He answered them:

Just because of this, let him turn to God on this very day, for
　　　　perhaps he must die on the morrow, and thus it will
　　　　come about that all his days will be days of turning to
　　　　God.

Judgment

When a man is led in to be judged,[29] he is asked:

Have you done your business faithfully?

Have you set yourself regular periods to study the Torah?

Have you begotten children after you?

Have you looked forward to redemption?

Have you used all your wits in the study of the Law?

Have you understood how one thing will follow from another?

Yet even so—if "the fear of the Lord is his treasure" (Isa.
　　　　33:6), it will go well with him,

if not, it will not.

Revelation and the Study of the Law

FROM THE TALMUD AND MIDRASH

The awesome event of the revelation on Mount Sinai lay in the past,
and the voice of the prophets, spokesmen of divine will, became silent in the
time of Ezra the Scribe, so taught the talmudic masters. However, the Scriptures are a living record of divine revelation. It is incumbent upon man to
penetrate the surface of what is written and to discover the divine thought and
will. That is the meaning of study: through immersion into the text of Torah,
the learner will perceive anew the word spoken on Sinai.

As a statue

"I am the Lord thy God" (Exod. 20:2):[30]

The Holy One, blessed be he, appeared as a statue which can
        be seen from everywhere.
A thousand men gaze at it, and it gazes back at all.
So looked the Holy One, blessed be he, when he was speaking
        to Israel.
Each and every one of Israel said to himself:
It is to me the Word is speaking.

All at one time

"And God spoke all these words" (Exod. 20:1).
—All at one and the same time:
taking life and giving life at one and the same time,
afflicting and healing at one and the same time.
Answering the woman in her travail,
those who go down to the sea and the desert farers,
those locked in the prison house,
one in the east and one in the west, one in the north, and one
        in the south;
"Forming the light, and creating darkness; making peace and
        creating evil'" (Isa. 45:7),
—all at one and the same time.

As the desert

Why was the Torah given in the desert [of Sinai]?
To teach you
that if a man does not hold himself as unpossessed as the
        desert,
he does not become worthy of the words of the Torah.

The Torah was given in public, for all to see, in the open.
For if it had been given in the land of Israel, Israel would have
        said to the nations of the world, You have no share
        in it;
therefore the Torah was given in the wilderness, in public, for
        all to see, in the open,
and everyone who wishes to receive it, let him come and re-
        ceive it.

Israel and the nations

When the Omnipresent revealed himself to give the Torah to
      Israel,
he revealed himself not to Israel alone, but to all the nations.
At first he went to the children of Esau, and said to them:
Will you accept the Torah?
They said to him: What is written in it?
He said to them: "Thou shalt not kill."
They said to him: Master of the Universe, our father was a
      killer by nature;
as it is said [. . .]: "And by the sword shalt thou live"
      (Gen. 27:40).
Then He went to the children of Ammon and Moab and said
      to them:
Will you accept the Torah?
They said to him: What is written in it?
He said to them: "Thou shalt not commit adultery."
They said to him: Master of the Universe, immorality is our
      nature [. . .].
He went and found the children of Ishmael, and said to them:
Will you accept the Torah?
They said to him: What is written in it?
He said to them: "Thou shalt not steal."
They said to him: Master of the Universe, our father was a
      thief by nature [. . .].
There was not a nation of all the nations to whom He did not
      go, and to whom he did not speak, and on whose
      threshold he did not knock, to ask whether they wished
      to receive the Torah. . . .
But even the seven commandments which the children of
      Noah did accept[31] they could not persevere in,
until he lifted their yoke off them, and gave the laws to Israel.

The children

When Israel stood to receive the Torah,
the Holy One, blessed be he, said to them:

I am giving you my Torah. Bring me good guarantors that you
     will guard it, and I shall give it to you.
They said: Our patriarchs are our guarantors.
The Holy One, blessed be he, said to them:
Your patriarchs are unacceptable to me,[32]
yet bring me good guarantors, and I shall give it to you.
They said to him:
Master of the Universe, our prophets are our guarantors.
He said to them:
The prophets are unacceptable to me:
"The rulers transgressed against Me; the prophets also proph-
     esied by Baal" (Jer. 2:8).
Yet bring me good guarantors, and I shall give it to you.
They said:
Behold, our children are our guarantors.
The Holy One, blessed be he, said:
They are certainly good guarantors.
For their sake I give the Torah to you.

The keepers of the city

Rabbi Judah the Prince asked Rabbi Dosa and Rabbi Ammi
     to go forth and inspect the cities in the Land of Israel.
They came to a city and said to the people: Have the keepers
     of the city brought before us.
They brought the overseer and the senator.
Then they said to them: Are these the keepers of the city?
     Why, these are the destroyers of the city!
Then the people asked them: Who are the keepers of the city?
Thereupon they answered: The teachers of the Scriptures and
     of the Tradition, who keep watch by day and by night,
     in accordance with the words:
"This book of the law shall not depart out of thy mouth, but
     thou shalt meditate therein day and night" (Josh. 1:8).

Witnesses

"And ye are My witnesses, saith the Lord, and I am God"
     (Isa. 43:12).

If ye are "my witnesses," I am the Lord,
and if ye are not my witnesses,
I am not, as it were, the Lord.

In thy heart

"For this commandment which I command thee this day, it is
      not too hard for thee, neither is it far off. It is not in
      heaven. . . . Neither is it beyond the sea . . ." (Deut.
      30:11-13).
They said to Moses:
Our master, lo, you say to us it is not in heaven and it is not
      beyond the sea;
then where is it?
He said to them:
In a place that "is very nigh unto thee, in thy mouth, and in
      thy heart, that thou mayest do it" (v. 14)—
It is not far from you, it is near to you.

What animals teach

Had the Torah not been given us, we could have learned
      modesty from the cat, the command not to rob from
      the ant, chastity from the dove, and propriety from
      the cock.

The core of the commandments

Six hundred and thirteen commandments were given to
      Moses, three hundred and sixty-five prohibitory laws,
      equaling the number of the days of the solar year,
and two hundred and forty-eight mandatory laws,
corresponding to the parts of the body.
David came and brought them down to eleven;
as it is written:
"Lord, who shall sojourn in Thy tabernacle? . . .
He that walketh uprightly, and worketh righteousness, and
      speaketh truth in his heart; that hath no slander upon
      his tongue, nor doeth evil to his fellow, nor taketh up

> a reproach against his neighbor; in whose eyes a vile person is despised, but he honoreth them that fear the Lord; he that sweareth to his own hurt, and changeth not; he that putteth not out his money on interest, nor taketh a bribe against the innocent" (Ps. 15:1-5).

Isaiah came and brought them down to six;
as it is written:

> "He that walketh righteously and speaketh uprightly; he that despiseth the gain of oppressions, that shaketh his hands from holding of bribes, that stoppeth his ears from hearing of blood, and shutteth his eyes from looking upon evil" (Isa. 33:15).

Micah came and brought them down to three;
as it is written:

> "It hath been told thee, O man, what is good . . .: Only to do justly, and to love mercy, and to walk humbly with thy God" (Mic. 6:8).

Isaiah came again and brought them down to two;
as it is said:

> "Thus saith the Lord,
> Keep ye justice, and do righteousness" (Isa. 56:1).

Amos came and brought them down to one;
as it is said:

> "For thus saith the Lord unto the house of Israel:
> Seek ye Me, and live" (Amos 5:4).

Or:
Habakkuk came and brought them down to one;
as it is said:

> "But the righteous shall live by his faith" (Hab. 2:4).

A greater principle

"Thou shalt love thy neighbor as thyself" (Lev. 19:18).
Rabbi Akiba says: This is the great principle of the Torah.
Ben Azzai says: "This is the book of the generations of Adam:

> In the day that God created man, in the likeness of God made He him" (Gen. 5:1)—

this is a principle greater than that.

The yoke of freedom

Had Israel gazed deep into the words of the Torah when it
        was given them,
no nation or kingdom could ever rule over them.
And what did it say to them?
Accept upon yourselves the yoke of the kingdom of heaven,
and subdue one another in the fear of heaven,
and deal with one another in charity.

Fire and light

"Now mount Sinai was altogether on smoke, because the Lord
        descended upon it in fire" (Exod. 19:18):
this tells us that the Torah is fire, and was given in the midst
        of fire, and is compared to fire.
As the way of fire is, that when a man is near it, he is burned,
        when far from it, chilled—
so the only way for a man to do is to warm himself in the
        light.

The Torah is called a "fiery law" (Deut. 33:2):
Let all who come to engage in the Torah
see themselves as standing in the midst of fire.

Not in heaven

. . . On that day Rabbi Eliezer [in dispute with other sages]
        brought all the proofs in the world [in support of his
        opinion], but the sages would not accept them.[33]
He said to them: If the law is according to me, let this locust
        tree prove it.
The locust tree moved a hundred cubits. (And some say: four
        hundred cubits.)
The sages said to him: The locust tree cannot prove anything.
Then he said to them: If the law is according to me, let this
        stream of water prove it.
The stream of water turned and flowed backward.
They said to him: The stream cannot prove anything.

Then he said to them: If the law is according to me, let the
walls of the House of Study prove it.

The walls of the House of Study began to topple.

Rabbi Joshua reprimanded the walls:

If scholars are disputing with one another about the law, what
business is it of yours?

They did not fall down out of respect for Rabbi Joshua, and
did not straighten up out of respect for Rabbi Eliezer,
and they are still inclined.

Then Rabbi Eliezer said to them: If the law is according to
me, let the heaven prove it.

A voice came forth from heaven and said:

Why do you dispute with Rabbi Eliezer? The law is according
to him in every case.

Thereupon Rabbi Joshua rose to his feet and said:

"It is not in heaven" (Deut. 30:12):

the Torah has already been given once and for all from Mount
Sinai;

we do not listen to voices from heaven.

For Thou hast already written in the Torah on Mount Sinai:
"After the majority must one incline" (Exod. 23:2).

[Later on] Rabbi Nathan came upon Elijah [the prophet].[34]

He said to him: What was the Holy One, blessed be he, doing
at that moment?

Elijah said to him:

He was smiling and saying: My children have defeated me,
my children have defeated me!

The trapper

[The Prophet] Elijah,[35] of blessed memory, said:

Once I was on a journey and came upon a certain man who
began to mock and scoff at me.

I said to him: What will you answer on the Day of Judgment,
since you have not learned Torah?

He said: I will be able to answer: I was given no understanding and knowledge and intelligence by heaven.

I said to him: What is your trade?

He said to me: I am a trapper of birds and fish.
I said to him:
Who gave you the knowledge and intelligence to take flax
 and to spin and to weave it, and to make nets, and to
 take fish and birds in them, and to sell them?
He said to me: The understanding and knowledge for that
 were given me by heaven.
I said to him: You were given understanding and knowledge
 to take the flax, to spin and to weave it, and to take fish
 and birds in the nets,
but you were given no understanding to gain Torah?
Yet it is written:
"But the word is very nigh unto thee, in thy mouth, and in
 thy heart that thou mayest do it" (Deut. 30:14).
At once he considered the matter in his heart, and lifted up
 his voice and wept.

The vessels

A parable:
A man came to the shopkeeper to buy a measure of wine.
The shopkeeper said to him: Bring me your vessel.
But the man opened his bag.
Then he said to the shopkeeper: Give me some oil.
The shopkeeper said to him: Bring me your vessel.
But the man opened the corner of his garment.
Said the shopkeeper to him: How can you buy wine and oil if
 you have no vessel at hand?
Similarly:
God says to the wicked:
You have no good deeds with you—how then do you wish to
 learn Torah!

They questioned Rabban Johanan ben Zakkai:
A sage who fears sin—what is he like?
He answered them: He is an artisan with the tools of his craft
 in his hands.
A sage who does not fear sin—what is he like?

He answered them: He is an artisan without the tools of his
    craft in his hands.
A man who fears sin, but is not a sage—what is he like?
He answered them: He is a man who is no artisan, but one
    who has the tools of the craft in his hands.

For love of Torah

Rabbi Johanan[36] was walking from Tiberias to Sepphoris, and
    Rabbi Hiyya bar Abba was supporting him.
They came to a certain field, and Rabbi Johanan said:
This field was mine, and I sold it in order to gain the Torah.
They came to a certain vineyard, and he said:
This vineyard was mine, and I sold it in order to gain the
    Torah.
They came to a certain olive grove, and he said:
This olive grove was mine, and I sold it in order to gain the
    Torah.
Rabbi Hiyya began to cry.
Rabbi Johanan said: Why are you crying?
He said to him: Because you left nothing for your old age.
He said to him: Is what I have done a small thing in your eyes?
For I have sold things which [belong to the world] created in
    the course of six days,
and I have gained a thing which was given in the course of
    forty days;
as it is said [of Moses]: "And he was there with the Lord forty
    days and forty nights" (Exod. 34:28).

Should you say:
Lo, I am learning Torah that I may become rich,
and that I may be called "Master,"
and that I may receive a reward
—therefore it is said: "to love the Lord your God" (Deut.
    11:13), all that you do you must do only out of love.

The free gift

. . . [God] showed Moses all the treasures that are the reward
    of the righteous for their deeds.

Moses asked: Whose treasure is this?

God answered: The masters of the Torah.

—And whose treasure is this?

—Those who honor them.

Then He showed Moses a treasure greater than all the rest.

Moses said: Master of the Universe, whose is this great treasure?

He said to him:

He who has good deeds, I give him his reward from his own treasure;

and he who has none of his own, freely give from this;

as it is said: "And I will be gracious to whom I will be gracious, and I will show mercy on whom I will show mercy" (Exod. 33:19).

The mark of a man's foot

"And the Lord said unto Moses . . . Behold I will stand before thee there upon the rock in Horeb" (Exod. 17:5-6).

The Holy One, blessed be he, said to him:

Wherever you find the mark of a man's foot,

there I am before you.

Equality

Should you say:

There are children of the elders,

and there are children of the great,

and there are children of the prophets,

—it is said:

"If ye shall diligently keep *all* this commandment" (Deut. 11:22):

Scripture tells us that *all* are equal in the Torah.

And so it is said:

"Moses commanded us a law, an inheritance of the congregation of Jacob" (Deut. 33:4).

—"Priests, Levites, and Israelites" is not written here, but: "the congregation of Jacob."

Why is it that sages do not have sons who are also sages?
So that no one shall think the Torah can be inherited.
Also:
So that they shall not consider themselves superior to the rest
of the community.
Rabbi Hanina said:

Much have I learned from my teachers,
and more from my comrades than from my teachers,
and from my disciples the most.

A man

Whence do we know that even a Gentile who engages in the
Torah is like a high priest?
We learn it from: "Ye shall therefore keep My statutes, and
Mine ordinances, which if a man do, he shall live by
them" (Lev. 18:5).
"Priests, Levites, and Israelites" was not said,
but "a man";
thus you may learn that even a Gentile who engages in the
Torah
—lo, he is like a high priest.

Humility

If a man lowers himself for the sake of Torah,
eats dried-out dates and wears mean clothing,
and sits diligently at the doors of the sages,
every passerby says: This might be a fool!
But in the end you will find that the whole Torah is within
him.

"The small and great are there [in afterlife] alike;
and the servant is free from his master" (Job 3:19):
Don't we know that "the small and great are there"?
The meaning is:
He who makes himself small for the sake of Torah in this
world,
will be great in the world to come;

he who makes himself a servant for the sake of Torah in this
    world,
will be a free man in the world to come.

Scholars and kings

A sage takes precedence over a king of Israel;
if a sage dies, we have none like him—
if a king dies, all Israel are eligible for kingship.

The gates

There is no creature the Holy One, blessed be he, rejects,
but he accepts them all.
The gates are open at every hour,
and all who wish to enter, may enter.
Therefore it is said:
"My doors I opened to the wanderer" (Job 31:32)
—meaning the Holy One, blessed be he, who suffers his crea-
    tures.

Israel: A Holy Community

FROM THE TALMUD AND MIDRASH

Is Israel a people, a nation or a religion? The argument persisted for
centuries and various definitions were put forward and rejected. The talmudic
Haggadah, in describing Israel, offers an indication of what the Jewish people
considered themselves to be after the loss of the last vestiges of national independence, and (in the passage, "Jacob's Ladder") how they interpreted
their precarious position in the framework of the nations of the world, which,
following the law of historic life, rise and fall.

Three signs

This people is known by three signs:
Being compassionate, shamefaced, and charitable.
Everyone who has these three signs is worthy of cleaving to
    this people.

Poverty

What is the meaning of the Scriptural verse:
"Behold, I have refined thee, but not as silver; I have tried
      thee in the furnace of poverty" (Isa. 48:10)?
It teaches that the Holy One, blessed be he, went over all the
      good qualities that he might give Israel, and found
      poverty the best.
That is what people say:
Poverty is becoming to Jews, like a red halter on a white horse.

Like oil

"Thy name is as oil poured forth" (Cant. 1:3).[37]
As oil is bitter to begin with, but sweet in the end,
so: "And though thy beginning was small, yet thy end should
      greatly increase" (Job 8:7).
As oil improves only through being pressed,
so Israel cannot turn from sin,
except through chastisement.
As oil which when a drop of water falls into a full cup of oil,
      a drop of the oil spills out,
so, when a word of Torah enters the heart, a word of scoffing
      leaves it;
when a word of scoffing enters the heart, a word of Torah
      leaves it.
As oil brings light to the world,
so Israel brings light to the world;
as it is said: "And nations shall walk at thy light, and kings at
      the brightness of thy rising" (Isa. 60:3).
As oil is soundless,
so Israel is soundless in this world.

Jacob and Esau

"The voice is the voice of Jacob, but the hands are the hands
      of Esau" (Gen. 27:22).
The nations of the world entered before Abnimos the weaver.[38]
They said to him:

Can we attack this nation?
He said to them:
Go and pass before their Houses of Study and Houses of
        Prayer.
If you there hear children chanting, you cannot attack them.
But if you do not hear children chanting, you can attack them.
For thus their father assured them:
"The voice is the voice of Jacob";
So long as the voice of Jacob is chanting in Houses of Study
        and Houses of Prayer,
the hands are not "the hands of Esau."[39]

Sharing

Every distress that Israel and the nations of the world share
is a distress indeed.
Every distress that is Israel's alone
is no distress.

In that night when Israel crossed the Red Sea,
the angels desired to sing a song before God.
But the Holy One, blessed be he, forbade it, and said to them:
My legions are in distress, and you would sing a song in my
        presence?

Jacob's ladder [40]

"And he dreamed, and behold a ladder set up on the earth,
        and the top of it reaching to heaven; and behold the
        angels of God ascending and descending on it" (Gen.
        28:12).
—Teaching us that Holy One, blessed be he, showed to our
        father Jacob
the lord of Babylonia[41] ascending and descending,
and the lord of Media ascending and descending,
and the lord of Greece ascending and descending,
and the lord of Rome ascending and descending.
The Holy One, blessed be he, said to him: Jacob, you must
        ascend too!
Then our father Jacob grew very fearful and said:

But perhaps, as they shall have to descend, I, too, shall have
    to descend.

The Holy One, blessed be he, said to him:

"Be not dismayed, O Israel" (Jer. 30:10). If you ascend, you
    shall never have to descend.

But Jacob did not have faith, and did not ascend.

The Holy One, blessed be he, said to him:

If you had had faith and ascended, you would never have
    descended again.

But now that you have not had faith, and have not ascended,
your children will be enslaved to four kingdoms in this world,
through duties, taxes in kind, fines and poll taxes.

Then Jacob grew very fearful and said to the Holy One,
    blessed be he: Will that last forever?

He said to him (*ibid.*): "Be not dismayed, O Israel,

for behold I will save thee from afar"—from Babylonia.

"And thy seed from the land of their captivity will return"—
    from Gaul and Spain and the neighboring lands.

"And Israel shall return"—from Babylonia.

"And be quiet"—from Media.

"And at ease"—from Greece.

"And none shall make him afraid"—from Rome.

Peace

FROM THE TALMUD AND MIDRASH

The very numerous sayings on the importance of peace in personal,
communal, political, or religious life, scattered over the talmudic and midrashic
literature, represent a tradition of some four centuries. They are documents of
nonpolitical Judaism in the form it took after the destruction of Judaea. Here
Israel apprehends its activities as culminating in peace, utilizing the Torah as
an instrument of peace and as a blueprint of the worship of God, conceived
as a God of peace. In addition to scattered sayings, certain portions within
the talmudic-midrashic works can be recognized as anthologies, or remnants of
anthologies on peace. As a rule the individual maxims are introduced by the
phrase, "Great is peace."

Great is peace, because peace is for the earth what yeast is for
      the dough.
If the Holy One, blessed be he, had not given peace to the
      earth,
it would be depopulated by the sword and by hosts of animals.

The world rests upon three things: On justice, on truth, on
      peace.
Yet, those three are one and the same thing.
For if there is justice, there is truth, and there is peace.
And these three are expressed in one and the same verse:
"Execute the judgment of truth and peace in your gates"
      (Zech. 8:16).
Wherever there is justice, there is peace, and wherever there is
      peace, there is justice.

See how great is his reward who makes peace between men.
It is written: "Thou shalt build the altar of the Lord thy God
      of unhewn stones" (Deut. 27:6).
If these stones which cannot hear and cannot see and cannot
      smell and cannot speak,
because they make peace between men through the sacrifices
      that are offered upon them
Scripture saves them from the sword and declares:
"Thou shalt lift no iron tool upon them" (*ibid.* v.5)
—man, who can hear and see and smell and speak,
how much more is this true of him, when he makes peace be-
      tween his fellow-men.

Great is peace,
for Aaron the priest was praised only because he was a peace-
      able man.
For it was he who loved peace, who pursued peace, who was
      first to offer peace, and who responded to peace;
as it is written:
"He walked with Me in peace and uprightness" (Mal. 2:6).
And what is written thereafter?
"And did turn many away from iniquity."
This teaches: If ever he saw two men who hated each other,

he went to one of them and said to him: "Why do you
hate that man? For he came to my house, and prostrated himself before me and said: 'I have sinned
against him!' Go and pacify him!"
And Aaron left him and went to the second man and spoke to
him as to the first.
Thus it was his wont to set peace and love and friendship between man and man, and he 'did turn many away from
iniquity.'

Great is peace,
for we seal all benedictions and all prayers with "peace."
The recitation of "Hear, O Israel" we seal with "peace":
"Spread the tabernacle of peace."
The benediction of the priests is sealed with "peace":
"And give thee peace" (Num. 6:26).

Thus spoke the Holy One, blessed be he, to Israel:
"You have caused my house to be destroyed and my children
to be banished—
but ask for Jerusalem's peace and I shall forgive you."
He, however, who loves peace, who pursues peace, who offers
peace first, and responds to peace,
the Holy One, blessed be he, will let him inherit the life of
this world and the world to come,
as it is written:
"But the humble shall inherit the land, and delight themselves in the abundance of peace" (Ps. 37:11).

Exile and Redemption

FROM THE TALMUD AND MIDRASH

That the fall of the Temple in the year 70 was proof that God had
forsaken Israel was an argument used by the early Christian community that
called itself the new Israel. The talmudic sages rejected this argument. It was
their contention that the divine presence (*Shekhinah*) never left Israel. It

accompanies Israel into exile, partakes in its sufferings, and will partake in its ultimate redemption. The date and the manner of redemption mattered less (especially in the first generations after the year 70) than people's internal preparedness. If they would "but hearken to His voice," Messiah would come today.

The keys of the Temple

When the Temple was about to be destroyed, the young
        priests assembled in bands with the keys of the Temple
        in their hands, and went up to the roof of the Temple,
        and said before Him:
Master of the Universe, seeing that we have not been worthy
        to be faithful treasurers, let the keys be given back to
        you,
and they threw them heavenwards.
Then something like a hand came forth and received the keys
        from them.
Whereupon they leaped and fell into the fire.

Love

"For I am love-sick" (Cant. 2:5).
The congregation of Israel said to the Holy One, blessed be
        he:
Master of the Universe, all the ills you bring upon me—are to
        bring me to love you the more.
Another interpretation:
The congregation of Israel said to the Holy One, blessed be he:
Master of the Universe, all the ills the nations of the world
        bring upon me—
are because I love you.

Divine Presence in exile

You find:
Every place where Israel was exiled, the Divine Presence was
        with them.
They were exiled to Egypt, the Presence was with them.
They were exiled to Babylon, the Presence was with them.
They were exiled to Elam, the Presence was with them.

They were exiled to Rome, the Presence was with them.
And when they shall return, the Presence, as it were, will be
with them.

Waiting

"For with thee is the fountain of life; in Thy light do we see
light" (Ps. 36:10).
As one who was journeying at the time of the sinking of the
sun,
and someone came and lit a candle for him, and it went out;
and another came and lit a candle for him, and it went out.
He said: From now on, I shall wait for the morning light
alone.
So, Israel said to the Holy One, blessed be he:
Master of the Universe, we made a lamp for you in the days of
Moses, and it went out;
ten lamps in the days of Solomon,[42] and they went out.
From now on we will wait for your light alone:
"In Thy light do we see light."

Today

Rabbi Joshua, son of Levi, came upon the prophet Elijah[43]
and asked him: "When will the Messiah come?"
The other replied: "Go and ask him yourself."
"Where is he to be found?"
"Before the gates of Rome."
"By what sign shall I know him?"
"He is sitting among poor lepers: the others unbind all their
sores at once, and then bind them up again, but he
unbinds one wound at a time, and binds it up again
straightway, thinking, should I perhaps be needed [to
appear as the Messiah] I shall not be delayed."
So he went and found him and said: "Peace be with you, my
master and teacher!"
He answered him: "Peace be with you, son of Levi!"
Then he asked him: "When are you coming, master?"
He answered him: "Today!"

Thereupon he returned to Elijah and said to him: "He has
    deceived me, he said he would come today, and he
    has not come."
Elijah answered: "This is what he meant: 'Today—if ye would
    but hearken to His voice' (Ps. 95:7)."[44]

The real redemption

Israel said to the Holy One, blessed be he:
Have you not redeemed us already through Moses and Joshua
    and all the judges and kings?
Yet now are we to return to be enslaved and be ashamed, as
    though we had never been redeemed?
The Holy One, blessed be he, said to them:
Seeing that your redemption was at the hands of flesh and
    blood,
and your leaders were men, here today, tomorrow in the
    grave;
therefore your redemption has been redemption for a space.
But in time to come I myself will redeem you;
I, who am living and enduring,
will redeem you with a redemption enduring forever;
as it is said:
"O Israel, that art saved by the Lord with an everlasting sal-
    vation" (Isa. 45:17).

The Messiah

The garment in which [God] will clothe the Messiah will
    shine forth from one end of the world to the other.
Those of Israel will make use of his light, and will say:
Blessed the hour in which the Messiah was created;
blessed the womb from which he came;
blessed the generation which sees him;
blessed the age that waited for him.
The opening of his lips is blessing and peace;
his speech is pleasure of spirit;
his garment is glory and majesty;
his words bring confidence and rest,

his tongue pardon and forgiveness;
his prayer is a sweet savor,
his supplication holiness and purity.
Blessed are you, Israel, for what is in store for you.

Messiah and the world to come

Samuel[45] said:
There is no difference between this world and the days of the
Messiah except [that they will be free of the] servitude
to the [foreign] kingdoms.
Rabbi Johanan[46] said:
All the prophets prophesied only for the days of Messiah, but
what concerns the world to come—
"no eye hath seen, oh God, beside Thee, what He will do for
him that waiteth for Him" (Isa. 64:3).[47]

Rav used to say:
Not like this world is the world to come.
In the world to come there is no eating nor drinking;
no procreation of children or business; no envy, or hatred, or
competition;
but the righteous sit, their crowns on their heads,
and enjoy the splendor of the Divine Presence.

Planting

Rabban Johanan ben Zakkai used to say:
If there be a plant in your hand when they say to you:
Behold the Messiah!
—Go and plant the plant, and afterward go out to greet him.[48]

Reflections on the Book of Job

FROM THE TALMUD AND MIDRASH

In contradistinction to the author of the Testament of Job, the talmudic
sages acknowledge Job as a rebel and an accuser of God who multiplies his

wounds "without cause." They contrast Job, whom they consider one of the heathen prophets, with Abraham, the lover of God. But, although Job is known as one "who feared the Lord" the talmudic masters try to understand this "fear" as implying the motive of "love." It is the Lord's work to inform Job that in spite of the apparent injustice and anarchy, He is still concerned with His creation and with man. The personal element, missing in God's answer to Job in the Bible, is restored by the sages.

Heathen prophets

Seven prophets prophesied to the nations of the world.
Balaam and his father, Job [and his friends] Eliphaz the Temanite, Bildad the Shuhite, Zophar the Naamathite, and Elihu the son of Barachel the Buzite.

Unaided knowledge

There are four persons who came to know the Holy One, blessed be he, out of their own thinking:
Abraham: There was no man who would have taught him how to know God; he reached this knowledge by himself;
Likewise Job, of whom it is said: "I have treasured in my bosom the words of His mouth" (Job 23:12).
Likewise Hezekiah, King of Judah, about whom it is said: ". . . when he knoweth to refuse the evil, and choose the good" (Isa. 7:15).
The King Messiah, too, by himself did he reach the knowledge of the Holy One, blessed be he.

Who can hinder Thee

". . . Although Thou knowest that I shall not be condemned; and there is none that can deliver out of Thy hand" (Job 10:7).
Raba said:
Job sought to free the whole world from judgment.
He said: Lord of the Universe, Thou hast created the ox with his cloven hoofs and Thou hast created the ass with his whole hoofs;
Thou hast created Paradise and Thou hast created Gehinnom;[49]

Thou hast created the righteous ones and Thou hast created
the wicked ones—
who is it that can hinder Thee?[50]
What did Job's friends answer him?
"Yea, thou doest away with fear, and impairest devotion before God" (15:4);
The Holy One, blessed be he, did create the evil impulse,
but he also created the Torah with which to season it.

Fear of God and love of God[51]

It is written of Job, "one that feared God" (1:1)
and it is written of Abraham, "Thou fearest God" (Gen.
22:12):
now, just as "fearing God" with Abraham implies [that he
acted] from love,
so "fearing God" with Job implies [that he acted] from love.

Rabbi Joshua ben Hyrcanus expounded:
Job served the Holy One, blessed be he, only from love,
as it is written: "Though He slay me, yet will I trust in Him"
(13:15),
or, clearer still: "Till I die I will not put away mine integrity
from me" (27:5)—
teaching that he acted from love.
Rabbi Joshua [ben Hananiah] said:
Who will remove the dust from your eyes, Rabban Johanan
ben Zakkai,
for all your life you have used to expound that Job served God
only from fear,
as it is said: "That man was whole-hearted and upright, and
one that feared God and shunned evil" (1:1)
and now, Joshua, the disciple of your disciple, taught us that
Job acted from love.

Abraham and Job

Rabbi Levi said:
The statement made by Abraham is like the statement made
by Job;

but Job expressed it rashly and Abraham deliberately.
Job said: "It is all one—therefore I say: He destroyeth the
      innocent and the wicked" (9:22);
but Abraham said: "Wilt Thou indeed sweep away the right-
      eous and the wicked?" (Gen. 18:23).

Rabbi Johanan said:
Greater is what is said of Job than what is said of Abraham.
Of Abraham Scripture says: "For now I know that thou fear-
      est God" (Gen. 22:12),
whereas of Job it is said: "That man was whole-hearted and
      upright, and one that feared God and shunned evil"
      (1:1).

Rabbi Levi said:
Satan [in speaking to God][52] acted out of a sacred intention:
When he saw that the Holy One, blessed be he, favored Job,
      he thought:
Far be it that He should forget the love of Abraham.
[Later,] when Rav Aha bar Jacob reported this interpretation
      in Papunia,
Satan came and kissed his feet.

Satan

Rabbi Yitzhak said:
The pain of the Satan[53] was stronger than that of Job;
the Satan can be compared to a servant to whom his master
      said: Break the barrel but preserve the wine therein.

No resurrection

"As the cloud is consumed and vanisheth away, so he that
      goeth down to the grave shall come up no more" (7:9);
this shows that Job denied the resurrection of the dead.

Job the rebel

"Oh that my vexation were but weighed, and my calamity
      laid in the balances altogether!" (6:2).
Rav said:

Dust should be put into the mouth of Job
[because he spoke as if there were] an equality with heaven
      [on the part of man].
"There is no arbiter betwixt us, that might lay his hand upon
      us both" (9:33).
Rav said:
Is there a servant who may argue against his master?

Enemy of God?

"He would break me with a tempest and multiply my wounds
      without cause" (9:17).
Job said to Him:
Master of the Universe, perhaps a tempest has passed before
      Thee and thus Thou confusest Iyob [Job] and Oyeb
      [enemy]? [54]
He answered him out of the tempest:
"Gird up now thy loins like a man; for I will demand of thee,
      and declare thou unto Me" (38:3):
Many hairs have I created in man, and for every hair I have
      created a groove of its own, so that two hairs should
      not suck from one groove . . .
I do not confuse grooves, how could I confuse Iyob and Oyeb?
"Who hath cleft a channel for the waterflood?" (38:25):
Many drops have I created in the clouds, and for every drop
      a mould of its own, so that two drops should not come
      forth from one mould; for should two drops come forth
      from one mould they would wash away the soil and it
      would not bring forth fruit.
I do not confuse drops, how could I confuse Iyob and Oyeb?
"Or a way for the lightning of the thunder" (*ibid.*):
Many thunderclaps have I created in the clouds, and for each
      clap a path of its own, so that two claps should not
      issue in the same path . . .
I do not confuse thunderclaps, how could I confuse Iyob and
      Oyeb?
"Knowest thou the time when the wild goats of the rock bring
      forth?" (39:1):

The wild goat is cruel to her young. When she crouches to
>   give birth, she goes up to the top of the mountain so
>   that the young should fall off and die; so I prepare an
>   eagle to catch it in his wings and put it before her;
>   should the eagle be one second too early or one second
>   too late the young would be killed.
I do not confuse the seconds, how could I confuse Iyob and
>   Oyeb?
"Or canst thou mark when the hinds do calve?" (*ibid.*)
The calf has a narrow womb. When she crouches to give birth,
>   I prepare a serpent that bites her at the opening of the
>   womb and she is delivered from her young; were the
>   serpent one second too early or too late, she would die.
I do not confuse the seconds, how could I confuse Iyob and
>   Oyeb?
"Job speaks without knowledge and his words are without
>   wisdom" (34:35).

The turning point

As long as Job stood against his friends and his friends against
>   him,
the attribute of divine justice[55] prevailed;
only after they made peace with each other and Job prayed
>   for his friends,
the Holy One, blessed be he, returned to him,
as it is said:
"And the Lord turned the fortune of Job, when he prayed for
>   his friends" (42:10).

Blessing

When Rabbi Johanan finished the Book of Job, he used to
>   say:
The end of man is death
the end of cattle is to slaughter—
all are doomed to die.
Blessed is he who has grown in the Torah
and whose toil is in the Torah,

and who is giving pleasure to his Maker;
who has grown up with a good name
and with a good name departs from this world.

Prayers of the Masters

FROM THE TALMUD TRACTATE BERAKHOT

In addition to the regular order of daily devotion it was the custom of
the talmudic masters to utter a self-composed private prayer. The following is
a brief collection quoted in the talmudic tractate Berakhot ("Benedictions").
As public worship developed, many such meditations were incorporated into
the regular prayer book.

May it be Thy will, O Lord our God,
to cause to dwell in our lot, love, brotherliness, peace and
        friendship;
to enrich our boundaries through disciples,
to prosper our goal with hope and with future,
to set us a share in Paradise,
to cause us to obtain good companions and good impulse in
        Thy world;
that we may rise in the morning and find
our heart longing to hear Thy name.

May it be Thy will, O Lord our God,
to look upon our shame,
to behold our misery;
clothe Thyself in Thy mercy,
and cover Thyself in Thy power,
and wrap Thyself in Thy love,
and gird Thyself in Thy grace;
may the attribute of Thy kindness and mildness
come before Thee.

May it be Thy will, O Lord our God,
that we do not sin,
so that we fall not into shame or disgrace before our fathers.

May it be Thy will, O Lord our God,
that Thy Torah be our occupation,
that our hearts be not grieved
nor our eyes darkened.

May it be Thy will, O Lord our God,
to grant us long life, a life of peace, of good,
a life of blessing, of sustenance, of bodily vigor;
a life in which there is fear of sin
a life free from shame and disgrace, a life of prosperity and
        honor,
a life in which we may have the love of Torah and the fear
        of heaven,
a life in which Thou shalt fulfil all the wishes of our heart for
        good.

Master of the Universe,
it is known and apparent before Thee
that it is our will to do Thy will.
But what hinders us?
The ferment in the dough,[56] and servitude to the [foreign]
        kingdoms.
May it be Thy will to save us out of their hands,
so that we may again do the commandments of Thy will
with a whole heart.

My God, before I was formed
I had no worth
and now that I am formed,
it is as though I had not been formed.
Dust I am in my life,
and how much more in my death!
Here am I, in Thy presence,
like a vessel filled with shame and disgrace.
May it be Thy will, O Lord my God,
that I sin no more,
and the sins I have committed before Thee
purge them away in Thy great mercy,
but not through suffering and grave disease,

My God,
Keep my tongue from evil,
and my lips from speaking guile.
To those who slander me, let my soul be silent,
my soul shall be to all as dust.
Open my heart to Thy Torah,
let my soul pursue Thy commandments.
And deliver me from evil schemes, from the evil impulse,
and from an evil woman,
from all evil that rushes to come into the world.
But as for those who think evil against me,
speedily break their plots and destroy their thoughts.
Let the words of my mouth
and the meditation of my heart
be acceptable in Thy presence,
O Lord, my rock, my redeemer.

O my God, the soul that Thou hast given me is pure!
Thou didst create it, Thou didst form it, Thou didst breathe
it into me, Thou preservest it within me,
In time Thou wilt take it from me, and return it to me in the
life to come.
As long as the soul is within me, I will give thanks unto Thee,
O Lord my God, and the God of my fathers,
master of all deeds, lord of all souls!

Reflections on Life

FROM SEDER ELIYAHU RABBA

Using older material, a tenth-century author, whose country of residence is in doubt (Palestine? Babylonia? Italy?), composed a collection of
teachings, maxims and parables on the wide scope of nonlegal talmudic-midrashic themes: Creation and world order; law and commandments; study and
teaching; repentance and charity; joy of life and humility; and divine love that

encompasses all His creatures. The title of the book, *Tanna debe Eliyahu*, or *Seder Eliyahu*, refers to the teachings of the prophet Elijah, whom the talmudic legend pictures as frequenting the academies of Palestine, imparting moral and religious advice. The book, written in Hebrew and divided into two parts (*Seder Eliyahu Rabba*, The Large Order of Elijah, and *Seder Eliyahu Zutta*, The Small Order of Elijah), is characterized by stylistic beauty and warm human appeal. Little known in the Middle Ages, it became popular when it appeared in print (Venice, 1598). A critical edition appeared in 1902, based on a manuscript in the Vatican Library dating from the year 1073.

Every day

Every day man is sold, and every day redeemed.
Every day man's spirit is taken from him and [. . .] returned to him in the morning.
Every day miracles are worked for him as for those who went out of Egypt.
Every day redemption is worked for him, as for those who went out of Egypt.
Every day he is fed on the breasts of his mother.
Every day he is chastised for his deeds, like a child by his teacher.

Surpassing both

King David said:
I, what am I in this world?
I have been fearful in the midst of my joy, and have rejoiced in the midst of my fear,
and my love has surpassed them both.

Preparation

Let a man do good deeds, and then ask Torah from the Omnipresent.
Let a man do righteous and fitting deeds, and then ask wisdom from the Omnipresent.
Let a man seize the way of humility, and then ask understanding from the Omnipresent.

Man's deeds

I call heaven and earth to witness:
whether it be heathen or Israelite,
whether it be man or woman, manservant or maidservant,
all according to his deeds
does the holy spirit rest upon a man.

Heaven and man

. . . The Holy One, blessed be he, continued to appease
        Moses.
He said to him:
Am I not your Father, and you my children,
you my brothers, and I your brother;
you my friends, and I your friend;
you my lovers, and I your lover;
Have I allowed you to lack?
All that I ask you in this, as I have examined myself and found
        eleven qualities,
so all I ask of you is eleven qualities;
and they are:
"He that walketh upright, and worketh righteousness,
And speaketh truth . . ." (Ps. 15:2-5).

The Holy One, blessed be he, continued to appease Moses.
He said to him:
Do I at all favor an Israelite or a Gentile,
a man or a woman, a manservant or a maidservant?
But whoever he is who keeps a commandment, the reward is
        at its heels.
Hence it was said:
He who honors heaven more, heaven's honor is more, and his
        own honor is more, as well.
He who honors heaven less, and honors himself more,
heaven's honor continues the same, but his own honor is less.

Provision

I call heaven and earth to be my witness,
that the Holy One, blessed be he, is sitting and dividing pro-

visions with his own hand
among all who come into the world,
and among all the handiwork that he created in the world;
from man to beast, to creeping thing, and to the bird in the
     sky.

Prayer

David, King of Israel, said:
My Father who art in heaven
blessed be Thy great Name for all eternity
and mayest Thou find contentment from Israel, Thy servants,
     wherever they may dwell.
Thou hast reared us, made us great, sanctified us, praised us;
Thou hast bound on us the crown of the words of Torah
they that reach from end to end of the world.
Whatever of Torah I have fulfilled, this came only through
     Thee;
whatever loving-kindness I have shown, this came only through
     Thee;
in return for the little of Torah that I have done before Thee
Thou hast given me a share in this world, in the days of the
     Messiah, and in the world to come.

In the midst of sorrow

When Moses descended from Mount Sinai, and saw the
     abominations of Israel,
he gazed at the tablets and saw that the words had flown away,
and broke them at the foot of the hill.
At once he fell dumb. He could not say a word.
At that moment a decree was passed concerning Israel,
that they were to study these same words
in the midst of sorrow and in the midst of slavery,
in migration, and in confusion,
in pressing poverty, and in lack of food.
For the sorrow they have suffered,

the Holy One, blessed be he, shall reward them during the
　　　days of the Messiah,
many times over.

Meeting

How does a man find his Father who is in heaven?
He finds him by good deeds, and study of the Torah.
And the Holy One, blessed be he, finds man
through love, through brotherhood, through respect,
through companionship, through truth, through peace,
through bending the knee, through humility,
through studious session, through commerce lessened,
through service of the masters, through the discussion of
　　　students,
through a good heart, through decency,
through No that is really No,
through Yes that is really Yes.

The Oral Law

Once I was on a journey, and I came upon a man who went
　　　at me after the way of heretics.
Now, he accepted the Written Law, but not the Oral Law.[57]
He said to me:
The Written Law was given us from Mount Sinai;
the Oral Law was not given us from Mount Sinai.
I said to him:
But were not both the Written and the Oral Law spoken by
　　　the Omnipresent?
Then what difference is there between the Written and the
　　　Oral Law? To what can this be compared?
To a king of flesh and blood who had two servants, and loved
　　　them both with a perfect love;
and he gave them each a measure of wheat, and each a bundle
　　　of flax.
The wise servant, what did he do?
He took the flax and spun a cloth.

Then he took the wheat and made flour.

The flour he cleansed, and ground, and kneaded, and baked, and set on top of the table.

Then he spread the cloth over it, and left it so until the king should come.

But the foolish servant did nothing at all.

After some days, the king returned from a journey and came into his house and said to them:

My sons, bring me what I gave you.

One servant showed the wheaten bread on the table with a cloth spread over it,

and the other servant showed the wheat still in the box, with a bundle of flax upon it.

Alas for his shame, alas for his disgrace!

Now, when the Holy One, blessed be he, gave the Torah to Israel,

he gave it only in the form of wheat, for us to extract flour from it,

and flax, to extract a garment.

To walk humbly

Thus said the Holy One, blessed be he, to Israel:

My children, have I allowed you to lack?

What do I seek of you?

All I ask is that you love one another,

and honor one another, and respect one another,

and let there be found in you neither transgression nor theft nor any ugly thing;

so that you never become tainted;

as it is said: "It hath been told thee, O man, what is good . . . and to walk humbly with thy God" (Mic. 6:8)

—do not read: "Walk humbly with thy God,"

but rather: "Walk humbly, and thy God will be with thee"

—as long as you are with Him in humility,

He will be with you in humility.

Notes to "The Rest Is Commentary"

1. I. F. Baer, "The Historical Foundations of the Halacha," *Zion*, XVII (1952); "The Ancient Hasidim in Philo's Writings and in Hebrew Tradition," *Zion*, XVIII (1953).

2. H. A. Wolfson, *Philo: Foundations of Religious Philosophy in Judaism, Christianity and Islam* (Cambridge: Harvard University Press, 1947).

3. E. Bickerman, *The Maccabees* (New York: Schocken Books, 1947).

4. W. F. Albright, *From the Stone Age to Christianity* (2d ed.; Baltimore: Johns Hopkins University Press, 1940), ch. VI.

5. E. Schürer, *A History of the Jewish People*, (New York: Schocken Books, 1961), p. 21.

6. *See* A. Kaminka, "Hillel's Life and Work," *The Jewish Quarterly Review*, N.S., XXX, 107-122.

7. W. Jaeger, *Paideia: the Ideals of Greek Culture*, trans. G. Highet (3 vols.; New York: Oxford University Press, 1939 seq.).

8. Flavius Josephus, *War*, II, 8:14.

9. Flavius Josephus, *ibid.*, II, 8:7.

I

1. Creation of man by God implies to the author that evil was not intended; evil resulted from man following freely his "inclination" (Hebrew, *Yetzer*). The theological difficulty still remains.

2. God knows what a man has chosen.

3. Comp. Prov. 13:24: "He that spareth his rod hateth his son."

4. The father lives on in his son.

5. The author tries to justify the physician's job before the adherents of the "old ways" who saw in the physician too modern a figure.

6. *See* Exod. 15:23 f.

7. Sickness is here considered a punishment for wrongdoing.

8. Note the emphasis on travel as aiding in the scribe's education.

9. Simon, surnamed "the Righteous" lived at the beginning of the second century B.C.

10. The Temple.

11. The Holy of Holies; the passage refers to the high priest's service on the Day of Atonement; *see* Lev. 16.

12. This refers to the ceremony of the Feast of Weeks; *see* Num. 28:26.

13. "A covenant of peace to maintain the sanctuary" and the promise of the high priesthood "for ever" (Ben Sira 45:24). Phinehas was the grandson of Aaron.

14. Note the Stoic idea of the world soul.

15. Man's actions are the cause of evil that befalls him.

16. God's mercy is to lead man to repentance.

17. According to a Stoic saying, quoted by Philodemus (*ca.* 50 B.C.)

"the wise are the friends of God and God of the wise."

18. Wisdom as a prerequisite of prophecy is also Stoic teaching.

19. Xenophon's *Memorabilia* (memoirs of Socrates), II, 1, offers a statement parallel to this section.

20. The four cardinal virtues according to Plato and the Stoics.

21. This refers to the temptation of Eve.

22. The righteous are immortal. "The wise man who appears to have departed from this mortal life lives in a life immortal" (Philo).

II

1. He was kept in Rome for twelve years after the defeat of Syria at Magnesia, 190 B.C.

2. The so-called "Seleucid Era" is counted from October 1, 312, on the accession of Seleucus I of Syria.

3. The reference is to the Jewish Hellenists.

4. An operation with the purpose of undoing circumcision by which the heathens recognized a Jew; the athletic exercises in the gymnasium were practiced in the nude.

5. However, Egypt rose again; Antiochus returned to besiege Alexandria and failed.

6. Apollonius (II Macc. 5:24).

7. This citadel was called Acra and was held by a Syrian detachment.

8. The policy of paganization was supported by Jewish Hellenists.

9. The term is taken from Dan. 12:11.

10. "The sons of Joarib" is one of the twenty-four classes of priests.

11. Modin lies east of Lydda (Lud).

12. Num. 25:7 f.

13. "The Pious," members of communities of peasants who adhered strictly to ideals of Torah and the prophets; seeing the threat to the practice of religion they abandoned their peace-loving tenets.

14. The "sacrifice" of Isaac, Gen. 22.

15. Gen. 39.

16. Num. 25:7 f.

17. Josh. 1:2 ff.

18. Num. 13:30 ff.

19. I Sam. 24:4 ff.

20. II Kings 2:1.

21. Dan. 3 and 6.

22. *Ibid*.

23. Judah and his men have won victories over superior Syrian armies; they defeated Apollonius, the governor of Samaria, and Seron, commander of Coele-Syria; they checked three Syrian generals with 40,000 foot soldiers and 7,000 horsemen near Emmaus. An attack by Lysias of Syria who came up from the south, at Beth Zur, was repelled.

24. Exod. 20:25; Deut. 27:5 f.; no iron could be used in cutting the stones.

25. First reference to the Hanukkah (Feast of Lights) celebration.

26. Idumaea, land of Edom, southern neighbor of Judaea.

27. That is, after Simon, Judah the Maccabee's brother, had achieved

the goal of the twenty-years' rebellion: independence from Syria. He captured the Citadel (Acra). The Jewish Hellenists submitted to the newly established government of Simon, or left the country.

28. The modern Jaffa. Simon's capture of the fortress Gazara (the Biblical Gezer) in the plain of Judaea, to assure an easy connection between Jerusalem and Jaffa.

29. After the death of Judah, his brother Jonathan carried on the cause of the rebellion.

30. Jonathan had concluded a treaty of "confederacy and friendship" with Sparta, and renewed the treaty Judah had made with Rome.

31. Approximate value of $35,000.

32. The high priestly office as a part of the Maccabean rule had started with Jonathan; the high priests preceding Jonathan were Hellenists.

33. Simon's descendants (John Hyrcanus, Aristobulus I, Alexander Jannaeus, Salome Alexandra, Aristobulus II, Hyrcanus) ruled the country up to 63 B.C. when Pompey made Judaea tributary to Rome.

III

1. Comp. "the day of the Lord," a term applied by the Biblical prophets to the final day of judgment.

2. The text of this line is possibly corrupt.

3. The netherworld.

4. Note in the following the arguments of "the sinners" (Sadducees?) and the writer's affirmation of the future bliss of the righteous.

5. This refers to the resurrection of the dead which doctrine was variously defined.

6. Title of the Messiah.

7. After "their punishment shall have come from the Lord." The new priesthood, which is to follow the immoral Hellenization of this sacred office, is pictured in Messianic terms.

8. A rare image in Jewish literature.

9. Beliar (Belial): angel of lawlessness, chief of evil spirits.

10. This most probably refers to the Hasmonaean ruling house.

11. The high priesthood.

12. Pompey, who in 63 B.C. entered Jerusalem and established Roman rule in Judaea.

13. *Ibid.*

14. Pompey carried the Hasmonaean Aristobulus II and his children captive to Rome.

15. The society of the Hasidim.

16. Political calamity gave rise to the renewed expectation of the Messianic kingdom.

IV

1. Considered the legitimate family of priests.

2. Or, multitude.

3. A surrogate for the name of God.

4. The perverse men, i.e., the non-sectarians, may not even after puri-

fication touch "the Purity" (food, vessels, rites) of the holy men, i.e., the sectarians.

5. The true Israel is identified with the sectarian brotherhood.

6. The term "Many" appears to be used as a technical term for the membership.

7. Or, as Brownlee suggests, religion.

8. In the original: HUHA, a surrogate of God.

9. In the original the word for "the Lord" is substituted by four dots.

10. The original has the Hebrew letter Aleph, possible esoteric reference to the name of God.

11. The members were to keep secret the teachings of the brotherhood.

12. Belial (Beliar): angel of lawlessness, chief of evil spirits.

13. By observing the laws governing ritual purity.

14. Philo introduces his presentation by contrasting the order of the Therapeutae with the Egyptian animal worship which caused the Egyptians to lose "the most vital of the senses, sight."

15. This notion is Platonic (_Phaedrus_) and goes back to Hesiod.

16. The corresponding Greek word suggests duties performed in rotation (F. H. Colson).

17. Without the aid of a midwife.

18. A Platonic phrase (_Timaeus_).

19. The reference is to the ancient Israelites crossing the Red Sea after the exodus from Egypt.

VI

1. The double meanings of _polis_ ("city" and "state"), and of _pheugein_ ("to flee," "to be exiled," hence "to be outlawed") clarify this passage. According to the Cynics and the Stoics, the wise man does not regard himself as a citizen of any single state, but as a member of the world state. Citizenship in this world state is based on the possession of reason; Philo interpreted this ethically.

2. This is an allusion to the third meaning of _polis_—the urban in contrast to the rural. The Greeks considered the peasant (_agroikos_) uneducated, just as the Jews so regarded the _Am ha-Aretz_, and the Romans the _rusticus_.

3. This is the reading of the Septuagint. The Hebrew text reads: "He [God] made them houses."

4. This and the following refers to Exod. 16, Num. 11, Exod. 15:22-25.

5. This refers to Herod and to the Hasmonaean kings who preceded Herod.

6. In A.D. 37, Caligula appointed Agrippa king over the northeastern districts of Herod's kingdom, previously ruled by Herod's son, Philip. His realm was expanded later.

7. Minister in the service of Emperor Augustus and friend of Herod. See Flavius Josephus, _War_ I, 20:4; _Antiquities_ XVI, 2:1; the visit took place in 15 B.C.

8. Comp. "In Praise of the High Priest Simon, Son of Johanan," from the Wisdom of Ben Sira.

9. Succeeding Augustus, Tiberius ruled from 14 to 37.

10. Pontius Pilate, procurator of Judaea (26 to 36) and judge in the trial of Jesus.

11. The residence of the Roman procurators.

12. Another instance of Pilate's outrages is reported by Josephus in *Antiquities* XVIII, 3:1 and *War* II, 9, 2-3.

13. The Day of Atonement. *See* Lev. 16.

14. Edicts of Augustus concerning the Jews' rights "to follow their own customs according to the law of their forefathers" are recorded by Josephus in *Antiquities* XVI, 6:1-3.

15. On other donations of Augustus to the Temple, *see* Josephus, *War* V, 13:6.

16. Julia Major, a daughter of Augustus, married emperor Tiberius, Caligula's grandfather.

17. Emperor Tiberius kept Agrippa in prison.

18. Teacher of rhetoric in Rhodes and in Rome; Cicero and Julius Caesar were his disciples.

19. Alexandrian writer.

20. *Nomos*, law, appears first in Hesiod.

21. In contradistinction to the Greek deities who are born.

22. An adaptation of the four cardinal virtues of the Platonic School.

23. The reference is to Skeptics.

24. The Epicureans.

25. Plato (*Timaeus*), in part followed by Philo, thought of God as creating the world with the aid of collaborators.

26. The Pentateuchal laws (Exod. 23:8, Deut. 16:19 and 27:25) do not impose the death penalty in this case; with some exceptions Josephus follows Scriptural laws.

27. Republic III, 398 A.

28. Fifth century B.C.

29. Fifth century B.C.; known as "the atheist."

30. Fifth century B.C.; he wrote: "Regarding the gods, I am unable to know whether they exist or do not exist."

31. Visited Athens in the time of Solon.

VII

1. The first destruction of Jerusalem (by Babylon) took place in 586 B.C. The author, however, uses the image of the first Temple period to suggest the second Temple, destroyed by Rome in A.D. 70. The date thus refers to A.D. 100.

2. Salathiel (Shealtiel) is the father of Zerubbabel, leader of the Jews, who returned to Zion after the Babylonian Exile, in 538 B.C. (Ezra 3:2; 5:2). The identification of Salathiel with Ezra is fictitious; Ezra appeared in Jerusalem a century later.

3. Babylon stands here for Rome.

4. The apocalyptic starts his argument with Adam, not with Abraham or the Exodus from Egypt.

5. The apocalyptic maintains the idea of the hereditary weakness of human nature. Comp. Romans 5:12 f. Classical Judaism has a more optimistic view of man.

6. The concept of angels (as distinct from "divine messengers") belongs to the late-Biblical and post-Biblical tradition.

7. The human body is the "vessel" of the mind.

8. Comp. the view of the pessimistic School of Shammai against the optimistic view of the School of Hillel, in "Man" (chapter "Hillel the Elder").

9. The habitations of the righteous dead.

10. Hebrew, Yerahmiel.

11. The end will come when the divinely pre-ordained number of the righteous has been completed.

12. The course of history is predetermined; man's action is not a factor.

13. The Antichrist, the eschatological arch-enemy.

14. "We who have received the Law and sinned must perish, together with our heart, which has taken it in: the Law, however, perishes not, but abides in its glory" (IV Ezra 9:36-37).

15. The three years count from Solomon's ascension to the throne to the building of the Temple. Mystically interpreted, the three years refer to three millennia from Creation to the foundation of the Temple.

16. This refers to the "heavenly Jerusalem" which is the model of Jerusalem on earth.

17. The interpretation is based on the inclusiveness implied in the word "all" in the verse quoted.

VIII

1. Over food, the promised land, and over Jerusalem.

2. The Mediterranean.

3. Probably refers to the Sadducees who rejected the belief in a future world.

4. At certain times it may be advisable to void or amend a law in order to preserve the Law as a whole.

5. About 3 P.M.

6. A communal institution for the support of the poorest.

7. This refers to every participant, not only to the poor.

8. A dish of nuts and fruit pounded together and mixed with vinegar. The bitter herbs were dipped into this to mitigate their bitterness.

9. Some texts add: "On other nights we eat all other manner of vegetables, but this night bitter herb."

10. Some texts add: "On other nights we dip but once, but this night twice."

11. Egyptian slavery and idolatry.

12. Son (or grandson) of Hillel the Elder.

13. Exod. 12:27 and 39; 1:14.

14. This refers to the "Hallel" Psalms, 113 to 118.

15. End of Ps. 113.

16. End of Ps. 114.

17. Hebrew *afikoman*, Greek *epi komon*, or *epikomios*, meaning festival procession. The solemn Passover meal with its symbolism must not be followed by an after-dinner revelry which was a customary sequel to the banquet in the Hellenist world, especially for the young.

IX

1. Leader, with Nehemiah, of the Judaean community after the establishment of the Second Temple (*see* Introduction).

2. Quoted from the "Sayings of the Fathers," Mishnaic collection of ethical maxims.

3. The phrase indicates conversion to Judaism.

4. This saying is an affirmation of divine justice; the victim of drowning must himself have drowned somebody. However, the first drowning and its cause remains unexplained and outside of human reasoning.

5. The negative version of the Golden Rule.

6. Seat of the central academy, established after the fall of Jerusalem.

7. Menahot 110a.

8. Prov. 15:1.

9. *Supra* note 7.

10. Learning and wealth.

11. Rabbi Johanan lost ten sons; he carried a bone (or a tooth) of the tenth son with him.

12. God. *See* Dan. 7:9.

13. In the talmudic tradition the term God (*Elohim*) is interpreted as referring to the divine attribute of stern justice, while "Lord" (JHVH) indicates the attribute of love and mercy.

14. Hebrew, *Shekhinah*: the divine element indwelling in the world; the presence of the divine among men.

15. This passage is part of the address by which the Court impressed the witnesses with the seriousness of their testimony.

16. Pico della Mirandola, a representative Renaissance thinker, borrowed this passage for his description of "modern man" (*De hominis dignitate*, Rome 1486).

17. "Evil desire" (Hebrew, *Yetzer ha-Ra*, an urge which is opposed to the desire to do good (*Yetzer ha-Tov*). It is not considered as evil per se, but as a power abused by men. It is rather the "passion" in which all human action originates. Man is called upon to serve God "with both desires."

18. This refers to the miraculous feeding of the Israelites in the wilderness.

19. On this verse later Jewish thought based the doctrine of the "thirteen attributes" of God.

20. Honi, or Onias, a Hasid and miracle worker in the Hasmonean period (*see also* Josephus, *Antiquities* XIV, 2:1).

21. Talmudic tradition considers him to be the youngest disciple of Hillel the Elder. He lived in the period of the destruction of the Second Temple.

22. Gifts to the poor.

23. Festival, liturgic, and ritual requirements.

24. According to the law, the negligent worker is responsible for the loss.

25. Rav (Babylonia, third century) applied the moral rather than the civil law.

26. Editor of the Mishnah, end of second century, and descendant of Hillel the Elder.

27. Be Hozae: Khuzistan, a province in southwest Persia.
Be Lapat: capital of Khuzistan in the Sasanian period.

28. After his ascent to heaven, Elijah, according to legend, continued to appear as a divine messenger, teaching, helping, befriending the pious.

29. The reference is to judgment after death.

30. The starting words of the first commandment.

31. Seven basic laws (prohibition against idolatry, incest, murder, profanation of the name of God, robbery, the duty to form instruments of justice, prohibition against eating parts cut from living animals) to be accepted by the descendants of Noah, i.e., by all men. Hugo Grotius (17th century) took the Noahide commandments as the foundation for his "natural law."

32. Biblical sentences are quoted to justify the rejection.

33. The discussion concerned the question whether an oven of a particular construction was liable of ritual uncleanness. Rabbi Eliezer declared it as clean, the sages as unclean. Both Rabbi Eliezer and Rabbi Joshua (mentioned later) were disciples of Johanan ben Zakkai.

34. *Supra* note 28.

35. *Ibid.*

36. Johanan bar Nappaha of Tiberias, a leading third century scholar.

37. The Song of Songs is interpreted by the Talmud as an allegory on the love between God and Israel.

38. Oinomaos of Gadara (second century A.D.), a member of the school of the younger Cynics. The Midrash (Lam. Rabba, Introd. 2) calls Biblical Balaam and Oinomaos *the* philosophers of the pagans.

39. That is, in this case the hands are without power.

40. This passage, attributed to Rabbi Meir (second century A.D.), should be read as an example of talmudic reflection on Israel's precarious position in world history, here represented by the "four kingdoms," and an expression of her hope in redemption.

41. Each nation is said to have its angelic representation in heaven.

42. The reference is to the desert sanctuary in the time of Moses and Solomon's temple in Jerusalem.

43. *Supra* note 28.

44. A strong affirmation of the belief that redemption depends on the action of man.

45. Leading scholar in Babylonia (third century A.D.).

46. Johanan bar Nappaha of Tiberias, a leading third century scholar.

47. Both sayings militate against a supernatural conception of the Messianic age. The "world to come," on the other hand, is a purely spiritual concept from which historical and national notions are removed. The following saying by Rav (Babylonia, third century A.D.) is especially significant for this understanding of the world to come.

48. For the understanding of this saying it should be remembered that its author lived around the period of the destruction of Jerusalem when many Jews engaged in Messianic and apocalyptic visions.

49. Gehenna; hell.

50. That is, there is no freedom of will and action.

51. Fear and love are considered to be the two possible human atti-

tudes to the divine, the two motives of man's moral action. Naturally, love ranks higher than fear.

52. The Tempter in the prose introduction to the Book of Job.

53. The Satan was given permission to put Job through various trials but was bidden to preserve his life.

54. That is, consider me as your enemy.

55. Strict justice and forgiving mercy are considered to be the two possible divine attitudes to man and world.

56. The evil impulse.

57. Written Law refers to Torah; Oral Law to Tradition; the Sadducees accepted the first, the Pharisees both.

Sources and Acknowledgments for
"The Rest Is Commentary"

I

IN PRAISE OF WISDOM: The origin of wisdom, Wisdom of Ben Sira, 1:1-10; The fear of the Lord is true wisdom, *ibid.*, 1:11-20 and 26-30; On free will, *ibid.*, 15:11-20; A man's duties, *ibid.*, 7:11-28 and 32-36; Of women, *ibid.*, 9:1-9 and 25:16-26:4; The training of children, *ibid.*, 30:1-13; The physician, *ibid.*, 38:1-15.

THE IDEAL SCRIBE: *Ibid.*, 39:1-11.

MANIFESTATION OF GOD IN NATURE: *Ibid.*, 43.

THE HIGH PRIEST, SIMON, SON OF JOHANAN: *Ibid.*, 50:1-24.

WISDOM AND THE ORDER OF THIS WORLD: Wisdom is a spirit that loveth man: Wisdom of Solomon, 1:1-15; God—lover of souls, *ibid.*, 11:21-12:2; Wisdom is a breath of the power of God, *ibid.*, 7:22-8:1; Solomon desired wisdom as a bride, *ibid.*, 8:2-18; Immortality, *ibid.*, 2:23-3:9.

II

THE ORIGIN OF THE MACCABEAN REBELLION: First Book of Maccabees, 1-2.

THE REDEDICATION OF THE TEMPLE: *Ibid.*, 4:36-61.

SIMON'S BENEFICENT RULE: *Ibid.*, 14:4-49.

MARTYRDOM OF THE SEVEN BROTHERS AND THEIR MOTHERS: Second Book of Maccabees, 7.

III

THE DAY OF JUDGMENT: Book of Enoch, 102:1-103:4.

THE VICTORY OF THE RIGHTEOUS: *Ibid.*, 50-51.

THE ELECT ONE: *Ibid.*, 49.

A NEW PRIESTHOOD: Testament of Levi, 18:2-14.

THOU ART OUR KING: Psalms of Solomon, 17.

IV

THE RULES OF THE DEAD SEA, OR QUMRAN, BROTHERHOOD: Manual of Discipline, column 5, line 1 to column 6, line 8, and col. 8, lines 1 to 19.

FROM THE SOURCE OF HIS KNOWLEDGE: A Psalm: *Ibid.*, col. 10, line 23 to col. 11, line 15.

HYMNS OF THE DEAD SEA BROTHERHOOD: Streams in dry ground, Thanksgiving Hymns, VIII, 4-12; They seek Thee with a double heart, IV, 5-37.

THE ORDER OF THE ESSENES: Philo, "Every Good Man Is Free" (Probus), XII-XIII.

THE SECT OF THE THERAPEUTAE: Philo, "On the Contemplative Life," II-IV and VIII-XI.

V

JOB THE SAINT: Testament of Job, edited and translated by K. Kohler, *Semitic Studies in Memory of Alexander Kohut*, Berlin, 1897.

VI

HELENISTIC EXPOSITION OF SCRIPTURE: On Hiding From the Presence of God: Philo, *Allegorical Commentary*, III, 1-6 and 28-31; Revelation in the Sinai desert, Philo: *The Decalogue*, I-IV and X; The Sabbath, *The Special Laws* II, ch. XV.

THE EMPEROR'S STATUE: Philo, *Legacy to Gaius*, XXXVI-XLII. (Translation based on C. D. Yonge, *The Works of Philo Judaeus*, vol. IV, London 1855.)

I TAKE REFUGE: Prayer of Asenath. P. Batiffol, Studia Patristica, Paris 1889–1890.

INSPIRED REASON: Fourth Book of Maccabees, 18.

IN DEFENSE OF JUDAISM: Flavius Josephus, *Against Apion*, II, 15-42. (Translation based on *The Works of Flavius Josephus*, by Whiston, revised by A. R. Shilleto, vol. V, London 1890.)

VII

THE HEROES OF MASADA: Flavius Josephus, *The Jewish War*, VII, 8:7.

THE VISION OF A NEW ERA: Fourth Book of Ezra, 3:1-5:15.

THE VISION OF THE DISCONSOLATE WOMAN: *Ibid.*, 9:38-10:57.

THE CONSOLATION OF ZION: Apocalypse of Baruch, 44-46.

THE TEN MARTYRS, Asarah Haruge Malkhut, in *Bet ha-Midrash*, ed. A. Jellinek, vol. VI; Midrash Ele Ezkera, Jellinek, *ibid.*, vol. II. Sanhedrin 14a, Abodah Zarah 17b-18b, Semahot VIII.

VIII

THE ORDER OF BENEDICTIONS: Mishnah Berakhot, VI and IX.

THE SEDER CEREMONY: Mishnah Pesahim, X, 1-8.

HILLEL THE ELDER: The re-established Torah, Sukkah 20a; Education, Soferim XVI, 9; Disciples, Abot de R. Nathan, First Version, III; On disseminating knowledge, Berakhot 63a; Peace, Abot I, 12; The ignorant cannot be a hasid, *ibid.* II, 6; Torah, *ibid.*, II, 8 and 5; With people, Tosefta Berakhot II, 21; cf. Derekh Eretz Zutta V; Teachings, Abot I, 14; II, 8; I, 13; II, 7; Lev. Rabba I, 5; The human body, Lev. Rabba XXXIV, 3; Beautiful bride, Ketubot 16b f; Disaster, Berakhot 60a; The poor man, Ketubot 67b; The wager, Shabbat 30b; The entire Torah on one foot, Shabbat 31a; Every day, Betzah 16a; Man, Erubin 13b; The rival schools, *ibid.*; The heavenly voice, Sotah 48b. (Translations from N. N. Glatzer, *Hillel the Elder*, Washington 1959.)

THE WAYS OF GOOD LIFE: Every day, Berakhot 63b; The gist of it, *ibid.*, 17a; The gates of Torah, *ibid.*; My neighbor, *ibid.*; Brothers, *ibid.*; The final goal, *ibid.*; Chastisements of love, *ibid.*, 5a; Old men, *ibid.*, 8b; Animals first, *ibid.*, 40a; Sinners, ibid., 10a; Far and near, *ibid.*, 34b and 60b f; Beauty, *ibid.*, 5b; The blessing, *ibid.*, 28b; In farewell, *ibid.*, 17a.

CREATION AND MAN: In its time, Gen. Rabba IX, 2; In the beginning, *ibid.*, XII, 15; Between heaven and earth, Tanhuma Gen. 2:4 (Buber, p. 11); Origins, Sanhedrin 38a f, Gen. Rabba XXII, 4; The crown of creation, Sanhedrin 38a; Singularity, Mishnah Sanhedrin IV, 5; For you, Eccles. Rabba VII, 28, Gen. Rabba V, 10; Grow!, Gen. Rabba X, 7; Evil desire, *ibid.*, IX, 9, Yoma 69b; Coming and going, Eccles. Rabba V, 21; Order, Yoma 38a f, Abot de R. Nathan, First Version, XXXIX.

GOD—MAN—WORLD: Justice, Gen. Rabba XXXIX, 6; Sustenance, Mekhilta 16:14 (47b); Ascent, Abodah Zarah 20b; The imitation of God, Sifre Deut. 11:22 (85a), Sotah 14a; Four answers, Pesikta de R. Kahana 158b; Of their own free will, Numbers Rabba VIII, 2; The heart, Midrash Hagadah Gen. 38:1, Sota 5a; Destiny, Erubin 13b; Rain, Taanit 23b; Mercy not sacrifice, Abot de R. Nathan, First Version, IV; Honor due to parents and to God, Yer. Peah I, 1, Kiddushin 30b. Captivity, Horayot 13a; The law and more, Baba Metzia 83a; Let everyone enter, Baba Batra 8a; The sufferings, Baba Metzia 85a; Jesters, Taanit 22a; The guardian of chastity, Yer. Taanit 64b; Demands, Erubin 100b; Blood, Pesahim 25b; Commendation, Mishnah Eduyot V, 7; They that love Him, Shabbat 88b; Today, *ibid.*, 153a; Judgment, *ibid.*, 31a.

REVELATION AND THE STUDY OF THE LAW: As a statue, Pesikta de R. Kahana 110a; All at one time, Tanhuma Exod. 20:1; As the desert, Pesikta de R. Kahana 107a; Mekhilta 19:2 (62a); Israel and the nations, Sifre Deut. 33:2 (142b); The children, Cant. Rabba I, 24; The keepers of the city, Pesikta de R. Kahana 120b; Witnesses, *ibid.*, 102b; In the heart, Deut. Rabba VIII, 7; What animals teach, Erubin 100b; The core of the commandments, Makkot 23b f.; A greater principle, Sifra 19:8 (89b); The yoke of freedom, Sifre Deut. 32:39 (138b); Fire and Light, Mekhilta 19:18 (65a); Pesikta de R. Kahana 200a; Not in heaven, Baba Metzia 59b; The trapper, Tanhuma Deut. 31:1; The vessels, Abot de R. Nathan, Second Version, XXXII, and First Version, XXII; For love of Torah, Lev. Rabba XXX, 1; Sifre Deut. 11:13 (79b); The free gift, Tanhuma Exod. 33:19; The mark of man's foot, Mekhilta 17:6 (52b); Equality, Sifre Deut. 11:22 (84b); Nedarim 81a; Taanit 7a; A man, Abodah Zarah 3a; Humility, Abot de R. Nathan, First Version, XI, and Baba Metzia 85b; Scholars and kings, Horayot 13a; The gates, Exod. Rabba XIX, 4.

ISRAEL: A HOLY COMMUNITY: Three signs, Yebamot 79a; Poverty, Hagigah 9b; Like oil, Cant. Rabba I, 21; Jacob and Esau, Pesikta de R. Kahana 121a; Sharing, Deut. Rabba II, 14; Jacob's ladder, Pesikta de R. Kahana 151; Lev. Rabba XXIX, 2.

PEACE: Perek ha-Shalom and Num. Rabba XI, 16-20.

EXILE AND REDEMPTION: The keys of the Temple, Taanit 29a; Love, Cant. Rabba II, 14; Divine presence in exile, Mekhilta 12:51; Waiting, Pesikta de R. Kahana 144a; Today, Sanhedrin 98a; The real redemption, Midrash Tehillim 31:2; The Messiah, Pesikta de R. Kahana 149a f; Messiah and the world to come, Berakhot 34b and 17a; Planting, Abot de R. Nathan, Second Version, XXXI.

REFLECTIONS ON THE BOOK OF JOB: Heathen prophets, Baba Bathra 15b; Unaided knowledge, Num. Rabba XIV, 7; Who can hinder Thee, Baba

Bathra 16a; Fear of God and love of God, Sotah 31a; Abraham and Job, Tanhuma Vayera 5; Baba Bathra 15b f; Satan, Baba Bathra 16a; No resurrection, *ibid.*; Job the rebel, *ibid.*; Enemy of God?, *ibid.*; The turning point, Pesikta Rabbati 165a; Blessing, Berakhot 17a.

PRAYERS OF THE MASTERS: Berakhot 16b to 17a.

REFLECTIONS ON LIFE: Every day, Seder Eliyahu Rabba II; Surpassing both, *ibid.*, III; Preparation, *ibid.*, VI; Man's deeds, *ibid.*, IX; Heaven and Man, *ibid.*, XIV; Provision, *ibid.*, XV; Prayer, *ibid.*, XVIII; In the midst of sorrow, *ibid.*, XIX; Meeting, *ibid.*, XXIII; The Oral Law, Seder Eliyahu Zutta II; To walk humbly, Seder Eliyahu Rabba XXVI.

Abbreviations employed in quotations from Scripture

Gen.	Genesis	Hos.	Hosea
Exod.	Exodus	Zeph.	Zephaniah
Lev.	Leviticus	Hag.	Haggai
Num.	Numbers	Zech.	Zechariah
Deut.	Deuteronomy	Mal.	Malachi
Josh.	Joshua	Prov.	Proverbs
Judg.	Judges	Lam.	Lamentations
Sam.	Samuels	Eccles.	Ecclesiastes
Isa.	Isaiah	Dan.	Daniel
Jer.	Jeremiah	Neh.	Nehemiah
Ezek.	Ezekiel	Chron.	Chronicles

Acknowledgments

Thanks are due to the following authors and publishers for permission to use their translations: American Schools of Oriental Research and Professor William Hugh Brownlee for passages from the latter's translation of the Dead Sea Manual of Discipline (Bulletin of the American School of Oriental Research, Supplementary Studies Nos. 10-12 [1951] and No. 135 [1954]); Harvard University Press for *Philo*, translated by F. H. Colson (Loeb Classical Library edition, vols. VII [*The Decalogue, The Special Laws*] and IX ["Every Good Man Is Free," "The Contemplative Life"]); Oxford University Press for selections from *Apocrypha and Pseudepigrapha of the Old Testament*, edited by R. H. Charles (Oxford, 1913) and the Mishnah, translated by Herbert Danby; Schocken Books, Inc. for selections by N. N. Glatzer, translated by Jacob Sloan, from *Hammer on the Rock* (New York, 1948), and from *In Time and Eternity* (New York, 1946); the Viking Press for excerpts from *The Dead Sea Scrolls*, by Millar Burrows (copyright 1955 by Millar Burrows).

PART TWO

Faith and Knowledge

Introduction to "Faith and Knowledge"

I

The Jews of Prague used to relate an ancient legend according to which their ancient synagogue, the *Altneushul,* was built with stones which exiles from Jerusalem carried away when the Temple was destroyed by the Romans. They promised themselves to dismantle the synagogue and carry the stones back to the Holy Land once the Messiah came. Style and structure, however, point to the eleventh century as the period in which the synagogue was built and to the twelfth as the time of renovation. Later plans at reconstruction are said to have been stopped by the sages, in order not to disturb the blood of the martyrs that adhered to the walls. At the Torah-reading platform is a lovingly preserved scarlet flag; it was presented to the Jewish community in recognition of its aid in the defense of Prague against the Swedes during the Thirty Years' War.

This is the legend and a few facts about the Prague synagogue. Independent of fact and fiction has been its function, unchanged throughout the ages: to provide the devout with a place to assemble and to offer thanks for the light of day and for the rest of night; to pray for insight, sustenance, and peace; to sanctify the seventh day and to remember, as a community, the great events of the Biblical past and to keep alive, together, the hope for a Messianic future; to repent sins and to pray for forgiveness on the Days of Awe; forever, to utter the praise of the Creator; and, forever to study the classical writings and to grow in knowledge.

The building grew older; the prayers and the studies retained the freshness and immediacy of youth. The building became a quaint relic of the past; but the assembly of the faithful and the studious converted the memories of the past and the hopes for the future into strength to master this day and every day.

The community of Israel in the period after the loss of its land, living among many nations yet separated from them, has these two faces. Symbol of the first is the exterior of an old building, hallowed but often odd to behold and anachronistic to its surroundings; symbolic of the other is a living community, giving voice to what it considers great, enduring, transcending the moment.

To focus on the external aspects of Jewish existence creates a gloomy, rueful picture historically, and a demonically distorted image theologically. Israel, then, would appear to be (or to have been) a ghostlike, weird, arid, rootless, eccentric, marginal group of people, and its faith retarded, present without future, question without answer, missed opportunity; a faith doomed and destined to fail. Only he who ventures to penetrate the surface will become conscious of forces that sustained Judaism and allowed it not only to survive medieval discrimination, persecutions, expulsions, misunderstanding, and hatred, but to keep alive the spirit of trust, of optimism, of cooperation, ready for the dawn of a new day.

At the core of this faith lie the convictions that historical success or failure is not the ultimate measure of things, that might is not necessarily right, and powerlessness and rejection by men is no evidence or sign of divine rejection. Yannai, an early medieval Hebrew poet expressed this in the following lines:

> Not everyone who is loved, is loved.
> Not everyone who is hated, is hated.
> Some are hated below, and loved above. . . .
> Hated we are, for you we love, O Holy One!

Those who, in view of historical realities—the fall of Zion and the rise of Rome in whatever form—doubted the reality of this "love above" left the community of Israel. Those who remained did so in the daily and hourly affirmation of that love; they did so, prepared to bear the paradox of the concluding line of Yannai's poem.

II

Although centuries-old Jewish communities continued to exist in Eastern countries (e.g., Palestine and Mesopotamia), the centers of Jewish life and thought in the Middle Ages were in the West; the most active part of Jewry had become European.

Jews lived in Rome from the second pre-Christian century, and in Spain from the first Christian centuries, first under the Romans, then under the Visigoths, the Moslems, and the Christians, respectively. They were known in France, in Germany, in the Balkans, in southern Russia, long before the barbarian invasions. Economically, the Jews underwent a transition from predominantly agricultural and artisan groups in Antiquity and the early Middle Ages to an even greater concentration in later periods on business, petty trade, and, finally, on moneylending. This concentration resulted from the legislation of the dominant society that excluded the Jew from landownership, from control of a working force, from craft-guilds and merchant guilds. The resolve of the Church to enforce the Biblical prohibition of usury among its adherents, left this economically necessary but morally reprehensible occupation to the Jew, the outsider, if not the outcast, in this society. On a different level, however, many Jews were employed as financial and political advisers by various rulers, especially in Spain, and many others followed the medical profession and were often called to serve at the courts of Spain and Italy. Nevertheless, the total occupational structure was abnormal and unhealthy; its cause was intolerance directed toward a people in dispersion that refused to conform to the dominant religion; its effect was still greater intolerance, deeper hostility.

Yet, despite all this, and despite restrictive laws, periods of pogroms and edicts of expulsion, an important positive aspect must not be overlooked. It is true that a vast gulf separated the Biblical religions: Judaism, Christianity, and Islam. But it was a common ground, and, in the case of Judaism and Christianity, a common document of faith, the Hebrew Bible, on which the religions disagreed. Both disagreement *and* the common source are determining factors in Western Jewish history and in the history of Judaeo-Christian relations; it was the latter that allowed for some measure of communication in the present and an expectation of reconciliation in the hoped-for future. The Jew had a rightful place in the universal scheme of things as seen by the Christian; the aim was not the Jew's annihilation, but his inclusion, for which end he was to be preserved (though in a state of degradation).

In the Jewish view, the Christian's rejection of Israel was temporary, just as the low state of Israel in dispersion was in appearance only and, as such, served a high purpose. In the words of the poet Judah ha-Levi: "God has a wise design concerning us, which may be likened to the seed that falls into the ground and to all appearances is transformed into earth, water, and dirt, retaining none of its qualities—or so it would seem to the ordinary observer—whereas actually it is the seed that transforms the earth and the water into its own substance. . . . And once the pure core appears and is ready to assume . . . the form of the first seed, then that tree produces fruit like that from which its own seed has come. So it is in the case of the law of Moses. All who come after it will yet be transformed to it by virtue of its essential truth, although to all appearances they would seem to reject it. The nations are a preparation and introduction to the awaited Messiah, who is the fruition. And they will all become his fruit once they recognize him, and the tree will be one. Then they will praise the root that they formerly despised."

This parable (*Kuzari* IV, 23) expresses the medieval Jew's belief that, in the final analysis, he lived in a world in which his role as the seed of the divine teaching will be realized, not in spite of, but through, his suffering; a world in which, at present, nation lifts up sword against nation and faith is set against faith, but in which, in the future, the relationship between the "seed" and the "fruit" will be recognized "and the tree will be one."

The philosopher Maimonides, too, saw Christianity and Islam as fulfilling the historical mission of spreading in the world essentially Judaic ideas, thus preparing the world for the Messianic era and for universal and pure monotheism.

Such views had no immediate, practical, institutional implications in the medieval scheme of things. But beneath all antagonism and the attitude of mutual exclusiveness there existed an unspoken, passive awareness of a common ground. It was one of the factors that prevented Judaism from assuming the character of a fossilized sect, a development that would have taken place if Judaism had had to survive, say, in a Far Eastern society.

III

There was one vast area of intellectual endeavor which allowed interaction and open communication between the members of different religious societies. This was the activity of transmitting and interpreting the knowledge and thought of Antiquity to the European West, of bringing Moslem science to the attention of the new centers of learning, of continuing these efforts, an activity through which the Middle Ages advanced into an age of broader scope. In this intellectually immensely important process, the Hebrew language played the role of intermediary between the Greek and the Arabic on the one hand, and Latin, the language of Christian scholarship, on the other. A few examples will illustrate the point.

Abraham bar Hiyya (Spain and Provence, 11th-12th cent.), mathematician and astronomer, together with the Italian Plato of Tivoli, translated Arabic treatises that introduced mathematics to the Latin world. Leonardo Pisano (Fibonacci) used bar Hiyya's work in the field of geometry in his *Practica Geometriae*. The Biblical commentator Abraham ibn Ezra (Spain, 12th cent.) translated philological and astronomical studies from Arabic into Hebrew; some of his mathematical treatises were translated into Latin and edited by Peter of Abano in Padua (13th-14th cent.).

Emperor Frederick II (1211-1250), who has been called the "first modern man," made his court a center of studies for Christian, Moslem, and Jewish scholars; he called Jacob ben Abba Mari Anatoli of Southern France to Naples, where Anatoli translated into Hebrew the Moslem philosopher's, Averroës (12th cent.), commentaries on Aristotle, Averroës' own and al-Farabi's (9th-10th cent.) works on astronomy and logic, and the *Almagest* by Ptolemy, the second-century Alexandrian astronomer and geographer. Among other scholars invited to join Frederick's Italian center was Judah ibn Makta of Toledo, author of a

Hebrew and Arabic scientific encyclopaedia based on Aristotle's
works. Charles of Anjou, King of Sicily, commissioned Faraj ben
Salim of Girgenti (13th cent.) to render into Latin the *Liber
continens,* the great medical work of Rhazes, the Persian-born
physician (9th-10th cent.), and other works. Robert of Anjou,
King of Naples and patron of scholarship, had Kalonymus ben
Kalonymus of Arles, Provence (13th-14th cent.) come to Rome to
translate from Arabic into Hebrew some of the works of the
philosophers Averroës, al-Kindi (9th cent.), al-Farabi, and Galen,
the second-century Greek physician.

Jewish astronomers were invited to compile the "Alfonsine
astronomical tablets" and to translate them into Spanish; im-
proved tablets were made by Joseph ibn Wakkar (1396), and
again by Abraham Zacuto, court astronomer to King Emanuel of
Portugal (1492); the latter work, in a Latin translation, accompanied the expeditions of Vasco da Gama and Columbus.
Cresques of Las Palmas, Majorca, drew the first world map
(1375), which the King of Aragon presented to Charles VI of
France; the map set forth the voyages of Marco Polo. Invited by
Henry the Navigator, Cresques assisted in the establishment of an
astronomical observatory in Portugal.

Once printing presses were established, major works of the
past were made available to the scholarly community. In 1520,
Aristotle's *Posterior Analytics* was published in Venice, accom-
panied by Averroës' "Major Commentary," in a translation by the
grammarian Abraham de Balmes, Jewish physician to the learned
Cardinal Domenico Grimani. De Balmes also translated (from the
Hebrew intermediate version) *Liber de mundo* by the Arab
astronomer al-Haytham (10th-11th cent.). A few years later,
Averroës' *Destructio destructionis,* a work in defense of ration-
alism was published in a Latin rendition by the physician Calo
Kalonymus, who also translated into Latin Moses ibn Tibbon's
Hebrew verison of *Theoria planetarium* by the Arab astronomer
al-Bitroji. The great eleven-volume Latin edition of the works of
Aristotle, with Averroës' commentaries, published in Venice in
the mid-sixteenth century, incorporated the renditions of many
Jewish translators and commentators, e.g., Gersonides, Jacob

Mantino, and Jacob Anatoli. Later in the sixteenth century, Aristotle's *De coelo* was issued in a Latin translation by Moses Alatino, a pupil of the philosopher Francesco Piccolomini in Perugia; the translation was based on a Hebrew rendition of an Arabic translation of the lost Greek original.

These examples (they could be multiplied) demonstrate the existence in the Middle Ages of a field of cultural interest in which, guided by Aristotle and his interpreters, many ages, countries, races, religions, and languages were involved. The search for rational knowledge, for rational confirmation of faith, for extension of the limits of the knowable, bridged, on some level at least, the gulf that separated medieval societies.

IV

Dedicated as medieval and early modern Jews were to this work of the transmission of knowledge of Antiquity to, and revival of learning in, the Western world, the main intellectual effort was quite naturally directed toward the cultivation of Israel's law, piety, and wisdom. These studies admitted contacts with extra-Judaic cultures (especially in the fields of philosophy and poetry), but the prime intention of the Jewish thinker and writer was to contribute his share to the instruction, strengthening, and growth of the community of Israel. The present volume does not attempt to cover all, or even most, of the aspects of medieval Jewish life and learning. Many other concerns, in addition to those contained in the title of this book, were characteristic of medieval Jewry: emphasis on community organization and its institutions, which gave the Jewish group the instruments of survival in a predominantly hostile world, and which permitted the preservation of its distinct religious civilization; cultivation of family life as the sacred core of the group organism; discipline of the law and the amenities of custom, which gave life the assurance of a meaningful order and a sense of proportion; cultivation of Hebrew, chiefly as a written language, which provided a means of communication, connecting the communities in various parts of the world and, at the same time, the present with the Hebraic past, thus strengthening the consciousness of continuity and the unity of Israel; and, finally, the Messianic belief, expressed either in the patient hope for redemption, or in activist movements designed to throw off the burden of exile.

Out of the many possible aspects, the present volume concentrates on two major themes: faith and knowledge. In the literature at hand we encounter attempts to correlate the two, to treat the one as the precondition of the other, to interpret the one in the light of the other. Ideally, the aim is the harmony between the realms of spiritual life; in reality, there is tension, crisis, tendency toward onesidedness; occasionally, however, the ideal becomes the real, and thought turns into life.

No attempt was made to idealize medieval Jewry; the selections include harsh self-criticism. But the reader is expected to gain some understanding of that element by which Jews maintained their dignity and sense of purpose in periods of degradation. He will realize, it is hoped, that the external appearance of medieval Jewish quarters, the weird, dreary, relic-like exterior of a house of prayer, or decayed tombstones are no fit symbols for a community that strove to preserve the breath of life in both faith and knowledge. "For you we love, O Holy One!"

Prelude

Abraham ibn Ezra, Joseph Caspi, and
Solomon ibn Gabirol

That knowledge is a prerequisite of faith, that knowledge of God pre-
supposed knowledge of the physical universe is a frequent theme in
medieval Hebrew literature. Equally recurrent is the theme of faith as
the summit of the Law. Of the three quotations that follow, the first is
from Abraham ibn Ezra's (Spain, 12th cent.) commentary on the Bible,
the second from *Sefer ha-Musar* (Treatise on Ethics) by Joseph Caspi
(South France, 13th–14th cent.), known especially for his commentary
on Maimonides' *Guide to the Perplexed*. The third quotation, on faith,
is from the *Choice of Pearls* by the poet Solomon ibn Gabirol (Spain,
11th cent.).

I

"And let us know, eagerly strive to know the Lord, his going
forth is sure as the morning" (Hosea 6:3).

This [knowledge of the Lord] is the aim of all wisdom and
solely to this end man was created. But man cannot know the
Lord unless he has studied many branches of wisdom which are
comparable to the steps of a ladder on which man ascends until
he reaches the highest rung. The reason [why Hosea uses the
image of] "the morning" is that like the morning commences
[with but a little] light which grows bigger and bigger, so does
the student [only gradually] recognize the Lord out of His works
until he [finally] sees the truth.

II

How can I know God and that He is one, unless I know what knowing means, and what constitutes oneness? [. . .] No one really knows the true meaning of loving God and fearing him, unless he is acquainted with natural science and metaphysics, for we love not God as a man loves his wife and children, nor fear we Him as we would a mighty man. I do not say that all men can reach this intellectual height, but I maintain that it is the degree of highest excellence, though those who stand below it may still be good.

III

A wise man said, "Everything requires a fence."

He was asked, "What is the fence?" He answered, "Trust." "What is the fence of trust?" he was asked; and he replied, "Faith." To the further question, "What is the fence of faith?" he answered, "To fear nothing." A wise man was asked, "What is the fence of faith?" and his reply was, "Trust in God, acceptance of His decrees, and self-surrender to Him."

There is nothing greater than faith; but few men endure patiently such misfortunes as poverty, sickness and terror. Yet know that all these [can be better endured when aid is derived] form the gates of faith.

O men, supplicate your God that He endow you with faith, for faith is the summit of the Law. Beg also tranquility from Him, for it is the summit of greatness; in cheerfulness seek it in this world and the hereafter. In faith is a sufficiency of riches; and in His service a sufficiency of occupation.

I. God

THE ONENESS OF GOD

Moses Maimonides

Within medieval Judaism, Maimonides (or, the Rambam, as he is traditionally called) made the most determined attempt to do justice to both faith and knowledge. Born in Cordoba, Spain, in 1135, he led a migratory life in Spain from 1148 to 1158; the following years the Maimonides family spent in Fez, Morocco, then established permanent residence in Egypt in 1165 or 1166, first in Alexandria, then in Fostat. Moses, "the marvel of the generation," was a rabbinical scholar, philosopher, leader of Jewry, and physician, and his writings encompass all these fields. For years he was physician at the Court of Saladin, the Sultan who in 1187 reconquered most of Palestine from the Crusaders. Maimonides died in 1204.

His major works include: *A Commentary on the Mishnah,* written in Arabic, concluded in 1168; *Mishneh Torah* (Code of Jewish Law), written in Hebrew, completed in 1180 (the first of the Code's fourteen books, *Sefer ha-Madda* [The Book of Knowledge] is a presentation of the principles of Judaism and a summary of the author's metaphysics and philosophical ethics); and *Moreh Nebukhim* (The Guide to the Perplexed), written in Arabic, completed about 1190, which is an exposition of his philosophy, a conciliation between the Bible and Aristotle, a synthesis of classical Jewish religion and Neoplatonic Aristotelianism. Among his shorter writings *The Epistle to Yemen* (*Iggeret Teman*), a treatise on Jewish persecution and the faith in redemption, should be mentioned. In addition he wrote hundreds of *responsa* and some twenty medical treatises. In his *Mishneh Torah,* Maimonides gave the traditional Jew a systematically arranged, all-comprising *Code* to facilitate both study and practice of the religious laws.

The passage that is here reprinted is from the first chapter and the beginning of the second in his *Code.* What was to become a major concern in his *Guide*, the oneness and incorporeality of God, is here stated in a clear, strong outline.

The first edition of the *Mishneh Torah* appeared in Italy about 1480, the second at Soncino in 1490. They were followed by numerous other editions, mostly with commentaries.

The foundation of foundations and the pillar of all wisdom is to know that there is a First Being who caused all beings to be. All beings from heaven and earth, and from between them, could not be save for the truth of His being.

If it could be supposed that He did not exist, nothing else could possibly exist.

If, however, it were supposed that all other beings were non-existent, He alone would still exist. Their non-existence would not involve His non-existence. For all beings are in need of Him; but He, blessed be he, is not in need of them nor of a single one of them. Hence, the truth of His being is incomparable to the truth of any other individual being. [. . .]

This God is one. He is not two nor more than two, but one; so that none of the things existing in the universe to which the term one is applied is like unto His oneness; neither such a unit as a species which comprises many [individual] units, nor such a unit as a body which consists of parts and dimensions. His one-ness is such that there is no other oneness like it in the uni-verse. [. . .]

That the Holy One, blessed be he, is incorporeal is clearly set forth in the Torah and in the Prophets, as it is said, "(Know therefore) that the Lord, He is God in heaven above, and upon the earth beneath" (Deut. 4:39); and a corporeal being is in-capable of being in two places at one time. Furthermore, it is said, "For ye saw no manner of form" (Deut. 4:15).

Since this is so, what is the meaning of the following expres-sions found in the Torah: "Beneath his feet" (Exod. 24:10); "Written with the finger of God" (Exod. 31:18); "The hand of God" (Exod. 9:3); "The eyes of God" (Gen. 38:7), "The ears of God" (Num. 11:1), and similar phrases? All such terminology is adapted to the conception of sons of man who have a clear per-ception of corporeal things only. The Torah speaks in the lan-guage of men. All these phrases are metaphorical. [. . .]

Since it has been demonstrated that He is incorporeal, it is clear that none of the accidents of matter can be attributed to Him; neither joining nor separation, neither place nor dimension, neither ascent nor descent, neither right nor left, neither front nor back, neither sitting nor standing. Nor does He exist in time, in the sense that either a beginning or an end or number of years can be attributed to Him. Nor does He change, for there is nought in Him that would cause any change in Him. He is neither subject to death nor to life like to the life of a living body. Folly cannot be attributed to Him, nor can wisdom, like that of a wise man; neither sleep nor awakening, neither passion nor frivolity; neither joy nor melancholy; neither silence nor speech like that of human beings. And so the sages have said, "Above, there is neither sitting nor standing, neither rigidity nor relaxation." [1]

This being so, the expressions in the Torah and in the words of the Prophets and others similar to these, are all of them metaphorical and figurative, as for example, "He that sitteth in the heavens shall laugh" (Ps. 2:4), "They have provoked me to anger with their vanities" (Deut. 32:21), "As the Lord rejoiced" (Deut. 28:63), etc. To all these applies the saying "The Torah speaks in the language of men." So too, it is said, "Do they provoke Me to anger?" (Jer. 7:19); and yet it is said "I am the Lord, I change not" (Malachi 3:6). If God could sometimes be angry and sometimes rejoicing, He would be subject to change. All these states exist in physical beings that are of lowly and mean condition, dwelling in houses of clay, whose origin is in the dust. Blessed and exalted above all this, is God, blessed be he.

This God, honored and revered, it is our duty to love and fear; as it is said, "Thou shalt love the Lord, thy God" (Deut. 6:5), and it is further said, "Thou shalt fear the Lord, thy God" (Deut. 6:13).

And what is the way that will lead to the love of Him and the fear of Him? When a person will contemplate His great and wondrous works and creatures and will behold through them His wisdom which is incomparable and infinite, he will spontaneously love Him, praise Him, glorify Him, and long with an exceeding longing to know the Great Name. And when he ponders these matters, he will be taken aback in a moment and stricken with awe, and realize that he is an infinitesimal creature, lowly and humble, endowed with slight and slender intelligence, standing in the presence of Him who is perfect in knowledge. In harmony with these matters, I shall explain some large, general aspects of the works of the Lord of the universe, that they may serve the intelligent individual as a door to the love of God, even as our sages have remarked in connection with the theme of the love of God, "Observe the universe and hence you will recognize Him who spoke and the world was called into existence." [2]

KNOWLEDGE OF GOD

Moses Maimonides

In Biblical thought the will of God is expressed in His laws and especially in the moral commandment; man worships God by fulfilling the commandment. Maimonides, while retaining the Biblical view, points to a higher form of communion between man and God: Knowledge. Knowledge of the physical world is the basis for the purely theoretical knowledge, which, in turn, culminates in the knowledge of God. In taking this position, Maimonides follows the lead of Aristotle, who considered the faculty of knowing to be man's supreme achievement, just as God, the highest mind, exists in the apprehension of Himself. And, again following Aristotle and his Moslem interpreters, Maimonides explained human reason and thought as becoming actualized by their contact with the cosmic source of all knowledge, the so-called "Active Intellect" which originates in God. Man, in developing his faculty of reason, is in contact with God. Knowledge of God is the road to God; in this knowledge, too, originates the love for God.

The excerpt below is from *Moreh Nebukhim* (The Guide to the Perplexed). To the intellectual, conscious of the rationalist trends in some parts of the Islamic and Christian world, and perplexed about the validity of revelation, Maimonides offered in the *Guide* a foundation from which it was possible to arrive at a harmony between the demands of reason and the principles of revealed faith. He envisaged intellectual self-perfection as the road—and the precondition—to a closeness to God, and interpreted the laws, ritual and ethical, as steps on that road.

The *Guide,* written in Arabic, was translated into Hebrew by

Samuel ibn Tibbon in the author's lifetime, and was first published in Italy before 1480. Another translation into Hebrew, by the poet Judah al-Harizi, became the basis for a translation into Latin by August Justinianus (Paris, 1520). Ibn Tibbon's version was rendered into Latin by Johannes Buxtorf (Basel, 1629). In 1580 the work appeared in an Italian translation. The Arabic original was published by Solomon Munk (Paris, 1856–66). The importance of the *Guide* was not restricted to Judaism; the work was studied by Christian scholastics, and is often quoted by Thomas Aquinas.

I will begin the subject of this chapter with a simile. A king is in his palace, and all his subjects are partly in the city, and partly abroad. Of the former, some have their backs turned towards the king's palace, and their faces in another direction. Others are making for the palace, seeking to obtain entry to it and to have audience with the king, but have not yet seen even the face of the wall of the house. Of those that are going towards the palace, some reach it, and go round about in search of the entrance gate; others have passed through the gate, and walk about in the ante-chamber; and others have succeeded in entering into the inner part of the palace, and being in the same room with the king in the royal palace. But even the latter do not immediately on entering the palace see the king, or speak to him; for, after having entered the inner part of the palace, another effort is required before they can stand before the king—at a distance, or close by—hear his words, or speak to him.

I will now explain the simile which I have made. The people who are abroad are all those that have no religion, neither one based on speculation nor one received by tradition. Such are the outlying tribes of the Turks that wander about in the distant north, the Kushites who live in the distant south, and those in our country who are like these. I consider these irrational beings, and not as human beings; they are below mankind, but above the apes, since they have the form and shape of man, and a mental faculty above that of the apes.

Those who are in the city, but have their backs turned towards the king's palace, are men of thought and speculation who have arrived at false doctrines, which they either adopted in consequence of great errors made in their own speculations, or received from others who misled them. Because of these doctrines they recede more and more from the royal palace the more they seem to proceed. These are worse than the first class.

Those who are making for the palace, and aim to enter it, but have never yet seen it, are the mass of religious people; the multitude that observe the divine commandments, but are ignorant.

Those who arrive at the palace, but go round about it, are those who devote themselves exclusively to the study of the practical law; they believe traditionally in true principles of faith, and learn the practical worship of God, but are not trained in philosophical treatment of the principles of their faith, and do not endeavor to establish the truth of their faith by proof.

Those who undertake to investigate the principles of religion, have come into the forecourts; and there is no doubt that these can also be divided into different grades. But those who have succeeded in finding a proof for everything that can be proved, who have a true knowledge of God, so far as a true knowledge can be attained, and are near the truth, wherever an approach to the truth is possible, they have reached the goal, and are in the presence of the king in the inner parts of the palace.

My son, so long as you are engaged in studying the mathematical sciences and logic, you belong to those who go round about the palace in search of the gate. When you understand physics, you have entered the hall; and when, after completing the study of natural sciences, you master metaphysics, you have entered the innermost court, and are with the king in the same palace. You have attained the degree of the wise men, who include men of different grades of perfection. There are some who direct all their mind toward the attainment of perfection in metaphysics, devote themselves entirely to God, exclude from their thought every other thing, and employ all their intellectual faculties in the study of the universe, in order to find in it guidance towards God, and to learn in every possible way how God rules all things; they form the class of those who have entered the audience chamber. This is the rank of the prophets.

One of these [Moses] has attained so much knowledge, and has concentrated his thoughts to such an extent in the idea of God, that it could be said of him, "And he was with the Lord"

(Exod. 34:28). During that holy communion he could ask Him, answer Him, speak to Him, and be addressed by Him, enjoying beatitude in that which he had obtained to such a degree that "he did neither eat bread nor drink water" (*ibid.*); his intellectual energy was so predominant that all coarser functions of the body, especially those connected with the sense of touch, were in abeyance. Some prophets are only able to see, and of these some approach near and see, whilst others see from a distance.

We have already spoken of the various degrees of prophets; we will therefore return to the subject of this chapter, and exhort those who have attained a knowledge of God, to concentrate all their thoughts in God. This is the worship peculiar to those who have acquired a knowledge of the highest truths; and the more they reflect on Him, and think of Him, the more are they engaged in His worship.

Those, however, who think of God, and frequently mention His name, without any correct notion of Him, but merely following some imagination, or some theory received from another person, are, in my opinion, like those who remain outside the palace and distant from it. They do not mention the name of God in truth, nor do they reflect on it. That which they imagine and mention does not correspond to any reality; it is a thing invented by their imagination. The true worship of God is only possible when correct notions of Him have previously been conceived. When you have arrived by way of intellectual research at a knowledge of God and His works, then commence to devote yourselves to Him, try to come near Him and strengthen the intellect, which is the bond that links you to Him. The Torah distinctly states that the highest kind of worship to which we refer in this chapter, is only possible after the acquisition of the knowledge of God: "To love the Lord your God, and to serve Him with all your heart and with all your soul" (Deut. 11:13). As we have shown several times, man's love of God is identical with His knowledge of Him. The divine service enjoined in these words must, accordingly, be preceded by the love of God. Our sages have pointed out to us that it is a service in the heart, which I understand to mean this that man concentrates all his thoughts upon Him, and is absorbed in these thoughts as much as possible.

It has thus been shown that after having acquired the knowledge of God, the aim should be complete devotion to God and constant exercising of intellectual thought in His love. He accomplishes this generally by seclusion and retirement. Every man of virtue should therefore seek seclusion, and should only in case of necessity associate with others.

IN THE PRESENCE OF GOD

Solomon ibn Gabirol

Solomon ibn Gabirol was born in Malaga about 1020 and died in Valencia about 1060. He wrote (in Arabic) *Mekor Hayyim* (Fons Vitae, Source of Life), a metaphysical and ontological system in the Neoplatonic tradition; ethical treatises, presented elsewhere in this volume; and religious and secular poetry. Some of his liturgic poems became a part of the prayer book, especially of the Sephardic and oriental rites. The most profound of them is the long hymn, *Keter Malkhut* (*The Kingly Crown*), selections from which are here reprinted.

While most of his poems, and indeed most creations by Hebrew poets in Spain, employed Arabic meters and stylistic forms, *The Kingly Crown* is free of this influence; it is composed in a freely flowing rhymed prose; an external unity of the sequence of stanzas is established by a Biblical quotation that concludes each stanza; the internal unity is provided by the poem's theme: the praise of God, the creator of the universe. From among the attributes of God, it is His will, manifested in the creation of the cosmic system, that the poet describes in terms of the astronomical knowledge of his age. The hymn concludes with a confession and a prayer from the humble man to whom the vision of the ultimate was granted. "*The Kingly Crown* is, by common consent, the greatest Hebrew religious poem of the Middle Ages, and indeed one of the major works of Hebrew literature since the completion of the Old Testament" (Bernard Lewis). Although it is not a part of the liturgy, it has been included in the prayer book for the Day of Atonement for private reading.

Translations of the hymn include Latin (1618), Yiddish (1674), Spanish (1769), French (1773), and Persian (1895).

Thine are the greatness and the strength and the splendor and the glory and the majesty.

Thine O God is the Kingdom and the rising above all things and the richness and the honor.

Thine are the higher and the lower creatures, and they bear witness that they perish and Thou dost endure.

Thine is the might whose secret our thoughts are wearied of seeking, for Thou art so much stronger than we.

Thine is the mystery of power, the secret and the foundation.

Thine is the name that is hidden from the wise, the strength that sustains the world over the void, the power to bring to light all that is hidden.

Thine is the mercy that rules over Thy creatures and the goodness preserved for those who fear Thee.

Thine are the secrets that no mind or thought can encompass, and the life over which decay has no rule, and the throne that is higher than all height, and the habitation that is hidden at the pinnacle of mystery.

Thine is the existence from the shadow of whose light every being was made to be, and we said "Under His shadow we shall live" (Lam. 4:20).

Thou art, but the hearing of ears and the seeing of eyes cannot reach Thee, and how and why and where have no rule over Thee.

Thou art, but for Thine own essence, and for no other with Thyself.

Thou art, and before all time was Thou wert, and without place Thou didst dwell.

Thou art, and thy secret is hidden and who can reach it—"far off, and exceeding deep, who can find it out?" (Eccles. 7:24).

Thou livest, but not from determined time or known epoch.

Thou livest, but not with soul or breath, for Thou art soul of the soul.[3]

Thou livest, but not as the life of man that is like vanity, its end in moths and worms.

Thou livest, and whoever attains Thy secret will find eternal delight—"and eat, and live for ever" (Gen. 3:22).

Thou art the supreme light, and the eyes of the pure of soul shall see Thee, and clouds of sin shall hide Thee from the eyes of sinners.

Thou art the light hidden in this world and revealed in the world of beauty, "In the mount of the Lord it shall be seen" (Gen. 22:14).

Thou art the eternal light, and the inward eye yearns for Thee and is astonished—she shall see but the utmost part of them, and shall not see them all.[4]

Who can contain Thy might, when from the abundance of Thy glory Thou didst create a pure radiance, hewn from the quarry of the Rock,[5] and dug from the mine of Purity? [6]

And on it Thou didst set a spirit of wisdom, and Thou didst call it
     the Soul.

Thou didst fashion it from the flames of fire of the Intelligence,[7] and
     its spirit is as fire[8] burning in it.

Thou didst send it into the body to serve it and to guard it, and it is
     as a fire within, and yet it does not burn it.

From the fire of the spirit it was created, and went forth from nothing-
     ness to being, "because the Lord descended upon it in fire" (Exod.
     19:18).

Who can reach Thy wisdom, when Thou gavest the soul the power of
     knowledge which inheres in her?

So that knowledge is her glory, and therefore decay has no rule over
     her, and she endures with the endurance of her foundation; this
     is her state and her secret.

Who can requite Thy bounties, when thou gavest the soul to the body,
     to give it life, to teach and show it the path of life, to save it from
     evil?

Thou didst form man out of clay,[9] and breathe into him a soul and
     set on him a spirit of wisdom, by which he is distinguished from
     a beast, and rises to a great height.

Thou didst set him enclosed in Thy world, while Thou from outside
     dost understand his deeds and see him,

And whatever he hides from Thee—from inside and from outside
     Thou dost observe.[10]

Who can know the secret of Thine accomplishments, when Thou
     madest for the body the means for Thy work?

Thou gavest him eyes to see Thy signs,

Ears, to hear Thy wonders,

Mind, to grasp some part of Thy mystery,

Mouth, to tell Thy praise,

Tongue, to relate Thy mighty deeds to every comer,

As I do to-day, I Thy servant, the son of Thy handmaid,

I tell, according to the shortness of my tongue, one tiny part of Thy
     greatness.

O my God, if my sin is too great to bear, what wilt Thou do for Thy
     great name?

If I cannot hope for Thy mercies, who but Thou will have pity on me?

Therefore, though Thou kill me, I shall hope in Thee,[11]

And if Thou search out my sin, I shall flee from Thee to Thee, and
     hide myself from Thy wrath in Thy shadow.

I shall hold on to the skirts of Thy mercy until Thou hast pity on me.
     "I will not let Thee go, except Thou bless me" (Gen. 32:26).

Let it be Thy will, O Lord our God and God of our fathers, sovereign
  of all the worlds, to have pity on me and be near to me.
To visit me with the visitation of Thy will, to bear to me the light of
  Thy countenance, to let me find Thy grace.
And do not recompense me according to my deeds, nor make me the
  reproach of the foolish,
In the midst of my days do not take me away, and do not hide Thy
  face from me.
Cleanse me of my sins, and do not cast me from Thy countenance,
Let me live with honor, and after that with honor take me,[12]
And when Thou shalt take me out of this world, bring me in peace to
  the life of the world to come,
Summon me on high, and let me dwell among saints,
Number me among those who have a portion in eternal life
And make me worthy to shine with the light of Thy countenance.
Give me new life, and from the depths of the earth raise me up again,
And I shall say: I praise Thee, Lord, for though Thou wert angry,
  with me Thou didst soften Thine anger and pity me,[13]
Thine is the mercy, O God, in all the good which Thou hast vouch-
  safed to me and which Thou wilt vouchsafe to me until the day I
  die.

LORD WHERE SHALL I FIND THEE?

Judah ha-Levi

Jewish prayer books of all rites contain a wealth of poetic creations by
Judah ha-Levi; they accompany the celebration of the Sabbath, the
Pilgrimage Festivals, the Days of Awe, fast days and the minor feasts.
They were chosen for inclusion because they gave profound expression
to the spiritual forces that affected Israel as a community of faith; the
presence of God, the sanctity of life, the meaning of exile and of the
return to Zion, the hope for redemption.

Not all of the several hundred pieces of Judah ha-Levi's religious
poetry were made a part of the liturgy and not all of his poetic work
was religious. We know of more than four hundred secular poems from
his pen—in praise of nature, friendship, love, beauty and wine—and
topical verse. Major libraries preserve collections of this poetry. An
edition in four volumes, based on manuscripts and early imprints, was
prepared by H. Brody (Berlin, 1901–1930); Franz Rosenzweig wrote a
theological and aesthetic commentary to ninety of the poems, which
appeared as an appendix to a translation into German.

Judah ben Samuel ha-Levi, born about 1080 in Toledo, Castile, combined Hebrew scholarship and poetry with the medical profession. "My heart is in the east, and I in the uttermost west," he wrote. His revolt against the social conditions in Spain and his longing for the Land of Israel made him leave his home, his only daughter, and his friends to start on a journey to Zion (about 1140), a goal he never reached. On the poet's philosophical work, *Kuzari,* see the preface to "The Servant of God."

My thought awaked me with Thy Name,
    Upon Thy boundless love to meditate;
       Whereby I came
The fullness of the wonder to perceive,
    That Thou a soul immortal shouldst create
To be embound in this, my mortal frame.
    Then did my mind, elate,
Behold Thee and believe;
    As though I stood among
    That hushed and awe-swept throng
And heard the Voice and gazed on Sinai's flame!

    I seek Thee in my dreams,
    And lo, Thy glory seems
To pass before me, as of old, the cloud
    Descended in his sight, who heard
    The music of Thy spoken word.
Then from my couch I spring, and cry aloud,
"Blest be the glory of Thy Name, O Lord!"

           ⸺

With all my heart, O Truth, with all my might
    I love Thee; in transparency, or night,
Thy Name is with me; how then walk alone?
    He is my Love; how shall I sit alone?
He is my Brightness; what can choke my flame?
    While He holds fast my hand, shall I be lame?
Let folk despise me; they have never known
    My shame for Thy sake is my glorious crown.
O Source of Life, let my life tell thy praise,
    My song to Thee be sung in all my days!

           ⸺

Let my sweet song be pleasing unto Thee—
    The incense of my praise—

O my Beloved that are flown from me,
　　Far from mine errant ways!
But I have held the garment of His love,
Seeing the wonder and the might thereof.
The glory of Thy name is my full store—
My portion for the toil wherein I strove:
Increase the sorrow:—I shall love but more!
　　Wonderful is Thy love!

⤸

Lord, where shall I find Thee?
High and hidden is Thy place;
And where shall I not find Thee?
The world is full of Thy glory.

Found in the innermost being,
He set up the ends of the earth:
The refuge for the near,
The trust for those far off.
Thou dwellest amid the Cherubim,
Thou abidest in the clouds;
Thou art praised by Thine hosts
Yet art raised above their praise.
The whirling worlds cannot contain Thee;
How then the chambers of a temple?

And though Thou be uplifted over them
Upon a throne high and exalted,
Yet art Thou near to them,
Of their very spirit and their flesh.
Their own mouth testifieth for them
That Thou alone art their Creator.
Who shall not fear Thee,
Since the yoke of Thy kingdom is their yoke?
Or who shall not call to Thee,
Since Thou givest them their food?

I have sought Thy nearness,
With all my heart have I called Thee,
And going out to meet Thee
I found Thee coming toward me,
Even as, in the wonder of Thy might,
In the sanctuary I have beheld Thee.
Who shall say he hath not seen Thee?—
Lo, the heavens and their hosts

Declare the fear of Thee,
Though their voice be not heard.

Doth then, in very truth,
God dwell with man?
What can he think—every one that thinketh,
Whose foundation is in the dust—
Since Thou art holy, dwelling
Amid their praises and their glory?
Angels adore Thy wonder,
Standing in the everlasting height;
Over their heads is Thy throne,
And Thou upholdest them all!

II. The Love for God

"Thou shalt love . . ."

Pascal's "The entire religion of the Jews consisted only of the love for God" points indeed to a core issue in Jewish thought from the Biblical "Thou shalt love the Lord thy God" to Franz Rosenzweig's interpretation of revelation as becoming conscious of divine love which is responded to by human love. Approaches and emphases vary from thinker to thinker. While Maimonides (twelfth century) considered knowledge an essential pre-condition to the love of God, Hasdai Crescas (fourteenth–fifteenth century) saw in love itself the way to God, who is pure love; his disciple, Joseph Albo (fifteenth century), spoke of the love of God as the highest possible love and emphasized God's love for man, though reason was not able to explain it.

Here follow four texts on the subject: one by Maimonides; another by Bahya ibn Pakuda, the eleventh-century moralist; a third from the *Zohar*, chief document of Kabbalah, and, in conclusion, a discussion by Moses Hayyim Luzzatto, eighteenth-century mystic and moralist (see "The House of Study in Padua," and "Humility"). Compare also "The Universality of Love."

Moses Maimonides

Let no man say, "I will observe the precepts of the Torah and occupy myself with its wisdom, so that I may receive all the blessings described in the Torah, or merit the life in the world to come; I will abstain from transgressions against which the Torah warns, so that I may be saved from the curses described therein, or that I may not be cut off from life in the world to come." It is not right to worship the Lord after this fashion, for whoever does so, worships Him out of fear. This is not the standard set by the prophets and sages. Only those serve God in this way, who are ignorant men, women or children whom one trains to serve out of fear, until their knowledge increases when they will worship out of love.

Whoever serves God out of love, occupies himself with the study of the Torah and the fulfilment of commandments and walks in the paths of wisdom, impelled by no external motive whatsoever, moved neither by fear of evil nor by the desire to inherit the good; such a man does the true thing because it is true and, ultimately, happiness comes to him as a result of his conduct. This standard is indeed a very high one; not every sage attained to it. It was the standard of Abraham our father, whom God called His lover, because he worshiped only out of love. It is the standard which God, through Moses, bids us achieve, as it is said, "And thou shalt love the Lord, thy God" (Deut. 6:5). When a person loves God with the proper love, he will momentarily observe all the commandments out of love.

What is the proper love of God? It is to love the Lord with a great and very strong love, so that one's soul shall be tied to the love of the Lord, and one should be continually enraptured by it, like a love-sick individual, whose mind is at no time free from his passion for a particular woman, the thought of her filling his heart at all times, when sitting down or rising up, even when he is eating or drinking. Still more intense should be the love of God in the hearts of those who love Him. And this love should continually possess them, even as He commanded us, "with all thy heart and with all thy soul" (Deut. 6:5). This, Solomon expressed allegorically, saying, "for I am sick with love" (Cant. 2:5). The entire Song of Songs is indeed an allegory on this subject.

The ancient sages said: "Peradventure you will say, 'I will study Torah, in order that I may become rich, that I may be called rabbi, that I may receive a reward in the world to come.' It is therefore said, 'To love the Lord,' meaning: Whatever you do, do it out of love only." [1] [. . .] So too, the greatest sages were wont to exhort particularly those among their disciples who were understanding and intelligent, "Be not like servants who minister to their master upon the condition of receiving a reward." But it is proper to be like servants who serve their master not for the sake of receiving aught.[2] Only because he is the master, it is right to serve him; that is, serve him out of love.

Whoever engages in the study of the Torah, in order that he may receive a reward or avoid calamities is not studying the Torah for its own sake. Whoever occupies himself with the Torah, neither out of fear nor for the sake of reward, but solely out of love for the Lord of the whole earth who enjoined us to do so, is occupied with the Torah for its own sake. The sages however said, "One should always engage in the study of the Torah, even if not for its own sake; for he who begins thus will end by studying it for its own sake."[3] Hence, when instructing the young, women or the ignorant generally, we teach them to serve God out of fear or for the sake of reward, till their knowledge increases and they have attained a large measure of wisdom. Then we reveal to them this secret, little by little, and train them by easy stages till they have comprehended it, and serve God out of love.

It is known and certain that the love of God does not become tied up in a man's heart till he is continuously and thoroughly possessed by it and gives up everything else in the world for it; as God commanded us, "with all thy heart and with all thy soul" (Deut. 6:5). One only loves God by the measure of knowledge that one knows Him. According to that knowledge will be that love; if the former be little or much, so will the latter be little or much. A person ought therefore to dedicate himself to the understanding and comprehension of those sciences and studies which will inform him concerning his Master, as far as it lies in human power to understand.

Bahya ibn Pakuda

Once the light of reason rises in the soul . . . she distinguishes truth from falsehood; the true face of her Creator and Guide is revealed to her. Once she understands the greatness of His power and the might of His awe, she bows to Him in fear and trembling. In this position she remains until the Creator calms her fear and dread. Then she drinks from the cup of divine love; she will be alone with God and dedicate herself to Him, love Him, trust Him, long for His will. If He deals kindly with her, she will be grateful; if He brings suffering upon her, she will suffer while her trust will grow even stronger.

Of one of the pious men they tell that he used to arise in the middle of the night and pray: "My God, thou hast made me hunger, and naked forsaken me, and set me in the darkmost of night, and taught me thy power and height. Though thou burn me in fire I shall but continue to love thee and to joy in thee, as Job said: 'Though He cut me down, to Him I shall aspire' (Job 13:15)."

The *Zohar*

"Thou shalt love the Lord thy God" (Deut. 6:5). This means that man should bind himself to Him with very strong love, and that all service performed by man to God should be with love, since there is no service like the love of the Holy One, blessed be he. Rabbi Abba said: These words are the epitome of the whole Law, since the Ten Commandments are summed up here. Nothing is so beloved of God as that a man should love Him in the fitting manner. How is this? As it is written, "with all thy heart," which includes two hearts, one good and one evil; "with all thy soul," one good and one evil; and "with all thy might." What lesson can be learnt from the word "all" here?

Rabbi Eleazar said: The word "might" refers to money, and "all" means both money which comes to a man from inheritance and money which a man earns himself. Rabbi Abba said: To return to the words "and thou shalt love": one who loves God is crowned with loving-kindness on all sides and does loving-kindness throughout, sparing neither his person nor his money. We know this from Abraham, who in his love for his Master spared neither his heart nor his life nor his money. He paid no heed to his own desires because of his love for his Master; he spared not his wife, and was ready to sacrifice his son because of his love for his Master; and he sacrificed his money also by standing at the cross-roads and providing food for all comers. Therefore he was crowned with the crown of loving-kindness. Whoever is attached in love to his Master is deemed worthy of the same, and what is more, all worlds are blessed for his sake.

Happy those to whom the love of their Master cleaves; there is no limit to their portion in the other world. Rabbi Isaac said: Many are the abodes of the righteous in the other world, one above another, and highest of all that of those to whom was attached the love of their Master, for their abode is linked with the palace that surpasses all, the Holy One, blessed be he, being crowned in this one. This Palace is called Love, and it is established for the sake of love. So it is too with the Holy Name, the forms of the letters of which are linked together, so that the whole is called "love"; wherefore he who loves his Master is linked to that Love. Hence it is written, "And thou shalt love the Lord thy God."

Moses Hayyim Luzzatto

To love God is to long passionately for His near presence, and to follow in the wake of His holiness, as we follow after anything which we passionately desire. To mention His name, or to discern His wonderful deeds, or to study His Torah, or His divine nature, is then as real a source of pleasure as the intense love of a husband for the wife of his youth, or of a father for an only son. Such is the love which renders communion a delight.

Such love must spring from no ulterior motive. A man must love the Creator, blessed be he, not because He bestows welfare, wealth and success upon him, but because to love God is as natural and as imperative to him, as for a son to love his father. In the words of Scripture, "Is not He thy father, that hath created thee?" (Deut. 32:6). And the test of this love is hardship and adversity. Commenting upon the commandment, "Thou shalt love the Lord thy God with all thy soul and with all thy might" (*ibid.* 6:5), our sages added, " 'With all thy soul' means, even at the cost of thy life, and 'with all thy might' means, even at the cost of thy possessions." [4]

Those who possess true knowledge do not think of themselves at all; what they pray for is that the glory of God be extolled, and that they may be able to afford Him joy. The greater the hindrances and, therefore, the greater the effort required to remove those hindrances, the more happy they are to prove the firmness of their faith.

The element of joy is one of the great essentials in the worship of God. "Serve the Lord with gladness," exhorted David, "come before His presence with singing" (Ps. 100:2). Elsewhere, "Let the righteous be glad: let them exalt before God: yea, let them rejoice with gladness (*ibid.* 68:4). "The Divine Presence," said our sages, "rests only upon one who finds joy in the performance of a commandment." [5] In commenting upon the verse, "Serve the Lord with gladness," Rabbi Aibu said, "Whenever thou art about to pray, let thy heart rejoice that thou art about to pray to a God who is without a peer." [6] Here, indeed, is cause for true rejoicing, that we are privileged to serve the Lord who is incomparable, and to occupy ourselves with His Torah and his commandments, which are means to the attainment of perfection and eternal glory. In the words of Solomon, "Draw me to Thee, we will run after Thee; the King hath brought me into His chambers; we will be glad and rejoice in Thee" (Cant. 1:4). The farther a man is permitted to penetrate into the innermost recesses of the knowledge of God's greatness, the greater will be his joy, and the more will his heart exult within him.

WHY IS MY LOVED ONE WROTH

Moses ibn Ezra

Moses ibn Ezra (born in Granada, *ca.* 1060, died in Castile, 1139) is one of the most productive of the classical Hebrew poets in Spain. His sacred poetry (much of which was incorporated into the liturgy) sings of the glory of creation, dwells upon the transitoriness of life and man's sinful state, prays for forgiveness and divine mercy, and for Israel's return to the Holy Land. Ibn Ezra was among the first to cultivate secular themes; using the style and forms of Arabic poetry, he wrote of nature, friendship, wine, and composed elegies occasioned by an unfortunate love for his niece. His outlook on life was gloomy: "The years of man are dreams and death is the interpreter."

> Why is my loved One wroth—
> That He should be disdainful of me,
> While my heart, in its yearning for Him,
> Is shaken like a reed?
> He hath forgotten the time
> When, joyously, I followed Him into the wilderness;
> Why do I cry this day,
> And He answer not?

> But though He slay me
> Yet will I trust in Him;[7]
> And if He hide His face,
> I will bethink me of His tenderness, and turn thereto.
> The loving-kindness of the Lord will not fail His servant
> For pure gold changes not, nor dims.[8]

THE UNIVERSALITY OF LOVE

Judah Abrabanel (Leone Ebreo)

Love as the all-pervading force in life temporal and eternal was one of the most pondered themes among Italian humanist writers. One of the first writings in this field was Marsilio Ficino's commentary on Plato's *Symposium* (1475). The motif of universal love penetrated Hebrew works of the period, such as *Heshek Shelomoh* (The Delight of Solomon), a commentary on the Song of Songs by Johanan Alemanno, teacher of Pico della Mirandola in Hebrew and Kabbalah.

Dialoghi d'Amore (The Dialogues of Love) is considered to be the most important document exemplifying this trend of thought. Written in 1501–1502, it presents three dialogues between Philo, the lover, and Sophia, wisdom, his beloved. The discussion of the nature of love (first dialogue) leads to the contemplation of the universality of love (second dialogue) and culminates in the appreciation of the cosmic significance of divine love. The author of the *Dialoghi*, Judah Abrabanel (Leone Ebreo), was born in Lisbon about 1460. He was a victim of the expulsion of the Jews from Spain and Portugal, and together with his famous father Isaac Abrabanel (statesman, Biblical scholar) he settled in Italy. Medicine was his profession; as philosopher he followed the Neoplatonic trend. His work (which, in certain respects, is reminiscent of Giordano Bruno's philosophical system) was published in 1535 in Rome and enjoyed considerable popularity; it was translated into French, Spanish, Latin, and Hebrew. Spinoza had a copy of the Spanish edition in his library.

Philo: You have heard from me ere now, O Sophia, that the whole Universe is one individual (i.e., like a single person), each one of these bodies and spirits, eternal or corruptible, being a member or part of this great individual. And all and every one of its parts was created by God with a purpose common to the whole as well as with a purpose peculiar to each part. It follows that whole and parts alike are perfect and happy in proportion as they rightly and completely discharge the functions for which they were designed by the Supreme Artificer. The purpose of the whole is the perfection in unity, as planned by the Divine Architect, of the entire Universe; but the purpose of each part is, not merely the perfection of that part in itself, but also the right promotion by that perfection of the perfection of the whole, which is the universal end and the first purpose of the Godhead.

For this general end, rather than for its own, each part was created, ordained and consecrated; so much so that failing in a portion of that service, whereof the activities appertain to the perfection of the Universe, would involve it in a graver fault and in greater unhappiness than if it failed in its own activity. So too it is made happier by the general, than by its own [weal], even as in a human individual the perfection of a part, e.g., the eye or hand, consists not merely nor even chiefly in the beauty of the eye or the hand, nor again in the ability of the eye to see much or of the hand to ply many crafts: but first and principally it consists in the eye's seeing and the hand's doing what is requisite for the weal of the whole person, and their worth and excellence are measured by their true service to the whole person, for their own beauty is their own activity. Wherefore the part often offers and exposes itself to immediate danger, as nature bids, for the protection of the whole person: e.g., an arm will encounter a sword to guard the head.

As then this law is constantly observed throughout the Universe, the intelligence finds more happiness in turning the heavenly spheres (such activity, though alien and corporeal, being necessary to the existence of the whole) than by its inward essential contemplation, which is its own activity. This is what Aristotle means by saying the intelligences move for the sake of a higher and more excellent cause, namely God: that they are realizing His plan of the Universe. Thus by loving and turning their spheres they bind the Universe in unity, and so properly win the divine love and grace, and even to union with God, that love and union being alike what holds the Universe together and their ultimate end and desired happiness.

Sophia: I am well pleased with this solution. And I suppose it is for the same reason that the spiritual intelligence of man unites with a body as frail as the human: to execute the divine plan for the coherence and unity of the whole Universe.

Philo: You have said well, and so it is in truth. For as our souls are spiritual intelligences, no benefit can accrue to them from association with the frail and corruptible body, but they would be far better off in their intimate and pure activity of intellect: but they coalesce with our bodies merely for love and service of the Supreme Creator of the World, taking intellectual life and knowledge and the light of God down from the upper world of eternity to the lower world of decay, that even this lowest part of the world may not be without divine grace and eternal life, and that this great animal may have every one of its parts as vital and intelligent as is the whole.

And as in this way our souls realize the unity of the whole Universe according to the divine plan, which was the general and chief end of the creation of things, they rightly enjoy the divine love, and after separation from the body achieve the union with God, which is their supreme happiness. But failing in its office, the soul is deprived of this divine love and union: and therein lies its supreme and eternal punishment: for, having the faculty to mount on high to Paradise by rightly governing its body, it is retained by its iniquity in the lowest hell, banned eternally from union with God and its own felicity, unless indeed the Divine Compassion were so great as to offer it an opportunity of atonement.

Sophia: God guard us from such aberration and make us upright in the execution of His holy will and divine plan!

Philo: Amen! But you already know, O Sophia, that it cannot be accomplished without love.

Sophia: Indeed love is not only common to all things in the world, but even supremely necessary, since none can be blessed without love.

Philo: Without love not only can there be no felicity; but the world would not exist nor would anything be found therein, if there were no love.

Sophia: Why all this?

Philo: Because the world and all in it can exist only insofar as it is wholly one, bound up with all it contains as an individual with his members. On the other hand, any division would involve its total destruction, and, as nothing unites the Universe with its different components save love alone, it follows that love itself is the condition of the existence of the world and all in it.

Sophia: Tell me how love animates the world and out of so many things forms a single unity.

Philo: From what has already been said you can easily understand that. God Most High creates and governs the world by love, and binds it together in unity: for as God is one with the most perfect simplicity of unity, that which derives from Him must needs be one with entire unity. For one derives from one, and from pure unity perfect union. Moreover, the spiritual world is united with the material by means of love: nor would the separate intelligences or angels of God ever unite with, or inform, or become animating souls of, the heavenly bodies, unless they loved them. Nor would intelligent souls unite with human bodies to make them rational, if love did not constrain them thereto. Nor [finally] would the soul of this world unite with this sphere of birth and decay, if it were not for love. Again, inferiors unite with superiors, the corporeal world with the spiritual, the corruptible with the eternal, and the whole Universe with its Creator, through the love it bears Him and its desire to unite with Him and be blessed in His divinity.

Sophia: It is even so. For love is a vivifying spirit penetrating all the world and a bond uniting the whole Universe.

Philo: Seeing that you feel thus about love, there is no need to tell you further of its universality, which we have spent all to-day in expounding.

SAINTLINESS

Moses Hayyim Luzzatto

Hasid is the Hebrew term here translated by "saint." Both this term and that designating saintliness, *Hasidut,* have different shades of meaning and emphasis, the variations depending on whether reference is to the period of the Second Commonwealth, the period of Judah the Pious and Eleazar Rokeah, or the great movement founded by the Baal Shem Tov. Underlying all the uses is the Biblical *Hesed,* "loving concern," a term applied both to God and to man. *Mesillat Yesharim* (Path of the Upright), Luzzatto's work on Jewish ethics, first published in Amsterdam in 1740, holds the sanctification of God to be the only proper motivation of human action and that man's duty is to bear the yoke with one's fellow-man. "Saintliness," he postulates, "is latent in the character of every normal person," yet this trait must be carefully cultivated. He counsels solitude, renunciation of material concerns, dedicated study of sacred writings, and concentration upon the divine. (See also "The Love for God.")

Luzzatto the moralist and the mystic (see the preface to "The House of Study in Padua") was also a poet. In his lyric and dramatic verse, he, well acquainted with Italian literature, employs purely human motifs: the beauty of nature, love, friendship. Heir of classical Judaism and its tensions, he is at the same time the forerunner of modern Hebrew secular poetry.

In all his works the saint's motive must be the furtherance of the well-being of his generation and securing for it divine favor and protection. Those who belong to the same generation as the righteous man, enjoy the fruit of his actions. It is, indeed, the will of God that Israel's saints should win atonement for those who are spiritually their inferiors. The Holy One, blessed be he, desires not the destruction of the wicked, and it is the task of the saint to strive to win for them divine grace and atonement. This should be his purpose in serving God, and this petition he should utter in his prayers. He should pray in behalf of the men of his generation that God grant forgiveness to all those who need forgiveness, and cause to repent all those who are in need of repentance. The true shepherds of Israel in whom the Holy One, blessed be he, takes delight are those who are ready to sacrifice themselves for the flock; who by every possible means earnestly strive to secure for it peace and well-being; who always stand in the breach and who, by means of prayer, seek to avert the evil decrees against it and to open for it the gates of blessing.

III. The Faith of Israel

THE DUTIES OF THE HEART

Bahya ibn Pakuda

The aim of the Arabic-written *Guide to the Duties of the Heart* was the reconstruction of the Jewish faith from within. The author, Bahya ibn Pakuda (Spain), who wrote his book between 1080 and 1090, realized that no Jewish work explored "the hidden wisdom" which (as distinct from "the visible wisdom" and the discussion of "the duties of the limbs") concerns itself with "the duties of the heart" and which constitutes the firm foundation of religion. Such duties (which are not bound to particular seasons or situations as are rituals and ceremonies) are belief in the one and incorporeal Creator, readiness to worship Him, ethical conduct, and purity of thought. Bahya is a rationalist, but he does not spend his intellectual energies on reconciling philosophy and revelation. In addition to Saadia, Bahya was also influenced by a Neoplatonically interpreted Aristotelianism and by Islamic mysticism (the "Faithful Brethren"). But Bahya is not a mystic; he is firmly rooted in the world of men—a world, however, that demands humility, conquest of passions, and a complete trust in divine mercy.

The work—one of the most popular in pre-modern Judaism—was translated into Hebrew by Judah ibn Tibbon in 1161 (*Torat Hovot ha-Levavot*), and was first printed in Naples in 1489. Another early translation into Hebrew was by Joseph Kimhi. Many imprints followed, also translations into Spanish (1569), Portuguese (1670), German (1836), Italian (1847), and other languages. The original Arabic text was edited by A. S. Yahuda in 1912.

The noblest of the gifts which God bestowed on His human creatures, next to having created them with mature faculties of perception and comprehension, is wisdom. This constitutes the life of their spirit, the lamp of their intellect.

All departments of science, according to their respective topics, are gates which the Creator has opened to rational beings, through which they may attain to a comprehension of the Torah and of the world. This knowledge affords instruction concerning the secrets of the physical world and the uses and benefits to be derived from it. They also furnish information concerning industries and arts conducive to physical and material well-being.

But essential to the understanding of Torah is the sublime knowledge of theology, which we are under an obligation to acquire. To acquire it, however, for the sake of worldly advantages is forbidden. The text, "To love the Lord, thy God, to listen to His voice, and to cleave to Him" (Deut. 30:20), has been thus expounded by our teachers: "Let not a man say, 'I shall read Scripture, in order that they may call me scholar, I shall study Mishnah that they may call me rabbi, I shall study Mishnah, that I may be a senior, entitled to a seat at the college.' Learn out of love and honor will follow." [1]

The avenues which the Creator has opened for the knowledge of His Torah are three. The first is a sound intellect; the second, the Book of His Law revealed to Moses, His prophet; the third, the traditions which we have received from our ancient sages, who received them from the prophets. These avenues have already been discussed at adequate length by our great teacher, Saadia.[2]

The science of the Torah, moreover, falls into two parts: The first aims at the knowledge of practical duties and is the science of external conduct. The second deals with the duties of the heart, namely, its sentiments and thoughts, and is the science of the inward life.

Of the duties of the heart, I shall mention a few that occur to me to serve as examples of those not cited. Among affirmative duties of the heart are: to believe that the world had a Creator, that He created it *ex nihilo,* and that there is none like unto Him; to accept His oneness; to worship Him with our hearts; to meditate on the wonders exhibited in His creatures, that these may serve us as evidences of Him; that we put our trust in Him; that we humble ourselves before Him, and revere Him; that we tremble and be abashed when we consider that He observes our visible and our hidden activities; that we yearn for His mercy; that we devote our works to the glory of His name; that we love

Him and love those that love Him, and thus draw nigh to Him; that we reject His adversaries—and similar duties, not apprehended by the senses.

Negative duties of the heart are the converse of those just mentioned. Also included among them are: that we shall not covet, avenge, nor bear a grudge; that our minds shall not dwell on transgressions, nor hanker after them, nor resolve to commit them; that we shall abstain from transgressions of a similar character—all which are purely mental and observed by none but the Creator; as it is written, "I, the Lord, search the heart; I try the reins" (Jer. 17:10); "The lamp of God is the soul of man, searching all the inward parts" (Prov. 20:27).

On closer study, I found that the class of the duties of the heart is in force continuously, throughout our lives, without intermission, and that we have no excuse for neglecting them; this applies to such duties, for example, as to confess the oneness of God with all our heart, to render Him service inwardly, to revere Him and to love Him, to yearn to fulfill the precepts obligatory upon us, to trust in Him and surrender ourselves to Him, to remove hatred and jealousy from our hearts, to abstain from the superfluities of this world which disturb and hinder us in the service of God. For all these are obligatory at all seasons, in all places, every hour, every moment, and under all circumstances, as long as we have life and reason.

After I had become convinced of the obligatory character of the duties of the heart and that we are bound to observe them; after I had noticed that these duties had been neglected and that no book had been composed specially treating of them and had further realized in what condition our contemporaries were as a result of their inability to comprehend, much less fulfil, these duties and occupy themselves with them, I was moved by the grace of God to inquire into the science of inward duties.

It became clear to me that all works done for God's sake must have as their roots purity of heart and singleness of mind. Where the motive is tainted, good deeds, however numerous and even though practised continuously, are not accepted; as Scripture says, "Yea, when ye make many prayers, I will not hear. Wash you, make you clean, put away the evil of your doings from before mine eyes" (Isa. 1:15–16). Further, "But the word is very nigh unto thee, in thy mouth and in thy heart, that thou mayest do it" (Deut. 30:14).

Again it is said, "But let him that glorieth glory in this, that he understandeth and knoweth Me, that I am the Lord, doing kindness, justice and righteousness" (Jer. 9:23). The meaning is that a man who glories should glory in comprehending God's ways, recognizing His beneficence, reflecting on His creation, realizing His might and wisdom, as manifested in His works.

All the texts here adduced are proofs of the obligatory character of the duties of the heart and the discipline of the soul. You should realize however that the aim and value of the duties of the heart consist in their securing the equal cooperation of body and soul in the service of God, so that the testimony of heart, tongue and the other bodily organs shall be alike, and that they shall support and confirm, not contradict or differ from, each other. This harmony it is which is called in Scripture wholeheartedness, or uprightness, in such texts as the following, "Thou shalt be whole-hearted with the Lord thy God" (Deut. 18:13). "He that walketh uprightly, and worketh righteousness and speaketh truth in his heart" (Ps. 15:2).

THE SERVANT OF GOD

Judah ha-Levi

Judah ha-Levi (see the preface to "Lord Where Shall I Find Thee") wrote his *Kuzari,* from which the chapter that follows is taken, against the historical and intellectual background of his time. In the eleventh century Israel, in exile, found herself betwixt Christianity and Islam, engaged in the crucial struggle for power. Intellectually, Judaism had to defend itself against the proud claims of Aristotelian philosophy and Karaite (anti-Rabbinic) criticism. Ha-Levi's Arabic-written work is entitled: *Book of Arguments and Proofs in Defense of the Despised Faith.* The title of the Hebrew translation, *Sefer ha-Kuzari,* refers to the pagan king of the Chazars searching for a new religion, whom the author presents in a dialogue with a Jewish sage (the Master) on the nature of Israel. Judah ha-Levi employs this setting for the propagation of his theory of Judaism as the road to an intuitive, prophetic knowledge of God, as opposed to the speculative, philosophical knowledge of the "First Cause."

The passage below is the master's answer to the king's request for a description of "a servant of God according to your conception." The discussion of the master's answer is followed by the rabbinic arguments against the Bible-centered and anti-talmudic Karaites.

The *Kuzari*, written during the last decade of the poet's life, was translated into Hebrew by Judah ibn Tibbon and was first printed in Fano in 1506, then in Venice in 1547. The Hebrew text with a Latin translation by Johannes Buxtorf appeared in Basel in 1660; a Spanish translation, in 1663. A critical edition of the Arabic text was published by H. Hirschfeld (Leipzig, 1887).

The Master: According to our view a servant of God is not one who detaches himself from the world, lest he be a burden to it, and it to him; or hates life, which is one of God's bounties granted to him. On the contrary, he loves the world and a long life, because it affords him opportunties of deserving the world to come. [. . .] He feels no loneliness in solitude and seclusion, since they form his associates. He is rather ill at ease in a crowd, because he misses the Divine Presence which enables him to dispense with eating and drinking. Such persons might perhaps be happier in complete solitude; they might even welcome death, because it leads to the step beyond which there is none higher.

Philosophers and scholars also love solitude to refine their thoughts, and to reap the fruits of truth from their researches, in order that all remaining doubts be dispelled by truth. They only desire the society of disciples who stimulate their research and retentiveness, just as he who is bent upon making money would only surround himself with persons with whom he could do lucrative business. Such a degree is that of Socrates and those who are like him.

There is no one nowadays who feels tempted to strive for such a degree, but when the Divine Presence was still in the Holy Land among the people capable of prophecy, some few persons lived an ascetic life in deserts and associated with people of the same frame of mind. They did not seclude themselves completely, but they endeavoured to find support in the knowledge of the Torah and in holy and pure actions which brought them near to that high rank. These were the disciples of prophets. He however, who in our time, place, and people, "whilst no open vision exists" (1 Sam. 3:1) the desire for study being small, and persons with a natural talent for it absent, would like to retire into ascetic solitude, only courts distress and sickness for soul and body. The misery of sickness is visibly upon him, but one might regard it as the consequence of humility and contrition. He considers himself in prison as it were, and despairs of life from disgust of his prison and pain, but not because he enjoys his seclusion. How could it be otherwise? He has no intercourse with the divine light, and cannot associate himself with it as did the prophets. He lacks the necessary learning to be absorbed in it and to enjoy it, as the philosophers did, all the rest of his life. [. . .]

The Kuzari: Give me a description of the doings of one of your pious men at the present time.

The Master: A pious man is, so to speak, the guardian of his country, who gives to its inhabitants provisions and all they need. He is so just that he wrongs no one, nor does he grant anyone more than his due. Then, when he requires them, he finds them obedient to his call. He orders, they execute; he forbids, they abstain.

The Kuzari: I asked thee concerning a pious man, not a prince.

The Master: The pious man is nothing but a prince who is obeyed by his senses, and by his mental as well as his physical faculties, which he governs corporeally. He is fit to rule, because if he were the prince of a country he would be as just as he is to his body and soul. He subdues his passions, keeping them in bonds, but giving them their share in order to satisfy them as regards food, drink, cleanliness, etc. He further subdues the desire for power, but allows them as much expansion as avails them for the discussion of scientific or mundane views, as well as to warn the evil-minded. He allows the senses their share according as he requires them for the use of hands, feet, and tongue, as necessity or desire arise. The same is the case with hearing, seeing, and the kindred sensations which succeed them; imagination, conception, thought, memory, and will power, which commands all these; but is, in its turn, subservient to the will of intellect. He does not allow any of these limbs or faculties to go beyond their special task, or encroach upon another.

If he, then, has satisfied each of them (giving to the vital organs the necessary amount of rest and sleep, and to the physical ones waking, movements, and worldly occupation), he calls upon his community as a respected prince calls his disciplined army, to assist him in reaching the higher or divine degree which is to be found above the degree of the intellect. He arranges his community in the same manner as Moses arranged his people round Mount Sinai. He orders his will power to receive every command issued by him obediently, and to carry it out forthwith. He makes faculties and limbs do his bidding without contradiction, forbids them evil inclinations of mind and fancy, forbids them to listen to, or believe in them, until he has taken counsel with the intellect. [. . .] He directs the organs of thought and imagination, relieving them of all worldly ideas mentioned above, charges his imagination to produce, with the assistance of memory, the most splendid pictures possible, in order to resemble the divine things sought after. Such pictures are the scenes of Sinai, Abraham and Isaac on Moriah, the Tabernacle of Moses, the Temple service, the presence of God in the Temple, and the like.

He, then, orders his memory to retain all these, and not to forget them; he warns his fancy and its sinful prompters not to confuse the truth or to trouble it by doubts; he warns his irascibility and greed not to influence or lead astray, nor to take hold of his will, nor subdue it to wrath and lust. As soon as harmony is restored, his will power stimulates all his organs to obey it with alertness, pleasure, and joy. [. . .]

The moment [of prayer] forms the heart and fruit of his time, whilst the other hours represent the way which leads to it. He looks forward to its approach, because while it lasts he resembles the spiritual beings, and is removed from merely animal existence. The three times of daily prayer are the fruit of his day and night, and the Sabbath is the fruit of the week, because it has been appointed to establish the connection with the Divine Spirit and to serve God in joy, not in sadness, as has been explained before. All this stands in the same relation to the soul as food to the human body. The blessing of one prayer lasts till the time of the next, just as the strength derived from the morning meal lasts till supper. The further his soul is removed from the time of prayer, the more it is darkened by coming in contact with worldly matters. [. . .] During prayer he purges his soul from all that has passed over it, and prepares it for the future.

According to this arrangement there elapses not a single week in which both his soul and body do not receive preparation. Darkening elements having increased during the week, they cannot be cleansed except by consecrating one day to service and to the physical rest. The body repairs on the Sabbath the waste suffered during the six days, and prepares itself for the work to come, whilst the soul remembers its own loss through the body's companionship. He cures himself, so to speak, from a past illness, and provides himself with a remedy to ward off any future sickness. He, then, provides himself with a monthly cure, which is "the season of atonement for all that happened during this period," [3] i.e., the duration of the month.

He further attends the Three Festivals and the great Fast Day,[4] on which some of his sins are atoned for, and on which he endeavors to make up for what he may have missed on the days of those weekly and monthly cycles. His soul frees itself from the whisperings of imagination, wrath, and lust, and neither in thought or deed gives them any attention. [. . .] The fast of this day is such as brings one near to the angels, because it is spent in humility and contrition, standing, kneeling, praising and singing. All his physical faculties are denied their natural requirements, being entirely abandoned to religious service, as if the animal element had disappeared. The fast of a pious man is such that eye, ear, and tongue share in it, that he regards nothing except that which brings him near to God. This also refers to his innermost faculties, such as mind and imagination. To this he adds pious works.

THE FAITH OF ABRAHAM

Moses Maimonides

Monotheism was known to earliest humanity, Maimonides believed (see "The Oneness of God"); polytheism, "the worship of stars and images," was a descent from an original knowledge of God. "As time passed the Name of God was forgotten by mankind," and recognized only by a few solitary individuals, such as the Biblical Enosh, Me- thuselah, Noah, Shem, and Eber. It was Abraham who found his way back from idolatry to monotheism. He is pictured as inquiring into the nature of the universe and finally postulating One God who "guides the celestial sphere and creates everything." Abraham realized "that the whole world was in error" and became the propagator of the truth at which he had arrived through reason and without the benefit of a teacher. Maimonides thus presents the patriarch as a philosopher turned theologian, and the Hebrews as a missionary people sent out to spread the knowledge of God. The excerpt below is from the *Mishneh Torah*. See also "The Proselyte."

Abraham was forty years old when he recognized his Creator. Having attained this knowledge, he began to refute the inhabit- ants of Ur of the Chaldees, arguing with them and saying to them, "The course you are following is not the way of truth." He broke the images and commenced to instruct the people that it was not right to serve any one but the God of the universe, to Whom alone it was proper to bow down, offer up sacrifices and make libations, so that all human creatures might, in the future, know Him; and that it was proper to destroy and shatter all the images, so that the people might not err like these who thought that there was no god but these images. When he had prevailed over them with his arguments, the king [of the country] sought to slay him. He was miraculously saved, and emigrated to Haran.

He then began to proclaim to the whole world with great power and to instruct the people that the entire universe had but one Creator and that Him it was right to worship. He went from city to city and from kingdom to kingdom, calling and gathering together the inhabitants till he arrived in the land of

Canaan. There too, he proclaimed his message, as it is said, "And he called there on the name of the Lord, God of the universe" (Gen. 21:33): When the people flocked to him and questioned him regarding his assertions, he would instruct each one according to his capacity till he had brought him to the way of truth, and thus thousands and tens of thousands joined him. These were the persons referred to as "men of the house of Abraham."

He implanted in their hearts this great doctrine, composed books on it, and taught it to Isaac, his son. Isaac, from his seat of learning, gave instructions and exhortations. He imparted the doctrine to Jacob and ordained him to teach it. He, too, at his seat of learning, taught and morally strengthened all who joined him. The patriarch Jacob instructed all his sons, set apart Levi, appointed him head and placed him in a house of study to teach the way of God and keep the charge of Abraham. He charged his sons to appoint from the tribe of Levi, one instructor after another, in uninterrupted succession, so that the learning might never be forgotten. And so it went on with ever increasing vigor among Jacob's children and their adherents till they became a people that knew God.

When Israel had stayed a long while in Egypt, they relapsed, learnt the practices of their neighbors and, like them, worshipped idols, with the exception of the tribe of Levi, which steadfastly kept the charge of the fathers. This tribe of Levi never practised idolatry. The root planted by Abraham would, in a very short time, have been uprooted, and Jacob's descendants would have relapsed into the error and perversities universally prevalent. But because of God's love for us and because He kept the oath made to our father Abraham, He appointed Moses to be our teacher and the teacher of all the prophets, and charged him with his mission. After Moses had begun to exercise his prophetic functions and Israel had been chosen by the Lord as His heritage, he crowned them with commandments and made known to them the way to worship Him.

DEVOTION

Moses Maimonides

Kavvanah (here translated as "devotion"), a term already employed
in talmudic literature, denotes direction of the mind, concentration,
attention (to the meaning of a religious law, especially of prayer),
devotion. Negatively, it means exclusion of extraneous, distracting
thoughts. The talmudic dictum, "A fulfilment of a commandment requires *Kavvanah*" (Berakhot 13a), was elaborated on by the various
branches of post-Biblical literature. Cultivation of *Kavvanah* was the
mark of the pious person. The Kabbalists went a few steps further by
probing into the hidden, mystic meanings underlying the sacred words
of prayer and enjoining concentration upon these meanings; an effect
upon "the upper worlds" was to result from such exercise; the Hasidim
adopted this system. Maimonides states the normative position of
Kavvanah; the quotation is from his *Mishneh Torah.*

Prayer without devotion is no prayer at all. He who has
prayed without devotion ought to pray once more. He whose
thoughts are wandering or occupied with other matters should
not pray before he has collected his thoughts. If he has returned
from a journey tired or troubled let him pray only after he has
collected his thoughts.

What then is devotion? One must free his heart from all
other thoughts and regard himself as standing in the presence
of God. Therefore, before engaging in prayer, a man ought to
go aside for a little in order to bring himself into a devotional attitude, and then he should pray quietly and with feeling, not like
one who carries a weight and goes away. Then after prayer the
worshipper ought to sit quiet for a little and then depart. The
early pious men [*Hasidim*] waited an hour before prayer and an
hour after, and engaged in prayer for a whole hour.

THE SEVEN BENEDICTIONS

AT THE MARRIAGE SERVICE

Prayer Book

In the traditional Jewish marriage service, the seven benedictions are recited by the celebrant following the ring ceremony, in which the bride becomes consecrated to the groom, and the reading of the marriage contract (*Ketubah*); upon the conclusion of the benedictions the cup of wine is presented to the bridegroom and the bride, and a glass is broken by the bridegroom in memory of the destruction of the Temple. Customarily, the service ends with the priestly blessing pronounced over the couple.

Blessed art thou, O Lord our God, king of the universe,
who createst the fruit of the vine.

Blessed are thou, O Lord our God, king of the universe,
who hast created all things to His glory.

Blessed are thou, O Lord our God, king of the universe,
Creator of man.

Blessed art thou, O Lord our God, king of the universe,
who hast made man in His image,
after His likeness,
and hast prepared unto him, out of his very self, a perpetual fabric of
    life.
Blessed art thou, O Lord,
Creator of man.

May Zion who was barren be exceeding glad and exult,
when her children are gathered within her in joy.
Blessed art thou, O Lord,
who makest Zion joyful through her children.

O make these loved companions greatly to rejoice,
even as of old thou didst gladden thy creature in the garden of Eden.
Blessed art thou, O Lord,
who makest bridegroom and bride to rejoice.

Blessed art thou, O Lord our God, king of the universe,
who hath created joy and gladness, bridegroom and bride,

mirth and exultation, pleasure and delight,
love, brotherhood, peace and fellowship.
Soon may there be heard in the cities of Judah, and in
    the streets of Jerusalem,
the voice of joy and gladness,
the voice of the bridegroom and the voice of the bride,
the jubilant voice of bridegrooms from their canopies,
and of youths from their feasts of song.
Blessed are thou, O Lord,
who makest the bridegroom to rejoice with the bride.

IV. Man

MAN—THE CENTER

OF THE UNIVERSE

Saadia Gaon

In the tenth century educated men in the Islamic East became fully aware of the philosophical heritage of classical Greece; Platonic and Aristotelian writings were now available in Arabic or Syriac translations. Both Moslem and Jewish thinkers were confronted with the need of reconciling faith and reason. For Islam, this reconciliation was affected by the free-thinking *Mutazilites;* for Judaism, by the writings of Saadia (892–942), the Gaon of Sura, Babylonia. Saadia's major work, *The Book of Doctrines and Beliefs* (933), written in Arabic and translated into Hebrew by Judah ibn Tibbon under the title *Sefer ha-Emunot ve-ha-Deot,* undertook to demonstrate that the teachings of Judaism conform to the principles of reason. However, revelation is necessary; it guides man before he can make full and unerring use of reason. Saadia departs from the philosophers only in his interpretation of Creation (which implies the concept of man's uniqueness). Ibn Tibbon's version was first printed in Constantinople in 1562 and frequently republished. The Arabic original was edited by S. Landauer in 1880.

I commence my discussion of this point with the following prefatory observation. In spite of the great multiplicity of created things, we need have no difficulty in deciding which of them is the most essential part of Creation, because this is a point which the science of nature is able to elucidate for us. From the teaching of science on this point we find that man is the most essential part of Creation, because it is the rule and habit of nature to place the most excellent [part of anything] in the center with things of less excellence surrounding it.

To take our first illustration from something very small: The grain is in the middle of the grain-sheaf because it is the most excellent part of the stalk; for the plant grows out, and is fed, from the grain. Likewise the kernel from which the tree grows is in the middle of the fruit, no matter whether the kernel is edible as in the case of an almond tree, or whether it is a stone as in the case of the date. In the latter case the edible part of the fruit is of less importance and left at the outside as a protecting shell for the kernel. Likewise the yolk is in the middle of the egg because the young of birds and the chickens develop from it. Likewise, the heart of man is in the middle of his chest because it is the seat of the soul and of the natural warmths. Likewise the pupil is in the middle of the eye because it is the chief organ of sight. We notice that the same observation applies to a great number of things besides.

Then we found that the earth occupied the center of the universe, entirely surrounded by the celestial spheres. This made it clear to us that the earth was the most essential part in the created universe. Then we examined everything which the earth contains, and observed that earth and water are both inanimate things; the beast we found to be lacking in reason; there remained nothing superior but man. This makes it certain for us that he is undoubtedly the ultimate object of Creation. We searched the Scriptures and found therein the divine proclamation, "I, even I, have made the earth, and created man upon it" (Isa. 45:12). Moreover, the opening chapter of the Torah first goes through all categories of creatures and at the end of them says, "Let us make man" (Gen. 1:26), just like an architect who builds a palace, furnishes it, puts everything in order, and then invites the owner to occupy it.

After these preliminary remarks I come to my subject proper.

Our Lord has informed us through His prophets that He endowed man with superiority over all His creatures. Thus He said, "And have dominion over the fish of the sea, and over the fowl of the air. . . ." (Gen. 1:38). This is also the theme of Psalm 8 from beginning to end. God further informed us that He gave man the ability to obey Him, placing it as it were in his hands, endowed him with power and free will, and commanded him to choose that which is good, as is said, "See, I have set before thee this day life and good . . .", and concludes, "Therefore choose life" (Deut. 3:15, 19).

Afterwards we studied well the question wherein man's superiority consisted, and we found that he was raised to superiority by virtue of the wisdom which God bestowed upon and taught him, as is said, "Even He that teacheth man knowledge" (Ps. 94:10). By virtue of it man preserves the memory of deeds that happened long ago, and by virtue of it he foresees many of the things that will occur in the future. By virtue of it he is able to subdue the animals so that they may till the earth for him and bring in its produce. By virtue of it he is able to draw the water from the depth of the earth to its surface; he even invents irrigating wheels that draw the water automatically. By virtue of it he is able to build lofty mansions, to make magnificent garments, and to prepare delicate dishes. By virtue of it he is able to organize armies and camps, and to exercise kingship and authority for establishing order and civilization among men. By virtue of it he is able to study the nature of the celestial spheres, the course of the planets, their dimensions, their distances from one another, as well as other matters relating to them.

If one imagines that the highest degree of excellence is given to some being other than man, let him show us such excellence or a similar one in any other being. He will not find it. It is therefore right and proper that man should have received commandments and prohibitions, and that he should be rewarded and punished, for he is the axis of the world and its foundation, as is said, "For the pillars of the earth are the Lord's . . ." (I Sam. 2:8), and furthermore, "The righteous is the foundation of the world" (Prov. 10:25).

When I reflected on these fundamental facts and what follows from them, I became convinced that our belief in man's superiority is not a mere delusion, nor the result of our inclination to judge in favor of man; nor is it out of vanity and boastfulness that we make such a claim for ourselves, but it is something demonstrably true and perfectly correct. The reason why God in His wisdom endowed man with this excellence can only be to make him the recipient of commandments and prohibitions, as it says, "Behold, the fear of the Lord, that is wisdom; and to depart from evil is understanding" (Job 28:28).

ON CREATION

Moses Maimonides

While Maimonides insisted on the rational character of the revealed laws, he opposed the philosophical (Aristotelian) concept of the eternity of the world in favor of the non-rational, Jewish doctrine of *creatio ex nihilo* (creation from nothing). He took this position, because the Judaic concept of Creation implied purpose, will, and a personal, free, God (His freedom expressing itself in His ability to do miracles), while the Aristotelian view suggested necessity, and an impersonal, mechanical law. In such a universe there was no room for freedom of will, for man choosing between good and evil. In respect to these concepts the rationalist Maimonides put himself in a scientifically weaker position in order to safeguard a definition of man fundamental in Judaism. On the other hand, he followed an anti-traditional trend by making immortality of the soul dependent on intellectual attainments.

The excerpt below is from *Moreh Nebukhim* (The Guide to the Perplexed). See preface to "Knowledge of God."

We do not reject the eternity of the universe, because certain passages in the Torah confirm the Creation; for such passages that indicate that the universe is created are no more numerous than those in which God is represented a corporeal being. The method of allegorical interpretation is no less possible or permissible in the matter of the universe being created than in any other. We might have explained them allegorically in the same manner as we did when we denied corporeality. We should perhaps have had an easier task in showing that those passages referred to are in harmony with the theory of the eternity of the universe if we accepted the latter, than we had in explaining the anthropomorphisms in the Bible when we rejected the idea that God is corporeal.

For two reasons, however, we have not done so, and have not accepted the eternity of the universe. First, the incorporeality

of God has been demonstrated by proof; those passages in the
Bible, which in their literal sense contain statements that can be
refuted by proof, must and can be allegorically interpreted. But
the eternity of the universe has not been conclusively proved. A
mere argument in favor of a certain theory is not sufficient reason
for rejecting the literal meaning of a Biblical text, and explaining it allegorically, when the opposite theory can be supported
by an equally good argument.

Secondly, our belief in the incorporeality of God is not contrary to any of the fundamental principles of our Torah; it is
not contrary to the words of any prophet. Only ignorant people
believe that it is contrary to the teaching of Scripture. We have
shown that this is not the case; on the contrary, this is the real
intention of the text. If, on the other hand, we were to accept
the eternity of the universe as taught by Aristotle, that everything in the universe exists by necessity, that nature does not
change, and that nothing deviates from its fixed behavior, we
should necessarily be in opposition to the foundation of our
religion, we should disbelieve automatically every miracle, and
certainly reject all hopes and fears derived from Scripture, unless
the miracles are also explained allegorically. The Allegorists
amongst the Moslems have done this, and have thereby arrived
at absurd conclusions.

If, however, we accepted the eternity of the universe and
assumed, with Plato, that the heavens are likewise transitory, we
should not be in opposition to the fundamental principles of
our Torah; this theory would not imply the rejection of miracles,
which, on the contrary, would be possible. The Scriptural text
might have been interpreted accordingly, and many expressions
might have been found in the Torah and in other writings that
would confirm and support this theory. But there is no necessity
for this expedient, unless that theory were proved. As there is no
proof sufficient to convince us, this theory need not be taken into
consideration [. . .]

Accepting Creation, all miracles become possible, the Torah
itself becomes possible, and any difficulty in this question is removed. We might be asked, Why has God inspired a certain person and not another? Why has He revealed the Torah to one

particular nation, and at one particular time? Why has He commanded this, and forbidden that? Why has He shown through a prophet certain particular miracles? What is the object of these laws, and why has He not made the commandments and the prohibitions part of our nature, if it was His object that we should live in accordance with them?

We answer to all these questions: He willed it so; or, His wisdom decreed it. Just as He created the world according to His will, at a certain time, in a certain form, and as we do not understand why His will or His wisdom decided upon these peculiar forms or that time, so we do not know why His will or wisdom determined any of the things mentioned in the preceding questions. But if we assume that the universe has the present form as the result of fixed laws, there is occasion for the above questions; and these could only be answered in a reprehensible way, implying denial and rejection of the Biblical texts, concerning which no intelligent person can doubt that they are to be taken in their literal sense.

Owing to the absence of all proof, we reject the theory of the eternity of the universe. It is for this very reason that people of worth have spent and will spend their days in speculating on this problem. For if Creation had been demonstrated by proof, even if only according to the Platonic hypothesis, all arguments of the philosophers against us would be of no avail. If, on the other hand, Aristotle had a proof for his theory, the whole teaching of the Torah would be rejected, and other manners of thinking would take its place. I have thus shown that all depends on this one point. Note it.

ON FREE WILL

Moses Maimonides

Biblical laws and the call to "choose life" (Deut. 30:19) tacitly presuppose man's free will; the prophets postulate man's moral responsibility, implying his freedom. The Talmud is more explicit: "Everything is in the hand of Heaven, except the fear of Heaven" (Berakhot

33b), which is the realm of human decision and action. Determinism is rejected; divine omniscience is assumed, but no attempt is made to resolve the contradiction between freedom of will and divine foreknowledge. This became a central issue in medieval Jewish religiophilosophical thought. Saadia Gaon maintained God's full and free knowledge of all events, including those in the future, but denied that this knowledge is the cause of human action; in order to be able to exercise his responsibility toward the laws, man must be considered free. Consequently, Saadia rejected the Islamic doctrine of predestination. He included freedom of will among the three central teachings of Judaism (the others being God and immortality). The Averroist Gersonides (thirteenth–fourteenth century), who accepted natural causality as the principle regulating the affairs of the world, had no difficulty separating divine knowledge from the realm of human action. On the other hand, Hasdai Crescas (fourteenth–fifteenth century), opponent of extreme rationalism, moved in the direction of determinism. Within this centuries-long thought process, and within the given limits, Maimonides' position is possibly the soundest. His statement on the issue, reprinted below, is from his *Mishneh Torah*.

Free will is bestowed on every human being. If he desires to turn towards the good path and be just, he has the power to do so. If he wishes to turn towards the evil path and be wicked, he is at liberty to do so. And thus is it written in the Torah, "Behold, the man is become as one of us, to know good and evil" (Gen. 3:22)—which means that the human species stands alone in the world—there being no other kind like him as regards this subject of being able of his own accord, by his reason and thought to know what is good and what is evil, with none to prevent him from either doing good or evil. And since this is so [there is reason to fear] "lest he put forth his hand etc." (*ibid*.).

Let not the notion, expressed by the foolish among other peoples and most of the senseless folk among Israelites, pass through your mind that at the beginning of a person's existence, the Holy One, blessed be he, decrees that he is to be just or wicked. This is not so. Every human being may become righteous like Moses, our teacher, or wicked like Jeroboam; wise or foolish, merciful or cruel; niggardly or generous; and so with all other qualities. There is no one that coerces him or decrees what he is to do, or draws him to either of the two ways; but every person turns to the way which he desires, with the consent of his mind and of his own volition. Thus Jeremiah said, "Out of the mouth of the Most High, proceedeth not evil and good" (Lam. 3:38); that is to say, the Creator does not decree either that a man shall be good or wicked.

Accordingly it follows that it is the sinner who has inflicted harm on himself. He should, therefore, weep for, and bewail what he has done to his soul—how he has mistreated it. This is expressed in the next verse, "Wherefore doth a living man complain, or a strong man? Because of his sins" (Lam. 3:39). The prophet continues: Since liberty of action is in our hands and we have, of our free will, committed all these evils, it behoves us to return in a spirit of repentance: "Let us search and try our ways, and return to the Lord" (Lam. 3:40).

This doctrine is an important principle, the pillar of the Torah and the commandment, as it is said, "See, I set before thee this day life and good, and death and evil" (Deut. 30:15); and again it is written, "Behold, I set before you this day, a blessing and a curse" (Deut. 11:26). This means that the power is in your hands, and whatever a man desires to do among the things that human beings do, he can do, whether they are good or evil; and, because of this faculty, it is said, "O that they had such a heart as this always" (Deut. 5:26), which implies that the Creator neither forces the children of men nor decrees that they should do either good, or evil, but it is all in their own keeping.

If God had decreed that a person should be either just or wicked, or if there were some force inherent in his nature which irresistibly drew him to a particular course, or to any branch of knowledge, as to a given view or activity, as the foolish astrologers, out of their own fancy, pretend, how would He have charged us through the prophets: "Do this and do not do that, improve your ways, do not follow your wicked impulses," when, from the beginning of his existence, his destiny has already been decreed, or his innate constitution drew him to that from which he could not set himself free? What room would there be for the whole of the Torah? By what right or justice could God punish the wicked or reward the just? "Shall not the Judge of all the earth act justly?" (Gen. 18:25).

Do not, however, wonder: How can a man do whatever he

desires, and act according to his discretion? Can aught in the world be done without the Master's will and pleasure? The Scripture itself says, "Whatsoever the Lord pleased, that hath He done in heaven and on earth" (Ps. 135:6). Know then that everything takes place according to His will, notwithstanding that our acts are in our power. How so? Just as it was the will of the Creator that fire and air shall ascend, earth and water descend, and that the sphere shall revolve in a circle, and all other things in the universe shall exist in their respective ways which He desired, so it was His will that man should have freedom of will, and all his acts should be left to his discretion; that nothing should force him or draw him to aught, but that, of himself and by the exercise of his own mind which God had given him, he should do whatever it is in a man's power to do. Hence, he is judged according to his deeds. If he does well, good is done to him; and if he does ill, evil is done to him.

Perchance you will say, "Does not the Holy One, blessed be he, know everything that will be before it happens?" He either knows that a certain person will be just or wicked, or He does not know. If he knows that he will be just, it is impossible that he should not be just; and if you say that He knows that he will be just and yet it is possible for him to be wicked, then He does not know the matter clearly. As to the solution of this problem, understand that "the measure thereof is longer than the earth and wider than the sea" (Job 11:9), and many important principles of the highest sublimity are connected with it. It is essential that you know what I am about to say.

We have already explained[1] that God does not know with a knowledge which exists outside of Himself, like human beings whose knowledge and self are separate entities, but He, blessed be His Name, and His knowledge are one. This, the human intellect cannot clearly apprehend. And just as it is not in human power to apprehend or discover the truth of the Creator, as it is said, "For there shall no man see Me and live" (Exod. 33:20), so it is not in human power to apprehend or discover the Creator's knowledge. We lack the capacity to know in what manner God knows all creatures and their actions. Yet we do know beyond doubt that a human being's actions are in his own hands and the Holy One neither draws him on, nor decrees that he should act thus or not act thus. It is not religious tradition alone by which this is known, but even by evidence of the words of wisdom. Hence, it is said in the prophetic writings that a man will be judged for all his deeds, according to his deeds, whether they be good or evil. And this is the principle on which all the words of prophecy depend.

THE CREATION OF MAN

Moses Nahmanides

In the chapter "Has the Messiah Come?" we shall meet Moses ben Nahman (Nahmanides, Ramban) as the Jewish spokesman at the Debate at Barcelona in 1263. The religious philosopher, talmudist, mystic, physician, is best known for his Commentary to the Pentateuch, which he wrote in his old age and which he completed in Palestine. Nahmanides believed that "in the Torah are hidden every wonder and every mystery, and in her treasures is sealed every beauty of wisdom," as he says in the Introduction; that, mystically, the entire text of the Torah is but a series of the unknown names of God; and on another level of reading, the Biblical stories are prefigurations of the later history of man. No wonder that he was opposed to the rationalist Biblical commentary of Abraham ibn Ezra and viewed with suspicion certain "unorthodox" opinions of Maimonides, whom he otherwise revered. Nahmanides, in turn, was criticized for having made mysticism accessible to the masses. The Commentary, first published in Lisbon in 1489, was later included in the editions of the Hebrew Bible and its classical expositions.

"And God said, Let us make man" (Gen. 1:26). The reason for this signal honor is that there was nothing comparable in the preceding creations to his being. The true interpretation of the word *na'aseh* ("Let us make") is that God created *ex nihilo* [out of nothing] only on the first day. From then on He used the elements [which He had created on the first day]. In the same way as He gave the waters the power to swarm with living creatures and brought forth beasts from the earth, He now said, "Let us . . . ," that is, I and the earth, make man. Out of the earth

shall come forth the material elements to make up the body of
man, just as is the case with animal and the wild beast, and I,
the Lord will give him spirit from above . . . Thus man is like
the lower creatures [in his physical structure], and like the higher
beings in appearance and beauty, which is evidenced by his urge
for wisdom, knowledge, and the doing of good deeds.

The eminence of the human soul, its distinction and superiority, lie in the fact, as the Torah informs us, that it was God
who "blew the soul of life into the nostrils" of man (Gen. 2:7).
This teaches us that man's soul does not originate in the material
elements of his body, as is the case with all lower living creatures,
nor is it even a substance evolved from the Separate Intelligences;
instead, it is of the essence of the Holy One, since he who blows
into the nostrils of another bestows upon him the breath of his
own soul. Man's powers of learning and understanding come thus
directly from Him.

Prior to his sin man performed his duties by inherent disposition; he was like the heavens and their hosts who [in the
words of the sages] "are creatures of truth, whose achievement
is truth, and who do not deviate from the path set for them."
Love and hatred do not enter into the performance of their functions. It was the eating of the fruit of the Tree of Knowledge
that brought desire and will into the heart of man. From then on
he began choosing between one mode of action and another in
accordance with his disposition for good or bad. [. . .] For
this reason prior to the sin all parts of the human body were to
Adam and Eve as the face and hands; they entertained no
thoughts of shame concerning any part of the body. But after
they ate of the tree they acquired the power to choose between
good and evil. The power is indeed divine; but as far as man is
concerned it also contains a potential of evil, since his deeds became dependent upon his desires and passions.

Consider it in your heart that the Holy One, blessed be he,
has created all lower creatures for the benefit and use of man,
since we know of no purpose for the creation of all objects who

have no recognition of the Creator, except this—that they serve man. Now man has been created for the prime purpose that he recognize his Creator. Should he fail to know his Creator altogether, and what is even worse, should he fail to gain a realization of the fact that certain deeds are pleasing to God and others are displeasing, then man becomes as the unknowing beast. If man shows no desire to acquire a knowledge of God, and the realization that there is a difference between good and bad, the whole purpose of the world is lost.

The intent of all the commandments is that we acquire a firm belief in God, and proclaim Him as the One who has created us all. This is, in fact, the very purpose of Creation. The Supreme Being desires of man only that he know Him and acknowledge that He is the Creator. The prayers we recite, the synagogues we build, the holy convocations we hold, are all designed to give us an opportunity to gather and give outward expression to our inner conviction that He is our Creator and that we are His creatures.

Argument for

THE IMMORTAL SOUL

Leone Modena

Kol Sakhal (The Voice of the Fool), a seventeenth-century book of uncertain authorship (Isaiah Sonne attributed it to the heretic Uriel da Costa), is primarily an attack on the authority of the Oral Law in Judaism. The author's position was refuted by Leone Modena (1571–1648), rabbi in Venice, a late Renaissance figure, in his *Shaagat Arye* (The Lion's Roar). Attack and refutation were published in 1852 by Isaac S. Reggio, who believed Leone Modena, the skeptic rabbi, to be the author of both. The section from which the excerpt that follows is taken precedes the polemic part and outlines the writer's personal beliefs.

Just as, from the point of view of sense perception, we have no reason to believe that man's soul was in existence before he

himself came into being, so we would be inclined to say that
with his death, his soul, too, must perish. No man has ever returned after his death and given us any compelling testimony to
his soul's immortality. He, therefore, who would not deceive himself must admit that no decisive proof of man's spiritual immortality has ever been furnished by either a Jewish or a Gentile
thinker. On the contrary, since the burden of proof is upon him
who would maintain a given belief, rather than on him who
denies it, it might almost be said that those who deny the belief
in immortality have positive proof of the soul's disintegration.

It is not my task here to enumerate the arguments on either
side. I merely wish to state my own conclusions, arrived at after
a careful consideration of all these arguments.

Most frightening for every Jew is the fact that, when we
read through the whole Pentateuch from the beginning of Genesis to the end of Deuteronomy, we fail to find in all the words
of Moses a single indication pointing to man's spiritual immortality after his physical death, or the existence of any world
beside this one. Even though Moses [. . .] on several occasions
speaks about how the observance of the commandments would
be duly rewarded, he contents himself with promising the people
physical rewards and success in this life—children, honor, and
wealth.

Not when he spoke, before the revelation of the Torah,
about God's promises to the patriarchs and saints, nor at the time
that the Torah was revealed through him, nor even after then,
did Moses say a single word to the effect that God has promised:
If you will walk in My statutes, then your soul will enjoy everlasting bliss after death. Moses speaks instead of seasonal rain,
bread, natural increase, life secure in the land, the defeat of enemies, and the like. Even in the Prophets and in the Writings
there are only vague hints concerning immortality; and all such
supposed hints might just as well be interpreted as having reference to physical life.

Nevertheless, when we contemplate our present existence,
reason inclines us (if it does not altogether compel us) to believe
that the soul continues on after our physical death. There is,
first, some sense of this in the fact that nature, doing nothing in

vain, has implanted in the human mind a desire for eternal life that is not realized in the life of the body. Then there is the evidence from the increase of our mental powers at the very time when old age brings with it a weakening of the body; if the connection between body and mind were absolute rather than incidental, we should expect the opposite to be true: the mind becoming weaker in proportion to the body's enfeeblement.

But what I consider to be the decisive proof is derived from our basic assumption that man is *sui generis,* neither like the angels nor like the beasts, and that he has been created for the purpose of giving God pleasure by his wide range of intelligent actions. How, then, can we say that ultimately man has no advantage over the beasts, and that the same fate, the same death, will befall him as them? How can we say that the creature who, by dint of his intellect, builds cities and moves mountains, changes the course of rivers, knows the paths of the high heavens, and can recognize his God—that this creature should come in the end to perish entirely like a horse, or a dog, or a fly?

Moreover, if this were so, then man's consciousness would be a sorry drawback. Animals are not troubled by anything about life or death other than by those things which they actually experience at a given moment. Man's consciousness, on the other hand, increases his pain by anticipating troubles yet to come, and dwelling on those already present. This is far more painful than the actual trouble: as it has rightly been said, the trouble of death is the thought of it before it comes.

Rather should it be said that the Creator Who, having joined man's soul to his body, takes pleasure in, or abhors, man's deeds, and bestows His rewards or punishments accordingly—that this Creator has made it possible for a man at his death to have his soul separated from his body, so that the soul may remain to receive the pleasure or the pain of which, in his lifetime, the man was judged deserving, in accordance with his deeds.

THE MAN AND HIS SOUL

A Midrash

The Talmud and the Midrash record popular tales about the Angel of Night and Conception, who brings the semen before God, who determines the future fate of the new being yet grants him freedom of will, and about the unborn being's journey through Paradise and Hell and all the places it is to inhabit on earth. An anonymous early medieval compiler gathered such material (some of which show Platonic and Stoic influence) and composed this dramatic story of the soul: *Midrash Yetzirat ha-Velad* (The Midrash of the Creation of the Child).

In what manner does the conformation of the child happen? In the hour when a man approaches his wife, the Holy One, blessed be he, calls out to His messenger, the one who is guardian over pregnancy, and says to him: "Know that this man tonight shall beget a child; go now and watch over the seed."

The messenger then does as he is bid. He takes the seed, brings it before the Holy One, blessed be he, and speaks to Him thus: "Lord of the universe, I have done as you told me, but what is to become of this seed? Make what disposition you choose."

Then the Holy One, blessed be he, determines at once whether it shall be strong or weak, tall or short, male or female, foolish or wise, rich or poor. But whether it is to be just or wicked He does not determine, for as we say: "Heaven ordains all, save the fear of heaven." [2]

At once the Holy One, blessed be he, beckons His messenger, him who holds sway over souls, and says to him: "Deliver that soul before me. For in this manner have all creatures been formed since the beginning and so shall it be unto the end."

At once the soul comes before the Holy One, blessed be he, and bows down before Him. At this hour He speaks to it thus: "Enter into that seed." On the instant the soul opens its mouth and declares: "Lord of the universe, the world in which I have resided from the day You made me is sufficient unto me;

give me leave, if this be Your pleasure, to remain without and not enter into that mortal seed, for I am holy and pure."

And the Holy One, blessed be he, speaks to the soul: "The world into which I would have you enter is better than the world in which you find yourself now. It was for this seed that you were meant on the day I made you."

At once He bids the soul enter that seed, though against its will. And the messenger returns and bids the soul enter into the womb of the mother. Then he summons thither two messengers to watch over the creature lest it fall. And over its head a light is kindled, as the Scripture has it: "When His candle shone upon my head" (Job 29:3), and it looks about and beholds the world from beginning to end.

And on the morrow the messenger takes this creature and leads it into the Garden of Eden and shows it the just, those who are dwelling in glory, and says to the creature: "Do you know whence this soul came?" And the creature makes answer and says: "No." Then the messenger speaks to the creature thus: "Him whom you behold in such glory and so exalted was formed like you in his mother's womb; and so was this one, and this one; and they all obeyed the laws and ordinances of the Holy One, blessed be he. If you do as they have done, after death—for they too have died—you will be exalted in glory, as they are. However, if you do not, your destiny will be to dwell in a place which I shall show you presently."

And in the evening he takes the creature to the place of the damned and shows it the sinners, those whom the minions of hell confound and strike with fiery rods until they cry: Woe is us!—but no one takes pity on them. And once more the messenger speaks to the creature: "My son, do you know who these are that the flames burn?" And the creature answers: "No." Whereupon the messenger says: "Know that these too were formed from mortal seed in the wombs of their mothers, but they failed to obey and bear witness to the Holy One, blessed be he; it is for this that they suffer so. Know, my child, that you are destined to leave your abode and die. Therefore, do not choose the path of the sinner but the path of the just: and thus you shall live eternally."

And he journeys with the creature from morning until night and shows it all the places where it will tread, and the place in which it will dwell, and the place in which it will be buried at last. And after this he shows it the world of the good and the ill.

Toward evening he returns the creature to the womb of its mother. But the Holy One, blessed be he, shuts it up with doors and bars, as it is written: "Or who shut up the sea with doors, when it brake forth, as it had issued out of the womb?" (Job 38:8) and it is written: "And I have put My words in thy mouth, and I have covered thee in the shadow of Mine hand" (Isa. 51:16). So the child lies in its mother's womb for nine months; for the first three months it dwells in the lower part, for the second three months in the middle part, for the last three months in the upper part. It partakes of all that its mother eats and drinks; its waste, however, it does not pass, for else its mother would die.

When the time has come for the creature to issue from the womb, that selfsame messenger visits it and says: "Come forth, for it is time now to enter the world." But the creature replies: "Did I not say once before to Him who spoke to me, Lord of the universe, that the world in which I have dwelt all this time is sufficient unto me?" The messenger replies: "The world which I would have you enter is more beautiful than that other one;" and he adds: "Perforce you were fashioned in the womb of your mother; perforce you are born and step forth into the world." The creature cries as it hears these words. And why does it cry? Because it must leave the world it has dwelt in. The moment it issues forth the messenger strikes it under the nose, and extinguishes the light that shone over its head and bids it step forth, unwilling; and the creature forgets all it has ever seen. And as it steps forth it cries. Why? Because at that hour seven worlds are led past it.

The first world resembles that of a king: every one inquires into the. child's pleasure; everyone desires to see and to kiss it, for this is the first year of his life.

The second world resembles that of a pig that is always completely surrounded by filth—and so is the child in his second year.

The third world resembles that of a kid gamboling in the pasture: so does the child frolic until his fifth year.

The fourth world resembles that of a horse proudly prancing along the road: so does the child bear himself proudly, flaunting his youth, until he has reached his eighteenth year.

The fifth world resembles that of a donkey on whose shoulders a pack-saddle is laid: in like manner burdens are placed upon him; he is given a wife, he begets sons and daughters, and has to provide for his children and servants.

The sixth world resembles that of a dog that must provide for itself: it snatches its food where it can, snatches from this one and pilfers from that one, and is not ashamed.

The seventh world resembles that of a scarecrow: for now he is utterly changed, even his servants curse him and wish him dead, and his children mock him to his face.

At last the time has come for his death. The messenger of the Lord appears before him and says: "Do you recognize me?" And he replies: "Yes." Then he adds: "What brings you to me today?" And the messenger says: "I have come to take you away from this world."

Then he cries, his voice resounding from one end of the world to the other, but not a creature can hear him. And he says to the messenger: "Did you not lead me out of two worlds and set me down in this world in which I dwell now?"

And the messenger says to him: "Have I not told you long since that perforce you were fashioned and born, and so you are destined to die, and at last will give account and reckoning before the King over kings of kings, the Holy One, blessed be he?"

THE BRIDGE OF TIME

Yedayah ha-Bedersi

In his *Behinat Olam* (The Examination of the World), of which a quotation appears below, Yedayah ha-Bedersi, thirteenth-fourteenth-century Provencal poet, physician, and philosopher, meditates about both the lofty state and the predicaments of the sage, about the transitoriness of worldly goods and the permanence of wisdom and goodness, and the triumph of truth. First published in Mantua, between 1476 and 1480, the work was republished about seventy times, and translated into Latin (1650), French (1629), and other languages.

The world is a tempestuous sea of immense depth and breadth, and time is a frail bridge constructed over it, the beginning of which is fastened with the cords of chaos that preceded existence, while the end thereof is to behold eternal bliss, and to be enlightened with the light of the King's countenance. The width of the bridge is a cubit and it lacks borders. And thou, son of man, against thy will art thou living, and art continually travelling over it, since the day thou hast become a man.

HEALING

Jacob ben Asher

It is an ancient Judaic view that the physician's art is not an act of interference with the divine will but a legitimate exercise of human knowledge and skill, even a duty. Among the formulations of this concept is the one quoted below, taken from *Arbaa Turim*, authoritative code of Jewish law compiled by Jacob ben Asher (1269–1343) of Germany and Spain. *Arbaa Turim* became the basis for the extensive work of Halakhah, *Bet Yosef*, and the definitive code, *Shulhan Arukh*, both by Joseph Caro (Safed, sixteenth century).

The school of Rabbi Ishmael derived from Exod. 21:19 ("and the offender shall cause the victim to be thoroughly healed,") that permission is granted the physician to heal. The physician may not say "Why borrow trouble? I may err and appear like one who killed a person unwittingly." He shall indeed be exceedingly careful in exercising his art even as a judge must be careful in deciding criminal cases. In like manner, the physician may not say: "God smites, and shall I heal?" This is not the way of men with regard to healing, as we find King Asa in his sickness consulting not God, but physicians (II Chron. 16:12). Hence Scripture came to teach us that the physician is permitted to heal. Indeed, healing is a duty; it is saving life. He who is zealous in the work of healing is praiseworthy; and he who refuses to heal is a shedder of blood.

THE END OF MAN

Prayer Book

The Jewish attitude to life is reflected in the attitude to death. Both come from God, and, therefore, both are affirmed as good. As life is lived in the consciousness of the Divine Presence, so the Jew hopes to die in full consciousness of the divine. He prays in life to express his communion with God, and so he prays when death approaches and dies with the affirmation of God on his lips. His body is returned to dust, but death and destruction are transcended in the glorification of God and the vision of a perfect world. The content of the *Kaddish* is this glorification and this vision rather than an expression of mourning. Even the phrase, "words of solace," does not refer to the mourners, but to Zion. But the reference to the quickening of the dead and to life eternal caused the *Kaddish*, originally intended as a closing prayer at study sessions, to be transferred to the burial liturgy. The liturgy that is here reprinted is taken from the traditional prayer book of the Ashkenazic ritual; there are, of course, other customs and variant liturgies.

Prayer to be said by a sick person

A prayer of the afflicted when he fainteth and poureth out his complaint before the Lord. Hear my prayer, O Lord, and let my cry come unto Thee. Hide not Thy face from me in the day of my distress: incline Thine ear unto me; in the day when I call answer me speedily.

O Lord, healer of all flesh, have mercy upon me, and support me in Thy grace upon my bed of sickness, for I am weak. Send me and all who are sick among Thy children relief and cure. Assuage my pain, and renew my youth as the eagle's. Vouchsafe wisdom unto the physician that he may cure my wound, so that my health may spring forth speedily.

Hear my prayer, prolong my life, let me complete my years in happiness, that I may be enabled to serve Thee and keep Thy commandments with a perfect heart. Give me understanding to know that this bitter trial hath come upon me for my welfare, so that I may not despise Thy chastening nor weary of thy reproof.

O God of forgiveness, who art gracious and merciful, slow to anger and abounding in loving-kindness, I confess unto Thee with a broken and contrite heart that I have sinned, and have done that which is evil in Thy sight. Behold, I repent me of my evil way, and return unto Thee with perfect repentance.

Help me, O God of my salvation, that I may not again turn unto folly, but walk before Thee in truth and uprightness. Rejoice the soul of Thy servant, for unto Thee, O Lord, do I lift up my soul. Heal me, O Lord, and I shall be healed, save me, and I shall be saved, for Thou art my praise. Amen.

Prayer on a death bed

I acknowledge unto Thee, O Lord my God and God of my fathers, that both my cure and my death are in Thy hands. May it be Thy will to send me a perfect healing. Yet if my death be fully determined by Thee, I will in love accept it at Thy hand.

May my death be an atonement for the sins, iniquities and transgressions of which I have been guilty against Thee. Vouchsafe unto me of the abounding happiness that is treasured up for the righteous. Make known to me the path of life; in Thy presence is fullness of joy; at Thy right hand are pleasures for evermore.

Thou who art the father of the fatherless and judge of the widow, protect my beloved kindred with whose soul my own is knit. Into Thy hand I commend my spirit; Thou hast redeemed me, O Lord God of truth. Amen.

When the end is approaching:

The Lord reigneth; the Lord hath reigned; the Lord shall reign for ever and ever.

Blessed be His name, whose glorious kingdom is for ever and ever.

The Lord he is God.

Hear, O Israel: the Lord our God, the Lord is one.

The Burial Service

The Rock, His work is perfect, for all His ways are judgment: a God of faithfulness and without iniquity, just and right is He. The Rock, perfect in every work, who can say unto Him, What workest Thou? He ruleth below and above; He killeth and maketh alive: He bringeth down to the grave, and bringeth up again. The Rock, perfect in every deed, who can say unto Him, What doest Thou? O Thou who speakest and doest, of Thy grace deal kindly with us, and for the sake of him who was bound like a lamb [Isaac], O hearken and do. Just in all Thy ways art Thou, O perfect Rock, slow to anger and full of compassion.

Spare and have pity upon parents and children, for Thine, Lord, is forgiveness and compassion. Just art Thou, O Lord, in causing death and in making alive, in whose hand is the charge of all spirits; far be it from Thee to blot out our remembrance: O let Thine eyes mercifully regard us, for Thine, O Lord, is compassion and forgiveness. If a man live a year or a thousand years, what profiteth it him? He shall be as though he had not been.

Blessed be the true Judge, who causes death and maketh alive. Blessed be he, for His judgment is true, and His eye discerneth all things, and He awardeth unto man his reckoning and his sentence, and all must render acknowledgment unto Him. We know, O Lord, that Thy judgment is righteous: Thou art justified when Thou speakest, and pure when Thou judgest, and it is not for us to murmur at Thy method of judging; just art Thou, O Lord, and righteous are Thy judgments.

O true and righteous Judge! Blessed be the true Judge, all whose judgments are righteous and true. The soul of every living thing is in Thy hand; Thy right hand is full of righteousness. Have mercy upon the remnant of the flock of Thy hand, and say unto the angel, Stay thy hand. Thou art great in counsel and mighty in deed; Thine eyes are open upon all the ways of the children of men, to give unto every one according to his ways, and according to the fruit of his doings. To declare that the Lord is upright; He is my Rock, and there is no unrighteousness in Him.

The Lord gave, and the Lord hath taken away; blessed be the name of the Lord. And He, being merciful, forgiveth iniquity and destroyeth not: yea, many a time He turneth his anger away, and doth not stir up all his wrath.

(Psalm 16 is read).

The coffin is borne to the burial ground. Those who have not visited the burial ground for thirty days, say the following:
Blessed be the Lord our God, King of the universe, who formed you in judgment, who nourished and sustained you in judgment, who brought death on you in judgment, who knoweth the number of you all in judgment, and will hereafter restore you to life in judgment. Blessed art Thou, O Lord, who quickenest the dead.

Thou, O Lord, art mighty for ever, Thou quickenest the dead, Thou art mighty to save.

Thou sustainest the living with loving-kindness, quickenest the dead with great mercy, supportest the falling, healest the sick, loosest the bound, and keepest Thy faith to them that sleep in the dust. Who is like unto Thee, Lord of mighty acts, and who resembleth Thee, O King, who killest and quickenest, and causest salvation to spring forth?

Yea, faithful art Thou to quicken the dead.

When the coffin is lowered into the grave, the following is said:
May he come to his place in peace.
Or, may she come to her place in peace.

On quitting the burial ground it is customary to pluck some grass, and to say one of the following sentences:
And they of the city shall flourish like the grass of the earth.
He remembereth that we are dust.

All those who have been present at the burial wash their hands, and say:

He will destroy death for ever; and the Lord God will wipe away tears from off all faces; and the rebuke of His people shall He take away from off all the earth: for the Lord hath spoken it (Isa. 25:8).

They then return from the burial ground and recite Psalm 91. Children after the burial of a parent recite the Kaddish.

The Kaddish

Exalted and sanctified be His great name
in the world that is to be created anew
where He will quicken the dead, and raise them up unto life eternal;
will rebuild the city of Jerusalem and establish His temple in the midst thereof;
and will uproot worship of idols from the earth and restore the worship of God.
O may the Holy One, blessed be he, reign in his sovereignty and glory
in the days of your lifetime
and in the life of the whole house of Israel
speedily and soon,
Let us say, Amen.
May His great name be blessed for ever and to all eternity.
Blessed and praised, honored, adored and extolled, glorified and lauded supremely,
be the name of the Holy One, blessed be he.
He is high above all blessings and hymns, praises and words of solace
that may be uttered throughout the world.
Let us say, Amen.
May there be abundant peace from heaven,
and life for us and for all Israel.
Let us say, Amen.
May he who maketh peace in His hights
bring peace to us and to all Israel.
Let us say, Amen.

Prayer in the House of Mourning, after the ordinary Daily Service and the reading of Psalm 49:

O Lord and King, who art full of compassion, in whose hand is the soul of every living thing and the breath of all flesh who causest death and makest alive, who bringest down to the grave and bringest up again, receive, we beseech Thee, in Thy great loving-kindness the soul of ——— who hath been gathered unto his [her] people. Have mercy upon him [her]; pardon all his [her] transgressions, for there is not a just man upon earth, who doeth good and sinneth not. Remember unto him [her] the righteousness which he [she] wrought, and let his [her] reward be with him [her], and his [her] recompense before him [her].

O shelter his [her] soul in the shadow of Thy wings. Make known to him [her] the path of life: in Thy presence is fulness of joy; at Thy right hand are pleasures for evermore. Vouchsafe unto him [her] of the abounding happiness that is treasured up for the righteous, as it is written, "Oh how great is Thy goodness, which Thou hast laid up for them that fear Thee, which Thou hast wrought for them that trust in Thee in the sight of the sons of men" (Psalm 31:20).

O Lord, who healest the broken-hearted and bindest up their wounds, grant Thy consolation unto the mourners: put into their hearts the fear and love of Thee, that they may serve Thee with a perfect heart, and let their latter end be peace. Amen.

"As one whom his mother comforteth, so will I comfort you, and in Jerusalem shall ye be comforted. Thy sun shall no more go down, neither shall thy moon withdraw itself; for the Lord shall be thine everlasting light, and the days of thy mourning shall be ended" (Isa. 66:13, 60:20).

He will destroy death for ever; and the Lord God will wipe away tears from off all faces; and the rebuke of His people shall He take away from off all the earth: for the Lord hath spoken it (Isa. 25:8).

V. Knowledge

THE STUDY OF TORAH

Moses Maimonides

In the following passages, quoted from the *Mishneh Torah*, Maimonides summarizes the attitude of classical Judaism to learning, its emphasis on the centrality of the knowledge of Torah as the key to religious faith and ethical behavior. His sources are mainly the talmudic writings; his aim, to keep this spirit alive.

When should a father commence his son's instruction in Torah? As soon as the child begins to talk, the father should teach him the text, "Moses commanded us a law" (Deut. 33:4), and [the first verse of] the *Shema* ("Hear O Israel, the Lord our God, the Lord is One," Deut. 6:4). Later on, according to the child's capacity, the father should teach him a few verses at a time, till he be six or seven years old, when he should take him to a teacher of young children.

If it is the custom of the country for a teacher of children to receive remuneration, the father is to pay the fee, and it is his duty to have his son taught, even if he has to pay for the instruction, till the child has gone through the whole of the Written Law [the Scriptures]. Where it is the custom to charge a fee for teaching the Written Law, it is permissible to take payment for such instruction. It is forbidden however to teach the Oral Law [the Tradition] for payment. [. . .] If a person cannot find one willing to teach him without remuneration, he should engage a paid teacher, as it is said, "Buy the truth" (Prov. 23:23). It should not however be assumed that it is permissible to take pay for teaching. For the verse continues, "And sell it not," the inference being, that even where a man had been obliged to pay for instruction [in the Oral Law], he is nevertheless forbidden to charge, in his turn, for teaching it.

Every man in Israel is obliged to study Torah, whether he be poor or rich, in sound health or ailing, in the vigor of youth or very old and of weakened vitality. Even a man so poor that he is maintained by charity or goes begging from door to door, as also a man with a wife and children to support, are obliged to set aside a definite period during the day and at night for the study of the Torah.

Among the great sages of Israel, some were hewers of wood, some, drawers of water, while others were blind. Nevertheless, they devoted themselves by day and by night to the study of the Torah. Moreover, they are included among the transmitters of the tradition in the direct line from Moses our master.

Until what period in life is one obliged to study Torah? Even until the day of one's death, as it is said, "And lest they [the precepts] depart from thy heart all the days of thy life" (Deut. 4:9). Whenever one ceases to study, one forgets.

The time allotted to study should be divided into three parts. A third should be devoted to the Written Law; a third to the Oral Law; and the last third a person should spend thinking and reflecting so that he may understand the end of a thing from its beginning, and deduct one matter from another and compare one matter to another, and reason out by the hermeneutical rules by which the Torah is interpreted till one knows which are the principal rules and how to deduce therefrom what is forbidden and what is permitted and other like matters which he has learnt from oral tradition. This is termed Talmud.

A woman who studies Torah has a reward coming to her, but not in the same measure as a man because she was not commanded to do so [. . .].

With three crowns was Israel crowned: the crown of the Torah, the crown of the priesthood and the crown of kingship. The crown of the priesthood was bestowed upon Aaron, as it is said, "And it shall be unto him and unto his seed after him, the covenant of an everlasting priesthood" (Num. 25:13). The crown of kingship was conferred upon David, as it is said, "His seed shall endure forever, and his throne as the sun before Me" (Ps. 89:37). The crown of the Torah, behold, there it lies ready within the grasp of all Israel, as it is said, "Moses commanded us a Law, an inheritance of the congregation of Jacob" (Deut. 33:4). Whoever desires it can win it. Do not suppose that the other two crowns are greater than the crown of the Torah, for it is said, "By me, kings reign and princes decree justice; by me, princes rule" (Prov. 8:15–16). Hence the inference, that the crown of the Torah is greater than the other two crowns.

The sages said, "A bastard who is a scholar takes precedence of an ignorant High Priest." [1]

Of all precepts, none is equal in importance to the study of the Torah. Nay, study of the Torah is equal to them all, for study leads to practice. Hence, study always takes precedence of practice.

At the judgment hereafter, a man will first be called to account in regard to his fulfillment of the duty of study, and afterwards concerning his other activities. Hence, the sages said, "A person should always occupy himself with the Torah, whether for its own sake or for other reasons. For study of the Torah, even when pursued from interested motives, will lead to study for its own sake." [2]

He whose heart prompts him to fulfill this duty properly, and to be crowned with the crown of the Torah, must not allow his mind to be diverted to other matters. He must not aim at acquiring Torah as well as riches and honor at the same time, "This is the way for the study of the Torah: A morsel of bread with salt thou shalt eat, and water by measure thou shalt drink; thou shalt sleep upon the ground and live a life of hardship, the while thou toilest in the Torah." [3] "It is not incumbent upon thee to complete the task; but neither art thou free to neglect it." [4]

Possibly you may say: When I shall have accumulated money, I shall resume my studies; when I shall have provided for my needs and have leisure from my affairs, I shall resume my studies. Should such a thought enter your mind, you will never win the crown of the Torah. "Rather make the study of the Torah your fixed occupation" [5] and let your secular affairs engage you casually, and do not say: "When I shall have leisure, I shall study; perhaps you may never have leisure." [6]

In the Torah it is written, "It is not in heaven . . . neither is it beyond the sea" (Deut. 30:12–13). "It is not in heaven," this means that the Torah is not to be found with the arrogant; "nor beyond the sea," that is, it is not found among those who cross the ocean.[7] Hence, our sages said, "Not he who engages himself overmuch in business is wise." [8] They have also exhorted us, "Engage little in business and occupy thyself with the Torah." [9]

The words of the Torah have been compared to water, as it is said, "O every one that thirsteth, come ye for water" (Is. 55:1); this teaches us that just as water does not accumulate on a slope but flows away, while in a depression it stays, so the words of the Torah are not to be found in the arrogant or haughty but only in him who is humble and lowly in spirit, who sits in the dust at the feet of the wise and banishes from his heart lusts and temporal delights; works a little daily, just enough to provide for his needs, if he would otherwise have nothing to eat, and devotes the rest of the day and night to the study of the Torah.[10]

One however who makes up his mind to study Torah and not work but live on charity, profanes the name of God, brings the Torah into contempt, extinguishes the light of religion, brings evil upon himself and deprives himself of life in the world to come, for it is forbidden to derive any temporal advantage from the words of the Torah. The sages said, "Whoever derives a profit for himself from the words of the Torah takes his own life away from the world." [11] They have further charged us, "Make not of them a crown wherewith to aggrandize thyself, nor a spade wherewith to dig." [12] They likewise exhorted us, "Love work, hate lordship." [13] "All study of the Torah, not conjoined with work, must, in the end, be futile, and become a cause of sin." [14] The end of such a person will be that he will rob people for his living.

It indicates a high degree of excellence in a man to maintain himself by the labor of his hands. And this was the normal practice of the early pious men [Hasidim]. Thus, one secures all honor and happiness here and in the world to come, as it is said,

"When thou eatest of the labor of thine hands, happy shalt thou be, and it shall be well with thee" (Ps. 128:2). Happy shalt thou be in this world, and it shall be well with these in the world to come, which is altogether good.[15]

The words of the Torah do not abide with one who studies listlessly, nor with those who learn amidst luxury, and high living, but only with one who mortifies himself for the sake of the Torah, enduring physical discomfort, and not permitting sleep to his eyes nor slumber to his eyelids. "This is the Law, when a man dieth in a tent" (Num. 19:14). The sages explained the text metaphorically thus: "The Torah only abides with him who sacrifices his life in the tents of the wise." [16]

While it is a duty to study by day and by night, most of one's knowledge is acquired at night. Accordingly, when one aspires to win the crown of the Torah, he should be especially heedful of all his nights and not waste a single one of them in sleep, eating, drinking, idle talk and so forth, but devote all of them to study of the Torah and words of wisdom. Whoever occupies himself with the study of the Torah at night—a mark of spiritual grace distinguishes him by day, as it is said, 'By day the Lord will command His loving-kindness, and in the night His song shall be with me, even a prayer unto the God of my life' " (Ps. 42:9).[17]

IN PRAISE OF LEARNING, EDUCATION,

AND THE GOOD LIFE

Judah ibn Tibbon

Judah ibn Tibbon is best known for his translations of philosophical and philological works from the Arabic into Hebrew. Born about 1120, Judah was forced to leave his native Granada and he settled in Lunel, Provence, where he practiced medicine. Among the works which his translations made accessible to the Hebrew reader were Saadia Gaon's *Doctrines and Beliefs*, Bahya ibn Pakuda's *Duties of the Heart*, Solomon ibn Gabirol's *Introduction to the Improvement of the Qualities of the Soul*, Judah ha-Levi's *Kuzari*, and grammatical treatises by Jonah ibn Janah. In his Preface to the translation of the *Duties of the Heart*, he discussed the problem of literalness versus readability, the crux of translators to this day. He died in 1190.

His son, Samuel ibn Tibbon (ca. 1150–1230), to whom the admonitions that follow are addressed, was also a physician. He continued the family's tradition of translating and is best known for his Hebrew rendition of Maimonides' *Guide to the Perplexed*.

Judah's "ethical will," a testimony to his broad culture, love of books, and humanism, has been preserved in manuscript in the Bodleian Library and was published in London and in Berlin, both in 1852.

Thou knowest, my son, how I swaddled thee and brought thee up, how I led thee in the paths of wisdom and virtue. I fed and clothed thee; I spent myself in educating and protecting thee, I sacrificed my sleep to make thee wise beyond thy fellows, and to raise thee to the highest degree of science and morals. These twelve years I have denied myself the usual pleasures and relaxations of men for thy sake, and I still toil for thine inheritance.

I have assisted thee by providing an extensive library for thy use and have thus relieved thee of the necessity of borrowing books. Most students must wander about to seek books, often without finding them. But thou, thanks be to God, lendest and borrowest not. Of many books, indeed, thou ownest two or three copies. I have besides procured for thee books on all sciences. Seeing that thy Creator had graced thee with a wise and understanding heart, I journeyed to the ends of the earth and fetched for thee a teacher in secular sciences. I neither heeded the expense nor the danger of the ways. Untold evil might have befallen me and thee on those travels, had not the Lord been with us!

But thou, my son, didst deceive my hopes! Thou didst not choose to employ thine abilities, hiding thyself from all the books, not caring to know them or even their titles. Hadst thou seen thine own books in the hand of others, thou wouldst not have recognized them; hadst thou needed one of them, thou wouldst not have known whether it was with thee or not, without asking me; thou didst not even consult the catalogue of the library.

All this thou hast done. Thus far thou hast relied on me to rouse thee from the sleep of indolence, thinking that I would live with thee for ever! Thou didst not bear in mind that death must divide us, and that there are daily vicissitudes in life. But who will be as tender to thee as I have been, who will take my place— to teach thee out of love and goodwill? Even if thou couldst find such a one, lo! thou seest how the greatest scholars, coming from the corners of the earth, seek to profit by my society and instruction, how eager they are to see me and my books. [. . .] May thy God endow thee with a new heart and spirit, and instill into thee a desire to retrieve the past, and to follow the true path henceforward!

Thou art still young, and improvement is possible, if Heaven but grant thee a helping gift of desire and resolution, for ability is of no avail without inclination. If the Lord please to bring me back to thee, I will take upon me all thy wants. For whom indeed do I toil but for thee and thy children? May the Lord let me see their faces again in joy!

Therefore, my son! stay not thy hand when I have left thee, but devote thyself to the study of the Torah and to the science of medicine. But chiefly occupy thyself with the Torah, for thou hast a wise and understanding heart, and all that is needful on thy part is ambition and application. I know that thou wilt repent of the past, as many have repented before thee of their youthful indolence. [. . .] Devote thyself to science and religion; habituate thyself to moral living, for "habit is master over all things." As the Arabian philosopher holds, there are two sciences, ethics and physics. Strive to excel in both!

Contend not with men, and meddle not "with strife not thine own" (Prov. 26:17). Enter into no dispute with the obstinate, not even on matters of Torah. On thy side, too, refrain from subterfuges in argument to maintain thy case even when thou art convinced that thou art in the right. Submit to the majority and do not reject their decision. Risk not thy life by taking the road and leaving thy city in times of disquiet and danger.

Show respect to thyself, thy household, and thy children, by providing decent clothing, as far as thy means allow; for it is unbecoming for any one, when not at work, to go shabbily dressed. Spare from thy belly and put it on thy back.

And now, my son! if the Creator has mightily displayed His love to thee and me, so that Jew and Gentile have thus far honored thee for my sake, endeavor henceforth so to add to thine honor that they may respect thee for thine own self. This thou canst effect by good morals and by courteous behavior; by steady devotion to thy studies and thy profession, as thou wast wont to do before thy marriage.

My son! Let thy countenance shine upon the sons of men: tend their sick, and may thine advice cure them. Though thou takest fees from the rich, heal the poor gratuitously; the Lord will requite thee. Thereby shalt thou find favor and good understanding in the sight of God and man. Thus wilt thou win the respect of high and low among Jews and non-Jews, and thy good name will go forth far and wide. Thou wilt rejoice thy friends and make thy foes envious.

My son! Examine regularly once a week thy drugs and medicinal herbs, and do not employ an ingredient whose properties are unknown to thee. I have often impressed this on thee in vain when we were together.

My son! If thou writest aught, read it through a second time, for no man can avoid slips. Let not any consideration of hurry prevent thee from revising a short epistle. Be punctilious in regard to grammatical accuracy, in conjugations and genders, for the constant use of the vernacular sometimes leads to error in this matter. A man's mistakes in writing bring him into disrepute; they are remembered against him all his days. Endeavor to cultivate conciseness and elegance, do not attempt to write verse unless thou canst do it perfectly. Avoid heaviness, which spoils a composition, making it disagreeable alike to reader and audience.

See to it that thy penmanship and handwriting are as beautiful as thy style. Keep thy pen in fine working order, use ink of good color. Make thy script as perfect as possible, unless forced to write without proper materials, or in a pressing emergency. The beauty of a composition depends on the writing, and the beauty of the writing, on pen, paper and ink; and all these excellencies are an index to the author's worth. [. . .]

[In the past] when thou didst write thy letters or compose

thine odes to send abroad, thou wast unwilling to show a word to me and didst prevent me from seeing. When I said to thee, "Show me!" thou wouldst answer: "Why dost thou want to see?" as if thinking that my help was unnecessary. And this was from thy folly, in that thou wast wise in thine own eyes.

If, my son, thou desirest to undo the past, the Creator will grant His pardon, and I shall forgive all without reserve or reluctance. Reject not my word in all that I have written for thee in this, my testament, and wherein thou hast not honored me heretofore, honor me for the rest of my days, and after my death! All the honor I ask of thee is to attain a higher degree in the pursuit of wisdom, to excel in right conduct and exemplary character, to behave in friendly spirit to all and to gain a good name, that greatest of crowns, to deserve applause for thy dealing and association with thy fellows, to cleave to the fear of God and the performance of His commandments—thus wilt thou honor me in life and in death!

My son! I command thee to honor thy wife to thine utmost capacity. She is intelligent and modest, a daughter of a distinguished and educated family. She is a good housewife and mother, and no spendthrift. Her tastes are simple, whether in food or dress. Remember her assiduous attendance on thee in thine illness, though she had been brought up in elegance and luxury. Remember how she afterwards reared thy son without man or woman to help her.

If thou wouldst acquire my love, honor her with all thy might; do not exercise too strict an authority over her; our sages have expressly warned men against this. If thou givest orders or reprovest let thy words be gentle. Enough is it if thy displeasure is visible in thy look, let it not be vented in actual rage.

My son! Devote thy mind to thy children as I did to thee; be tender to them as I was tender; instruct them as I instructed thee; keep them as I kept thee, try to teach them Torah as I have tried, and as I did unto thee do thou unto them! Be not indifferent to any slight ailment in them, or in thyself (may God deliver thee and them from all sickness and plague), but if thou dost notice any suspicion of disease in thee or in one of thy limbs, do forthwith what is necessary in the case. As Hippocrates has said: "Time is short, and experiment is dangerous." Therefore be prompt, but apply a sure remedy, avoiding doubtful treatment.

Examine thy Hebrew books at every new moon, the Arabic volumes once in two months, and the bound codices once every quarter. Arrange thy library in fair order, so as to avoid wearying thyself in searching for the book thou needest. Always know the case and chest where the book should be. A good plan would be to set in each compartment a written list of the books therein contained. If, then, thou art looking for a book, thou canst see from the list the exact shelf it occupies without disarranging all the books in the search for one. Examine the loose leaves in the volumes and bundles, and preserve them. These fragments contain very important matters which I have collected and copied out. Do not destroy any writing or letter of all that I have left. And cast thine eye frequently over the catalogue so as to remember what books are in thy library.

Never refuse to lend books to anyone who has not means to purchase books for himself, but only act thus to those who can be trusted to return the volumes. Cover the bookcase with rugs of fine quality; and preserve them from damp and mice, and from all manner of injury, for thy books are thy good treasure. If thou lendest a volume make a note of it before it leaves thy house, and when it is returned, draw thy pen over the entry. Every Passover and Feast of Booths call in all books out on loan.

Make it a fixed rule in thy home to read the Scriptures and to peruse grammatical works on Sabbaths and festivals, also to read Proverbs and the Ben Mishle.[18] Also I beg of thee, look at the chapter concerning Jonadab son of Rechab[19] every Sabbath, to instill in thee diligence to fulfill my commands. [. . .]

May He who gives prudence to the simple, and to young men knowledge and discretion, bestow on thee a willing heart and a listening ear! Then shall our soul be glad in the Lord and rejoice in His salvation!

THE GIFT OF THE LAW

Obadiah ben Abraham

The passage that follows is part of a treatise attributed to Rabbi Obadiah, grandson of Moses Maimonides. In it Obadiah offers an introduction to the perfect spiritual life which is to lead to a union with God. Maimonides considered reason to be a bond between God and man (*Guide* III, 51); but in contradistinction to the grandfather's intellectualism, the grandson, using a similar phrase, gives it a mystical turn. The treatise is contained in the Judaeo-Arabic manuscript, Oriental 666, of the Bodleian Library.

Know, my son, that reason forms the bond between God and thyself. The food which nourishes it is the science of the unalterable things; without these it is unable to subsist or to maintain itself. Just as the body cannot subsist except by the healthy food that suits it, so reason is only maintained by the true sciences, whose permanency guarantees its own. But [for] him who studies the sciences whose meaning he is ignorant of, [the object of his study] so to speak lacks consistency and serves no useful purpose either in this world or in the next [. . .]. As for us, God has made us a gift of the Law, perfect in itself and giving perfection, that Law which we now possess. It lends us mastery over our moral qualities as well as intellectual vigor, for sound reason is the perfect Law and the divine Law is sound reason.

PROPOSED JEWISH ACADEMY

IN MANTUA

David Provenzal

In the Renaissance period Jews in Italy found it possible to study—mainly medicine—at the universities of that country. In Sicily the Jewish communities were authorized in 1466 to establish a *studium gene-*

rale (university) for the training of medical men and jurists. Little more is known about this project. There are records of Jewish teachers at Italian schools of higher learning; in 1529 Jacob Mantino (Giacobbe Giudeo) was appointed Lecturer in Medicine at the University of Bologna and, a few years later, Professor of Practical Medicine at the "Sapienza" in Rome.

Some staunch traditionalists opposed such "modernist" tendencies. Other community leaders realized the futility and unreality of opposition and wished to counteract Jewish assimilation to secular society by establishing an academy in which the curriculum would combine the study of sciences with Hebrew training. Such was the proposal of 1566, here reprinted. The graduates were expected to complete their studies at a regular university.

Authors of the proposal were Rabbi David Provenzal of Mantua and his son Abraham, a physician. David Provenzal was a talmudist with considerable knowledge of Latin and philosophy. His curious collection of some two thousand Latin and Greek words, which he tried to trace back to a supposedly original Hebrew, has not been preserved. Provenzal's friend was the literary historian Azariah de Rossi.

The Hebrew text was originally a Mantua broadside; it was published in *Ha-Lebanon* V, 1868.

Now these are the rules that we intend to observe with the aid of God who will help us as He helps anyone whose purpose is lofty. The following requirements, though they be many, will be fulfilled in every sense of the word, without fail. Man has a will whereby he can accomplish anything he wishes if he but have God's help, and so with His aid do we intend to proceed at all times.

Young students who come from out of town to board in my house will be provided with a bed, table, chair, and lamp, and will be completely free from providing for their bodily needs. At the table they will always speak of both religious and secular matters so that there will be imparted to them intellectual and social qualities to be employed in all their conduct, and thus "they will behold God while eating and drinking" (Exod. 24:11). Those who come to register in my home shall not be transients but shall come for a period of five years until they show good progress in their studies, or they must at least stay three years, for one must labor at least that length of time to maintain his grasp on knowledge.

In studying the Bible we will read the best of the old and the new commentators both for the purpose of explaining the basis for the commandments, judgments, and laws, and for the purpose of understanding the science of the Torah which many call divine philosophy. We will also add new interpretations which have not yet been published, in accordance with the point of view that investigation is always worth while, for there is no study that does not result in something new. With God's help we will pursue the same method a part of the time with the Prophets and the Writings as well as with those Midrashim that are useful and valuable for furthering knowledge.

We will fix periods for the study of Hebrew grammar in order to get into its spirit and to know its rules. For many fundamental questions are dependent upon this: both the true meaning of the Biblical verses as well as the understanding of the secrets hidden in them like apples of gold in frames of silver. We will also study the Masorah.[20]

While studying grammar they can also learn to speak idiomatically and write correctly—whether they say little or much —as for instance when dealing with a matter of law. When studying poetry they will be taught the methods of the best of the poets.

At special hours the students will learn Latin, which is almost indispensable now in our country, for no day passes by that we do not require this knowledge in our relations with the officials. We have a precedent for this since even the members of the household of Judah the Prince were allowed to trim their hair like the pagans because they had frequent contact with the Roman government. The students shall also write themes in Hebrew and in good Italian and Latin with the niceties and elegances of style that are characteristic of each language and the knowledge of which redounds to one's fame and reputation.

Those who are versed in Latin can read the scientific books dealing with logic, philosophy, and medicine and thus get acquainted with them step by step, so that any one who wishes to become a physician need not waste his days and years in a university in sinful neglect of Jewish studies. On the contrary, through his own reading he should inform himself gradually of all that he need know, and then if he should study in a university for a brief period he can, with God's help, get his degree. After this he may enter practice with competent Jewish and Christian physicians. But even those who do not as yet know any Latin may read those scientific books which have already been translated into Hebrew, and thus save time, for the basic thing in knowledge is not language but content, for everything depends on what the mind really grasps.

Furthermore, by the aid of competent men the students will be made proficient in the different types of Christian scripts. And likewise in the science of arithmetic and calculation they will do many problems. And they will get many-sided instruction in the various forms of arithmetic, geometry, and fractions. They will also be taught and made familiar with the usual studies such as arithmetic and geometry, which have already been mentioned, as well as with geography and astrology. All these disciplines will be taught by us to the limits of our capacity, and no student will have to go anywhere else to study, for we will carry them as far as we can. For more advanced instruction we will find a competent scholar to work with us.

At fixed periods the students will engage in debates in our presence both in matters of Jewish law and in the sciences, in order to sharpen their minds. Each young man will learn more or less in accordance with his individual capacity—the main thing is that they be religious in spirit. Also they will gradually be taught to speak in public and to preach before congregations.

If God will grant us the merit of having a great many pupils, we will secure more instructors who will look after them properly, to give each student his just due. "May the graciousness of the Lord our God be upon us and mayest Thou establish the work of our hands" (Ps. 90:17). Amen. May it be Thy will.

THE INNER LIFE
OF THE JEWS IN POLAND

Nathan Hannover

This somewhat idealized portrayal of Jewish life in seventeenth-century Poland is the concluding chapter of *Yeven Metzulah* (The Deep Mire), a chronicle of the Chmielnicki massacres in 1648, 1649, and 1652. The author, Nathan Hannover of Ostrog, Volhynia, was an eyewitness to the Cossack uprisings of 1648 which brought ruin to the Jewish communities of the region. Hannover managed to flee Ostrog; he sojourned in Germany, Holland, Venice (where he published his chronicle), Livorno, Jassy and Focsani (Rumania), and finally, in Ungarisch-Brod (Moravia), where he met a martyr's death in 1683. Mystically inclined (he published a collection of Kabbalistic prayers, Prague, 1662), he believed the tragic events in Eastern Europe to be the required preparation for the advent of the Messiah. A spirit of warm humaneness permeates his description of the economic and religious life of Polish Jews, their high regard for scholarship, education, community cohesion, and social welfare.

And now I will begin to describe the practices of the Jews in the Kingdom of Poland, which were founded on principles of righteousness and steadfastness.

It is said in the Sayings of the Fathers: "Simeon the Just used to say: 'Upon three things the world is based: Upon the Torah, upon divine service, and upon the practice of charity.' " [21] Rabban Simeon, the son of Gamaliel said: "By three things is the world preserved: by truth, by judgment and by peace." [22] All the six pillars upon which the world rests were in existence in the Kingdom of Poland.

The Pillar of the Torah: Throughout the dispersions of Israel there was nowhere so much learning as in the Kingdom of Poland. Each community maintained academies, and the head of each academy was given an ample salary so that he could maintain his school without worry, and that the study of the Torah might be his sole occupation. The head of the academy did not leave his house the whole year except to go from the house of study to the synagogue. Thus he was engaged in the study of the Torah day and night. Each community maintained young men and provided for them a weekly allowance of money that they might study with the head of the academy. And for each young man they also maintained two boys to study under his guidance, so that he would orally discuss the Talmud, the commentaries of Rashi and the Tosafot,[23] which he had learned, and thus he would gain experience in the subtlety of talmudic argumentation. The boys were provided with food from the community benevolent fund or from the public kitchen. If the community consisted of fifty householders it supported not less than thirty young men and boys. One young man and two boys would be assigned to one householder. And the young man ate at his table as one of his sons. Although the young man received a stipend from the community, the householder provided him with all the food and drink that he needed. Some of the more charitable householders also allowed the boys to eat at their table, thus three persons would be provided with food and drink by one householder the entire year.

There was scarcely a house in all the Kingdom of Poland where its members did not occupy themselves with the study of the Torah. Either the head of the family was himself a scholar, or else his son, or his son-in-law, or one of the young men eating at his table. At times, all of these were to be found in one house. Thus there were many scholars in every community. A community of fifty householders had twenty scholars who achieved the title Morenu[24] or Haver.[25] The head of the academy was above all these, and the scholars accepted his authority and would go to his academy to attend his discourses.

The program of study in the Kingdom of Poland was as follows: The term of study consisted of the period which required the young men and the boys to study with the head of the academy. In the summer it extended from the first day of the month of Iyar [ca. May] till the fifteenth day of the month of Ab [ca. August], and in the winter, from the first day of the month of Heshvan [ca. November], till the fifteenth day of the month of Shevat [ca. February]. After the fifteenth of Shevat or the fifteenth of Ab, the young men and the boys were free to study wherever they preferred. From the first day of Iyar till the Feast of Weeks, and in the winter from the first day of Heshvan till Hanukkah, all the students of the academy studied Talmud, the commentaries of Rashi and Tosafot, with great diligence. Each day they studied one page of the Talmud with the commentaries.

All the scholars and the young students of the community as well as all those who showed inclination to study the Torah assembled in the academy. The head of the academy alone occupied a chair and the scholars and the other students stood about him. Before the head of the academy appeared they would engage in a discussion, and when he arrived each one would ask him that which he found difficult in the Law and he would offer his explanation to each of them.

They were all silent, as the head of the academy delivered his lecture and presented the new results of his study. After discussing his new interpretations the head of the academy would discuss a *chilluk*,[26] which proceeded in the following manner: He would cite a contradiction from the Talmud, or Rashi, or Tosafot, he would question deletions and pose contradictory statements and provide solutions which would also prove perplexing; and then he would propose solutions until the Law was completely clarified.

In the summer they would not leave the academy before noon. From the Feast of Weeks till the New Year, and from Hanukkah till Passover, the head of the academy would not engage in so many discussions. He would study with the scholars the Codes such as the *Arbaah Turim*[27] and their commentaries. With young men he would study Rav Alfas[28] and other works. In any case, they also studied Talmud, Rashi, and Tosafot, till the first day of Ab or the fifteenth day of Shevat. From then on until Passover or the New Year they studied the codes and similar works only. Some weeks prior to the fifteenth day of Ab or the fifteenth day of Shevat, the head of the academy would honor each student to lead in the discussion in his stead. The honor was given both to the scholars and the students. They would present the discussion, and the head of the academy would listen and then join in the disputation. This was done to exercise their

intellect. The same tractate [of the Talmud] was studied throughout the Kingdom of Poland in the proper sequence of the Six
Orders.

Each head of an academy had one inspector who daily went
from school to school to look after the boys, both rich and poor,
that they should study. He would warn them that they should
study and not loiter in the streets. On Thursdays all the boys had
to be examined by the superintendent on what they had learned
during the week. [. . .] Likewise on Sabbath Eve all the boys
went in a group to the head of the academy to be questioned on
what they had learned during the week, as in the aforementioned
procedure. In this manner there was fear upon the boys and they
studied with regularity. Also during the three days preceding the
Feast of Weeks and during Hanukkah, the young men and the
boys were obliged to review what they had studied during that
term, and for this the community leaders gave specified gifts of
money. Such was the practice till the fifteenth of Ab or the fifteenth of Shevat. After that the head of the academy, together
with all his students, the young men and the boys, journeyed to
the fair. In the summer they travelled to the fair of Zaslaw and
to the fair of Jaroslaw; in the winter to the fairs of Lwow and
Lublin. There the young men and boys were free to study in any
academy they preferred. Thus at each of the fairs hundreds of
academy heads, thousands of young men, and tens of thousands
of boys, and Jewish merchants, and Gentiles like the sand on the
shore of the sea, would gather. For people would come to the fair
from one end of the world to the other. Whoever had a son or
daughter of marriageable age went to the fair and there arranged a match. For there was ample opportunity for everyone
to find his like and his mate. Thus hundreds and sometimes
thousands of such matches would be arranged at each fair. And
Jews, both men and women, walked about the fair, dressed in
their best garments. For they were held in esteem in the eyes of
the rulers and in the eyes of the Gentiles, and the children of
Israel were many like the sand of the sea, but now, because of our
sins, they have become few. May the Lord have mercy upon
them.

In each community great honor was accorded to the head of

the academy. His words were heard by rich and poor alike. None questioned his authority. Without him no one raised his hand or foot, and as he commanded so it came to be. [. . .] Everyone loved the head of the academy, and he that had a good portion such as fatted fowl, or capons or good fish, would honor the head of the academy, with half or all, and with other gifts of silver and gold without measure. In the Synagogue, too, most of those who bought honors would accord them to the head of the academy. It was obligatory to call him to the Torah reading third, on the Sabbath and the first days of the Festivals. And if the head of the academy happened to be a Kohen or a Levite, he would be given preference despite the fact that there may have been others entitled to the honor of Kohen or Levi, or the concluding portion of the reading. No one left the Synagogue on the Sabbath or the Festival until the head of the academy walked out first and his pupils after him; then the whole congregation accompanied him to his home. On the Festivals the entire congregation followed him to his house to greet him. For this reason all the scholars were envious and studied with diligence, so that they too, might advance to this state, and become an academy head in some community; out of doing good with an ulterior motive, there came the doing good for its own sake, and the land was filled with knowledge.

The Pillar of Divine Service: At this time prayer has replaced sacrificial service, as it is written: "So we will render for bullocks, the offering of our lips" (Hosea 14:3). At the head was the fellowship of those who rose before dawn, called "they that watch for the morning," to pray and to mourn over the destruction of the Temple. With the coming of dawn the members of the "Society of Readers of Psalms" would rise to recite Psalms for about an hour before prayers. Each week they would complete the recitation of the entire Book of Psalms. And far be it, that any man should oversleep the time of prayer in the morning and not go to the Synagogue, except for unusual circumstances. When a man went to the Synagogue, he would not depart thence to his business until he had heard some words of the Torah expounded by a scholar or a passage from the commentary of Rashi on the Torah, the Prophets, the Writings, the Mishnah or some laws of ritual, whatever his heart desired to learn; for in all Synagogues there were many groups of scholars who taught others in the Synagogue immediately after evening and morning prayers.

The Pillar of Charity: There was no measure for the dispensation of charity in the Kingdom of Poland, especially as regards hospitality. If a scholar or preacher visited a community, even one which had a system of issuing communal tickets to be offered hospitality by a householder, he did not have to humiliate himself to obtain a ticket, but went to some community leader and stayed wherever he pleased. The community beadle then came and took his credentials to collect funds to show it to the Synagogue official or the community leader for the month, and they gave an appropriate gift which was delivered by the beadle in dignified manner. He was then the guest of the householder for as many days as he desired. Similarly all other transients who received tickets, would be the guests of a householder, whose turn it was by lot, for as many days as he wished. The guest was given food and drink, morning, noon and evening. If they wished to depart they would be given provisions for the road, and they would be conveyed by horse and carriage from one community to another. If young men or boys or older men or unmarried girls, came from distant places, they would be forthwith furnished with garments. Those who wanted to work at a trade would be apprenticed to a tradesman, and those who wanted to be servants in a house would be assigned to serve in a house.

Those who wanted to study would be provided with a teacher, and afterwards, when he became an important young man, a rich man would take him to his house and give him his daughter in marriage as well as several thousand gold pieces for a dowry, and he would clothe him in the finest. After the wedding he would send him away from his home to study in great academies. When he returned home after two or three years, his father-in-law would maintain a study group for him in his home and he would spend much money among the householders who were prominent scholars that they should attend his study group for a number of years, until he also will become a head of an academy in some community. Even if the lad was not yet an important student at that time but had a desire to study, enabling him to become a scholar after he had studied, there would at times come a rich man who had a young daughter, and give him food and drink and clothes, and all his needs, as he would to his own son, and he would hire a teacher for him until he was ready with his studies, then he would give him his daughter in marriage. There is no greater benevolence than this.

Similarly there were very praiseworthy regulations for poor unmarried girls in every province. No poor girl reached the age of eighteen without being married, and many pious women devoted themselves to this worthy deed. May the Lord recompense them and have compassion upon the remnant of Israel.

The Pillar of Justice was in the Kingdom of Poland as it was in Jerusalem before the destruction of the Temple, when courts were set up in every city, and if one refused to be judged by the court of his city he went to the nearest court, and if he refused to be judged by the nearest court, he went before the great court. For in every province there was a great court. Thus in the capital city of Ostrog there was the great court for Volhynia and the Ukraine, and in the capital city of Lwow there was the great court for Little Russia. There were thus many communities each of which had a great court for its own province.

If two important communities had a dispute between them, they would let themselves be judged by the heads of the Council of the Four Lands[29] (may their Rock and Redeemer preserve them) who would be in session twice a year. One leader would be chosen from each important community, added to these, were six great scholars from the land of Poland, and these were known as the Council of the Four Lands. They would be in session during every fair in Lublin between Purim and Passover, and during every fair at Jaroslaw in the month of Ab [ca. August] or Elul [ca. September]. The leaders of the Four Lands had the authority to judge all Israel in the Kingdom of Poland, to establish safeguards, to institute ordinances, and to punish. Each difficult matter was brought before them and they judged it. And the leaders of the Four Lands selected judges from the provinces to relieve their burden, and these were called judges of the provinces. They attended to cases involving money matters; fines, titles, and other difficult laws were brought before them. [. . .]

The Pillar of Truth: Every community appointed men in charge of weights and measures, and of other business dealings, so that everything would be conducted according to truth and trustworthiness.

The Pillar of Peace, for it is said: "The Lord will give strength unto His people; the Lord will bless His people with peace" (Ps. 29:11). There was in Poland so much interest in learning that no three people sat down to a meal without discussing Torah, for throughout the repast everyone indulged in talks of Torah and puzzling passages in the Midrashim, in order to fulfill the words: "Thy law is in my inmost parts" (Ps. 40:9). And the Holy One blessed be he, recompensed them so that even "when they were in the land of their enemies, He did not despise them and did not break his covenant with them" (Lev. 26:44). And wherever their feet trod the ground among our brothers of the House of Israel they were treated with great generosity, above all, our brethren who were in distress and in captivity among the Tartars. For the Tartars led them to Constantinople, a city that was a mother in Israel, and to the famed city of Salonica, and to other communities in Turkey and Egypt, and in Barbary and other provinces of Jewish dispersion where they were ransomed for much money, as mentioned above. To this day they have not ceased to ransom prisoners that are brought to them each day.

Those who escaped the sword of the enemy in every land where their feet trod, such as Moravia, Austria, Bohemia, Germany, Italy, were treated with kindness and were given food and drink and lodging and garments and many gifts, each according to his importance, and they also favored them with other things. Especially in Germany did they do more than they could. May their justice appear before God to shield them and all Israel wherever they are congregated, so that Israel may dwell in peace and tranquility in their habitations. May their merit be counted for us and for our children, that the Lord should hearken to our cries and gather our dispersed from the four corners of the earth, and send us our Redeemer speedily in our day. Amen, Selah.

The house of study

in padua

An Eighteenth-Century Document

Moses Hayyim Luzzatto (1707–1746) is best known for his ethical work *Mesillat Yesharim* (Path of the Upright), passages of which appear elsewhere in this volume ("The Love for God," "How to Attain Saintliness," "Humility"). In his time, however, he was noted for his mysticism and his strongly accentuated Messianic thought. Following the tragic turn in the Sabbatianic movement of the seventeenth century a mystic was easily suspected of heretic leanings, and leading rabbis saw in Luzzatto's mystical writings a threat to middle-of-the-road Judaism. They forbade him further study of Kabbalah, and, when he disregarded the prohibition, excommunicated him in 1735. Luzzatto left his native Padua, lived for a while in Amsterdam, then moved on to Palestine. Shortly after his arrival, he and his family died during a plague in 1746.

The study group which young Luzzatto founded in Padua, the regulations of which are here presented, was actually a community of mystics. One among them drew up these rules, and the text indicates that the members of the group had more in mind than the study of the *Zohar*. Uninterrupted study and saintly conduct of life aimed at "the restoration of the Divine Presence and . . . of all Israel."

With the help of God may we begin and prosper, Amen.

These are the words of the covenant, the laws and ordinances and teachings, which the holy associates hereunto subscribing have taken upon themselves for the unification of the Holy One and the Divine Presence all acting as one, because "Jephthah in his generation is even as Samuel in his generation" [30]—to perform this service of God, which shall be reckoned to the account of all. The following are the obligations which they have accepted:

First, to prosecute in this House of Study a continuous uninterrupted study of the holy book of *Zohar*, each man his portion, one after another, daily, from the morning until the Evening

Prayer, except for the Sabbaths, Festivals, Purim, the Ninth of Ab,[31] the eve of the Ninth of Ab, and except for the Friday afternoons, according to the condition which we have stipulated before God:

1. That this study shall not be reckoned a vow. That is to say, an omission shall not, God forbid, become a stumbling block to the comrades and be considered a default of a vow. But it shall be imposed upon them with all the power and stringency that mouth can utter and heart can feel.

2. That the study shall never be interrupted, and when one man takes the place of his comrade, he is to begin before his comrade has finished, so that the study shall never be interrupted.

3. If a comrade shall be absent on a journey, be it near or far, the remaining comrades shall complete his study, and it shall be reckoned to his account, as if he had studied with them.

4. This study shall not be performed for the purpose of receiving any reward, of whatever nature, not even, God forbid, in thought. But it is to be performed only for the purpose of the "restoration" of the Divine Presence, the "restoration" of all Israel, the people of the Lord, that they may bring joy to their Creator; this study shall entail no reward but the merit of doing more such deeds for the purpose of the unification of the Holy One and the Divine Presence and the "restoration" of all Israel.

5. If (God forbid!) it should happen that the study is interrupted in any manner, either through duress or error or forgetfulness, may such interruption produce no evil impression whatsoever, either on earth or on high. The object of the comrades in prosecuting this study is solely perfection, and not any iniquity whatsoever.

6. The general teachings of our teacher and master, Rabbi Moses Hayyim, which he teaches in the House of Study at noontime daily, may be reckoned as part of this study.

7. Each of the comrades may upon occasion honor one who does not belong to the holy brotherhood by allowing him to study in his place and at his hour; and it shall be considered as if it was one of the holy members doing the reading.

8. The comrades have also undertaken to combine day and night in this study.

9. This study may not be undertaken for the individual perfection of any one of the comrades, nor even in atonement for a sin; its sole meaning is the "restoration" of the Divine Presence, and the "restoration" of all Israel.

10. No one of the comrades shall be assigned any fixed hours for this study, but each shall study as his heart dictates, whenever he is able.

Those who have concluded this sure covenant subscribe hereunto: [signed] Israel Hezekiah Trevis, Isaac Marini, Yekutiel of Vilna, Jacob Israel Forte, Solomon Dina, Michael Terni, Jacob Hayyim Castel Franco.

The following regulations are subjoined to the above, that the new comrades may serve God in truth and with a whole heart. The comrades have taken the following upon themselves:

1. They will perform their service before God in truth, with humility and perfect love, with no expectation of reward for themselves, but only for the sake of the "restoration" of the Divine Presence, and the "restoration" of all Israel. Any reward due them for their fulfillment of the commandments and their good deeds they offer up as a gift to all Israel, to show their love of the holy Presence, and to bring joy to their Creator.

2. The comrades have all united to serve their Creator as one man with a simple and a pure service; when any comrade fulfills any commandment, it shall be considered as fulfilled by all the comrades for the sake of the perfection of the holy Presence. But any sin or fault committed by any single comrade shall not be reckoned to the community at large. For the community has been formed to share perfection, not iniquity.

3. The comrades have taken upon themselves to love one another, and to treat one another kind-heartedly and with brotherly love, and to accept remonstrances from one another with great love, without anger or hate, but in a loving spirit, and in a peaceful manner, so that they may be accepted before the Lord.

4. The comrades have undertaken to keep all the words of the Holy Book [the *Zohar*], which they have learned, a sealed secret, and to reveal nothing except with the permission of the master.

5. They shall all endeavor to come to the study of the *Zohar* every day at whatever hour they find it possible.

6. They are all under obligation to be present, unless detained by an accident, at the holy House of Study every Sabbath after the Afternoon Prayer for instruction by their master, may his light shine.

7. They shall make themselves resolute to perform their service before the Lord, and to pay heed neither to the jesting nor to the laughter of others.

8. The newly consecrated comrades have undertaken to leave the room without objections, in the event that the holy comrades who subscribed to the original regulations find it necessary to transact any business the nature of which cannot be revealed to others in the House of Study.

9. If any person wishes to join their company afterwards, all conditions hitherto obtaining among them shall apply to him as well.

10. The comrades shall guard their mouths and tongues from evil speech, and transact their affairs and fill their needs with all respect and reverence for the holy Presence. Far be it from them to treat lightly any stringent law or usage in Israel. But they will add observance to observance in their wish to remain pure before the Lord God of Israel.

The following are the signatures wherewith they subscribe to these regulations: [signed] Isaiah ben Joseph, Isaiah ben Abraham, Mordecai ben Rephael, Solomon ben Samuel, Moses ben Michael, Abraham ben Jacob, Isaac Hayyim ben Jacob Isaac Katz, Simeon ben Jacob Vita, Mordecai ben Benzion.

These are the statutes of this holy House of Study:

The comrades have taken it upon themselves to speak nothing but what concerns the Torah at the holy table of study of their master, Rabbi Moses Hayyim. Nor shall they linger in conversation in other houses of study, when the hour of study approaches, but they shall seat themselves at the table with reverence and awe. And Rabbi Israel, son of Rabbi Michael, one of the comrades who has been chosen for this special duty, is to raise his voice and announce: "Give glory to the Lord God of Israel!"

Immediately the holy comrades are to bow their heads, and no further word is to escape their lips. They are required to break off their conversation and to remain silent in great awe. If the comrades engage in unnecessary talk, even if it is not the hour of study and they are not at the study table, Rabbi Yekutiel has the right to motion to Rabbi Israel, and Rabbi Israel shall say, "Give glory to the Lord God of Israel!" Then everyone is immediately required to fall silent. If quarrels should break out among the comrades (God forbid) even outside the House of Study, Rabbi Israel can bring any comrade to silence by saying to him, "Give glory to the Lord God of Israel!"—and the comrade must become silent. The other statutes dealing with silence are indeed written in the book of the covenant to which the comrades have subscribed with their own hands.

In their pursuit of saintly living the comrades have taken it upon themselves not to utter any idle word whatsoever anywhere in the whole House of Study. And they have further taken the following upon themselves:

Whenever any comrade shall come into this House of Study, his head should be bowed and he should give greeting with the words, "Let the glory of the Lord endure forever!" Then those sitting in the House of Study will reply, "Blessed be the name of the Lord from this time forth and forever!"

Whenever any comrade leaves the House of Study, he must go backwards, saying, "Praised be the Lord out of Zion!"

When the master Rabbi Moses Hayyim shall enter the House of Study, he shall say, "May the Lord our God be with us!" Then those sitting in the House of Study shall reply, "May the Lord give strength unto his people!"

When the master Rabbi Moses Hayyim shall seat himself at his table, he shall say, "The Lord is high above all nations," and the comrades shall reply, "Who is like unto the Lord our God, that dwelleth so high, that looketh down so low upon the heavens and the earth?" Then Rabbi Israel shall say, "Give glory to the Lord God of Israel!" and the comrades shall immediately bow their heads and fall silent, prepared to study before the holy Presence in fear and trembling and awe. Then Rabbi Yekutiel shall say to all the holy comrades, "Apply your minds!"

The comrades have also taken it upon themselves not to raise their voices in the holy House of Study in the course of their studies, even where they may, except for talmudic dissertation. They have also taken it upon themselves to do nothing in the House of Study without the permission of their master, Rabbi Moses Hayyim, may his light shine.

Furthermore, all the holy comrades, both of the first company and of the second, have agreed to guard themselves closely against speaking any falsehoods, and to make it their endeavor to allow only truth to pass their lips, forever. Consequently, when one comrade shall say to another, "Speak the truth!"—it shall be considered the most binding oath possible.

The comrades have further taken it upon themselves that one of the comrades shall daily recite, first the Ten Commandments and then the Six Hundred and Thirteen Precepts, and then Psalm 119 from verse 9, "Wherewithal shall a young man keep his way pure," until the end of the section.

They have further taken it upon themselves to read all through the Bible, and some comrades all through the Mishnah, every month.

They have further taken it upon themselves to tithe their days before the Lord in fasting. Every tenth day shall be holy, and one of the comrades shall fast on that day. The comrades are all to fast in rotation.

Further they have taken it upon themselves to perform absolution of all reproaches and absolution of all ill will every month.

The comrades have further added to the regulation concerning the daily study of the holy *Zohar* the provision that they shall study all day until the sixth hour of the night, with the exception of the nights from the close of the Day of Atonement until after the Feast of Booths, and the nights of the fourteenth and the fifteenth of Adar,[32] and also the nights from the day of preparation for the Passover festival until after the festival, and the nights from the day of preparation for the Feast of Weeks until after the festival. Nor are they to study during the nights preceding and following the fast days of the Seventeenth of Tammuz, the Ninth of Ab, and the Day of Atonement. But if the requirements of the hour dictate the necessity of study, the decision is to lie in the hands of the master, Rabbi Moses Hayyim. [. . .]

The Lord has helped them to this point; may he nevermore forsake them, until the Messiah shall come whose coming is proper, unto whom "shall the gathering of the people be" (Gen. 49:10), as it is written, "For then will I turn to the people a pure language, that they may all call upon the name of the Lord, to serve Him with one consent" (Zeph. 3:9); "and the Lord shall be King over all the earth; in that day shall the Lord be One, and His name one" (Zech. 14:9).

VI. The Ways of Good Life

A POET'S ETHICAL COUNSEL

Solomon ibn Gabirol

Solomon ibn Gabirol (see the preface to "The Kingly Crown") wrote two popular works on morals. The one, *Improvement of Moral Qualities,* written in 1045 and translated from the original Arabic into Hebrew by Judah ibn Tibbon (*Tikkun Middot ha-Nefesh*) in 1167, relates human behavior to the five senses and four humors of medieval psychology and avoids references both to metaphysics and to Jewish law. The Hebrew version appeared first in Constantinople about 1550 (as an appendix to Bahya's *Duties of the Heart*), and in Riva di Trento in 1562. The original Arabic text was published by Stephen S. Wise, 1901.

The other work, *Choice of Pearls,* is extant in a Hebrew version (*Mivhar ha-Peninim*); of the Arabic original only two pages survive. The little book is a collection of wise, pithy sayings and ethical aphorisms, culled mainly from Arabic writings. It appeared first in Soncino in 1484, then in Cremona in 1558. A Latin translation was published in 1591, 1612, and 1630; a Yiddish rendition, in 1739.

From *Improvement of Moral Qualities*

The divine Socrates said: "From whom doth disappointment never part? He who seeks a rank for which his ability is too feeble." Again he said, "He who sets himself up as wise will be set down by others for a fool." I hold that bad manners are attributable to superciliousness.

Socrates said, "Aversion is always felt for him who has an evil nature, so that men flee away from him." Aristotle says, "As the beauty of form is a light for the body, so is beauty of character a light for the soul." Again he said in his testament to Alexander his pupil, "It does not show much nobility of purpose on the part of a king to lord it over men; [the less so] for one man over a fellow-man." [. . .]

It is told of Ardeshir, the king, that he gave a book to a man accustomed to stand at his side, and said unto him, "When thou seest me become violently angry give it to me," and in the book [was written], "Restrain thyself, for thou art not God, thou art but a body, one part of which is on the point of consuming the other, and in a short while it will turn into the worm and dust and nothingness."

The greatest riches are contentment and patience. One of the sages has said, "He who desires of this world only that which is sufficient for him, will be content with the very least thereof." Another sage was wont to admonish his son, "He who cannot bear with one word, will be compelled to listen to many. He who esteems his rank but slightly, enhances men's estimation of his dignity." In holding the view that it may be right [at times] to repudiate this quality, I mean thereby that a man should not abuse himself before the wicked. With reference to such a case it is said, "A righteous man, falling down before the wicked, is as a troubled fountain and a corrupt stream" (Prov. 25:26). It was said concerning this, "He who deserves [the greatest] compassion is the wise man lost among fools." In the ethical sayings of Lokman [we find], "when the noble man forsakes the world, he becomes humble: the ignoble in forsaking the world becomes haughty." In the book of al-Kuti [it is said], "Be humble without cringing, and manly without being arrogant. Know thou that arrogance is a wilderness and haughtiness a taking refuge therein, and, altogether, a going astray."

A wise man was asked, "What is intelligence?" and he answered, "Modesty." Again he was asked, "What is modesty?" and he replied, "Intelligence." This quality, although like unto meekness and agreeing therewith, is of a nobler rank than the latter, for it is kindred to intelligence. To every man of understanding the nobility of intellect is patent, for it is the dividing line between man and beast, in that it masters man's natural impulses and subdues passion. With the help of intelligence man realizes the benefit of knowledge and gets to understand the true nature of things; he comes to acknowledge the oneness of God, to worship his Master, and to bear a striking resemblance to the character of the angels. Since this precious quality is of so noble a kind, it follows that modesty which resembles it is almost equally so. The proof of its being thus related is, that thou wilt never see a modest man lacking intelligence, or an intelligent man devoid of modesty. This being so, man must direct all his efforts to the attainment of this wonderful and highly considered quality. [. . .]

It was said that, "Pudency and faith are interdependent, and either cannot be complete without the other." A poet said, "Keep guard over thy modesty: truly pudency marks the countenance of a nobleman." It is said that "Impudence and a lack of pudency are offshoots of unbelief." He who wishes to acquire pudency should associate with those who are modest with respect to him. An Arab was wont to say, "Pay no regard to any man unless he show thee that he cannot do without thee, even when thou needest him most, so that, if thou sin, he will forgive and act as though he were the sinner; and, if thou wrong him, he will demean himself as though he had been the offender." Another said, "Finally, one learns from the words of prophecy, 'If thou art not pudent, do whatsoe'er thou wilt.'" In the course of a characterization of modesty, the poet said, "Upon him reposes the mantel of piety: and, in truth, a light streams from between his eyes."

Al-fadil says: "By reason of belief and piety, men dwell together for a time. Afterward they are kept together by reason of modesty, pudency, and blamelessness." Aristotle said in his discourse, "As a result of modesty [one's] helpers are multiplied." He was accustomed to say, "In chaste children modesty clearly rules over their countenance." [. . .] A philosopher said, "Modesty asserts itself in the midst of wrath." Again it was said, "The enmity of the modest man is less harmful to thee than the friendship of the fool."

With reference to valor and patience in facing danger, the poet spake: "There came a day in the heat of which some people warmed themselves, but though there was no fire, they acted as if in the fire's midst. But we had patience until the day was done. Likewise, a case of misfortune can be brought to a close only through patience."

Among the things which have been said in order to encourage the use of valor is: "Crave death, and life will be granted thee." The Arabs were accustomed to call the man of valor "safe." Among the things which have been said on the emboldening of the spirit in combat is the word of the poet: "I went to the rear to preserve my life [in battle], but I found that I could not preserve my life unless I went forward."

From *Choice of Pearls*

Love

If to his complete love for thee one adds good advice, do thou add to thy pure love for him the self-imposed duty of listening to him.

When the roots [of love] are deeply set in the heart, the branches manifest themselves upon the tongue; and true love can only manifest itself to thee from a perfect heart.

The sage was asked, "What is love?" He replied, "The mutual attraction of hearts and their close association."

The eye of a needle is not narrow for two friends, but the world is not wide enough for two enemies.

Wouldst thou know who is thy friend and who thine enemy, note what is in thine heart.

Who cast his troubles upon thee but withheld from thee his happiness, believe not in his love.

The sage was asked, "Whom lovest thou most?" He replied, "The person whose kindnesses towards me are many; otherwise it is the person towards whom my sins are many [and he forgave me]." [. . .]

Give freely to thy friend of thy soul and wealth, to thine

acquaintance of thy kindness and fair words, to everybody affability and friendly greeting, and to thine enemy fairness. Have regard to what thou hast learnt from the divine Law, be pure to all in thine actions, and [take care of] thy reputation with all men. [. . .]

No man has loved me, without my sincerely returning his love for ever; nor can anyone be mine enemy without my praying that the Creator will set him right [towards me]. Nobody confided a secret to me which I disclosed; never have I set my hand to anything which was not honorable; nor have I consented to anything and then retracted, even if it involved the loss of all my wealth.

Silence

If I speak, I may experience regret, but should I not speak, I shall not experience regret.

If I utter a word, it becomes my master; but should I not utter it, I am its master.

I am better able to retract what I did not say than what I did say.

What use is it to me to speak a word which, if it be repeated against me, may do me injury, but if unrepeated would not be of advantage to me!

Sometimes a word may involve the loss of something considerable.

The indolence of silence is better than the indolence of loquacity; die of the disease of silence, but not of the disease of loquacity.

The best worship is silence and hope.

Through silence thou mayest experience one regret, but through loquacity two regrets.

A man's silence is preferable to inopportune speech.

In much silence, reverence develops.

Treasure thy tongue as thou treasurest thy wealth.

Lackest thou instruction, cleave to silence.

The bait by which a man is caught lies concealed beneath his tongue; a man's death is between his cheeks.

The preponderance of speech over intellect leads to deception, that of intellect over speech to blame; but it is good when one graces the other.

When one's words exceed his intellect, they overpower him; but when one's intellect exceeds his words, he overpowers them.

It is related that a man from Arabia entered a company and preserved a lengthy silence. Somebody said to him, "Rightly do they call thee one of the noble men of Arabia." He replied, "My brethren, the portion of a man from his ear belongs to himself, but the portion of a man from his tongue, belongs to others."

Perception

He is not clever who carefully considers a matter after he has stumbled in it, but he who comprehends it and gives it close consideration so as not to stumble.

The summit of intellect is the perception of the possible and impossible, and submission to what is beyond his power.

The clever man, through the words he utters, arrives at the goal of his effort.

Evidence of a man's mind is his choice; and his faith is not perfected until his mind has been perfected.

It is meet for an intelligent man to be aware of his age, guard his tongue, and attend to his business.

What a man writes is an index of his intellect, and his [selection of a] representative is an index of his discrimination.

When the righteousness of a person is being recounted to thee, ask, "What is his mind?"

The mind of a man is hidden in his writings, but through criticism it is brought to light.

SIMPLE PIETY

Judah the Pious

The *Sefer Hasidim* (Book of the Pious), from which the passages that follow are taken, gives an insight into the inner life of the Jewish community in Germany in the twelfth and thirteenth centuries. The work is not a learned system in the manner of the religio-philosophical

books of the Spanish Jews, but a loosely arranged compilation of utterances on practically all aspects of Jewish life and thought. But back
of them all is a definite concept of the *Hasid*, the pious man, the ideal
type of the period. The *Hasid* (a quite different *Hasid* from that of the
Second Commonwealth and talmudic periods) is a man who has withdrawn from the affairs of the world; leading an ascetic life, he has
achieved equanimity and inner peace; he worships God in utter simplicity of the heart and surrender; his love embraces all that God has
created; he is ready to bear humiliation and insult. This concept of
the conduct of the "Pious men of Germany" (*Haside Ashkenaz*) is
rooted in a mystic concept of God and His relationship to world and
man. I. F. Baer has pointed to the fascinating parallel between Judah
the Pious, chief spokesman of German Hasidim, and Francis of Assisi,
his Christian contemporary.

Most of the material in the *Book of the Pious* comes from Judah
the Pious (died 1217); some was written by his father, Samuel the Pious
(mid-twelfth century); and some originated with Eleazar ben Judah
Rokeah of Worms, Judah's greatest disciple. The compilation was effected at the end of the thirteenth century and appeared first at Bologna in 1538.

Be not jealous of the man who is greater than thou and
despise none who is smaller than thou.

If thou hast a guest, never speak to him about learned matters unless thou knowest he is able to partake in the conversation.

Never put to shame thy man-servant or thy maid-servant.

The man who is cruel to animals will have to answer for it
on the Day of Judgment, and the very drivers will be punished
for applying the spur too often.

Those who constantly fast are not in the good way. Scribes,
teachers, and workmen are altogether forbidden to inflict penance
upon themselves. If the Holy One, blessed be he, had any particular delight in much fasting, He would have commanded it
to Israel; but, He only asked of them that they should worship
Him in humility.

If a man should ask: "Behold, I have money; shall I buy
a Scroll of the Torah for it or shall I distribute it to the destitute
poor?" Answer him with the words of Isaiah: 'When thou seest
the naked, that thou cover him, and hide not thyself from thine
own flesh' (Isa. 58:7).

If a man sees a non-Jew committing a sin, let him protest
against it if he has the power to do so; for behold, did not the

Holy One, blessed be he, send the prophet Jonah to the people
of Nineveh that they may do repentance?

The Holy One, blessed be he, executes the judgment of the
oppressed, whether Jew or Christian, hence cheat not anybody.

A BRIEF SUMMARY OF

ETHICAL RULES

Yehiel ben Yekutiel

The simple, modest statement on ethical behavior that follows here was
written by a thirteenth-century Roman copyist (among other manuscripts, his copy of the Palestinian Talmud is still preserved) and
moralist. His book, *Bet Middot* (Constantinople, 1511), later published
under the title *Sefer Maalot ha-Middot* (Cremona, 1556), is based on
classical Hebrew sources and, in addition, on Christian ethical writings
current at the time.

And now, my children, I shall make brief mention of the
various ethical principles so that you may consider them with
great care, with the help of God.

Know your Creator who created you *ex nihilo,* who brought
you forth from nothingness, who has vouchsafed all good unto
you in the past and does it every day. His knowledge implies
cleaving unto Him, to follow in His ways, to fulfill his commandments. The service of the Creator has to be rooted in love.
All your deeds should be done and your words spoken out of
love for Him, not out of an ulterior motif, such as expecting reward or fearing punishment. All must stem from love, just as the
Holy One, blessed be he, loves those who love Him and fulfills
their desire. My children, love humility, as the Holy One, blessed
be he, loves the humble, the meek and those of a broken spirit.
Reject the attitude of pride and haughtiness which is a mode
hated alike by God and men. Pride prepares many a stumbling-
block and those who are haughty fall into snares.

My children, love modesty and thus be protected from sin.
The Holy One, blessed be he, created the world in modesty, gave

the Torah in modesty; he loves dearly the modest ones and gives them their due reward. Be on your guard against boisterousness and impudence which are but roads to harlotry. Also, love simplicity—God has delight in the simple ones. Whosoever walks in simplicity with God and man is protected from transgression. Reject deception, a trait that leads to lie and fraud—a denial of God who is truth.

My children, love mercy which is one of the divine attributes. The world could not stand had not God brought into it the quality of mercy. He who has mercy with the human creatures brings goodness into the world and earns heavenly mercy. Contrariwise, he who is cruel with people brings wrath even upon himself and upon the world at large and exposes himself to divine retribution.

And, my children, love peace. Wherever is peace there is awe of the divine. Even the realms above are in need of peace, and all the more the lower realms. Even the dead need peace, and all the more those alive. Thus seek peace and pursue it, as the Holy One, blessed be he, loves peace. When He started His work of creation, He occupied himself with creating an object of peace, and that was light. All good blessings and consolations in the sacred writings that the Lord gives Israel conclude on a note of peace. Contrariwise, flee strife which is a very hateful thing in the eyes of God. We find that He may overlook idolatry but will not overlook strife.

HUMILITY

Moses Hayyim Luzzatto

On Luzzatto see the preface to "How to Attain Saintliness." See also "The House of Study in Padua." *Mesillat Yesharim* (Path of the Upright), from which the following is quoted, has become one of the most popular ethico-religious writings in Judaism. It takes its place with such works as *The Book of the Pious* by Judah the Pious, *Duties of the Heart* by Bahya ibn Pakuda, and *The Lamp of Illumination* by Israel ibn al-Nakawa (see "The Sabbath Bride"). The famous talmudic academy (*Yeshivah*) at Slobodka (near Kovno), which emphasized the study of ethics, used Luzzatto's work as a basic text.

Humility means that a man should be wholly persuaded of his unworthiness to be the recipient of praise and glory. A man of this sort will surely find it impossible to consider himself superior to any others. This attitude toward himself he will have not only because he is aware of his failings, but also because he realizes the insignificance of his attainments.

That in the awareness of his shortcomings a man should be humble is self-evident. It is impossible for any man to be altogether without faults, which may be due to nature, to heredity, to accidents, or to his own doings. "For there is not a righteous man upon earth that doeth good, and sinneth not" (Eccles. 7:20). Such defects leave no room for self-esteem, despite the many excellent traits that one may otherwise possess. The defects are sufficient to eclipse the virtues. The possession of learning, for example, makes dangerously for pride and self-esteem, since it is an advantage that accrues wholly to the intellect, which is the highest faculty of the human being. Yet there is no one so learned who does not make mistakes, or who is not in need of learning from his equals, and at times even from his disciples. How, then, shall a man dare to boast of his learning?

The man of understanding will, upon reflection, realize that there is no justification for pride or vainglory, even if he was privileged to become very learned. A man of understanding, who has acquired more knowledge than the average person, has accomplished nothing more than what his nature impelled him to do, as it is the nature of the bird to fly, or of the ox to pull with all its strength. Hence, if a man is learned, he is indebted to natural gifts which he happens to possess. And any one gifted by nature with a mind like his would be just as learned. The man who possesses great knowledge, instead of yielding to pride and self-esteem, should impart that knowledge to those who are in need of it. As Rabbi Johanan ben Zakkai said, "If thou hast learned much Torah, take not any merit, for thereunto wast thou created." [1] If a man is rich, let him rejoice in his portion and help those who are poor; if he is strong, let him help those who are weak, and redeem those who are oppressed. For indeed we are like the servants of a household. Every one of us is appointed to some task and is expected to remain at his post and do the work of the household as well as possible. In the scheme of life there is no room for pride.

So must he conclude whose understanding is sound and unperverted. And insofar as he is firmly and permanently of this mind, he may be called truly humble, for his humility is based on conviction. "How great are those who are lowly in spirit," said our sages.[2] A man of upright heart does not allow himself to be misled by the fact that he possesses good traits. He is fully aware that he is nonetheless unworthy, since he is bound to have some faults. Even the commandments which he succeeded in fulfilling could scarcely have enabled him to attain perfection. Whatever good a man possesses is due to the divine grace accorded to him, in despite of the inherent imperfection of his physical nature. He should be grateful to God who has thus been gracious to him, and for this very reason be humble. [. . .]

Moreover, the company of the humble is very sweet, and people find delight in him. He is not given to anger or to strife; he does everything calmly and peacefully. Happy is he who is privileged to possess this virtue; all the wisdom in the world cannot compare with humility.

AT PEACE WITH THE WORLD

Joel ben Abraham Shemariah

The following excerpts from a will of an eighteenth-century Jew of Vilna (first printed in 1799 or 1800) is one of the many expressions of what truly mattered in the secluded Jewish society of the medieval and early modern periods: life according to the commands of the Torah, observance of the sacred seasons, study and prayer, charity and an ethical attitude toward one's neighbor, and—peace with the world, which is the Lord's.

To be at peace with all the world, with Jew and Gentile, must be your foremost aim in this terrestrial life. Content with no man. In the first instance, your home must be the abode of quietude and happiness; no harsh word must be heard there, but over all must reign love, amity, modesty, and a spirit of gentleness and reverence. This spirit must not end with the home, however. In your dealings with the world you must allow neither money nor ambition to disturb you. Forego your rights, envy no man. For the main thing is peace, peace with the whole world. Show all men every possible respect, deal with them in the finest integrity and faithfulness. For Habakkuk summed up the whole Torah in the one sentence: "The righteous shall live by his faith" (Hab. 2:4).

The root of all the commandments consists of the two hundred and forty-eight affirmative and the three hundred and sixty-five negative precepts. But the branches, which include all virtuous and vicious habits, extend into countless thousands of thousands. To specify them is impossible, but the Scriptures have in several places reduced them to general categories. One of these is: "In all thy ways acknowledge Him" (Prov. 3:6). Another: "Keep thy feet in an even path" (*ibid.*, 4:26).

When, in the course of the prayers, you come to the "Sanctification," [3] fulfill the text: "I will be hallowed among the children of Israel" (Lev. 22:32). But you must at the same moment resolve to uphold the duty to love thy neighbor as thyself. For in the "Sanctification" we use the phrase: "We will sanctify Thy name in the world, even as they sanctify it in the highest heavens." We must indeed strive to imitate the angels on high, and as they are in a state of perfect love and unison, such must also be our condition.

It was oft my way at assemblies to raise my eyes and regard those present from end to end, to see whether in sooth I loved everyone among them, whether my acceptance of the duty to love my fellow-men was genuine. With God's help I found that indeed I loved all present. Even if I noticed one who had treated me improperly, then, without a thought of hesitation, without a moment's delay, I pardoned him. Forthwith I resolved to love him. If my heart forced me to refuse my love, I addressed him with spoken words of friendship, until my heart became attuned to my words. So, whenever I met one to whom my heart did not incline, I forced myself to speak to him kindly, so as to make my heart feel affection for him.

What if he were a sinner? Even then I would not quarrel with him, for I wonder whether there exists in this age one who is able to reprove another! On the other hand, if I conceived that he would listen to advice, I drew near to him, turning towards him a cheerful countenance. If, however, I fancied that he would resent my advances, I did not intrude on him. As there is a duty to speak, so is there a duty to be silent.

THE MIDDLE COURSE

Solomon Ganzfried

The *Shulhan Arukh* by Joseph Caro (sixteenth century), a compilation of Jewish Law, came to be accepted as the definitive code in all aspects of life; scholars of the subsequent periods wrote merely commentaries and supplements to the *Shulhan Arukh*. The need for abridgments for the use of laymen and for quick reference was filled by a number of works; the most widely accepted of them has been the *Kitzur Shulhan Arukh* by the Hungarian rabbi, Solomon Ganzfried (1804–1886), first published in 1864. In this manual Ganzfried condensed the first of the four parts of the major code, which deal with practical religious life, adding to it chapters based on other sections of the code, such as laws concerning charity, mourning, marriage, and business; this he supplemented by chapters on ethical conduct, selected mainly from the *Mishneh Torah* by Maimonides. The passages that follow are an abridgment of its *Hilkhot Deot* (Laws Relating to Moral Dispositions).

People differ widely with respect to their natures. There is one of an angry disposition who is always angry, and there is another who is sedate and never becomes angry, or becomes angry once in many years; there is a one who is unduly haughty, and there is another who is unduly humble; one is voluptuary, his soul is never satiated with desire, another possesses a pure heart and has no desire even for small things which are the necessities of life; one possesses an unbounded greed who is not satisfied with all the wealth the world possesses, another one is a shiftless fellow who is satisfied with little which does not even suffice for him, and he does not seek to earn enough for his necessities; one afflicts himself with hunger, keeps on saving, and whatever he eats of his own he does so with grief, another who spends all his money freely; and the same is true with all dispositions and views; e.g., the gay and the melancholy, the villain and the noble, the cruel and the compassionate, the gentle and the hardhearted, and the like.

The good and right path to follow is the middle course to which one should become habituated. He should desire only the things which are requisite for the body, and it is impossible to live without them; neither should a man be too much occupied with his business, but only sufficient to obtain things that are required for the immediate necessities of life; neither should he be tight-fisted too much, nor should he spend his money freely, but should give alms according to his means, and lend liberally to the needful; and he should not be too jocular and gay, nor morose and melancholy, but should be happy all his days with satisfaction and with friendliness. Relating to all other ethical principles also he who adopts the middle course is called a sage.

Pride is an extremely bad vice, and a person is not to become accustomed to it even to the slightest degree, but he should train himself to be humble of spirit. And how can you train yourself to be humble and low of spirit? All your words shall be quietly uttered, your head bent down, your eyes shall look downward and your heart upwards, and every man shall be considered in your estimation as greater than you are; if he is more learned than you, then you must honor him [. . .].

Anger is likewise an extremely bad vice, and it is proper that one should keep away from it, and he should accustom himself not to get angry even at things that would justify anger. But when necessary to exercise his authority over his children and his household, he may pretend to be angry in their presence in order to chastise them, while inwardly he should retain his composure. He who becomes angry it is accounted to him as if he had worshipped idols, and all kinds of Gehenna have dominion over him. The life of those who are wont to become angry is not considered life at all. [. . .] This is the proper path and the path of the just that they are insulted and do not insult; they hear themselves reviled, and answer not; they do things for love's sake and rejoice even when suffering pain.

A man should always cultivate the faculty of silence, and should converse only on matters concerning Torah, or of the necessities of life, and even then he should not talk too much.

A man should neither be gay and jocular nor should he be melancholy, but he should be happy. Neither should a man possess greed for wealth, nor should he go idle; but he should have a benevolent eye, do less business and engage himself in the study of the Torah, and he shall be happy with that little which is his portion.

Perhaps a man will say: "Since envy, voluptuousness and ambition and their like take a man away from the world, I will entirely keep away from them even to the extreme," with the result that he would not partake of meat, nor drink wine, nor marry a woman, nor live in a comfortable abode, and not put on respectable clothes, but he will put on sack cloth or the like; this also is an improper path. Our sages ordered that a man should abstain himself only from those things which the Torah forbade us, and he shall not vow abstinence from things which are permitted. They forbade to torment oneself with fast days more than is required; and concerning all these things and the like, King Solomon said: "Be not righteous over much; neither show thyself over wise: why wouldst thou destroy thyself?" (Eccles. 7:16).

One should not be ashamed of the people who mock him when engaged in the service of the Lord, blessed be His Name; nevertheless he should not answer them harshly, in order that he may not acquire a disposition of being boldfaced, even in matters not concerning the service of God. [. . .]

It is the nature of man to follow his friends and neighbors and town folks in his actions. Therefore one should associate himself with the just and stay always with the sages so that one may learn their actions, and keep away from the wicked who talk in the dark. And if one dwell in a place where its leaders are wicked and its inhabitants do not walk in the right path, he should move away from there to dwell in a place where its inhabitants are just men and follow in the path of the good.

One should associate himself with the learned in order to learn their deeds, as it is written: "And unto Him thou shalt cleave" (Deut. 10:20). Is it then possible for a man to cleave to the Divine Presence? But thus did our sages explain: "Cleave unto the learned in the Torah. Therefore should a man make an endeavor to marry the daughter of a scholar, to give his daughter in marriage to a learned man, to eat and drink with the learned, do business with the learned, and to associate with them in every possible connection, for it is written "And to cleave unto Him" (Deut. 11:22).[4]

VII. The Community of Israel

THE GOD OF ABRAHAM AND THE GOD OF ARISTOTLE

Judah ha-Levi

Certain aspects of Judah ha-Levi (see the preface to "Lord Where Shall I Find Thee" are reminiscent of the Moslem mystic and moralist Ghazali: both men attempted to free religion from dependency on philosophy, both emphasized the autonomous aspects of faith. The rationalist philosopher, Ha-Levi theorizes, "seeks Him that he may be able to describe Him accurately"; to the believer, God is an issue of personal concern; not speculation but love motivates his quest (*Kuzari* IV, 13, 16). In the section from the *Kuzari* reprinted below (see the preface to "The Servant of Gód"), Judah ha-Levi applies to his theory the two Biblical terms for the deity, *Adonai*, Yahve, commonly translated as "the Lord," and *Elohim*, usually rendered as "God." However, what is the basis for religious faith? It is, says Ha-Levi, the revelation on Sinai, an event that took place in the bright light of history and has been remembered as such throughout the ages.

The Kuzari: Now I understand the difference between *Elohim* and *Adonai*, and I see how far the God of Abraham is different from that of Aristotle. Man yearns for *Adonai* as a matter of love, taste, and conviction; whilst attachment to *Elohim* is the result of speculation. A feeling of the former kind invites its votaries to give their life for His sake, and to prefer death to His absence. Speculation, however, makes veneration only a necessity as long as it entails no harm, but bears no pain for its sake. I would, therefore, excuse Aristotle for thinking lightly about the observation of the law, since he doubts whether God has any cognizance of it.

The Master: Abraham bore his burden honestly, viz., the

life in Ur of the Chaldees, emigration, circumcision, the removal of [his son] Ishmael, and the distress of the sacrifice of Isaac, because his share of the Divine Influence had come to him through love, but not through speculation. He observed that not the smallest detail could escape God, that he was quickly rewarded for his piety and guided on the right path to such an extent that he did everything in the order dictated by God. How could he do otherwise than deprecate his former speculation? The sages explain the verse: "And He brought him [Abraham] forth abroad" (Gen. 15:5) as meaning: "give up thy horoscopy!" [1] That is to say, He commanded him to leave off his speculative researches into the stars and other matters, and to follow faithfully the object of his inclination, as it is written: "Taste and see that the Lord is good" (Ps. 34:9). [. . .] He who follows the divine law, follows the representatives of this view. His soul finds satisfaction in their teachings, in spite of the simplicity of their speech and ruggedness of their similes. This is not the case with the instructions of philosophers, with their eloquence and fine teachings, however great the impressiveness of their arguments. The masses do not follow them, because the human soul has a presentiment of the truth.

The Kuzari: I see thee turning against the philosophers, attributing to them things of which just the opposite is known. Of a person who lives in seclusion, and acts rightly, it is said, he is a philosopher, and shares the views of philosophers. Thou deprivest them of every good action.

The Master: Nay, what I told thee is the foundation of their belief, viz., that the highest human happiness consists in speculative science and in the conception by reason and thought of all intelligible matters. [. . .] This cannot, however, be obtained except by devoting one's life to research and continual reflection, which is incompatible with worldly occupations. For this reason they renounced wealth, rank, and the pleasure of children, in order not to be distracted from study. As soon as man has become acquainted with the final object of the knowledge sought for, he need not care what he does. They do not fear God for the sake of reward, nor do they think that if they steal or murder that they will be punished. They recommend good and dissuade from evil in the most admirable manner from the point of view of propriety and praiseworthiness, and in order to resemble the Creator who arranged everything so perfectly; they have contrived laws, or rather regulations without binding force, and which may be over-ridden in times of need. The law of the Torah, however, is not so, except in its social parts, and the law itself sets down those which permit exceptions and those which do not.

The Kuzari: The light [of Israel] of which thou speakest has now gone out without hope of its being re-kindled. It has completely disappeared, and no one is able to trace it.

The Master: It is only extinguished for him who does not see us with an open eye, who infers the extinction of our light from our degradation, poverty, and dispersion, and concludes from the greatness of others, their conquests on earth and their power over us, that their light is still burning.

The Kuzari: I will not use this as an argument, as I see two antagonistic religions prevailing, although it is impossible that the truth should be on two opposite sides. It can only be on one or on neither. You have explained to me in connection with the verse: "Behold My servant shall prosper" (Isa. 52:13), that humility and meekness are evidently nearer to the Divine Influence than glory and eminence. The same is visible in these two religions. Christians do not glory in kings, heroes and rich people, but in those who followed Jesus all the time, before his faith had taken firm root among them. They wandered away, or hid themselves, or were killed wherever one of them was found, suffered disgrace and slaughter for the sake of their belief. These are the people in whom they glory, whose ministers they revere, and in whose names they build churches. In the same way did the friends of Islam bear much poverty, until they found assistance. In these, their humility and martyrdom do they glory; not in the princes who boasted of their wealth and power, but rather in those clad in rags and fed scantily on barley bread. Yet they did so in the utmost equanimity and devotion to God. Had I ever seen the Jews act in a like manner for the sake of God, I would place them above the kings of David's house. For I am well aware

of what thou didst teach me concerning the words: "with him
also that is of a contrite and humble spirit" (Isa. 57:15), as well
as that the light of God only rests upon the souls of the humble.

The Master: Thou art right to blame us for bearing our
exile without compensation. But if I think of prominent men
amongst us who could escape this degradation by a word spoken
lightly, become free men, and turn against their oppressors, but
do not do so out of devotion to their faith: is not this the way
to obtain intercession and remission of many sins. [. . .] Besides
this, God has a secret and wise design concerning us, which
should be compared to the wisdom hidden in the seed which
falls into the ground, where it undergoes an external transformation into earth, water and dirt, without leaving a trace for him
who looks down upon it. It is, however, the seed itself which
transforms earth and water into its own substance, carries it from
one degree to another, until it refines the elements and transfers
them into something like itself, casting off husks, leaves, etc. and
allowing the pure core to appear, capable of bearing the Divine
Influence. The original seed produced the tree bearing fruit re-
sembling that from which it had been produced. In the same
manner the Torah of Moses transforms each one who comes after
him, though he may externally reject it. The nations merely serve
to introduce and pave the way for the expected Messiah, who is
the fruition, and they will all become his fruit. Then, if they
acknowledge him, they will become one tree. They will revere
the origin which they formerly despised, as we have observed
concerning the words: "Behold My servant shall prosper."

THE EVENT ON SINAI

Moses Maimonides

About 1165 the Jewish community in faraway Yemen found itself in a
critical situation. The fanatical Shiite ruler of Yemen initiated a forced
conversion to Islam and started on a course of persecutions; a recent
Jewish convert to Islam propagandized for his new religion; another
Jew inaugurated a Messianic movement, with himself as the precursor

of the redeemer. The thrice-troubled community turned to Moses
Maimonides for guidance. In his *Iggeret Teman* (Epistle to Yemen),
written about 1172, Maimonides offered sober arguments against the
apostate's contention that the Bible alluded to the rise of Muhammad;
he cautioned against premature Messianism, warned against pretenders,
but upheld the hope of ultimate redemption. Above all, he expressed
the trust that Israel would survive suffering and persecution; the
strength for such survival, he stated, comes from realization of the
revelation on Sinai. The selection that follows refers to this aspect of
the Epistle. The Epistle, written in Arabic, was translated into Hebrew by Samuel ibn Tibbon and others.

The sages, of blessed memory, frequently allude to persecutions in the following manner: "Once the wicked government
passed the following decree of persecution," or, "they decreed so
and so." After a while God would make the decree null and
void by destroying the power which issued it. It was this observation that led the sages to affirm that persecutions are of short
duration.

The divine assurance was given to Jacob our father, that
his descendants would survive the people who degraded and discomfited them as it is written: "And thy seed shall be like the
dust of the earth" (Gen. 28:14). That is to say, although his offspring will be abased like dust that is trodden under foot, they
will ultimately emerge triumphant and victorious, and as the
simile implies, just as the dust settles finally upon him who tram-
ples upon it, and remains after him, so shall Israel outlive its
persecutors.

The prophet Isaiah has long ago predicted that various
peoples will succeed in vanquishing Israel and lording over them
for some time. But that ultimately God will come to Israel's assistance and will put a stop to their woes and affliction.

We are in possession of the divine assurance that Israel is
indestructible and imperishable, and will always continue to be
a pre-eminent community. As it is impossible for God to cease
to exist, so is Israel's destruction and disappearance from the
world unthinkable, as we read, "For I the Lord change not, and
ye, O sons of Jacob, will not be consumed." (Malachi 3:6). Similarly, He has avowed and assured us that it is unimaginable that
He will reject us entirely even if we disobey Him, and disregard

His behests, as the prophet Jeremiah avers, "Thus saith the Lord: If heaven above can be measured, and the foundations of the earth searched out beneath, Then will I also cast off all the seed of Israel for all that they have done, saith the Lord" (Jer. 31:36). Indeed this very promise has already been given before through Moses our master who says, "And yet for all that, when they are in the land of their enemies, I will not reject them, neither will I abhor them, to destroy them utterly, and to break My covenant with them; for I am the Lord their God" (Lev. 26:44).

Put your trust in the true promises of Scripture, brethren, and be not dismayed at the series of persecutions or the enemy's ascendency over us, or the weakness of our people. These trials are designed to test and purify us so that only the saints and the pious ones of the pure and undefiled lineage of Jacob will adhere to our religion and remain within the fold, as it is written, "And among the remnant are those whom the Lord shall call" (Joel 3:5). This verse makes it clear that they are not numerous, being the descendants of those who were present on Mount Sinai, witnessed the divine revelation, entered into the covenant of God, and undertook to do and obey as is signified in their saying, "we will do, and obey" (Exod. 24:7). They obligated not only themselves but also their descendants, as it is written, "to us and to our children forever." (Deut. 29:28). We have been given adequate divine assurance that not only did all the persons who were present at the Sinaitic revelation believe in the prophecy of Moses and in his Torah, but that their descendants likewise would do so, until the end of time, as it is written, "Lo, I come unto thee in a thick cloud, that the people may hear when I speak with thee, and may also believe thee forever" (Exod. 10:9).

Consequently it is manifest that he who spurns the religion that was revealed at that theophany, is not an offspring of the folk who witnessed it. For our sages have insisted that they who entertain scruples concerning the divine message are not scions of the people that were present on Mount Sinai. May God guard us and you from doubt, and banish from our midst confusion, suspicion, which lead to it.

Now, my brethren, all Israel in the diaspora, it behooves you to hearten one another, the elders to guide the youth, and the leaders to direct the masses. Give your assent to the truth that is immutable and unchangeable, and to the following postulates of a religion that shall never fail. God is one in a unique sense of the term, and Moses is His prophet and spokesman, and the greatest and most perfect of the seers. To him was vouchsafed by God what has never been vouchsafed to any prophet before him, nor will it be in the future. The entire Torah was divinely revealed to Moses of whom it was said, "with him do I speak mouth to mouth" (Num. 12:8). It will neither be abrogated nor superseded, neither supplemented nor abridged. Never shall it be supplanted by another divine revelation containing positive and negative duties. Keep well in mind the revelation on Sinai in accordance with the divine precept to perpetuate the memory of this occasion and not to allow it to fall into oblivion. Furthermore we were enjoined to impress this event upon the minds of our children, as it is written, "Only take heed to thyself, and keep thy soul diligently, lest thou forget the things which thine eyes saw, and lest they depart from thy heart all the days of thy life; but make them known unto thy children and thy children's children" (Deut. 4:9).

It is imperative, brethren, that you make this great event on Sinai appeal to the imagination of your children. Proclaim at public gatherings its momentousness. For this event is the pivot of our religion, and the proof which demonstrates its veracity. Evaluate this phenomenon at its true importance for Scripture has pointed out its significance in the verse, "For ask now of the days past, which were before thee, since the day that God created man upon the earth, and from the one end of heaven unto the other, whether there hath been any such thing as this great thing is, or hath been heard like it?" (Deut. 4:32).

Remember, my brethren in this covenant, that this great, incomparable and unique historical event, is attested by the best of evidence. For never before or since, has a whole nation witnessed a revelation from God or beheld His splendor. The purpose of all this was to confirm us in the faith so that nothing can change it, and to reach a degree of certainty which will sustain us in these trying times of fierce persecution and absolute tyranny, as it is written, "for God is come to test you" (Exod.

20:17). Scripture means that God revealed Himself to you thus
in order to give you strength to withstand all future trials. Now
do not slip nor err, be steadfast in your religion, and persevere in
your faith and its duties.

THE PROSELYTE

Moses Maimonides

Although Judaism, after the loss of Jerusalem, refrained from missionary zeal, it always considered itself a universal religion; periods of
complete exclusivity were relatively few. Individuals who, like Abraham
of old, found their way to the faith of Israel were welcomed in the
community; they were included in the prayer for God's mercy. There
are known examples of proselytes who shared the fate of the imperiled
community and ended their life as martyrs. The text that follows is a
responsum by Maimonides (see "Moses Maimonides") addressed to a
proselyte who invited an authoritative opinion on his status.

I received the question of the wise and erudite scholar,
Obadiah the proselyte. You ask as to whether you, being a proselyte, should utter the prayers: "Our God and God of our fathers;
Who has separated us from the nations; Who has brought us
out of Egypt," and the like.

Pronounce all prayers as they are written and do not change
anything. Your prayer and blessing should be the same as that
of any other Israelite, regardless of whether you pray in private
or conduct the service of the community. The explanation is as
follows: Abraham, our father, taught mankind the true belief
and the oneness of God, repudiating idolatry; through him many
of his own household and also others were guided "to keep the
way of the Lord, to do righteousness and justice" (Gen. 18:19).
Thus he who becomes a proselyte and confesses the oneness of
God, as taught in the Torah, is a disciple of Abraham, our father.
Such persons are of his household. Just as Abraham influenced
his contemporaries through his word and teaching, so he leads
to belief all future generations, through the testament he gave to
his children and his household. In this sense Abraham is the

father of his descendants who follow his ways, and of his disciples, and of all the proselytes.

You should therefore pray, "Our God and God of our fathers," for Abraham is also your father. In no respect is there a difference between us and you. And certainly you should say, "Who has given unto us the Torah," because the Torah was given to us and the proselytes alike, as it is said: "As for the congregation, there shall be one statute both for you and for the stranger who lives with you; as ye are, so shall the stranger be before the Lord. One law and one ordinance shall be both for you and for the stranger that lives with you" (Num. 15:16f.). Keep in mind that most of our ancestors who left Egypt were idol worshipers; they mingled with the Egyptian heathen and imitated their ways, until God sent Moses, our teacher, the master of all the prophets. He separated us from these nations, initiated us into the belief in God, us and all the proselytes, and gave us one Law.

Do not think little of your origin: we are descended from Abraham, Isaac, and Jacob, but your descent is from the Creator, for in the words of Isaiah, "One shall say: 'I am the Lord's'; and another shall call himself by the name of Jacob" (Isa. 44:5).

BENEDICTION WHEN

FACING MARTYRDOM

Medieval Jewish chronicles, especially those from Central Europe, are replete with reports of individuals and communities that, when faced by the choice between death and apostasy, chose martyrdom. The saints of the Maccabean period, the defenders of Masada, Rabbi Akiba and other sages of the era of the Hadrianic persecution, offered examples for the "Sanctification of the Name" (*Kiddush ha-Shem*), as such martyrdom was termed. German Jewry gave rise to a special benediction for such occasions. The appended quotation is from a *responsum* by Meir of Rothenburg, a thirteenth-century German rabbi.

> Blessed art Thou, O Lord, our God, king of the universe,
> who has sanctified us by Thy commandments
> and bade us love Thy glorious and awful Name
> Who was and is and will be,

> with all our heart and all our soul,
> and to sanctify Thy Name in public.
> Blessed art Thou, O Lord,
> who sanctifies Thy Name among the many.

Once a person has made the decision to die for the sanctification of the divine Name, then people may inflict upon him all imaginable pain yet he will remain numb. That this is indeed the case is proven by the fact that no man can touch fire without crying out at the slightest contact, even if he decides to keep back his cry; yet we know that the martyrs do not cry.

WHY CATASTROPHES COME

Solomon Alami

On March 15, 1391, anti-Jewish riots broke out in Seville and spread over Castile; Jewish quarters were sacked, synagogues ruined, lives destroyed. Conversion was a possible escape, but the greed for Jewish wealth was greater than the desire for converts. Christians who were discovered sheltering Jews were punished. By the time passions subsided, some seventy communities had been attacked and over seventy thousand Jews had perished. Spanish Jewry was broken.

An eyewitness of the persecutions, Solomon Alami, scholar and community leader, addressed in 1415, his *Iggeret Musar* (Epistle of Ethical Admonition) to one of his disciples. In the spirit of Biblical prophecy, Alami interpreted the events of 1391 as occasioned by Israel's moral and religious failings. Only honest self-criticism and radical improvement of one's inner life will lead to a better future, he counseled.

The *Iggeret Musar* (the concluding part of which is here reprinted) was first printed in 1510 in Constantinople and went through several editions. In 1946, A. M. Haberman edited the Parma manuscript of the Epistle from a photostat in the Schocken Library in Jerusalem.

"Rejoice not, O Israel! Exult not like the peoples" (Hosea 9:1). Forget not the evil decrees hurled against us since the year 4908 [1148], when the Almohades made themselves masters in Spain and persecuted our communities and seats of learning. A few years later destruction came to the eastern countries. Moses Maimonides lived at that time; both in his youth and in his old age he witnessed the hardships of his people. Because of our many sins the community of Lucena was reduced to ruins, Lucena "a city and a mother in Israel," a center of learning for many generations.

The next period brought the expulsion from England [1290], from France [1306], and from other realms. From that time on we sank deeper and deeper, and our Torah was delivered unto flames. Our wives and daughters were defiled; the others were deprived of their honor. Deep calls to deep, calls for sword, famine, and captivity. Death seems preferable to such a life. Very recently, in the year 5151 [1391], we suffered much destruction in all the provinces of Castile and in the kingdom of Catalonia. Our communities in Aragon, too, were gravely tried and had to endure famine and thirst, homelessness and the death of many children.

This we cannot forget. But if we ask ourselves why all this happened to us, then we have to accept the truth: we ourselves are at fault. God is just and righteous and it was in His power to help us. We and our own iniquities caused this evil to happen.

Our sages were jealous of each other and disrespectful. Their main attention was given to minor details, to novel explanations, clever elucidations. They did not pay much attention to the Book before them, and its counsel of justice and sanctity. There was much quarreling among the wise men. What the one proved, the other disproved; what the one forbade, the other permitted. Thus the Torah, which was one, fell apart. People did not feel obliged to follow such blind leadership, and no wonder.

Then there were those scholars who attempted to interpret the Scriptures in the Greek manner and clothe it in a Greek dress. They believed that Plato and Aristotle had brought us more light than Moses our master.

Now, if a man should not be able to "live by his faith," why should he suffer death for it and endure the yoke and the shame of dispersion among the nations? It serves no good purpose to quote Scriptures as support for philosophical opinions; the way of reason and the way of faith are too far apart and will never meet. No prophets are found among the followers of Aristotle, while many prophets, young and old, arose in Israel's ancient land. Those who read a few columns in a book of Greek philosophy will soon tear to shreds the scroll of the Torah, scoff at the laws, and dispute the validity of tradition. They will never know the thought of the Lord, never understand His counsel.

The next in line of decadence were the leaders of the communities and those favored and trusted by the kings. Their riches and high position made them forsake humility and forget the general misery. "Israel hath forgotten his Maker and builded palaces" (Hosea 8:14). They acquired costly wagons and horses, dressed in precious garments; the wives and daughters of these leaders carried themselves like princesses, and proudly displayed their jewelry.

They gave up study and industry, and cultivated idleness, vainglory, and inordinate ambition. Law and wisdom, our ancient heirloom, no longer counted for them. Everyone chased after coveted positions; envy estranged a man from his fellow and they didn't mind denouncing one another before the Court. Little did they realize that their souls were the price they paid and that they faced a bitter end. They oppressed the wretched, and the poor became the victims of their tyranny. The burden of taxation they shifted to the poorer class. In the end, the Court itself found them despicable and removed them from their power. No Jew was left who could represent the cause of the people before the king and say a good word in behalf of a fellow Jew in need. Down to the ground fell the glory of the "mighty." It is time to wake up from the slumber of foolishness.

There are still other reasons for our miseries and hardships. Our heart lacks faith and modesty; we refuse to admit our failings; our good deeds lack sincerity; our prayers are light-hearted. If you take from your face the mask of hypocrisy and if you have eyes to see you will recognize that the majority of our nation have abandoned truth.

The Sabbath is being profaned and those who try to voice admonition are quickly silenced; no one likes the moralist. The seer shall not see. "Speak to us smooth things, prophesy illusions" (Isaiah 30:10).

There are many among us who repudiate the belief in divine providence, and only few who retain the idea of reward and punishment.

There is no communal spirit among us. People quarrel over trifles. Strict honesty is no longer observed; there is over-reaching, and deceit is practiced even in dealing with the people at large: thus do we desecrate in their midst the Holy Name of our God.

Who among us is ready to give up the love of the world and to consider his end? Who will repent his treason and return to his God with a perfect heart? Who will again dedicate himself to the Covenant of Israel, and in his youth or, later, in his maturity enter the service of his God? Not one man will you find among us who will seriously reflect on the fall of our own kingdom, the decline of wisdom, the cessation of prophecy, the destruction of our Temple, and the desecration of the Name of God who is our glory. Not one will divest himself of his orna-ments in mourning over the disgrace of the Torah, the mar-tyrdom of our sages—events which our eyes have seen and our ears have heard—the loss of our congregation and our homes.

Surrounded by people suffering persecution, expulsion, forced conversion, some there are who manage to hold banquets, listen to music, and imitate the Gentiles in their clothes and hairdress.

The nation in whose land we sojourn offers tithes and gen-erous contributions for the support of their scholars, and this strengthens their religion; princes and noblemen desire to dedi-cate their children to the service of the church. Our own emi-nences, on the other hand, keep their sages on bread and water; no one can maintain even this meager subsistence without suf-fering humiliation; utterly disgraceful is the way in which the secretaries in charge of charity are dealt with. Our notables are not at all eager to have their sons become scholars. The word of God is not wanted by these proud men. Seeing the low state of scholars, simple people, too, prefer to let their sons learn the humblest of crafts rather than enter into the humiliating world of learning.

If you look around you in a place of worship where a

teacher expounds the Law, you will find the rich people asleep, the others engaged in idle talk, and the women in chatter. Should the speaker reprimand them the situation would grow worse. Here we could learn much from our Christian neighbors, who listen quietly and reverently to their preacher, and who are responsive to his scolding; no one will nap while he delivers his sermon.

Much ado is made about charity; the rich talk a lot and do little; what they pledge on the Sabbath they regret on Sunday; the collectors call on them ten times before they receive the promised donation. Woe unto the poor who depend on their kind hearts. The prophet had them in mind when he said: "And He looked for justice, but behold violence; for righteousness, but behold a cry" (Isaiah 5:7).

Often I hear you, my brethren, complaining about having been snubbed. It serves you right. Rarely do you yourselves respect each other. Quite often is the wise man excluded from your circles; instead, you welcome dandies and bearers of titles. In Andalusia I knew rich Jews who never invited anyone but equally rich Jews; they played hosts to monks, imams, government officials, dance masters, court contractors, comedians, circus proprietors, doubtful characters of all colors and creeds; but no Jewish scholar was ever invited, no serious author, no teacher of the ancient nobility of Israel, Jewish issues are discredited and renounced; people forget that this leads to the rejection of the human.

The imitation of the customs of the ruling Church assumed frightful proportions, especially in Mallorca. Some Jews avoided speaking the word "Jew" in the presence of Christian servants. Presents were exchanged on Christmas, not on Purim as Scripture and ancestral usage decreed. Parties were tendered on Easter; Passover, the holiday commemorating Israel's liberation from slavery, was treated like a weekday. The Sabbath was no longer observed, at least not as a day of joyous rest. Grace after meals was interrupted in honor of any Christian acquaintance who entered the door. The daughters of rich families could no longer read Hebrew. Indeed, not much remained of these families; in my youth most of them had already joined the Church.

Others were satisfied with preserving the outer forms of religion while disregarding its inner content. On a day of penitence they got rid of their prayers but not of their vices. They used adulatory words in the street; at home you heard only incessant squabbling and quarreling. There is no understanding between father and son; mothers are despised by their "educated" daughters. In the prayers on the Day of Atonement, the only true things are the listings of sins; the transgressions enumerated must sound familiar.

Much time was needed for the pursuit of pleasure, especially by the rich families of exuberant Seville; no time was left in which to pay attention to the poor, to friends, to teachers, or scholars. Festivities and banquets ate up leisure, money, and— mercy. Luxurious living bred egoism, arrogance, a negative attitude to the Torah of our fathers, and a callousness towards Israel's needs.

Among the scholars, teachers of the laws, authors of books, you find vanity and contentiousness competing with scholarship and piety. Many study in order to get a position, they teach for the fee; pretense rates higher than quiet work; the handsome speaker displaces the solid one, the flatterer pushes aside the honest man. Simple teachings are made complicated by unproductive sophistry, just in order to parade something "novel." Little men, poor of mind, write books of no use to anybody; they carry copies to their sponsors, who give them some money; they should be ashamed to disgrace our ancient writings.

Worse, of course, is the half-educated crowd, philosophers in their bedrooms who, blind to true knowledge, believe that the world stands and falls on their doings. What they read but don't understand, they reject as of no value; what they do grasp, they have known all along. In Portugal, I found a whole class of semi-scholars who had put their noses into various books; yet before they had time to learn anything they already felt qualified to judge others. They appeared as the protagonists of whatever was being much talked about; they memorized pertinent quotations from fashionable philosophers and from writers in vogue; they were the heralds of every newest craze. Recently, in Elvas, a man was ready to found a society for the support of some latest rage, sure of the acclaim of the young ladies.

The right way is to listen to the teachings of the prophets and of the sages of old; to advance humility, loving-kindness, and virtue; to love Israel and its Torah, and to be forbearing with the faults of our brethren. May they learn to act out of true fear of God and not out of worldly vanity. If people could be taught to restrain their desires, to be content, and to trust in divine providence, then much of what saddens my heart would be overcome and our good would increase with the good of man. May what happened to our philosophers in Catalonia not happen to us: their strength of faith was surpassed by simple people, by women and children.

The promise of our Scriptures upholds me; so great is the power of this promise, so deep the fountain of our hope, that I do not despair of the future of Israel, which one day will recognize its failings and receive forgiveness.

THE PARABLE OF
THE PRECIOUS STONES

Solomon ibn Verga

The work *Shevet Yehudah* (The Rod of Judah) by Solomon ibn Verga and his son Joseph is a compilation of popular traditions, reports on Jewish persecutions in the Middle Ages, religious disputations between Jews and Christians, and an inquiry into the causes of anti-Jewish sentiment, especially in Spain. The elder ibn Verga lived at the time of the expulsion of the Jews from Spain, went to Portugal, became a Marrano, and fled the country in 1506; Joseph emigrated as a Marrano to Turkey, where he completed his father's work. It is dedicated to a relative, Judah ibn Verga, whose records the authors may have used.

The parable reprinted below is testimony to a spirit of religious liberalism with an admixture of philosophic skepticism. It first appeared in Italian collections of anecdotes and stories (*novelle*), e.g., in Boccaccio's *Decamerone*. Later we find it in G. E. Lessing's *Nathan the Wise* (1779), the dramatic poem on tolerance.

The book was first printed in Turkey about 1550; it later appeared in Spanish (Amsterdam, 1640), and in Latin (Amsterdam, 1651).

Once, King Don Pedro the Elder had a Jewish sage, Ephraim ben Sancho, brought before him. He asked him: "Which religion is, in your opinion, the better one, the religion of Jesus or yours?" Answered the sage: "My religion is better for me, in view of my condition: I was a slave in Egypt and God has miraculously delivered me from there; but your religion is better for you, as it was always the dominant one." Said the king: "My question refers to the religions themselves, without regard to their adherents."

The sage answered: "After three days' deliberation I shall give answer to my lord—if this is acceptable." The king agreed.

After three days the sage returned and appeared to be perturbed and in a dejected mood. The king inquired about the reason for this state of mind and the sage answered: "I have been slandered today without having done anything wrong and I come to you, our Lord, for your judgment. This is what happened. A month ago my neighbor went on a long journey; in order to comfort his two sons he left them two precious stones. Now the two brothers came to me to inquire about the value of the stones and the difference between them. I told them: 'Who would know this better than your father, the *lapidario*, who is a great authority in the field of precious stones; send to him and he will tell you the truth.' Thereupon they hit me and slandered me."

Said the king: "They have done wrong and deserve to be punished."

Replied the sage: "O our king, do notice what you yourself just said. Behold, Esau and Jacob[2] were brothers each of whom received a precious stone. Now, our lord had asked which is the better one; may he send a messenger to our Father in heaven, the great *lapidario;* he will surely explain the difference between the two."

Equality

Jacob ben Abba Mari Anatoli

The quotation that follows is from *Malmad ha-Talmidim,* a collection of expositions on the Pentateuch in which the author, Jacob ben Abba Mari Anatoli (France-Italy, thirteenth century) demanded a thorough knowledge of the sacred texts and their backgrounds as a precondition for piety and religious practice. Anatoli was a physician, preacher, translator, admirer of Maimonides' philosophy, and opposed to a narrow view of Judaism; in his sermons he quotes Plato, Aristotle, Averroes and Christian contemporaries, Michael Scotus and Emperor Frederick II (who sponsored his translating activity).

With regard to [the idea of] man having been created in the image of God [it must be said that] all peoples are equal and it cannot be maintained that only the people of Israel has been granted a soul [. . .]. In truth, all men are created in the image of God and this is the will of God. Israel has been distinguished as the recipient of the revealed teachings. By its dedication to them Israel is better prepared to represent this quality. Yet a Gentile who dedicates himself to Torah is greater than a Jew who turns his back upon it.

The hebrews

among the nations

Simone Luzzatto

Simone (Simhah) ben Isaac Luzzatto (1583–1663), rabbi in Venice, planned a work on the beliefs and customs of Judaism; a treatise on the status of the Jews among the nations, with emphasis on the conditions in Venice, was to become an appendix to this work. The larger plan probably never materialized, but the treatise is extant: *Discorso circa il stato degli Ebrei* (1638), dedicated to the Venetian doge and the Senate. This dedication explains the apologetic nature of the treatise; however, the author displays impartiality and discusses both Jewish merits and faults with equal candor. His approach is historical and socio-economical, rather than theological. (As a theologian, Luzzatto was opposed to mysticism and to Messianic speculations, and advocated a middle course between reason and revelation).

Peoples and nations have their days numbered no less than all other sublunary things. Once they have reached the very apogee of their grandeur, their plunge into the abyss of oblivion is not far:

> Muoiono le Città, muoiono i Regni
> Copre is fasti e le pompe arena e herba

> (Cities die, Kingdoms die
> And under sand and weeds their pomp and ostentation lie).

Since things come to their end in one of two ways, either by decaying utterly, or by transforming themselves, i.e., retaining their essence while breaking into fragments and losing their simple configuration (as in the instance of shattered glass and divided waters), so, in the same wise, are nations unmade and their existence concluded. Chaldea, Persia, Greece, Rome, and all the Gentilic nations were utterly abolished; they were dissolved and transformed by new metamorphoses; only the names of some of these have come down to us; and of others, only an occasional fragment of their history, which has been preserved for us like stray timbers from some shipwreck.

The Hebrew nation did not undergo such mutation and chance, but rather was shattered and divided into an infinity of pieces, and dispersed over the orb. Yet it retained in great measure its essential identity. We cannot doubt that of itself it could not have summoned up the strength to stay the ravening appetite of time, successfully to withstand its fierce onset over a space of 1600 years; but that it depended upon the will of Divine Majesty to preserve it, for ends best known to Itself.

Though captivity and dispersion be the worst scourge that can befall a people or nation, rendering it lowly and abject, and the scorn and mockery of others, it is nonetheless a sovereign remedy for its duration and preservation, for it relieves the ruling

Princes of their envy and suspicion, and the distracted people of pride and vanity, making them to become humble and compliant. [. . .]

The diaspora not only served them [the Hebrews] well by rendering them obedient to those more mighty than they, but it saved them from dogmatic new fangles, which cannot easily penetrate and invade the whole of the nation, since the integrant parts are divided and dispersed.

As for the number of Hebrews, it cannot be precisely ascertained, for there is not even a trustworthy record at hand, of the places they inhabit. As for the Ten Tribes [of Israel] who were led into captivity by Shalmaneser before the destruction of the First Temple,[3] no certain news of them is to be had, though by now the world has been thoroughly investigated and discovered.

Beginning with the Eastern parts, we know that under the king of Persia a great number of Hebrews have found asylum and a small measure of liberty. In the Turkish state is the principal domicile of the nation, not only because they have long been there, but also because the vast concourse of Hebrews dismissed from Spain found their way thither. The cause of such an influx rested, first and foremost, on liberty to practice their religion, for the Turk is tolerant toward alien faiths. Also, because there is to be found there an infinite quantity of Greeks, who also practice alien rite; hence, no reflection is made on those of the Hebrews. Beyond this, they are allowed to own houses and lands, to lend money, and to exercise whatsoever other profession. No obstacle is placed in the way of owning lands, since there is no nobility. Though the Greeks own a considerable portion of lands, most of them busy themselves with the crafts, whilst the Turks apply themselves to the militia and government of the people; whence it comes about that no occasion is given for hatred and conflict.

It might be supposed that like customs of circumcision must occasion a certain friendly correspondence. Such is not the case, for experience has shown that peoples whose religious practices are in part alike, in part dissimilar, are less congenial to one another than those absolutely divided and distinct therein. In Constantinople and Salonica, there is a greater number of them [the Hebrews] than in other cities. It is thought that these two cities alone have some 80,000; and it is estimated that in the Turkish Empire, they count more than 1,000,000. In the Holy Land and in Jerusalem, in particular, there come annually not only a considerable number of Hebrews from all the nations of the world, but also vast sums in annual revenues which are offered there for the nourishing of the poor and the support of academies.

In Germany, under the Emperor, are also a considerable number, but many more in Poland, Russia, and Lithuania, where there are academies and universities whither thousands of youths repair to study the civil and canon law of the Jews. In those regions they are freely empowered to pronounce upon any difference or dispute, whether civil or criminal, that may arise amidst the nation.

In the dominions separated from the Roman Church, Jews do not reside for the most part. It is a certainty that the Hebrew nation inclines more toward the Roman opinion than that of others. The Jews hold that Holy Writ is in many passages impenetrable without the light of tradition, by which last they set great store, as I have already shown. Further, they believe that good works are very important in the sight of God, and they practice them diligently, though ever joining them to faith. They affirm free will and judge it to be the chief article of their belief. They affirm, similarly, that the merits of others may be a prop to those deficient in virtue; hence, the living pray for the dead. They believe the purification of the penitent to be real—not putative, as Calvin hath held. And though the word Purgatory rarely figures in their authors, they make a three-fold distinction among souls: the beatified, those condemned to finite temporal punishment, and those eternally so condemned; for they hold that God absolves guilt yet exacts the penalty. Their sermons are in Hebrew, not in the vernacular.

In the Low Countries they are treated with great charity and affection, notably in Amsterdam, Rotterdam, and Hamburg. They are lands where mercantile pursuits are so flourishing that all may find an asylum there.

In the Western lands there remains only Italy; and on the

African littoral, the kingdoms of Fez and Morocco. As for Italy, they are universally protected and favored by princes; and their rights and privileges are inalterably respected. These are things under the eyes of all, and I speak no further of Italy. I believe I may give 25,000 as their number.

In Morocco, Fez, and other nearby cities not subject to the sway of the Turk, there are a great number, many of them having removed thither from Castile and Portugal because of the short distance.

A vast number of Jews are reputed to inhabit the interior countries of Africa, but about these regions so little is known that no number can be determined with any certainty.

Though divided, riven, and dismembered, the opinions and dogmas of the whole of this nation are uniform, the ceremonial rites identical, and in certain non-essential things barely dissimilar.

The foregoing is what I have been moved to report concerning this nation and those aspects thereof which appertain to the interest of the princes and peoples who harbor it; in particular, to the Most Serene Venetian Republic, which receives the Jew within her state with such benignity and protects him with wonted justice and clemency, showing by her every action how she detests and abhors that unjust and monstrous sentiment voiced by the impious statesman Photinus to the young and inexperienced King Ptolemy—as Lucan[4] sings:

> *Dat poenas laudata fides, cum susitinet inquit*
> *Quos fortuna premit, fatis accede deisque,*
> *Et cole felices, miseros fuge, sidera terra,*
> *Ut distant, et flamma mari, sic utile recto.*

(We praise loyalty but it pays the price when it supports those whom Fortune crushes. Take the side of destiny and Heaven, and court the prosperous but shun the afflicted. Expediency is far from the right as the stars from earth or fire from water.)

The which utterance brought about the betrayal of the greatest captain of that century; I mean the murder of Magnus Pompey, whose decapitation strangled and severed the neck of Roman liberty, and reared a monument of eternal infamy to him who assented to that execrable utterance. The admonitory prophecy (as feigned by Virgil) and uttered by a most prudent father to a pious son who was to give birth to the grandeur and the glory of the Roman people—this I would commend to this Serene Republic, so that perhaps one day, through the benevolence of Heaven, she may be the emulator of the triumphs, too, of that republic with whose virtues she vies:

> *Tu regere Imperio populos Romane memento.*
> *Hae tibi erunt artes pacisque imponere morem*
> *Parcere subiectis et deballare superbos.*

(Remember, O Roman, with might to rule the nations. These be thy arts: to impose the ways of peace, to spare the humble, to humble the proud.)

VIII. The Sabbath

SHIELD OF OUR FATHERS

Prayer Book

The two main themes of the celebration of the Sabbath, the remembrance of Creation and the memory of Israel's exodus from Egypt, recur in many places within the Sabbath liturgy and rituals. The prayer before us, which refers to the first of the two themes, is recited at the traditional Friday Evening Service, as a summary of the "seven benedictions" of the *Amidah* (Prayer of Benedictions).

> He was a shield of our fathers with His word,
> and by His bidding He will quicken the dead.
> He is the holy God, there is none like him.
> He gives rest to His people on his holy Sabbath day,
> for it pleased Him to grant them rest.
> Him we will worship with reverence and awe,
> and daily and constantly we will praise His name
> in the fitting forms of blessings.
> He is the God of our praise, the Lord of peace,
> Who hallows the Sabbath and blesses the seventh day,
> and in holiness gives rest unto a people abounding with joy,
> in remembrance of His work of Creation.

THE SANCTITY OF THE SABBATH

The *Zohar*

The mystics saw in the Sabbath the mysterious root of all faith, the hidden ground out of which the world renews itself; it is "the door through which a man enters the world to come" (Joseph Gikatila, thirteenth century). The Sabbath, which concluded the work of Creation, is more than a symbol of redemption; it is a foretaste of a perfected, redeemed world. It is "the root of all types of holiness" (Elijah de Vidas, sixteenth century). The excerpt that follows is from the *Zohar* (the Book of Splendor). On the *Zohar,* see "Mystical Understanding of Jewish Concepts."

"Remember the Sabbath Day, to sanctify it" (Exod. 20:8). Said Rabbi Isaac: It is written, "And God blessed the seventh day" (Gen. 2:3); and yet we read of the manna, "Six days ye shall gather it, but on the seventh day, the Sabbath, in it there shall be none" (Exod. 16:26). If there was no food on that day what blessing is attached to it? Yet we have been taught that all blessings from above and from below depend upon the seventh day. Why, then, was there no manna just on this day? The explanation is that all the six days of the transcendent world derive their blessings from it, and each supernal day sends forth nourishment to the world below from what it received from the seventh day. Therefore he who has attained to the grade of Faith must needs prepare a table and a meal on the eve of the Sabbath so that his table may be blessed all through the other six days of the week. For, indeed, at the time of the Sabbath preparation there is also prepared the blessing for all the six days that shall follow, for no blessing is found at an empty table. Thus one should make ready the table on Sabbath night with bread and other food.

Said Rabbi Hiyya: Because all things are found in the Sabbath it is mentioned three times in the story of Creation: "And on the seventh day God ended his work"; "and he rested on the seventh day"; "and God blessed the seventh day" (Gen. 2:2, 3). Rav Hamnuna the ancient, when he sat at his Sabbath meals, used to find joy in each one. Over one he would exclaim: "This is the holy meal of the Holy Ancient One, the All-hidden." Over another he would say: "This is the meal of the Holy One, blessed be he." And when he came to the last one he would say: "Complete the meals of the Faith." Rabbi Simon used always to say when the time of the Sabbath meal arrived: "Prepare ye the meal of the supernal Faith! Make ready the meal of the King!" Then he would sit with a glad heart. And as soon as he had finished the third meal it was proclaimed concerning him: "Then shalt thou delight thyself in the Lord, and I will cause thee to ride upon the high places of the earth and feed thee with the heritage of Jacob thy father" (Isa. 58:14).

Also mark this. On all festivals and holy days a man must both rejoice himself and give joy to the poor. Should he regale himself only and not give a share to the poor, his punishment will be great. [. . .] On this day—so we have been taught—the Fathers crown themselves and all the Children imbibe power and light and joy, such as is unknown even on other festive days. On this day sinners find rest in Gehenna. On this day punishment is held back from the world. On this day the Torah crowns herself in perfect crowns. On this day joy and gladness resound throughout two hundred and fifty worlds.

Mark also this. On all the six days of the week, when the hour of the Afternoon Prayer arrives, the attribute of Justice is in the ascendant, and punishment is at hand. But not so on the Sabbath. When the time of the Sabbath Afternoon prayer arrives benign influences reign, the loving-kindness of the Holy Ancient One is manifested, all chastisements are kept in leash, and all is satisfaction and joy. In this time of satisfaction and goodwill Moses, the holy, faithful prophet, passed away from this world, in order that it should be known that he was not taken away through judgment, but that in the hour of grace of the Holy Ancient One his soul ascended, to be hidden in Him. Therefore "no man knows of his sepulchre unto this day" (Deut. 36:6). As the Holy Ancient One is the All-hidden One, whom neither those above nor those below can comprehend, so was this soul of Moses hidden in the epiphany of God's good will at the hour of the Sabbath Afternoon Prayer. This soul is the most hidden of all hidden things in the world, and judgment has no dominion over it. Blessed is the lot of Moses.

On this day the Torah crowns herself with all beauty, with all those commandments, with all those decrees and punishments for transgressions—in seventy branches of light which radiate on every hand. What it is to behold the little twigs which constantly emanate from each branch—five of which stand in the Tree itself, all the branches being comprised in it!

What it is to behold the gates which open at all sides, and through which bursts forth in splendor and beauty the streaming,

inexhaustible light! A voice is heard: "Awake, ye supernal saints!
Awake, holy people, chosen from above and from below! Awake
in joy to meet your Lord, awake in perfect joy! Prepare yourselves
in the threefold joy of the three Patriarchs! Prepare yourselves
for the Faith, the joy of joys! Happy are ye, O Israelites, holy in
this world and holy in the world to come."

THE SABBATH BRIDE

Israel ibn al-Nakawa

Already the Talmud calls the Sabbath "the bride of the Congregation
of Israel" (Genesis Rabba XI, 9). This motif lent itself to further elaborations by poets, mystics, and ethical writers. The excerpt that follows
is from *Menorat ha-Maor* (The Lamp of Illumination), by Israel ibn
al-Nakawa, an ethical writer of Toledo, Spain, who died a martyr's
death in 1391.

We learn in the Midrash that the Sabbath is like unto a
bride. Just as a bride when she comes to her groom is lovely,
bedecked and perfumed, so the Sabbath comes to Israel lovely
and perfumed, as it is written: "And on the seventh day He
ceased from work and He rested" (Exod. 31:17) and immediately
afterwards we read: "And He gave unto Moses *kekhalloto*
["when he finished," but the word may be translated as] as his
bride," to teach us that just as a bride is lovely and bedecked,
so is the Sabbath lovely and bedecked; just as a groom is dressed
in his finest garments, so is the man on the Sabbath day dressed
in his finest garments; just as a man rejoices all the days of his
wedding feast, so does man rejoice on the Sabbath; just as the
groom does no work on his wedding day, so does a man abstain
from work on the Sabbath day; and therefore the sages and the
early pious men called the Sabbath a bride.

There is a hint of this in the Sabbath prayers. In the Friday
Evening Service we say: "Thou hast sanctified the seventh day,"
referring to the marriage of the bride to the groom ["sanctification" being the Hebrew word for marriage]. In the Morning

Service we say: "Moses rejoiced in the gift [of the Sabbath] bestowed upon him" which corresponds to the groom's rejoicing with the bride. In the Additional Prayer we make mention of "the two lambs, the fine flour for a meal offering, mingled with oil and the drink thereof" referring to the meat, the bread, the wine, and the oil used in the wedding banquet. In the Afternoon Prayer we say: "Thou are one" to parallel the consummation of the marriage by which the bride and groom are united.

THE SABBATH AND THE DAYS

OF THE WEEK

Judah Loew ben Bezalel

Judah Loew (Liva) ben Bezalel ("the Maharal"), *ca*. 1525–1609, rabbi in Prague, is popularly known from the legend that describes him as the creator of the "Golem," a mysterious robot. In his writings he appears as a talmudic scholar, a mildly mystical interpreter of the true meaning of Torah (Torah as the means by which the "lower" and "upper" worlds meet in the human intellect), an opponent of philosophical studies, and as early advocate of the basic natural rights of nations. The passage that follows is from *Tiferet Yisrael*, Venice, 1599.

The statement that God rested on the seventh day of the creation means that He created and completed all. The heavens also are in action, but their activity does not bring any completion and therefore they have no rest for interruption.

One may be surprised at God being linked with the idea of rest, because "The Lord . . . fainteth not, neither is weary" (Isa. 90:78), but one must consider the following: Whoever requires time for his work must finally rest. Of course the creation of the world in time is only as it appears to the recipient, man. For it is impossible that the plants should have appeared at the same moment that the earth was created, when according to the order of the creation the earth itself was to bring them forth. The same applies to all the other creations, and therefore the time had to be extended. Thus if the time required for the creation of the

world is regarded from the human point of view, then also the
rest is meant as a human conception. It is as if it were stated that
God created everything within the time stated for the sake of the
recipient, man, because the latter would faint and grow weary
if he were to receive everything at once. Hence the rest on the
seventh day.

Why there are six days of work and a seventh day of rest
can be explained in the following manner. The world is corporeal, and every body has six different sides, through which it
becomes complete, namely above, below, and the extensions to
the four quarters of the compass. These sides bound the body,
but in every body there is one point set neither to the right nor
the left, neither to the front nor to the back, and which has no
spatial extension like the six sides, namely, the middle. The
middle is not subject to space, therefore it is not corporeal. When
God created the corporeal world, He did so in six days corresponding to the six corporeal extensions. The seventh day was the
day of rest, corresponding to the incorporeal middle.

The seventh day is holy, because holiness can be attributed
only to the incorporeal. When our sages said that on the Sabbath man acquired a special soul, they meant by it that the incorporeal soul increased in strength. Therefore that day is sanctified by the kindling of lights, because light is entirely different
from other corporeal objects.

SANCTIFICATION

Prayer Book

In the liturgy of the Synagogue, the Reader's repetition of the *Amidah*
(Prayer of Benedictions) contains the insertion of the *Kedushah* (Sanctification), a series of Biblical passages spoken by the congregation, introduced and concluded by the Reader. The Biblical verses are Isa.
6:3, Ezek. 3:12, and Ps. 146:10; the *Musaf* (Additional Prayer for Sabbath and Holidays) provides for the insertion of Deut. 6:4 ("Hear, O
Israel") and Num. 15:41 ("I am the Lord"). The introduction presents
the community's glorification of God as corresponding to, and imitat-

ing, the glorification on the part of the heavenly hosts. The liturgy
concludes on the theme of the kingdom of God. The core of the *Kedushah* originated in the talmudic period; various elaborations are the
work of the early Middle Ages. The version that follows is from the
Musaf Service.

Reader
We will revere thee and sanctify thee in the mystic utterance
of the holy Seraphim. They hallow thy name in the heavenly
sanctuary, as it is written by the hand of thy prophet, And they
called unto one another saying:

Congregation
"Holy, holy, holy, is the Lord of hosts: the whole earth is full of
His glory."

Reader
His glory pervades the universe; His ministering angels ask one
another, Where is the place of His glory? In response they say,
Blessed—

Congregation
"Blessed be the glory of the Lord from His place."

Reader
From His place may He turn in mercy and be gracious unto a
people that evening and morning, twice daily, proclaim in love
the unity of His name, saying, Hear—

Congregation
"Hear, O Israel: the Lord our God, the Lord is One."

Reader
One is our God; he is our Father; he is our King; he is our
Savior. He will save and redeem us a second time. In his mercy
He will let us hear in the presence of all living, Behold I have
now redeemed you in the latter times, as at the beginning: "To
be your God.

Congregation
I am the Lord your God."

Reader
And in thy Holy Words it is written, saying,

Congregation
"The Lord shall reign for ever, thy God, O Zion, unto all generations. Hallelujah."

Reader
Unto all generations we will declare thy greatness, and to all eternity we will proclaim thy holiness. Thy praise, O our God, shall never depart from our mouth; for thou, O God, art a great and holy king.
Blessed art thou, O Lord, the holy God.

IX. The Ways of the Mystics

MYSTICAL UNDERSTANDING

OF JEWISH CONCEPTS

The *Zohar*

Jewish mysticism in thirteenth-century Spain, and especially in Castile, can be interpreted, at least in some of its aspects, as a reaction against overemphasis on rationalism in thought and against secularization of life; against Judaism becoming the sole domain of technical scholarship or of the rich and the socially prominent. Mysticism (*Kabbalah,* i.e., tradition) pointed to the deeper layers of Jewish religion, which it represented as the authentic tradition of Israel. It penetrated into the mysteries of the divine being and the miracle of Creation; it applied itself to the problem of Israel's suffering in exile; it focused the adept's attention upon the origins of the world rather than upon the process of history and the "end of days"; it taught purity of thought and the right intention in prayer, study of Torah, and repentance; possibly under the influence of the Franciscan movement, it extolled the poor, the meek, and the ascetic; and it guided to the love of the living God.

The chief work of Kabbalah is the *Zohar* (the Book of Splendor). It was written toward the end of the thirteenth century by Moses de Leon, a man who in his youth had studied Maimonides' philosophical work, then turned toward Neoplatonism and Kabbalah (G. G. Scholem). Composed in Aramaic, the *Zohar* imitated the form of the midrashic works of the early Christian centuries. For three centuries after about 1500 the *Zohar* "came to fulfill the great historical task of a sacred text supplementing the Bible and Talmud on a new level of religious consciousness" (G. G. Scholem).

The work was first published (three volumes) in Mantua, in 1558–1560; there followed many editions of the text and commentaries. Portions of the *Zohar* were translated into Latin by the Christian Kabbalist Knorr von Rosenroth (*Kabbala denudata,* 1677), who was instrumental in acquainting the philosopher Leibniz with Jewish mysticism.

Body and Soul

"Ye shall be holy for I the Lord am holy" (Lev. 19:2). When God came to create the world and reveal what was hidden in the depths and disclose light out of darkness, they were all wrapped in one another, and therefore light emerged from darkness and from the impenetrable came forth the profound. So, too, from good issues evil, and from mercy issues judgment, and all are intertwined, the good impulse and the evil impulse, right and left, Israel and other peoples, white and black—all depend on one another.

Said Rabbi Abba: Why does the section of "holiness" [in Leviticus] follow immediately upon the section dealing with sexual offences? Because we have learnt that whoever preserves himself from these offences shows that he was begotten in holiness; all the more so if he sanctifies himself with the holiness of his Master. The Companions have indicated the proper time of marital intercourse for all classes. He who desires to sanctify himself according to the will of his Master should not have intercourse save from midnight onwards, or at midnight, for at that time the Holy One, blessed be he, is in the Garden of Eden, and greater holiness is abroad, wherefore it is a time for a man to sanctify himself. This is the rule for the ordinary man. But students who know the ways of the Torah should rise at midnight to study and to join themselves with the Community of Israel to praise the holy Name and the holy King; and their time of intercourse is at that hour on the night of the Sabbath when grace abounds, that they may obtain favor from the Community of Israel and the Holy One, blessed be he, and those are called holy.

Rabbi Abba quoted here the verse: "Who is like thy people Israel, one nation in the earth?" (1 Sam. 7:23). God, he said, chose Israel and made them a unique nation in the world and called them "one nation," after His own name. He gave them many precepts to be crowned withal, including the phylacteries of the head and the arm, wherewith a man becomes one and complete. For he is only called "one" when he is complete, and not if he is defective, and therefore God is called One when He is consummated with the Patriarchs and the Community of Israel. When, therefore, the Israelite puts on his phylacteries and wraps himself in the fringed garment, he is crowned with holy crowns after the supernal pattern and is called "one," and it is fitting that One should come and attend to one. And when is a man called "one"? When he is male with female and is sanctified with a high holiness and is bent upon sanctification; then alone he is called one without blemish. Therefore a man should rejoice with his wife at that hour to bind her in affection to him, and they should both have the same intent. When they are thus united, they form one soul and one body: one soul through their affection, and one body, as we have learnt, that if a man is not married he is, as it were, divided in halves, and only when male and female are joined do they become one body. Then God rests upon "one" and lodges a holy spirit in it: and such are called "the sons of God."

The Ten Words

The Ten Words contain the essence of all the commandments, the essence of all celestial and terrestrial mysteries, the essence of the Ten Words of Creation.[1] They were engraved on tables of stone, and all the hidden things were seen by the eyes and perceived by the minds of all Israel, everything being made clear to them. At that hour all the mysteries of the Torah, all the hidden things of heaven and earth, were unfolded before them and revealed to their eyes, for they saw eye to eye the splendor of the glory of their Lord. Never before, since the Holy One created the world, had such a revelation of the Divine Glory taken place. Even the crossing of the Red Sea, where, as has been said, even a simple maid-servant saw more of the Divine than the prophet Ezekiel,[2] was not so wonderful as this.

For on this day all the earthly dross was removed from them and purged away, and their bodies became as lucent as the angels above when they are clothed in radiant garments for the accomplishment of their Master's errands; in which garments they penetrate fire without fear, as we read concerning the angel who appeared to Manoah (Jud. 13:20). And when all the fleshly impurity was removed from the Israelites their bodies became, as we have said, lucent as stars and their souls were as resplendent as the firmament, to receive the light. Such was the state of the Israelites when they beheld the glory of their Lord.

It was not thus at the Red Sea, when the filth had not as yet been removed from them. There, at Mount Sinai, even the embryos in their mothers' wombs had some perception of their Lord's glory, and everyone received according to his grade of perception. On that day the Holy One, blessed be he, rejoiced more than on any previous day since He had created the world, for Creation had no proper basis before Israel received the Torah. But when once Israel had received the Torah on Mount Sinai the world was duly and completely established, and heaven and earth received a proper foundation, and the glory of the Holy One was made known both above and below, and He was exalted over all. Blessed be the Lord for ever. Amen and Amen.

The Poor and the Lowly

Rabbi Eleazar asked Rabbi Simeon, his father: "We've been taught that there are three sins which cause famine to be visited upon the earth, and all three are to be found among the rich, because of their arrogance, and are not found among the poor. Why is it then that God lets the poor perish and preserves the rich? They will only multiply their sins against Him!"

Rabbi Simeon replied: "You have asked a good question. [. . .] Observe, now! Of all the inhabitants of the earth none are as close to the Supreme King as those who serve as His 'vessels.' And who are they? 'A broken and contrite heart' (Ps. 51:19) and 'he who is of a contrite and humble spirit' (Isa. 57:15), these are the vessels of the King. And when famine strikes the world and hunger and privation bear down upon the poor, they weep and cry before the King; and the Holy One, blessed be he, feels closer to them than to anyone else, as is written, 'For He has not despised nor loathed the affliction of the poor man, nor has He hidden His face from him, but whenever he cried to Him, He listened' (Ps. 22:25). And then the Holy One, blessed be he, takes note of that which causes famine to descend upon the earth. Woe unto the wicked, who are the cause of it all, when God is moved to scrutinize the world upon hearing the cries of the poor! God save us from ever offending them, for it is written, 'I will be certain to hear his cry' (Exod. 22:22). [. . .] Woe unto the rich when there is famine in the world, and the voice of the poor reaches to God. The poor man's offering, you see, comes closest to God, for his heart is contrite.''

When the Holy One, blessed be he, visits judgment upon the world, it is for the sin of the heads of the people, the sin of subverting justice and of distorting it. Do not wonder why God allows the lowly to expire through the failure of the mighty to do justice, for the poor are God's vessels and are close to him and when famine comes they cry to Him and He listens to them and He calls before the bar of justice those who brought this suffering upon the poor, as is written, "And when he will cry to me I will listen, for I am kind" (Exod. 22:26).

"A prayer of the poor man, when he grows faint and pours out his complaint before the Lord" (Ps. 102:1): The prayer of the poor man is received by God ahead of all other prayers.

"Happy is he who is considerate of the poor" (Ps. 41:2): How great is the reward that the poor merit of the Lord for they are closest to God, as is written, "A broken and contrite heart, O God, Thou wilt not despise" (Ps. 51:19).

The poor man is closer to God than anyone else, as is written, "And when he will cry to Me, I will listen," for God abides in these broken vessels, as is written, "I dwell on high, amid holiness, but also with the contrite and humble in spirit" (Isa. 57:15). Therefore, we have been taught that he who reviles the indigent scoffs at the Divinity. And it is also written, "Do not rob the poor because he is poor, or crush the needy at the gate; for the Lord will defend their cause and despoil of life those who despoil them" (Prov. 12:22f.). Their Guardian is mighty and He holds sway over all. He requires no witnesses and no associate judge, nor does He take a bond as do other judges.

He who looks after the welfare of the poor man, God sees to his welfare and prolongs his life even when his day comes to depart this world. "The wages of a hired man shall not remain with thee overnight" (Lev. 19:13). He who withholds the poor man's hire from him, in effect deprives him and his family of their life. Just as he reduces their vitality, God reduces his days and shortens his life in this world. Even if long life and many good things had been decreed for that man, they are all withdrawn from him. What is more, his soul does not rise aloft.

Happy is he who encounters a poor man, for this poor man is a gift sent to him by God.

Material Wealth

One day a young man approached his teacher and said to him, "Master, where is the wealth?" "It is obvious," reasoned the teacher, "that he is not motivated in the pursuit of learning by any lofty ideal," so he retired to his chamber. There he heard a voice saying to him, "Do not frown upon the young man, for he shall yet be great." The master went back to the student and said to him, "Sit down, my son; sit, and I will give you riches." Presently, a very rich man came along and gave the student some of his wealth, and the love of Torah waxed stronger in the young man's heart. One day the teacher found the young man sitting and weeping; whereupon he asked him, "Why do you weep?" The student replied, "Will I forfeit my share of the world to come because of this wealth? I seek only the spiritual rewards for good deeds." Thought the master, "It is evident that his study is now heaven-intentioned." He summoned the rich man and said to him, "Take your wealth and distribute it to the poor and the orphaned."

THE PRACTICE OF

MYSTICAL MEDITATION

Abraham Abulafia

Abraham Abulafia was born in Saragossa, Aragon, in 1240. One of the major figures in medieval Jewish mysticism, he became the representative of what G. G. Scholem terms "prophetic Kabbalah," an originator of a method leading to an intuitive, "prophetic," knowledge of God and an ecstatic communion with Him. The method consisted in a contemplation upon the letters of the Hebrew alphabet, which in certain mystical computations and combinations (*Tzeruf*) constitute the name of God. "The systematic practice of meditation as taught by him [Abulafia], produces a sensation closely akin to that of listening to musical harmonies. The science of combination is a music of pure thought, in which the alphabet takes the place of the musical scale" (G. G. Scholem). The Kabbalist succeeded in reconciling his mystic doctrine with the religious philosophy of Maimonides, whom he greatly revered. In the last analysis, the latter's *Guide to the Perplexed* leads to mystic knowledge. In 1280, the visionary, in response to an "inner voice," journeyed to Rome, to call Pope Nicholas III to account for the sufferings of the Jews and to propose to him a conversion to Judaism. Abulafia was condemned to the stake; the Pope's death soon thereafter gained Abulafia a stay of execution. Among his many writings is the apocalypse *Sefer ha-Ot* (The Book of the Sign), published by A. Jellinek in 1887. His chief disciple was Joseph ben Abraham Gikatila. Abulafia died in Barcelona about 1292. Our first selection deals with the practice of meditation; the second describes the mystical experience.

I

Know that the method of *Tzeruf* [the combination of letters] can be compared to music; for the ear hears sounds from various combinations, in accordance with the character of the melody and the instrument. Also, two different instruments can form a combination, and if the sounds combine, the listener's ear registers a pleasant sensation in acknowledging their difference. The strings touched by the right or left hand move, and the sound is sweet to the ear. And from the ear the sensation travels to the heart, and from the heart to the spleen,[3] and enjoyment of the different melodies produces ever new delight. It is impossible to produce it except through the combination of sounds, and the same is true of the combination of letters. It touches the first string, which is comparable to the first letters, and proceeds to the second, third, fourth and fifth, and the various sounds combine. And the secrets, which express themselves in these combinations, delight the heart which acknowledges its God and is filled with ever fresh joy.

II

Be prepared for thy God, oh Israelite! Make thyself ready to direct thy heart to God alone. Cleanse the body and choose a lonely house where none shall hear thy voice. Sit there in thy closet and do not reveal thy secret to any man. If thou canst, do it by day in the house, but it is best if thou completest it during the night. In the hour when thou preparest thyself to speak with the Creator and thou wishes Him to reveal His might to thee, then be careful to abstract all thy thought from the vanities of this world. Cover thyself with thy prayer shawl and put phylacteries on thy head and hands that thou mayest be filled with awe of the Divine Presence which is near thee. Cleanse thy clothes, and, if possible, let all thy garments be white, for all this is helpful in leading the heart towards the fear of God and the love of God. If it be night, kindle many lights, until all be bright. Then take ink, pen and a table to thy hand and remember that thou art about to serve God in joy of the gladness of heart. Now begin to combine a few or many letters, to permute and to combine them until thy heart be warm. Then be mindful of their movements and of what thou canst bring forth by moving them.

And when thou feelest that thy heart is already warm and when thou seest that by combinations of letters thou canst grasp new things which by human tradition or by thyself thou wouldst not be able to know and when thou art thus prepared to receive the influx of divine power which flows into thee, then turn all thy true thought to imagine the Name and His exalted angels in thy heart as if they were human beings sitting or standing about thee. And feel thyself like an envoy whom the king and his ministers are to send on a mission, and he is waiting to hear something about his mission from their lips, be it from the king himself, be it from his servants. Having imagined this very vividly, turn thy whole mind to understand with thy thoughts the many things which will come into thy heart through the letters imagined. Ponder them as a whole and in all their detail, like one to whom a parable or a dream is being related, or who meditates on a deep problem in a scientific book, and try thus to interpret what thou shalt hear that it may as far as possible accord with thy reason.

And all this will happen to thee after having flung away tablet and quill or after they will have dropped from thee because of the intensity of thy thought. And know, the stronger the intellectual influx within thee, the weaker will become thy outer and thy inner parts. Thy whole body will be seized by an extremely strong trembling, so that thou wilt think that surely thou art about to die, because thy soul, overjoyed with its knowledge, will leave thy body. And be thou ready at this moment consciously to choose death, and then thou shall know that thou hast come far enough to receive the influx. And then wishing to honor the glorious Name by serving it with the life of body and soul, veil thy face and be afraid to look at God. Then return to the matters of the body, rise and eat and drink a little, or refresh thyself with a pleasant odor, and restore thy spirit to its sheath until another time, and rejoice at thy lot and know that God loveth thee!

THE SEARCH FOR TRUTH

Solomon ibn Adret

Solomon ibn Adret (*ca.* 1235–1310), disciple of Jonah Gerondi and Moses Nahmanides (see "Has the Messiah Come?"), rabbi of Barcelona, and widely recognized rabbinical authority and leader of Spanish Jewry ("El Rab d'Espagña"), was compelled to take a stand on two crucial issues of his day: philosophy and mysticism. Although he greatly respected both the rationalist Maimonides and the mystic Nahmanides, he saw the Jewish community imperiled by the trends the two men represented. Philosophical enlightenment bred religious skepticism; mysticism gave rise to visionaries, blindly followed by the credulous. To counteract the first, he issued (1305) a ban against those who would study philosophy before reaching the age of twenty-five (i.e., before having undergone a thorough training in the traditional talmudic discipline). To meet the second danger, he released a long and sharply worded *responsum* (Nr. 548) against the untutored and unrestrained mystics, and especially against Abraham Abulafia (see "The Practice of Mystical Meditation"). The passage that follows appears at the end of this *responsum*.

To Israel, the heir of the religion of truth, the children of Jacob, the man of truth. [. . .] it is easier to bear the burden of exile than to believe in anything before it is thoroughly and repeatedly examined and all its dross has been purged away, even though it appears to be a sign or a miracle. The undeniable evidence for Israel's love of truth and rejection of anything which is doubtful can be seen in the relation of the people of Israel to Moses. In spite of the fact that they were crushed by slavery, yet when Moses was told to bring them tidings of their redemption, he said to the Lord: "Behold, they will not believe me, nor hearken to my voice, for they will say: 'The Lord hath not appeared unto me'" (Exod. 4:1). Moses had to bring evidence. Thus it is characteristic of our people not to be satisfied unless exhaustive examination has proven a matter to be true.

LIFE IN SAFED

Solomon Shloemel ben Hayyim Meinstrl

The Land of Israel, which never ceased to attract Jewish pilgrims and settlers, gained added importance when, in the sixteenth century, the mystic doctrines of Isaac Luria of Safed spread throughout the Jewish world. The sages of Safed planned the reinstitution of the ancient rite of ordination (*Semikhah*) and of the Sanhedrin, in preparation for the Messianic age. In the same period of time, Rabbi Judah Loew (Liva) ben Bezalel of Prague propagated the basic rights of nations, declared exile and dispersion to be unnatural, and postulated a return to the land of Israel (1599). Such is the background of the decision of a little-known writer of the report that follows to leave his native Moravia and make his home in Safed. A few years later (1621), a younger contemporary of Loew ben Bezalel, Isaiah ha-Levi Horovitz, author of *Shene Luhot ha-Berit* (The Two Tablets of the Covenant) and popularizer of Kabbalah, came to settle in Safed. Politically, Safed enjoyed an era of peaceful development under the Druse ruler Fakhr ed-Din, who, except for some brief interruptions, controlled southern Lebanon and northern Galilee from 1584 to 1635.

I have come to inform you that the God of blessing in his great loving-kindness has vouchsafed me the merit of making my dwelling in the Holy Land, here in Safed, may she be rebuilt speedily and in our days, in the Upper Galilee; and I have now been here for five years in the midst of the Land, thank God, with no business other than the study of the Torah and the service of His blessed Name. The day I became twenty-two my

Maker moved me and awakened my heart and said to me: "How long, O sluggard, wilt thou sleep in the slumber of idleness? Rise now, gird up thy loins like a warrior and pursue the knowledge of the Torah and of the commandments, and become an understanding youth."

Thereupon I arose and took courage and put away all worldly affairs from me; and I prepared myself to seek and know the God of my fathers with all my heart and with all my soul; and I sat before the Lord my God and repented with all my heart.

And when my Maker brought me to my twenty-eighth year, tidings reached me of the awesome, holy, and wonderful wisdom to be gained in the Land of the Living, where are to be found the seats of Torah and Testimony; and the light of their Torah causes the Holy Spirit to shine forth over his flock, our people, so that their actions accord with their love of the will of their Maker. At once I girded my loins to run the course; and I sent my wife away with a divorce as she did not wish to go with me. I also paid her all that was due her in accordance with her marriage contract, and also left our one daughter who was at that time thirteen years old with her. So, of all that had been mine not so much as a hair was left, not even my clothes and books, for I left them behind for her alimony and for the dowry of my daughter; but I trusted in the God of Jacob and entrusted my welfare to him. So I did depart from the land of my birth, in complete destitution.

I arrived in the holy city of Safed in the mid-days of the Feast of Booths of 5363 [autumn, 1602], arriving in peace and finding a holy congregation. For this is a great city before God with close on to three hundred great rabbis, all of them pious and men of works. Eighteen talmudic academies I found here, as well as twenty-one synagogues and a large House of Study with close on to four hundred children in the charge of four teachers, who give them free instruction. For there are wealthy folk in Constantinople who pay the hire of the teachers, and likewise send them clothes every year. And in all the synagogues, after the Morning and Evening Prayer, the entire congregation gather together and sit before their rabbis, five or six groups in every synagogue, each group engaging in study before they forsake the synagogue. One group regularly studies the works of Maimonides, another studies *En Yaakov*,[4] while the third makes the [talmudic] tractate Berakhot their set study; others regularly study a daily chapter of the Mishnah with commentary; and yet another group study the Talmud with the commentaries of Rashi and Tosafot;[5] and another group regularly studies the holy *Zohar* [the Book of Splendor]; and another group regularly studies the Scriptures.

In this way there is no one who goes forth in the morning to his trade or business without having first learned his measure of the Torah. Everybody does the same in the evening, after the Evening Prayer. Then on the Sabbath day all the people go to hear the sermons of the rabbis. And every Thursday they all gather together in one great synagogue after the Morning Prayer, where they pray to his Name; an awesome prayer for the welfare of all Israel wherever they may be, and mourn the exile of the Divine Presence and of Israel, and the destruction of the house of our God. And they bless all those who send their money to aid the poor of the Land of Israel that the Holy One, blessed be he, may prolong their days and their years and make their affairs prosper and guard them against every trouble and distress.

Before they begin to pray, the great and pious rabbi, our master Rabbi Moses Galante,[6] may his Rock and Maker guard him, ascends the pulpit and utters mighty words and rouses Israel to fear of the Name and brings them to love the Creator, by means of his sweet tongue, great wisdom, and erudition and vast sanctity. Afterward there ascend two heads of academies, great and pious scholars and men of good deeds. [. . .]

Then they begin to pray in awe and fear and great dread. Who has ever seen the like of those great and bitter prayers and outcries of all Israel that weep and as one man let tears fall over the exile and the destruction because of our many sins; how they confess their iniquities!

Then every New Moon's eve they follow the practices of the eve of the Day of Atonement until midnight, proclaiming a stoppage of work until that hour. And all Israel gather together in one great synagogue or proceed to the grave of Hosea ben Beeri the prophet, over which there is a magnificent building formed like a dome, and they enter inside; or else they proceed to the cave of the divine teacher, Abba Saul,[7] may he rest in peace; or else they assemble before the grave of Rabbi Judah bar Ilai;[8] all of which saints are buried near the city. There they pray an awesome prayer until the noon, sometimes spending the entire day there praying and preaching.

Now the Gentiles who dwell on the soil of Israel are all subject to the holiness of Israel. Even though we stand all day long in the field, wearing our prayer shawls and phylacteries and calling upon the Lord our God in a great voice at the graves of the saints, not a single Gentile would approach a congregation of Jews when they are praying, or open his mouth to mock at the prayer. But they all go their ways. On the contrary, they hold the graves of our holy masters in great reverence, as well as the synagogues; and they kindle lights at the graves of the saints and vow to supply the synagogues with oil.

The villages of En Zetim and Meron contain ruined synagogues, but because of our many sins no Jews dwell there. There are countless Torah Scrolls within the Arks in the synagogues which the Gentiles treat with much honor. The keys to the synagogues are in their hands, and they clean them and light candles before the Arks, and no one would approach to touch a Torah Scroll. Sometimes we go unto those villages to pray, and recite our prayers in those synagogues.

Apart from this, I found that the entire Holy Land is filled with the blessing of the Lord, with great plenty and a great cheapness which is beyond all estimation and imagining and telling. Now when I perceived the great plenty to be found in the Holy Land, and saw that all this bounty is being consumed by the nations of the world while Israel are dispersed and have not the merit to eat of its fruits or to be sated with its goodness, I wept greatly and I said: Would that our brethren the children of Israel knew but a tenth of all this plenty and goodness and great satiety which are now to be found in the Land of Israel! For then they would weep day and night over their exile and over this pleasant, good and spacious land which they have lost, which even in its ruins brings forth fruits and oil and wine and silk for a third of the world; so that men come in ships from the ends of the world, from Venice and Spain, and France, and Portugal, and Constantinople, and load up with corn and olive oil, raisins, and cakes of figs, and honey, and silk, and good soap, all of which are as plentiful as the sand of the seashore. [. . .]

Poultry and eggs are very cheap, a chicken costing five or six kreutzer, and five or six eggs can be had for a coin which is worth about two of the smallest coins of our land. [. . .] Then there are the fine fruits: carobs, oranges, lemons, and melons, and watermelons which are as sweet as sugar, and cucumbers, and pumpkins, and lettuces and all sorts of other greens which are unknown to you, so there is no advantage in my mentioning them. There is a quality in the fruits and greens and desserts of the Land of Israel whose like is not to be found in your parts, like gold compared with silver or wheaten bread with barley; so that he who has merited of the Name, be it blessed, to make his home in the Land of Israel, and has a little money with which to support himself, happy is he and happy his portion; for he can win himself life in the world to come by joining the company of the great men of piety and good deeds who are in the Land, and can also take pleasure before the Lord and give pleasure to his spirit in these good and fat pastures, eating of its fruits and having his fill of its goodness. All this he can achieve here in the Land of Israel, at a third of the expenses and costs at home, and live the life of a king. Apart from this, there are the clear and wholesome air and the healthgiving water which prolong a man's days. For this reason most of the inhabitants of this country, almost all of them, live very long lives up to eighty or ninety or a hundred or a hundred and ten years.

Now the Lord who is the true God and King of the universe knew my heart and saw my good intention, how with all my heart and all my soul I entreated the Lord to answer me in my time of trouble and to deliver me. So He gave me all I desired of Him, and He brought me in peace to the Land of Israel, on the Feast of Booths in the year 5364 [1603], where he had appointed for me as my helpmeet a good and God-fearing woman, the daughter of a great and very exalted and pious scholar, whose vast holiness and tremendous piety are known to all Israel. He is the sage, our honored master, Rabbi Israel Sarug[9] of blessed memory.

The Holy One, blessed be he, has given me the merit of possessing all the writings prepared by that holy and godly man and teacher of all Israel, our master Rabbi Isaac Luria of blessed memory; more than are in the possession of any of the sages of the Land of Israel. I came to them through the wife I married in the Land of Israel, who inherited them from her honored father, our master Rabbi Israel Sarug of blessed memory, who tirelessly sought them out all his life long and expended more than two hundred thalers on them until he obtained them all.

I now have them, praise God, and I delight in them every day; and the blessed Name has caused me to find favor and friendship among all the sages of Safed. My rabbi and teacher, before whom I sit and from whom I learn Torah, particularly the wisdom of the Kabbalah, is the perfect and very humble sage, our honored master Rabbi Masud, the Great Light[10] of Fez. He is famous in all Israel by reason of his great holiness and vast knowledge and erudition in the entire Torah, may the blessed Name guard and preserve him.

So now I have no other business than the business of the Torah and the service of the blessed Name. Praises and thanksgiving to God who brought me here and has given me the merit of all this until now. The woman whom your servant married did not bring me either gold or silver, but a house and its vessels and the Kabbalah writings of our master Rabbi Isaac Luria and the little clothing she had; and nothing more. For I married the daughter of a pious scholar for the sake of heaven, to obtain those holy writings, for without her I could never have obtained them at all, since they are to be found only in the hands of a few rare and singular individuals, men of lofty soul and extraordinarily pious. The Creator, taking pity on me, has permitted me to obtain them, by which means He has caused me to find favor and friendship in the eyes of all sages of Safed, may it be rebuilt and established speedily and in our days; and they do not withhold from me any of all the secrets concealed in the Torah.

Written by Solomon Shloemel, son of my noble father, Rabbi Hayyim, known as Meinsterl, of blessed memory, and written in haste here at Safed, may she be rebuilt and established speedily and in our days, in the Upper Galilee, which is in "the Land of Beauty," on the twenty-fourth day of Tammuz 5367 [1607].

THE LIFE OF

RABBI ISAAC LURIA

Solomon Shloemel ben Hayyim Meinsterl

The "Lurianic Kabbalah," the mystic teachings associated with the name of Isaac Luria (1534–1572), taught comprehension of the process of Creation as a form of divine exile, dealt with the origin of evil, and assigned to men the task of "restoration of the primordially planned order of things in their relation to God" (G. G. Scholem). It provided a profound answer to the pressing problem of exile, strongly accentuated by the catastrophe of the expulsion of the Jews from Spain; it made not merely the inner circles of mystics but the people of Israel as a whole participants in a mystically understood Messianism. Isaac Luria was not a writer; he left the formulation of his doctrine to his disciples, and especially to Hayyim Vital Calabrese (1543–1620). The saintly personality of the master (who died at the age of thirty-eight) survived in many legends. Solomon Shloemel ben Hayyim Meinsterl, who came to Palestine in 1602, wrote letters containing a short life of Luria (the "Ari," abbreviated from *Adonenu* [our master] Rabbi Isaac), which incorporates the revered traditions about the man. The letters were first printed in *Taalumot Hokhmah,* by Samuel Ashkenazi, Basel, 1629. (See also "A Godly Life.")

During his youth, the Ari, of blessed memory, lived in Egypt although he was born in Jerusalem. At his birth the prophet Elijah appeared to his father—for he was very pious, as was his mother too—and said to him: "Take heed, now, on the day of the circumcision, not to circumcise this child until you see me standing beside you in the synagogue."

Now when the eighth day came and they took the child to the synagogue for the circumcision the father looked around on all sides for Elijah but did not see him there. By some sort of a pretext, the father delayed for about a half an hour or more and kept the congregation standing. They wondered why he held off so long and finally they all rebuked him. He, however, paid no attention to their complaint but waited till finally Elijah did come. He said to the father: "Sit down on the chair," and the father sat down with the infant in his arms. Then Elijah came, took the child from the parent, put him on his own lap and held him with his own two arms. The man who performed the circumcision went ahead with his work and saw nothing, of course, but the father. After the child had been circumcised Elijah returned him to the father, saying: "Here is your child. Take good care of him for a great light shall shine forth from him upon all the world."

Later when he was still a lad his father died. Because of poverty he went down to Egypt to the home of his uncle who was a very rich man. Luria developed into a brilliant student noted for his keenness, powers of argumentation, and sound reasoning, so that by the time he was fifteen years of age he was superior to all the sages of Egypt in his understanding of and his ability to debate in talmudic law. His uncle then gave him his daughter to wife. After the marriage he studied alone with our honored teacher, Rabbi Bezalel Ashkenazi,[11] for seven years, and after this he studied by himself for six years. In addition to this, for two years in succession, he kept himself in seclusion in a certain house built along the Nile river and sanctified himself by an unusual piety. He was altogether alone and spoke with no one. On the eve of the Sabbath, just before it grew dark, he would return to his home, but even here, too, he would talk to no one, not even his wife, except when it was absolutely necessary, and then only in Hebrew and very briefly.

It was there on the banks of the Nile that he merited for himself the descent of the Holy Spirit. At times Elijah the prophet revealed himself to him and taught him the secrets of the Torah, and he was found so worthy that throughout the night his soul would mount on high, and hosts of ministering angels would come to guard him on the way till they had led him into the heavenly assembly, and there they would ask of him in which academy he wished to study. [. . .]

After these two years of extreme asceticism in Egypt, Elijah

appeared to him. Luria was at that time only thirty-six years of
age; and he was thirty-eight years old when, from here in Safed
he was summoned to the Academy on High, because of our many
sins. Elijah had said to him: "The time of your death is approaching. And now go up to Safed. There you will find a certain scholar whose name is Rabbi Hayyim Calabrese;[12] anoint
him in your stead; lay your hands upon him and teach all your
lore for he will take your place. The sole purpose of your coming
into the world has been to "restore" the soul of Rabbi Hayyim,
for it is a precious one. Through you he will merit wisdom,
and a great light shall shine forth from him upon all Israel. I
assure you that I will reveal myself to you whenever you need
me; I will lay bare before you the secrets of the upper and the
nether worlds, and God, too, will pour out upon you his Holy
Spirit a thousand times more than you are able to acquire here in
Egypt."

All these things did our Master Luria, of blessed memory,
reveal to our teacher Rabbi Hayyim Calabrese, and he in turn
revealed them intimately to a chosen few of his associates in the
land of Israel. But our teacher Hayyim, however, wrote in the
book which he composed that it appeared to him that Luria was
the Messiah ben Joseph[13] but the Master would not admit it to
him because of his exceeding humility. However, his disciples
could surmise it from what Luria had told them. [. . .]

Luria knew all the deeds of men and even their thoughts.
He could read faces, look into the souls of men, and recognize
souls that migrated from body to body. He could tell you about
the souls of the wicked which had entered into trees and stones
or animals and birds; he could tell you what commandments a
man had fulfilled and what sins he had committed since youth;
he knew wherein a sinful man had been punished by God and
would prescribe acts of "restoration" to remove a moral blemish,
and knew just when such a moral defect had been corrected. He
understood the chirping of birds, and through their flight he
divined strange things, as is referred to in the verse: "For a bird
of the air shall carry the voice, and that which hath wings shall
tell the matter" (Eccles. 10:20). All of this he acquired because

of the piety, asceticism, purity, and holiness that he had exercised since his youth.

In the presence

of the divine

Moses Cordovero

In the sixteenth century, Safed, situated in the hills of Galilee, was the home of a group of mystics who rallied around Isaac Luria (see also "The Life of Rabbi Isaac Luria" and "Life in Safed"). In this period Safed was the home of Joseph Caro, author of the *Shulhan Arukh,* code of Jewish law, and of *Solomon Alkabetz,* who wrote the Sabbath hymn *Lekha Dodi;* here Israel Najara, outstanding Kabbalist poet, spent his youth; here Hayyim Vital Calabrese (1543-1620), Luria's outstanding disciple and author of *Etz Hayyim* (Tree of Life), was born; here, too, flourished Moses Cordovero (1522-1570), mystical theologian, and his disciples, Elijah de Vidas, author of *Reshit Hokhmah* (Beginning of Wisdom), and Abraham Galante.

Cordovero's major works include *Pardes Rimmonim* (Orchard of Pomegranates), written in 1548, which is a comprehensive exposition of mystical theology and a work comparable in scope and importance to Maimonides' *Guide to the Perplexed.* His minor treatises include *Tomer Deborah* (The Palm Tree of Deborah, an allusion to Judges 4:5), a mystic's statement on ethics. He taught the classical doctrine of *imitatio dei:* in his acts and thoughts man is to imitate divine qualities (such as mercy and compassion), represented in the ten *Sephirot,* emanations through which God, the Infinite (*En Sof*), and as such beyond human knowledge, becomes manifest. (Such *Sephirot* are "Sovereignty" and "Loving-kindness" mentioned in the texts that follow.) In "imitating" divine qualities man acts upon the *Sephirot* and contributes to their functioning; man's life is of cosmic significance. The *Tomer Deborah,* from which the passages that follow are taken, was first printed in Venice in 1589 and became very popular among Jewish moralists, both mystical and non-mystical.

Who is a God Like Unto Thee? (Micah 7:18)

This refers to the Holy One, blessed is he, as a patient King Who bears insult in a manner that is above human understanding. For behold, without doubt, there is nothing hidden from His providence. Furthermore, there is no moment when man is not nourished and does not exist by virtue of the divine power which flows down upon him. It follows that no man ever sins against God without the divine affluence pouring into him at that very moment, enabling him to exist and to move his limbs. Despite the fact that he uses it for sin, that power is not withheld from him in any way. But the Holy One, blessed is he, bears this insult and continues to empower him to move his limbs, even though he uses the power in that very moment for sin and perversity offending the Holy One, blessed be he, who, nonetheless, suffers it. Nor must you say that He cannot withhold that good, for it lies in His power in the moment it takes to say the word 'moment' to wither the sinner's hand or foot, as He did to [King] Jeroboam. And yet though it lies in His power to arrest the divine flow— and He might have said: "If you sin against Me do so under your own power, not with Mine"—He does not, on this account, withhold His goodness from man, bearing the insult, pouring out His power and bestowing of His goodness. This is to be insulted and bear the insult, beyond words. This is why the ministering angels refer to the Holy One, blessed is he, as "the patient King." And this is the meaning of the prophet's words: "Who is a God like unto Thee?" He means: "Thou, the good and merciful, art God, with the power to avenge and claim Thy debt, yet Thou art patient and bearest insult until man repents." Behold this is a virtue man should make his own, namely, to be patient and allow himself to be insulted even to this extent and yet not refuse to bestow of his goodness to the recipients.

The Disease of Pride

Now I have found a cure by which a man can be cured of the disease of pride and enter the gates of humility. It is that he accustom himself to flee honor as much as possible, for if he allows honor to be paid him he will become attuned to such matters of pride and his nature will find satisfaction in it and he will find it difficult to be cured.

I have further found a good medicine, though not as effective as the other. This is that man should train himself to do two things: first, to honor all creatures, in whom he recognizes the exalted nature of the Creator Who in wisdom created man. And so it is with all creatures, that the wisdom of the Creator is in them. He should see for himself that they are therefore exceedingly to be honored for the Creator of all, the most exalted Wise One has busied Himself with them and if man despises them he touches upon the honor of their Creator.

The second is to bring the love of his fellow-men into his heart, even loving the wicked as if they were his brothers and more so until the love of his fellow-men becomes firmly fixed in his heart. He should love even the wicked in his heart saying: "Would that these were righteous, returning in repentance, so that they were all great men, acceptable to the Omnipresent; as the faithful lover of all Israel [Moses] said: 'Would that all the people of the Lord were prophets'" (Num. 11:29).

How can he love them? By recalling in his thoughts the good qualities they possess, by covering their defects and refusing to look at their faults and looking only at their good qualities. He should say to himself: "If this loathsome beggar were very rich how much then would I rejoice in his company, as I rejoice in the company of some other. But if he were to don the splendid garments of some other there would be no difference between him and his superior; why then should his honor be less in my eyes? Behold, in God's eyes he is superior to me for he is plagued with suffering and poverty and cleansed from sin and why should I hate one whom the Holy One, blessed is he, loves?" In this way man's heart will turn towards the good and he will accustom himself to ponder on all the good qualities we have mentioned.

Loving-kindness

How shall a man train himself to acquire the quality of loving-kindness? The main way in which man can enter into the secret of loving-kindness is to love God with perfect love so as not to forsake His service for any reason whatsoever for nothing has any value at all for him compared with the Blessed One's love. Therefore, he should primarily attend to the requirements of God's service and the rest of his time may be for other needs.

This love should be firmly fixed in his heart whether he receives good at the hands of the Holy One, blessed is he, or whether he receives sufferings and rebukes. These latter, too, he should look upon as tokens of God's love. As it is written: "Faithful are the wounds of a friend" (Prov. 27:6). And it is written: "With all thy might" (Deut. 6:5) which the sages explain as, "For whichever measure He measures out to thee," in order to include all measures under "Loving-kindness." It will then be found that the secret of his life's direction will be from "Sovereignty," but even when "Sovereignty" acts in judgment it is still bound to "Loving-kindness." This was the quality of Nahum of Gamzu who used to say: "This, too, is good," [14] namely, to bind it constantly to the side of "Loving-kindness" which is called "Good." He used to say: "Also this, which appears to belong to the Left bound to 'Power,' is for nothing but good, that is bound to 'Loving-kindness.'" He concentrated on the good side of the quality and concealed its judgment. This is a great method of constantly binding oneself to "Loving-kindness."

In the *Tikkunim*[15] it is explained: "Who is a saint? He who does loving-kindness to his Creator." For in the acts of benevolence man carries out in the lower worlds after the same pattern and this is what is meant by doing loving-kindness to his Creator. It is necessary, therefore, to know the types of benevolence practised among men, all of which he should do on his Creator's behalf in the upper worlds, if he wants to acquire the quality of loving-kindness.

X. The Ways of the Hasidim

ISRAEL BEN ELIEZER,

THE BAAL SHEM TOV

Hasidic Accounts

The Hasidism that rose in Eastern Europe in the eighteenth century was a reaction against an overemphasis on talmudic learning on the one hand, and on radical mystical Messianism (which had expressed itself in the Sabbatian movement) on the other. Hasidism popularized older Kabbalist ideas; it taught the immanence of God in all existence; it cultivated religious enthusiasm and stressed simple piety and ethics; it considered prayer to be a "cleaving" to God; it produced a type of charismatic leader (the *Zaddik*), around whom the hasidic fellowship centered.

Israel ben Eliezer, the Baal Shem Tov (Master of the Holy Name, *ca.* 1700–1760), founder of Hasidism, lived in Medzibozh, Podolia, from where the new movement spread. His teachings were orally transmitted; foremost among his disciples were Dov Baer of Mezrich ("The Great Maggid") and Jacob Joseph of Polnoy, the recorder of early hasidic teachings. The Baal Shem Tov's saintly life and miraculous deeds became the subject of many legends, reverently preserved by the hasidic communities. The opposition to Hasidism on the part of the orthodox community culminated in a ban of excommunication, pronounced in 1772 by Elijah, the Gaon of Vilna, spokesman of the Mitnagdim ("the opponents"). Hasidism, however, continued to function as a vital force in Judaism.

The first part of the material that follows is taken from the legendary tradition that developed around the Baal Shem Tov, as restated by Martin Buber, the modern interpreter of Hasidism. The second part consists of quotations from *Tzavaat ha-Rivash* (The Testament of the Baal Shem).

Legends

The Tree of Knowledge

They say that once, when all souls were gathered in Adam's soul, at the hour he stood beside the Tree of Knowledge, the soul of the Baal Shem Tov went away, and did not eat of the tree.

His Father's Words

Israel's father died while he was still a child.

When he felt death drawing near, he took the boy in his arms and said: "I see that you will make my light shine out, and it is not given me to rear you to manhood. But, dear son, remember all your days that God is with you, and that because of this, you need fear nothing in all the world."

Israel treasured these words in his heart.

Themselves

The Baal Shem said:

In the prayers we say: "God of Abraham, God of Isaac, and God of Jacob," and not: "God of Abraham, Isaac, and Jacob," for Isaac and Jacob did not base their work on the searching and service of Abraham; they themselves searched for the unity of the Maker and his service.

The Torah is Perfect

Concerning the verse of the psalm: "The law of the Lord is perfect" (Ps. 19:8), the Baal Shem said:

It is still quite perfect. No one has touched it as yet, not a whit and not a jot of it. Up to this hour, it is still quite perfect.

Without the World to Come

Once the spirit of the Baal Shem was so oppressed that it seemed to him he would have no part in the coming world. Then he said to himself: "If I love God, what need have I of the world to come!"

Simplicity

Once the Baal Shem said to his disciples: Now that I have climbed so many rungs in the service of God, I let go of all of them and hold to the simple faith of making myself a vessel for God. It is, indeed, written: "The simple believeth every word" (Prov. 14:15) but it is also written: "The Lord preserveth the simple" (Ps. 116:6).

To One Who Admonished

The Baal Shem said this to a zaddik who used to preach admonishing sermons: What do you know about admonishing! You yourself have remained unacquainted with sin all the days of your life, and you have had nothing to do with the people around you—how should you know what sin is!

With the Sinners

The Baal Shem said:

I let sinners come close to me, if they are not proud. I keep the scholars and the sinless away from me if they are proud. For the sinner who knows that he is a sinner, and therefore considers himself base—God is with him, for He "dwelleth with them in the midst of their uncleannesses" (Lev. 16:16). But concerning him who prides himself on the fact that he is unburdened by sin, God says, as we know from the Talmud: "There is not enough room in the world for myself and him."

Love

The Baal Shem said to one of his disciples:

The lowest of the low you can think of, is dearer to me than your only son is to you.

The Temptation

It is told:

Sabbatai Zevi, the "false Messiah" long dead, came to the Baal Shem and begged him to redeem him. Now it is well known that the work of redemption is accomplished by binding the stuff of life to the stuff of life, by binding mind to mind, and soul to soul. In this way, then, the Baal Shem began to bind himself to that other, but slowly and cautiously, for he feared he might try to harm him. Once, when the Baal Shem lay asleep, Sabbatai Zevi came and tried to tempt him to become as he himself was. Then the Baal Shem hurled him away with such vigor that he fell to the very bottom of the nether world. When the Baal Shem spoke of him, he always said: "A holy spark was within him, but Satan caught him in the snare of pride."

The Testament

Equality

The principle of equality is of major importance. This means that every person should be equal in a man's eyes whether that person lacks knowledge or whether he knows the whole Torah. How does one attain this attitude of equality? It is attained by constant clinging to God, for out of a constant concern to cling to God, one has no time to think of other matters.

If one serves God with great attachment, he should not consider himself greater than his fellow, for he himself is simply like other beings, created to serve God. God has given his neighbor intelligence, just as He has given it to him. Moreover, how is he more important than a worm, for the worm, too, serves God with all its understanding and power? Indeed, man, himself, is even a worm and grub, as it is said: "For I am a worm and not a man" (Ps. 22:7), and if God had not given man intelligence, he would only be able to serve Him as the worm does. Therefore, if man is no more important to God than a worm, can he be more important to God than other men? A man should think of himself as a worm, and should realize that all other such small creatures are just as important to God as men are, for all of them are His creations and the only ability men possess beyond the lower animals is only that which the Creator has given them.

Prayer

When a man is on a low plane of attachment to God, it is better that he pray from the prayer book, because when he reads the written words and concentrates, he will then be able to pray with more intention. But when he has already a high plane of attachment to God, it is better to close his eyes so that sight should not interfere with his attachment to the upper world of God. The Baal Shem Tov said that the upper world was revealed to him, not because he had studied much Talmud and commentaries, but because of the prayers which he always uttered with great intensity.

Sometimes the evil inclination will mislead a man by telling him that he committed a great sin even though the transgression involved nothing more than a severe application of the law or may not have been a sin at all; in which case, the evil inclination simply wishes to sadden him and thus prevent him from worshipping God. One must be careful to detect this deceit and say to the evil inclination: "I do not pay attention to the severe law you accuse me of having transgressed, for your intention is simply to keep me from serving God. But if in truth it was a sin, then God will have more joy on my account if I pay it no heed and refuse to be saddened by my transgression. On the contrary! I shall worship Him, in joy, for it is an important principle that one should avoid sadness as much as possible during the service of God.

Do not increase detailed observances in any matter, for it is the intention of the evil inclination to cause a man to fear that he has not properly fulfilled his obligation in this particular matter in order to cause a man to grow sad, and sadness severely restrains a man from serving God properly. Even if he stumbles into sin, he should not be overly sad, for this might make him neglect his worship altogether. He should only be regretful and then return to rejoice in his Creator. Even if he knows that he has not properly fulfilled an obligation because of circumstances beyond his control, he should not be sad, but rather should he consider that God inquires into man's inner intentions, and God knows that he wishes to fulfill his obligations even perfectly, but he simply cannot.

The Sinner and Repentance

"The words of his mouth are iniquity and deceit, he has ceased to be wise, to do good" (Ps. 36:4). There are two kinds of people: One is a complete sinner who knows his Master, but rebels against Him. As for the second, the evil impulse closes his eyes and he deems himself a completely righteous man and is so regarded by others. He may even study, pray and fast in self-affliction. Yet, for nothing does he toil for he possesses no genuine attachment to God, no complete faith as is required in order to be attached to God at all times. Nor does he know the main principle of worship: the proper way to study, to pray, to fulfill a commandment for its own sake.

The difference between these two men is that for the complete sinner there is a possibility of a cure, for when he comes to the awakening or repentance, he returns to God with all his heart and will beseech the Lord to lead him in the "path dwelling with light" (Job 38:19). But for the second type of man, there is no possibility for improvement, for his eyes are barred from seeing God, His greatness and works. For, he is righteous in his own eyes, so how can he return in repentance?

COMMUNION WITH GOD AND MEN

Abraham Kalisker

The following two passages are from letters of Abraham Kalisker (died 1810), a disciple of Dov Baer of Mezritch, who, however, pursued an independent course of thought; the letters were written from Palestine, whither he had emigrated in 1777. The first passage expounds the mystical *nihil* (*ayin*, naught, nothingness), self-abasement before God, thus making room for God and fellow man; the second is in praise of fellowship; true membership in a community of faith is seen as a way to the communion with God.

I

[. . .] The final aim of Torah and *Hokhmah* [i.e., wisdom] [. . .] is to attain the perfect *ayin,* everywhere a man should render his self non-existent; the very source of wisdom is *ayin.* *Ayin* is its very root and from this root grow humility and lowliness, even as our sages said: "The Torah is fulfilled only by him who makes himself like the desert," [1] free to poor and rich alike, and who regards himself as no greater than his fellow man, but feels "non-existent" before him. In this way they [man and his fellow man] are integrated one into the other, for *ayin* combines a thing and its opposite, and therefrom results the straight lines which encompasses peace and blessing.

II

[. . .] Whoever is smitten by his conscience let him, for the sake of God and for his own sake, act as follows: Let him seek peace and fortify it [. . .] and if, Heaven forbid, his heart urges him to separate himself from the fellowship of men, let him hasten swiftly to his spiritually stronger brethren who truly and intently obey the voice of God, and say to them, "My brethren-in-soul, save me and let me hear the word of God, that He may heal my broken heart." Moreover, let this man school himself to fill his heart with love for his fellows even if it should lead to the departure of the soul. Let him persevere in this until his soul and the soul of his brethren cleave together. And when they have all become as one, God will dwell in their midst, and they will receive from Him an abundance of salvation and consolation. [. . .]

THE TEACHINGS
OF MENDEL OF KOTZK

Hasidic Accounts

Mendel of Kotzk, who died in 1859, was a disciple of the hasidic master Yaakov Yitzhak of Pshysha ("the Yehudi"), who had studied under Yaakov Yitzhak, "the Seer" of Lublin, who in turn belonged to the group of disciples of Dov Baer of Mezritch, a successor to the Baal Shem, founder of Hasidism. But with Mendel of Kotzk traditional hasidic leadership and the idea of the communion between rabbi and congregation underwent a crisis. In contradistinction to the ideals of love, mercy, religious group life, stressed by his predecessors, Mendel emphasized the tragic side of life, the chaotic element in man; he called for rigid discipline of learning, individual effort toward spiritual growth, and withdrawal from the crowd. The way to truth, he argued, demands solitude, suffers no imitation, and no compromise. Mendel himself spent the last twenty years of his life in virtual isolation; his disciples had left him.

After Waking

One morning after prayer the rabbi of Kotzk said:

When I woke up today, it seemed to me that I was not alive. I opened my eyes, looked at my hands, and saw that I could use them. So I washed them. Then I looked at my feet and saw that I could walk with them. So I took a few steps. Now I said the blessing: "Blessed art thou who quickenest the dead," and knew that I was alive.

The Lord of the Castle

Rabbi Mendel once spoke to his hasidim about a certain parable in Midrash: How a man passed by a castle and, seeing it on fire and no one trying to put out the blaze, thought that this must be a castle without an owner, until the lord of the castle looked down on him and said: "I am the lord of the castle." [2] When Rabbi Mendel said the words: "I am the lord of the castle," all those around him were struck with great reverence, for they all felt: "The castle is burning, but it has a lord."

To What Purpose Was Man Created?

Rabbi Mendel of Kotzk once asked his disciple Rabbi Yaakov of Radzimin: "Yaakov, to what purpose was man created?" He answered: "So that he might perfect his soul."

"Yaakov," said the zaddik, "is that what we learned from our teacher, Rabbi Bunam? No, indeed! Man was created so that he might lift up the Heavens."

The Ladder

Rabbi Mendel of Kotzk said to his disciples:

The souls descended from the realms of Heaven to earth on a ladder. Then it was taken away. Now up there they are calling the souls home. Some do not budge from the spot, for how can one get to Heaven without a ladder? Others leap and fall, and leap again and give up. But there are those who know very well that they cannot make it, but try and try over and over again until God catches hold of them and pulls them up.

Man's Advantage

This is what Rabbi Mendel said about the words in the Scriptures: "This is the law of the burnt-offering" (Lev. 6:2):

Why does God demand sacrifice of man and not of the angels? That of the angels would be purer than that of man could ever be. But what God desires is not the deed but the preparation. The holy angels cannot prepare themselves; they can only do the deed. Preparation is the task of man who is caught in the thicket of tremendous obstacles and must free himself. This is the advantage of the works of man.

Immersion

This is what the rabbi of Kotzk said concerning Rabbi Akiba's saying that "God is the waters of immersion of Israel":[3] "The waters of immersion only purify a man if he is wholly immersed, so that not a hair is showing. That is how we should be immersed in God."

God's Dwelling

"Where is the dwelling of God?"

This was the question with which the rabbi of Kotzk surprised a number of learned men who happened to be visiting him.

They laughed at him: "What a thing to ask! Is not the whole world full of his glory!"

Then he answered his own question:

"God dwells wherever man lets him in."

Fathers and Sons

A man came to the rabbi of Kotzk and complained of his sons who refused to support him, though he was old and no longer able to earn his own livelihood. "I was always ready to do anything at all for them," he said, "and now they won't have anything to do with me."

Silently the rabbi raised his eyes to Heaven. "That's how it is," he said softly. "The father shares in the sorrow of his sons, but the sons do not share in the sorrow of their father."

No Strange God

They asked the rabbi of Kotzk: "What is new about King David's saying, 'There shall no strange God be in thee' (Ps. 81:10)? For was it not specifically stated in the decalogue: 'Thou shalt have no other gods before Me' " (Exod. 20:3).

He replied: "The meaning is this: God ought not to be a stranger to you."

Worry

A hasid told the rabbi of Kotzk about his poverty and troubles. "Don't worry," advised the rabbi. "Pray to God with all your heart, and the merciful Lord will have mercy upon you."

"But I don't know how to pray," said the other.

Pity surged up in the rabbi of Kotzk as he looked at him. "Then," he said, "you have indeed a great deal to worry about."

Holiness

It is written: "And ye shall be holy men unto Me" (Exod. 22:30).

The rabbi of Kotzk explained: "Ye shall be holy unto me, but as men, ye shall be humanly holy unto me."

Afar Off

This is how Rabbi Mendel expounded the verse from the Scriptures: "Am I a God near at hand . . . and not a God afar off" (Jer. 23:23)?

"Afar off" refers to the wicked. "Near at hand" refers to the righteous. God says: "Do I want him who is already close to me, do I want the righteous? Why, I also want him who is afar off, I want him who is wicked!"

Great Guilt

Rabbi Mendel said:

He who learns the Torah and is not troubled by it, who sins and forgives himself, who prays because he prayed yesterday—a very scoundrel is better than he!

Comparing One to Another

Someone once told Rabbi Mendel that a certain person was greater than another whom he also mentioned by name.

Rabbi Mendel replied: "If I am I because I am I, and you are you because you are you, and you are you because I am I, then I am not I, and you are not you."

What Cannot Be Imitated

The rabbi of Kotzk said:

Everything in the world can be imitated except truth. For truth that is imitated is no longer truth.

First Prize

Rabbi Yehiel Meir, who was a poor man, went in to his teacher, the rabbi of Kotzk, with a beaming face and told him he had won the first prize in a lottery. "That wasn't through any fault of mine," said the zaddik. Rabbi Yehiel went home and distributed the money among needy friends.

Different Customs

A hasid of the rabbi of Kotzk and a hasid of the rabbi of Tchernobil were discussing their ways of doing things.

The disciple of the rabbi of Tchernobil said: "We stay awake all night between Thursday and Friday, on Friday we give alms in proportion to what we have, and on the Sabbath we recite the entire Book of Psalms."

"And we," said the man from Kotzk, "stay awake every night as long as we can; we give alms whenever we run across a poor man and happen to have money in our pockets, and we do not say the psalms it took David seventy years of hard work to make, all in a row, but according to the needs of the hour."

Thou Shalt Not Steal

Rabbi Yehiel Meir of Gostynin had gone to his teacher in Kotzk for the Feast of Weeks. When he came home, his father-in-law asked him: "Well, did your people over there receive the Torah differently than anywhere else?"

"Certainly!" said his son-in-law.

"What do you mean?" asked the other.

"Well, to give you an instance," said Rabbi Yehiel. "How do you here interpret 'thou shalt not steal' " (Exod. 20:15)?

"That we shall not steal from our fellow men," answered his father-in-law. "That's perfectly clear."

"We don't need to be told that any more," said Rabbi Yehiel. "In Kotzk this is interpreted to mean: You shall not steal from yourself."

Speak unto the Children of Israel

When a disciple of the rabbi of Lentshno visited the rabbi of Kotzk, his host said to him: "Give my greetings to your teacher. I love him very much. But why does he cry to God to send the Messiah? Why does he not rather cry to Israel to turn to God? It is written: 'Wherefore criest thou unto Me? Speak unto the children of Israel' " (Exod. 14:15).

The Three Pillars

Rabbi Mendel said:

Three pillars support the world: Study, worship, and good deeds, and as the world approaches its end the two first will shrink, and only good deeds will grow. And then what is written will become truth: "Zion shall be redeemed with justice" (Isa. 1:27).

IN PREPARATION FOR

THE DAY OF ATONEMENT

A Hasidic Account

Shmelke, rabbi of Nikolsburg in Moravia (died 1778), was a disciple of Dov Baer, the Maggid of Mezrich, chief disciple of the Baal Shem. The piece that follows, taken from *Divre Torah,* collected hasidic teachings (Josefow, 1852), describes a "revivalist" sermon. In addition to the actual address, the preacher's accompanying action and the people's reaction are also given: the people are not passive listeners; they are participants in the drama of *Teshuvah* ("turning," return to God, repentance); the whole being is involved in the response to the Zaddik's (hasidic leader's) words.

We all entered the old House of Prayer fearful and trembling, and the entire hall was filled an hour and a half before the prayer. When our rabbi reached the threshold of the House of Prayer wrapped in a prayer shawl he went up to the Ark, crying as he went in a loud voice the verse: "For on this day shall atonement be made for you, to cleanse you; from all your sins shall ye be clean before the Lord" (Lev. 16:30); and he quoted Rabbi Akiba: "Happy are you, O Israel; before whom do you purify yourselves and who is it that purifies you—if not your Father who is in heaven." [4]

At once all the people burst into tears. When the Zaddik reached the Ark, he began to recite various verses to awaken the people to repentance, such as: "Against Thee, Thee only, have I sinned, and done that which is evil in Thy sight" (Ps. 51:6); "For I do declare mine iniquity; I am full of care because of my sin" (Ps. 38:19); "Purge me with hyssop, and I shall be clean; wash me, and I shall be whiter than snow" (Ps. 51:9); "And I will sprinkle clean water upon you, and ye shall be clean; from all your uncleannesses, and from all your idols, will I cleanse you" (Ezek. 36:35).

Afterwards he began to expound the loftiness of the holy

and awesome Day of Atonement, on which every man can find help and redemption to enable him to redeem his soul:

"Come, my beloved brothers, my heart's companions, let us purify ourselves before him, for on this Day of Atonement His compassion will certainly be moved in our favor. But you must know, my brothers, that the reciting of, 'Hear, O Israel' is one of the principles of repentance. Let us recite, 'Hear, O Israel,' as though we were giving our lives for the sanctification of the Name of God. For indeed Abraham our father offered up his life for the sanctification of the Name of God and threw himself into the fiery furnace, and Isaac his son offered himself at the Binding. If we follow their footseps and do as they did and sanctify his great Name with love, and cry all together, 'Hear, O Israel,' with devotion, they will stand and intercede for us on the holy and awesome day."

At once all the people burst into tears and cried, "Hear, O Israel, the Lord our God, the Lord is one."

Then our master and rabbi continued and said: "After having merited the sanctification and proclamation of the unity of his Name out of His great love for us, we have no doubt merited the purification of our hearts for His service and for his fear. But we must still fulfill a great principle of repentance, which is the acceptance of the commandment, 'Thou shalt love thy neighbor as thyself' " (Lev. 19:18).

At once all the people cried after him, "Thou shalt love thy neighbor as thyself."

Then our rabbi continued and said: "Since we have merited the sanctification of His Name and the unification of our souls to love our neighbors, God will help us to find forgiveness, and we shall merit the purification of our thoughts as the Blessed One has commanded us in His holy Torah; the Torah itself will intercede for us."

At once all the people began to make confession of their iniquities. After they had finished, our rabbi took a scroll and expounded the verse, "Behold, I was brought forth in iniquity, and in sin did my mother conceive me" (Ps. 51:7). He said, "Who can hear these words without his heart being torn to shreds? Even a heart of stone would melt."

Our rabbi also expounded as follows: "The principle behind our purification is alluded to in the Mishnah, 'Heave-offering seedlings that have become unclean become clean again if replanted, for they do not carry uncleanliness,'[5] that is to say, heave-offering seedlings that became unclean when detached from the earth lose their uncleanliness when replanted. For as long as seedlings are attached to the earth they are clean. When plucked from the earth they can become unclean. But if they are attached to their source again, their uncleanliness stops.

"So it is with us. Our souls are hewn from the pure place under the throne of glory, and when our souls come to this world they become unclean because of our iniquities. But when a man attaches his thoughts to the Name of God, the soul returns and attaches itself to its source, and is cleansed of its uncleanliness, as the Scripture says, 'But ye that cleave unto the Lord your God are alive every one of you this day' (Deut. 4:4). For when a man clings to God with all his soul, he revives his soul by cleansing it of its uncleanliness, as it is said, 'are alive every one of you this day.' It is also said, 'Light is sown for the righteous, and gladness for the upright in heart' (Ps. 97:11); for when we have cleansed our soul like a seedling that returns to its source, there will be 'gladness for the upright in heart.' "

Our master continued and said: "But you must know that the weeping on this day will not avail if there is sadness in it, for 'the Divine Presence does not rest . . . in the midst of sadness . . . but in the midst of joy at keeping a commandment.'[6] Indeed, this day on which we merit the stripping of all the crookedness from the hearts, and the approach to the King over all kings, the Holy One, blessed be he, and the return of our souls to their source—this day is indeed a day of joy, when his hand is opened to receive those who return, to make atonement for us and cleanse our souls. Therefore, let all the tears we shed on this day be tears of joy, for we have merited the attachment unto the Lord, we who 'are alive every one of us this day.'

DEATH

Hasidic Teachings

A person's or a group's attitude to death is indicative of his attitude to life. In a special sense this is particularly true of Hasidism, which, more than other religious trends in Judaism, realized the preciousness of life. The following reports, pertaining to a variety of hasidic masters' thoughts on death, are culled from a wide range of sources.

The Purpose of Creation

In the hour of his death the Baal Shem said: "Now I know the purpose for which I was created."

The End of Rabbi Susya

Rabbi Susya lived to a great age. For seven years before his death, he was bedridden and in pain, in atonement, it was said, for the sins of Israel. His gravestone is inscribed: "Here lieth he who served God in love, rejoiced in pain, and turned many away from guilt."

The Divine Nothing

Just before he died, Rabbi Shneur Zalman of Ladi asked his grandson: "Dost thou see aught?"

The grandson looked at the rabbi in surprise. Thereupon the dying man said: "I see as yet only the Divine Nothing that gives life to the universe."

Learning to Die

When Rabbi Bunam was lying on his deathbed, his wife wept bitterly. Thereupon he said: "Why dost thou weep? All my life has been given me merely that I might learn to die."

Optimism and Faith

When Rabbi Elimelekh of Lizensk perceived that his end was approaching, he made himself master of an extraordinary cheerfulness. One of his disciples inquired the reason for his unusual mood. The rabbi thereupon took the hand of his faithful disciple into his own, and said: "Why should I not rejoice, seeing that I am about to leave this world below, and enter into the higher worlds of eternity? Do you not recall the words of the Psalmist (23:4): 'Yea, though I walk through the valley of the shadow of death, I will fear no evil, for Thou art with me.' Thus does the grace of God display itself."

The Time of Confession

When Rabbi Zalman Hasid was nigh unto death, his friends came to his bedside, and asked him to recite the "Confession," enjoined for the occasion. The Rabbi smiled and said: "Friends, do you really believe a death-bed confession contains much merit? No, friends! A man should 'confess' when he is seated at his dining table, and eating the good food thereon."

God's Partner

Rabbi David Leikes lived more than a hundred years. He was esteemed as an authority in the civil law of the rabbis, and his decisions were admired by all the *Dayyanim* [religious judges]. Once a very complicated case arose, when the aged rabbi was on his death-bed. His demise was expected hourly. The *Dayyanim* hoped that the ancient rabbi's mind might still be sufficiently clear to aid them, perhaps for the last time. They visited his home and stated their request. The rabbi's children protested vigorously, and argued against troubling him, lest thereby his end be hastened. Suddenly the door opened, and the dying rabbi entered. "Do you know," he said, "that we are taught by the Talmud that one who judges a case correctly becomes thereby God's partner? Yet you wish to deprive me of this opportunity."

He gave his decision in the difficult case in a manner so remarkable that it left no doubt of its correctness; he returned to his bed with the help of his children, and a moment later he died.

Why We Fear to Die

The Gerer Rabbi said: "Why does a man fear to die? Is he not returning to his Father in Heaven? The reason lies in this:

in the world to come, a man obtains a clear retrospect of all his deeds upon earth. When he perceives the senseless errors he has committed, he cannot abide himself. Therein lies his Purgatory."

When the Gerer was undergoing his last illness, the physician who attended him advised him to gain a little strength by more sleep.

The rabbi replied: "Does not the wise physician know that it is Torah and prayer, not sleep, which grants strength unto a Jew?"

XI. The Land of Israel, Exile, and Redemption

JERUSALEM

Benjamin of Tudela

Much of our knowledge of the twelfth-century Jewish communities the world over is owed to the *Itinerary* of Benjamin of Tudela, Navarre. The actual purpose of Benjamin's travels which lasted several years and ended in 1173, is unknown; perhaps it was a Jew's urge to gain a comprehensive firsthand view of his dispersed people and to make a pilgrimage to the land of Israel. From Spain, Benjamin went to Rome, from there to Otranto and Corfu and across Greece to Constantinople. He visited the Greek Archipelago, Rhodes, and Cyprus, and went to Antioch. A journey through Palestine followed; from there he went to Damascus, Bagdad, and Persia, and from there home by way of Aden, Assouan, Egypt, and Sicily. Germany and France (beyond its southern part) were not included in his tour. His descriptions (based on notes made on the spot) cover the structure of a community, its leaders, and the occupational life of its members; there are also references to religious life and lore and to the sects of the time. Only a part of his travel diary is extant.

Our selection consists of the notations on his visit to Jerusalem. As a result of the First Crusade (1099) and the establishment of the Christian Kingdom of Jerusalem, the Jewish community in Palestine was greatly diminished in size and importance. But Benjamin came to the country not only to study the sorry present; mainly, he wanted to relive the glories of Israel's past and to behold its remains.

The *Itinerary*, written in Hebrew (*Masaot Benjamin*), was first published in Constantinople in 1543, then, from a better manuscript, in Ferrara in 1556. A Latin translation (Antwerp) appeared in 1575, and in 1633, the Hebrew text with a Latin rendition. An English translation was published in London (1625), a Dutch, in Amsterdam (1666), a Yiddish, in Amsterdam (1691), and a French, in Haag (1735).

Jerusalem [. . .] is a small city, fortified by three walls. It is full of people whom the Mohammedans call Jacobites, Syrians, Greeks, Georgians and Franks, and of people of all tongues. It contains a dyeing-house, for which the Jews pay a small rent annually to the king, on condition that besides the Jews no other dyers be allowed in Jerusalem. There are about two hundred Jews who dwell under the Tower of David in one corner of the city. The lower portion of the wall of the Tower of David, to the extent of about ten cubits, is part of the ancient foundation set up by our ancestors, the remaining portion having been built by the Mohammedans. There is no structure in the whole city stronger than the Tower of David.

The city also contains two buildings, from one of which—the hospital—there issue forth four hundred knights; and therein all the sick who come thither are lodged and cared for in life and in death. The other building is called the Temple of Solomon; it is the palace built by Solomon the king of Israel. Three hundred knights are quartered there, and issue therefrom every day for military exercise, besides those who come from the land of the Franks and the other parts of Christendom, having taken upon themselves to serve there a year or two until their vow is fulfilled. In Jerusalem is the great church called the Sepulchre, and here is the burial-place of Jesus, unto which the Christians make pilgrimages.

Jerusalem has four gates—the gate of Abraham, the gate of David, the gate of Zion, and the gate of Gushpat, which is the gate of Jehoshaphat, facing our ancient Temple, now called Templum Domini. Upon the site of the sanctuary Omar ben al Khataab erected an edifice with a very large and magnificent cupola, into which the Gentiles do not bring any image or effigy, but they merely come there to pray. In front of this place is the Western Wall, which is one of the walls of the Holy of Holies.[1] This is called the Gate of Mercy, and thither come all the Jews to pray before the wall of the court of the Temple. In Jerusalem, attached to the palace which belonged to Solomon, are the stables built by him, forming a very substantial structure, composed of large stones, and the like of it is not to be seen anywhere in the world. There is also visible up to this day the pool used by the priests before offering their sacrifices, and the Jews coming thither write their names upon the wall. The gate of Jehoshaphat leads to the valley of Jehoshaphat, which is the gathering-place of nations.[2] Here is the pillar called Absalom's Hand, and the sepulchre of King Uzziah.

In the neighborhood is also a great spring, called the Waters of Siloam, connected with the brook of Kidron. Over the spring is a large structure dating from the time of our ancestors, but little water is found, and the people of Jerusalem for the most part drink the rain-water, which they collect in cisterns in their houses. From the valley of Jehoshaphat one ascends the Mount of Olives;[3] it is the valley only which separates Jerusalem from the Mount of Olives. From the Mount of Olives one sees the Sea of Sodom,[4] and at a distance of two parasangs from the Sea of Sodom is the Pillar of Salt into which Lot's wife was turned; the sheep lick it continually, but afterwards it regains its original shape. The whole land of the plain and the valley of Shittim as far as Mount Nebo[5] are visible from here.

In front of Jerusalem is Mount Zion,[6] on which there is no building, except a place of worship belonging to the Christians. Facing Jerusalem for a distance of three miles are the cemeteries belonging to the Israelites, who in the days of old buried their dead in caves, and upon each sepulchre is a dated inscription, but the Christians destroy the sepulchres, employing the stones thereof in building their houses. These sepulchres reach as far as Zelzah in the territory of Benjamin. Around Jerusalem are high mountains.

On Mount Zion are the sepulchres of the House of David, and the sepulchres of the kings that ruled after him. The exact place cannot be identified, inasmuch as fifteen years ago a wall of the church of Mount Zion fell in. The Patriarch commanded the overseer to take the stones of the old walls and restore therewith the church. He did so, and hired workmen at fixed wages; and there were twenty men who brought the stones from the base of the wall of Zion. Among these men there were two who were sworn friends. On a certain day the one entertained the other;

after their meal they returned to their work, when the overseer said to them, "Why have you tarried to-day?" They answered, "Why need you complain? When our fellow workmen go to their meal we will do our work." When the dinner-time arrived, and the other workmen had gone to their meal, they examined the stones, and raised a certain stone which formed the entrance to a cave. Thereupon one said to the other, "Let us go in and see if any money is to be found there." They entered the cave, and reached a large chamber resting upon pillars of marble overlaid with silver and gold. In front was a table of gold and a sceptre and crown. This was the sepulchre of King David. On the left thereof in like fashion was the sepulchre of King Solomon; then followed the sepulchres of all the kings of Judah that were buried there. Closed coffers were also there, the contents of which no man knows. The two men essayed to enter the chamber, when a fierce wind came forth from the entrance of the cave and smote them, and they fell to the ground like dead men, and there they lay until evening. And there came forth a wind like a man's voice, crying out: "Arise and go forth from this place!" So the men rushed forth in terror, and they came unto the Patriarch, and related these things to him. Thereupon the Patriarch sent for Rabbi Abraham el Constantin, the pious recluse, who was one of "the mourners for Jerusalem," [7] and to him he related all these things according to the report of the two men who had come forth. Then Rabbi Abraham replied, "These are the sepulchres of the House of David; they belong to the kings of Judah, and on the morrow let us enter, I and you and these men, and find out what is there." And on the morrow they sent for the two men, and found each of them lying on his bed in terror, and the men said: "We will not enter there, for the Lord doth not desire to show it to any man." Then the Patriarch gave orders that the place should be closed up and hidden from the sight of man unto this day. These things were told me by the said Rabbi Abraham.

Mystic Drama of Jerusalem

The *Zohar*

The *Zohar* (The Book of Splendor; see "Mystical Understanding of Jewish Concepts") and other medieval mystical writings present a drama wherein the phenomena of life on earth serve as mere symbols of what takes place between the human soul and its Creator, between the Community of Israel and the Holy One. In this drama, Zion and Jerusalem play a significant role. Jerusalem's position in the past, its fall and hoped-for restoration, are intricately bound up with the destiny of Israel and of the world. The destruction of Jerusalem causes a critical disruption of unity in the whole of the universe; the restoration of Zion will bring about harmony even within the Deity. The following passages, culled from various parts of the *Zohar*, illustrate the drama of the fall and the return, which takes place simultaneously on two levels, one upper, one lower: a blend of the rational and the supernatural, the heavenly and the earthly, which is Jerusalem.

I

One day the friends were walking with Rabbi Simeon. He said: "I see all other nations raised and Israel humiliated. Why so? Because the King, God, has sent away the Queen, Israel, and has put the handmaid, the alien Crown, in her place." He wept and continued: "A king without a queen is no king; if the king is attached to the handmaid of the queen, where is his glory? The handmaid rules over Zion as the Queen once ruled over it. But one day the Holy One will restore the Queen to her rightful place; who shall then rejoice like the King and the Queen?—the King because he has returned to her, and has separated from the handmaid, and the Queen because she is reunited to the King. Hence it is written: "Rejoice exceedingly, O daughter of Zion" (Zech. 9:9).

II

The souls of the Lower Paradise at times go forth and roam about the world. They behold those suffering who have been afflicted for the sake of their belief in the oneness of God. The souls return, and report to the Messiah what they have seen. The Messiah weeps aloud; he enters the Hall of the Afflicted, and there takes upon himself entirely the pain and the sufferings of Israel. So long as Israel was in the Holy Land, the service in the Sanctuary and the offerings averted afflictions from the world; now it is the Messiah who spares mankind.

III

The Messiah shall reveal himself first in the land of Galilee: it was here in the Holy Land that the destruction began. All the rulers will gather to wage war against him, and even from among Israel some evil ones will join the battle against the Messiah. The Messiah lifts up his eyes and he sees the Patriarchs standing at the ruins of God's Sanctuary. He sees Mother Rachel with tears in her eyes. The Holy One tries to comfort her, but she refuses to be comforted.

The day will come when a fire shall flame in Great Rome [Constantinople] and it will consume the towers and turrets; many among the great and powerful shall perish in it. The rulers will take counsel together and issue decrees for the destruction of Israel. The Messiah sees an image of the destruction of the Sanctuary and of all the martyred saints. The saintly fathers will then rise and gird the Messiah with weapons of war—Abraham at his right, Isaac at his left, Jacob in front of him. Whereupon the Messiah will take ten garments of holy zeal and go into hiding for forty days; no eye shall be permitted to look at him.

The Holy One will behold the Messiah thus attired, and He will take him and kiss him upon his brow and crown him with the crown that He Himself wore when the children of Israel were freed from the Egyptian bondage; with this same crown will He crown King Messiah.

Then the Messiah will enter one of the sanctuaries and there see the angels who are called "the mourners for Zion" [8] weeping over the destruction of the Holy Temple. They will give him a robe of deep red that he may begin his work of vengeance.

After having been crowned on high, the Messiah will be

crowned on earth, by the grave of Mother Rachel, to whom he will offer happy tidings; now she will let herself be comforted and will rise and kiss him.[9]

His army will consist of those who are diligent in the study of the Torah, but there will be only a few of these in the world. Yet his army will gain strength: through the merit of the infants for whose sake the Divine Presence dwells in the midst of Israel in exile. It is the young who will give strength to the Messiah.

That day, the Messiah will begin to gather the exiles from one end of the world to the other. From that day on, the Holy One will perform for Israel all the signs and wonders which He performed in Egypt.

IV

After the destruction of the Temple, blessings were withheld from the world, both on high and here below, so that the baser forces were strengthened and could exercise control over Israel who had sinned. When the Temple was destroyed and the people driven into dispersion, the Divine Presence left her home to accompany Israel into exile. Before leaving, the Divine Presence took one last look at the Holy of Holies and the places where the Priests and the Levites worshipped.

Entering the lands of dispersion, the Divine Presence saw how the people were oppressed and tyrannized over by the heathen nations. But in the days to come, the Holy One will recall the Community of Israel, and the Divine Presence will return from exile. The Holy One will speak to the Community of Israel: "Shake thyself from the dust, arise, O captive Jerusalem" (Isa. 52:2). He will erect the Sanctuary, restore the Holy of Holies, build the city of Jerusalem, and raise Israel from the dust.

TEN KINGS

A Midrash

The Midrash known as *Pirke de Rabbi Eliezer* (The Chapters of Rabbi Eliezer), based on earlier materials but compiled no earlier than the eighth century (according to L. Zunz), contains this short sketch of a history of world dominions. But the original and only true lord of the world is God, and to him the kingdom will return. This Midrash was popular in the Middle Ages and in the early modern period. The first edition was printed at Constantinople in 1514; a Latin version, with an extensive commentary, appeared in 1644.

Ten kings ruled from one end of the world to the other. The first king was the Holy One, blessed be he, who rules in heaven and on earth, and it was His intention to raise up kings on earth, as it is said, "And he changeth the times and the seasons; he removeth kings, and setteth up kings" (Dan. 2:21).

The second king was Nimrod,[10] who ruled from one end of the world to the other, for all the creatures were dwelling in one place and they were afraid of the waters of the flood, and Nimrod was king over them.

The third king was Joseph, who ruled from one end of the world to the other, and the Egyptians brought their tribute and their presents to Joseph to buy [corn]; for forty years he was second to the king, and for forty years he was king alone.

The fourth king was Solomon, who reigned from one end of the world to the other, as it is said, "And Solomon ruled over all the kingdoms" (1 Kings 4:21); and it says, "And they brought every man his present, vessels of silver, and vessels of gold, and raiment, and armour, and spices, horses, and mules, a rate year by year" (10:25).

The fifth king was Ahab, king of Israel, who ruled from one end of the world to the other, as it is said, "As the Lord thy God liveth, there is no nation or kingdom, whither my lord hath not sent to seek thee" (18:10). All the princes of the provinces were controlled by him; they sent and brought their tribute and their presents to Ahab.

The sixth king was Nebuchadnezzar, who ruled from one end of the world to the other. Moreover, he ruled over the beasts of the field and the birds of heaven, and they could not open their mouth except by the permission of Nebuchadnezzar, as it is said, "And wheresoever the children of men dwell, the beasts of the field and the fowls of the heaven hath he given into thine hand" (Dan. 2:38).

The seventh king was Cyrus, who ruled from one end of the world to the other, as it is said, "Thus saith Cyrus king of Persia, All the kingdoms of the earth hath the Lord, the God of heaven, given me." (2 Chron. 36:23).

The eighth king was Alexander of Macedonia, who ruled from one end of the world to the other, as it is said, "And as I was considering, behold, an he-goat came from the west over the face of the whole earth" (Dan. 8:5). And not only that, but he wished to ascend to heaven in order to know what is in heaven, and to descend into the depths in order to know what is in the depths, and not only that, but he attempted to go to the ends of the earth in order to know what was at the ends of the earth.

The ninth king is King Messiah, who, in the future, will rule from one end of the world to the other, as it is said, "He shall have dominion also from sea to sea" (Ps. 72:8); and another Scripture text says, "And the stone that smote the image became a great mountain, and filled the whole earth" (Dan. 2:35).

The tenth king will restore the sovereignty to its owner. He who was the first king will be the last king, as it is said, "Thus saith the Lord, the King . . . I am the first, and I am the last; and beside me there is no God" (Isa. 46:6); and it is written, "And the Lord shall be king over all the earth" (Zech. 14:9).

THE SUFFERING OF THE MESSIAH

A Midrash

The concept of the redemptive quality of suffering, most profoundly expressed in the enigmatic "Servant of the Lord" sections in Isaiah (especially chapter 53), became one of the significant motifs in the talmudic and midrashic eschatological thought. We find records of this motif (some with reference to Isaiah 53) in the third century, but the idea may be even older. A fully developed statement is preserved in the *Pesikta Rabbati* (chapters 36 and 37), a midrash compiled probably in the ninth century. The version below is from *Bereshit Rab-*

bati, by Moses ha-Darshan of Narbonne (eleventh century), as quoted by the Dominican Raymond Martini of Barcelona in his *Pugio Fidei* (The Dagger of Faith).

Said Satan to the Holy One, blessed be he: "Let me accuse the Messiah and his generation."

The Holy One answered: "You cannot prevail against him."

Satan insisted: "O Lord of the universe, give me permission and I shall succeed."

But the Holy One answered: "I shall drive Satan from the world rather than allow one soul of that generation to perish."

Thereupon the Holy One turned to the Messiah: "Messiah, my righteous one, the day will come when the sins of those that are preserved near you will impose a heavy yoke on you. Your eyes will not see the light, your ears will hear the nations of the world emit invectives, your nose will smell decay, your mouth feel a bitter taste, your tongue cleave to the roof of your mouth, your skin shrivel upon your bones, your body languish in sighs and in sadness. Are you prepared to assume these burdens? If you take these sufferings upon yourself, well and good; if not, I shall eradicate those [future sinners]."

Answered the Messiah: "Lord of the universe, happily will I take upon myself these sufferings if I know that you will restore to life all those who have died since the days of the first man. And that all those should see salvation who have been devoured by wild animals, and all those who have drowned in oceans and rivers. And that your salvation be extended also to those who have been born prematurely and to those whom you plan to create but have not yet created."

Thereto the Holy One said: "So be it."

Then took the Messiah lovingly all the sufferings upon himself, as it is said: "He was oppressed but he humbled himself" (Isa. 53:7).

CREATION AND WORLD'S HISTORY

Moses Nahmanides

The concept that the history of the world is presaged in the Biblical story of the six days of creation occupied the medieval mind. This concept, in its manifold formulations, introduced order into the chaos of events and the promise of redemption and resolution of conflicts in a final, Sabbatical, era. The account that follows is from Nahmanides' Commentary to the Pentateuch (see "Has the Messiah Come?" and "The Creation of Man").

On the first two days [of Creation] nothing reached perfection, as the world was still full of water. This suggests that the first two thousand years of world history were marked with imperfection, as there was no one who proclaimed the name of God to the children of man. It is as the sages have said, "The first two thousand years were *Tohu* (unformed)." [11] Light, however, was created on the first day, which suggests the thousand years of Adam who was the light of the world, since he recognized his Creator.

On the second day God said, "Let there be a firmament in the midst of the waters and let it divide the waters" (Gen. 1:6); this indicates the division between Noah and his children on the one hand, and the wicked ones of their generation on the other.

On the third day dry land appeared, as well as all kinds of vegetation and fruits; these intimated the events of the third millenium which commenced when Abraham was forty-eight years old, at which time, according to tradition, he began proclaiming to the world the name of God.[12] This process continued until his descendants accepted the Torah at Mount Sinai, and the Temple was built. At that time all the commandments of the Torah which are "the fruits of the world" were proclaimed.

The fourth day which marked the creation of the luminaries, large and small, symbolized the fourth millenium in world history. It began 72 years after the building of the First Temple, and was completed 172 years after the destruction of the Second

Temple. This was the era when "the children of Israel had light in their dwellings" (Exod. 10:23), as the Glory of God filled the House. The smaller luminary, the moon, symbolized the era of the Second Temple, when the Light over it was smaller. Finally, the two luminaries disappeared. The Temple was destroyed.

On the fifth day—corresponding to the fifth millenium in world history—the waters began swarming with living creatures. This indicates the time in world history when power came to the new nations that appeared upon the face of the earth. It is the era when "men are made like fishes in the sea, like swarms without a chief" (Hab. 1:14).

The sixth day, corresponding to the sixth millenium marked two creations: in the early part of the day, before sunrise, the earth gave forth living creatures, and then man was created. This was an allusion to the fact that during a part of this millenium power will still be in the hands of the kingdoms which are likened to the beasts [in the vision of Daniel], but ultimately the redeemer, as symbolized by Adam, will come.

The seventh day, the Sabbath, suggests the world to come, "the day" that shall be all Sabbath and rest in a life everlasting.

MESSIAH THE TEACHER

The Messianic hope, which originated in Biblical times, developed in the course of the centuries until it encompassed the hope for individual, national, and universal redemption. Belief in the coming of the Messiah inspired fighters and dreamers, militants and escapists, rationalists and mystics; it gave meaning to martyrdom. Messianic impatience gave rise to nihilists and revolutionaries. Since there was no dogma to stabilize the functions and the features of the Messiah, many possibilities opened themselves to thought, imagination, and fancy. There was Messiah, the arbiter of the world, and Messiah, the miraculous redeemer. It is not surprising that among the Messianic texts there appear some that speak of him as a teacher and attribute to learned discourse a redemptive quality. The first selection below is from the early medieval *Alphabet of Rabbi Akiba;* the second selection is based on a medieval Yemenite manuscript. Compare also "The Sufferings of Messiah," "Mystic Drama of Jerusalem," and "Ten Kings."

I

At that future time, the Holy One, blessed be he, will sit down in the Garden of Eden and teach, and all the righteous ones will sit before Him. The Celestial Family will be present there: to His right the sun and the planets, to His left the moon and all the stars. The Holy One, blessed be he, will explain the principles of the new Torah which He is about to issue through the Messiah.

When He reaches the homily, Zerubbabel the son of Sealtiel [13] will rise and proclaim: "Exalted and sanctified be His great name." His voice will reach from one corner of the world to the other and all people will respond and say: "Amen!" Even those from among the Israelites and the heathens who are still confined in Gehenna, the place of punishment, even they will respond and say "Amen!" out of Gehenna, and their Amen will shake the world and will be heard by the Holy One, blessed be he.

The Lord will ask: What is this frightful voice which I have heard? The ministering angels will answer Him: Master of the universe, this was the voice of people in Gehenna, faithfully responding with Amen. Whereupon the Lord's compassion will be moved strongly toward them, and he will say: Why should I punish them beyond what they have already endured? The Evil Impulse caused them to fail.

In that hour will the Lord take the keys of Gehenna, hand them over to Michael and Gabriel in the presence of all the righteous ones, and say: Go and open the gates of Gehenna and let them come out. As it says: "Open ye the gates that the righteous people that keepeth faith may enter in" (Isa. 26:2).

Then go forth Michael and Gabriel, open the gates of Gehenna, grasp each person by his hand and lead him out of Gehenna, wash him, anoint him, heal him from the wounds of Gehenna, clothe him with beautiful and good garments, grasp each one by his hand and bring him before the Holy One, blessed be he, and before all the righteous ones.

Scripture says: "Let Thy priests, O Lord God, be clothed

with salvation, and let Thy pious ones rejoice in good" (II Chron. 6:41). By "priests" Scripture means the righteous among the Gentiles who serve God as priests in this world; by "pious ones" Scripture means those who formerly were wicked in Israel [and who have repented].

II

In the Messianic future the Holy One, blessed be he, will call the Garden of Eden "Zion" and Zion He will call Garden of Eden. The desolate places in Zion He will make bloom like Paradise. He will build a Jerusalem in Heaven and call it "the throne of the Lord." The just ones who remained in Zion and the pious ones who were found there will all be placed on thrones of glory, and a crown will be put on the head of every one, and the divine splendor will be reflected in their faces.

The Holy One, blessed be he, will write down the name of every just one for a good life, and for blessed years in the Messianic age, so that he may take part in the joy of Zion and the gladness of Jerusalem. As Scripture says: "Rejoice ye with Jerusalem, and be glad with her, all ye that love her" (Isa. 66:10).

The Messiah, son of David, will be given his seat in the Academy on High; they will call him "Lord" just as they call his Master, as it is written: "And this is his name whereby he shall be called, the Lord our righteousness" (Jer. 23:6).

And as the Messiah sits in his Academy, all the people will come and sit before him to listen to the new teaching and new laws and profound wisdom which he will teach Israel. Elijah the prophet—may he be remembered for blessing—will stand as an interpreter before the Messiah, whose voice will reach from one end of the world to the other.

What will come to pass in that hour? It will come to pass that Abraham, Isaac, and Jacob, Joseph and all the tribes, Moses and all the prophets, Aaron and all the Temple servants, Samuel and all the seers, David and all the kings, Solomon and all the wise men, Daniel and all the pious, Mordecai and all the sages, Ezra and all the scribes, the Hasmonean and all the heroes, Nehemiah and all the enlightened ones, yes, all the just ones, all of them will rise from their graves by the power of the Holy Spirit,

and come and take their seats in the Academy of the Messiah
and listen to his discourse on the Torah and the commandments.

And the Holy One, blessed be he, will reveal to them
through Elijah—may he be remembered for blessing—laws of
life, laws of peace, laws of zeal, laws of purity, laws of restraint,
laws of piety, laws of justice. Whosoever hears the discourse
issuing from the mouth of the Messiah, he will never forget it,
because it is the Holy One, blessed be he, who makes himself
manifest in the Academy of the Messiah, and it is he who pours
from His Holy Spirit over all the human beings in that Academy
so that the Holy Spirit rests upon each and every one.

In that Academy man's own reason will make him understand the commandments, the exegesis, the deliberations, the
lore, and the traditions; each one will know out of his own knowledge; as Scripture says: "And it shall come to pass afterward,
that I will pour out My spirit upon all flesh; and your sons and
your daughters shall prophesy, and old men shall dream dreams,
your young men shall see visions" (Joel 3:1).

Even men servants and maid servants which were bought
from the heathen nations will be endowed with the Holy Spirit
and be able to engage in a discourse; as it says: "And also upon
the servants and upon the handmaids in those days will I pour
out My spirit" (Joel 3:2). And each one will have a study room
in his home, a room for the Divine Presence.

THE DANCE OF THE RIGHTEOUS

Judah Loew ben Bezalel

Concerning the author see "The Sabbath and the Days of the Week."
The selection that follows is from his *Be-er ha-Golah*, Prague, 1598.

In the last paragraph of the talmudic tractate Taanit the
following statement is made in the name of Rabbi Eleazar: "A
time will come when God will arrange a dance for the righteous
in paradise. He will sit in their midst and everyone will point a
finger at Him, as it is written: 'Lo, this is our God; we have

waited for Him, and He will save us; this is the Lord: we have waited for Him, we will be glad and rejoice in His salvation'" (Isa. 25:9).[14]

People point to this statement and say that it is against all reason to suppose that there could be young maidens and men dancing in a holy place like the world to come, detached as it is from everything material. One must, however, understand that those words are meant to reveal a great blessing reserved for the righteous, and that deep wisdom is contained in this saying.

The dance is specially suitable for young maidens, as it is written: "Then shall the virgin rejoice in the dance, both young men and old together" (Jer. 31:13). The dance is joy expressed through action, not joy remaining in the heart. Women, and especially young maidens, are less thoughtful than men, and thought keeps back the full expression of joy. Since one day joy will find pure expression in paradise, joy itself is called the dance of the righteous. This will be the joy in God, as it is written: "Rejoice in the Lord, ye righteous" (Ps. 97:12). Therefore it is said that God will sit in their midst and everyone will point a finger at Him. This means that the righteous have no other joy except in God. He is the perfection of themselves. So far there is a simple explanation of the words of the sages.

But one must understand also what really is meant by the dance. Joy is something psychical, it is the expression of a perfection in man which belongs only to the soul but not to the material body. The body has only potential power, but no independence. Without this there is no perfection. The body is kept down by the weight of nature; it is oppressed. When therefore a man dances he experiences a greater joy, because he feels the perfection of the soul as power. Therefore it is said that God arranges a dance of the righteous in paradise, because all that is depressing and material is taken from them and only the soul has power. When it is said that God is in their midst, it means that they are freed from the material, which formed a barrier between them and God.

The dance spoken of is not any kind, but a round dance, in a circle. Every circle has a center, equidistant from any point of the circumference. Therefore it says that God sits in the center

of the righteous, as all points of the circumference are joined
to the center by the radii, turned towards it and attracted by it.
And just as the center is apart from the circumference, so He, the
Holy One, remains apart, although in their midst.

The dance has to be a round one, so that no one can say
that every righteous person adheres to God in his own manner.
As the dance proceeds round and round, every righteous one is
joined to God not from one place only, but from all places. Pointing a finger at God means that one points out something that is
separate from the rest. The righteous learn to know wherein lies
God's oneness and His difference from all else that is. The pointing with the finger is the recognition of this truth.

One can only write little about such mighty matters. The
wise one will add to it out of his own wisdom and knowledge.
May God forgive us and make us the last participants in this
holy dance.

HAS THE MESSIAH COME?

Moses Nahmanides

The debate at Barcelona in 1263 was one of the major religious disputations between Christians and Jews in the Middle Ages. It was preceded by the debate at Paris in 1240, and followed by one at Avila in
1375; the most impressive—and longest—disputation took place at
Tortosa, in 1413–1414. The aim of the Christian initiators of such public meetings was to demonstrate the superiority of the Church and to
gain converts to Christianity. At the Barcelona debate an attempt was
made for the first time to interpret talmudic-midrashic statements in
support of Christian teachings. The initiative for this disputation came
from Fra Paulo (or Pablo) Christiani, a converted Jew who had become a Dominican monk; some scholars assume that he taught the
Hebrew Bible and rabbinic writings to the scholarly Dominican, Raymond Martini. The disputation was sponsored by King James I of
Aragon and was attended by Raymond Martini, Raymond de Peñaforte, the King's confessor, also a Dominican, by the Franciscan Peter
de Janua, and the aristocracy and representatives of the population.
The spokesman for Judaism was Moses ben Nahman (Nahmanides,
Bonastrug de Porta, 1195–1270), rabbi in Gerona, Bible commentator,

and mystic. Upon the conclusion of the debate (that lasted four days) Nahmanides wrote a Hebrew report of the proceedings, in order to counteract a possible misrepresentation of his position in the discussion. Upon the intervention of Pope Clement IV, Nahmanides was banished from Aragon. He went to Palestine (1267), where he spent the last three years of his life.

Nahmanides' account appeared in print first in Wagenseil's *Tela ignea satanae*, 1681, together with a Latin translation; both text and translation are corrupt. A more reliable text appeared in Constantinople in 1710. The best edition is by M. Steinschneider (Berlin, 1860). The following are only selected parts from the report.

Our lord the king had commanded me to debate with Fra Paulo in his majesty's palace, in the presence of himself and his council, in Barcelona. To this command I replied that I would accede if I were granted freedom of speech, whereby I craved both the permission of the king and of Fra Raymond of Peñaforte and his associates who were present. Fra Raymond of Peñaforte replied that this I could have so long as I did not speak disrespectfully. [. . .]

Then Fra Paulo began by saying that he would prove from our Talmud that the Messiah of whom the prophets had witnessed had already come. I replied, that before we argued on that, I would like him to show and tell me how this could possibly be true. [. . .] Did he wish to say that the scholars who appear in the Talmud believed concerning Jesus that he was the Messiah, and that they believed that he was completely man and truly God in accordance with the Christian conceptions of him? Was it not indeed a known fact that Jesus existed in the days of the Second Temple, being born and put to death before the destruction of that Temple? But the scholars of the Talmud were later than this destruction. [. . .] Now, if these scholars had believed in the Messiahship of Jesus and that he was genuine and his religious belief true; and if they wrote those things which Fra Paulo affirms he is going to prove that they wrote; then how was it that they continued to hold by the Jewish faith and their original religious usage? For they were Jews and continued to abide in the religion of the Jews all their days. They died as Jews, they and their children, and their disciples who heard all the words they uttered. Why did they not apostatize and turn to the religion of Jesus as has done Fra Paulo who understands from their saying that the Christian faith is the true faith? [. . .]

Fra Paulo took up the debate and claimed that in the Talmud it was stated that the Messiah had already come. He brought forward that haggadic story, contained in the Midrash to the Book of Lamentations,[15] about the man who was ploughing when his cow began lowing. An Arab was passing by and said to the man: "O Jew, O Jew, untie your cow, untie your plough, untie your coulter, for the temple has been destroyed." The man untied his cow, his plough, and his coulter. The cow lowed a second time. The Arab said to the man: "Tie your cow, tie your plough, tie your coulter, for your Messiah has been born."

To this I answered: "I do not give any credence at all to this Haggadah but it provides proof of my argument." At this the fellow shouted: "See how the writings of his fellow-Jews are denied him!" I replied: "I certainly do not believe that the Messiah was born on the day of the destruction of the Temple and as for this Haggadah, either it is not true or it has another interpretation of the sort called the mystical explanations of the wise. But I shall accept the story's plain literal statement, which you have put forward, since it furnishes me with support. Observe then that the story says that at the time of the destruction of the Temple, after it had been destroyed, on that very day, the Messiah was born. If this be so, then Jesus is not the Messiah as you affirm that he is. For he was born and was put to death before the destruction of the Temple took place, his birth being nearly two hundred years before that event according to the true chronology and seventy-three years previous to that event according to your reckonings." At these words of mine my opponent was reduced to silence.

Master Gilles who was the king's justiciary,[16] then replied to me with the remark: "At the present moment we are not discussing about Jesus, but the question rather is: whether the Messiah has come or not? You say that he has not come, but this Jewish book says that he has come."

To this I said: "You are, as is the practice of those of your profession, taking refuge in a subtlety of retort and argument.

But nevertheless I shall answer you on this point. The scholars have not stated that the Messiah has come, but they have said that he has been born. For, for example, on the day when Moses our teacher was born he had not come, nor was he a redeemer, but when he came to Pharaoh by the commandment of the Holy One and said to Pharaoh, 'Thus saith the Lord, Let my people go,' (Exod. 8:1) then he had come. And likewise the Messiah when he shall come to the Pope and shall say to him by the commandment of God: 'Let my people go,' then he shall have come. But until that day comes, he shall not have come, nor [till then] will there be any Messiah at all. For David the king, on the day when he was born, was not a king nor was he a Messiah, but when Elijah shall anoint one to be a Messiah by the commandment of the deity he [the anointed one] shall be called Messiah and when, afterwards, the Messiah shall come to the Pope to redeem us, then it shall be announced that a redeemer has come."

Hereupon my opponent Fra Paulo urged that the Biblical section Isaiah 52:13 beginning with the words "Behold, my servant shall deal wisely" [17] treats of the subject of the death of the Messiah, of his coming into the power of his enemies and that they set him among the wicked as happened also in the case of Jesus. "You do believe," asked Fra Paulo, "that this section is speaking of the Messiah?"

I answered him: "According to the real meaning of the passage the section speaks only of the community of Israel the people. For thus the prophets address them constantly, as in Isaiah 41:8: 'Thou Israel my servant' and as in Isaiah 44:1: 'O Jacob my servant.'"

Fra Paulo then rejoined: "But I can shew you from the statements of the scholars that in their view the Biblical section is speaking of the Messiah."

I replied to this as follows: "It is true that our teachers in the Haggadic books do interpret the servant, in the Biblical section referred to, as indicating the Messiah. But they never assert that he was slain by his enemies. For you will never find in any of the writings of Israel, neither in the Talmud nor in the haggadic works, that the Messiah the son of David will be slain or that he will ever be delivered into the hands of his foes or buried among them that are wicked.

My opponent, Fra Paulo, returned again to the point discussed, with the assertion that in the Talmud it was distinctly stated that Rabbi Joshua ben Levi had asked Elijah when the Messiah would come and Elijah had given him the reply: Ask the Messiah himself. Joshua then asked: And where is he? Elijah said: At the gates of Rome among the poor. Joshua went there and found him and put a question to him, etc.[18] "Now," said Fra Paulo, "if what the Talmud here says be so, then the Messiah has already come and has been in Rome—but it was Jesus who was the ruler in Rome."

I said to him in reply to this: "And is it not plain from this very passage you cite that the Messiah has not come? For you will observe that Joshua asked Elijah when the Messiah would come. Likewise also the latter himself was asked by Joshua: when will the Master come? Thus he had not yet come. Yet, according to the literal sense of these haggadic narratives, the Messiah has been born; but such is not my own belief."

At this point our lord the king interposed with the question that if the Messiah had been born on the day of the destruction of the Temple, which was more than a thousand years ago, and had not yet come, how could he come now, seeing that it was not in the nature of man to live a thousand years?

My answer to him was: "Already the conditions of discussion have been laid down which preclude me from disputing with you and you from interposing in this debate—but among those who have been in former times, Adam and Methuselah were well nigh a thousand years old, and Elijah and Enoch more than this since these are they who [yet] are alive with God."

The king then put the question: "Where then is the Messiah at present?"

To this I replied: "That question does not serve the purposes of this discussion and I shall not give an answer to it but perchance you will find him, whom you ask about, at the gates of Toledo if you send thither one of your couriers." This last remark I made to the king in irony. The assembly then stood adjourned, the king appointing the time for the resumption of the debate to be the day after next.

On the day appointed, the king came to a convent that was within the city bounds, where was assembled all the male population, both Gentiles and Jews. There were present the bishop, all the priests, the scholars of the Minorities [i.e., the Franciscans] and the Preaching Friars [i.e., the Dominicans]. Fra Paulo, my opponent, stood up to speak, when I, intervening, requested our lord the king that I should now be heard. The king replied that Fra Paulo should speak first because he was the petitioner. But I urged that I should now be allowed to express my opinion on the subject of the Messiah and then afterwards, he, Fra Paulo, could reply on the question of accuracy.

I then rose and calling upon all the people to attend said: "Fra Paulo has asked me if the Messiah of whom the prophets have spoken has already come and I have asserted that he has not come. Also a haggadic work, in which someone states that on the very day on which the Temple was destroyed the Messiah was born, was brought by Fra Paulo as evidence on his behalf. I then stated that I gave no credence to this pronouncement of the Haggadah but that it lent support to my contention. And now I am going to explain to you why I said that I do not believe it. I would have you know that we Jews have three kinds of writings —first, the Bible in which we all believe with perfect faith. The second kind is that which is called Talmud which provides a commentary to the commandments of the Torah, for in the Torah there are six hundred and thirteen commandments and there is not a single one of them which is not expounded in the Talmud and we believe in it in regard to the exposition of the commandments. Further, there is a third kind of writing, which we have, called Midrash, that is to say sermonic literature of the sort that would be produced if the bishop here should stand up and deliver a sermon which someone in the audience, who liked it should write down. To a document of this sort, should any of us extend belief, then well and good, but if he refuses to do so no one will do him any harm. For we have scholars who in their writings say that the Messiah will not be born until the approach of the End-time when he will come to deliver us from exile. For this reason I do not believe in this book [which Fra Paulo cites] when it makes the assertion that the Messiah was born on the day of the destruction of the Temple."

My opponent now stood up and said: "I shall bring further evidence that the Messianic age has already been." But I craved my lord the king to be allowed to speak a little longer and spoke as follows: "Religion and truth, and justice which for us Jews is the substance of religion, does not depend upon a Messiah. For you, our lord the king, are, in my view, more profitable than a Messiah. You are a king and he is a king, you a Gentile, and he [to be] king of Israel—for a Messiah is but a human monarch as you are. And when I, in exile and in affliction and servitude, under the reproach of the peoples who reproach us continually, can yet worship my Creator with your permission, my gain is great. For now I make of my body a whole-burnt offering to God and thus become more and more worthy of the life of the world to come. But when there shall be a king of Israel of my own religion ruling over all peoples then I would be forced to abide in the law of the Jews, and my reward would not be so much increased.

But the core of the contention and the disagreement between Jews and Christians lies in what you Christians assert in regard to the chief topic of faith, namely the deity, for here you make an assertion that is exceedingly distasteful. And you, our lord the king, are a Christian born of a Christian and all your days you have listened to priests and they have filled your brain and the marrow of your bones with this doctrine and I would set you free again from that realm of habit and custom. Of a certainty the doctrine which you believe and which is a dogma of your faith cannot be accepted by reason. Nature does not admit of it. The prophets have never said anything that would support it. Also the miracle itself cannot be made intelligible by the doctrine in question as I shall make clear with ample proofs at the proper time and place. That the Creator of heaven and earth and all that in them is should withdraw into and pass through the womb of a certain Jewess and should grow there for seven months and be born a small child and after this grow up to be handed over to his enemies who condemn him to death and kill him, after which, you say, he came to life and returned to his former abode —neither the mind of Jew nor of any man will sustain this. Hence vain and fruitless is your arguing with us, for here lies the root of our disagreement. However, as it is your wish, let us further discuss the question of the Messiah."

Fra Paulo then said to me: "Then you do believe that the Messiah has come?"

I replied: "No, but I believe and am convinced that he has not come and there never has been anyone who has said concerning himself that he was Messiah—nor will there ever be such who will say so [concerning themselves]—except Jesus. And it is impossible for me to believe in the Messiahship of Jesus, because the prophet says of the Messiah that 'he shall have dominion from sea to sea and from the River until the ends of the earth' (Ps. 72:8). Jesus, on the other hand, never had dominion, but in his lifetime he was pursued by his enemies and hid himself from them, falling finally into their power whence he was not able to liberate himself. How then could he save all Israel? Moreover, after his death dominion was not his. For in regard to the Empire of Rome, he had no part in the growth of that. Since before men believed in him the city of Rome ruled over most of the world and after faith in him had spread, Rome lost many lands over which it once held sovereign power. And now the followers of Muhammad possess a larger empire than Rome has. In like manner the prophet Jeremiah declares that in the Messianic age 'they shall teach no more every man his neighbor, and every man his brother, saying, Know the Lord: for they shall all know me' (31:34), while in Isaiah it is written, that 'the earth shall be full of the knowledge of the Lord, as the waters cover the sea' (11:9). Moreover the latter prophet states that, in this time, 'they shall beat their swords into ploughshares . . . nation shall not lift up sword against nation, neither shall they learn war any more' (2:4). But since the days of Jesus up to the present the whole world has been full of violence and rapine, the Christians more than other peoples being shedders of blood and revealers likewise of indecencies. And how hard it would be for you, my lord the king, and for those knights of yours, if they should learn war no more!" [. . .] Afterwards on the same day I had audience of the king who remarked: "The debate still remains to be concluded. For I have never seen anyone who was in the wrong argue so well as you have." Then I heard in the palace-court that it was the will of the king and of the Preaching Friars [the Dominicans] to visit the synagogue on the Sabbath. So I tarried in the city for eight days.

When they came to the synagogue on the following Sabbath I addressed our lord the king in words that were worthy of the occasion and of his office. [. . .]

Fra Raymond of Peñaforte rose up and gave a discourse on the subject of the Trinity and asserted that the Trinity was wisdom and will and power. "And had not also the master," he said, "in a synagogue in Gerona assented to what Fra Paulo had said on this point?"

At this I got to my feet and spoke as follows: "I ask both Jews and Gentiles to give me their attention on this matter. When Fra Paulo asked me in Gerona if I believed in the Trinity, I replied: 'What is the Trinity? Do you mean that three material bodies, of the sort that men have, constitute the Godhead?' He said: 'No.' Then I asked: 'Do you mean that the Trinity consists of three subtle substances such as souls or that it is three angels?' He said: 'No.' 'Or do you mean,' I enquired, 'that the Trinity is one substance which is a compound of three substances such as are those bodies which are compounded of the four elements?' He said: 'No.' 'If that is the case' said I, 'then what is the Trinity?' He answered: 'Wisdom and will and power.' To which I replied that I acknowledged that the deity was wise and not foolish, and will without passibility, and powerful and not weak, but that the expression Trinity was entirely misleading. For wisdom in the Creator is not an unessential quality but He and His wisdom are one and He and His will are one and He and His power are one —and, if this be so, the wisdom and the will and the power are one whole. And even if these were unessential qualities of God, the thing which is the Godhead is not three but is one, bearing three unessential qualities."

Then Fra Paulo stood up and said that he believed in the perfect unity of the Deity but that nevertheless there was in that unity a Trinity, and this was a doctrine very profound for neither the angels nor the princes of the upper regions could comprehend it.

My answer to this was: "It is clear that no person believes what he does not know. Hence it is that the angels do not believe in a Trinity." The associates of Fra Paulo made him remain silent. Our lord the king rose up and he and those with him descended from the place where the prayer-desk was, each going their several ways.

On the morrow, I had audience of our lord the king whose words to me were: "Return to your city in safety and in peace." Then he gave me three hundred dinars and I took my leave of him with much affection. May God make him worthy of the life of the world to come. Amen.

A VISIT TO PARADISE

Immanuel ben Solomon of Rome

Immanuel ben Solomon ha-Romi (ca. 1270–ca. 1330) was born in Rome, lived in various Italian cities, and is known in Italian as Manoello Guideo. He wrote Biblical commentaries and poetry, occasionally in Italian, but chiefly in Hebrew. Influenced by his country, he introduced the sonnet form into Hebrew poetry, but wrote also in the style of the Spanish Hebrew poets. His themes range from the sensual and frivolous to the lofty and religious, from witty satire to sublime prayer. He collected his poems in a Diwan, entitled Mahbarot (Makamat, miscellanies). The concluding poem (from which a section is here reprinted), a vision of the "world beyond" called Ha-Tofet ve-ha-Eden (Hell and Paradise), is patterned on Dante's Divine Comedy. Guided by Daniel (Dante?), Immanuel meets in Hell such men and women as the daughters of Lot, the Biblical Pharaoh, the wife of Potiphar, Aristotle, and Galen. In Paradise he finds a throne prepared for "Daniel," another possible allusion to Dante. The Diwan was first printed at Brescia in 1491. The author and his work are of interest as products of their time and surroundings; in the history of Jewish thought Immanuel occupies a very minor place.

While we walked to and fro through the streets of Eden, and looked upon the gallery of the men of wisdom, I perceived men full of splendor and majesty, compared to whose beauty the sun and moon are dark; a place was given them in the world of angels. Not recognizing any one of them, I asked the man who talked with me, that I might know concerning them. And he said unto me: "These are the pious of the Gentiles, who prevailed with their wisdom and intellect, and ascended the degrees of the ladder of wisdom in accordance with their ability. They were not as their fathers, a stubborn and rebellious generation; but they investigated with their intellect as to who is the Maker, and who the Creator that fashioned them with His loving-kindness, took them out from nothingness to existence, and brought them to this world; and as to what is the purpose for which He created them. When they asked their fathers, and considered their answers, they knew that they were worthless; they despised their creed, and set their mind to investigate the creed of other nations.

"Having investigated all the creeds, and having found that the hands of each of them are steadfast in strengthening its own foundations and in disparaging other creeds, they did not say: 'Let us remain in our creed, for it has been handed down to us by our fathers,' but out of all creeds they chose those doctrines which are true, and concerning which the wise men did not differ; these doctrines they accepted, and to them they clung. But to those opinions which all nations disparage they turned their back, not their face. As regards God, they arrogantly call Him by a name at which our heart trembles and shudders, for every nation calls Him by a special name.

"We, however, say: 'Let His name be what it may, we believe in the truly First Existence, that produced life; that was, is, and will be; that created the universe, when His wisdom so decided; that is hidden from us through the intensity of His revelation; that faints not, and is not weary, and of whose understanding there is no searching; that has mercy upon His creatures, and feeds them, as a shepherd tends his flock; who will call us unto Him, when our end draws nigh, and whose glory will gather us together.'" [. . .]

[Then] I remembered the rank of Daniel my brother, who had led me in the right way, and directed my path, and who had been near me when I fled. He is the plate of the holy crown upon my forehead, the life of my flesh and the breath of my spirit. I thought of the full account of his greatness, of his generosity and excellence, of his prudence and understanding, of his humility and righteousness, and of his renown which fills the ends of the earth. I then said unto the man who held my right hand: "I pray thee, my lord, show me the place of Daniel and his habitation; what manner of house do ye build for him, and what place is his rest?"

And he said unto me: "Know of a certainty that his rank is very high, and that the ends of the earth are full of his renown; even thy rank is too low to reach him. 'For he bore the sin of many, and made intercession for the transgressors' (Isa. 53:12). But because the Highest Wisdom knew that without thee he would find no rest and no repose, it placed thy booth near his booth, though thy worth is less than his; for the Highest Wisdom knew that he will have delight in thy company: he would be Moses, and thou wouldst be Joshua unto him; in order that all may declare, as it is said: Your souls are united, they cling together, and cannot be sundered. 'Will two walk together, except they have agreed?'" (Amos 3:3).

There is nothing to marvel at that I was joyful, for I knew that my lot fell in pleasant places, being aware that I shall have redemption on account of him. And I said unto the man: "As thou livest, show me the splendor of his throne, where he rests. For I know that its height mounts up to the heavens, and its head reaches unto the clouds."

And the man said unto me: "Come with me, and I shall show thee his joy and the glory of his resting-place." So I went after him [. . .]. Angels kept on bringing material for the work, and were making pleasant and beautiful canopies that shone like the brightness of the firmament, whose covering was of every precious stone, and whose structure was of sapphire, and tables, lamps, thrones, and crowns for the pure souls. We saw there a big ivory throne overlaid with gold, which gave life to him that finds it, and health to all his flesh. Crown stones glittered upon it, and garments of blue and purple and scarlet were spread over it; they sparkled like burnished brass, the glory of all lands. Upon the top of the throne was a crown, the weight of which was a *kikkar* of gold, and a precious stone that cannot be obtained for fine gold, nor can silver be weighed for the price thereof.

A voice was saying: "Proclaim that the merchandise thereof shall be for them that dwell before the Lord." And the man that talked with me said: "Hast thou seen the crown and the lofty throne whereupon thy brother Daniel rises as a lion, and lifts himself up as a lioness? This is his resting-place for ever, and here shall he dwell, because he hearkened to the word of the Lord, and there is no sage or thinker like him in all the earth."

Thereupon I rendered praise and thanks unto my Lord, because He brought him to the rest and to the inheritance; and I said: "Blessed be the Lord who is one, and who has no second, because He has not forsaken His loving-kindness and His truth toward my master."

When we ascended to the higher steps of Eden, we saw a thing whereat we marvelled; for there we saw men who during their life were ravenous beasts, bad to God and bad to men; they died as wicked men the death of them that are slain; their blood was poured out as water, and their flesh as dung. When I saw them shine like the brightness of the firmament, their height mounting up to the heavens, and their head reaching unto the clouds, I said in my heart: "Behold, the Lord has forgiven the sin of many, and makes intercession for the transgressors." I then inquired of the man that talked with me, that I might know the reason why these men deserved this lofty rank.

And he said unto me: "These men sinned, dealt perversely, and transgressed; for their sin they perished before their time, and were filled with bitterness; they were delivered into the hands of cruel people, and fell wounded, having been pierced through, into the lions' dens and upon the mountains of the leopards; they were left together unto the fowl of heaven and unto the ravenous birds of the mountains. When they approached the bitterness of death, they recalled the wickedness they had done, and accepted the bitterness of death with love, knowing that it came to them as a just retribution. Death was more pleasant unto them than life, because they considered that

they deserved a greater calamity, and that through these sufferings they were redeemed from a severer punishment than death.
When at the point of dying they showed their joy and delight
with their mouth and heart; and because they had received part
of their punishment in the corrupt world, wrath was averted from
their souls. Their death having been cruel and bitter, it was accounted as a crown of glory and a diadem of beauty upon the
head of their souls. It is, therefore, because of their death that
they deserved this glorious rank."

THE MESSIANIC AGE

Moses Maimonides

Maimonides rejected the various popular conceptions of Messianic
Utopia that persisted for centuries and—in the concluding chapters
of the *Mishneh Torah*—presented a natural, rational, historical, political view of the Messianic era. In contradistinction from the Messianic
age, Maimonides defined the classical Jewish concept of "the world to
come" as a state of incorporeal, spiritual bliss into which the souls of
persons worthy of this state enter "after the life of the present world
in which we now exist with body and soul" (*Mishneh Torah, Hilkhot
Teshuvah* VIII). The Messianic age appears to him as a period of preparation for the life in the world to come. Compare also "The Event on
Sinai."

The Messianic king will in time arise and establish the kingdom of David in its former position and in the dominion it
originally had. He will build up the sanctuary and gather the
scattered of Israel. In his day, the laws will become what they
were in olden times. They will bring offerings, they will observe
years of release and years of jubilee, according to the commandment given in the Torah.[19]

The Torah testifies to the Messianic king, as it is written:
"The Lord thy God will turn thy captivity, and have compassion
upon thee, and will return and gather thee from all the peoples,
whither the Lord thy God hath scattered thee. If any of thine
that are dispersed be in the uttermost parts of heaven, from

thence will the Lord thy God gather thee, and from thence will He fetch thee. And the Lord thy God will bring thee into the land which thy fathers possessed, and thou shalt possess it" (Deut. 30:3–5).

Do not think, however, that the Messianic king must give signs and miracles and create new things in this world, or bring the dead back to life, and the like. It will not be so. For see: Rabbi Akiba, who was a great sage among the sages of the Mishnah, it was he who carried arms for ben Koziba,[20] the king, and it was he who said of him that he was the Messianic king. He and all the sages of his generation thought that this was the Messianic king, until he was slain in his guilt. And after he was slain they all knew that he was not the Messianic king. But never had the sages asked him for a sign or for miracles. The root of these things is the following: This Torah, its statutes and its laws, are for all times. There is nothing one could add to it, and nothing one could take away.

If a king should arise out of the house of David, one who meditates upon the Torah, and like his ancestor, David, occupies himself with the commandments according to the written and the oral law, who has bent Israel to go in the ways of the Torah and to restore its breach, and who has fought the battles of the Lord, then it might be presumed that he is the Messiah. If he has succeeded, if he has built up the sanctuary in its place, if he has gathered the scattered of Israel, behold, then he is surely the Messiah. He will perfect the whole world, so that all together may serve the Lord, as it is written: "For then will I turn to the peoples a pure language, that they may all call upon the name of the Lord, to serve Him with one consent" (Zeph. 3:9).

Do not think in your heart that in the days of the Messiah something will be changed in the ways of the world, or that an innovation will appear in the work of Creation. No! The world will go its ways as before, and that which is said in Isaiah, "And the wolf shall dwell with the lamb, and the leopard shall lie down with the kid" (Isa. 11:6) is but a parable, and its meaning is that Israel will dwell in safety with those who were lawless among the heathen, and all will turn to the true faith; they will not rob, nor destroy, and they will eat only what is permitted, in peace, like Israel, as it is written: "The lion shall eat straw like the ox" (Isa. 11:7). And everything else like this that is said concerning the Messiah is also a parable. In the days of the Messiah all will know what the parable signified and what it was meant to imply.

The sages said: "Nothing, save the cessation of the servitude to the nations, distinguishes the days of the Messiah from our time." [21] From the words of the prophets we see that in the early days of the Messiah, "the war of Gog and Magog" will take place,[22] and that before this war, a prophet will arise who will make straight the people of Israel and prepare their hearts, as it is written: "Behold, I will send you Elijah the prophet before the coming of the great and terrible day of the Lord" (Mal. 3:23). But he comes only to bring peace into the world, as it is written: "And he shall turn the heart of the fathers to the children" (Mal. 3:24).

Among the sages there are some who say Elijah will come before the coming of the Messiah. But concerning these things and others of the same kind, none knows how they will be until they occur. For in the prophetic books these things are veiled, and the sages have no tradition concerning them, save what they have deduced from the Scriptures, and so herein their opinion is divided. At any rate, neither the order of this event nor its details are the root of religion. A man must never ponder over legendary accounts, nor dwell upon midrashic interpretations dealing with them or with matters like them. He must not make them of primary importance, for they do not guide him either to fear or to love God. Nor may he seek to calculate the Messianic end. The sages said: "Let the spirit of those breathe its last, who seek to calculate the end." [23] Rather let him wait and trust in the matter as a whole, as we have expounded.

The sages and the prophets did not yearn for the days of the Messiah in order to seize upon the world, and not in order to rule over the heathen, or to be exalted by the peoples, or to eat and drink and rejoice, but to be free for the Torah and its wisdom, free from oppression and intrusion, so that they may become worthy of life in the world to come.

When that time is here, none will go hungry, there will be

no war, no zealousness, and no conflict, for goodness will flow abundantly, and all delights will be plentiful as the numberless motes of dust, and the whole world will be solely intent on the knowledge of the Lord. Therefore those of Israel will be great sages, who will know what was concealed and they will attain what knowledge of their Creator it is in man's power to attain, as it is written: "For the earth shall be full of the knowledge of the Lord, as the waters cover the sea" (Isa. 11:9).

Epilogue

THE HOLY ONE IS

WITHIN THEE

Eleazar ben Judah

Eleazar ben Judah of Worms, called also Eleazar Rokeah, *ca.* 1160–*ca.* 1230, talmudist, liturgic poet, moralist, is important chiefly as a disciple of Judah the Pious (see "Simple Piety") and, with him, promulgator of the mystic doctrine of the "Pious Men of Germany." His God "maintains His silence and carries the universe"; but He reveals himself through the appearance of His Glory (*Kavod*), which acts as mediator between Creator and Creation. Eleazar wrote *Rokeah* (Dealer in Spices), a treatise on Jewish teachings and laws (first appearance in Fano, 1505). The extract that follows is based on Hosea 11:9, "The Holy One is within thee."

Let thy life be one of holiness and self-denial. [. . .] Fix thy mind upon the Almighty when thou standest before Him in prayer; should some alien thought come to thee in thy devotions, be silent until thy heart is joined once more in reverence to thy Creator. Say to thyself whilst thou prayest, "How honored am I in being suffered to offer a crown to the King of Glory! In awe and humility will I enter the divine gates."

Love the Lord thy God. Let thy heart know Him, and declare His oneness. Do thy work until eventide; but remember to love Him at all times. See, He stands before thee! He is thy Father, thy Master, thy Maker, submit thyself to Him. Ah, happy is he whose heart trembleth with the joy of God and is forever singing to its Maker! He bears patiently the divine yoke, he is humble and self-denying, he scorns the world's vain pleasure, he lives by his faith, he has gentle speech for all, he rejoices in the joys of others, he loves his neighbor, and does charity in secret.

Notes to "Faith and Knowledge"

I

1. Hagigah 15b.
2. Cf. Sifre on Deut. 11:22.
3. I.e., the universal soul, from which all human souls derive.
4. Cf. Num. 23:13.
5. I.e., God.
6. A play on words on Isa. 41:1; *bor* in Hebrew means both pit and purity.
7. The Soul emanates from the Intelligence, as the latter emanates from the Will (of God).
8. Cf. Isa. 30:33.
9. Cf. Job 33:6.
10. Cf. Exod. 25:11.
11. Cf. Job 13:15.
12. Cf. Ps. 73:24.
13. Cf. Isa. 12:1.

II

1. Sifre on Deut. 11:13.
2. Sayings of the Fathers I, 3.
3. Pesahim 50b.
4. Berakhot 54a.
5. Shabbat 30b.
6. Midrash Psalms 100:2.
7. Cf. Job 13:15.
8. Cf. Lam. 4:1.

III

1. Nedarim 62a.
2. Saadia Gaon (ninth–tenth century), religious philosopher, author of *Sefer ha-Emunot ve-ha-Deot* (The Book of Doctrines and Beliefs).
3. From the Additional Service for the New Moon.
4. The Day of Atonement.

IV

1. _Mishneh Torah,_ The Fundamentals of the Torah II.
2. Berakhot 33b.

V

1. Horayot 13b.
2. Pesahim 50b.
3. Sayings of the Fathers VI, 4.
4. _Ibid.,_ II, 21.
5. _Ibid.,_ I, 15.
6. _Ibid.,_ II, 5.
7. Erubin 55a.
8. Sayings of the Fathers II, 6.
9. _Ibid.,_ IV, 12.
10. Taanit 7a.
11. Sayings of the Fathers IV, 7.
12. _Ibid._
13. _Ibid.,_ I, 10.
14. _Ibid.,_ II, 2.
15. Gittin 67a.
16. Berakhot 63b.
17. Abodah Zarah 3b.
18. "The Son of Proverbs," aphorisms in the form of the Biblical Book of Proverbs, by Samuel ha-Nagid, Spain, eleventh century.
19. Jer. 35.
20. The system of critical notes on the accepted Biblical text.
21. Sayings of the Fathers I, 2.
22. _Ibid.,_ I, 18.
23. Rashi: Rabbi Solomon ben Isaac (France, eleventh century), commentator of Bible and of Babylonian Talmud. Tosafot: Explanatory notes on the Talmud; the period of the Tosafists began immediately after Rashi. Both the commentary of Rashi and the notes of the Tosafists are printed on the margin of a typical page of the Talmud.
24. Our teacher; a rabbinical title.
25. Fellow; a title of distinction.
26. A difference in the point of view of two authorities.
27. Presentation, in four parts, of the rabbinical law, by Jacob ben Asher (Germany–France, thirteenth–fourteenth century).
28. Isaac Alfasi (North Africa–Spain, eleventh century), author of a compendium of the Talmud.
29. Central governing organization of Polish Jewry, from 1580 to 1764; the "four lands" were Great Poland, Little Poland, Red Russia (Podolia and Galicia), and Volhynia.
30. Rosh ha-Shanah 25b.

31. Fast day commemorating the destruction of Jerusalem.
32. Purim.

VI

1. Sayings of the Fathers II, 9.
2. Sotah 5b.
3. The *Kedushah*.
4. Ketubot 111b.

VII

1. Shabbat 156a.
2. Symbolically, the ancestors of Christianity and Israel.
3. Israel fell in 721 B.C., after the death of Shalmaneser V of Assyria.
4. Roman poet (first century); in his epic *Pharsalia* he described the civil war between Caesar and Pompey.

IX

1. "With ten words (sayings) the world was created" (Sayings of the Fathers V, 1).
2. Mekhilta on 15:2.
3. The center of emotion.
4. A compilation of the non-legal (aggadic) material from the Babylonian Talmud, by Jacob ben Solomon ibn Habib (Spain–Turkey, fifteenth–sixteenth century).
5. *See* note V, 23.
6. Moses ben Mordecai Galante (Rome–Safed, sixteenth century), talmudist and mystic, successor of Joseph Karo in the rabbinate of Safed.
7. A Tannaite.
8. Disciple of Rabbi Akiba (second century).
9. Disciple of Isaac Luria, head of the mystics of Safed.
10. Euphemistically so called because he was blind.
11. Bezalel ben Abraham Ashkenazi (sixteenth century), disciple of David ibn Zimra and his successor as chief rabbi in Cairo; author of *Shitta Mekkubetzet,* collection of talmudic annotations.
12. *See* preface to this chapter.
13. Predecessor of the Messiah, son of David.
14. Taanit 21a.
15. A part of the *Zohar*.

X

1. Numbers Rabba I, 6.
2. Genesis Rabba XXXIX, 1.
3. Mishnah Yoma VIII, 9.
4. *Ibid*.
5. Mishnah Terumot IX, 7.
6. Shabbat 30b.

XI

1. The Western (or "Wailing") Wall is a part of a wall surrounding the Temple Mount.
2. *See* Joel 4.
3. Part of its slopes were used as a burial field outside of the eastern wall of Jerusalem.
4. The Dead Sea.
5. *See* Deut. 34:1.
6. *See* II Sam. 5:7.
7. Name of various sects of men fasting and praying for the coming of the Messiah and the restoration of Zion.
8. *See* preceding note.
9. Cf. Jer. 31:14f.
10. Cf. Gen. 10:8f.
11. Sanhedrin 97a.
12. Genesis Rabba XCV, 2. *See also* "The Faith of Abraham."
13. Who once led the exiles from Babylon to Jerusalem.
14. Taanit 31a.
15. Lamentations Rabba I, 57.
16. The king's *justiciar* was, next to the king, the most important officeholder in Aragon; he presided over the *Cortes*.
17. Or, "My servant shall prosper."
18. Sanhedrin 98a.
19. Deut. 15:1-4; Lev. 25:8-24.
20. Ben Koziba ("Son of Lies") and Bar Kokhba ("Son of the Star"): names applied to the leader of the Jewish revolt against the Romans in 132 to 135.
21. Sanhedrin 91b.
22. Ezek. 38-39.
23. Sanhedrin 97b.

Sources and Acknowledgments for
"Faith and Knowledge"

Prelude

KNOWLEDGE AND FAITH: Abraham ibn Ezra, Commentary on Hosea 6:3, tr. N. N. G.*; Joseph Caspi, *Sefer ha-Musar*, in Eleazar Ashkenazi, *Taam Zekenim*, tr. I. Abrahams, *Jewish Life in the Middle Ages*, London, 1932, p. 394; Solomon ibn Gabirol, *Choice of Pearls*, tr. A. Cohen, New York, 1925, pp. 45f.

I

THE ONENESS OF GOD: Maimonides, *Mishneh Torah, Hilkhot Yesode ha-Torah* I, 1–II, 2 abridged; the translations from *Mishneh Torah* throughout this volume are based on Moses Hyamson, *The Mishneh Torah*, New York, 1937, and Simon Glazer, *Book of Mishneh Torah*, New York, 1927.

KNOWLEDGE OF GOD: Maimonides, *Moreh Nebukhim* III, 51, tr. based on M. Friedländer, *The Guide for the Perplexed*, London, 1904.

IN THE PRESENCE OF GOD: Solomon ibn Gabirol, *Keter Malkhut* 1, 3, 4, 6, 29-32, 38, 40, abridged, tr. Bernard Lewis, *The Kingly Crown*, London, 1961.

LORD WHERE SHALL I FIND THEE?: My Thought Awakened Me: *Diwan of Jehuda Halevi*, ed. H. Brody, III, 65, tr. S. Solis Cohen, *United Synagogue Recorder* I, 1921, 3; With All My Heart, O Truth: ed. H. Brody, II, 221, tr. Judah Goldin, *Menorah Journal* XXXI, 1945, p. 196; Let my Sweet Song: ed. H. Brody, *Mivhar ha-Shirah ha-Ivrit*, p. 170, tr. Nina Salaman, *Selected Poems of Jehuda Halevi*, Philadelphia, 1928, p. 117; Lord, Where Shall I Find Thee: *Diwan*, ed. H. Brody, III, 150, tr. N. Salaman, *op. cit.*, pp. 134f.

II

"THOU SHALT LOVE . . .": Maimonides, *Mishneh Torah, Hilkhot Teshuvah* X; Bahya ibn Pakuda, *Hovot ha-Levavot* X, 1; *Zohar* on Deut. 6:5, tr. M. Simon and H. Sperling, *The Zohar*, London, 1934, V, pp. 357ff.

WHY IS MY LOVED ONE WROTH: Moses ibn Ezra, tr. S. Solis-Cohen, Philadelphia, 1934, p. 101.

* The initials refer to the editor of this volume.

THE UNIVERSALITY OF LOVE: Judah Abrabanel, *The Philosophy of Love* (Dialoghi d'Amore), tr. F. Friedeberg-Seeley and J. H. Barnes, London, 1937, pp. 188-191.

SAINTLINESS: M. H. Luzzatto, *Mesillat Yesharim XIX*, tr. M. M. Kaplan, Philadelphia, 1936, pp. 180f.

III

THE DUTIES OF THE HEART: Bahya ibn Pakuda, *Hovot ha-Levavot* Introduction, tr. M. Hyamson, *Duties of the Heart*, 1925, pp. 1-12, abridged.

THE SERVANT OF GOD: Judah ha-Levi, *Kuzari* III, 1-5, tr. H. Hirschfeld, London, 1905, pp. 119-124.

THE FAITH OF ABRAHAM: Maimonides, *Mishneh Torah, Hilkhot Abodah Zarah* I, 3.

DEVOTION: *Ibid., Hilkhot Tefillah* IV, 15-16.

THE SEVEN BENEDICTIONS AT THE MARRIAGE SERVICE: Prayer Book, ed. S. Singer, New York, 1915, p. 299.

IV

MAN—THE CENTER OF THE UNIVERSE: Saadia Gaon, *Sefer ha-Emunot ve-ha-Deot* IV, beginning, tr. A. Altmann, *Saadya Gaon, The Book of Doctrines and Beliefs*, Oxford, 1946, pp. 115ff.

ON CREATION: Maimonides, *Moreh Nebukhim* II, 25, tr. M. Friedländer, *op. cit.*

ON FREE WILL: Maimonides, *Mishneh Torah, Hilkhot Teshuvah* V.

THE CREATION OF MAN: Nahmanides, Commentary on Gen. 1:26; 2:7, 2:9; *Torat Hashem Temimah;* Commentary on Exod. 13:16, tr. Ch. B. Chavel, *Ramban*, New York, 1960, pp. 75, 78f.

ARGUMENT FOR THE IMMORTAL SOUL: Leone Modena, *Kol Sakhal* I, tr. Jakob J. Petuchowski, *Commentary* XX (1955), pp. 462f.

THE MAN AND HIS SOUL: *Midrash Yetzirat ha-Velad*, Jellinek, *Bet ha-Midrash* I, tr. N. N. G., *Commentary* XIV (1952), pp. 369ff.

THE BRIDGE OF TIME: Yedayah ha-Bedersi, *Behinat Olam*, quoted in *Judaism* II (1953), p. 224.

HEALING: Jacob ben Asher, *Arbaa Turim, Yore Deah* 336, quoted in Samuel S. Cohon, *Judaism: A Way of Life*, Cincinnati, 1948, p. 93.

THE END OF MAN: Prayer Book, ed. S. Singer, New York, 1915, pp. 317-324.

V

THE STUDY OF TORAH: Maimonides, *Mishneh Torah, Hilkhot Talmud Torah* I, 6-13; III.

IN PRAISE OF LEARNING, EDUCATION, AND THE GOOD LIFE: Judah ibn Tibbon, in I. Abrahams, *Hebrew Ethical Wills*, Philadelphia, 1926, III, abridged.

THE GIFT OF THE LAW: Obadiah ben Abraham, in G. Vajda, "The

Mystical Doctrine of R. Obadyah, Grandson of Moses Maimonides," *The Journal of Jewish Studies* VI (1955), p. 215.

PROPOSED JEWISH ACADEMY IN MANTUA: David Provenzal, in Jacob R. Marcus, *The Jew in the Medieval World,* Cincinnati, 1938, No. 78.

THE INNER LIFE OF THE JEWS IN POLAND: Nathan Hannover, *Yeven Metzulah* XVI, tr. A. J. Mesch, *Abyss of Despair,* New York, 1950, pp. 110-121.

THE HOUSE OF STUDY IN PADUA: Text, S. Ginzburg, *The Life and Works of M. H. Luzzatto,* Philaldelphia, 1931, tr. N. N. G., *Commentary* XI (1951), pp. 480-483.

VI

A POET'S ETHICAL COUNSEL: Solomon ibn Gabirol, *Tikkun Middot ha-Nefesh,* ed. and tr. S. S. Wise, New York, 1901, I, 1-3, III, 3 (pp. 58f., 61-64, 99); *Mivhar ha-Peninim,* tr. A. Cohen, New York, 1925, pp. 69, 78-80, 58f.

SIMPLE PIETY: Judah the Pious, *Sefer Hasidim,* quoted in S. Schechter, *Studies in Judaism* III, Philadelphia, 1924, pp. 19f.

A BRIEF SUMMARY OF ETHICAL RULES: Yehiel ben Yekutiel, *Sefer Maalot ha-Middot* XXIII, tr. N. N. G.

HUMILITY: M. H. Luzzatto, *Mesillat Yesharim* XXII, tr. M. M. Kaplan, Philadelphia, 1936, pp. 192-196, 204, abridged.

AT PEACE WITH THE WORLD: Joel ben Abraham Shemariah, in I. Abrahams, *Hebrew Ethical Wills,* Philadelphia, 1926, XXIII, abridged.

THE MIDDLE COURSE: Solomon Ganzfried, *Kitzur Shulhan Arukh* XXIX, 1-11, tr. H. E. Goldin, *Code of Jewish Law,* New York, 1927.

VII

THE GOD OF ABRAHAM AND THE GOD OF ARISTOTLE: Judah ha-Levi, *Kuzari* IV, 17-23, tr. H. Hirschfeld, *op. cit.,* pp. 196-200.

THE EVENT OF SINAI: Maimonides, *Iggeret Teman,* ed. A. S. Halkin, tr. B. Cohen, *Epistle to Yemen,* New York, 1952, pp. Vff.

THE PROSELYTE: Maimonides, *Teshuvot (Responsa),* ed. A. H. Freimann, Jerusalem, 1934, No. 42, tr. N. N. G., in *Maimonides Said,* New York, 1941, pp. 57ff.

BENEDICTION WHEN FACING MARTYRDOM: Quoted in S. Schechter, *Studies in Judaism* III, Philadelphia, 1924, p. 17. The appended quotation: Meir of Rothenburg, *Responsa,* Prague, 1608, No. 517.

WHY CATASTROPHES COME: Solomon Alami, see preface, tr. N. N. G., *Commentary* XIX (1955), pp. 480-483.

THE PARABLE OF THE PRECIOUS STONES: Solomon ibn Verga, *Shevet Yehudah,* ed. Y. Baer, Jerusalem, 1947; tr. N. N. G.

EQUALITY: Jacob ben Abba Mari Anatoli, *Malmad ha-Talmidim,* Lyck, 1866, 28b; tr. N. N. G

THE HEBREW AMONG THE NATIONS: Simone Luzzatto, *Discorso circa il Stato degli Ebrei,* Venice, 1638, Considerations XVII-XVIII, tr. F. Giovanelli, *Commentary* III (1947), pp. 474-478.

VIII

SHIELD OF OUR FATHERS: Prayer Book, ed. S. Singer, *op. cit.*, p. 120.

THE SANCTITY OF THE SABBATH: *Zohar* on Exod. 20:8 (II, 88a-89a), tr. Simon and Sperling, *op. cit.*, III, pp. 268-273, abridged.

THE SABBATH BRIDE: Israel ibn al-Nakawa, *Menorat ha-Maor*, ed. H. G. Enelow, New York, 1930, II, 191, tr. A. J. Heschel, *The Sabbath*, New York, 1951, pp. 54f.

THE SABBATH AND THE DAYS OF THE WEEK: Judah Loew ben Bezalel, *Tiferet Yisrael*, Venice, 1599, X, tr. F. Thieberger, *The Great Rabbi Loew*, London, 1955, pp. 112f.

SANCTIFICATION: Prayer Book, ed. S. Singer, *op. cit.*, pp. 160f.

IX

MYSTICAL UNDERSTANDING OF JEWISH CONCEPTS: Body and Soul: *Zohar* on Lev. 19:2 (III, 80b-81b), tr. Simon and Sperling, *op. cit.*, V, pp. 91-94, abridged; The Ten Words: *ibid.*, II, 93b-94a, tr. *op. cit.*, III, pp. 280f.; The Poor and the Lowly: *ibid.*, III, 8b-9a, *Midrash ha-Neelam* to Ruth in *Zohar Hadash*, 94b, *Zohar* I, 168b, II, 61a, 86b, III, 85a, II, 198a, tr. in Y. Baer, *A History of the Jews in Christian Spain*, I, Philadelphia, 1961, pp. 263ff.; Material Wealth: *Zohar* I, 88a f., tr. Y. Baer, *op. cit.*, pp. 265f.

THE PRACTICE OF MYSTICAL MEDITATION: Abraham Abulafia, tr. from unpublished writings in G. G. Scholem, *Major Trends in Jewish Mysticism*, New York, 1954, pp. 134, 136f.

THE SEARCH FOR TRUTH: Solomon ibn Adret, *Sheelot u-Teshuvot*, Bene Berak, 1958, No. 548, tr. Gunther W. Plaut.

LIFE IN SAFED: Solomon Shloemel ben Hayyim Meinstrl, in *Sefer Taalumot Hokhmah*, Basle, 1629, tr. I. M. Lask, in K. Wilhelm, *Roads to Zion*, New York, 1948, pp. 57-64.

THE LIFE OF RABBI ISAAC LURIA: Solomon Shloemel ben Hayyim Meinstrl, *op. cit.*, pp. 37a-38b, tr. in Jacob R. Marcus, *The Jew in the Medieval World*, Cincinnati, 1938, No. 52.

IN THE PRESENCE OF THE DIVINE: Moses Cordovero. Who is a God Like Unto Thee? *Tomer Deborah* I, tr. Louis Jacobs, *The Palm Tree of Deborah*, London, 1960, pp. 47f.; The Disease of Pride: *ibid.*, II, tr. Jacobs, *op. cit.*, pp. 77ff.; Loving-kindness: *ibid.*, V, tr. Jacobs, *op. cit.*, pp. 90ff.

X

ISRAEL BEN ELIEZER, THE BAAL SHEM TOV: Legends: M. Buber, *Tales of the Hasidim: The Early Masters*, New York, 1947, pp. 35-78, selected; The Testament: *Tzavaat ha-Rivash*, tr. Sanford D. Shanblatt, *Judaism* IX (1960), pp. 282ff.

COMMUNION WITH GOD AND MEN: Abraham Kalisker, quoted in J. G. Weiss, "R. Abraham Kalisker's Concept of Communion with God and Men," *The Journal of Jewish Studies* VI (1955), pp. 89, 96.

THE TEACHINGS OF MENDEL OF KOTZK: M. Buber, *Tales of the Hasidim: The Later Masters*, New York, 1948, pp. 275-287, selected.

IN PREPARATION FOR THE DAY OF ATONEMENT: *Divre Torah*, Josefow, 1852, tr. M. T. Galpert and J. Sloan, in S. Y. Agnon, *Days of Awe*, New York, 1948, pp. 204-208.

DEATH: Louis Newman and Samuel Spitz, *The Hasidic Anthology*, New York, 1944, ch. XXIX, selected.

XI

JERUSALEM: *The Itinerary of Rabbi Benjamin of Tudela*, ed. M. N. Adler, London, 1907, pp. 22-25.

MYSTIC DRAMA OF JERUSALEM: *Zohar*. I: III, 69a; II: II, 212a; III: II, 7b-9a; IV: I, 134a, tr. *Commentary* XXI (1956), pp. 365f., based on tr. by Simon and Sperling (*op. cit.*).

TEN KINGS: *Pirke de Rabbi Eliezer* XI, tr. Gerald Friedländer, London, 1916, pp. 80-83, abridged.

THE SUFFERINGS OF THE MESSIAH: *See* preface; tr. N. N. G.

CREATION AND WORLD'S HISTORY: Nahmanides, Commentary on Gen. 2:3, tr. Charles B. Chavel, *Ramban*, New York, 1960, pp. 75ff.

MESSIAH THE TEACHER: I: A. Jellinek, *Bet ha-Midrash* III, Leipzig, 1853; II: Yehuda Ibn Shmuel, *Midreshe Geulah*, Jerusalem, 1954. *Commentary* XVIII (1954), pp. 466f.; tr. N. N. G.

THE DANCE OF THE RIGHTEOUS: Judah Loew ben Bezalel, *Beer ha-Golah* IV, tr. F. Thieberger, *op. cit.*, pp. 100ff.

HAS THE MESSIAH COME? *See* preface, tr. O. S. Rankin, *Jewish Religious Polemic*, Edinburgh, 1956, pp. 179-210, abridged.

A VISIT TO PARADISE: Immanuel ben Solomon, *Ha-Tofet ve-ha-Eden (Mahberot* XXVIII), tr. B. Halper, *Post-Biblical Hebrew Literature*, Philadelphia, 1921, pp. 188-193.

THE MESSIANIC AGE: Maimonides, *Mishneh Torah, Hilkhot Melakhim* XI-XII, tr. N. N. G., abridged.

Epilogue

THE HOLY ONE IS WITHIN THEE: Eleazar ben Judah, *Rokeah, Hilkhot Hasidut*, tr. S. Schechter, in *Studies in Judaism* III, pp. 22f.

ACKNOWLEDGMENTS

Thanks are due to the following authors and publishers for permission to use their translations referred to under "Sources": American Academy for Jewish Research for excerpts from *Moses Maimonides' Epistle to Yemen*, edited by Abraham S. Halkin, translated by Boaz Cohen (1952); *Commentary* for permission to reprint six "Cedars of Lebanon"; East and West Library, London, for excerpts from *Saadya Gaon: The Book of Doctrines and*

Beliefs, edited and translated by Alexander Altmann (1946), and *The Great Rabbi Loew of Prague,* by F. Thieberger (1955); Philipp Feldheim, New York, for selections from *Ramban: His Life and Teachings,* by Charles B. Chavel (1960); Abraham J. Heschel and Farrar, Strauss and Cudahy for a quotation from *The Sabbath,* pp. 54f. (1951); the estate of Moses Hyamson for the use of his *The Mishneh Torah, Book I* (1937), as the basis for the rendition of the respective selections, and for excerpts from his *Duties of the Heart* (1925); The Jewish Publication Society of America for excerpts from *Selected Poems of Jehudah Halevi,* translated by Nina Salaman (1928), *Selected Poems of Moses ibn Ezra,* translated by S. Solis-Cohen (1934), *Mesillat Yesharim,* translated by Mordecai M. Kaplan (1936), *Hebrew Ethical Wills,* edited by I. Abrahams (1926), *Studies in Judaism III,* by S. Schechter (1924), *Post-Biblical Hebrew Literature,* edited by B. Halper (1921); *The Journal of Jewish Studies* for quotations from vol. VI (1955), pp. 89, 96, and 215; Bloch Publishing Co., for a selection from *The Hasidic Anthology,* by L. I. Newman (1944) and *Abyss of Despair,* translated by A. J. Mesh, ch. XVI (1950); Schocken Books Inc., New York, for selections from *Days of Awe* by S. Y. Agnon, translated by M. T. Galpert and J. Sloan (1948), *Major Trends of Jewish Mysticism,* by G. G. Scholem (1954), *Roads to Zion,* edited by K. Wilhelm, translated by I. M. Lask (1948), *Tales of the Hasidim* I-II, by M. Buber (1947-48); The Sonzino Press, London, for quotations from *The Zohar,* III, V, translated by Harry Sperling, Maurice Simon and P. P. Levertoff (1934, 1949), and from *The Philosophy of Love,* translated by F. Friedeberg-Seeley and Jean H. Barnes (1937); The Union of American Hebrew Congregations for passages from *The Jew in the Medieval World,* by Jacob R. Marcus, Nos. 52 and 78 (1938); University Press, Edinburgh, for the translation of the Barcelona Debate in *Jewish Religious Polemic,* by O. S. Rankin (1956); Vallentine, Mitchell, London, for selections from *Solomon ibn Gabirol: The Kingly Crown,* translated by Bernard Lewis (1961), and *Rabbi Moses Cordovero: The Palm Tree of Deborah,* translated by Louis Jacobs (1960).

PART THREE

The Dynamics of Emancipation

Introduction to "The Dynamics of Emancipation"

THE JUDAISM of the modern era differs radically from that of preceding periods, because—for the first time in its history—it is an active element in the world-historic order. A combination of separateness *and* universalism, which determined Jewish existence and historical thinking in earlier periods, no longer provides the comfort that a dialectical tension between them had granted. No longer can separateness be accepted as fact and universalism as the ideal for a distant future.

While some form of separateness is affirmed by all who desire the continued existence of Judaism, the challenge of "the world" is real, and its political, social, cultural, and intellectual issues of tremendous impact.

To some, the dilemma between being a Jew and being a Western man appears to be beyond repair, and the abnegation of Judaism, or its reduction to a bare minimum of ethnic descent or cultural background, the only possible solution. Others cultivate some aspects of separate Jewish life as a self-respecting response to anti-Semitism and the exclusivity of the majority groups. A small but determined group of Jews perpetuates the pre-modern isolation of Judaism in order to be able to lead a life guided entirely by the Law (*halakhah*), allowing only unavoidable contact with "the world."

Those who cannot but assume responsibility toward both the Torah of Judaism and the affairs of the world face prodigious difficulties of reconsidering inherited values and adjusting to the new conditions. Ultimately, there is no contradiction between these two forces, Judaism and "the world." But we do not live in the sphere of the ultimate; we live instead in constant contact with the provisional and temporary, in contact with practical exigencies and demands of the hour, where a theory, even a good one, is of no avail.

It was the German-Jewish philosopher Hermann Cohen who

said: "He who, as a matter of principle, reserves the fundamental teachings of Judaism for the Jewish people, denies the One God of Messianic humanity." [1] And the French writer Edmond Fleg maintained that "assimilation is indispensable for the spread of the Jewish truth and to incorporate it with reality, while for preserving and fortifying the soul of Israel, Zionism and orthodoxy are no less indispensable." [2] These are noble sentiments, but they presuppose for their realization conditions which do not exist. The philosopher Nathan Rotenstreich, who views Judaism as "opposed to secular movements which deprive the real world of meaning," suggests "a reserved acceptance of the actual world, an acceptance united with the attempt to shape it in the light of principles not derived from man alone."[3] This notion points to the complexity of the task confronting a modern man who happens to maintain a distinct Judaic orientation. The precariousness lies in the "reservation" with which, in this proposal, the "actual world" is to be accepted. The challenge of the world may prove more powerful and irresistible than anticipated. It is to be expected that our experience in this world will, in time, suggest a bolder synthesis.

In the view of the historian of philosophy Alexander Altmann, modern Jewish thought "reflects the fundamental change in outlook that characterizes modern thought in general. It no longer seeks to harmonize the truth of revelation with those of authoritative pagan thinkers, but is concerned with the significance of the Jewish religion as a manifestation of the human spirit, and its place within the larger framework of thought, be it conceived as universal reason, the dialectic of the mind, the system of culture, or the human existence as such." [4] This statement on present-day thought can be applied to other spheres of life; it indicates a meeting of the two realms—Judaism and "the world."

Most of the texts gathered in this volume mirror the emancipated Jew's conviction of his being rooted in the life of the historical world and, at the same time, his concern with the ways of meaningful preservation of Judaism. Jewish history is reinterpreted in the light of Israel's relationship to humanity (Heinrich Graetz, Moses Hess, Simon Dubnov, Erich Kahler, Salo W. Baron); the rise of modern Judaic scholarship is reviewed as an emancipatory force (Leopold Zunz); Jewish faith is re-examined with keen sensitivity (Abraham Geiger, Leo Baeck, Martin Buber); the ideological and institutional structure of Jewish religion in the modern era is scrutinized (Samuel Hirsch, I. M. Wise, Mordecai M. Kaplan, Louis Finkelstein, Samuel Belkin); tradition is recalled and reaffirmed (S. R. Hirsch, A. I. Kook, Franz Rosenzweig); the catastrophe of the Nazi period is reacted to with a trembling heart, in faith, and in quiet heroism (Robert Weltsch, Leo Baeck, A. J. Heschel, Judah L. Magnes, Anne Frank, Albert Einstein, Elie Wiesel); rebirth of the national idea and the new State of Israel is noted both from the viewpoint of their significance for the Jew and for the modern world he entered therewith (Theodor Herzl, A. D. Gordon, Chaim Weizman, David Ben-Gurion); the American experience is recorded, both affirmatively and critically (Louis D. Brandeis, Waldo Frank, Ludwig Lewisohn, Salo W. Baron, Abram L. Sachar, Joachim Prinz).

All these and other such expressions of opinion or commitment —some representative and official, others personal—are a testimony to a vitality and dynamism that, it is hoped, justify the title of this volume. This too is significant: notwithstanding the pronounced change in subject-matter and style, motivation and sensitivity, that sharply distinguish the modern Jewish thinker from his predecessors in past periods, there is much to indicate a continuity of historical consciousness and of certain guiding values that persist throughout the ages.

The historian Salo W. Baron speaks of the Jewish people today as "passing through one of the greatest of their historical crises"; never before were there "more dangers for Jewish survival than are contemporary developments." [5] Obviously, as in the past, not every person of Jewish origin will have the strength, or the determination, to face the dangers. But again, as in the past, this historical crisis is being met by many with a dynamic affirmation of the task at hand.

The "modern age" in Judaism is in its initial stage (especially on this continent)—which explains the uncertainties, the contradictoriness, the immaturity one often encounters in Jewish discussions. These are but the growing pains of a group which is undergoing a transformation from a community of faith, withdrawn from the scene of active history, to a community conscious of these roots and of this past, yet squarely facing "the world." Only a future generation will be in a position to define this synthesis and to give it a name.

I. *In the Perspective of Emancipation*

A DEFINITION OF JUDAISM

MOSES MENDELSSOHN

Enlightened, westernized, Jewry traces its intellectual origin to the philosopher Moses Mendelssohn (1729-1786). This German Jew, who made the transition from the ghetto to the free Western society, arrived at a reformulation of religion and of Judaism, whose intent was to free the ancient faith of its restrictive character and to enable the Jew to live meaningfully in a new liberal and secular world—which to be sure never came into being. Mendelssohn believed that true faith is based on reason alone and thus is equally accessible to all men; it is not based on a divine revelation to any one religious community; thus all men of reason are able to unite in their knowledge of God and of eternal truths. Here Mendelssohn follows the lead of Locke, Shaftesbury, and Leibnitz. Revelation, as taught by Judaism, pertains to precepts of conduct and laws of action, not to principles of faith. Mendelssohn wished Jews to remain fully loyal to these commandments, as he himself remained an observant Jew. Beyond this special province of Judaism he envisaged a brotherhood of men, bound by the tenets of reason and free from religious compulsion and from the state's intervention in matters of faith. He was one of the first—if not the first—to demand separation of church and state. He expected the Christian world to effect a similar reinterpretation of religion. His definition of Judaism failed to create a school, but he himself became a symbol of the synthesis between Judaism and Europeanism.

Mendelssohn's works include *Phaedon* (1767), a philosophical treatise on the immortality of the soul widely read at the time; a translation of the Pentateuch into German (1783); *Jerusalem* (1783), a work on Judaism and religion; and *Morgenstunden* (1785), a study of Spinoza and rational religion. The excerpt that follows is taken from *Jerusalem*; it is translated by Alfred Jospe.

[. . .] I recognize no eternal verities save those which not only can be comprehended by the human intellect but can also be demonstrated and confirmed by man's faculties. It is, however, a misconception of Judaism if Mr. Moerschel [1] were to assume that I cannot take this position without deviating from the religion of my fathers. On the contrary, I consider this view an essential aspect of the Jewish religion and believe that this teaching represents one of the characteristic differences between Judaism and Christianity. To sum it up in one sentence: I believe Judaism knows nothing of a *revealed religion* corresponding to the way Christians define the meaning of this term. The Israelites possess a *divine legislation:* laws, commandments, statutes, rules of conduct, instruction in God's will and in what they are to do to attain temporal and eternal salvation. Moses, in a miraculous and supernatural way, revealed to them these laws and commandments, but not dogmas, eternal verities or self-evident propositions. These the Lord reveals to us as well as to all other men at all times through nature and events, never through the spoken or written word. [. . .]

One applies the term "eternal verities" to those principles which are not subject to time and remain eternally unchanged. [. . .] Besides these eternal verities, there exist also temporal, historical truths—events which occurred at a certain point in time and may never recur, or principles which, by the processes of cause and effect, became accepted as truth at a certain time and place and whose claim to be truth is relative to this point in time and space. To this category belong all truths in history—events of former times which once took place, of which we were told by others but which we ourselves can no longer observe.

[. . .] I do not believe that man's intellect is incapable of perceiving those eternal truths which are indispensable to man's happiness and that God, therefore, was compelled to reveal them in a supernatural way. Those who cling to this notion deny the omnipotence or the goodness of God. [. . .] They think that He was good enough to disclose to men those truths on which their happiness depends but that He was neither omnipotent nor good enough to grant them the capacity of discovering these truths for themselves. [. . .] If the human race, without revelation, cannot be but depraved and miserable, why should by far the larger part of mankind have been compelled to live without the benefit of true revelation from the beginning? [. . .]

According to the tenets of Judaism, all people can attain salvation; and the means to attain it are as widespread as mankind itself, as liberally dispensed as the means of satisfying one's hunger and other natural needs.

[. . .] Judaism does not claim to possess the exclusive revelation of immutable truths which are indispensable to salvation. It is not a revealed religion as this term is commonly understood. Revealed religion is one thing; revealed legislation, another. The voice that was heard on that great day at Sinai did not proclaim, "I am the Eternal, thy God, the necessary self-evident Being, omnipotent and omniscient, Who rewards men in a future life according to their deeds." This is the universal religion of reason, not Judaism. This kind of universal religion was not, and in fact could not have been, revealed at Sinai; for who could possibly have needed the sound of thunder or the blast of trumpets to become convinced of the validity of these eternal verities? [. . .] No, all this was supposed to be already known or taught and explained by human reason and certain beyond all doubt. [. . .] The divine voice that called out, "I am the Lord thy God who led thee out of the land of Egypt" (Exodus 20:2)—this is a historical fact, a fact on which the legislation of that particular people was founded; laws were to be revealed here, commandments and judgments, but no immutable theological truths.

[. . .] Among the precepts and statutes of the Mosaic law there is none saying "Thou shalt believe" or "Thou shalt not believe"; all say "Thou shalt do" or not do. Faith accepts no commands; it accepts only what comes to it by way of reasoned conviction. All commandments of the divine law are addressed to the will, to man's capacity to act. In fact, the original Hebrew term [*emunah*] which is usually translated as "faith" means in most instances merely "trust" or "confidence," e.g., "And he trusted in the Lord, and He counted it to him for righteousness" (Genesis 15:6); "And Israel saw . . . and trusted the Lord and His servant Moses" (Exodus 14:31). Whenever the text refers to eternal verities it does not use the term "believe," but "understand" and "know." "Know this day and meditate upon it in thy heart that the Lord is God . . . there is none else" (Deuteronomy 4:39).

Nowhere does a passage say, "Believe, O Israel, and thou wilt be blessed; do not doubt, Israel, lest thou wilt be punished." Command and prohibition, reward and punishment apply only to acts of commission or omission which depend on a man's will power; and these are governed by his notions of good and evil and affected by his hopes and fears. Beliefs and doubts, however, intellectual assent or dissent, are governed neither by our wishes or desires, nor by our fears or hopes, but by what we perceive to be true or false.

For this reason, ancient Judaism has no symbolical book, no articles of faith. No one had to be sworn to credal symbols or subscribe by solemn oath to certain articles of faith. We do not require the affirmation of religious doctrines by oath and consider this practice incompatible with the true spirit of Judaism.

THE JEWISH COMMUNITY AND THE STATE
Doctrinal Decisions of the Grand Sanhedrin

In 1807 Napoleon I convened a Jewish high court (patterned after the Palestinian Sanhedrin of Antiquity) in order to lend legal authority to the declaration of loyalty to the State issued previously by an Assembly of Jewish Notables. Among the questions the French authorities put before the Assembly was, "In the eyes of Jews are Frenchmen not of Jewish religion considered as brethren or as strangers?" Both the Assembly and the Sanhedrin availed themselves of this opportunity to affirm the Jewish position. The answer to a number of such questions was prefaced by a general declaration, which asserted the distinction between religious and political laws; this declaration is here reproduced. The transactions of the Sanhedrin (which lasted one month) helped to clear the air of prejudices concerning Jews. Napoleon himself soon lost interest in the entire matter.

Blessed for ever be the name of the Lord, God of Israel, who has placed upon the thrones of France and of the Kingdom of Italy a prince after His heart. God has seen the humiliation of the descendants of Jacob of old, and He has chosen Napoleon the Great as the instrument of His compassion. The Lord judges the thoughts of men, and He alone commands their conscience, and His anointed one permits all men to worship Him according to their belief and faith. Under the shadow of his name security has come into our hearts and our dwellings and from this time on we are permitted to build, to sow, to reap, to cultivate all human knowledge, to be one with the great family of the State, to serve him and to be glorified in his lofty destiny. His high wisdom permits this assembly, which shall be illustrious in our annals, and the wisdom and virtue of which shall dictate decisions, to reconvene after the lapse of fifteen centuries, and to contribute to the welfare of Israel. Gathered this day under his mighty protection, in the good city of Paris, we, learned men and leaders in Israel, to the number of seventy-one, constitute ourselves the Grand Sanhedrin to the end that we may find the means and the strength to promulgate religious decrees which shall conform to the principles of our sacred laws and which shall serve as a standard to all Israelites. These decrees shall teach the nations that our dogmas are in keeping with the civil laws under which we live, and that we are in no wise separated from the society of men.

We therefore declare that the divine Law, the precious heritage of our ancestors, contains within itself dispositions which are political and dispositions which are religious: that the religious dispositions are, by their nature, absolute and independent of circumstances and of the age; that this does not hold true of the political dispositions, that is to say, of the dispositions which were taken for the government of the people of Israel in Palestine when it possessed its own kings, pontiffs and magistrates; that these political dispositions are no longer applicable, since Israel no longer forms a nation; that in consecrating a distinction which has already been established by tradition, the Grand Sanhedrin lays down an incontestible truth; that an assembly of Doctors of the Law, convened as a Grand Sanhedrin, is alone competent to determine the results of this distinction: that, if the Sanhedrin of old did not establish this distinction, it is because the political situation did not at that time call for it, and that, since the dispersion of Israel, no Sanhedrin has ever been assembled until the present one.

Engaged in this holy enterprise, we invoke the divine light, from which all good emanates, and we feel ourselves called upon to contribute, as far as in our power lies, to the completion of the moral regeneration of Israel. Thus, by virtue of the right vested in us by our ancient usage and by our sacred laws, which have determined that the assembly of the learned of the age shall possess the inalienable right to legislate according to the needs of the situation, and which impose upon Israel the observance of these laws—be they written or contained in tradition—we hereby religiously enjoin on all obedience to the State in all matters civil and political.

SCHOLARSHIP AND EMANCIPATION

LEOPOLD ZUNZ

Leopold Zunz (1794-1886), one of the founders of the *Wissenschaft des Judentums* (Science of Judaism) movement and one of the greatest Jewish scholars in the modern era, aimed at a reconstruction of Judaism through the cultivation of the methods and the spirit of modern historical scholarship. Such an approach to the Jewish past and its literature would, he postulated, reveal the deepseated, if not always realizable, tendency in Judaism to be an integral part of world history and to cooperate with Western humanity in its intellectual and universally human endeavors. Conscious of his place and function in the past, the contemporary Jew would be all the more ready to join in the life of new, enlightened, Europe. Another, equally important, function of Jewish historical scholarship was to acquaint the Western world and its leaders with the true nature of Judaism, to remove old prejudices, and to promote civic equality. Zunz's books and essays in the field of Hebrew literary history reflect this latter tendency; however, predominantly they are works of sober, objective, painstaking, orderly research; they became the solid foundation upon which future historians could safely build. The excerpts here presented (for the first time translated by Harry Zohn) are parts of the introduction to Zunz's first major work, *Die gottesdienstlichen Vorträge der Juden* (*The Liturgical Addresses of the Jews*), published in 1832. Zunz the scholar was deeply involved in the political events of Germany of his time; in the revolutionary year 1848, and later, he was a passionate spokesman for democracy and liberalism.

Permit me to preface the necessary information about the contents and the meaning of the book which is herewith presented to my readers with a few remarks about Jewish affairs in general and the problems to whose solution I should like to contribute in particular. In doing so I appeal the judgments of authorities which recognize prejudice and abuses to places where the verdict pronounced is truth and justice. For when all around us freedom, scholarship, and civilization are fighting for and gaining new ground, the Jews too are entitled to make claim to serious interest and untrammeled justice. Or shall the arbitrariness of club-law and of medieval madness retain a foothold only in the laws applying to Jews, at a time when clericalism and Inquisition, despotism and slavery, torture and censorship are on their way out?

It is high time that the Jews of Europe, particularly those of Germany, be granted right and liberty rather than rights and liberties—not some paltry, humiliating privileges, but complete and uplifting civil rights. We have no desire for stingily apportioned rights which are balanced by an equal number of wrongs; we derive no pleasure from concessions born of pity; we are revolted by privileges obtained in an underhanded manner. Any man should blush with shame whom a patent of nobility from the powers-that-be raises above his *brothers in faith*, while the law, with stigmatizing exclusion, assigns to him a place below the lowest of his *brothers in fatherland*. Only in lawful, mutual recognition can we find satisfaction, only irrevocable equality can bring our suffering to an end. However, I see no love or justice in a freedom which removes the shackles from the hand only to apply them to the tongue, in a tolerance which takes pleasure in our decline rather than our progress, in a citizenship which offers protection without honor, burdens without prospects. Such noxious elements can only produce serious sickness in the body politic, harming the individual as well as the community. [. . .]

The neglect of Jewish scholarship goes hand in hand with civil discrimination against the Jews. Through a higher intellectual level and a more thorough knowledge of their own affairs the Jews could have achieved a greater degree of recognition and thus more justice. Furthermore, much bad legislation, many a prejudice against Jewish antiquity, much condemnation of new endeavors are a direct consequence of the state of neglect in which Jewish literature and Jewish scholarship have been for about seventy years, particularly in Germany. And even though writings about the Talmud and against the Jews mushroomed overnight and several dozen Solons offered themselves to us as reformers, there was no book of any consequence which the statesmen could have consulted, no professor lectured about Judaism and Jewish literature, no German learned society offered prizes in this field, no philanthropist went traveling for this purpose. Legislators and scholars, not to mention the rabble among writers, had to follow in the footsteps of the 17th-century authorities, Eisenmenger,[2] Schudt,[3] Buxtorf,[4] and others like beggars, or had to borrow from the dubious wisdom of modern informants. Indeed, most people frankly admitted their ignorance of this area or betrayed it with their very first words. The (supposed) knowledge of Judaism has not progressed beyond the point where Eisenmenger left off 135 years ago, and philological studies have made almost no progress in 200 years. This explains the fact that even estimable writers assume an entirely different character—one is tempted to call it spectre-like—when the subject of the Jews comes around: all quotations from the sources are copied from the subsidized works of the 16th and 17th centuries; statements that were successfully refuted long ago are served up like durable old chestnuts; and given the lack of any scholarly activity, or any up-to-date apparatus, the oracle of the wretches is consulted. Out of ignorance or malice, some people have blended an imaginary Judaism and their own Christianity into a sort of system of conversion or concluded that regressive laws were necessary. Although excellent men have already spoken out in favor of Jewish studies and worked for them, on the whole there has been little improvement in this regard. [. . .]

In the meantime, however, the Jews have not been completely idle. Since the days of Mendelssohn[5] they have worked and written in behalf of civil rights, culture and reform, as well as their trampled-upon ancient heritage. A new era has revealed its strength in life and scholarship, in education and faith, in ideas, needs, and hopes; good seeds have been sown, excellent forces have been developed. But what is still needed is a protective institution which can serve as a support for progress and scholarship and as a religious center for the community. The physical needs and public safety of Jewish communities are being met by hospitals and orphanages, poorhouses and burial grounds. However, religion and scholarship, civil liberty, and intellectual progress require schools, seminaries, and synagogues; they must enlist the efforts of capable community leaders, competent teachers, well-trained rabbis. If emancipation and scholarship are not to be mere words, not some tawdry bit of fancy goods for sale, but the fountainhead of morality which we have found again after a long period of wandering in the wilderness, then they must fecundate institutions—high-ranking educational institutions, religious instruction for everyone, dignified religious services, suitable sermons. Such institutions are indispensable for the needs of the congregational totality of the Jews; but to establish them we need religious zeal and scholarly activity, enthusiastic participation in the entire project, benevolent recognition from the outside.

Free, instructive words are something not to be denied. Mankind has acquired all its possessions through oral instruction, through an education which lasts a lifetime. In Israel, too, the words of teaching have passed from mouth to mouth in all ages, and any future flourishing of Jewish institutions can derive only from the words that diffuse knowledge and understanding. [. . .]

Apart from all present-day efforts in this field and any personal connection I may have with them, the institution of the liturgical addresses of the Jews seemed to me to deserve and require a strictly historical investigation. The substance of my research on the origin, development, and fortunes of this institution, from the

time of Ezra[6] to the present, is now presented in this book. [. . .]
I hope that in addition to their main purpose, the recognition of
the right and the scholarship of the Jews, my investigations will
stimulate interest in related studies and win for the nobler endeavors of our time the favor of the mighty, the benevolence of
the prudent, the zeal of the pious. Such a reward will be sweeter
to me than any literary acclamation.

THE HEBREWS AND THE GREEKS

HEINRICH GRAETZ

Heinrich Graetz (1817-1891), historian, Biblical scholar,
member of the faculty of the (conservative) Jewish Theological
Seminary in Breslau, Germany, editor of the prestigious *Monats-
schrift für die Wissenschaft des Judentums*, is best known for
his *History of the Jews*. This eleven-volume work, which appeared from 1853 to 1876, quickly replaced an earlier, and first,
attempt to tell the story of Judaism, that by I. M. Jost (1793-
1860), and became one of the most influential works in modern
enlightened Jewry.

The pages of Jewish history reveal to Graetz the meaning of
Jewish existence. The radical opposition to idolatry marks the
appearance of Israel on the stage of world history. The free,
transcendent, merciful Creator-God is the negation of the pagan
deification of nature, its determinism and human bondage. The
concept of man, which results from the Israelite idea of God,
calls for a social, political, organism in which this concept and
this idea can be translated into reality. Israel lives in this Messianic mission. Its sufferings in the course of history serve only
to confirm this calling. It is the suffering of the Deutero-
Isaiahnic "Servant of the Lord," and like the latter it has a universalist meaning. Thus Jewish history is to Graetz religious,
spiritual, history, the story of a people of religion.

The general influence of German Idealism on Graetz's
philosophy of history is obvious. However, Hegel's notion which
confined Israel to the ancient Orient is strongly opposed by
Graetz, the self-conscious West European. Graetz's *History* displays many weaknesses. He had no understanding of the social

and economic factors in history, no appreciation of East European Jewry, no grasp of Jewish mysticism and Hasidism. The biographical aspects are overplayed; the political background of events underplayed. Nevertheless, the *History*, composed with verve and passion, was an immensely attractive popularization of the work done by the learned members of the school of modern Judaic studies, and by the author's own scholarly contributions.

An English translation of the *History* appeared in London in 1891. For this edition Graetz wrote an Epilogue ("Retrospect"), which is here reprinted.

The history of a people has here been narrated, which, dating from primeval times, continues to possess all the vitality necessary for its continued existence. Having entered the arena of history more than three thousand years ago, it shows no desire to depart therefrom.

This people, then, is both old and young. In its features the traces of hoary age remain indelibly impressed; and yet these very features are fresh and youthful, as if they were but of recent development. A nation, a relic of ages immemorial, which has witnessed the rise and decay of the most ancient empires, and which still continues to hold its place in the present day, deserves, for this fact alone, the closest attention. It must be borne in mind that the subjects of this History—the Hebrews, Israelites, or Jews— did not spend their existence in seclusion and contemplative isolation. Far from it! During all epochs they were dragged along in the fierce whirl of passing events. They struggled much, and suffered severely. The life of the people during more than three thousand years received many shocks and injuries. It still bears the trace of its many wounds, while no one can deny its right to the crown of martyrdom; and nevertheless it lives to the present day! It has accomplished much useful work, a fact that is gainsaid by none except pessimists and malignant cavilers. Had it only succeeded in disillusioning the cultured portion of mankind from those deceptions of idolatry which end in moral and social corruption, it would deserve special attention for this alone; but it has rendered far greater services to the human race. [. . .]

The Greeks and the Hebrews were the sole originators of a higher culture. If the modern Roman, German, and Sclavonic nations, both on this side and on the other side of the ocean, could be despoiled of what they received from the Greeks and the Israelites, they would be utterly destitute. This idea, however, is a mere fancy; the nations can no longer be deprived of what they once borrowed, and what has since then become welded into their very nature. The participation of the Greeks in the regeneration of civilized races is conceded without a dissenting voice and without a suspicion of envy. It is freely admitted that the Greeks scattered abroad the budding blossoms of art, and the ripe fruits of a higher intelligence; that they opened up the domain of the beautiful, and diffused the brightness of Olympic ideas. It is also acknowledged that their intellectual genius found its embodiment in their whole literature, and that from this literature and the surviving relics of their ideals in the fine arts, there still issues forth new life-giving energy. [. . .]

The people of Israel proclaimed a God at one with Himself, and unchangeable; a holy God, who requires holiness from mankind, the Creator of heaven and earth, of light and darkness. He, though mighty and exalted, is yet near to humanity, especially protecting the poor and the oppressed, a jealous but not a vengeful God, to whom the moral conduct of man is not a matter of indifference, although he is a God of mercy, and regards all mankind with love as the work of His hands. To this God evil is an abomination, for He is a God of justice, a Father to the orphan, and a Defender of the widow. These words of world-wide import penetrated deep into the heart of man, and, at a later period were the means of hurling the beautiful gods of the heathen into the dust.

The thought and desire that men should be equal before the law as before God, that the stranger should have equal rights with the native, also grew from the idea of man's resemblance to the divine image, and became established amongst the Israelites as a fundamental law of the state. This was the first recognition of the rights of man, for, among the nations of old, even the leaders of civilization never conceded that right which has now become an established rule. [. . .]

Israel's dominant idea became of far-reaching importance in its ethical tendency. It is by no means a matter of indifference in the moral conduct of man, as regards both great and small things, whether the earth, the scene of action, is governed by one Power or by several mutually antagonistic forces. The one conception ensures unity and peace, the other unveils a picture of dissension and discord, and leads to barbarism. The likeness of man to God —in opposition to the blasphemous idea of God's likeness to man —and the train of thought arising from monotheism impresses man with self-respect and with a regard for his fellow-man. Thereby the life of even the humblest of men is placed under religious and moral protection. [. . .]

The Israelite nation alone effected the emancipation of man by proclaiming holiness of life, the equal rights of aliens and home-born, and all that is included in the term humanity. It is not superfluous to point out that the foundation-stone of culture, "Thou shalt love thy neighbor as thyself" (Leviticus 19:18), was laid by this people. Who prayed that the poor might be raised from the dust; the suffering, the orphan, and the helpless from the dung-hill? The Israelite people. Who declared that everlasting peace was the holy ideal of the future, "when one nation should no longer draw sword against the other, and should no longer learn the art of war" (Isaiah 2:4)? Israel's prophets. That people has been called a wandering mystery, but it should rather be called a wandering revelation. It has revealed the secret of life, and the art of all arts—how a nation may guard itself against being given up to destruction. [. . .]

The prophets knew no higher ideal than that the earth should be filled with the knowledge of God as the sea covers its bed (Isaiah 11:9). Life is highly prized, but it must be a pure and holy life. Only after a long and unhappy course of history did a gloomy and ascetic theory of life creep in, and produce a sad and misanthropic order, which stamped out pure gladness as a sin, and regarded the earth as a valley of tears, and to this condition it actually became, to some extent, reduced. [. . .]

The Israelites decidedly have great faults; they have greatly erred, and have been severely punished for their shortcomings.

History describes and reveals these errors, their origin, their eventful results, and the consequences which resulted from them. Many of these faults were acquired, and were to some extent the effect of their surroundings; but there were also peculiar and original features in the character of this people. Why should they be more perfect than all other nationalities, not one of which has ever attained to perfection in all directions?

Those who eagerly endeavor to show the failings and shortcomings of the Israelite people as through a magnifying glass unconsciously pay them high honor by making greater demands upon them than upon other nations. It is a decided defect on the part of the Israelites that they left behind neither colossal buildings nor architectural memorials. Possibly the race did not possess any talent for architecture; or perhaps, owing to its ideals of equality, the kings and warriors were not so highly esteemed that it was considered necessary to erect in their memory stupendous palaces, pyramids, or marble monuments. The hovels of the poor ranked higher. The Israelites did not even erect a temple to God (Solomon's Temple being built by the Phœnicians), for the heart was God's temple. The Israelites neither sculptured nor painted gods, for they did not consider the Deity a subject for pleasant pastime, but gave Him pious and earnest devotion. Nor did the Israelites excel in artistic epics, and still less in drama or comedy. This may have been a want in their idiosyncrasy, and is also connected with their strong distaste for mythological births and scandals. They evinced a similar dislike to all dramas, public games, and theatrical displays. However, in compensation, they had poetical conceptions which adequately reflect the ideals of life, as these are described in the Psalms and in the poetically fashioned eloquence of the prophets. Both possess this trait in common, that their fundamental quality is truth and not fiction, whereby poetry instead of being a mere toy and plaything for the imagination, became the instrument for attaining ethical culture.

Their literature, though it does not treat of the drama, is yet full of dramatic vigor; and, if not actually humorous, is nevertheless replete with irony, and from its ideal pedestal proudly contemplates all delusions. The Israelite prophets and psalmists, whilst developing a beautiful poetic form, never sacrificed the truth of the subject for the sake of style. The Israelites also introduced a historical style of their own, which pictured events according to the canons of truth, and without any endeavor to excuse or hide the shortcomings of heroes, kings, or nations. [. . .] If Greek literature elevated the dominion of art and its perceptions, Hebrew literature idealized the domain of holiness and morality. The history of a nation which has achieved so much has a decided right to full appreciation.

Judged superficially, the course of history from the entry of the Israelites into Canaan until far into the times of the kings may easily give rise to misconception, for the most striking events seem to bear a political character. Invasions, battles, and conquests, occupy the foreground of history. [. . .] Most of the kings, and also their sons and courtiers, acted as arbitrarily as if there had been no code of law to set limits to their despotic will, and as if they had never even heard of the Ten Commandments of Sinai.

For centuries the people wore the bonds of wild idolatry, and differed only in a slight degree from the heathen world which surrounded it. Was the race in its beginnings actually of no importance? Did the people for a considerable time keep pace with its Semitic kinsmen, and only at a given period become stamped with those peculiarities which caused it to contrast so strongly with its neighbors? Did not Sinai illumine its very cradle? or was this fact stated to have been the case only in after-days and by historians? Sceptics have said as much, but the fragments of Israelite poetry, dating from primeval times, give the lie to this assertion. Several centuries before the inception of kingly rule, and in the first days of the hero-judges, in the days of Deborah, "the mother in Israel," a poet sang of the marvels of the revelation; at Sinai he described the people of God as contrasting strikingly with their environment, and ascribed their lapses to the fact that they had followed "false gods," and thereby fallen away from their widely different origin. Even if one were inclined to doubt the veracity of history, yet credence must be given to poetry as a trustworthy eye-witness. It is not to be denied, that the spiritual birth of the Israelite people was simultaneous with their actual birth, and that Sinai was the scene of the one event, as Egypt was of the other; and that the Ark of the Covenant with the sacred Ten Commandments was its faithful attendant from the earliest days. [. . .]

In the law God is the Holy Will, determining whatever is ethical and good. He is the sacred Type which indicates the way, but not the cause for which actions are to be performed, in order that some definite advantage may accrue. The Israelite creed is, therefore, by no means a dogmatic doctrine, but one of duty. Though a law of deliverance, it has no mystic admixture. But this religion or law of redemption was certainly beyond the comprehension of the people while yet in its infantine stage, and the ideal which was intended to endow it with significance and vitality remained for a long time an enigma to the people. This enigma was first solved by the prophets. A considerable period elapsed even after the prophets had spoken their burning words of fire, before the nation became the guardian of the teachings heard at Sinai, and before they erected a temple for it in their own hearts.

But as soon as this maturity was attained, and the "heart of stone had become a heart of flesh" (Ezekiel 11:19), as soon as the prophetic body were able to dispense with the intervention of the priesthood, they could depart from the scene; they had become superfluous, for the nation itself had attained to a complete comprehension of its own being and its own mission. History shows how this twofold transformation was effected; how the family of a petty sheik became the nucleus of a people; how this small people was humiliated to the condition of a horde; how this horde was trained to become a nation of God through the law of self-sanctification and self-control; and how these teachings, together with a spiritual ideal of God, became breathed into it as its soul.

This national soul likewise grew into the national body, was developed and took the form of laws, which, though they were not subjected to the fluctuations of time, were yet suited to the occurrences of the age. The transformation was effected only amidst severe struggles; obstacles from within and without had to be overcome, and errors and relapses to be amended, before the nation's body could become a fitting organ for the nation's soul. The hidden things had to be revealed, the obscure to be illumined, vague notions to be brought into the light of certainty, before that ideal Israel (as foreshadowed by the prophets in the far distance of time, and which had been expressly distinguished by them from Israel as it then existed with all its defects) might become a "light unto the nations" (Isaiah 49:6). Assuredly, there is no second people now dwelling upon the globe, or hidden within the stream of time, which, like Israel, has carried with it a pre-ordained law. This people not alone possessed such a law, but also the full conviction that it existed only on account of this law, and in order to be the exponent of this law, and that its sole importance lay in its vocation to announce the truths of salvation. These were to be inculcated not by violence and compulsion, but by example, by action, and by the realization of those ideals which as a people the Israelites were to proclaim.

The profound insight afforded by history has proved that it was the mission of the Greeks to bring to light the ideals of art and science, but the Greeks themselves had no knowledge of this fact.

It was otherwise with the Israelites. Not only was their task apportioned to them, but the revelation was made to them that it was their task, and that without it they were of no more significance than "a drop in the pitcher, or a mote of dust in the balance" (Isaiah 40:15). Only on this account did the men of God call the Israelites a chosen people. The fact of being chosen imposed on the nation heavier and more important responsibilities, and a greater measure of duty; and when their mission, as the exponents of a special and religious moral conception, became clear to them, the people prized their task beyond all things—more highly than their fatherland and nationality, and even more than life itself. And because they sacrificed themselves, the idea which dominated them attained to enduring existence and to immortality.

ISRAEL WITHIN THE ORGANISM
OF HUMANITY

MOSES HESS

Moses (originally, Moritz) Hess (1812-1875), the first German Socialist, in 1841 recognized the intellectual potential of Karl Marx and introduced him to the doctrine of communism. He advised contemporary Judaism to disappear from the stage of history, "that out of its death might spring a new, more precious life" (*Die heilige Geschichte der Menschheit*, A *Sacred History of Mankind*, 1837). In *Die europäische Triarchie* (*The European Triarchy*, 1841), he reiterated his advice, in the belief that an all-encompassing world society (the Socialist utopia) should adhere not to a national, historically conditioned, religion, but to a universal one. On behalf of a new, reconstructed, world, he collaborated with P. J. Proudhon, Bruno Bauer, Étienne Cabet, Max Stirner (all of whom were later dismissed by Marx as metaphysical moralists), and with Michael Bakunin, the Russian revolutionary, and Ferdinand Lassalle.

Then—Isaiah Berlin suggests the possibility of "a transfiguring experience"—Hess began to apprehend the importance of national communities, to view them as natural, historical, phenomena, analogous to those of the family unit. Without abandoning his Socialist involvement he decided to revise his position on Judaism. *Rom und Jerusalem*, which appeared in 1862, is an account of his revised position and a profession of his new faith. In it he advocates the re-establishment of the Jewish nation, regaining the Land of Israel, and a radical reconsideration of the teachings of classical Judaism, e.g., the unity of all creation, which, to him, is the basis of socialism and of the equality of men. Thus, in addition to assimilationist Reform and dogmatic Neo-Orthodoxy, a new voice began to be heard, a voice that became the intellectual foundation of modern Zionism. The piece which follows is the ninth of the twelve letters in *Rom und Jerusalem*.

You confronted me with the dilemma, that we must either agree with the Luxemburg Hirsch,[7] that the goal and essence of Judaism is humanitarianism, in which case it is not national regeneration, but the realization of humanitarian ideals which is the aim worth striving for;—and Judaism, like every religious or political society, must ultimately become absorbed and disappear in the larger fellowship of humanity;—or we must agree with the Frankfort Hirsch,[8] who sees in Judaism the only salvation; in which case, we disagree with the modern humanitarian aspirations and, like orthodox Christianity, we need make little appeal to public opinion of the century; for public opinion will receive such an appeal with the same feeling that it would receive a Chinese Proclamation or a Papal Bull.

I believe, dear friend, that the opinions I have heretofore expressed in my correspondence with you have little in common with either horn of the dilemma. They do not agree with the conceptions of either extreme faction, but belong to a different order of ideas. I believe that not only does the national essence of Judaism not exclude civilization and humanitarianism, but that the latter really follow from it, as necessarily as the result follows from the cause. If, in spite of this, I emphasize the national side of Judaism, which is the root, rather than the humanitarian aspect, which is the bloom and flower, it is because in our time people are prone to decorate themselves with the flowers of culture rather than cultivate them again in the soil on which they grew. It is out of Judaism that our humanitarian view of life sprang. There is not a phase in Christian morality, nor in the scholastic philosophy of the Middle Ages, nor in modern philanthropy, and, if we add the latest manifestation of Judaism, Spinozism, not even in modern philosophy, which does not have its roots in Judaism. Until the French Revolution, the Jewish people was the only people in the world which had, simultaneously, a national as well as a humanitarian religion. It is through Judaism that the history of humanity became a sacred history. I mean by that, that process of unified organic development which has its origin in the love of the family and which will not be completed until the whole of humanity becomes one family, the members of which will be united by the holy spirit, the creative genius of history, as strongly as the organs of a body are united by the creative natural forces. As long as no other people possessed such a national, humanitarian cult, the

Jews alone were the people of God. Since the French Revolution, the French, as well as the other peoples which followed them, have become our noble rivals and faithful allies.

With the final victory of these nations over medieval reaction, the humanitarian aspirations, with which I am greatly in sympathy, so long as they do not express themselves merely in hypocritical, flowery words, will be realized and bear fruit. Anti-national humanitarianism is just as unfruitful as the anti-humanitarian nationalism of medieval reaction. In theoretical anti-national humanitarianism I can only see, mildly speaking, an idealistic dream, but not a semblance of reality. We become so saturated with spiritualistic love and humanistic chloroform that we ultimately become entirely unconscious of the pain and misery that the antagonism which still exists between the various members of the great human family causes in real life. This antagonism will not be eradicated by enlightened sermons, but only by a process of historical development based on laws as unchangeable as the laws of nature. Just as nature does not produce flowers and fruits of a general character, nor general plants and animals, but produces particular plant and animal types, so does the creative power in history produce only folk types. In mankind, the plan of the plant and animal kingdoms finds its perfection; but humanity, as a separate life sphere, as the sphere of social life, is still in the process of development. We find in the history of social life a primal differentiation of folk-types which at first, plant-like, existed side by side with each other; then, animal-like, fought each other and destroyed or absorbed one another, but which will finally, in order to become absolutely free, live not only in friendly fashion with one another, but live *each for the other*, preserving, at the same time, their particular type identity.

The laws of universal history, I mean the history of the universe, namely, those of the cosmic, organic and social life, are as yet little known. We have particular sciences, but not a science of the universe; we still do not know the unity of all life. One thing, however, is certain, that a fusion of cults, an ideal to which so many aspire, and which was realized, at least in part, for thousands of years by Catholic Rome, will as little establish a lasting peace in human society as the philanthropic but unscientific belief in the absolute equality of men. In their attempt to base the granting of equal rights to all men on the primitive uniformity of all races and types, the humanitarians confound the organization of social life on the basis of solidarity, which is the result of a long and painful process of historical development, with a ready-made, inorganic equality and uniformity, which becomes rarer and rarer the farther back we go in history. The reconciliation of races follows its own natural laws, which we can neither arbitrarily create nor change. As to the fusion of cults, it is really a past stage in the development of social life. It was the watchword of that religion which owes its existence to the death of the nations of antiquity, i.e., Christianity. To-day the real problem is how to free the various oppressed races and folk-types and allow them to develop in their own way. The dangerous possibility that the various nationalities will separate themselves entirely from each other or ignore each other, is to be feared as little as the danger that they will fight among themselves and enslave one another.

The present-day national movement not only does not exclude humanitarianism, but strongly asserts it; for this movement is a wholesome reaction, not against humanism, but against the things that would encroach upon it and cause its degeneration, against the leveling tendencies of modern industry and civilization which threaten to deaden every original organic life-force, by introducing a uniform inorganic mechanism. As long as these tendencies were directed against the antiquated institutions of a long-passed historical period, their existence was justified. Nor can this nationalistic reaction object to them, insofar as they endeavor to establish closer relations between the various nations of the world. But, unfortunately, people have gone so far in life, as well as in science, as to deny the typical and the creative; and as a result the vapor of idealism, on the one hand, and the dust of atomism on the other, rest like mildew on the red corn, and stifle the germinating life in the bud. It is against these encroachments on the most sacred principles of creative life that the national tendencies of our time react, and it is against these destructive forces that I appeal to the original national power of Judaism.

Like the general universal cosmic life which finds its termination in it, and the individual microcosmic life in which all the buds and fruits of the spirit finally ripen, humanity is a living organism, of which races and peoples are the members. In every organism changes are continually going on. Some, quite prominent in the embryonic stage, disappear in the later development. There are organs, on the other hand, hardly noticeable in the earlier existence of the organism, which become important only when the organism reaches the end of its development.

To the latter class of members of organic humanity (which class is really the creative one) belongs the Jewish people. This people was hardly noticeable in the ancient world, where it was greatly oppressed by its powerful, conquering neighbors. Twice it came near being destroyed; namely, in the Egyptian and Babylonian captivities; and twice it rose to new spiritual life and fought long and successfully against the mightiest as well as the most civilized peoples of antiquity—the Greeks and the Romans. Finally, in the last struggle of the ancient world, it was this people which fertilized the genius of humanity with its own spirit, so as to rejuvenate itself, along with the regeneration of humanity. To-day, when the process of rejuvenation of the historical peoples is ended and each nation has its special function in the organism of humanity, we are for the first time beginning to conceive the special significance of the various organs of humanity.

England, with its industrial organization, represents the nerve-force of humanity which directs and regulates the alimentary system of mankind; France, that of general motion, namely, the social; Germany discharges the function of thinking; and America represents the general regenerating power by means of which all elements of the historical peoples will be assimilated into one. When we observe that every modern people, every part of modern society, displays in its activity as an organ of humanity a special calling, then we must also determine the importance and function of the only ancient people which still exists to-day, as strong and vigorous as it was in the days of old, namely, the people of Israel.

In the organism of humanity there are no two peoples which attract and repel each other more than the Germans and the Jews; just as there are no two mental attitudes which are simultaneously akin to each other and still diametrically opposed, as the scientific-philosophical and the religious-moral. Religion, in its higher form, is the spiritual tie which binds the creature to the Creator, the infinite thread, the end of which returns to its source, the bridge which leads from one creation to the other, from life to death, and from death back to life. It not only brings man to know the Absolute more intimately, but it inspires and sanctifies his whole life with the divine spirit. In religion, as in love, especially in a religion like Judaism, which is neither one-sidedly materialistic nor one-sidedly spiritualistic, body and spirit merge into one another. The greatest and most dangerous enemy of the Jewish religion in antiquity was the religion of gross sensualism, the material love of the Semites, namely, Baal worship. In medieval ages, the enemy was represented by the embodiment of spiritualistic love—Christianity. The Jewish people which, thanks to its prophets of antiquity and rabbis of the Middle Ages, kept its religion from both extremes of degeneration, was, and is still today, that organ of humanity which expresses the living, creative force in universal history, namely, the organ of unifying and sanctifying love. This organ is akin to the organ of thought, but is, at the same time, opposed to it. Both draw their force from the inexhaustible well of life. But, while the religious genius individualizes the infinite, philosophic, scientific thought abstracts from life all its individual, subjective forms and generalizes it. Objective philosophy and science have no direct connection with life; religious teaching is intimately united with it, for either religion is identical with the national, social and moral life, or it is mere hypocrisy.

I have wandered from my trend of thought. I merely wanted to explain to you why I do not ally myself with the humanitarian aspirations which endeavor to obliterate all differentiation in the organism of humanity and in the name of such catch words as liberty and progress, build altars to arbitrariness and ignorance, on which our light-minded youth offers its best energies and sacrifices.

AUTO-EMANCIPATION

LEO PINSKER

The pamphlet *Auto-Emancipation* is the first statement by a modern Jew whose hope that assimilation was the natural solution of the Jewish problem failed him and who turned to nationalism as providing a just and honorable answer. Leo Pinsker (1821-1891), a native of Russian Poland, was a respected physician in Odessa and a member of the assimilationist "Society for the Dissemination of Culture Among the Jews in Russia." When, in 1881, violent pogroms broke out in Russia, he realized the depth of "Judaeophobia" and the precariousness of life of the Jewish minority. Further attempts at assimilation seemed both futile and dishonest; the Jewish problem was to be approached from a political angle. He joined the *Hoveve Zion* (Lovers of Zion) movement and convened its first conference (in Kattowitz, 1884). Opposition to Pinsker's idea of self-aid and self-determination came mainly from the ranks of the liberals outside Russia, who continued to believe in social progress, but Herzl's Zionism lent it new and decisive force.

The nations of the earth could not destroy us bodily, yet they were able to suppress in us every sense of national independence. So now we look on with fatalistic indifference when in many countries we are refused such recognition as would not lightly be denied to Zulus. [. . .] We were the shuttle-cock which the peoples tossed in turn to one another. The cruel game was equally amusing whether we were caught or thrown, and was enjoyed all the more as our national respect became more elastic and yielding in the hands of the peoples. [. . .]

When we are ill-used, robbed, plundered and dishonored, we dare not defend ourselves, and, worse still, we take it almost as a matter of course. When our face is slapped, we soothe our burning cheek with cold water; and when a bloody wound has been inflicted, we apply a bandage. When we are turned out of the house which we ourselves built, we beg humbly for mercy, and when we fail to reach the heart of our oppressor we move on in search of another exile.

When an idle spectator on the road calls out to us: "You poor Jewish devils are certainly to be pitied," we are most deeply touched; and when a Jew is said to be an honor to his people, we are foolish enough to be proud of it. [. . .] If no notice is taken of our descent and we are treated like others born in the country, we express our gratitude by actually turning renegades. For the sake of the comfortable position we are granted, for the flesh-pots which we may enjoy in peace, we persuade ourselves, and others, that we are no longer Jews, but full-blooded citizens. Idle delusion! Though you prove yourselves patriots a thousand times, you will still be reminded at every opportunity of your Semitic descent. This fateful *memento mori* will not prevent you, however, from accepting the extended hospitality, until some fine morning you find yourself crossing the border, and you are reminded by the mob that you are, after all, nothing but vagrants and parasites, without the protection of law.

But even humane treatment does not prove that we are welcome.

Indeed, what a pitiful figure we cut! We are not counted among the nations, neither have we a voice in their councils, even when the affairs concern us. Our fatherland—the other man's country; our unity—dispersion; our solidarity—the battle against us; our weapon—humility; our defense—flight; our individuality—adaptability; our future—the next day. What a miserable role for a nation which descends from the Maccabees!

Do you wonder that a people which allowed itself for dear life's sake to be trampled upon, and has learned to love these very feet that trample upon them, should have fallen into the utmost contempt!

Our tragedy is that we can neither live nor die. We cannot die despite the blows of our enemies, and we do not wish to die by our own hand, through apostasy or self-destruction. Neither can we live; our enemies have taken care of that. We will not recommence life as a nation and live like the other peoples, thanks to those over-zealous patriots, who think it is necessary to sacrifice every claim upon independent national life to their loyalty as citizens—which should be a matter of course. Such fanatical patriots deny their ancient national character for the sake of any other nationality, whatever it may be, of high rank or low. But they deceive no one. They do not see how glad one is to decline Jewish companionship.

Thus for eighteen centuries we have lived in disgrace, without a single earnest attempt to shake it off! [. . .]

Today, when our kinsmen in a small part of the earth are allowed to breathe freely and can feel more deeply for the sufferings of their brothers; today, when a number of other subject and oppressed nationalities have been allowed to regain their independence, we, too, must not sit a moment longer with folded hands, we must not consent to play forever the hopeless role of the "Wandering Jew." It is a truly hopeless one, leading to despair.

When an individual finds himself despised and rejected by society, no one wonders if he commits suicide. But where is the deadly weapon to give the *coup de grace* to the scattered limbs of the Jewish nation, and then who would lend his hand to it? The destruction is neither possible nor desirable. Consequently, we are bound by duty to devote all our remaining moral force to reestablishing ourselves as a living nation, so that we may ultimately assume a more fitting and dignified role among the family of the nations.

If the basis of our argument is sound, if the prejudice of mankind against us rests upon anthropological and social principles, innate and ineradicable, we must look no more to the slow progress of humanity. And we must learn to recognize that as long as we lack a home of our own, such as the other nations have, we must resign forever the noble hope of becoming the equals of our fellowmen. We must recognize that before the great idea of human brotherhood will unite all the peoples of the earth, millenniums must elapse; and that meanwhile a people which is at home everywhere and nowhere, must everywhere be regarded as alien. The time has come for a sober and dispassionate realization of our true position.

With unbiased eyes and without prejudice we must see in the mirror of the nations the tragi-comic figure of our people, which with distorted countenance and maimed limbs helps to make universal history without managing properly its own little history. We must reconcile ourselves once and for all to the idea that the other nations, by reason of their inherent natural antagonism, will forever reject us. We must not shut our eyes to this natural force which works like every other elemental force; we must not complain of it; on the contrary, we are in duty bound to take courage, to rise, and to see to it that we do not remain forever the Cinderella, the butt of the peoples.

EMANCIPATION

JAMES DARMESTETER

The French Orientalist and humanist James Darmesteter (1849-1894) is known for his research in Iranian literature and religion and for his French translation of the *Avesta*. As a Jew he lived estranged from the Synagogue; but his religious philosophy drew from Biblical and Hebraic sources. He envisaged the religion of the future as a blend of scientific truth and prophetic ethics (essays in *Les Prophètes d'Israel*, 1892). In his "Essay on the History of the Jews," from which the following excerpt is taken, Darmesteter, a disciple of Ernest Renan, pointed to the distinctive place this history occupies within world history. It is, he states, a history of contacts "with nearly all the great civilizations and with nearly all the great religious ideas that have left their impress on the civilized world"; it is concerned "with the ideas, the religions, the social factors, in short with the living forces of humanity." The Jewish people is closely identified with them in action or in suffering. Jewish history "accompanies universal history throughout its entire range and is closely interwoven with it." The most significant meeting of the two occurs in the period of the Emancipation.

This era, which terminates the material history of the Jewish people, opens a new and strange phase in the history of its thought. For the first time this thought finds itself in accord, and no longer in conflict, with the general tendency of humanity. Judaism, which from its first hour has always been at war with the dominant religion, whether that of Baal, of Jupiter, or of Christ, at length encounters a state of thought which it need not combat because it finds there the reflex of its own instincts and traditions. The [French] Revolution is, in fact, only the echo in the political world of a much vaster and deeper movement which wholly transforms thought and which, in the realm of speculation, ends with the substitution of the scientific conception of the world for the mythical, and on the practical side brings to the fore the notion of justice and progress.

In this great downfall of mythical religion, the crash of which fills our age, Judaism, such as the centuries have made it, has had the least to suffer and the least to fear because its miracles and rites constitute no essential and integral part of it. As a consequence, it does not fall with the rest. Judaism has not made the miraculous the basis of its dogma nor installed the supernatural as a permanent factor in the progress of events. Its miracles from the time of the Middle Ages are but a poetic detail, a legendary recital, a picturesque decoration; and its cosmogony—borrowed in haste from Babylon by the last compiler of the Bible, with the stories of the apple and the serpent over which so many Christian generations have labored—never greatly disturbed the imagination of the rabbis nor weighed very heavily upon the thought of the Jewish philosophers. Its rites were never "an instrument of faith," an expedient to "lull" rebellious thought into faith; they are merely cherished customs, a symbol of the family, of transitory value, and destined to disappear when there shall be but *one* family in a world converted to the *one* truth.

Set aside all these miracles, all of these rites, and behind them will be found the two great dogmas which, ever since the prophets, constitute the whole of Judaism: the divine unity and Messianism, unity of law throughout the world and the terrestrial triumph of justice in humanity. These are the two dogmas which at the present time illuminate humanity in its progress both in the scientific and the social order of things, and which are termed in modern parlance, unity of forces and belief in progress.

For this reason, Judaism is the only religion that has never entered into conflict, and never can, with either science or social progress, and that has witnessed, and still witnesses, all their conquests without a sense of fear. These are not hostile forces that it accepts or submits to merely from a spirit of toleration or policy in order to save the remains of its power by a compromise. They are old friendly voices which it recognizes and salutes with joy, for it has heard them resound for centuries already, in the axioms of free thought and in the cry of the suffering heart. For this reason, the Jews in all the countries which have entered upon the new path have begun to take a share in all the great works of civilization, in the triple field of science, of art, and of action; and that share, far from being an insignificant one, is out of all proportion to the brief time that has elapsed since their enfranchisement.

Does this mean that Judaism should nurse dreams of ambition and think of realizing one day that "invisible church of the future" invoked by some in prayer? This would be an illusion, whether on the part of a narrow sectarian or on that of an enlightened individual. The truth, however, remains that the Jewish spirit can still be a factor in this world, making for the highest science for unending progress and that the mission of the Bible is not yet complete.

The Bible is not responsible for the partial miscarriage of Christianity, due to the compromises made by its organizers, who in their too great zeal to conquer and convert paganism, were themselves converted by it. But everything in Christianity which comes in a direct line from Judaism lives, and will live; and it is Judaism which through Christianity has cast into the old polytheistic world, to ferment there until the end of time, the sentiment of unity and an impatience to bring about charity and justice.

The reign of the Bible and also of the Evangelists in so far as they were inspired by the Bible can become established only in proportion as the positive religions connected with it lose their power. Great religions outlive their altars and their priests. Hellenism, abolished, counts less skeptics today than in the days of Socrates and Anaxagoras. The gods of Homer died when Phidias carved them in marble, and now they are immortally enthroned in the thought and heart of Europe. The cross may crumble into dust, but there were words spoken under its shadow in Galilee, the echo of which will forever vibrate in the human conscience.

And when the nation who made the Bible shall have disappeared
—the race and the cult—though leaving no visible trace of its
passage upon earth, its imprint will remain in the depth of the
heart of generations who will unconsciously, perhaps, live upon
what has thus been implanted in their breasts. Humanity, as it is
fashioned in the dreams of those who desire to be called free-
thinkers, may with the lips deny the Bible and its work; but
humanity can never deny it in its heart without the sacrifice of
the best that it contains, faith in unity and hope for justice, and
without a relapse into the mythology and the "might makes right"
of thirty centuries ago

EMANCIPATION AND JUDAISM

SAMSON RAPHAEL HIRSCH

S. R. Hirsch (1808-1888) is the most distinguished modern
reinterpreter of Jewish tradition. He counteracted the identification of Jewish orthodox thought and life with adherence to old-
fashioned, outmoded, concepts and blindness to enlightenment.
Against this image, envisaged by the emancipated in the post-
Mendelssohnian era, he counterposed his idea of a Jew as a
man versed in the languages, literatures, and sciences of the
West, an informed and active citizen of his country, yet one
who adhered to the Jewish law in its totality and without compromise. He attributed a symbolic meaning to Jewish ritual,
liturgy, and customs, and stressed their spiritual aspects and their
sanctification of life. Judaism thus became the perfection and
fulfillment of that which was initiated in classical antiquity and
in modern humanism. Such understanding of Judaism, Hirsch
thought, can be attained through selfless study of its literary
sources and a life of religious practice.

Hirsch's *magnum opus* is *Horeb* (1837), which presents his
doctrine in systematic fashion. Other works are *Neunzehn Briefe
über Judentum* (*Nineteen Letters of Ben Uziel*, 1836), commentaries on the Pentateuch (1867-1878), *Psalms* (1882), the
Hebrew Prayer Book (1895), and six volumes of essays (1902-
1912). As rabbi of the separatist orthodox community in Frankfurt-am-Main (from 1851 on) he established a school system in

the spirit of Neo-Orthodoxy. Though limited to a segment of Jewry, his influence has been deep.

Emancipation was a life issue when Hirsch wrote *Nineteen Letters of Ben Uziel*; the excerpt that follows is the sixteenth of the letters. After the July revolution of 1830, German Jews resumed the struggle for civil rights, whose promise was glimpsed early in the nineteenth century, but was severely curtailed at the Congress of Vienna (1815). Gabriel Riesser (1806-1863) became the great champion of equal rights for Jews, who were ready to assume equal duties and to identify themselves with the cause of Germany. His organ, *Der Jude* (*The Jew*), founded in 1832, led this struggle with courage and determination. His opponents, such as the Protestant theologian H. E. G. Paulus, insisted on conversion as a precondition of emancipation. Even less extreme political leaders viewed Jewish emancipation as a religious rather than a purely civic issue, a fact the Jews tried to overlook. Hirsch (then rabbi in the Grand Duchy of Oldenburg, which, by the way, maintained a liberal policy toward its Jews) sensed the complex nature of emancipation, and its possible negative effect on Jewish spiritual life. He felt that emancipation should never be viewed as ending *galut*, the state of being in exile, and as altering the Jew's prime obligation, namely, to lead a life according to Torah. Orthodoxy was willing to accept emancipation but only on its own terms.

You ask me for my opinion on the question which at present agitates so greatly the minds of men, emancipation; whether I consider it feasible and desirable, according to the spirit of Judaism, our duty to strive to attain it. [. . .]

When Israel began its great wandering through the ages and nations, Jeremiah proclaimed the following as its duty:

"Build houses and dwell therein; plant gardens and eat the fruit thereof; take wives unto yourselves, and beget sons and daughters, and take wives for your sons and give your daughters in marriage that they bear sons and daughters, and that you multiply there and diminish not. And seek the peace of the city whither I have exiled you, and pray for it to the Lord, for in its peace there will be unto you peace" (Jeremiah 29:5-7).

To be pushed back and limited upon the path of life is, therefore, not an essential condition of the *galut*, Israel's exile state among the nations, but, on the contrary, it is our duty to join ourselves as closely as possible to the state which receives us into its midst, to promote its welfare and not to consider our well-being as in any way separate from that of the state to which we belong.

This close connection with all states is in nowise in contradiction to the spirit of Judaism, for the former independent state life of Israel was not even then the essence or purpose of our national existence; it was only a means of fulfilling our spiritual mission.

Land and soil were never Israel's bond of union, but only the common task of the Torah; therefore, it still forms a united body, though separated from a national soil; nor does this unity lose its reality, though Israel accept everywhere the citizenship of the nations amongst which it is dispersed. This coherence of sympathy, this spiritual union, which may be designated by the Hebrew terms *am* and *goy*, but not by the expression "nation," unless we are able to separate from the term the concept of common territory and political power, is the only communal band we possess, or ever expect to possess, until the great day shall arrive when the Almighty shall see fit, in His inscrutable wisdom, to unite again His scattered servants in one land, and the Torah shall be the guiding principle of a state, an exemplar of the meaning of divine revelation and the mission of humanity.

For this future, which is promised us in the glorious predictions of the inspired prophets, whom God raised up for our ancestors, we hope and pray; but actively to accelerate its coming were sin, and is prohibited to us, while the entire purpose of the Messianic age is that we may, in prosperity, exhibit to mankind a better example of "Israel" than did our ancestors the first time, while, hand in hand with us, the entire race will be joined in universal brotherhood through the recognition of God, the All-One.

Because of this purely spiritual nature of the national character of Israel it is capable of the most intimate union with states, with, perhaps, this difference, that while others seek in the state only the material benefits which it secures, considering possession and enjoyment as the highest good, Israel can only regard it as a means of fulfilling the mission of humanity.

Summon up, I pray you, the picture of such an Israel, dwelling in freedom in the midst of the nations, and striving to attain unto its ideal, every son of Israel a respected and influential exemplar priest of righteousness and love, disseminating among the nations not specific Judaism, for proselytism is interdicted, but pure humanity. What a mighty impulse to progress, what a luminary and staff in the gloomy days of the Middle Ages had not Israel's sin and the insanity of the nations rendered such a *galut* impossible! How impressive, how sublime it would have been, if, in the midst of a race that adored only power, possessions, and enjoyment, and that was oft blinded by superstitious imaginings, there had lived quietly and publicly human beings of a different sort, who beheld in material possessions only the means of practicing justice and love towards all; whose minds, pervaded with the wisdom and truth of the law, maintained simple, straightforward views, and emphasized them for themselves and others in expressive, vivid deed-symbols.

But it would seem as though Israel was to be fitted through the endurance of harsh and cruel exile for the proper appreciation and utilization of its milder and gentler form.

When *galut* will be comprehended and accepted as it should be, when in suffering, the service of God and His Torah will be understood as the only task of life, when even in misery God will be served, and external abundance esteemed only as a means of this service, then, perhaps, Israel will be ready for the greater temptations of prosperity and happiness in dispersion.

Just as it is our duty to endeavor to obtain those material possessions which are the fundamental condition of life, so also is it the duty of every one to take advantage of every alleviation and improvement of his condition open to him in a righteous way; for, the more means, the more opportunity is given to him to fulfill his mission in its broadest sense; and no less than of the individual is it the duty of the community to obtain for all its members the opportunities and privileges of citizenship and liberty. Do I consider it desirable?

I bless emancipation, when I see how the excess of oppression drove Israel away from human intercourse, prevented the cultivation of the mind, limited the free development of the noble sides of character, and compelled many individuals to enter, for the sake of self-support, upon paths which, to be sure men filled with the true spirit of Judaism would have shunned even in the extremest necessity, but the temptation to enter upon which they were too weak to withstand.

I bless emancipation when I notice that no spiritual principle, even such as are born of superstitious self-deception, stands in its way, but only those passions degrading to humanity, lust for gain and narrow selfishness; I rejoice when I perceive that in this concession of emancipation, regard for the inborn rights of men to live as equals among equals, and the principle that whosoever bears the seal of a child of God, unto whom belongs the earth, shall be willingly acknowledged by all as brother, are freely acknowledged without force or compulsion, but purely through the power of their inner truth and demand, as a natural consequence, the sacrifice of the base passions, love of self and gain. I welcome this sacrifice, wherever it is offered, as the dawn of reviving humanity in mankind, as a preliminary step to the universal recognition of God as the only Lord and Father, of all human beings as the children of the All-One, and consequently brethren, and of the earth as soil common to all, and bestowed upon them by God to be administered in accordance with His will.

But for Israel I only bless it if at the same time there awakes in Israel the true spirit, which, independent of emancipation or non-emancipation, strives to fulfill the Israel-mission; to elevate and ennoble ourselves, to implant the spirit of Judaism in our souls, in order that it may produce a life in which that spirit shall be reflected and realized.

I bless it, if Israel does not regard emancipation as the goal of its task, but only as a new condition of its mission, and as a new trial, much severer than the trial of oppression; but I should grieve if Israel understood itself so little, and had so little comprehension of its own spirit that it would welcome emancipation as the end of the *galut*, and the highest goal of its historic mission. If Israel regards this glorious concession merely as a means of securing a greater degree of comfort in life, and greater opportunities for the acquisition of wealth and enjoyments, it would show that Israel had not comprehended the spirit of its own Law, nor learnt aught from the *galut*. But sorrowfully, indeed, would I mourn, if Israel should so far forget itself as to deem emancipation—freedom from unjust oppression and greater opportunity for possession and pleasure—as not too dearly purchased through capricious curtailment of the Torah, capricious abandonment of our inner life. We must become Jews, Jews in the true sense of the word, permitting the spirit of the Law to pervade our entire being, accepting it as the fountain of life spiritual and ethical; then will the spirit of Judaism gladly welcome emancipation as affording a greater chance for the fulfillment of its task, the realization of an ideal life.

A SPIRITUAL NATION

SIMON DUBNOV

Heinrich Graetz (1817-1891), the German-Jewish historian, depicted Jewish history as an intellectual, religious, and literary record of a people and as the annals of suffering and martyrdom. But to Simon Dubnov (1860-1941), his East European counterpart, the Jewish people were "a living national organism," and he saw its Diaspora history as a persistent attempt to maintain and develop internal self-government, or autonomy, and to place cultural, religious, and literary activity in the service of the people's collective existence. By so doing the Jewish people "remained the subject and creator of its history, and this not only in the spiritual sphere but no less in the sphere of its social life in general."

After a series of preparatory works, concentrating especially on the history of Jews in Eastern Europe, Dubnov undertook the presentation of Jewish history in its universality; translated into German from the Russian manuscript, it appeared in ten volumes in 1925 to 1929, under the title *Weltgeschichte des jüdischen Volkes* (*World History of the Jewish People*). His secularist, nationalist, orientation is clearly evident; e.g., in his interpretation of the various Messianic movements as attempts at national liberation and restoration of autonomy. Though conscious of the world historical background of Jewish history, he failed to elaborate on the relationship between the two. His *Die jüdische Geschichte. Ein geschichtsphilosophischer Versuch* (*Jewish History: An Essay in the Philosophy of History*, 1898) discusses the essence of the various historical periods and concludes with the general statement here reprinted.

In 1922, Dubnov left his native country and settled in Germany; in 1933, he fled Germany and moved to Riga, Latvia. When the Germans occupied Riga in 1941, the eighty-one year-old scholar was relegated to the ghetto and shortly afterwards shot to death.

Jewish history possesses the student with the conviction that Jewry at all times, even in the period of political independence, was pre-eminently a spiritual nation, and a spiritual nation it continues to be in our own days, too. Furthermore, it inspires him with the belief that Jewry, being a spiritual entity, cannot suffer annihilation: the body, the mold, may be destroyed, the spirit is immortal. Bereft of country and dispersed as it is, the Jewish nation lives, and will go on living, because a creative principle permeates it, a principle that is the root of its being and an indigenous product of its history. This principle consists first in a sum of definite religious, moral, or philosophic ideals, whose exponent at all times was the Jewish people, either in its totality, or in the person of its most prominent representatives. Next, this principle consists in a sum of historical memories, recollections of what in the course of many centuries the Jewish people experienced, thought, and felt in the depths of its being. Finally, it consists in the consciousness that true Judaism, which has accomplished great things for humanity in the past, has not yet played out its part, and, therefore, may not perish. In short, the Jewish people lives because it contains a living soul which refuses to separate from its integument, and cannot be forced out of it by heavy trials and misfortunes such as would unfailingly inflict mortal injury upon less sturdy organisms.

This self-consciousness is the source from which the suffering Jewish soul draws comfort. History speaks to it constantly through the mouth of the great apostle who went forth from the midst of Israel eighteen hundred years ago: "Call to remembrance the former days, in which, after ye were enlightened, ye endured a great conflict of sufferings; partly, being made a gazing-stock both by reproaches and afflictions; and partly, becoming partakers with them that were so used. [. . .] Cast not away therefore your confidence, which hath great recompense of reward." [9]

Jewish history, moreover, arouses in the Jew the desire to work unceasingly at the task of perfecting himself. To direct his attention to his glorious past, to the resplendent intellectual feats of his ancestors, to their masterly skill in thinking and suffering, does not lull him to sleep, does not awaken a dullard's complacency or hollow self-conceit. On the contrary, it makes exacting demands upon him. Jewish history admonishes the Jews: "Noblesse oblige. The privilege of belonging to a people to whom the honorable title of the 'veteran of history' has been conceded, puts serious responsibilities on your shoulders. You must demonstrate that you are worthy of your heroic past. The descendants of teachers of religion and martyrs of the faith dare not be insignificant, not to say wicked. If the long centuries of wandering and misery have inoculated you with faults, extirpate them in the name of the exalted moral ideals whose bearers you were commissioned to be. If, in the course of time, elements out of harmony with your essential being have fastened upon your mind, cast them out, purify yourselves. In all places and at all times, in joy and in sorrow, you must aim to live for the higher, the spiritual interests. But never may you deem yourselves perfect. If you become faithless to these sacred principles, you sever the bonds that unite you with the most vital elements of your past, with the first cause of your national existence."

The final lesson to be learned is that in the sunny days of mankind's history, in which reason, justice, and philanthropic instinct had the upper hand, the Jews steadfastly made common cause with the other nations. Hand in hand with them, they trod the path leading to perfection. But in the dark days, during the reign of rude force, prejudice, and passion, of which they were the first victims, the Jews retired from the world, withdrew into their shell, to await better days. Union with mankind at large, on the basis of the spiritual and the intellectual, the goal set up by the Jewish prophets in their sublime vision of the future (Isaiah 2, and Micah 4), is the ultimate ideal of Judaism's noblest votaries. Will their radiant hope ever attain to realization?

If ever it should be realized—and it is incumbent upon us to believe that it will—not a slight part of the merits involved will be due to Jewish history. We have adverted to the lofty moral and humanitarian significance of Jewish history in its role as conciliator. With regard to one-half of Jewish history, this conciliatory power is even now a well-established fact. The first part of Jewish history, the Biblical part, is a source from which, for many centuries, millions of human beings belonging to the most diverse denominations have derived instruction, solace, and inspiration. It is read with devotion by Christians in both hemispheres, in their houses and their temples. Its heroes have long ago become types, incarnations of great ideas. The events it relates serve as living ethical formulas. But a time will come—perhaps it is not very far off—when the second half of Jewish history, the record of the two thousand years of the Jewish people's life after the Biblical period, will be accorded the same treatment. This latter part of Jewish history is not yet known, and many, in the thrall of prejudice, do not wish to know it. But ere long it will be known and appreciated. For the thinking portion of mankind it will be a source of uplifting moral and philosophical teaching. The thousand years' martyrdom of the Jewish people, its unbroken pilgrimage, its tragic fate, its teachers of religion, its martyrs, philosophers, champions, this whole epic will in days to come sink deep into the memory of men. It will speak to the heart and the conscience of men, not merely to their curious mind. It will secure respect for the silvery hair of the Jewish people, a people of thinkers and sufferers. It will dispense consolation to the afflicted, and by its examples of spiritual steadfastness and self-denial encourage martyrs in their devotion. It is our firm conviction that the time is approaching in which the second half of Jewish history will be to the noblest part of thinking humanity what its first half has long been to believing humanity, a source of sublime moral truths. In this sense, Jewish history in its entirety is the pledge of the spiritual union between the Jews and the rest of the nations.

WHAT ARE THE JEWS?

ERICH KAHLER

Erich Kahler (born in Prague, 1885) is one of the great contemporary humanists. In *Man the Measure* (1943) he sketched the development of the human element in man and the enfoldment of history, which is to him the biography of man. He believes in "the unity of humanity and the unity of history," in "the consistent development of an organic being that is man." In this belief, he opposes current cynical pessimism. In *The Meaning of History* (1964), he endeavors to restore to modern man "the background of communal memory and the sense of his national, or human, identity, which is history." Within the framework of world history, Kahler turns his attention to the character and the instinctive function of the Jewish people, past the present. In *Israel unter den Völkern* (*Israel Among the Nations*, 1936) he discusses Jewish religion, nationalism, emancipation, assimilation, Westernization, and contribution to history. The excerpt that follows is taken from the essay "Forms and Features of Anti-Judaism" (*Social Research* VI, 1939).

Kahler's other works include *Das Geschlecht Habsburg* (*The Habsburg Dynasty*, 1919), *Der deutsche Character in der Geschichte Europas* (*The German Character in European History*, 1937), *The Tower and the Abyss* (1957), and two volumes of poetry (1903, 1905). In 1938 Kahler came to the United States and taught history at the New School for Social Research in New York; since 1949 he has been a member of the Institute of Advanced Study in Princeton.

We have surveyed the mutations of hatred against the Jews through thousands of years, we have seen how it began and how it developed. Yet none of this can furnish a completely satisfactory explanation of a phenomenon unique in history. Not all the single motivations we have encountered in the course of our review— whether real or spurious—can account for it, but only the composite character, the unique social structure of the people to which it attaches.

This people has offended, to begin with, simply by the unusual fact that it still exists, that it has maintained itself beyond its territorial existence; that is to say, that it has at the same time remained intact and been absorbed by the rest of the world. The great peoples of the Far East, the Chinese and the Hindus, are as old as the Jews, but they have their own enormous countries where their tremendous inexterminable populations have stayed forever. Buddhism became a world religion, yet retained its own wide territories, as has Arabic Islam.

The Jews have always been numerically a small people, which despite the most stubborn defense, could not maintain its tiny homeland against the conquering nations which overran it. Their territorial destruction would have been inevitable even if their religion had not from the very outset had so spiritual a basis, so inimical to the power of the state. By virtue of this spiritual basis, however, they raised themselves, for all their weakness, above the nations by which they were subdued. They gave birth to one world religion, Christianity, and to a large extent shaped a second, that of Islam. They had an alternative—to be absorbed by these universal religions and missions. They did not accept it, not only because of the unconditional spirituality of their religious idea, but also because of their stubborn insistence on their ritual laws. The fact that the Jews, dispersed over the entire globe, have maintained themselves to the present day is based solely on the indissoluble union of a strictly spiritual and universal religious idea with strict physical adherence to ritual. The ritual was the means to the physical survival of the people because an abstract law, particularly one of such ethical severity, cannot possibly hold the masses together. Some physical prompting is needed, some magic sign in the midst of daily life. Yet the ritual alone, without the consecration of the spiritual law, would have become meaningless and obsolete; it would have perished like any pagan cult.

The union of the two, however, cannot have been brought about by any rational deliberations on the part of the founders and priests of Israel. It is an elemental fact, beyond any rational plans. It is the expression of a definite folk structure. The Jewish people is a social organism which has its roots in the earliest strata of

human society, and which in its ramifications extends into the ultimate, into an almost utopian future of mankind. This does not
mean that there is such a thing as a Jewish "race." The conception
of race is in itself untenable—a pure original race of the genus
Homo has never been proved to exist. The Jewish people is in any
case a mixture of diverse anthropological components. But it is no
nation either. For "nation" is a term that can be applied only to a
purely secular folk organism whose life centers not in a special
inherited religion or a theocratic realm, but in a completely
worldly form of government and cultural development. Nations
are folk structures which came about *after* the development, and
under the aegis of, a world religion, as did France, England and
Germany. The substance of the French nation has nothing to do
with religion, however great the influence of Christianity on its
development. Its basic elements are its language, its countryside,
its forms of government, its folk type and the manifestations of its
social and intellectual civilization.

A common substratum for Jewry, however, is unthinkable without its inherited religion, for to Jewry religion is not a creed existing independent of it and apart from it, but developed step by
step with the development of this folk type itself. A social structure such as this may be called a tribe. Lévy Bruhl in his investigations of the mentality of primitive peoples accurately describes
the development of religion from the life of primitive man. He
shows how the entire existence of the early tribes is permeated by
a mystic and magical "participation" of its individual members
with each other, with the tribe as a whole, and with the cosmic
forces in the world, and how every gesture of daily life assumes a
mystic, a magical and sacred significance. [10] The creation of what
we call religion is equivalent to the objectivation of a life source,
a world-governing and life-giving deity, and to the differentiation
and separation of man from this objectified life center. And ritual
preserves for us the magical and mystic formalities of the relation
between man and deity.

The revelation and the Law of the Jewish God as well as the
covenant he makes with Israel are nothing but such an objectiva-

tion. The rite of circumcision, for example, the consecration of the genitals, is the sign of man's surrender to the deity, of the covenant sealed with blood which he makes with deity.[11] The life of the orthodox Jew is completely enveloped in ritual forms the original meaning of which he no longer knows at all, but which have become so much part and parcel of him that even an involuntary violation causes a profound disturbance in the very foundation of his life. To understand the life of the orthodox Jew one must appreciate the full spiritual power of taboo, one must realize that among primitive tribes a man who violates a dietary law really dies as a result.[12] The life cycle of the Jewish people goes way back to this primitive time, and it is because their roots go so deep that the Jews have been able to preserve their universal God and their ethical Law through all of time and all their exile.

All ancient peoples, the Chinese, the Indians, the Arabs, reach back into that early time, but not one of them lives scattered among the western nations, and not one of them has at the same time a vanguard at the farthest front of modern civilization. The Jewish people as it exists at present combines within itself every stage of human development. Today at the northern edge of the Sahara there are still Bedouin Jews living like their patriarchal ancestors. They celebrate the great feast days at the burial mound of a celebrated rabbi, together with Tunisian, Moroccan, Egyptian Jews, they gallop up, shoot their rifles into the air and shout "Shalom!" (Peace!)[13] There are talmudic Jews living in the midst of European peoples and in America; one can recognize them by their special garb, their kaftans, beards and side curls, and by their minute observance of the ritual law. There are the scholar scribes who continue to interpret and expound the Law as has been the custom since Babylonian times. And there are the scholars of modern science: Einstein, Freud, Ehrlich[14] and Bergson.[15] There are the small dealers and peddlers from the time of the ghetto, and the bankers and industrialists of our own era. There are the members of the international aristocracy, the Rothschilds and Sassoons,[16] and the masses of the Jewish proletariat in eastern Europe and in New York, laborers and handworkers, as well as the farmers in the new Palestine. There are extreme nationalists, European and Zionist, there are Christians and there are Marxists.

When one considers these many differences of a social, ethical and intellectual kind and realizes the gulf the Jews have bridged from the tenacious kernel of orthodoxy to world wide principles of social betterment in which all peculiarly Jewish features have been even more completely obliterated than in Christendom; when one bears in mind the status of hopeless minority in which the Jews have lived everywhere and at all times, and the collective responsibility which they have perpetually borne; when one thinks of the fanatic spirituality which the Jews have translated from the severity of their Law into their modern theories and even into all their sacrifices for the welfare of humanity—when one views all this in its entirety and remembers at the same time the violent attack of paganism even against the patient Christian churches, one can appreciate what an enormous field of attack Judaism offers to a world racked by hatred and economic crises.

The suffering of the Jews was prophesied from the beginning;[17] their history, strangely enough, begins with an exodus. The prophecy at the same time heralds the meaning of their suffering, of their mission in behalf of mankind: they are to fulfil God's kingdom of brotherly love on earth. Under this twofold sign stands Israel's covenant with the Creator, that fusion of tribal particularity and abstract universality. Herein is the full, the only significance of Israel's vocation as God's "chosen people," which has been set down to a prideful aloofness from the rest of the world for which the Jews have been tormented all the more. It is all an endless circle in which cause and effect can no longer be distinguished.

The Jews, on the average, are no better than other peoples—that was never the meaning of "chosen." But they have suffered more than all other peoples, and the more they are made to suffer, the greater the distinction conferred upon them. Such an excess of suffering through thousands of years must have special historical significance. But here we face the bounds where understanding ends and faith begins.

JACOB-ISRAEL AND THE WORLD

YITZHAK LAMDAN

The Russian-born Yitzhak Lamdan (1900-1954), who settled in Palestine in 1920, belongs to the group of outstanding
post-World War I Hebrew poets that includes such men as
Avigdor Hameiri, Uri Zevi Greenberg, Abraham Shlonsky, and
Sh. Shalom. Lamdan's poem "Masada" (1927) portrays the
Jewish pioneer (*Halutz*) as the last-ditch fighter for Jewish survival. His "For the Sun Declined," from which our quotation is
taken, has the Biblical Jacob rebel against the special divine
love which must bring upon him isolation from "the world,"
a fate resulting from Israel's election. The excerpt is translated
by Simon Halkin.

Thou hast plucked me out of the heart of the world,
　　away from all its hues and tinges,
So that I be yours alone, and only with you, with you!
Let me be! I will not be dragged perforce any more
To the gallows of thy love, O Lover and Seducer!
As one, the only chosen one, I am called to thee,
And by the time I come—I am misshapen—crippled;
"Jacob, Jacob!" No, I will not come and listen,
And be once more scorned of man, yet beloved of God.

If you have some matter to impart to me, a great and
　　precious matter of love—
Stretch it at my feet as a verdant carpet of spring;
Light it up over my head as a blazing morning-rose.
Let its music sing in a myriad voices that all, that
　　all, may hear;
Bejewel with it thy stars at night; thy sun by day,
And let the butterflies of all thy world frolic with it.

Otherwise, neither love, thy love, nor the pain it
　　spells!
Let me be, that I may move among the least of the world;
Unaware, like all of them, let me walk the roads of life,

A slave to the toil of day, free—to night's rest;
One thread out of many, woven unbeknown,
Into the web of being, both radiant and somber.

JUDAISM AND MANKIND

ABRAHAM GEIGER

The German-Jewish theologian Abraham Geiger (1810-1874) is justly considered to be the most important exponent of religious reform in nineteenth century Central Europe. He defined modern Judaism as a community of faith that has freed itself of the vestiges of the past, peoplehood, ritual laws, and dependence on tradition. Central in his concept of Judaism is prophetic humanism and Messianic universalism. Only later in his life did he admit, in ever greater measure, the relevance of the Jewish historic experience as a basis of reform. In Jewish intellectual history he recognized gradually unfolding religious ideas; there is no set and ready system of Judaism, he counseled, only constant change, adaptation, and refinement. Approaching Judaism and its basic documents, the Bible and the Talmud, in this spirit, he endeavored to effect not merely certain changes in religious practice, but a sweeping religious renaissance of German Jewry; at the same time, he wished to free Judaism from its isolation from the rest of civilized humanity.

Geiger's work as a reformer was grounded in broad and solid scholarship. He is the author of *Urschrift und Übersetzungen der Bibel* (*The Original Text and Translations of the Bible in Their Relation to the Inner Development of Judaism*, 1857, rev., 1928), *Salomon Gabirol und seine Dichtungen* (*Solomon ibn Gabirol and His Poems*, 1867), and numerous essays in the *Jüdische Zeitschrift für Wissenschaft und Leben*, a periodical which he edited from 1863 to 1874. He served as liberal rabbi in various communities and, finally, in Berlin. Through his efforts, an Academy for Jewish Research (Hochschule für die Wissenschaft des Judentums) was established in Berlin in 1872. There he taught Jewish history and literature. His *Allgemeine Einleitung in die Wissenschaft des Judenthums* (*General Introduction to the Science of Judaism*) is based on lectures in this

Academy. His influence on Jewish religious liberalism in Western Europe and America has been profound and lasting. To a wider audience Geiger addressed his *Das Judenthum und seine Geschichte* (1864 and 1871, partly translated in *Judaism and Its History* [1911]). In the concluding chapter, Geiger points to the mid-eighteenth century as the turning point from an age of hostility and persecution to an age of humanism. Then he continues:

How the time will develop farther, how mankind will form itself in that wrestling, is not in doubt for the presentient eye, spying into the distance. The mind of mankind is striving upward, the nations altogether as individual members of one great body of humanity will be illuminated by the real, divine spirit, all mutually promoting, strengthening, and purifying each other, and religion will appear as the energy of life, rejuvenated as the noblest flower of wisdom in the minds. Whether it will be that religion which has inherited the power, whether it will be able to work up to the full height of accomplishing its reconciliation with the live, political spirit and with science—to render a final verdict on that, may be left to the future. At any rate, Judaism, since it is permitted to enter into the full movement of the world's history, has rejuvenated its spirit, received science, and has partly broken through the bars which excluded it as mere national faith from the rest of mankind. That change of form and mental transformation of Judaism is a fact which it has already accomplished during the narrow, only gradually widening opening of its jail gates, a fact out of the history of the last, painful century which is graven with shining lines into the tablets of history.

Animated by the breath of complete liberty, constantly more and more imbued with the spirit of science and widening and deepening the view, Judaism of the present will steadily become more and more conscious of its task and strive for its accomplishment, a task which corresponds as much to all deeper endeavor of the present as it is deeply rooted in its own basic essence: to become the religion of mankind. Only that religion which is reconciled with free thought has the justification, but at the same time also, the guarantee of its continuance. On the contrary, every religion which makes battle against the right of the mind will be crushed under the wheels of time. Only that religion which carries the guarantee of its future within itself, which considers it its task to spend its blessings to all mankind, and therefore presents itself to the totality in a form fit for it, not one that confines itself to a narrow circle, withdraws into a cell, bars itself from the rest of mankind as if that were a soulless or alien body and is absorbed by preference into its own petty interests. Judaism will always bear in mind that it is called to strive for the goal, even if that can not be brought about by us alone, that God will be acknowledged as one, and His name as one

FAITH

ABRAHAM ISAAC KOOK

Abraham Isaac Kook (1865-1935), Russian-born talmudic scholar, became rabbi of Jaffa, Palestine, in 1904; Chief Rabbi of Jerusalem in 1919; and in 1921, Ashkenazic Chief Rabbi of Palestine. During this period the country changed from a land of pious old pilgrims and sacred memories to a land of modern young men and women, the majority of whom were indifferent to religion. Kook "became the link between the two worlds; he bridged them in his own personality" (Samuel H. Bergman). Behind the differences of background and outlook, behind the diversity and contradiction manifested in the visible world, he sensed an underlying spiritual unity. "Everything is part of a larger order and of a realm of which God is King." Separation between men, and within man, and man's separation from God, he taught, are occasioned by one cardinal sin: forgetfulness. Man forgets God as the source of all reality, and, with this forgetfulness forgets also his own roots. But "the power of *teshuvah* (return) permits everything to return and to reunite with the full reality of divine perfection." Kook believed that every nation had developed a special talent; Israel—and that includes each and every Jew—"has the capacity for discovering the divine light in every aspect of reality."

This mystic doctrine (based, in part, on hasidic teachings)

had an important practical effect: it helped to reduce the tension between the old world and the new.

Among Kook's works are *Orot ha-Kodesh* (*The Lights of Holiness*) and a *Commentary to the Prayer Book*. We quote a collection of excerpts from his works.

Faith is the song of life. Woe to him who wishes to rob life of its splendid poetry. The whole mass of prosaic literature and knowledge is of value only when it is founded on the perception of the poetry of life.

Faith and love are the very essence of life. There would be nothing of value left in the travail of life if these two luminaries, faith and love, were taken from it.

Contemporary civilization throughout the world is founded entirely on unbelief and hate, forces which nullify the essence of life. It is impossible to overcome this disease of modern society unless we discover the good that is contained in faith and love. The Torah and the divine precepts are the channels through which faith and love flow unceasingly.

All the troubles of the world, especially the ills of the soul such as sadness, impatience, disgust with life and despair are due only to the failure of knowing how to face the majesty of God in utter surrender.

Death is an illusion. Fear of death, the universal disease of mankind, stems from sin. All the labors of man center round his desire to escape death, but he cannot achieve his goal without first enriching his soul in the direction of its inner source.

The Torah and all its precepts form a great and mighty divine poem of trust and love. Because of our reverence and affection for the people of Israel, we lovingly observe the customs of Israel, even if they are not wholly based on divine revelation. This affection of ours is sacred, derived from a high and divine source.

The basic principle of the observance of the rules and regulations introduced by our sages is the fact that all Israel has accepted them. The honor of our nation and its historical influence are embodied in them. Hence, whatever is more ancient is more beloved, since the will and the general character of the people are revealed in it.

A wonderful vital force is hidden in the heart of each Jew, which impels him to attach himself to his people, whose life stream flows within him. This subconscious impulse makes him share the powerful yearning for the pure and uplifting light of truth and divine equity, a yearning that is bound to be realized some day in actual life.

The Jewish precepts, practices and customs are the vessels which contain a few sparks from the great light from above. The vital force of the Torah will do its work in the innermost being of him who clings to its precepts, even though that person remains unaware of its operation. The moment a man desires to have a share in the spirit of Israel, the divine spirit enters his aspirations, even in spite of himself. All the possessions of Israel are suffused with the indwelling spirit of God: its land, its language, its history and its customs.

Prayer is an absolute necessity for us and for the whole world; it is also the most sacred kind of joy. The waves of our soul beat ceaselessly on the shores of consciousness. We desire of ourselves and of the whole world the kind of perfection that the limitation of existence renders impossible. In our despair and frustration we are likely to turn against our better judgment and against our Creator. But before this cancer of the spirit has had time enough to grow in our midst, we come to pray. We give utterance to our thoughts and are uplifted to a world of perfect existence. Thus our inner world is rendered perfect in truth, and restful joy fills our consciousness.

Every plant and bush, every grain of sand and clod of earth, everything in which life is revealed or hidden, the smallest and the biggest in creation—all longs and yearns and reaches out toward its celestial source. And at every moment, all these cravings are gathered up and absorbed by man, who is himself lifted up by the longing for holiness within him. It is during prayer that all these pent-up desires and yearning are released. Through his prayer, man unites in himself all being, and lifts all creation up to the fountainhead of blessing and life.

Every sin brings about a particular type of trembling in the soul (which does not cease until repentance has been made). It is possible to detect this trembling in the lines of the face, in gestures, in the voice, in the handwriting or style of language and speech. The defect is to be observed precisely where the sin has walled off the light. When man repents out of love, the cosmic light of the world of unity shines upon him and everything is joined in oneness; evil joins with the good and raises it to even a higher value.

The sage is more important than the prophet. What prophecy, with all its militant and fiery weapons, failed to do, the sages accomplished by developing many students and by the repeated study of the Torah and all its laws. In time, the efforts of the sages overshadowed the words of the prophets, and prophecy itself disappeared. But it shall come to pass in the latter days that the light of prophecy shall return, as it is written: "I shall pour forth my spirit upon all flesh" (Joel 3:1). Prophecy shall recognize the great accomplishments of the sages and declare: "The sage is greater than the prophet." [2]

THE VOICE OF JACOB

RICHARD BEER-HOFMANN

The Vienna-born poet, dramatist, and novelist Richard Beer-Hofmann (1866-1945) was one of the very few of his class and country to whom Judaism was a living force, a persistent spiritual challenge. What he wrote of Theodor Herzl is true of himself: "At last, once again a human being who does not bear his Judaism resignedly as a burden or as a misfortune, but who, on the contrary, is proud to be among the legitimate heirs of an ancient culture." Among his few but exquisite writings are the novel *Der Tod Georgs* (*The Death of George*, 1900); the tragedy *Der Graf von Charolais* (*The Count of Charolais*, 1904); *Jaakobs Traum* (*Jacob's Dream*, 1915), and *Der junge David* (*Young David*, 1933), both Biblical dramas. The theme of *Jacob's Dream* is Israel's election. Jacob is the visionary, the seeker; he wrestles with God; he suffers with all suffering creatures and meets them in boundless compassion. His brother

Edom, on the other hand, is firmly rooted in the earth; he has
power; he rejoices in the certainty of his knowledge and his
satiety. But, in the divine scheme of things, both are essential.
And: "Only because you are Edom may I be Jacob." To be
Jacob means to give a divine answer to man's questions.

JACOB

[*Trembling with grief*]

Must ye ask indeed?
Do ye not know—does God not know of me?
Did I not grow up ever turned towards Him
Ready for Him—a chalice—opened wide?
Three generations He has hovered round us . . .
Knows He not yet my blood? Would He insist
That shameless now my stammering lips avow
What He must know?
[*With deeply hurt pride*]
Was't but to heap gifts on us
He chose us, promised glory, power and wealth?
Finds He no use for us but to be kings?
I will not rule! Does He not know?
Mitzraim,³ Babel and the sea-land's princes—
Can He believe I envy them their gain?
NAUGHT do I envy—not your bliss, nor you . . .
[*His voice filled with pain*]
Could I rejoice when all things suffer pain?
All come to me, by day, by night in dreams,
Green herbage of the earth, man, beast and stone
Plead for an answer with dumb eyes complaining,
Asking me—yet all answer is His own!
[*He looks to the Angels, as if asking help*]
'T was but for this—it seemed—to me, a boy,
That He sent all on earth that suffers pain.
[*Softly, as if sharing a secret*]
Majestic, fearful in His far seclusion,
He to remotest heavens himself exiled . . .
So has He chosen my seed to be a plant,

To flourish through all time and proudly grow—
  [*With growing confidence*]
That from my mouth—renewed for ever more
The word of His eternal will may flow!
For this He broke asunder bridge and path
'Twixt me and the uncaring bloom of youth,
That I—a man—may tread for aye on earth
The distant way God treads, the way of truth,
And with His word resolving every pain
Speak ever for Him and proclaim His worth!

A MINORITY RELIGION

LEO BAECK

Rabbi, scholar, and religious thinker, Leo Baeck (1873-1956) was destined to become chief spokesman and representative of German Jewry during the Hitler years. Imbued with deep, quiet faith and unafraid, he set an example of courage and dignity to the imperiled Jewish communities and, from 1943 onward, in the concentration camp in Theresienstadt. During this period he put into practice the tenets which in previous years he had formulated in his writings, sermons, and lectures at the Berlin *Hochschule für die Wissenschaft des Judentums*, a liberal theological seminary.

In 1905 Baeck published *Das Wesen des Judentums* (*The Essence of Judaism*) in response to Adolf von Harnack's *Das Wesen des Christentums* (*The Essence of Christianity*, 1900). Influenced by Kant and Neo-Kantianism, he affirmed the central position of the ethical commandment in Judaism and its stress on the realization of this commandment in life—private, communal, and political. In Jewish religious experience, he wrote, "commandment" (*Gebot*) is complemented by "mystery" (*Geheimnis*). The root of Judaism's vitality is the tension between order and freedom, God's nearness (in the commandment) and His otherness (in the mystery); the commandment itself points to mystery as its origin. Yet, "the primary quality of Judaism is moral action."

After his liberation from the concentration camp at the end of the war, Baeck lived in England and in the United States, taught, helped in the postwar reconstruction, and continued writing on the religious meaning of Jewish experience.

Only through this personal connection with and working for the task of religion, can the individual become a true member of the community. To belong to it fully he must realize his faith through his actions. Thus alone can a minority be equal to its religious task, which is why the commandment to sanctify God's name occupies a central position in Judaism. Upon each individual is imposed the full weight of missionary duty; he holds in his hands the reputation of the entire community; and to him applies that saying of Hillel: "If I am here, then everyone is here." [4] The commandment has a claim on everyone and refers to everyone, including the most humble. And the fact of always being in the minority intensifies and spiritualizes the ethical task: each single member is to conduct his life so that the "kingdom of priests" is realized on earth.

Every individual thus creates the religion and establishes its significance. Here we find again that peculiarity of Jewish religiousness—it commands man and attributes to him the power of creation. In Christianity, the individual is borne by the Church; it existed prior to him and is more than he; he stands in its faith and lives through it. But in Judaism there is no Church, there is only the community which takes shape through the actions of the individual; it is subsequent to and exists through him; he is its bearer. Wherever there are Jews, no matter how few, fulfilling the commandments of their religion, there is a Jewish community; the whole of Judaism exists there. A Church always tries to be a Church of the many and in the end it yields to the temptation of power; thus far no Church has escaped that fate. But the community can always be a community of the few, each and every one of whom share their religion. The community is a union of strength for the sanctification of God's name; its genius is to be small in order to be great.

Often it seems that the special task of Judaism is to express the idea of the community standing alone, the ethical principle of the minority. Judaism bears witness to the power of the idea as against the power of mere numbers and worldly success; it stands for the enduring protest of those who seek to be true to their own selves, who assert their right to be different against the crushing pressure of the vicious and the leveling. This too is a way of constant preaching to the world.

By its mere existence Judaism is a never silent protest against the assumption of the multitude that force is superior to truth. So long as Judaism exists, nobody will be able to say that the soul of man has surrendered. Its very existence through the ages is proof that conviction cannot be mastered by numbers. The mere fact that Judaism exists proves the invincibility of the spirit, and though it may sometimes assume the appearance of an extinct volcano—Judaism has often been depicted in that image—there yet dwells a power in it which quietly renews itself and stirs it to fresh activity. From the few, who remain so for the sake of God, there emanate the great and decisive tendencies in history. With regard to this fact alone one is often tempted to adapt a well-known phrase by saying: "If Judaism did not exist, we should have to invent it." Without minorities there can be no world-historic goal.

And just because it was always a minority, Judaism has become a standard of measurement of the level of morality. How the Jewish community was treated by the nations among which it lived has always been a measure of the extent to which right and justice prevailed; for the measure of justice is always its application to the few. What Israel, which gave its faith to mankind, receives in turn is also a measure of the development of religion. In Israel's lot one can see how far off are the days of the Messiah. Only when Israel can live securely among the nations will the promised time have arrived, for then it will be proved that belief in God has become a living reality. Not only its ideas and its character indicate the significance of Judaism; its history among the nations is equally important. This history is itself a deed.

It requires religious courage to belong to a minority such as Judaism always has been and always will be; for many days will come and go before the Messianic time arrives. It requires ethical courage to be a Jew when all worldly comforts, honors and prizes lure him to the other side, and often the Jew has to fight the battle between ideas and interests, between belief and unbelief.

If it is the peculiarity of the Jewish spirit to be rooted in conscience and in the fear of God, not merely to want to see but to see the right, not merely to know but to know the good; if it therefore has the capacity of not surrendering to passing days or ages; if it has the strength of resistance against all powers and multitudes which seek only to rule and oppress; if its peculiar nature is thus always to continue seeking, never believing that it has found the end; if it implies that persistence in the knowledge of the commandment, that never tiring will for the ideal, that gift to comprehend the revelation of God, to see the future and call men toward it, to rally the many into unity—if indeed all this is peculiar to the Jewish spirit, then there is here the ultimate meaning of Jewish religiousness.

But this peculiarity has been developed through the lives of those who in the name of their God always had the will to live in opposition to the many, and who, in order not to become estranged from him, endured estrangement upon earth. Whoever is a Jew has long lived contrary to his advantage and under difficulties with regard to his life's career. If he remains loyal to his religion, it can only be for the sake of the religion. In the mere adherence to Judaism there is a core of idealism; it means—with all the tension and paradox that is in Jewish character—a style of its own in the world.

Humanity is possessed of different styles, by whose variety it seeks to express itself. Personalities have arisen, now in this people and now in that, through whom mankind strove to speak. Many of these men lived at the periphery of the life of their people, despising them; many have fought for their people; and many wearied of the fight. The great men of the Jewish people have fought for it to the last; they penetrated their people to the marrow, imposing on them a distinctive stamp. No people is heir to such a revelation as the Jews possess; no people has had such a weight of divine commandment laid upon it; and for this reason no people has been so exposed to difficult and exacting times. This in-heritage has not always been realized, but it is one that will endure, awaiting its hour. Judah ha-Levi,[5] who saw into the soul of the Jewish people and the Jewish religion as few men have, meant just this when he said that the prophecy is alive in this people and that for this reason this people will live. The Jews are a nation, and at the same time, in their innermost being, a community—it is impossible for them to be the one without being the other; it is not enough that communities should exist among them —they must themselves, all of them together, be the community. The Jews exist in and for Judaism; the great We of knowledge and will finds its utterance in it.

Judaism lies open for all to see. We acknowledge the treasures possessed by other religions, especially by those that sprung from our midst. He who holds convictions will respect the convictions of others. Filled with reverence for its tasks, we Jews realize what our religion really means. We know that there can be applied to it the words of one of the old Jewish sages: "The beginning bears witness to the end, and the end will at long last bear witness to the beginning." [6]

THOU SHALT

LEO BAECK

On Leo Baeck, see the prefaces to *Judaism: A Minority Religion*, and *A Prayer Before Kol Nidre, Germany, 1935*. The passages here reproduced are from an article, "Why Jews in the World? A Reaffirmation of Faith in Israel's Destiny," which was one of the first Baeck wrote after his liberation from the Theresienstadt concentration camp.

It was through Judaism that ethical dynamism entered the world. Judaism first experienced that great unconditional "thou shalt" which the one God speaks. This "thou shalt" arises from the very foundation of reality, and it presents reality to man, the full and fundamental reality. One can and may doubt everything—and what is there that has not been doubted in Judaism?—except "thou shalt." Everything may be questioned—and what is there that has not been questioned in Judaism, or submitted to varying interpretations?—except "thou shalt."

The one God is known and understood in the "thou shalt"; when the "thou shalt" is denied and rejected God is denied and rejected. And because the great "thou shalt" contains the reality, it also contains the great hope: thus hope itself becomes a commandment, hope too becomes an unconditional, categorical postulation. Thou shalt hope! Revelation, ethical task, and promise are here one. This is the revelation, the "logos" of God, the totality of the commandment, the Torah, which, according to ancient simile, was "before the creation of the world." [7] [. . .]

The *one* God says to man "thou shalt." Double morality, double law, the double way are equal to polytheism, idolatry. The foundation is in the one God, fully in him and in nothing else but him, and no utility, no power, no politics, no convenience, may claim to be that foundation. In the "thou shalt" man experiences most intensely who he is, and comes to know most vividly his own personality, his individual self, and the peculiarity or uniqueness of his own life.

This is the deepest root of the Jewish religion: the individuality, the personality, the identity is bound up with the foundation of all being and all commandment. That is why this religion can never be a mere matter that is administered—neither a matter of state, as it was deemed in former times, nor a private matter, as was held later on, in the justifiable struggle against state religion. This religion cannot be something next to something else, for it expresses the substance and essence of man and of the individual. What is at stake in this religion is the self, the I, the ever-growing self, which has the certainty of possessing not simply a sequence of days but an individual life of its own. The great "thou shalt" which the one God speaks to everyone makes man truly man, makes his life truly *the* life. [. . .]

The *whole* man is the man who has "the whole heart, the whole soul, the whole might," [8] the man wholly himself, with an individuality, a personality. There is only one individuality, the one that is creative, and the man who fulfills God's commandment is creative, for he makes reality real, creates reality. And everyone is endowed with this genius, this creative power, this possibility of creating reality. And this too is the freedom vested in everyone, for there is only one fundamental freedom—ethical freedom, the freedom that creates reality. There is no freedom by gift—only the possibility of such freedom is given, only this creative, ethical freedom, this fulfillment of the individuality. Without it political and civic freedom would lack all foundation. And it is in this fundamental thing, in the demand that individuality and freedom be acquired and proven, that Judaism pre-eminently expresses its peculiarity—even more, its formative principle.

GOD AND MAN

MARTIN BUBER

The work of Martin Buber (b. 1878) is both a reinterpretation of classical Judaic thought and an affirmation of a modern thinker's personal philosophy, with the two components subtly blended and interrelated. To neglect or diminish the importance of either is to misrepresent Buber's uniqueness in modern intellectual history. He finds in Judaic sources (Biblical, talmudic and hasidic) a pivotal concern with individual man and his need to enter into relationship to the other person and, ultimately, to God, and to establish a community in which such relatedness can be realized; he discerns the same need as man's focal aspiration in modern society, where the individual is imperiled by forces which tend to make him expendable, replaceable, a mere cipher. In this point Buber's investigations of the spiritual history of Judaism have a natural continuation in his works on present-day problems, and *vice versa*.

Furthermore, Buber cuts across the time-honored distinction between the sacred and the secular, the life of faith and the life of the frail moment. His concept of man is a genuinely religious one; but he does not confine its realization to the realm called "religious" or to special seasons called "sacred." Such realization is to encompass the whole range of human life.

A bibliography of Buber's writings (1897-1957) enumerates

857 titles. Possibly the best known of these are his *I and Thou* (1937; the original German edition appeared in 1923) and *The Tales of the Hasidim* (1947-1948; German, 1906 seq.). The article that follows is an address he delivered at a Christian conference in 1930.

I see the soul of Judaism as elliptically turning round two centers.

One center of the Jewish soul is the primeval experience that God is wholly raised above man, that he is beyond the grasp of man, and yet that he is present in an immediate relationship with these human beings who are absolutely incommensurable with him, and that he faces them. To know both these things at the same time, so that they cannot be separated, constitutes the living core of every believing Jewish soul: to know both, "God in heaven," that is, in complete hiddenness, and man "on earth," that is, in the fragmentation of the world of his senses and his understanding; God in the perfection and incomprehensibility of his being, and man in the abysmal contradiction of this strange existence from birth to death—and between both, immediacy!

The pious Jews of pre-Christian times called their God "Father": and when the naively pious Jew in Eastern Europe uses that name today, he does not repeat something which he has learned, but he expresses a realization which he has come upon himself of the fatherhood of God and the sonship of man. It is not as though these men did not know that God is also utterly distant; it is rather that they know at the same time that however far away God is, he is never unrelated to them, and that even the man who is farthest away from God cannot cut himself off from the mutual relationship. In spite of the complete distance between God and man, they know that when God created man, he set the mark of his image upon man's brow, and embedded it in man's nature, and that however faint God's mark may become, it can never be entirely wiped out.

According to hasidic legend, when the Baal Shem[9] conjured up the demon Sammael, he showed him this mark on the forehead of his disciples, and when the master bade the conquered demon begone, the latter prayed, "Sons of the living God, permit me to remain a little while to look at the mark of the image of

God on your faces." God's real commandment to man is to realize this image.

"Fear of God," accordingly, never means to the Jews that they ought to be afraid of God, but that, trembling, they ought to be aware of his incomprehensibility. The fear of God is the creaturely knowledge of the darkness to which none of our spiritual powers can reach, and out of which God reveals himself. Therefore, "the fear of God" is rightly called "the beginning of knowledge" (Ps. 111:10). It is the dark gate through which man must pass if he is to enter into the love of God. He who wishes to avoid passing through this gate, he who begins to provide himself with a comprehensible God, constructed thus and not otherwise, runs the risk of having to despair of God in view of the actualities of history and life, or of falling into inner falsehood. Only through the fear of God does man enter so deep into the love of God that he cannot be cast out of it.

But fear of God is just a gate; it is not a house in which one can comfortably settle down—he who should want to live in it in adoration would neglect the performance of the essential commandment. God is incomprehensible, but he can be known through a bond of mutual relationship. God cannot be fathomed by knowledge, but he can be imitated. The life of man, who is unlike God, can yet be an *imitatio Dei*. "The likeness" is not closed to the "unlike." This is exactly what is meant when the Scripture instructs man to walk in God's way and in his footsteps. Man cannot by his own strength complete any way or any piece of the way, but he can enter on the path, he can take that first step, and again and again that first step. Man cannot "be like unto God," but with all the inadequacy of each of his days, he can follow God at all times, using the capacity he has on that particular day—and if he has used the capacity of that day to the full, he has done enough. This is not a mere act of faith; it is an entering into the life that has to be lived on that day with all the active fulness of a created person. This activity is within man's capacity; uncurtailed and not to be curtailed, the capacity is present through all the generations. God concedes the might to abridge this central property of decision to no primordial "fall," however far-reaching in its effects, for the intention of God the Creator is mightier than the sin of men. The Jew knows from his knowledge of creation and of creatureliness that there may be burdens inherited from prehistoric and historic times, but that there is no overpowering "original sin" which could prevent the late-comer from deciding as freely as did Adam; as freely as Adam let God's hand go, the late-comer can clasp it. We are dependent on grace; but we do not do God's will when we take it upon ourselves to begin with grace instead of beginning with ourselves. Only our beginning, our having begun, poor as it is, leads us to grace. God made no tools for himself, he needs none; he created for himself a partner in the dialogue of time, and one who is capable of holding converse.

In this dialogue, God speaks to every man through the life which he gives him again and again. Therefore man can only answer God with the whole of life—with the way in which he lives this given life. The Jewish teaching of the wholeness of life is the other side of the Jewish teaching of the unity of God. Because God bestows not only spirit on man, but the whole of his existence, from its "lowest" to its "highest" levels, man can fulfil the obligations of his partnership with God by no spiritual attitude, by no worship, on no sacred upper story; the whole of life is required, every one of its areas and every one of its circumstances. There is no true human share of holiness without the hallowing of the everyday. Whilst Judaism unfolds itself through the history of its faith, and so long as it does unfold itself through that history, it holds out against that "religion" which is an attempt to assign a circumscribed part to God, in order to satisfy him who bespeaks and lays claim to the whole. But this unfolding of Judaism is really an unfolding, and not a metamorphosis.

To clarify our meaning, we take the sacrificial cultus as an example. One of the two fundamental elements in Biblical animal sacrifice is the sacralization of the natural life: he who slaughters an animal consecrates a part of it to God, and so doing hallows his eating of it. The second fundamental element is the sacramentalization of the complete surrender of life. To this element belong those types of sacrifice in which the person who offers the sacrifice puts his hands on the head of the animal in order to identify himself with it; in doing so he gives physical expression to the thought that he is bringing himself to be sacrificed in the person of the animal. He who performs these sacrifices without having this intention in his soul makes the cult meaningless, yes, absurd; it was against him that the prophets directed their attack upon the sacrificial service which had been emptied of its core. In the Judaism of the Diaspora, prayer takes the place of sacrifice; but prayer is also offered for the reinstatement of the cult, that is, for the return of the holy unity of body and spirit. And in that consummation of Diaspora Judaism which we call hasidic piety, both fundamental elements unite into a new conception which fulfils the original meaning of the cult. When the purified and sanctified man, in purity and holiness, takes food into himself, eating becomes a sacrifice, the table an altar, and man consecrates himself to the deity. At that point, there is no longer a gulf between the natural and the sacral; at that point, there is no longer the need for a substitute; at that point the natural event itself becomes a sacrament.

The holy strives to include within itself the whole of life. The law differentiates between the holy and the profane, but the law desires to lead the way toward the Messianic removal of the differentiation, to the all-sanctification. Hasidic piety no longer recognizes anything as simply and irreparably profane; "the profane" is for Hasidism only a designation for the not-yet-sanctified, for that which is to be sanctified. Everything physical, all drives and urges and desires, everything creaturely, is material for sanctification. From the very same passionate powers which, undirected, give rise to evil, when they are turned toward God, the good arises. One does not serve God with the spirit only, but with the whole of his nature, without any subtractions. There is not one realm of the spirit and another of nature; there is only the growing realm of God. God is not spirit, but what we call spirit and what we call nature hail equally from the God who is beyond and equally conditioned by both, and whose kingdom reaches its fulness in the complete unity of spirit and nature.

The second focus of the Jewish soul is the basic consciousness that God's redeeming power is at work everywhere and at all times, but that a state of redemption exists nowhere and at no time. The Jew experiences as a person what every open-hearted human being experiences as a person: the experience, in the hour when he is most utterly forsaken, of a breath from above, the nearness, the touch, the mysterious intimacy of light out of darkness; and the Jew, as part of the world, experiences, perhaps more intensely than any other part, the world's lack of redemption. He feels this lack of redemption against his skin, he tastes it on his tongue, the burden of the unredeemed world lies on him. Because of this almost physical knowledge of his, he cannot concede that the redemption has taken place; he knows that it has not. It is true that he can discover prefigurations of redemption in past history, but he always discovers only that mysterious intimacy of light out of darkness which is at work everywhere and at all times; no redemption which is different in kind, none which by its nature would be unique, which would be conclusive for future ages, and which had but to be consummated. Most of all, only through a denial of his own meaning and his own mission would it be possible for him to acknowledge that in a world which still remains unredeemed, an anticipation of the redemption had been effected by which the human soul—or rather merely the souls of men who in a specific sense are believers—had been redeemed. [. . .]

Though robbed of their real names, these two foci of the Jewish soul continue to exist for the "secularized" Jew too, insofar as he has not lost his soul. They are, first, the immediate relationship to the Existent One, and second, the power of atonement at work in an unatoned world. In other words, first, the *non-incarnation* of God who reveals himself to the "flesh" and is present to it in a mutual relationship, and second, the unbroken continuity of human history, which turns toward fulfilment and decision. These two centers constitute the ultimate division between Judaism and Christianity.

We "unify" God when living and dying we profess his unity; we do not unite ourselves with him. The God in whom we believe, to whom we are pledged, does not unite with human substance on earth. But the very fact that we do not imagine that we can unite with him enables us the more ardently to demand "that the world shall be perfected under the kingship of the Almighty." [10]

We feel redemption happening, and we feel the unredeemed world. No redeemer with whom a new redeemed history began has appeared to us at any definite point in history. Because we have not been stilled by anything which has happened, we are wholly directed toward the coming of that which is to come.

A NEW LEARNING

*Draft of the Address at the Opening
of the Freies Jüdisches Lehrhaus in Frankfurt*

FRANZ ROSENZWEIG

Franz Rosenzweig (1886-1929), a native of Germany, was an accomplished historian and political philosopher before he turned to serious consideration of religion. To him, an assimilated, enlightened, Jew, religion meant Christianity, and more specifically, Protestantism. It was a dramatic event in his personal life (in 1913) that brought him back to his ancestral faith. Once he encountered this faith in its depth nothing mattered more than to live it and to teach it. His *Stern der Erlösung* (*Star of Redemption*), which he began on the Balkan front during the First World War, is an exposition of religious philosophy as seen by a former follower of Kant and Hegel. Shortly after the end of the war (1920), he accepted the leadership of the Jüdisches Lehrhaus in Frankfurt-am-Main, a house of Jewish studies which offered courses in the literature of Judaism and provided an open forum for the discussion of Jewish, philosophical, sociological, and simply human, issues. The Lehrhaus, inaugurated by Rosenzweig's address that is here reprinted, became a center of the Jewish intellectual and religious renaissance in Germany. In 1922 Rosenzweig was afflicted with progressive paralysis. Heroically, he adjusted his life to the most adverse physical conditions and spent his remaining years working on a translation and commentary of poems by Judah ha-

Levi, a translation (with Martin Buber) of the Bible, and in writing essays on religious philosophy, education, Biblical and historical problems. In thousands of letters he kept a close and lively contact with friends, colleagues, and disciples.

Today, as the Lehrhaus opens its doors to carry on the series of Jewish adult education courses which were held here during the past winter and summer, I shall not attempt to emulate the revered man[11] whose splendid address launched our last winter's activities by taking a subject from the vast field of Jewish scholarship. Nor would you expect it of me, younger and unknown as I am. I intend only to give you an account of the task we have set ourselves and the goals we have in mind, and I shall try to formulate these in the simplest of words.

Learning—there are by now, I should say, very few among you unable to catch the curious note the word sounds, even today, when it is used in a Jewish context. It is to a book, the Book, that we owe our survival—that Book which we use, not by accident, in the very form in which it has existed for millennia: it is the only book of antiquity that is still in living use as a scroll. The learning of this book became an affair of the people, filling the bounds of Jewish life, completely. Everything was really within this learning of the Book. There have been "outside books," [12] but studying them was looked upon as the first step toward heresy. Occasionally such "outside" elements—Aristotle, for example—have been successfuly naturalized. But in the past few centuries the strength to do this would seem to have petered out.

Then came the Emancipation. At one blow it vastly enlarged the intellectual horizons of thought and soon, very soon afterwards, of actual living. Jewish "studying" or "learning" has not been able to keep pace with this rapid extension. What is new is not so much the collapse of the outer barriers; even previously, while the ghetto had certainly sheltered the Jew, it had not shut him off. He moved beyond its bounds, and what the ghetto gave him was only peace, home, a home for his spirit. What is new is not that the Jew's feet could now take him farther than ever before—in the Middle Ages the Jew was not an especially sedentary, but rather a comparatively mobile element of medieval society. The new feature is that the wanderer no longer returns at dusk. The gates of the ghetto no longer close behind him, allowing him to spend the night in solitary learning. To abandon the figure of speech—he finds his spiritual and intellectual home outside the Jewish world.

The old style of learning is helpless before this spiritual emigration. In vain have both Orthodoxy and Liberalism tried to expand into and fill the new domains. No matter how much Jewish law was stretched, it lacked the power to encompass and assimilate the life of the intellect and the spirit. The *mezuzah* may have still greeted one at the door, but the bookcase had, at best, a single Jewish corner. And Liberalism fared no better, even though it availed itself of the nimble air squadron of ideas rather than trying to master life by engaging it in hand-to-hand combat with the Law. There was nothing to be done apparently, except dilute the spirit of Judaism (or what passed for it) as much as possible in order to stake off the whole area of intellectual life; to fill it in the true sense was out of the question. High-sounding words were always on tap, words that the Judaism of old had had, but which it was chary of uttering for fear of dulling their edges with too frequent use. High sounding words, like "humanity," "idealism," and so forth, which those who mouthed them thought as encompassing the whole world. But the world resists such superficial embraces. It is impossible to assimilate to Judaism a field of intellectual and spiritual life through constantly reiterating a catchword and then claiming it to have kinship with some Jewish concept or other. The problems of democracy, for instance, cannot be Judaized merely by referring to the sentence in the Torah: "One law and one ordinance shall be both for you and for the stranger that sojourneth with you" (Numbers 15:16), nor those of socialism by citing certain social institutions or social programs in ancient Israel. If we insist on trying, so much the worse for us! For the great, the creative spirits in our midst, have never allowed themselves to be deceived. They have left us. They went everywhere, they found their own spiritual homes, and they created spiritual homes for others. The Book around which we once gathered stands forlorn in this world, and even for those who regard it as a beloved duty to return to it at regular intervals, such a return is nothing but a turning away from life, a turning one's back on life. Their world remains un-Jewish even when they still have a Jewish world to return to. "Learning"—the old form of maintaining the relationship between life and the Book—has failed.

Has it really? No, only in the old form. For down at heel as we are, we should not be a sign and a wonder among the peoples, we should not be the eternal people, if our very illness did not beget its own cure. It is now as it has always been. We draw new strength from the very circumstance that seemed to deal the death blow to "learning," from the desertion of our scholars to the realms of the alien knowledge of the "outside books," from the transformation of our erstwhile *talmide hakhamim*[13] into the instructors and professors of modern European universities. A new "learning" is about to be born—rather, it has been born.

It is a learning in reverse order. A learning that no longer starts from the Torah and leads into life, but the other way round: from life, from a world that knows nothing of the Law, or pretends to know nothing, back to the Torah. That is the sign of the time.

It is the sign of the time because it is the mark of the men of the time. There is no one today who is not alienated, or who does not contain within himself some small fraction of alienation. All of us to whom Judaism, to whom being a Jew, has again become the pivot of our lives—and I know that in saying this here I am not speaking for myself alone—we all know that in being Jews we must not give up anything, not renounce anything, but lead everything back to Judaism. From the periphery back to the center; from the outside, in.

This is a new sort of learning. A learning for which—in these days—he is the most apt who brings with him the maximum of what is alien. That is to say, not the man specializing in Jewish matters; or, if he happens to be such a specialist, he will succeed, not in the capacity of a specialist, but only as one who, too, is alienated, as one who is groping his way home.

It is not a matter of pointing out relations between what is Jewish and what is non-Jewish. There has been enough of that. It is not a matter of apologetics, but rather of finding the way back into the heart of our life. And of being confident that this heart is a Jewish heart. For we are Jews.

That sounds very simple. And so it is. It is really enough to gather together people of all sorts as teachers and students. Just glance at our prospectus. You will find, listed among others, a chemist, a physician, a historian, an artist, a politician. Two-thirds of the teachers are persons who, twenty or thirty years ago, in the only century when Jewish learning had become the monopoly of specialists, would have been denied the right of teaching in a Jewish House of Study. They have come together here as Jews. They have come together in order to "learn"—for Jewish "learning" includes Jewish "teaching." Whoever teaches here—and I believe I may say this in the name of all who are teaching here —knows that in teaching here he need sacrifice nothing of what he is. Whoever gathers—and all of us are "gatherers"—must seize upon that which is to be gathered wherever he finds it. And more than this: he must seize upon himself as well, wherever he may find himself. Were we to do otherwise, we should continue in the errors of a century and perpetuate the failure of that century: the most we could do would be to adorn life with a few "pearls of thought" from the Talmud or some other source, and—for the rest—leave it just as un-Jewish as we found it. But no: we take life as we find it. Our own life and the life of our students; and gradually (or, at times, suddenly) we carry this life from the periphery where we found it to the center. And we ourselves are carried only by a faith which certainly cannot be proved, the faith that this center can be nothing but a Jewish center.

This faith must remain without proof. It carries further than our word. For we hail from the periphery. The oneness of the center is not something that we possess clearly and unambiguously, not something we can be articulate about. Our fathers were better off in that respect. We are not so well off today. We must search for this oneness and have faith that we shall find it. Seen from the periphery, the center does not appear invariably the same. In fact, the center of the circle looks different from each point of the periphery. There are many ways that lead from the outside in. Nevertheless, the inside is oneness and harmony. In the final analysis, everyone here should be speaking about the same thing. And he who speaks as he should, will in the end really have spoken about exactly what everyone else has spoken about. Only the outset, only the point of departure, will be different for everyone.

So, and only so, will you be able to understand the divisions and contrasts in our prospectus.[14] The contrasts are put in solely for the purpose of being bridged. Today what is classical, historical, and modern in Judaism may be placed side by side, but this ought not to be so and in the future will not be so. It is up to us to discover the root-fibers of history in the classical phase, and its harvest in the modern. Whatever is genuinely Jewish must be all three simultaneously. Such has been the case in Judaism in all its productive periods. And we shall leave it to those who stand on the outside to consider contrasts such as that between the Torah and the Prophets, between *Halakhah*[15] and *Haggadah*,[16] between world and man, as real contrasts which cannot be reconciled. So far as we are concerned, which one of us is not certain that there could be no Torah without the prophetic powers of Moses, father of all prophets before him and after him? And—on the other hand —that there could be no prophets without the foundation of a Law and an order from which their prophecy derived its rule and measure? As for any contrast between *Halakhah* and *Haggadah* —every page of the Talmud shows the student that the two are inseparably intertwined, and every page of Jewish history confirms that the same minds and hearts are preoccupied with both: scholarly inquiry and meditation, legal decision *and* scriptural exegesis. And, finally, the Jewish world! Who could imagine that it would be possible to build it up without man, Jewish man! And what—in the long run—will become of Jewish man if, no matter where he lives, he is not surrounded by an atmosphere Jewish to some degree, by a Jewish world?

So, all of this hangs together. More than that: it is one and the same within itself, and as such it will be presented to you here. You should regard every individual aspect, every individual lecture or seminar you attend, as a part of the whole, which is offered to you only for the sake of the whole.

It is in this sense that now, at the opening of the new term in this hall, I bid you welcome. May the hours you spend here become hours of remembrance, but not in the stale sense of a dead piety that is so frequently the attitude toward Jewish matters. I mean hours of another kind of remembrance, an inner remembering, a turning from externals to that which is within, a turning that, believe me, will and must become for you a returning home. Turn into yourself, return home to your innermost self.

A DEMOCRATIC THEOCRACY

SAMUEL BELKIN

Orthodox Judaism places primary emphasis on *Halakhah*, translation into day-to-day practice of Judaism's religious tenets. Theology and doctrinal fundamentals remain in the background, but the attentive student will discover the theory underlying the practice, the faith that inspires conduct. An excellent study of such concepts as implied in the laws is Samuel Belkin's *In His Image: The Jewish Philosophy of Man as Expressed in Rabbinic Tradition* (1960). Belkin, born in Poland in 1911 and since 1929 living in the United States, is a rabbi and a scholar in the field of Jewish Hellenism. In 1943 he assumed the presidency of Yeshiva University, which under his leadership became the center of modern American Orthodoxy. The essay that follows is the introduction to *In His Image*.

Many attempts have been made to formulate a coherent and systematic approach to Jewish theology. All such attempts, however, have proved unsuccessful, for Judaism was never overly concerned with logical doctrines. It desired, rather, to evolve a corpus of practices, a code of religious acts, which would establish a mode of religious living. True, these acts and practices stem from basic theological and moral concepts, but most significantly, these theological theories of Judaism always remain invisible, apprehensible only through the religious practices to which they gave birth. Great rabbinic scholars and philosophers, therefore, found a greater measure of agreement among themselves in their *minyan hamitzvot*, the classification of the 613 religious duties which the Torah places upon the Jew, than in their attempts to present basic Jewish dogma in the form of articles of faith. Moses Maimonides[1] lists thirteen basic dogmas but Joseph Albo[2] lays down only three.[3] It is, therefore, futile to attempt to discover an articulate and organized body of doctrines which can be characterized as "Jewish

Theology," in the full sense of the term. In Judaism, articles of faith and religious theories cannot be divorced from particular practices.

Probably the first Jew to endeavor to present a Jewish theology was the great Alexandrian philosopher Philo Judaeus;[4] but even he was more concerned with a philosophy of Judaism, or better still, a philosophy of Jewish practice, than with mere theological dogma. Philo followed neither the Stoics, who considered theology a branch of physics, nor Aristotle, who considered theology a branch of philosophy. In his view, theology is part of the highest branch of philosophy, ethics, and is concerned with the worship of God and the regulation of human life in accordance with the divine laws of the Torah.[5] Thus, in a sense, Philo gave voice to the fundamental Jewish concept that theology and the rules of human conduct are almost indivisible.

Josephus, the great historian, defining Judaism to a non-Jewish world, was so aware of this fundamental concept that he felt it necessary to coin a new term to express the uniqueness of the Jewish religion. The word he chose was theocracy, and he wrote: "Some people have entrusted supreme political powers to monarchies, others to oligarchies, and still others to the masses. Our lawgiver, Moses, was attracted to none of these forms of polity, but gave to his constitution the form which—if a forced expression is permitted—may be termed a theocracy." [6] This, he explains, means "placing all sovereignty in the hands of God." [7]

Within the terms of his own definition, Josephus' characterization of Judaism as a theocracy is a true one. Judaism maintains that the sovereignty of man is dependent upon the sovereignty of God; that a man should view every act which he performs as the fulfillment of the wish of the Kingdom of Heaven. This is the meaning of the oft-repeated talmudic injunctions that man should act "for the sake of Heaven," and take upon himself "the yoke of the Kingdom of Heaven." [8]

Accepting this as a fundamental concept of Judaism, it becomes clear why it is wasteful for researchers in historic Judaism to seek to uncover or investigate abstract theological dogmas. Research ought rather seek to uncover the religious motives which underlie the body of Jewish practice and Judaism's concept of morality. The philosophy, or if you will, the theology, of Judaism is contained largely in the *Halakhah*—in the Jewish judicial system—which concerns itself not with theory but primarily with practice. It is in the *Halakhah*, therefore, that the philosophy of Judaism is to be sought.

Unfortunately, this is not the direction modern research in Judaism has taken. Instead of seeking to plumb the spiritual and religious motives which determine rabbinic thought, modern Jewish scholarship has tried to explain Judaism in terms which are alien and do not apply to it, and has attempted to force even those practices and rituals which define the relationship of man to God into the molds of current sociological and economic theories. One sage suddenly becomes a "New Dealer," and another a "conservative Republican"; one is credited with a "liberal" approach to life while another is stamped a "reactionary."

Of course the disagreements between the Pharisees and the Sadducees had a profound impact upon the sociological and economic life of the community, and the same is true of the halakhic differences among the Tannaim, the mishnaic sages. For the most part, however, these disagreements did not spring from social or economic causes, nor were the disputants interested in championing one social class against another. The tannaitic sages were, above all, concerned with devising a code of living through which man, in his daily practices, could best serve God, and in such a system the duties of man to his fellow man are an organic part of his duties to his Maker.

Our sages' chief concern was finding a system by which man, in his conduct, would apply the basic religious principles laid down in the Torah. Measured against practical western concepts of social justice, talmudic laws—recorded in the Mishnah, the Tosefta, the halakhic midrashim, and the Gemara—appear quite impractical. Indeed approached from a secular and social point of view, many rabbinic laws are difficult to understand or appreciate. This is so, however, only because the underlying principles, and even the rules of procedure of rabbinic law spring from profound religious and theological concepts, and are not based at all on social theories.

The laws pertaining to "crime" for example, often result from the religious concept of "sin," and the laws governing community life arise directly from the rabbinic concept of the sacredness of the individual personality. The laws of "the court of man" are seen as reflections of "the laws of Heaven" and the norms for the conduct of man in his relations with his fellow man are governed by man's relation to God. Human or social "practicality" was never accepted as a determining factor in Jewish law.

Our sages did occasionally institute practical laws, but only when they felt that the ordinances would strengthen religious belief and practice, bring man closer to God, and help him reach the ultimate goal of penitence. Invoking rabbinic authority, they sometimes passed laws to help the poor or to insure fair conduct in the market place; at times they enacted rigorous laws for the protection of women. Such practical laws, however, they classified as *takkanot*, that is, innovations necessary to protect and aid the penitent, the poor and the weak. The classical example of a *takkanah*, the *Prosbol*,[9] was enacted to aid the debtor in need of a loan and not to protect the creditor.

As one studies these rabbinic innovations or *takkanot*, it becomes quite apparent that the sages were reluctant to enact them. They would have much preferred to preserve intact the practices set forth in the laws of the Torah, and enacted *takkanot* when compelled, primarily to bolster and strengthen the religious conduct of the community.

Given this understanding of the Jewish corpus of practice as divine law designed for the protection and defence of the individual, Judaism may well be characterized a "democratic theocracy," using the term "theocracy" as Josephus did, and not as understood by scholars today. It is a *theocracy* because the animating force of Jewish morality is not the protection of the state or community in the abstract, or of any mundane form of government. The entire system of Jewish morality derives from and is founded upon the concept of the sovereignty of God. It is a *democracy* because, unlike any other legal system, the rabbinic code places all emphasis upon the infinite worth and sacredness of the human being. In Judaism, the recognition of the *demos*, the individual and the infinite worth of his personality, are but a necessary outgrowth of the acceptance of God's *theos* (rulership), a relationship succinctly summed up in the phrase "democratic theocracy."

If the second element in this phrase is to be understood in the sense given it by Josephus, the first element is used as defined by Philo, who sought to explain the polity of the Torah to a non-Jewish world. According to Philo, democracy is "the most law-abiding and best of constitutions." [10] Understandably, Philo did not use the term "democracy" in the modern sense of a government elected by the whole populace, one in which every person is entitled to hold office.[11] To Philo, democracy, as an ideal form of government, "honors equality and has law and justice for its rulers." [12] It mattered little to Philo whether in the ancient polity of Judaism the functional government was vested in a monarchy, aristocracy or priesthood. Judaism to him meant the sovereignty of God as revealed in the Torah, the divine constitution which has as its goal the extension of justice to all. In this sense Philo characterized Judaism as a democracy and, as Professor Harry Wolfson has pointed out, he almost coined the term "theocracy" later used by Josephus to describe the Mosaic state.[13]

Upon these twin principles—the sovereignty of God and the sacredness of the individual—the religious philosophy of Judaism rests. Enunciated not merely as a theory, this philosophy is clearly reflected in the *Halakhah*. In fact, only by properly understanding the Jewish concept of divine kingship and human worth can we fully understand many legal and spiritual institutions in Judaism. It is also true, however, that since Judaism is interested in practice rather than in theory, only a close examination of Jewish law can reveal its philosophic foundations.

THE NEED FOR REFORM

SAMUEL HIRSCH

Samuel Hirsch (1815-1889) represented the radical wing of the Jewish reform movement. He served as rabbi in various communities in Germany and Luxemburg before coming to the United States as rabbi in Philadelphia (1866). His major work is *Die Religionsphilosophie der Juden* (*The Jewish Religious Philosophy*, 1842); in it, using Hegelian terminology, he presented Judaism as "absolute religion." He expostulated his reformist thinking in a number of works, among them in *Die Reform im Judenthum* (*The Reformation of Judaism*, 1844), from which the passages that follow are excerpted.

The need of the time is the highest law in Judaism; all ceremonies are but means for the fulfillment of this highest law; the means must however everywhere be subservient to the end, therefore also in Judaism. The demand that everything which hinders us from working for the maintenance and prosperity of civil society, with all our spiritual and material powers, be removed from our ceremonial practice is therefore religiously justified. [. . .] It is a serious misdemeanor against, and not an indifferent action towards, the spirit of Judaism if anything be retained which in any way prevents us from the fulfillment of duties incumbent upon the citizen as such. It matters not whether any ceremony which is not to be retained for the above-mentioned reason be prescribed in the Bible or the Talmud. [. . .] Even the most biased cannot deny that in the regulation of the ceremonial law the Bible had only the Jewish state in view. True, it foresees the downfall of the Jewish state as a divine punishment, but it conceives the event to have been possible of prevention by the Jews through a change of conduct, and therefore it gives no precepts as to how the religious life was to be arranged thereafter. When the Jewish state disappeared, the people, as Holdheim[14] correctly remarks, had no guiding principle to determine what, under the changed circumstances, should be retained and what must be abrogated. [. . .]

The ceremonies became meaningless, *i.e.* their meaning was no longer understood, and they passed current as the incomprehensible commands of God. Therefore to observe as many of the prescribed ceremonies as possible became the one and important principle. What was no longer possible of observance, as the temple service and everything connected with the possession of Palestine, naturally had to be relinquished. Yet this was regarded only as a punishment of God. God had abolished our sacrifices, our Sabbath and jubilee-years, because we are unworthy to fulfill these commands. Therefore the ever-repeated sigh, "Lead us back to Palestine in order that"—possibly to found there a state that should serve for the glorification of God? No, but—"we may pay our penalty there, that we may offer the prescribed number of sacrifices, etc." This is always and again the heathenish conception (so opposed to our time as well as to the Jewish spirit), that by the practice of ceremonies a service is rendered to God, and as though only the service in the temple at Jerusalem could be perfect because only there everything that God commands could be carried out. But our standpoint today is entirely different. We, and the world with us, have arrived at the threshold of the future that the prophets foresaw. A world-temple must be built unto God, for His name shall be praised from the rising of the sun to the setting thereof.[15] The freedom of every man must be not merely proclaimed but realized, for all were created in the image of God. The sanctity of labor must be declared, for man has been placed on earth to work, to employ and develop his powers. God's activity in the history of the individual and of nations must be recognized and acknowledged. God gives the individual and nations the opportunity to use their powers rightly. If they undertake this high task they will live; if not, and they prefer mental sloth and material luxury to hard work, they will go to ruin.

Finally, we must bear testimony to the world, through our cult and through appropriate symbols and ceremonies, that this truth is confirmed in sacred history, inasmuch as there is shown in it how, in a rude, material age, a people, ruder and more sensual than others, was trained until it recognized and taught for all time to come the rule of spirit over nature, and how the spirit can retain this superiority only by free, spiritual activity. Therefore symbols must be retained in Judaism, symbols which shall give this testimony in a fitting manner both to the Jews and to the world. But the Jews of the present day must, before all else, participate in the work of the age with all their powers; for this work is the object of Jewish history, yes, it is the be-all and the end-all of Judaism. The high aim sanctified by time and by Judaism is, that all men be free, all recognize God, all employ their spiritual and material powers with full and free desire, so that a throne be built for truth and justice on this earth, a throne which shall adorn the lowliest hut as well as the most glorious palace. Therefore no symbol can hereafter pass as Jewish which prevents the Jew from participating in and working towards the fulfillment of this object with all his powers. He may not be a mere spectator of the work of the modern age, but must give himself heart and soul to it, for this is the command of the God of his fathers, who only wishes to have right and love realized on earth, and therefore called Abraham from the other side of the river, and desired to make him and his descendants a blessing for the world through their deeds and their sufferings.

NECESSITY OF CHANGE
APPEAL BY BERLIN REFORMERS, 1845

Under the impact of modern industrial, cultural, and political developments, and the modicum of civil liberties granted German Jewry, Jewish traditions and institutions faced a severe crisis. The two worlds—the ancestral heritage and modern civilization—seemed unrelated to each other, and frequently evoked open conflict. It was incumbent upon Judaism to undergo a process of transformation and adaptation; the alternative, rejection of European culture, was out of the question. Even Neo-Orthodoxy, with its insistence on loyal adherence to the Jewish law *in toto*, required a measure of adaptation.

The most extreme call for "a change" within the framework of Judaism came from the groups that had founded German Jewish Reform. A "Society of the Friends of Reform" (*Verein der Reformfreunde*) was founded in Frankfurt-am-Main in 1842, and a similar organization in Berlin in 1845. The aim of both was to recall into the community those who had become indifferent to Judaism, and both dissociated themselves, the Berlin group less definitively than the Frankfurt society, from traditional, rabbinical, Israel. Following is the appeal (*Aufruf*) of the Berlin group, published in various Berlin newspapers in the beginning of April, 1845. It formed the basis for the establishment, in 1845, of a Reform congregation in Berlin which radically revised both doctrine and ritual.

From the time that we ceased to suffer from political oppression in our German fatherland and the soaring spirit cast off its fetters; from the time that we became identified with our surroundings in culture and custom, our religion failed gradually to give us that satisfaction which was the comfort and the happiness of our ancestors. Our religion clung to the forms and prescriptions that had been handed down for centuries, but our convictions and our sentiments, our inner religion, is no longer in harmony with this interpretation. Hence we are in a state of conflict with ourselves, and there is a contradiction between our inner life and faith and the external life, the given law.

True, our savants and teachers are engaged in a combat in the field of theology for and against a reconciliation of this contradiction; but how long has this been the case! and the end of the combat is not in sight. In the meantime, however, life has superseded scholarship; in the meantime the overwhelming majority of the cultured members of our community has renounced the greatest portion of our religious prescriptions, and even those which they still keep are observed without belief and without enthusiasm. The confusion is great. Nowhere union, nowhere a support, nowhere a limit. The old rabbinical Judaism with its firm basis has no basis any longer in us. In vain are the efforts of those who aim to preserve it artificially. The petrified doctrine and our life are divorced forever. The doubt which has begun to negate threatens to transgress all limits. It begets indifference and unbelief and delivers us over to a state of helplessness in which we are compelled to witness with pain how, together with the antiquated forms, the eternal holy kernel of true Judaism threatens to be lost for our descendants.

These are facts which speak for themselves, which only those do not see who will not see—facts which fill our hearts with glowing zeal, which call forth all our energy and embolden us to issue the call to you, our German coreligionists who feel as do we, who feel that it is incumbent on us not to view idly the ruin and the vain artificial varnishing of the breach but to take steps together after coming to a mutual understanding, to save out of the chaos what can continue to exist in our spiritual development and in our German life, and to repudiate openly what has died in us.

With this sentiment we have come together, feeling our justification to declare openly and decidedly the necessity of a change, a justification which we assume and may assume because our holiest interests are threatened with immediate danger, although we are conscious at the same time that we are not the elect who are to carry out this change. Therefore we wish to assure ourselves of the sympathy and agreement of our German coreligionists and in conjunction with them convene a synod in order to fix that aspect of Judaism which corresponds with our age and the sentiments of our heart.

We desire: *faith*; we desire: *positive religion*; we desire: *Judaism*. We hold fast to the spirit of Sacred Scripture, which we recognize as a testimony of divine revelation by which the spirit of our fathers was illumined. We hold fast to everything which is necessary for the true worship of God, rooted in the spirit of our religion. We hold fast to the conviction that Judaism's doctrine of God is eternally true and to the prediction that the knowledge of God as proclaimed by Judaism will at some time become the possession of all mankind. But we desire to interpret Holy Writ according to its divine spirit; we cannot sacrifice our divine freedom to the tyranny of the dead letter. We cannot pray sincerely for an earthly Messianic dominion which is to lead us to the home of our ancestors out of the fatherland to which we cling with all the bonds of love as though this were a strange land to us. We can no longer observe commands which have no spiritual hold on us and can no longer recognize a code as immutable lawbook according to which the essence and the mission of Judaism consist in blind adherence to forms and prescriptions which owe their origin to a time long past and forever vanished.

Permeated with the holy content of our religion we cannot preserve it in the bequeathed form, much less bequeath it in this form to our descendants and so, placed between the graves of our ancestors and the cradles of our children, the cornet-call of the age thrills us, the latest recipients of a great heritage in its antiquated form to be also the first who, with undaunted courage, with true fraternization by word and act, lay the foundation of this new structure for ourselves and the generations which come after us.

However, we do not wish to dissociate ourselves by this step from the community to which we belong; nay, we extend the hand of brotherhood in love and tolerance to all, also to those of our coreligionists who differ with us. We desire no schism. But upon you, who sympathize with us, we call confidently for the closest union that shall make for truth within, indulgence without, endurance in the fight with others and faithfulness towards ourselves.

And thus our appeal goes forth to you, German coreligionists, far and near,

That you associate yourselves with us by name and assure us by word and act of your support and aid in order that we in great number can convene a synod which shall renew and establish Judaism in the form in which it is capable and worthy of continuing as a living force for us and our children.

INTELLIGENT RELIGION

ISAAC MAYER WISE

Born in Bohemia, Isaac Mayer Wise (1819-1900) came to the United States in 1846, to become a major force in American reform Judaism. He consolidated the divergent liberal congregations into the Union of American Hebrew Congregations, founded in 1873; established, in 1875, the Hebrew Union College in Cincinnati, Ohio, a seminary for reform rabbis; and, in 1889, organized the Central Conference of American Rabbis. He also composed a modernized prayer book, *Minhag America* (*American Ritual*), which was used in many liberal congregations until replaced by the *Union Prayer Book*, issued by the Central Conference of American Rabbis. "He was the embodiment of the free democratic spirit . . . tirelessly active in the cause of freedom in religion. For him American Judaism represented a new phase in the history of the ancestral faith. . . . He taught the ultimate triumph of the principles of prophetic Judaism as reinterpreted by the theology of the reform movement" (David Philipson). The following passage is taken from an article written in 1854.

Our religion contains better elements than a mere controversial and casuistical rabbinism, and these better elements must be considered the primary cause of its self-preservation. The Jew had the consciousness that he alone possesses the most philosophical views of the existence and nature of the deity; of the nature, duties, and hopes of mankind; of justice, equity, and charity; of the several relations between God and his creatures, and between man and his fellow-man. With this sublime conviction he first stood in the midst of degraded and superstitious heathenism, then by the side of persecuting Catholicism, and finally opposed to a ridiculous mysticism. [. . .] The Jew, however, felt conscious of the verities of his religion, and therefore he loved them better than his life and worldly interests; he saw himself alone in the world, alone with his sublime ideas, and therefore he lived in his faith and for it, and the thousand forms which he observed only led him to his sublime ideas. It was this elevating and inspiring consciousness, and not rabbinism, which preserved Judaism. But now the idea, the sublime cardinal elements, are almost lost sight of in the multitude of thoughtless observances of rabbinical forms. [. . .] Judaism has become a set of unmeaning practices, and the intelligent Jew either mourns for the fallen daughter of Zion or has adopted a course of frivolity and indifference. Therefore we demand reforms. All unmeaning forms must be laid aside as outworn garments. The internal spirit of Judaism must be expounded, illustrated, and made dear again to the Jew. We must inform our friends and opponents that there is a Judaism independent of its forms, and that this is Judaism emphatically. It is therefore our principle of reform: "All forms to which no meaning is attached any longer are an impediment to our religion, and must be done away with." Before we propose to abolish anything we should inquire: What is its practical benefit? If there is none it is time to renounce it, for one dead limb injures the whole body. Another principle of reform is this: "Whatever makes us ridiculous before the world as it now is, may safely be and should be abolished," for we are in possession of an intelligent religion, and the nations from our precept and example should be led to say, "This is a wise and intelligent people" (Deuteronomy 4:6).

A third principle of reform is this, "Whatever tends to the elevation of the divine service, to inspire the heart of the worshiper and attract him, should be done without any unnecessary delay," for the value of divine service must be estimated according to its effect upon the heart and understanding.

A fourth principle of reform is this, "Whenever religious observances and the just demands of civilized society exclude each other, the former have lost their power"; for religion was taught for the purpose "to live therein and not to die therein";[16] our religion makes us active members of civilized society, hence we must give full satisfaction to its just demands.

Last, or rather first, it must be remarked, the leading star of reform must be the maxim, "Religion is intended to make man happy, good, just, active, charitable, and intelligent." Whatever tends to this end is truly religious, and must be retained or introduced if it does not yet exist. Whatever has an effect contrary to the above must be abolished as soon as possible.

CONSERVATIVE JUDAISM

ALEXANDER KOHUT

Conservative Judaism occupies a middle position between Orthodoxy and Reform. The concept was formulated in Germany, in the mid-nineteenth century, as a protest against the rising Reform tendencies. Its foremost spokesman was Zacharias Frankel (1801-1875), whose "positive-historical school" aimed at a synthesis of tradition and modernity through a historic approach to Jewish law and the literary sources of Judaism. As a religious movement Conservative Judaism took roots in

America. Its center is the Jewish Theological Seminary in New York, founded in 1887 and (in 1902) reorganized by Solomon Schechter (1850-1915). The structure of Conservatism's thinking was first coherently formulated by Alexander Kohut (1842-1894), Hungarian-born rabbi and Semitic scholar who came to the United States in 1885. In his lectures on *The Ethics of the Fathers* (1885), from which the passages that follow are taken, Kohut defined the position of what was to become a major religious movement in the United States.

The chain of tradition continued unbroken from Moses through Joshua, the Elders, the prophets and the Men of the Great Synagogue,[17] down to the latest times. On this tradition rests our faith, which Moses first received from God on Sinai. On this foundation rests Mosaic-rabbinical Judaism to-day; and on this foundation we take our stand. [. . .]

But you may ask: Shall the fence around the garden, shall reverence be extended around everything that the past hedged in . . . ? "Remember the days of old," said Moses, "and have regard to the changes of each generation" (Deuteronomy 32:7). The teaching of the ancients we must make our starting-point, but we must not lose sight of what is needed in every generation. [. . .]

And as these elders did, so can—yes, so must we, the later Epigoni—do in the exigencies of our own day. If the power to make changes was granted to the Elders, is not the power given equally to us? "But they were giants," we are told, "and we, compared with them, are mere pygmies." Perhaps so; let us not forget, however, that a pygmy on a giant's shoulder can see further than the giant himself.

Let us now revert to the question raised at the outset: Is Judaism definitely closed for all time, or is it capable of and in need of continuous development? I answer both Yes and No. I answer Yes, because religion has been given to man; and as it is the duty of man to grow in perfection as long as he lives, he must modify the forms which yield him religious satisfaction, in accordance with the spirit of the times. I answer No, in so far as it concerns the Word of God, which cannot be imperfect. [. . .]

You Israelite, imperfect as you are, strive to perfect yourself in the image of your perfect God. Hold in honor His unchangeable Law and let it be your earnest task to put new life into the outward form of our religion. [. . .]

Our religious guide is the Torah, the Law of Moses, interpreted and applied in the light of tradition. But inasmuch as individual opinion cannot be valid for the whole community, it behooves individuals and communities to appoint only recognized authorities as teachers; such men, that is to say, as acknowledge belief in authority, and who, at the same time, with comprehension and tact, are willing to consider what may be permitted in view of the exigencies of the times, and what may be discarded, without changing the nature and character of the foundations of the faith. [. . .]

A Reform which seeks to progress without the Mosaic-rabbinical tradition is a deformity—a skeleton without flesh and sinew, without spirit and heart. It is suicide; and suicide is not reform. We desire a Judaism full of life. We desire to worship the living God in forms full of life and beauty; Jewish, yet breathing the modern spirit. Only a Judaism true to itself and its past, yet receptive of the ideas of the present, accepting the good and the beautiful from whatever source it may come, can command respect and recognition. [. . .]

I do not know whether it will be my good fortune to have your sympathy in my religious attitude—that of Mosaic-rabbinical Judaism, freshened with the spirit of progress, a Judaism of the healthy golden mean. I hope I shall. [. . .]

CREATIVE JUDAISM

MORDECAI M. KAPLAN

Among the modern approaches to Judaism, Kaplan's (born 1881) is the most typically American. America's democracy, pragmatism, notions of tolerance, and readiness to change are reflected in his conception of Judaism as an evolving religious civilization and in the philosophy of "Reconstructionism," a movement he founded and of which he is chief exponent. For him, religion, which concerns itself with the highest good and with life's meaning, is the maturest expression of a civilization. In contradistinction to the personal God of classical Judaism, he defines God as that force in the universe that makes for the highest human aspirations—justice, truth, mercy—a force reflected in the world of man as ethical responsibility. Not supernatural revelation, as taught in classical Judaism, but reason, intuition, and experience are the sources of religious knowledge and of that which becomes recognized as true. Kaplan rejects the concept of Israel as a chosen people and replaces it by a "doctrine of vocation, of divine calling in which all peoples can have a share." He accepts the law of the Torah as central in Judaism, but admits revision, adaptation, and change; rituals are to be understood as symbols of the people's *sancta*. The land of Israel is focal in Kaplan's thinking because only there can Judaism as a civilization comprising all facets of life be realized. Hence, recognizing Zion as its nucleus, world Jewry should reorganize itself into a "trans-national" organic community with emphasis on religious and educational institutions. The aim of Kaplan's teachings is "to help American Jews achieve self-fulfillment both as Americans and as Jews."

From 1909 onward Kaplan taught at the Jewish Theological Seminary in New York. His major works are *Judaism as a Civilization* (1934), *The Meaning of God in Modern Jewish Religion* (1936), *The Future of the American Jew* (1948), and *The Greater Judaism in the Making* (1960). In 1935 he launched the *Reconstructionist*, the movement's periodical. What follows is a (somewhat abridged) chapter from *Judaism as a Civilization*, brought up to date by Professor Kaplan.

The differences between the world from which the Jew has emerged and that in which he now lives are so sharp and manifold that they almost baffle description. The Jew shared with the rest of the ancient world the universal belief that salvation meant the attainment of bliss in the hereafter as a result of having lived according to the will of God in this life. Consequently he was free from all self-questioning and doubt. He was sure of his privileged position in the scheme of divine redemption. But all such conceptions together with the reasoning upon which they are based are alien to the modern world. In the short time that the Jew has lived in the modern world, these conceptions have become almost unintelligible to him. He thus finds himself deprived of what had been the principal justification for his loyalty to Judaism.

The only adequate substitute for other-worldly salvation which formerly motivated the loyalty of the Jew to his social heritage is a creative Judaism. This means that Judaism must be so reconstructed as to elicit from him the best that is in him. It must be so conditioned as to enlarge his mental horizon, deepen his sympathies, imbue him with hope and enable him to leave the world better for his having lived in it.

The Jews who are likely to assume the task of thus conditioning Judaism are they who cannot do without it, and yet cannot do with it as it is. As a rule, they are those with whom Judaism is a habit. Coming from intensely Jewish homes, they have had Judaism bred into their very bones. Jewish modes of self-expression and association with fellow-Jews are as indispensable to them as the very air they breathe. They would like to observe Jewish rites, but so many of those rites appear to them ill-adapted to the conditions and needs of our day. They are affiliated with congregations, but they are bored by the services. They take an active part in Jewish organization, but are revolted by the futility, waste and lack of sincerity. They cannot help feeling that many an opportunity for reaching into the soul of the Jew, improving his character and eliciting his powers for good is thoughtlessly neglected. Anachronisms abound where cogency and relevance could prevail. Much that might be rendered beautiful and appealing is allowed to remain stale and flat. The teachers and scholars, instead of following the example of Moses, the teacher of all teachers, who went down to the people, ensconce themselves in the ivory tower of abstract learning.

Others, again, cannot do without Judaism because it is a nostalgia with them. It haunts them and gives them no rest. But as it is constituted at present, it offers no field for the expression of their innermost selves. Such Jews may never have seen anything Jewish in their homes, but some atavistic yearning or childhood memory has awakened within them. Now they want to become reunited with their people. If they are of a romantic temperament they may idealize their people's failings. Otherwise they may be repelled by the petrifaction of many of its lauded traditions and institutions and the aimlessness of most of its collective activities.

What must these Jews do to render Judaism creative?

1. In the first place they must rediscover Judaism; they must learn to know its true scope and character. The rediscovery of Judaism implies the lifting of the fog of pious sentimentalities and the mists of wish-thoughts which have enveloped it since the days of the emancipation. For fear lest Jews be charged with hyphenating their loyalties to the countries in which they are citizens, timid leaders and teachers have made it appear that Judaism is nothing more than a religion, or a cult. The Neo-Orthodox have taught that it is a revealed religion which so transcends all laws of social life as to be in no way affected or determined by them. As a revealed religion, Judaism is final and authoritative, destined to transform the environment but not to be transformed by it. The Reformists have interpreted Judaism as a historically evolved religion. According to them, the only bond which unites Jews is the mission to promulgate the truth about the unity of God and the brotherhood of mankind. These conceptions of Judaism have so emptied it of content that it has come to mean to most Jews nothing more than a medley of antiquated ideas and archaic practices which persist as an irrational hangover from the past.

A number of Jews who could not reconcile themselves to the vacuity of Reformism, or the intransigeance of Neo-Orthodoxy, are advocating the elimination of religion from Jewish collective life, and are staking the future of the Jewish people upon the spirit of nationalism. They point to nationalism as the most potent social energy in the modern world, and therefore conclude that it should be fostered as a means of solidifying and fructifying the life of the Jewish people. They forget, however, that, if nationalism is to unite the Jews, it must be rooted in the history and spirit of the Jewish people, otherwise the Jews would be merely playing at the kind of nationhood which has balkanized the world. Thus have the Secularists added to the general confusion of ideas which has obscured the true character of Judaism.

There must be an end to all these misconceptions and misunderstandings. The quality and quantity of life that spell Judaism must be rediscovered and reemphasized. It must be recognized as nothing less than a civilization. It must figure in the consciousness of the Jew as the *tout ensemble* of all that is included in a civilization, the social framework of national unity centering in a particular land, a continuing history, a living language and literature, religious folkways, mores, laws and art.

As a civilization, Judaism is that dynamic pattern of life which enables the Jewish people to be a means of salvation to the individual Jew. In the past when salvation meant attainment of bliss in the hereafter, the Jewish civilization was other-worldly in its entire outlook, content and motivation. Now when salvation depends on making the most of the opportunities presented by this world, the form of social organization, the language, literature, religion, laws, folkways and art must so function that through them the Jewish people will help to make the life of the Jew creative and capable of self-fulfillment. Jewish life must not depend upon syllogistic rationalization. It must have body and substance. It must function through vital institutions and articulate itself in a plastic and creative ideology.

The only way in which Jews will ever be able to coordinate their own mode of life satisfactorily with the life which they must share with their neighbors will be by rethinking their beliefs, reorganizing their institutions and developing new means of self-expression as Jews. To that end it will be necessary for them to operate with Judaism not merely as a religion but as a civilization. [. . .]

For Judaism to become creative once again, it must assimilate the best in contemporary civilizations. In the past this process of assimilating cultural elements from the environment was carried on unconsciously. Henceforth that process will have to be carried on in deliberate and planned fashion. Therein Judaism will, no doubt, have to depart from its own tradition. But conscious and purposeful planning is coming to be part of the very life process of society. No civilization, culture, economy or religion that is content to drift aimlessly has the slightest chance of surviving. It is in the spirit, therefore, of adopting the best in other civilizations and cooperating with them, and not in the spirit of yielding to their superior force or prestige, that Judaism should enter upon what will constitute a fourth stage in its development.

This development in Judaism necessarily presupposes many changes in its ideology, sanctions, practices and social organization. The criterion which is to determine whether a suggested change is beneficial or detrimental to Judaism is the extent to which it helps Judaism to retain its *continuity*, its *individuality* and its *organic character*.

The continuity of Judaism is maintained so long as the knowledge of Israel's past functions as an integral part of the Jew's personal memory, and is accompanied by some visible form or action symbolic of that fact. [. . .]

The individuality of Judaism is maintained so long as the newly instituted custom, sanction, idea or ideal helps to keep alive the element of otherness in the Jewish civilization. Not separatism must henceforth be the principle of living as a Jew, but otherness. Separatism is the antithesis of cooperation, and results in an ingrown and clannish remoteness which leads to cultural and spiritual stagnation. Otherness thrives best when accompanied by active cooperation and interaction with neighboring cultures and civilizations, and achieves an individuality which is of universal significance.

The organic character is maintained so long as all the elements that constitute the civilization play a rôle in the life of the Jew. Any attempt to live or transmit only certain elements in Judaism to the neglect of others is bound to end in failure, since in Judaism as a civilization the normal functioning of each element is bound up with and conditioned by the normal functioning of every other. [. . .]

2. To render Judaism creative it is essential to redefine the national status and reorganize the communal life of the Jews. Fundamental to the reconstitution of the Jewish people is national

unity. That unity is not determined by geographic boundaries; it is cultural rather than political. The Jews are an international people, functioning as such by virtue of their consciousness of a common past, their aspiration toward a common future and the will-to-cooperate in the achievement of common ends.

The State of Israel should serve as the symbol of the Jewish renascence and the homeland of Jewish civilization. Without such a center upon which Jews throughout the world might focus their interest, it is impossible for Jews to be conscious of their unity as a people. Without the spiritual aid and example of the adjustment of Judaism to modern life in the new Jewish environment possible only in the State of Israel, the efforts at similar adjustment by other Jewries of the world would be without impelling stimulus. Judaism cannot maintain its character as a civilization without a homeland. There essential Jewish creativeness will express itself in Hebraic forms not so easily developed in other lands. There Jews will attain sufficient autonomy to express their ideas and social will in all forms of organized life and thought. [. . .]

As a result of a peculiar conjuncture of historic forces, the citizen of a modern state is not only permitted but encouraged to give allegiance to two civilizations: one, the secular civilization of the country in which he lives, and the other, the Christian civilization which he has inherited from the past. He turns to the civilization of his country for his literary and esthetic values. From his national life arise those duties of civic allegiance which are the substance of patriotism. He turns to the Christian civilization for his moral and spiritual sanctions. The separation of church from state has put into the class of hyphenates all who adhere to both organizations. The necessity which justifies the Christian in hyphenating his Christianity with Americanism, justifies also the Jew in hyphenating his Jewishness with Americanism.

Jewish communal life is the *sine qua non* of cooperation among Jews. In America, particularly, Jews will need a measure of communal autonomy if American-Jewish life is to develop along broad and inclusive lines. Jewish organization should embrace all the activities of Jews, and integrate those activities into an organic unity. To such communities will belong all Jews who feel physical or spiritual kinship with the Jewish people, no matter what their personal philosophy may be.

Congregations will be units in these communities, units consisting of groups of Jews who wish to express their Judaism through common worship. The community, however, is larger than its congregations and must of necessity provide for needs and activities that do not fall within the scope of the congregation. There should also be other units consisting of groups and individuals who wish to express their Jewishness and their creativity through literature, the arts and activities for the furtherance of social welfare and social justice.

The community should direct Jewish economic life into productive occupations. The position of middleman, which history has imposed upon the Jew, is becoming economically insecure and unsound. For the sake of greater economic security, and because of the dignity and moral worth of engaging in productive labor, Jews should endeavor to enter the fields of industry and agriculture wherever opportunities permit.

The community should establish centers where the religious, philanthropic, social and educational problems of each neighborhood would be dealt with specifically. These centers, subsidized by the community, will stimulate Jewish creative effort among writers, scholars, artists, musicians and social workers.

The community should institute such civic activities as the establishment of Jewish arbitration courts, the recognition and recording of births, marriages, divorces and deaths, the representation of Jews before the non-Jewish community and the defense of Jewish rights.

Among the functions of Jewish communal life, priority should be given to Jewish education. In relief work and social service, the community discharges nothing more than an elementary human duty. But it is in the socialization of its members through the transmission and enrichment of a spiritual heritage that a community lives up to the highest purpose of its existence. Jewish education in its widest sense as applying to children, adolescents and adults must become one of the main functions of the Jewish community. [. . .] The school must be further supplemented by the home. If the home is to possess the requisite Jewish atmosphere, the adults as well as the young must continue their interest in Jewish study.

The Jewish community must foster institutions of higher learning. It must so apportion the duties of those engaged in communal work as to leave time and leisure for them to grow in the knowledge of their respective callings. It must stimulate in the home, in the synagogue and in the construction of Jewish public buildings the creative arts expressive of Jewish interests and ideals.

3. To render Judaism creative, its tradition must be revitalized. The main reason Jews display such a negative attitude to their tradition is no doubt the fact that they labor under the assumption that it is inextricably bound up with a theology which has ceased to have any vital meaning for them. They conceive tradition as a series of fixed and static ideas which either have to be accepted in the form in which they have come down, or be ignored entirely. This erroneous idea must be offset by the realization that the only way tradition will ever come into its own as an active factor in the Jewish consciousness is to disengage from it the element of past interpretation, and to identify the way it functioned socially and spiritually.

The future of Judaism is contingent upon the formulation of a Jewish ideology which will make it possible for Jews, despite their unlike-mindedness, to accept the intrinsic value of Jewish life. Only through a participation in Jewish interests and aspirations which elicits the best that is in him will the individual Jew find salvation through his people. But if such participation is to have a truly redeeming or saving influence, it must be accompanied by a clear perspective on the whole of Jewish life.

The crux of the problem of how to foster a constructive and unifying Jewish ideology at the present time is to disabuse the average person of the deeply rooted preconception that for a people or community to function as an instrument of salvation, all who compose it must think alike and behave alike. Out of this preconception stems the intolerance which is by no means confined to the historic churches. Modern nations are no less adept in intolerance. An inference which some wrongly draw from this hitherto unquestioned assumption is that, since it is impossible to get people to think and behave alike, there can be no such thing as a group acting as an instrument of salvation. Salvation, they maintain, is purely an individual achievement. Such a conclusion is tantamount to nihilism, yet it is the inevitable one to which any sincere and conscientious person is driven, so long as the churches and nations continue in their refusal or inability to reconcile the salvation they proffer with tolerance of credal differences. It is doubtful whether they will change their attitude. With the Jewish people, however, this synthesis is a matter of life and death. Its very existence depends upon its making a virtue of the necessity of giving its individual men and women wide scope in views, and at the same time extending salvation to all of them alike.

A people does not offer itself to the individual as an instrument of salvation, in the same way as a system of philosophy usually does, by appealing to his reason to accept certain general principles or abstract truths. It always comes to him with a story about itself which he is made to feel is in a deeper and truer sense his story than the experiences that are confined to his person. In the course of that story there figure certain events, persons, places, objects, or, in brief, *sancta*, which come to possess a vital interest for him, since they belong to a history that he comes to look upon as his own. These *sancta* the people interprets, and these interpretations form the ideology and rationale of its existence and strivings. In the past, when everybody thought alike, one type of interpretation or ideology was enough to enable the *sancta* to help the individual orient himself to the world about him. One ideology, uniform and unchangeable, thus came to be regarded as indispensable to salvation.

Now that such uniformity is no longer possible, there is the alternative of permitting different ideologies to be developed whereby the *sancta*, which have played an important part in the history of the people or church, may retain their place as sources of and occasions for ethical motivation and spiritual exaltation for individuals with different philosophies of life. The sense of unity and even of like-mindedness is not contingent upon the sameness of interpretation, but upon the sameness of the constellation of realities interpreted. [. . .]

Assuming, therefore, that multiple ideologies are compatible with unity of group spirit, there remains the task of formulating in outline, at least, an ideology for those Jews who cannot align themselves with any of the existing groups, and who experience the need of such salvation as the Jewish people in its proper capacity might afford them. Such Jews are sufficiently numerous and influential to deserve this consideration.

The principle underlying the ideology that would meet their need is that the traditional *sancta* must be kept within the focus of the Jewish consciousness. The interpretation, however, which is to be given to those *sancta* cannot be the one which they received in the past. Since any interpretation, to be valid, must coincide with the rest of one's thinking, it is essential that the ideas which form part of the Jewish social heritage be reinterpreted in the light of the modern world-outlook. If such reinterpretation is to succeed in bridging the gap between tradition and modernism, it must seek out from among the implications of tradition those which would reenforce the highest social and spiritual strivings of our day—the complete self-realization of the personality of the individual and the maximum cooperation among human beings irrespective of racial, political and historical divisions.

It is from the standpoint of the foregoing postulates with regard to the need of revitalizing Jewish tradition that religion must continue to be the central identifying characteristic of Jewish civilization. The Jewish genius has always sought to express itself in religious terms; it has always sought to interpret every individual act and process, both natural and human, in the light of reality regarded as creative and meaningful. Like all other phases of human life, religion is subject to the process of evolution. Jewish religion should ally itself with the modern orientation toward religion as the spiritual reaction of man to the vicissitudes of life, and as the expression of the highest needs of his being.

The problem of Jewish religion will be considerably clarified, if we will take into account the distinction between personal religion and folk religion. Jewish folk religion consists in all those expressions of Jewish life, and all those forms of custom and law, through which the individual identifies himself with the life and strivings of his people. It is therefore to be expected that Jews will find in folk religion a common spiritual denominator. Personal religion, on the other hand, is essentially the world-outlook which each one is taught and encouraged to achieve for himself. Such an outlook every individual Jew should be free to develop in accordance with his own personal convictions regarding life and the universe.

Jewish religion as a folk religion should find expression in the practice of the maximum possible number of Jewish religious customs and folkways compatible with one's circumstances. There can be no Jewish life without the use of Jewish symbols in the home and without the observance of Sabbaths, festivals and customs connected with birth, marriage and other vital events.

Yet traditional Jewish customs and folkways must be subject to modification, both in form and in motive, so that they may be observed sincerely and wholeheartedly by modern Jews. New folkways and customs should also be developed and sanctioned to give Jewish significance to numerous occasions in individual and social life at present not invested with spiritual meaning.

Jewish folk religion should find expression in the endeavor to render public worship as significant as possible by relating it to the ideology of the modern Jew and basing it upon the Jewish traditional forms as far as they are consistent with spiritual appeal.

It is a far cry from the simple Judaism of the past to the intricate program called for by Judaism as a civilization. Accustomed to think of Judaism as a form of truth, whether divinely revealed or humanly achieved, we conclude that complexity is a sign of artificiality. It is therefore necessary to recall that Judaism as a civilization is not a form of truth, but a form of life. The higher the organism is in the scale of life, the more intricate and complex its structure. To survive, Judaism must become complex. It must absorb some of the very forces and tendencies that threaten it, effect new syntheses on higher levels of national life, and enter upon a career which will set up new goals in the evolution of civilizations. [. . .]

TOWARDS A KINGDOM OF PRIESTS

LOUIS FINKELSTEIN

Few men have done more to widen the scope and deepen the meaning of Conservative Judaism than did Louis Finkelstein. The American-born (1895) rabbi and scholar succeeded (1940) Dr. Cyrus Adler in the presidency of the Jewish Theological Seminary in America and, since 1951, has been its chancellor. He has been responsible for the growth of Conservative Jewry's leadership and for the education of its laity. He emphasizes the tradition of Judaic scholarship in full awareness of the needs of our time and the condition of modern man. As a scholar he is best known as the author of *The Pharisees, the Sociological Background of Their Faith* (two volumes, 1938) and editor of *The Jews: Their History, Culture and Religion* (four volumes, 1949). The article that follows refers to the 1955 Convention of the United Synagogue of America, the association of over six hundred Conservative congregations in this country and Canada.

The perils to which man is exposed in the nuclear age differ from those of earlier times in their depth and in their extent. It is a truism to say that the world is becoming a neighborhood and that unless we can learn to be good neighbors we shall end in mutual destruction. It is in just such an age that the message of Bible and Talmud is so urgent and significant. This message requires each of us to transform himself into a master of the art of life so that each of us can become the means of helping the world and fulfilling the will of God.

The task which Conservative Judaism sets before itself in this age is the raising of the level of conduct by its members so that they may achieve the standards set by the great teachers of Judaism of old. Ethical life is too vital a matter to be left to specialists. This movement will not have fulfilled itself until the man of affairs, no less than the specialized student of the sacred texts, sees the fulfillment of his life in the achievement of saintliness.

In Judaism, the life process is one of continuous education for character and, therefore, requires not only practice of good deeds but constant preparation through study for situations which cannot be anticipated. The discovery of what is right under complicated conditions is not easy and does not come from intuition. It comes from a discernment born out of continuous concern with precedents established generation after generation by dedicated spirits.

We are fortunate in having in the literature bequeathed us by our fathers a vast storehouse of religious and ethical experience. The more we study the cases with which our ancestors dealt the better we will be able to handle the complications of our time, as individuals and as a group. The code of conduct now adopted at this convention is an important step in raising the level of conduct of our members. But an even greater step will be taken when each of us, following in the footsteps of our great teachers, sets aside time each day for the contemplation of man's moral dilemmas and tries to prepare himself to achieve greatness in the art which alone is common to all people—the art of the good life.

Nothing we can do for our fellow men outranks in importance the transformation of ourselves into "a kingdom of priests." The world today needs, as Solomon Schechter[18] said in his day, a sprinkling of saints, whose very example will help the rest of mankind in its struggle to attain spiritual life.

IV. *The Dark Years*

WEAR THE YELLOW BADGE WITH PRIDE

ROBERT WELTSCH

The article here reprinted (in a translation by Harry Zohn) appeared in April 1933 as an editorial in the prestigious Zionist periodical *Jüdische Rundschau* in Berlin. It brought a message of courage to the thousands of Jews who found themselves attacked and humiliated by the Nazi assumption of power. In the tradition of Jewish response to persecutions in the past, the editorial called for rededication, self-respect, and an acceptance of the challenge, so that the day designated by the Nazis to terrorize the Jew be turned "to a day of awakening and rebirth."

The writer, Robert Weltsch (born in Prague in 1891), was from 1919 to 1938 the editor-in-chief of the *Jüdische Rundschau*. Under his leadership, this journal was the organ of progressive, liberal Zionist thought, in both its political and cultural aspects. Weltsch's exquisite style and literary taste contributed much to the periodical's high reputation. Since 1940, Weltsch has been a member of the editorial staff of the daily newspaper *Haaretz* (Tel Aviv), and, since 1956, editor of the *Yearbooks* of the Leo Baeck Institute (London).

At the time, the "Yellow Badge" editorial gave inner strength to a shocked community. The new Jewish consciousness it created enabled German Jews to conduct their cultural affairs during the following ten years, as well as to organize emigration. In retrospect, however, Weltsch thinks "this article was based on a mistake"; it underestimated the true character and intentions of the enemy. One could not foresee that ten years after the appearance of the article the yellow badge would become a label for dispatch to concentration camps and gas chambers.

The first of April, 1933, will remain an important date in the history of German Jewry—indeed, in the history of the entire Jewish people.[1] The events of that day have not only political and economic aspects, but moral and psychological ones as well. The political and economic implications have been widely discussed in the newspapers, although the requirements of agitation have frequently obscured an objective understanding of them. To speak about the moral aspects is our task. For no matter how often the Jewish question is discussed these days, we ourselves are the only ones who can express what is going on in the hearts of German Jews, what can be said about events from the Jewish point of view. Today Jews can speak only as Jews; anything else is utterly senseless. The spectre of the so-called "Jewish press" has been dispelled. The fatal misconception of many Jews that Jewish interests can be represented under some other cloak has been eliminated. On the first of April German Jewry was taught a lesson that goes much deeper than even its bitter and currently triumphant adversaries suppose.

Moaning is not our style. We leave it to those Jews of a bygone generation who have learned nothing and forgotten everything to react to events of such impact with sentimental twaddle. Today there must be a new note in the discussion of Jewish affairs. We live in a new era. The national revolution of the German people is a widely visible signal that the old world of concepts has collapsed. This may be painful for many, but only those who face realities can hold their own in this world. We are in the midst of a vast transformation of intellectual, political, social, and economic life. Our concern is: How does Jewry react?

The first of April, 1933, can be a day of Jewish awakening and Jewish rebirth—*if the Jews want it to be*; if the Jews are ripe for it and possess inner greatness; if the Jews are *not* as they are depicted by their adversaries.

Having been attacked, Jewry must avow its faith in itself.

Even on this day of extreme excitement, when the most tempestuous emotions fill our hearts in the face of the unprecedented phenomenon of the entire Jewish population of a great civilized country being universally outlawed, the one thing we must preserve is our composure. Even though we are staggered by the events of recent days, we must not be dismayed, but must take stock without self-deception. What should be recommended at this time is that the work which witnessed the infancy of Zionism,

Theodor Herzl's *The Jewish State*,[2] be disseminated among Jews and non-Jews in hundreds of thousands of copies. If there is still left any feeling for greatness and nobility, gallantry and justice, then every National Socialist who looks into this book is bound to shudder at his own blind actions. Every Jew who read it would also begin to understand and would be consoled and uplifted by it. Page after page of this booklet, which first appeared in 1896, would have to be copied to show that Theodor Herzl was the first Jew dispassionate enough to examine anti-Semitism in connection with the Jewish question. And he recognized that an improvement cannot be effected by ostrich-like behavior, but only by dealing with facts frankly and in full view of the world. [. . .]

We Jews who have been raised in Theodor Herzl's spirit want to ask ourselves what our own guilt is, what sins we have committed. At times of crisis throughout its history, the Jewish people has faced the question of its own guilt. Our most important prayer says, "We were expelled from our country because of our sins." Only if we are critical toward ourselves shall we be just toward others.

Jewry bears a great guilt because it failed to heed Theodor Herzl's call and even mocked it in some instances. The Jews refused to acknowledge that "the Jewish question still exists." They thought the only important thing was not to be recognized as Jews. Today we are being reproached with having betrayed the German people; the National Socialist press calls us the "enemies of the nation," and there is nothing we can do about it. It is not true that the Jews have betrayed Germany. If they have betrayed anything, they have betrayed themselves and Judaism.

Because the Jews did not display their Jewishness with pride, because they wanted to shirk the Jewish question, they must share the blame for the degradation of Jewry. [. . .]

The leaders of the boycott gave orders that signs "with a yellow badge against a black background" be affixed to the boycotted stores. Here is a powerful symbol. This measure is intended as an act of stigmatization, of disparagement. We accept it and propose to turn it into a badge of honor.

Many Jews had a shattering experience last Saturday. Suddenly they were Jews—not out of inner conviction, nor out of pride in a magnificent heritage and contribution to mankind, but through the affixing of a red slip and a yellow badge. The squads went from house to house, pasting them on store fronts and business signs and painting them on windows; for twenty-four hours German Jews were put in a pillory, as it were. In addition to other marks and inscriptions one frequently saw on the shopwindows a large *Magen David*, the Shield of King David. This was supposed to be a disgrace. Jews, pick up the Shield of David and wear it honorably!

For—and this is the first task of our spiritual stock-taking—if today this shield is stained, it has not been entirely the work of our enemies. There have been many Jews whose undignified self-mockery knew no bounds. Judaism was regarded as something outmoded; people did not give it their serious attention; they wanted to free themselves of its tragic aspects by smiling. However, today there is a new type: the new, free Jew, a kind as yet unknown to the non-Jewish world. If today the National Socialist and German patriotic newspapers frequently refer to the type of the Jewish scribbler and the so-called Jewish press, if Jewry is held responsible for these factors, it must be pointed out again and again that they are not representative of Jewry, but at most have tried to derive a financial profit from the Jews. At a time of middle-class self-righteousness, these elements could expect acclamation from Jewish audiences if they lampooned and made light of Jews and Judaism. Quite frequently these circles preached to us nationally oriented Jews the ideals of an abstract cosmopolitan in an effort to destroy all deeper values of Judaism. Upright Jews have always been indignant at the raillery and the caricature directed by Jewish buffoons against Jews to the same extent, or even a greater extent, than they aimed them at Germans and others. Jewish audiences applauded their own degradation, and many attempted to create an alibi for themselves by joining in the mockery. [. . .]

As recently as thirty years ago it was considered objectionable in educated circles to discuss the Jewish question. In those days the Zionists were regarded as trouble-makers with an *idée fixe*. Now the Jewish question is so timely that every small child, every schoolboy as well as the man in the street have no other topic of conversation. All Jews throughout Germany were branded with the word "Jew" on April first. If there is a renewed boycott, the new directives of the boycott committee provide for a uniform designation of all shops: "German business" in the case of non-Jews, the simple word "Jew" for Jewish places. They know who is a Jew. There no longer is any evading or hiding it. The Jewish answer is clear. It is the brief sentence spoken by the prophet Jonah: *Ivri anokhi*, I am a Hebrew. Yes, a Jew. The affirmation of our Jewishness—this is the moral significance of what is happening today. The times are too turbulent to use arguments in the discussion. Let us hope that a more tranquil time will come and that a movement which considers it a matter of pride to be recognized as the pacemaker of the national uprising will no longer derive pleasure from degrading others, even though it might feel that it must fight them. As for us Jews, we can defend our honor. We remember all those who were called Jews, stigmatized as Jews, over a period of five thousand years. We are being reminded that we are Jews. We affirm this and bear it with pride.

A PRAYER BEFORE KOL NIDRE, GERMANY, 1935

LEO BAECK

In 1935, when the anti-Jewish legislation in Germany was well advanced (the "Nuremberg laws") and the Jewish community there harassed and humiliated, Rabbi Leo Baeck wrote the prayer that follows. It was sent to all rabbis in Germany to be read from the pulpit as part of the solemn service which ushers in the Day of Atonement. The Nazi police discovered the text and apprehended its author. The prayer was not uttered at the time. It was, however, read into the record of the Eichmann trial in Jerusalem.

At that time, Baeck was president of the *Reichsvertretung der Juden in Deutschland*, the official representative organization of the Jews in Germany. Established in 1933, this body engaged in social service, founded schools, organized cultural programs, and facilitated emigration.

On Leo Baeck, see preface to "A Minority Religion."

In this hour all Israel stands before God, the judge and the forgiver.

In His presence let us all examine our ways, our deeds, and what we have failed to do.

Where we transgressed, let us openly confess: "We have sinned!" and, determined to return to God, let us pray: "Forgive us."

We stand before our God.

With the same fervor with which we confess our sins, the sins of the individual and the sins of the community, do we, in indignation and abhorrence, express our contempt for the lies concerning us and the defamation of our religion and its testimonies.

We have trust in our faith and in our future.

Who made known to the world the mystery of the Eternal, the One God?

Who imparted to the world the comprehension of purity of conduct and purity of family life?

Who taught the world respect for man, created in the image of God?

Who spoke of the commandment of righteousness, of social justice?

In all this we see manifest the spirit of the prophets, the divine revelation to the Jewish people. It grew out of our Judaism and is still growing. By these facts we repel the insults flung at us.

We stand before our God. On Him we rely. From Him issues the truth and the glory of our history, our fortitude amidst all change of fortune, our endurance in distress.

Our history is a history of nobility of soul, of human dignity. It is history we have recourse to when attack and grievous wrong are directed against us, when affliction and calamity befall us.

God has led our fathers from generation to generation. He will guide us and our children through these days.

We stand before our God, strengthened by His commandment

that we fulfil. We bow to Him and stand erect before men. We worship Him and remain firm in all vicissitudes. Humbly we trust in Him and our path lies clear before us; we see our future.

All Israel stands before her God in this hour. In our prayers, in our hope, in our confession, we are one with all Jews on earth. We look upon each other and know who we are; we look up to our God and know what shall abide.

"Behold, He that keepeth Israel doth neither slumber nor sleep" (Psalm 121:4).

"May He who maketh peace in His hights
bring peace upon us and upon all Israel." [3]

THE MEANING OF THIS HOUR

ABRAHAM JOSHUA HESCHEL

A. J. Heschel (born 1907) is one of the most significant religious philosophers and interpreters of Judaism today. As author of numerous books and studies, as professor of Jewish ethics and mysticism at the Jewish Theological Seminary of America, as a tireless lecturer from coast to coast, Heschel enunciates the relevance of religion, and expounds the teachings of Judaism—prophetic, rabbinic, philosophical, mystical, the faith of scholars, saints, martyrs, poets, Messianists, and of the simple pious worshipper. In Heschel's thinking, in which immense learning is paired with the sensitivity of a true artist, these various strains form a coherent, integrated, whole. What moves him to speak and to write is a keen awareness of the precarious situation of modern man and deep belief that faith is the answer. A faith that is not a set pattern, form, convention, but a "living in a holy dimension," in which traditional rituals and creeds are transformed into elements of a "spiritual order."

Heschel calls his method "depth theology," a theology that speaks for the individual, that "seeks to meet the person in moments in which the whole person is involved." Religion understands man's life as an answer to God's question, addressed to him, a fulfillment of God's eternal expectation. "God is in search of man" and the Bible is the revelation of that search.

Heschel's works (among them, *Man Is Not Alone*, 1951, *Man's Quest for God*, 1954, *God In Search of Man*, 1955) are primarily directed to the Jew, but, in a sense, to all men to whom religion is a life issue. A recent work of scholarly interpretation is *The Prophets*, 1962.

The reprint that follows is based on a speech, delivered in March, 1938, at a conference of Quaker leaders in Frankfurt-am-Main; its final version appeared in *Man's Quest for God*.

Emblazoned over the gates of the world in which we live is the escutcheon of the demons. The mark of Cain in the face of man has come to overshadow the likeness of God. There has never been so much guilt and distress, agony, and terror. At no time has the earth been so soaked with blood. Fellow men turned out to be evil ghosts, monstrous and weird. Ashamed and dismayed, we ask: Who is responsible?

History is a pyramid of efforts and errors; yet at times it is the Holy Mountain on which God holds judgment over the nations. Few are privileged to discern God's judgment in history. But all may be guided by the words of the Baal Shem: If a man has beheld evil, he may know that it was shown to him in order that he learn his own guilt and repent; for what is shown to him is also within him.

We have trifled with the name of God. We have taken the ideals in vain. We have called for the Lord. He came. And was ignored. We have preached but eluded Him. We have praised but defied Him. Now we reap the fruits of our failure. Through centuries His voice cried in the wilderness. How skillfully it was trapped and imprisoned in the temples! How often it was drowned or distorted! Now we behold how it gradually withdraws, abandoning one people after another, departing from their souls, despising their wisdom. The taste for the good has all but gone from the earth. Men heap spite upon cruelty, malice upon atrocity.

The horrors of our time fill our souls with reproach and everlasting shame. We have profaned the word of God, and we have given the wealth of our land, the ingenuity of our minds and the dear lives of our youth to tragedy and perdition. There has never been more reason for man to be ashamed than now. Silence hovers mercilessly over many dreadful lands. The day of the Lord is a day without the Lord. Where is God? Why didst Thou not halt the trains loaded with Jews being led to slaughter? It is so hard to rear a child, to nourish and to educate. Why dost Thou make it so easy to kill? Like Moses, we hide our face; for we are afraid to look upon *Elohim*, upon His power of judgment.[4] Indeed, where were we when men learned to hate in the days of starvation? When raving madmen were sowing wrath in the hearts of the unemployed?

Let modern dictatorship not serve as an alibi for our conscience. We have failed to fight *for* right, *for* justice, *for* goodness; as a result we must fight *against* wrong, *against* injustice, *against* evil. We have failed to offer sacrifices on the altar of peace; thus we offered sacrifices on the altar of war. A tale is told of a band of inexperienced mountain climbers. Without guides, they struck recklessly into the wilderness. Suddenly a rocky ledge gave way beneath their feet and they tumbled headlong into a dismal pit. In the darkness of the pit they recovered from their shock only to find themselves set upon by a swarm of angry snakes. For each snake the desperate men slew, ten more seemed to lash out in its place. Strangely enough, one man seemed to stand aside from the fight. When indignant voices of his struggling companions reproached him for not fighting, he called back: "If we remain here, we shall be dead before the snakes. I am searching for a way of escape from the pit for all of us."

Our world seems not unlike a pit of snakes. We did not sink into the pit in 1939, or even in 1933. We had descended into it generations ago, and the snakes have sent their venom into the bloodstream of humanity, gradually paralyzing us, numbing nerve after nerve, dulling our minds, darkening our vision. Good and evil, that were once as real as day and night, have become a blurred mist. In our everyday life we worshiped force, despised compassion, and obeyed no law but our unappeasable appetite. The vision of the sacred has all but died in the soul of man. And when greed, envy and the reckless will to power came to maturity, the serpents cherished in the bosom of our civilization broke out of their dens to fall upon the helpless nations.

The outbreak of war was no surprise. It came as a long expected sequel to a spiritual disaster. Instilled with the gospel that truth is mere advantage and reverence weakness, people succumbed to the bigger advantage of a lie—"the Jew is our misfortune"—and to the power of arrogance—"tomorrow the whole world shall be ours," "the peoples' democracies must depend upon force." The roar of bombers over Rotterdam, Warsaw, London, was but the echo of thoughts bred for years by individual brains, and later applauded by entire nations. It was through our failure that people started to suspect that science is a device for exploitation, parliaments pulpits for hypocrisy, and religion a pretext for a bad conscience. In the tantalized souls of those who had faith in ideals, suspicion became a dogma and contempt the only solace. Mistaking the abortions of their conscience for intellectual heroism, many thinkers employ clever pens to scold and to scorn the reverence for life, the awe for truth, the loyalty to justice. Man, about to hang himself, discovers it is easier to hang others.

The conscience of the world was destroyed by those who were wont to blame others rather than themselves. Let us remember. We revered the instincts but distrusted the prophets. We labored to perfect engines and let our inner life go to wreck. We ridiculed superstition until we lost our ability to believe. We have helped to extinguish the light our fathers had kindled. We have bartered holiness for convenience, loyalty for success, love for power, wisdom for information, tradition for fashion.

We cannot dwell at ease under the sun of our civilization as our ancestors thought we could. What was in the minds of our martyred brothers in their last hours? They died with disdain and scorn for a civilization in which the killing of civilians could become a carnival of fun, for a civilization which gave us mastery over the forces of nature but lost control over the forces of our self.

Tanks and planes cannot redeem humanity, nor the discovery of guilt by association nor suspicion. A man with a gun is like a beast without a gun. The killing of snakes will save us for the moment but not forever. The war has outlasted the victory of arms as we failed to conquer the infamy of the soul: the indifference to crime, when committed against others. For evil is indivisible. It is the same in thought and in speech, in private and in social life. The greatest task of our time is to take the souls of men out of the pit. The world has experienced that God is involved. Let us forever remember that the sense for the sacred is as vital to us as the light of the sun. There can be no nature without spirit, no world without the Torah, no brotherhood without a father, no humanity without attachment to God.

God will return to us when we shall be willing to let Him in— into our banks and factories, into our Congress and clubs, into our courts and investigating committees, into our homes and theaters. For God is everywhere or nowhere, the Father of all men or no man, concerned about everything or nothing. Only in His presence shall we learn that the glory of man is not in his will to power, but in his power of compassion. Man reflects either the image of His presence or that of a beast.

Soldiers in the horror of battle offer solemn testimony that life is not a hunt for pleasure, but an engagement for service; that there are things more valuable than life; that the world is not a vacuum. Either we make it an altar for God or it is invaded by demons. There can be no neutrality. Either we are ministers of the sacred or slaves of evil. Let the blasphemy of our time not become an eternal scandal. Let future generations not loathe us for having failed to preserve what prophets and saints, martyrs and scholars have created in thousands of years. The apostles of force have shown that they are great in evil. Let us reveal that we can be as great in goodness. We will survive if we shall be as fine and sacrificial in our homes and offices, in our Congress and clubs, as our soldiers are on the fields of battle.

There is a divine dream which the prophets and rabbis have cherished and which fills our prayers, and permeates the acts of true piety. It is the dream of a world, rid of evil by the grace of God as well as by the efforts of man, by his dedication to the task of establishing the kingship of God in the world. God is waiting for us to redeem the world. We should not spend our life hunting for trivial satisfactions while God is waiting constantly and keenly for our effort and devotion.

The Almighty has not created the universe that we may have opportunities to satisfy our greed, envy and ambition. We have not survived that we may waste our years in vulgar vanities. The martyrdom of millions demands that we consecrate ourselves to the fulfillment of God's dream of salvation. Israel did not accept the Torah of their own free will. When Israel approached Sinai, God lifted up the mountain and held it over their heads, saying: "Either you accept the Torah or be crushed beneath the mountain." [5]

The mountain of history is over our heads again. Shall we renew the covenant with God?

THE SLAIN IN THE VALLEY OF DEATH

On the day of memorial for the Jewish victims of Nazi persecution, December 2, 1942

JUDAH L. MAGNES

Even before the full extent of Nazi persecution became known to the free world, there was enough evidence of the catastrophe; Jews everywhere rallied to express their profound concern. There were acts of saintly heroism on the part of individual non-Jews, in Germany and elsewhere. But those in power were silent. The appeals to the conscience of the world were but helpless outcries of the afflicted.

Judah L. Magnes (1877-1948), one of the men who gave voice to the impact of events on the Jewish community, was an American-born liberal rabbi who, in 1921, settled in Palestine. He devoted himself to the upbuilding of the Hebrew University in Jerusalem; when the University was opened in 1925, he became its chancellor, and in 1936, its president. He represented the highest prophetic-humanist ideals of Jewish faith and attempted to translate them into concrete action. Through the *Brit Shalom* (Covenant of Peace) and *Ihud* (Unity) movements, in which he played a leading part, he worked for Arab-Jewish understanding and for a binational commonwealth in Palestine. A religious group *Ha-Ol* (The Yoke), which Magnes

founded during World War II, strove for "acceptance of all
suffering in love, but not in joy; acceptance of the yoke even
unto the death of martyrdom; public sanctification of His Name;
to be the servant of God."

It is hard to believe, yet one must.
But should it be so hard for us?
The whole world is but a valley of slaughter, and the earth is filled
with violence. Each day, each hour those slain with the sword
fall in thousands and in myriads.
Yet it is hard to believe the reports that come to us.
But why?
From the very beginnings of our history our Bible speaks of:

> The voice of thy brother's blood which crieth unto me from
> the ground (Genesis 4:10);
> and the ever-lasting question,

> Am I my brother's keeper? (*Ibid.* 4:9)

The prophet likewise asked:

> Who hath believed our report?

while picturing his people's estate as,

> despised and rejected of men, a man of sorrows, stricken,
> smitten of God and afflicted (Isaiah 53:1, 3 f.).

No book is so close to the soul of a people as the book of Psalms
to Israel. Throughout its pages there is lamentation, mourning,
woe, because,

> They say of Jerusalem, rase it, rase it even to the foundation
> thereof; and because they dash thy little ones against the
> stones (Psalm 137:7, 9).

We commemorate the persecutions of the Roman Emperor
Trajan[6] each year as we read among the Atonement prayers:

> Let me remember the slain of the Kingdom.

Thus also in each period of our history—thus also in that very

Germany where, as we read in the thirteenth century Memor-buch,[7] holy congregations were sacrificed, Sanctifying the Name.

Yet it is hard for us to believe what we hear to-day, because we do not want to believe that man, created in the Image of God, is this devouring beast. It seems, we must learn this anew with each generation. It is the eternal warfare between the Image and the beast. Not much advance can be recorded. Mankind remains sunk in his uncleanness.

From Zion, the Hebrew University looks to the Universities of the world and says:

> The voice of the blood of your brothers cries to you from the ground (Genesis 4:10). Woe is me now, my soul is wearied of the murderers (Jeremiah 4:31). Have we not all one Father, hath not one Father created us? (Malachi 2:10)

Will the Universities of the world lift their voice? Or will they say:

> Am I my brother's keeper?

There is no healing for the world, except that Israel be healed; and Israel can be healed only if, with his full strength, he fulfil his noblest task, bringing healing to mankind.

As for us, we lift our voice on high:

> Awake, cast us not off for ever.
> Wherefore hidest Thou Thy face, and forgetest
> our affliction and our oppression? (Psalm 44:24 f.)
> Lord God, to whom vengeance belongeth,
> God, to whom vengeance belongeth, appear (Psalm 94:1).

And as we utter these terrifying words, let us remember that,

> To Me belongeth vengeance and recompense (Deuteron-omy 32:35), to Him Who putteth on the garments of vengeance. For, He judgeth the peoples righteously, for He cometh, for He cometh to judge the world with righteous-ness, and the peoples with his truth (Psalm 96:13).

IF GOD LETS ME LIVE

ANNE FRANK

Anne Frank was born in Germany in 1929; her family emigrated to Holland in 1933. She wrote her diary, from which the following excerpt is taken, between 1942 and 1944, while in hiding in an attic during the Nazi occupation in Holland. In August 1944 she and her family were led away; in March 1945 she died in the concentration camp of Bergen-Belsen. Later, her diary was discovered.

[. . .] We have been pointedly reminded that we are in hiding, that we are Jews in chains, chained to one spot, without any rights, but with a thousand duties. We Jews mustn't show our feelings, must be brave and strong, must accept all inconveniences and not grumble, must do what is within our power and trust in God. Sometime this terrible war will be over. Surely the time will come when we are people again, and not just Jews.

Who has inflicted this upon us? Who has made us Jews different from all other people? Who has allowed us to suffer so terribly up till now? It is God that has made us as we are, but it will be God, too, who will raise us up again. If we bear all this suffering and if there are still Jews left, when it is over, then Jews, instead of being doomed, will be held up as an example. Who knows, it might even be our religion from which the world and all peoples learn good, and for that reason and that reason only do we have to suffer now. We can never become just Netherlanders, or just English, or representatives of any country for that matter, we will always remain Jews, but we want to, too.

Be brave! Let us remain aware of our task and not grumble, a solution will come, God has never deserted our people. Right through the ages there have been Jews, through all the ages they have had to suffer, but it has made them strong too; the weak fall, but the strong will remain and never go under!

During that night I really felt that I had to die, I waited for the police, I was prepared, as the soldier is on the battlefield. I was eager to lay down my life for the country, but now, now I've been saved again, now my first wish after the war is that I may become Dutch! I love the Dutch, I love this country, I love the language and want to work here. And even if I have to write to the Queen myself, I will not give up until I have reached my goal.

I am becoming still more independent of my parents, young as I am, I face life with more courage than Mummy; my feeling for justice is immovable, and truer than hers. I know what I want, I have a goal, an opinion, I have a religion and love. Let me be myself and then I am satisfied. I know that I'm a woman, a woman with inward strength and plenty of courage.

If God lets me live, I shall attain more than Mummy ever has done, I shall not remain insignificant, I shall work in the world and for mankind!

And now I know that first and foremost I shall require courage and cheerfulness!

Yours, Anne

I BELIEVE

Inscription on the walls of a cellar in Cologne, Germany, where Jews hid from Nazis.

I believe in the sun even when it is not shining.
I believe in love even when feeling it not.
I believe in God even when He is silent.

ON THE AGENDA: DEATH

A Document of the Jewish Resistance

In February, 1943, Mordecai Tannenbaum, an "inmate" of the Vilna ghetto, was sent, with a few others, to organize the resistance in the ghetto of Bialystok. The reprint that follows is the record of a meeting held at the time by the executive committee of the *Hechalutz*, organization of Palestinian pioneers, Bialystok branch. Six months later, Nazi troops entered the ghetto; they met with fierce resistance, which continued until the middle of September, when the Nazis "won" the battle of Bialystok. Among the estimated forty thousand Jews who fell in the battle was Mordecai Tannenbaum. The record of the meeting, originally in Yiddish, was preserved by a Polish peasant.

MORDECAI: I'm glad that at least we're in a good mood. Unfortunately, the meeting won't be very gay; this meeting is historic or tragic, as you prefer, but certainly sad. The few people sitting here are the last *halutzim* in Poland. We are entirely surrounded by the dead. You know what has happened in Warsaw: no one is left. The same is true of Bendin and Czestochowa, and probably everywhere else. We are the last. It's not a particularly pleasant feeling to be the last; on the contrary, it imposes a special responsibility on us. We have to decide what to do tomorrow. There is no point in sitting together in the warmth of our memories, and there is no point in waiting for death together, collectively. What shall we do?

We can do two things: decide that with the first Jew to be deported now from Bialystok, we start our counter-attack, that from tomorrow on nobody is allowed to hide during the action. Everybody will be mobilized. We can see to it that not one German leaves the ghetto alive, that not one factory is left standing.

It is not out of the question that after we have finished our task some of us may even be still alive. But it must be a fight to the finish, till we fall.

Or we could decide to escape to the woods. We must consider the possibilities realistically. Two of our comrades were sent today to make a place ready; in any event, as soon as the meeting is over a military alert will be instituted. We must decide now, because our fathers can't do our worrying for us. This is an orphanage.

There is one condition; our approach must be based on an idea, and our thinking must be related to the movement. Whoever imagines or thinks that he has a real chance to stay alive, and wants to use his chance—fine, we'll help him in whatever way we can. Each one of us will have to decide for himself about his own life or death. But together we have to find a collective answer to the common question. I don't want to impose my opinion on anybody, so for the time being I won't express myself on the question.

ISAAC: What we're really debating is two different kinds of death. Attack means certain death. The other way means death two or three days later.

We ought to analyze both ways; perhaps something can be done. I don't have enough precise information, and I should like to hear the opinions of better informed comrades.

If comrades think that they could remain living, we ought to think about it.

HERSHL: It's still too early to strike a balance on everything we've lived through in the past year and a half. Nevertheless, in the light of the fateful decision confronting us, we must form a clear idea of what we have lived through.

Hundreds of thousands of Jews have perished in the last year; with great subtlety the enemy has succeeded in demoralizing us and leading us like cattle to the slaughterhouses of Ponar, Chelmno, Beloszyz, and Treblinka. The extermination of the Jewish communities of Poland will be not only the most tragic but also the ugliest chapter in Jewish history, a chapter of Jewish impotence and cowardice. Even our movement has not always stood on the required high level. Instead of giving the signal for desperate resistance, we have everywhere put off making a decision. Even in Warsaw the resistance would have had a different result if it had been started not at the end but at the beginning of the liquidation.

Here in Bialystok it is our fate to live through the last act of the bloody tragedy. What can we do, what ought we do? The way I see it, this is the objective situation. The great majority of the ghetto, of our own family, have been sentenced to death. We are condemned. We have never looked on the woods as a hiding place; we have seen the woods as a base for combat and revenge. But the tens of young people now escaping to the woods are not seeking a battlefield; most of them are living a beggar's life and will doubtless find a beggar's death. In the conditions in which we now find ourselves, our fate would be to lead the same beggar's and vagrant's life.

Only one thing remains for us: to organize collective resistance in the ghetto, at any cost; to consider the ghetto our Musa Dagh,[8] to write a proud chapter of Jewish Bialystok and our movement into history.

I can imagine how others would have reacted if their families had been subjected to what ours have been. The lowest Gentile peasant would have spat on his own life, and stuck a knife into the guilty one. The only emotion dominating him would have been the thirst for revenge.

Our duty is clear: with the first Jew to be deported, we must begin our counter-action. If anyone succeeds in taking arms from the murderer and going into the woods—fine. A young person with weapons can find his place in the woods. We still have time to prepare the woods as a place for combat and revenge.

I have lost everything, all those near to me; still, there persists the desire to live. But there is no choice. If I thought that not only individuals could save themselves, but fifty or sixty per cent of the ghetto Jews, I would say that our decision should be to remain alive at any cost. But we are condemned to death.

SARAH: Comrades! If we are concerned about honor, we have long since lost it. In most of the Jewish communities the extermination activities were carried out smoothly, without counter-action. It is better to remain living than to kill five Germans. In a counter-action we will all die, without any possible doubt. On the other hand, in the woods forty or fifty per cent of our people can be saved. That will be our honor and that will be our history. We are still needed; we shall yet be of use. Since in any event we do no longer have honor, let it be our duty to remain alive.

ENOCH: No illusions! We have nothing to expect but liquidation to the last Jew. We have a choice of two kinds of death. The woods won't save us, and certainly rebellion in the ghetto won't. There remains for us only to die honorably.

The prospects for our resistance are not good. I don't know whether we have adequate means for combat. It's the fault of all of us that our means are so small, but that's water over the dam

—we'll have to use what we have. Bialystok will be liquidated completely, like all the other Jewish cities.

In the first operation the factories were spared, but no one can believe that the Nazis will let them go this time.

It is obvious that the woods offer greater opportunities for revenge, but we must not go there to live on the mercy of peasants, to buy our food and lives for money. Going to the woods should mean going to become active partisans, but that requires arms.

The weapons we have aren't suited to the woods. If we do have enough time left, we should acquire arms and go to the woods.

But if the Nazi action intervenes, we must answer as soon as they touch the first Jew.

CHAIM: There are no Jews left, there are only remnants. There is no more movement, there are only remnants. There is no point in talking about honor; if we can, we must try to save ourselves, and not worry how we'll be judged. We must hide in the woods, and maintain systematic communication among the comrades.

MORDECAI: If we wanted to hard enough, and made up our minds that it was our duty, we could make sure our people were safe to the very end, as long as there were any Jews left in Bialystok. I ask an extreme question: do the comrades who are for the woods propose that we should hide and not react at the next Nazi action, so that we can escape into the woods later?

(VOICES FROM ALL SIDES: No, No!)

There are two opinions, one represented by Sarah and Chaim, and the other by Hershl and Enoch. Make your choice. One thing is sure—we won't go to the factories and pray to God that the Nazis catch the people who have hidden, so that we can be saved. And we won't watch passively from our factory windows when comrades from another factory are led away.

We can have a vote: Hershl or Chaim.

FANYA (*of the Branch*): I agree with Enoch. We have to choose between one big action here, or a series of much smaller actions, which in the end will have a much greater significance—I mean escaping into the woods. Because we aren't sufficiently well equipped and don't have the opportunity to go to the woods, and because the situation is very tense, we must emphasize counter-action right here; as soon as the first Jew is seized for deportation, we must attack with all our strength.

But if nothing happens for a few more weeks, we must make every effort to leave.

ELIEZER SUCHANITZKY (*of the Branch*): Comrades! I think it would be wrong for us to try to work in two directions at the same time. Taking to the woods is a good idea; it gives us some chance to remain alive. But at the present moment, when action is so imminent, going to the woods is an illusion. Even if we have another three or four weeks, we won't be able to assemble all the necessary material and take it with us.

I think there is only one thing for us to do: to answer a Nazi action with our counter-action. I think we should work only along this line, so that we can give the most forceful possible answer with the limited means at our disposal.

JOCHEBED: Why is there all this talk about death? It isn't natural. Even a soldier at the front, or a partisan in the woods, in the greatest danger keeps on thinking about life.

We know what the situation is, but why frighten everybody with all this talk about death? If that's what we should do, let's take to the woods, or remain here and fight it out. That doesn't mean that we must necessarily be killed. Everything we've been saying here is opposed to our most basic instincts.

CHAIM: I don't agree with Jochebed. We must be consistent, we dare not give anyone the moral dispensation to run away. This will be for keeps, not for fun. When we fight, it will have to be to the last. And to fight means to be killed. I think we would be accomplishing more if we remained alive, by taking to the woods.

[*He suggests setting up a base outside the ghetto, so that sabotage can be carried on inside the city even after the Nazis act.*]

MOSES: In the order of importance, the counter-action comes first; then, if possible, organization of partisan activity in the woods. Everyone here, without exception, should speak his mind, because the lives of all the comrades depend on the decisions made at this meeting. If necessary, let the meeting last until morning.

CHAIM: You want everybody to speak so the meeting should decide against counter-action in the ghetto. (*Protest.*)

DORKE (*of the Branch*): I think our position must be the position of people in a movement, of people with full consciousness of what they're doing, who know what has happened to our nearest relatives and friends.

We will die a worthy death. The chances for revenge are greater in the woods, but we cannot go there as vagrants, only as active partisans. Since the necessary preparation for the woods is impossible now, we must devote all our energy to the counter-action.

ZIPPORAH: It's hard to say anything, it's hard to choose the manner of your own death. There's a kind of argument going on inside me between life and death. It's not important for me whether I or somebody else will remain alive. After what we have lived through and seen with our own eyes, we shouldn't have too high a notion of the value of our lives. I am trying to think a little more deeply of the question of our movement.

We're proud of the fact that our movement lived through the most difficult period in the history of the Jewish community in Poland. I was brought here from Vilna, and so were many others. There were certainly more important people to save. It wasn't I who was brought here, and it wasn't you; it was the movement. Now the question has been posed: will the movement be destroyed entirely? Does the movement have the right to be destroyed? We are a movement of the Jewish people; we must, and we do in fact, undergo all the sorrows and persecutions of the people.

When we consider the right to stay alive, I say yes, we have every right. Perhaps our movement may have to be the only one to speak up, when that is needed. Take the example of Warsaw. That was certainly a proud and manly death, but it wasn't the kind of thing a movement should do.

The decision of a movement should be to remain alive.

I don't mean we should hold on to life for its own sake, but for continued work, for extending the chain that was not broken even in the darkest days.

Our chances are as small as they can be, but if we put everything we have into our effort, we can succeed.

SHMULIK: This is the first time we have had to hold a meeting about death. We are going to undertake our counter-action not to write history, but to die an honorable death, as young Jews in our times should. And if our history is ever written, it will be different from the history of the Spanish Jews, who leaped into the flames with "Hear, O Israel!" on their lips.

Now, as to the action. All our experience teaches us that we can't trust the Germans, in spite of their assurances that the artisans will be protected, that only those who don't work will be deported, and so on. They have succeeded in driving thousands of Jews to the slaughter only by deception and demoralization.

And yet we have a chance to come out of the impending action safely. Everyone is playing for time, and so should we. In the short time that remains, we can work to improve our small and impoverished store of weapons.

We should also do what we can about the woods, where we can fulfill two functions.

I don't want to be misunderstood. We shouldn't interpret our hiding while the action is taking place as cowardice.

No! Man's instinct for life is so great, and here we must be selfish. I don't care if others are deported in our place. We have a greater claim on life than others, rightly.

We have set an aim in life for ourselves—to remain living at any cost! We were brought here from Vilna because there was a smell of liquidation there, and living witnesses had to remain. We must therefore do everything we can, if there is no liquidation immediately, to wait and gain time.

But if the liquidation starts now, then let it be all of us together in the counter-action, and "let me die with the Philistines." [9]

SARAH: I want the comrades to know that I will do whatever is decided. But I'm amazed by the calmness with which we're talking about all this.

When I see a German, I begin to tremble all over. I don't know whether the comrades, and especially the girls, will have enough strength and courage. I said what I said before because I don't have any faith in my own strength.

EZEKIEL: I don't agree with Sarah. In the face of death you can become weak and powerless, or you can become very strong, since there is nothing to lose. I agree with Shmulik that we should begin our counter-action only in the event of a definite liquidation.

ETHEL: Concretely—if an action is started in the next few days, then our only choice can be a counter-action; but if we are granted more time, we should work along the lines of taking to the woods.

I hope I can be equal to the duties that will be imposed on us. It may be that in the course of events I shall be strengthened. In any case, I am resolved to do everything that needs to be done.

Hershl spoke rightly. We are going to perform a desperate act, whether we want to or not. Our fate is sealed, and there remains for us only the choice between one kind of death and another. I am calm.

MORDECAI: The position of the comrades is clear. We will do everything we can to help as many people as possible escape into the woods for partisan combat. Every one of us who is in the ghetto when the Nazis start their action must react as soon as the first Jew is seized for deportation. We are not going to haggle about our lives; we must understand objective conditions.

The most important thing is this: to maintain until the very end the pride and dignity of the movement.

JEWISH DESTINY AS THE DP'S SEE IT
The Ideology of the Surviving Remnant
SAMUEL GRINGAUZ

European Jews who endured the 1939-1945 disaster in concentration camps or as underground fighters and survived to become "displaced persons" in the postwar period formed specific views on their position as Jews and on Judaism in general. The essay that follows is an attempt, based on observation and personal participation, to describe the intellectual, psychological, and historical orientation of *She-erit Hapletah* (or *Sherit Hapleita*), the surviving remnant. The author, Dr. Samuel Gringauz (b. 1900), was a DP himself, head of the camp in Landsberg, Germany, and, after his liberation, president of the Congress of Liberated Jews in the U.S. Zone of Germany. Prior to 1933, he was scientific assistant at the Heidelberg Institute of Social Sciences; later he became judge in the District Court of Appeals in Memel and a leader in that city's Jewish community. In 1947 he came to the United States.

What above all distinguishes the outlook of the Jewish DP's is *its Judeocentrism and its intra-Jewish universalism and unity*.

For the Jewish DP, Jewishness is a given fact of existence that plays the deciding role in life and death, in attitude and feeling, and influences and governs every aspect of his life. During the most crucial years of his recent experience, it was the mere fact of his Jewishness that determined the physical circumstances of his existence, and it was this fact essentially that lay behind the danger of death in which he stood daily, and behind every important step he took.

The Jewish problem, for the Jewish DP, became a psychic and existential one. His Jewishness became the substance of consciousness, became fate. Just as his enemy showed day in and day out an all-embracing, extremely intense, and omnipresent anti-Jewish attitude, making the Jewishness of the Jew the center of all his attention, so too the Jew, in self-defense, made of his Jewishness the foundation of his consciousness. The results of this experience are what distinguish the Sherit Hapleita from the Jews of countries untouched by the catastrophe, and also from the Jews of Palestine, whose Jewish feeling is indeed strong and central, having been hardened and strengthened in battle, but remains nevertheless normal and healthy. The Judeocentrism of the Sherit Hapleita, as the fundamental factor in its ideology, exceeds in its nationalist intensity and all-embracingness all other tendencies.

The Sherit Hapleita sees it as its task to symbolize the Jewish national tragedy and be the protagonist of Jewish retribution. And although it is generally admitted that the individual Jewish DP is prey to spiritual weaknesses having their origin in the catastrophic conditions of the last years, this task is viewed by the Sherit Hapleita as one laid upon it by destiny and history regardless of the strength of its bearers, and for this very reason alone the task seems all the more urgent. Through the Sherit Hapleita the entire Jewish people is to measure the extent of its historical tragedy: the Sherit Hapleita must demonstrate to all Jews everywhere their involvement in the common fate. The Sherit Hapleita is to be a herald of the indivisibility of Jewish destiny; it shall, by its existence and its struggles, arouse and strengthen Jewish awareness of the national tragedy.

More than any other group in the Jewish nation, *the Sherit Hapleita feels itself charged with a great obligation to the dead* such as no unveiling of monuments can discharge: they have seen centuries-old monuments destroyed in an instant. Women on the way to the crematoria, children in their final agonies, comrades on the point of martyrdom—all those who screamed for retribution and revenge—have left behind a legacy whose executor the Sherit Hapleita feels itself to be, and whose accomplishment is the substance of its ideology. But the mission of retribution is not directly conceived in the sense of "an eye for an eye"; the enormity of the crime makes this unthinkable. The retributive mission of the Sherit Hapleita takes instead the form of a defiant affirmation of life and national rebirth. Nothing must permit Hitler a final triumph by the destruction of the Jews through the circumstances of the postwar world or through inner disintegration. Judaism, as a nation and a collectivity, must be preserved despite all its enemies, and shall emerge from the great catastrophe healthier and morally purified, shall experience a new renaissance and shall lead a normal life on its own soil. This is to be the retribution and the revenge.

Empowered by its own martyrdom and the legacy left it by the dead, the Sherit Hapleita—in the name of the everlasting awful majesty of one and a half million martyred children, two and a half million crucified mothers and wives, two million fallen fathers and brothers, a quarter of a million DP's still wasting away in the camps—demands of the Jewish people a single and united national-political attitude. This is the basic foundation of the Zionism of the survivors. It is no party Zionism; it is a historical-philosophical Zionism felt as an historical mission, as a debt to the dead, as retribution toward the enemy, as a duty to the living. It is, moreover, a Zionism of warning, because the Sherit Hapleita feels that the continuation of Jewish national abnormality means the danger of a repetition of the catastrophe.

A further essential element in the ideology of the Jewish DP's is *Jewish universalism*. The DP's are the surviving remnant of those Jews who, regardless of origin, culture, social position, ideology, class, yes, even religion, were condemned to death *only* because they were Jewish. American and Swiss citizens, heroes of the First World War, the most respected representatives of European culture, manual laborers and bankers, Zionists and Socialists, Orthodox Jews and Catholics, all were collectively stripped of every attribute and, nameless and nondescript, were tortured and killed—as "Jew X." A Jewish tailor from Rhodes who could find no one in the camp to understand him, and a Hungarian druggist baptized thirty years before, lay in the same wooden bunk with me, shared their experience as Jews with me, and died only because they were Jewish. This is why the Sherit Hapleita feels itself to be the embodiment of the unity of Jewish experience: Jewish unity for them is no political program but an actual and living fact of experience. This is why they feel themselves prophets of a national rebirth, charged with the task of symbolizing this unity and this rebirth, and of being the backbone of its realization.

The belief in these extraordinary tasks intensifies the group consciousness of the Sherit Hapleita and makes it see itself as a "chosen group" within the "chosen people." They feel that the historical experience of those "who were in Treblinka" is greater and deeper than the experience of those who only read about Treblinka. And when they hear it said that what happened in Germany could not be repeated in another country, they remember what a flourishing family were the German Jews, and how they said that what had happened in Russia could not be repeated in another country. In the hour of the imminence of death, when the tranced gaze stares into eternity, the eyes grow larger and the vision deeper. This is the Sherit Hapleita's inner justification for taking the prophet's rod in hand and coming forth as monitors and warning visionaries to the Jews of the countries untouched by the catastrophe.

Life in the Diaspora, for the Jewish DP's, is synonymous with the danger of recurrence. No sociological argument can obliterate from their minds what experience has stamped on it. For they have seen not only Germany. Eastern Europe and Central Europe are part of their experience. And they have seen the countries of Western Europe. The majority of the nations of Europe were represented among the oppressors in the concentration camps, and the only difference was that in this confusion of nationalities one was more strongly represented than the others. And they have watched these different nations *after* the end of the war, especially those who found their number of surviving Jews too high, and also those who met the influx of Jews with a cold antipathy. And they have seen the growth of a new anti-Semitism in Germany, in Europe, and among the occupation troops. The eyes of the Sherit Hapleita are large and deep, for they have looked on eternity.

The Sherit Hapleita is extraordinarily sensitized to and apprehensive of anti-Semitism. They have experienced how insignificant manifestations of hatred and exclusiveness, so easily disregarded at first, could bear the seeds of catastrophe, and they are only too ready today to generalize and exaggerate every anti-Semitic manifestation, to see in every incident the sign of a future explosion.

The Sherit Hapleita therefore undertakes the prophetic mission of warning the Jews of unaffected countries. Neither equality of rights, nor a constitution, nor patriotism is security against persecution, to their minds. One cannot escape one's Jewishness— either by assimilation, baptism, or mixed marriage. With satisfaction they heard Richard H. S. Crossman, a radical representative of the British Labor party, say that the Jews who denied their Jewishness contributed most to anti-Semitism. And they say to the Jews of countries untouched by the catastrophe: "It can happen again. And therefore we demand of you to build up Palestine not only for us, but as an ultimate place of refuge in general."

There are other considerations. The Sherit Hapleita has the conviction that today it is the sole force working for unity within the body of Jewry, and that it constitutes the only important political argument for the solution of the Jewish question that still carries some weight in the forum of international debate. The DP's are the only group within Jewish life toward whom everybody feels an obligation. They are the only ones for whose sake the Jews of different countries, of different points of view, of different organizations, will unite in common action.

The fate of the Sherit Hapleita, they consider, unites all Jewry in the battle for Palestine. For international Zionism the Sherit Hapleita is an argument, a strength, a reserve. On the one hand, the group would face complete ruin if it were left to its own resources; on the other hand, the Yishuv would be condemned to stagnation and despair were it not for the immigration of the DP's. Without the situation of the DP's as a basis of appeal, American Jewry could not be mobilized so effectively for the up-building of Palestine, nor could the Jews of other lands be nationally awakened and united. Thus the Sherit Hapleita feels today that it is the dynamic force of the Jewish future.

It has always been clear to us that the task laid upon us by destiny greatly exceeds our strength. We are deeply aware that a profound contradiction exists between what destiny has made of us and the task it has laid upon us. Ourselves the products of an unheroic and culpable relapse into barbarism, we are called upon to be the champions of a heroic renaissance. Victims of an outer and inner process of demoralization, we are called upon to accomplish a national and moral revival. End-products of a process of corruption unique in history, we are called upon to provide Jewish culture with a deeper and clearer content and theme. Victims of a psychic upheaval, we are called upon to re-establish the psychological stability of our people. Ourselves the product of the barbaric relationship of the environment to the Jews, it is our task to create a more humane relationship to the environment. This enormous discrepancy between what has been given us to do and what has been granted us to do it with, extraordinarily increases the difficulty of our task, yet does not release us from our obligation. This task history has assigned to us, and it cannot be put off on someone else. But simply to make our feelings known may serve to awaken understanding and make our task easier.

With the end of the great catastrophe, a fundamental change has become apparent in the inner structure of the Jewish people, one that marks the end of an old epoch—European, German-Polish—and the beginning of a new—American-Palestinian. Until the catastrophe, the European Jew—in his two branches, Eastern and Western—represented the Jewish dynamics and the Jewish consciousness. Jews outside Europe functioned either as cultural offshoots or as a cultural periphery. But now European Jewry is destroyed. If one excludes the Jews of Soviet Russia, who are isolated from the body of Jewry, and the Sherit Hapleita, a splinter group without a country and *in statu emigrandi*, then American Jewry represents seventy-five per cent of active Jewry. Therefore the new epoch in Jewish history will be an American-Palestinian one.

The enlistment of American Jewry in the struggle for Palestine, in the economic effort to build it up, and in the effort to preserve the surviving remnant in Europe, fosters a new Jewish unity that will leave its stamp on every future development. The Sherit Hapleita feels itself to be the connecting link in this new unity, the force that gives it meaning and substance. By uniting the efforts of the Jewish people, the Sherit Hapleita lays the basis for a new epoch in Jewish history.

Only in this context can we understand the general tendency to say "Adieu Europe." In the first months following the liberation, this tendency was simply a response to what had been the attitude of the European peoples during the years of the great catastrophe. When the first cultural lecture was given in the Landsberg camp in June 1945, I gave it the title "Adieu Europe." It was the prevailing mood that supplied this title—I was ignorant of the general situation. Later, when the great disillusionment came, when we saw that the tiny remnant of surviving Jews was an annoyance to the nations, when we observed that, though they condemned the annihilation of the Jews, in secret they were not dissatisfied with its results, this tendency to break with Europe acquired a firmer hold on us. Only later, after the entire situation became clear to us, after we realized the historic change that had taken place in the structure of world Jewry, after the end of the European period became obvious historically and philosophically too, only then did the movement "Adieu Europe" acquire a constructive form. And now, because of its objective historical reality, it has become a constituent part of our ideology. If, historically considered, the European epoch of our history is ended, it follows that our place is no longer in Europe, that we must carry with us the legacy of our millennial history to where a new Jewish history is being acted out, to Palestine and America, and give it over with reverence and hope to the makers of the new history, so that the secular continuity of our ethical and cultural values may be assured.

But the renunciation of Europe in no way signifies for us the renunciation of European culture. Quite the contrary. Our resolve to quit Europe is based precisely on the conviction that Europe itself has betrayed the legacy of European culture, and that European culture must be carried forward outside of Europe. We have been too much a part of European culture to abandon it now. As we once expressed it: "We leave Europe because Europe has injured us in our very quality as Europeans."

At the beginning of the modern period, when the Jew left the narrow alleys of the ghetto, he was, as a cultural type, no longer Oriental but European in the full cultural meaning of that term. The Europeanization of Jewish culture, which began with Alexandrian Hellenism, spread from Toledo, Naples, and French Provence through Spain, Portugal, Italy, and France and later to Central and Eastern Europe, was a process that stamped essential traits on the whole of Jewish culture. The Europeanization of Jewish culture was closely joined to the parallel process of the penetration of European culture by Jews. And if we today, after twelve hundred years of European history, quit the ground of Europe, then we do so in full awareness that we are the standard-bearers of Western culture. And in this spirit we intend to create our new homes.

There was a moment in our first reaction when we wanted to make all Western civilization responsible for Auschwitz. It should be borne in mind that for the Eastern European Jew—and he makes up ninety per cent of the Jewish DP's—Germany was the representative of Western civilization; everything the Eastern European acquired of Latin and Anglo-Saxon culture came to him through Germany. For this reason, Germany's relapse into barbarism meant, to him, the collapse of all Western civilization.

At the beginning of 1946, when I was called upon to present the Jewish point of view at a meeting of the Allied nations, I stated it as follows:

"The history of humanity is rich in horror. And if the annihilation of the Jewish people belongs among the most horrible events of history, still, we know—this too will be forgotten. Grass will grow where inexpressible suffering and martyrdom were earlier enacted. Where once the mass graves were, children will play their games and fathers will pursue their occupations. But in the hearts of Jews this question will never cease to be asked—how was it possible? How was it possible after two thousand years of Occidental and Christian culture, after Michelangelo and Leonardo da Vinci, after Molière and Victor Hugo, after William Shakespeare and Lord Byron, after Alexander von Humboldt and Immanuel Kant? How was it possible that professors and writers, priests and philosophers, artists and judges—how was it possible that almost the entire intellectual élite of Germany rapturously cheered on the blood-drunk murderers? And if it was possible once, where is the assurance that it won't happen again tomorrow . . . ?"

But in the summer of 1946, in an article "On the Tasks of the Jewish Remnant of Europe" [10] I expressed our position as follows:

"History has given us the task of symbolizing to the entire world the Jewish problem in modern civilization. We are the surviving remnant of those Jews who, amid rivers of blood and under the shadow of martyrdom, aroused the attention of the world to that problem. We, who are the victims of this civilization, have been called upon to discover the positive basis on which we can unite with it. We have a bill of indictment to prefer against this civilization. At the same time we know that we are part of it and must therefore bear a responsibility for it. We cannot and will not turn away from it. But we must make new contributions. Our experience must serve to redirect the Jewish people. Our tragedy must become the starting point of a new humanism."

And today this still remains the ideal of the Sherit Hapleita. We do not turn away from Occidental culture. We do seek, however, to contribute to its wider moral development. For it was not the civilization of Western Europe that betrayed us, but the monstrous discrepancy between its moral and its technical culture. While its moral culture has had a very slow development in time, with a very restricted extension in society, its technical culture has developed at a furious tempo and its extension in society has been enormous. In this way, that narrow section of society which possessed moral cultivation lost control of the democratic process and was vanquished by a mass technical culture. The free personality lost its command of the social destiny. Thus the moral underworld, and even unabashed mass criminals, were able to win control over the masses and the technical apparatus of society, and defile European civilization with blood and shame. It is precisely the man of the Sherit Hapleita, who in his fateful hours met both the beast of technical perfection and the true individual representatives of Western civilization, who is in the best position to distinguish between the free, civilized human being and the mass Moloch.

The man of the Sherit Hapleita has felt the negative and positive aspects of Western civilization on his own body. And he does not impeach civilization as such, but only its incapacity to subject the broad masses to its moral imperatives. The ideal of Jewish culture—the perfecting, on this earth, of every individual human being, both in his daily behavior and in his general moral and social attributes—coincides with the ideal of Western European culture at many points. And so the Sherit Hapleita accepts a neohumanism as its cultural ideal—the ideal of the moral and social perfection of humanity, the perfection of the broadest possible mass of the population in its practical and daily activities, which would create a community that would resist the pressure of its instincts as well as the oppression of the state, and follow its conscience only, a community that would be able to cast aside evil and make the good prevail. The Sherit Hapleita believes that the tragedy of the great catastrophe, and the Jewish problem itself within the framework of modern civilization, can contribute to a reorientation of Occidental civilization in the direction of the moral perfection of the individual. And the Sherit Hapleita believes that the Jewish people can best fulfill its great task in a country of its own, by the practical example of its social order, a social order whose core is the agricultural collectives of Palestine, which are probably alone in the world in reconciling the principle of personal freedom with that of social justice. [. . .][11]

Two thousand years ago, when the heroes of Jerusalem were defending the city against the Roman legions, Johanan ben Zakkai left the city to go to Jabneh. There, on strange ground, he founded the academy of Jabneh as a center of religious and social law by which to unite the scattered nation. Now as then, the task with which we are confronted is a double one: political struggle in and for Palestine, and the spiritual and social unification of the Jews of the rest of the world. We are confident that the Jewish people will stand the historical test, and that the historical genius of this ancient people will emerge strengthened and purified from this period of trial.

Such is the bold and hopeful ideology of the people of the Sherit Hapleita, who, during the years of horror and the fight for life, during the years of crematoria and partisan battles, even on the verge of almost certain death, expressed the hopes of the eternal people in the tragic but courageous words of this partisan song:

> *Never say that this road is the last;*
> *Though the gray of heaven cover the blue day,*
> *Yet our appointed hour will arrive,*
> *And the marching tread will echo: we are here!*

BEFORE THE MONUMENT TO THE MARTYRED JEWS OF THE WARSAW GHETTO

ALBERT EINSTEIN

On Einstein, see the preface to "On Zionism, the Land of Israel, and the Arabs." The statement that follows was read at the unveiling of the Memorial for the Battle of the Warsaw Ghetto, dedicated at Warsaw, April 19, 1948.

The monument before which you have gathered today was built to stand as a concrete symbol of our grief over the irreparable loss our martyred Jewish nation has suffered. It shall also serve as a reminder for us who have survived to remain loyal to our people and to the moral principles cherished by our fathers. Only through such loyalty may we hope to survive this age of moral decay.

The more cruel the wrong that men commit against an individual or a people, the deeper their hatred and contempt for their victim. Conceit and false pride on the part of a nation prevent the rise of remorse for its crime. Those who have had no part in the crime, however, have no sympathy for the sufferings of the innocent victims of persecution and no awareness of human solidarity. That is why the remnants of European Jewry are languishing in concentration camps and the sparsely populated lands of this earth close their gates against them. Even our right, so solemnly pledged, to a national homeland in Palestine is being betrayed. In this era of moral degradation in which we live the voice of justice no longer has any power over men.

Let us clearly recognize and never forget this: That mutual cooperation and the furtherance of living ties between the Jews of all lands is our sole physical and moral protection in the present situation. But for the future our hope lies in overcoming the general moral abasement which today gravely menaces the very existence of mankind. Let us labor with all our powers, however feeble, to the end that mankind recover from its present moral degradation and gain a new vitality and a new strength in its striving for right and justice as well as for a harmonious society.

THE INDICTMENT OF ADOLF EICHMANN

GIDEON HAUSNER

The indictment, dated Jerusalem, February 21, 1961, and headed "The Attorney-General of the Government of Israel (Gideon Hausner) *versus* Adolf, the son of Adolf Karl Eichmann, aged 54, at present under arrest," consisted of fifteen counts of "crimes against the Jewish people" and "crimes against humanity." "The Particulars of Offence" stated that "the accused, together with others, during the period 1939 to 1945, caused the killing of millions of Jews, in his capacity as the person responsible for the execution of the Nazi plan for the physical extermination of the Jews, known as 'the final solution of the Jewish problem.'" The Attorney-General's Opening Speech, delivered over three sessions of the Court, consisted of eleven chapters; the text that follows here comprises chapters one ("Introduction") and eleven ("The Charge and the Evidence"). The Court found Eichmann guilty on all counts, rejecting his denial of responsibility for the crimes. In March 1962, the case was reviewed by the Supreme Court of Israel, which confirmed the original verdict. Eichmann was executed in Ramleh Prison on the night of May 31, 1962; his body was cremated and the ashes thrown into the Mediterranean.

I

When I stand before you here, Judges of Israel, to lead the Prosecution of Adolf Eichmann, I am not standing alone. With me are six million accusers. But they cannot rise to their feet and point an accusing finger towards him who sits in the dock and cry: "I accuse." For their ashes are piled up on the hills of Auschwitz and the fields of Treblinka, and are strewn in the forests of Poland. Their graves are scattered throughout the length and breadth of Europe. Their blood cries out, but their voice is not heard. Therefore I will be their spokesman and in their name I will unfold the awesome indictment.

The history of the Jewish people is steeped in suffering and tears. "In thy blood, live!" (Ezekiel 16:6) is the imperative that has confronted this nation ever since its first appearance on the stage of history. Pharaoh in Egypt decided to "afflict them with their burdens" and to cast their sons into the river; Haman's decree was "to destroy, to slay, and to cause them to perish" (Esther 3:13); Chmielnicki[12] slaughtered them in multitudes; they were butchered in Petlura's pogroms.[13] Yet never, down the entire blood-stained road travelled by this people, never since the first days of its nationhood, has any man arisen who succeeded in dealing it such grievous blows as did Hitler's iniquitous regime, and Adolf Eichmann as its executive arm for the extermination of the Jewish people. In all human history there is no other example of a man against whom it would be possible to draw up such a bill of indictment as has been read here. The most terrible crimes of those fearful figures of barbarism and blood-lust, Nero, Attila, or Genghis Khan, the telling of which curdles our blood and makes our hair stand on end with horror, deeds that have become "a proverb and a taunt" (Jeremiah 24:9) and an "everlasting abhorrence" (Daniel 12:2) to the nations—these almost seem to pale into insignificance when contrasted with the abominations, the murderous horrors, which will be presented to you in this trial.

At the dawn of history, there were examples of wars of extermination, when one tribe assaulted another with intent to destroy, when, in the heat and passion of battle, peoples were slaughtered, massacred or exiled. But only in our generation has an organized State set upon an entire defenceless and peaceful population, men and women, grey-beards, children and infants, incarcerated them behind electrified fences, imprisoned them in concentration camps, and resolved to destroy them utterly.

Murder has been with the human race since the days when Cain killed Abel; it is no novel phenomenon. But we have had to wait till this twentieth century to witness with our own eyes a new kind of murder: not the result of the momentary surge of passion or mental black-out, but of a calculated decision and painstaking planning; not through the evil design of an individual, but through a mighty criminal conspiracy involving thousands; not against one victim whom an assassin may have decided to destroy, but against an entire people.

In this trial, we shall also encounter a new kind of killer, the kind that exercises his bloody craft behind a desk, and only occasionally does the deed with his own hands. Indeed, we know of only one incident in which Adolf Eichmann actually beat to death a Jewish boy, who had dared to steal fruit from a peach tree in the yard of his Budapest home. But it was his word that put gas chambers into action; he lifted the telephone, and railway trains left for the extermination centres; his signature it was that sealed the doom of thousands and tens of thousands. He had but to give the order, and at his command the troopers took to the field to rout Jews out of their homes, to beat and torture them and chase them into ghettoes, to pin the badge of shame on their breasts, to steal their property—till finally, after torture and pillage, after everything had been wrung out of them, when even their hair had been taken, they were transported en masse to the slaughter. Even the corpses were still of value: the gold teeth were extracted and the wedding rings removed.

We shall find Eichmann describing himself as a fastidious person, a "white-collar" worker. To him, the decree of extermination was just another written order to be executed; yet he was the one who planned, initiated and organized, who instructed others to spill this ocean of blood, and to use all the means of murder, theft, and torture. He is responsible, therefore, as though he with his own hands had knotted the hangman's noose, had lashed the victims into the gas-chambers, had shot in the back and pushed into the open pit every single one of the millions who were slaughtered. Such is his responsibility in the eyes of the law, and such is his responsibility by every standard of conscience and morality. His accomplices in the crime were neither gangsters nor men of the underworld, but the leaders of a nation—including professors and scholars, robed dignitaries with academic degrees, linguists, educated persons, the "intelligentsia." We shall encounter them—the doctors and lawyers, scholars, bankers and economists, in those councils which resolved to exterminate the Jews, and among the officers and directors of the work of murder in all its terrible phases.

This murderous decision, taken deliberately and in cold blood, to annihilate a nation and blot it out from the face of the earth, is so shocking that one is at a loss for words to describe it. Words exist to express what man's reason can conceive and his heart contain, and here we are dealing with actions that transcend our human grasp. Yet this is what did happen: millions were condemned to death, not for any crime, not for anything they had done, but only because they belonged to the Jewish people. The development of technology placed at the disposal of the destroyers efficient equipment for the execution of their appalling designs.

This unprecedented crime, carried out by Europeans in the twentieth century, led to the definition of a criminal concept unknown to human annals even during the darkest ages—the crime of Genocide.

The calamity of the Jewish people in this generation was considered at a number of the trials conducted in the wake of Germany's defeat in the Second World War, when mankind resolved to set up instruments of defence, through the establishment of courts and execution of judgments, to ensure that the horrors of war which our generation has witnessed shall not recur. But in none of those trials was the tragedy of Jewry as a whole the central concern. It was among the subjects treated; sometimes it was given great weight, always it evoked sentiments of horror; but it was never at the centre, since the accused at these trials were indicted for crimes against members of many and various nations. There was only one man who had been concerned almost entirely with the Jews, whose business had been their destruction, whose role in the establishment of the iniquitous regime had been limited to them. That was Adolf Eichmann. If we charge him also with crimes against non-Jews, committed as it were by the way, this is because we make no ethnic distinctions. But we should remember that the mission of the accused, in which for years he saw his destiny and calling, and to which he devoted himself with enthusiasm and endless zeal, was the extermination of the Jews.

Men still ask themselves, and they will certainly continue to ask in days to come: How could it have happened? How was it possible in the middle of the twentieth century? The judges at the Nuremberg trials also asked themselves this question, examined its various aspects, and arrived at interesting formulations; yet it would be difficult to claim that a full or satisfactory answer was given. I doubt whether in this trial we on our part will succeed in laying bare the roots of the evil. This task must remain the concern of historians, sociologists, authors and psychologists, who will try to explain to the world what happened to it. But we shall nevertheless endeavor, however briefly, to describe the background, in an attempt to explain what is perhaps altogether inexplicable by the standards of ordinary reason.

Hitler, his regime and crimes, were no accidental or transient phenomenon. He did not come to power as a result merely of a unique combination of circumstances. Historical processes are usually the product of many developments, like many streams flowing each in its own channel until they combine into a mighty river. They will come together only if their flow is in the same general direction.

No doubt various events contributed to the rise of Nazism: the defeat of Germany in the First World War; the subsequent economic difficulties; lack of leadership and futile party divisions; fratricidal strife and disunion—all these impelled the German people, disoriented and groping, to turn its eyes towards the false prophet. But Hitler would not have been able to remain in power, and to consolidate in his support all the strata of the German people, including most of the intellectuals—to win the support of so many university professors and professional men, the civil service and the whole army—if the road to his leadership had not already been paved. Not even the oppressive regime of the concentration camps, and the atmosphere created by the terror so rapidly activated against all opposition by the hooligans of the S.S. and the S.A., are adequate alone to explain the enthusiastic and devoted support he received from the majority of the nation, unless it had been preceded by an extensive spiritual preparation. When we read today the declarations of the scientists, authors, and journalists—including many who had not been among his adherents before—who chanted his praises and willingly gave him their support and backing, how they willingly and joyfully accepted his yoke, we must reach the conclusion, however reluctantly, that the people were ready and prepared to crown him as their leader. [. . .]

Hitler denied the existence of a common basis for all humanity. According to his doctrine, there is no mutual responsibility between men. In place of the injunction "And thou shalt love thy neighbor as thyself" (Leviticus 19:18), we find "Crush him that is unlike thyself!" Instead of the ideal of human brotherhood, we have the principle of race superiority. [. . .]

Only those whose blood was Aryan were worthy of citizenship. This was established by the Nuremberg laws. The preamble to the "Law for the Preservation of the German Blood and the German Honor" stated:

> "Imbued with the consciousness that the purity of German blood is essential to the continued existence of the German people, and animated by the inflexible resolve to secure the security of the German Nation for all time, the Reichstag has unanimously adopted the following law . . ." [. . .]

Institutes were established in Nazi Germany, devoted to racial research and the determination of the hierarchical pyramid of racial superiorities. The Jews found themselves at the bottom of the list, followed only by the Gipsies and the Negroes. [. . .]

And Hitler did free the hatred of the Jew which was latent in the hearts of large sections of the German people, intensify it and stimulate it into greater activity. The germ of anti-Semitism was already there; he stimulated it and transformed it into the source of an epidemic. For the purposes of Nazi Germany's internal policy, the Jew was a convenient object of hatred; he was weak and defenceless. The world outside remained silent when he was persecuted, and contented itself with verbal reactions that did little harm. The Jew was pilloried as a supporter of Communism—and therefore an enemy of the German people. In the same breath he was accused of being a capitalist—and therefore an enemy of the workers. National-Socialism had found in the Jew an object of hostility appropriate to both halves of its name, and it set him up as a target for both national enmity and class hatred. The Jew was also a ready target through which the attention of the public could be diverted from other problems. This too was an age-old weapon, which had been used by many anti-Semites down the ages. On this point we shall find the accused himself saying:

> "The Jewish Question was a welcome tactic to divert attention from other reverses . . . Whenever any difficulties of another sort arose, they took refuge, at least at this time, in the Jewish Question, and immediately the diversion was created. This was done not only by Himmler[14] himself, not only by the Gauleiters; this was the practice of every one among the so-called high leadership."

A confused and blinded world was not alarmed by this campaign of hatred and the denial of human rights. It did not understand that the persecution of the Jews was only the beginning of an onslaught on the entire world. The man whose henchmen howled the infamous words:

> "When Jewish blood spurts from the knife,
> Then all goes doubly well!"
> (*Wenn Judenblut vom Messer spritzt—*
> *Dann geht's nochmal so gut!*)

—the same man would soon, by a natural development and led by the same master-feeling of hate, proclaim that all the cities of England would be subjected to the same fate as bombed Coventry.

In order to complete the picture, we should point out that there were in Germany tens of thousands of scientists and ecclesiastics, statesmen and authors and ordinary people, who dared to help the Jews, to raise their heads in opposition to the iniquitous regime, and even to rebel against it, and among these were men whose names were famous in German science and culture. Thousands of opponents of the bloody regime were imprisoned and were later destined to suffer greatly in concentration camps before the Nazi monster was brought low. Thousands of these died without seeing the day of liberation. Hundreds of ecclesiastics were arrested and imprisoned. There were also examples of personal bravery—like that of the priest who was sent by Eichmann to a concentration camp for intervening openly on behalf of the Jews. There were

Germans who hid Jews and shared their rations with them and who at the risk of their lives helped them to hide or obtain "Aryan" papers, and there were others who maintained an anti-Hitler underground. During the War there were Germans who even protested to Hitler at the disgrace the Gestapo was bringing on the German people by acting like beasts of prey, as they described the extermination of the Jews. There were also soldiers who tried to frustrate the killings by direct intervention.

But after all is said and done, these were a very small minority. The decisive majority of the German people made peace with the new regime; and were phlegmatic witnesses of the most terrible crime ever perpetrated in human history. And when Goebbels, the Nazi Propaganda Minister, made a public bonfire of the creations of men of the spirit, Jewish and non-Jewish—the works of such men as Heinrich Heine, Thomas Mann, [Jakob] Wassermann, [Albert] Einstein, [Sigmund] Freud, Upton Sinclair, H. G. Wells, [Emile] Zola, Havelock Ellis, and scores of others, because they were "in opposition to the German spirit," he proclaimed:

"The soul of the German people can again express itself. These flames not only illuminate the final end of an old era; they also light up the new."

The majority of German intellectuals were ready to warm themselves at those bonfires, and to accept as their spiritual guide the false glitter of their flames.

Nazi Germany became the scene of an anti-Jewish campaign directed and spurred on by brutish passions of hate. The slogan, "Germany awaken—Jewry die!" (*Deutschland erwache—Juda verrecke!*) appeared on the walls. The Jews were accused of every fault and defect in existence. A poisonous diet of bestial incitement was published weekly in *Der Stuermer*, that odious newspaper edited by Julius Streicher, who was eventually executed by sentence of the International Military Tribunal.

In order to denigrate the Jew, all his works had to be denounced. For this purpose, the Nazis defiled the greatest Jewish creation of all the ages—the Bible. Alfred Rosenberg,[15] one of the "thinkers" of the Movement, demanded that the Holy Scriptures be removed from any sphere where they could be a spiritual influence or source of religious faith. He considered it a prime defect of the Protestant faith that it sanctifies the Old Testament. There was talk of "the redemption of Jesus" from his connections with Judaism, in order to make it possible to degrade the people into which he was born. [. . .]

Even before the power was firmly in their hands, the Nazis initiated official measures of persecution against the Jews. On April 1, 1933, only two months after they obtained power, they organized the "Day of Boycott," to give symbolic form to the goal of uprooting the Jews and driving them out of the German Reich. Jews were beaten and imprisoned in concentration camps; Aryan customers were forbidden to enter Jewish places of business. It was then that Robert Weltsch wrote his unforgettable article in the *Jüdische Rundschau*, the organ of German Zionism: "Wear the Yellow Badge with Pride!" [16] But even Weltsch could not foresee that the yellow badge could become the distinctive sign which, a few years later, would be forced upon all the Jews in countries ruled by the Nazis, so that they might be more easily identified for the purpose of the blood-bath. [. . .]

After the Nazis had succeeded in using anti-Semitism as an important instrument for securing their power in Germany itself, they planned to use the same poison of hate to bind together the enemies of the Jews throughout the world, in order, by this means, to undermine opposition to the hegemony of Nazi Germany. And while German military might cast its shadow of terror on peoples and lands, silencing the voice of reason, anti-Semitism was exploited as a deliberate expedient to undermine the conscience of the nations, to excite the basest of passions, and to encourage Quisling[17] and other collaborators. The Jew was described, in the official publications of the Party and the German Reich, as an enemy to the peace of the world, and there was a proposal for a league of nations against Jewry, *ein Völkerbund gegen Juda*.

Wherever the Nazi conqueror set foot, there awaited him a prepared group of adventurers, traitors to their country, under-

world characters—sometimes plain assassins, who cast lustful eyes
on Jewish property and lent their unclean hands to the task of
destruction. Wherever the German legions trod, they introduced the suppression of human freedom and whipped up Jew-
hatred. [. . .]

There is a Hebrew saying: "The wicked, even at the gate of
Hell, do not repent." [18] In April 1945, at the moment of his death
agonies, when the Soviet cannon were thundering in the streets of
Berlin, when Hitler sat imprisoned in the cellar of the Reichs-
kanzlei, his entire world in ruins and his country stricken, over
the corpses of six million Jews—at that moment, the Führer wrote
his political last will and testament. He bequeathed to his people
the injunction of eternal hatred for the Jews, and he concluded:

> "Above all, I enjoin the government and the people to up-
> hold the racial laws to the limit and to resist mercilessly the
> poisoner of all nations, international Jewry."

Even from beyond the grave, Hitler was still trying to sow the
seeds of hatred and destruction for the Jewish people.

II

Adolf Eichmann's guilt lies in the planning, initiation, organization and execution of the crimes specified in the indictment.
We shall prove his guilt as planner, initiator, organizer and executor of the crime known as "the final solution of the Jewish problem," his direct part in the implementation of this criminal program, his role as administrator, director and commander of the
operation, as well as the part he played as partner and accomplice
in the implementation of the program by others. He was the pivot
of the criminal conspiracy to exterminate the Jewish people, wholly
or in part, and he was partner in the crimes committed by the
S.S., the S.D., the Gestapo, including the members of the *Einsatz-
gruppen*, the Security Police commanders, senior S.S. and police
officers, their emissaries and branch offices, and all those who were
under their command and carried out their instructions in respect
of all the acts of murder, plunder, torture and persecution specified
in the indictment.

We shall prove that Eichmann performed all these deeds with the intention of destroying the Jewish people.

We shall prove that his deeds were crimes against the Jewish people, crimes against humanity, and war crimes, as specified in the indictment.

We shall also prove the offences he committed against persons of other nationalities. [. . .]

We shall call witnesses who met Eichmann at the time of these acts and others who will describe his actions and crimes as they experienced them in their own persons and will give evidence of what they saw and heard during the period of the Holocaust. The extermination of millions of Jews means the extermination of millions of witnesses, but witnesses still survive who can report what they saw with their own eyes, heard with their own ears and suffered in their own persons.

To the best of our ability, we shall try to demonstrate to this Court in full what Adolf Eichmann did to the Jewish people, but we shall not be able to bring proof as to the fate of each community or the destruction of each Jewish group. This will remain the task of the historian. Accordingly, we shall bring before the Court all the evidence at our disposal on the decisions made to carry out the extermination program, the methods by which these decisions were carried out, and evidence as to the role and responsibility of the accused therein. [. . .] It is beyond our power to give a complete description of this terrible disaster in all its depth.

I am afraid that even after submitting all the evidence and material which is in our possession, we shall not be able to do more than give a pale reflection of the enormous human and national tragedy which beset Jewry in this generation.

Adolf Eichmann will enjoy a privilege which he did not accord to even a single one of his victims. He will be able to defend himself before the Court. His fate will be decided according to law and according to the evidence, with the burden of proof resting upon the prosecution.

And the judges of Israel will pronounce true and righteous judgment.

A PLEA FOR THE DEAD

ELIE WIESEL

Elie Wiesel was born in Hungary in 1928. His memoir *Night* deals with his imprisonment in the concentration camps of Auschwitz and Buchenwald. After the war he turned to Paris, where he studied at the Sorbonne. Since 1956 he has resided in New York, writing for an Israeli newspaper. He has, in addition to his memoir, written two novels: *Dawn* and *The Day*. In the article here reprinted, he implores us to be silent and not to judge those who went to their death during the dark period in recent history.

I was barely fifteen when I first took part in a strange discussion about dignity and death and their possible relationship. People who were already dead and did not know it were debating the necessity rather than the possibility of being killed in what they called a dignified manner.

The reality of certain words escaped me; around me people were arguing; I heard everything and understood nothing. They said: we are going to die. I didn't believe it. They insisted: we must fight. I didn't see why.

I am twenty years older now and familiar with all the paths leading to the graveyards. And the discussion is still in progress. Only the participants have changed. Those of twenty years ago are dead. And I understand even less of it all.

It was spring, 1944. The first Hungarian "transports" had reached their destination: Auschwitz. The name was unfamiliar; we did not know that it had already entered history, that it had already destroyed history.

From the railway station, surrounded by police dogs and barbed wire, we marched toward the unknown. Far off, wreaths of red and yellow flame rose from factory chimneys into a moonless sky. It was then that some young men called for an uprising. Without arms? Pocket knives, fists and fingernails would do. There was nothing to lose, and nothing to gain, save honor.

Older people spoke up against it: God may intervene even at the very last moment; one must not precipitate matters. The argument spread. Then it was too late.

The uprising did not take place. And the Almighty did not intervene.

Lately, we have all begun to ponder the problem posed by the incomprehensible, or at least enigmatic, behavior of the Jews in the concentration camps. Why did they go like cattle to the slaughter? Important, if not essential, because it touches on eternal verities, that question has begun to nag at previously clear consciences; they suddenly need quick reassurance, need to have the guilty identified and their crimes specified, need to see isolated the meaning of events they lived through only vicariously.

The subject has become fashionable. It replaces Brecht,[19] Kafka[20] and Communism, all hackneyed now, worn out. In intellectual circles in New York, San Francisco, elsewhere, no evening is a success without Auschwitz. Psychiatrists, novelists, actors all have an opinion; each is ready to supply all the answers, to explain away all the mysteries: the executioner and the victim, even the destiny that brought them together on the same stage, in the same cemetery. It's simple. One need only understand history, politics, psychology, economics (take your choice); one need only accept the primary truth that always and everywhere $A + B = C$. If the dead are dead, it's that they desired death. Beyond the diversity of theories, set forth with outrageous certainty, is the unanimous conclusion that the victims because they were part of the game, must share in the responsibility of their own fate.

This is strikingly novel. Until now the Jews have been held responsible for everything that happened in this world: for the death of Jesus, for war and poverty, for famine, unemployment, revolutions and counter-revolutions. Now they are the cause of their own tragedy.

Our generation is full of sages and renowned teachers who have studied all the books and all the theories. They "know." I ought to admire them. I am still not capable of interpreting the terrified smile of that child torn from its mother and transformed into a flaming torch; nor can I comprehend the night which, in that instant, darkened the mother's eyes. Job chose questions and not answers and certainly not speeches. He never understood his own tragedy, which was, after all, only that of one man betrayed by God and his friends.

These thinkers and philosophers refuse to understand that the events of those days flowed from no law and no law flows from them. The prime material here is composed of death and mystery; it outruns our perceptions. One question leads to another and all are the same, and have nothing to do with the answers, whatever they are. A whole generation of fathers and sons couldn't have disappeared without creating, by their very disappearance, a mystery that passes our comprehension and represents our defeat. I still do not understand what happened, or how, or why. And my calculations always produce the same obstinate number: six million.

When the attorney-general asked the witnesses at the Eichmann trial [21] why they offered no resistance, many answered simply: "Whoever wasn't 'there' will never understand."

Well, I "was" there. And I still don't understand. What helped me survive and for what purpose? How did the Jews in Galicia manage to remain calm while digging their own graves? Why did that woman remain sane, having seen her child thrown in the air and used as a target for a German marksman? Why, and in the name of what, with what right, did she not go mad?

I don't know why. But who are we to ask her that question? The world was silent when Jews were massacred; let it have the elementary decency to be silent now, too. Its questions come a bit late; they should have been addressed to the executioner then or to his accomplices, those who knew and said nothing. In London, Stockholm, Geneva and Washington, and in the Vatican, too, the upper levels of government were aware of each transport bearing its human cargo to the end of the night. Yet no voice was raised. In the newspapers of that period Auschwitz and Buchenwald took up less space than traffic accidents.

The prisoners inside their barbed-wire universe were not unaware of their total abandonment. They knew themselves excluded, denied by the rest of humanity. In 1940-44 the conspiracy of silence seemed universal. Great Britain shut Palestine's gates, the

Swiss accepted only the rich and later the children. "Even if I had been able to sell one million Jews, who would have bought them?" Eichmann asked, not without truth. "What would you expect us to do with one million Jews?" echoed Lord Moyne in Cairo.[22]

There is no one left to count on: this was the feeling that prevailed in Auschwitz, Treblinka and Maidanek. We have been erased from history. Not only men died in Auschwitz but also the idea of Man, created in His image. The world burned its heart out there.

These observations are made without hatred, but not without anger. I find it more than shocking. I find it indecent to have to come to this: to have to plead in defense of the dead.

They are indicted now from having behaved as they did; they should have acted otherwise, if only to reassure the living, who might then go on believing in man's glory and grandeur.

I plead for the dead and I do not even say that they are innocent. I say simply that I do not confer upon myself the right to judge them.

Let them rest in peace. Do not ask them the meaning of their death. It might prove dangerous. These dead have their questions and theirs might well be more disturbing than our own. Their questions survived them. They will survive us.

My plea would be incomplete if I said nothing of the armed battles that many Jews "did" fight during the holocaust. But there is no need; so much has been written about the active fighting elite composed of men, women and children who with their pitiful tools stood up to the Germans in Warsaw, in Bialystok,[23] in Grodno and—God knows how!—even in Treblinka, Sobivor and Auschwitz.

If we were capable of enough sincerity, enough humility, we would offer these heroes unreserved admiration and make legends of their deeds; we are incapable of it.

The lesson of the holocaust, if any, is that strength is illusory and that within each of us there is a victim who is afraid, cold and hungry. And ashamed. You wish to understand? There is no longer anything to understand. You wish to know? There is no longer anything to know. It is not by playing with words or with corpses that you will understand or know.

The Talmud teaches man never to judge his friend as long as he has not stood in his place.[24]

But the murdered Jews are not your friends; they never were. It is because they had no friends that they were dissipated with the wind and the smoke somewhere near a peaceful spot in Silesia named Auschwitz.

The time has come for all of us to learn and to be silent.

v. *Zionism and the Land of Israel*

ON THE RETURN TO THE LAND OF ISRAEL

MOSES MONTEFIORE

In 1839, when Sir Moses Montefiore revisited Palestine (his first visit was in 1827), its Jewish population numbered about 10,000, including Jerusalem with 5,000; Safed with 1,500; Hebron with 750; Tiberias with 600; and some 400 Jews in the villages. All communities lived in dire poverty, depending in the main on charitable contributions from Jews in the Diaspora (*Halukkah*). Especially bad were conditions in Safed, which had suffered a plague epidemic in 1812 and an earthquake in 1837. The land was ruled by the Egyptian pasha Muhammad Ali who, in 1832, wrested Palestine from the Turks. The political unrest and the conflict between Turkey and Egypt led to British-inspired projects to restore Palestine to the Jews. But the needs of the Jews were more basic ones. Moses Montefiore (1784-1885), the great Anglo-Jewish philanthropist, tried to make the Palestine Jewish community self-supporting and productive through agriculture and manual labor. On several visits to Palestine he bolstered existing farming enterprises, founded agricultural settlements near Safed, Tiberias, and Jaffa, established a girls' school in Jerusalem, which stressed household economy, and built model dwellings in Jerusalem. His efforts were continued in the last two decades of the nineteenth century by the colonization plans of Baron Edmond de Rothschild and the *Hoveve Zion* (Lovers of Zion) groups.

Moses Montefiore participated in the founding of the Alliance Assurance Company, the Imperial Continental Gas Association, and the Provincial Bank of Ireland. In 1837 he was elected sheriff of the city of London and knighted by Queen Victoria; in 1846 he was created a baronet and the following year became high sheriff for Kent. As a Jew he was a leader of his community, serving as president of the Board of Deputies of British Jews from 1838 to 1874; cooperated in the movement for emancipa-

tion of the Jews; and fought for the rights of the oppressed
everywhere. His diaries (from which the following excerpt is
taken), edited by his secretary and adviser, Louis Loewe, were
published in 1890.

Safed, Friday, May 24, 1839

From all information I have been able to gather, the land in this
neighborhood appears to be particularly favorable for agricultural
speculation. There are groves of olive trees, I should think, more
than five hundred years old, vineyards, much pasture, plenty of
wells and abundance of excellent water; also fig trees, walnuts,
almonds, mulberries, &c., and rich fields of wheat, barley, and
lentils; in fact it is a land that would produce almost everything
in abundance, with very little skill and labor. I am sure if the
plan I have in contemplation should succeed, it will be the means
of introducing happiness and plenty into the Holy Land. In the
first instance, I shall apply to Muhammad Ali[1] for a grant of land
for fifty years; some one or two hundred villages; giving him an
increased rent of from ten to twenty per cent., and paying the
whole in money annually at Alexandria, but the land and villages
to be free, during the whole term, from every tax or rate either of
Pasha or governor of the several districts; and liberty being accorded to dispose of the produce in any quarter of the globe. This
grant obtained, I shall, please Heaven, on my return to England,
form a company for the cultivation of the land and the encourage-
ment of our brethren in Europe to return to Palestine. Many Jews
now emigrate to New South Wales, Canada, &c.; but in the Holy
Land they would find a greater certainty of success; here they will
find wells already dug, olives and vines already planted, and a
land so rich as to require little manure. By degrees I hope to induce
the return of thousands of our brethren to the Land of Israel. I
am sure they would be happy in the enjoyment of the observance
of our holy religion, in a manner which is impossible in Europe.

THE UNIVERSAL SIGNIFICANCE OF ZION

HENRY PEREIRA MENDES

Early Zionism found an ardent supporter in the United States in the English-born Henry Pereira Mendes (1852-1937), minister at the Sephardic congregation Shearith Israel in New York. His vision of a Jewish state transcended the aim of establishing a refuge for the oppressed; the state he advocated was to "aim at the spiritual interests of the Jews and of all humanity." His views were shared by many members of the "Historical School" in American Judaism. In harmony with his Messianic outlook on history, he envisaged a union between England and America (*England and America: the Dream of Peace,* 1897).

When we speak of "Palestine" we mean the ideals it stands for in prophetic vision.

By the restoration of Palestine to the Hebrews, we mean the establishment of a spiritual center for the world, and ultimately the establishment of the Kingdom of God on earth.

The realization of the prophetic ideals for the benefit and blessing of the world at large, and not for us Hebrews only, constitutes what is called "Prophetic Zionism," or "Bible-Zionism," or "Spiritual Zionism." These ideals are:

1) The establishment of a central spiritual influence for the world at large, for all mankind. [. . .]

2) A House of Prayer for all nations, and consequent gradual world-recognition of the Universal Fatherhood of God and the Universal Brotherhood of Man. [. . .]

3) Universal Knowledge of the Lord, with a center World-University for inspiration, help and guidance thereto. [. . .]

4) Universal Peace, secured by the establishment of a World's Court of International Arbitration, to whose decisions all nations will pledge their loyalty and honor.

Said court shall include representatives of Religion, Law and Science as prescribed by the Bible for the Highest Court of Appeal. [. . .]

We Hebrews humbly believe that God selected Abraham in order that through his descendants "all the families of the earth should be blessed";[2] that at Sinai He constituted us a nation of priests to lead all mankind to Him; that although our ancestors were expelled from their land and have for centuries been persecuted, slain, imprisoned or exiled, nevertheless they cherished, as we cherish today, the hope that the prophetic ideals associated with Palestine will be one day realized for mankind's happiness, that earth's wrongs shall be righted and the world at last be at rest. [. . .]

THE JEWISH STATE

THEODOR HERZL

"The restoration of the Jewish State"—this was Theodor Herzl's (1860-1904) answer to the problem of anti-Semitism in the Western world and the sense of homelessness experienced by many Jews in Eastern Europe. A successful Viennese journalist, essayist, and playwright, Herzl was led to realization of the instability and ambivalence of the Jewish situation chiefly by the impact of the "Dreyfus affair," which he "covered" for the *Neue Freie Presse*. His Zionism differed from the nationalist and cultural orientation of the East-European *Hoveve Zion* (*Lovers of Zion*) by its emphasis on political action and its use of diplomatic means in dealing with the great powers. He propagated his program in *Die Welt* (*The World*), official organ of the Zionist movement, in his pamphlet *Der Judenstaat* (*The Jewish State*, 1896), his novel *Altneuland* (*The Old-New Land*, 1904), and in his extensive diaries.

Der Judenstaat, an English edition of which appeared in 1896 under the title *The Jewish State: An Attempt at a Modern Solution of the Jewish Question*, envisages an exodus of Jews from the countries which humiliate or persecute them, the concentration in a country of their own, and the formation of an autonomous state; the propelling force of this far-reaching plan is the Jewish tragedy. The book outlines the creation of two organs of the movement: "The Society of the Jews," to function as legal representative of the Jewish people, and authorized to negotiate in its name, and "The Jewish Company," a stock company based on English law, to function as the economic instrument for migration and resettlement. The structure of the future state was to be predicated on the latest achievements of science and technology; private initiative was to be encouraged; work assured for everyone; and a working day was to consist of seven hours. "We shall at last live as free men on our own soil." The essay that follows is the short book's introductory chapter. See also "Opening Address, First Zionist Congress."

The understanding of economics among men actively engaged in business is often astonishingly slight. This seems to be the only explanation for the fact that even Jews faithfully parrot the catchword of the anti-Semites: "We live off 'host-nations'; and if we had no 'host-nation' to sustain us we should starve to death." This is one case in point of the undermining of our self-respect through unjust accusations. But how does this theory of "host-nations" stand up in the light of reality? Where it does not rest on narrow physiocratic views, it reflects the childish error which assumes that there is a fixed quantity of values in continuous circulation. But it is not necessary to be Rip van Winkle, and wake from long slumber, in order to realize that the world is considerably altered by the continuous production of new values. The technical progress achieved in our own wonderful era enables even the dullest of minds with the dimmest of vision to note the appearance of new commodities all around him. The spirit of enterprise has created them.

Without enterprise, labor remains static, unaltering; typical of it is the labor of the farmer, who stands now precisely where his forebears stood a thousand years ago. All our material welfare has been brought about by men of enterprise. I feel almost ashamed of writing down so trite a remark. Even if we were a nation of entrepreneurs—such as absurdly exaggerated accounts make us out to be—we would require no "host-nation." We are not dependent upon the circulation of old values; we produce new ones.

We now possess slave labor of unexampled productivity, whose appearance in civilization has proved fatal competition to handcrafts; these slaves are our machines. It is true that we need work-men to set our machinery in motion; but for this the Jews have manpower enough, too much, in fact. Only those who are ignorant of the condition of Jews in many countries of Eastern Europe would dare assert that Jews are unfit or unwilling to perform man-ual labor.

But in this pamphlet I will offer no defense of the Jews. It would be useless. Everything that reason and everything that sentiment can possibly say in their defense already has been said. Obviously, arguments fit to appeal to reason and sentiment are not enough; one's audience must first of all be able to understand or one is only preaching in a vacuum. But if the audience is already so far advanced, then the sermon itself is superfluous. I believe that man is steadily advancing to a higher ethical level; but I see this ascent to be fearfully slow. Should we wait for the average man to be-come as generously minded as was Lessing when he wrote *Nathan the Wise*,[3] we would have to wait beyond our own lifetime, be-yond the lifetimes of our children, of our grandchildren, and of our great-grandchildren. But destiny favors us in a different respect. The technical achievements of our century have brought about a remarkable renaissance; but we have not yet seen this fabulous advance applied for the benefit of humanity. Distance has ceased to be an obstacle, yet we complain of the problem of congestion. Our great steamships carry us swiftly and surely over hitherto un-charted seas. Our railways carry us safely into a mountain world hitherto cautiously scaled on foot. Events occurring in countries undiscovered when Europe first confined Jews in ghettos are known to us in a matter of an hour. That is why the plight of the Jews is an anachronism—not because over a hundred years ago there was a period of enlightenment which in reality affected only the most elevated spirits.

To my mind, the electric light was certainly not invented so that the drawing rooms of a few snobs might be illuminated, but rather to enable us to solve some of the problems of humanity by its light. One of these problems, and not the least of them, is the Jewish question. In solving it we are working not only for our-selves, but also for many other downtrodden and oppressed beings.

The Jewish question still exists. It would be foolish to deny it. It is a misplaced piece of medievalism which civilized nations do not even yet seem able to shake off, try as they will. They proved they had this high-minded desire when they emancipated us. The Jewish question persists wherever Jews live in appreciable numbers. Wherever it does not exist, it is brought in together with Jewish immigrants. We are naturally drawn into those places where we are not persecuted, and our appearance there gives rise to persecution. This is the case, and will inevitably be so, everywhere, even in highly civilized countries—see, for instance, France—so long as the Jewish question is not solved on the political level. The unfortunate Jews are now carrying the seeds of anti-Semitism into England; they have already introduced it into America.

Anti-Semitism is a highly complex movement, which I think I understand. I approach this movement as a Jew, yet without fear or hatred. I believe that I can see in it the elements of a cruel sport, of common commercial rivalry, of inherited prejudice, of religious intolerance—but also of a supposed need for self-defense. I consider the Jewish question neither a social nor a religious one, even though it sometimes takes these and other forms. It is a national question, and to solve it we must first of all establish it as an international political problem to be discussed and settled by the civilized nations of the world in council.

We are a people—*one* people.

We have sincerely tried everywhere to merge with the national communities in which we live, seeking only to preserve the faith of our fathers. It is not permitted us. In vain are we loyal patriots, sometimes superloyal; in vain do we make the same sacrifices of life and property as our fellow citizens; in vain do we strive to enhance the fame of our native lands in the arts and sciences, or her wealth by trade and commerce. In our native lands where we have lived for centuries we are still decried as aliens, often by men whose ancestors had not yet come at a time when Jewish sighs had long been heard in the country. The majority decides who the "alien" is; this, and all else in the relations between peoples, is a matter of power. I do not surrender any part of our prescriptive right when I make this statement merely in my own name, as an individual. In the world as it now is and will probably remain, for an indefinite period, might takes precedence over right. It is without avail, therefore, for us to be loyal patriots, as were the Huguenots, who were forced to emigrate. If we were left in peace [. . .].

But I think we shall not be left in peace.

Oppression and persecution cannot exterminate us. No nation on earth has endured such struggles and sufferings as we have. Jew-baiting has merely winnowed out our weaklings; the strong among us defiantly return to their own whenever persecution breaks out. This was most clearly apparent in the period immediately following the emancipation of the Jews. Those Jews who rose highest intellectually and materially entirely lost the sense of unity with their people. Wherever we remain politically secure for any length of time, we assimilate. I think this is not praiseworthy. Hence, the statesman who would wish to see a Jewish strain added to his nation must see to it that we continue politically secure. But even a Bismarck could never achieve that.

For old prejudices against us are still deeply ingrained in the folk ethos. He who would have proof of this need only listen to the people where they speak candidly and artlessly: folk wisdom and folklore both are anti-Semitic. The people is everywhere a great child, which can be readily educated; but even in the most favorable circumstances its education would be such a long-drawn-out process that we could far sooner, as already mentioned, help ourselves by other means.

Assimilation, by which I understand not only external conformity in dress, habits, customs, and speech, but also identity of attitude and deportment—assimilation of Jews could be achieved only by intermarriage. But the need for intermarriage would have to be felt by the majority; mere legislative sanction would never suffice. [. . .]

Those who really wish to see the Jews disappear through interbreeding can hope to see it come about in one way only. The Jews must first rise so far in the economic scale that old social prejudices against them would be overcome. How this might happen is shown by the example of the aristocracy, with whom the highest proportion of intermarriage occurs. The old nobility has itself refurbished with Jewish money, and in the process Jewish families are absorbed. But what form would this process take in the middle classes, where (the Jews being a bourgeois people) the Jewish question is mainly centered? The prerequisite growth in economic power might here be resented as economic domination, something which is already falsely attributed to the Jews. And if the power the Jews now possess evokes rage and indignation among the anti-Semites, to what outbursts would a further increase lead? The first step toward absorption cannot be taken, because this step would mean the subjection of the majority to a recently despised minority, which, however, would possess neither military nor administrative authority of its own. I, therefore, hold the absorption of Jews by means of their prosperity to be unlikely. In countries which now are anti-Semitic my view will be seconded. In others, where Jews are for the moment secure, it will probably be passionately challenged by my coreligionists. They will not believe me until they are again visited by Jew-baiting; and the longer anti-Semitism lies dormant, the more violently will it erupt. The infiltration of immigrating Jews attracted to a land by apparent security, and the rising class status of native Jews, combine powerfully to bring about a revolution. Nothing could be plainer than this rational conclusion.

Yet, because I have drawn this conclusion with complete indifference to everything but the truth, I shall probably be opposed and rejected by Jews who are in comfortable circumstances. Insofar as private interests alone are held by their anxious or timid possessors to be threatened, they may safely be ignored, for the concerns of the poor and oppressed are of greater importance than theirs. But I wish from the very beginning to deal with any mistaken ideas that might arise: in this case, the fear that if the present plan is realized, it could in any way damage property and interests now held by Jews. I will, therefore, thoroughly explain everything connected with property rights. If, on the other hand, my plan never becomes anything more than literature, things will merely remain as they are.

A more serious objection would be that I am giving aid and comfort to the anti-Semites when I say we are a people—*one* people. Or that I am hindering the assimilation of Jews where there are hopes of achieving it, and endangering it where it is already an accomplished fact, insofar as it is possible for a solitary writer to hinder or endanger anything.

This objection will be brought forward especially in France. It will probably also be made in other countries, but I shall first answer only the French Jews, who afford the most striking example of my point.

However much I may esteem personality—powerful individual personality in statesmen, inventors, artists, philosophers, or leaders, as well as the collective personality of a historic group of human beings, which we designate "nation"—however much I may esteem personality, I do not mourn its decline. Whoever can, will, and must perish, let him perish. But the distinctive nationality of the Jews neither can, will, nor must perish. It cannot, because external enemies consolidate it. It does not wish to; this it has proved through two millennia of appalling suffering. It need not; that, as a descendant of countless Jews who refused to despair, I am trying once more to prove in this pamphlet. Whole branches of Jewry may wither and fall away. The tree lives on.

Hence, if any or all of French Jewry protest against this scheme, because they are already "assimilated," my answer is simple: The whole thing does not concern them at all. They are Israelitic Frenchmen? Splendid! This is a private affair for Jews alone.

However, the movement for the creation of the State which I here propose would harm Israelitic Frenchmen no more than it would harm those who have "assimilated" in other countries. It would, rather, be distinctly to their advantage. For they would no longer be disturbed in their "chromatic function," as Darwin puts it, but would be able to assimilate in peace, because present-day anti-Semitism would have been stopped for all time. For it would certainly be believed that they are assimilated to the very depths of their being if they remained in their old homes, even after the new Jewish State, with its superior institutions, had become a reality.

The departure of the dedicated Jews would be even more to the advantage of the "assimilated" than of the Christian citizens; for

they would be freed of the disquieting, unpredictable, and inescapable competition of a Jewish proletariat driven by poverty and
political pressure from place to place, from land to land. This
drifting proletariat would become stabilized. Certain Christians
today—whom we call anti-Semites—feel free to offer determined
resistance to the immigration of foreign Jews. Jewish citizens cannot do this, although it affects them far more severely; for it is
they who first feel the competition of individuals who engage in
similar fields of enterprise, and who besides give rise to anti-
Semitism where it does not exist, and intensify it where it does.
This is a secret grievance of the "assimilated" which finds expression in their "philanthropic" undertakings. They organize emigration societies for incoming Jews. The ambiguous character of this
project would be comical if it did not involve human suffering.
Some of these charity institutions are created not for but against
the persecuted Jews: Remove the paupers as quickly and as far
away as possible. And thus, many an apparent friend of the Jews
turns out, on closer examination, to be no more than an anti-Semite
of Jewish origin in philanthropist's clothing.

But the attempts at colonization made even by truly well-mean-
ing men, interesting attempts though they were, have so far been
unsuccessful. I do not think that one or another person took up
the matter merely as an amusement, that they sent Jews off on
their journeys in the same spirit as one races horses. The matter
was too grave and too painful for that. These attempts were
interesting, to the extent that they may serve on a small scale as
an experiment foreshadowing the Jewish State idea. They were
even useful, for out of their mistakes we may learn how to proceed
in a large-scale project. They have, of course, also done harm. The
transplantation of anti-Semitism to new areas, which is the inevitable consequence of such artificial infiltration, seems to me the
least of these aftereffects. Far worse is the fact that the unsatis-
factory results inspire doubt among the Jews themselves as to the
capacity of Jewish manpower. But the following simple argument will suffice to dispel this doubt for any intelligent person:
What is impractical or impossible on a small scale need not be
so on a larger one. A small enterprise may result in loss under the

same conditions that would make a large one pay. A rivulet is not navigable even by boats; the river into which it flows carries stately iron vessels.

No human being is wealthy or powerful enough to transplant a people from one place of residence to another.[4] Only an idea can achieve that. The State idea surely has that power. The Jews have dreamed this princely dream throughout the long night of their history. "Next year in Jerusalem" is our age-old motto. It is now a matter of showing that the vague dream can be transformed into a clear and glowing idea.

For this, our minds must first be thoroughly cleansed of many old, outworn, muddled, and shortsighted notions. The unthinking might, for example, imagine that this exodus would have to take its way from civilization into the desert. That is not so! It will be carried out entirely in the framework of civilization. We shall not revert to a lower stage; we shall rise to a higher one. We shall not dwell in mud huts; we shall build new, more beautiful, and more modern houses, and possess them in safety. We shall not lose our acquired possessions; we shall realize them. We shall surrender our well-earned rights for better ones. We shall relinquish none of our cherished customs; we shall find them again. We shall not leave our old home until the new one is available. Those only will depart who are sure thereby to improve their lot; those who are now desperate will go first, after them the poor, next the well to do, and last of all the wealthy. Those who go first will raise themselves to a higher grade, on a level with that whose representatives will shortly follow. The exodus will thus at the same time be an ascent in class.

The departure of the Jews will leave no wake of economic disturbance, no crises, no persecutions; in fact, the countries of emigration will rise to a new prosperity. There will be an inner migration of Christian citizens into the positions relinquished by Jews. The outflow will be gradual, without any disturbance, and its very inception means the end of anti-Semitism. The Jews will leave as honored friends, and if some of them later return they will receive the same favorable welcome and treatment at the hands of civilized nations as is accorded all foreign visitors. Nor will their exodus in any way be a flight, but it will be a well-regulated movement under the constant check of public opinion. The movement will not only be inaugurated in absolute accordance with the law, but it can nowise be carried out without the friendly co-operation of the interested governments, who will derive substantial benefits.

To see that the idea is carried out responsibly and vigorously, the kind of guarantee is required which can be provided by the kind of corporate body which legal terminology calls a "moral" or "legal" person. I should like to distinguish clearly between these two designations, which are frequently confused. As "moral person," to deal with all but property rights, I propose to establish the "Society of Jews." As "legal person," to conduct economic activities, there will be a parallel "Jewish Company."

Only an impostor or a madman would even pretend to undertake such a monumental task on his own. The integrity of the "moral person" will be guaranteed by the character of its members. The capacity of the "legal person" will be demonstrated by its capital funds.

These prefatory remarks are intended merely as an immediate reply to the mass of objections which the very words "Jewish State" are certain to arouse. Hereafter we shall proceed more deliberately in our exposition, meeting further objections and explaining in detail what has only been outlined as yet, though we shall try, in the interest of a smoothly reading pamphlet, to avoid a ponderous tone. Succinct, pithy chapters will best serve the purpose.

If I wish to replace an old building with a new one, I must demolish before I construct. I shall therefore adhere to this natural sequence. In the first, the general, section, I shall clarify my ideas, sweep away age-old preconceptions, establish the politico-economic premises, and unfold the plan.

In the special section, which is subdivided into three principal sections, I shall describe its execution. These three sections are: The Jewish Company, Local Groups, and the Society of Jews. The Society is to be created first, the Company last; but in this exposition the reverse order is preferable, because it is the financial soundness of the enterprise which will chiefly be called into question, and doubts on this score must be removed first.

In the conclusion, I shall try to meet every further objection that could possibly be made. My Jewish readers will, I hope, follow me patiently to the end. Some will make their objections in another order than that chosen for their refutation. But whoever finds his reservations rationally overcome, let him offer himself to the cause.

Although I speak here in terms of reason, I am well aware that reason alone will not suffice. Long-term prisoners do not willingly quit their cells. We shall see whether the youth, whom we must have, is ripe; the youth—which irresistibly draws along the aged, bears them up on powerful arms, and transforms rationality into enthusiasm.

OPENING ADDRESS
FIRST ZIONIST CONGRESS, 1897

THEODOR HERZL

On Herzl and his political program, see the preface to *The Jewish State*. In convening a congress of delegates from wherever Jews dwelled for deliberation of the Jewish question, Herzl expressed a wish "to put the question in the arena and under the control of free public opinion." After two millennia of dispersion, the Jews stood before the world as one people, formulating its needs and its rights. The Zionist Congress, which became a permanent annual or biannual institution, met in Basel, Switzerland, August 29 through 31, 1897; it was attended by 197 delegates, reporters from Jewish and general newspapers, and some Christian Zionists, who were guests of the Congress. Herzl, the president of the Congress, gave the Opening Address, here reprinted. The program of the movement opened with the words: "Zionism seeks to establish for the Jewish people a legally secured homeland in Palestine." The term "state," favored by Herzl, was avoided; "homeland" (*Heimstätte*) was meant to imply the notion of cultural Zionism. Herzl's thinking is revealed in his diary: "In Basel I created the Jewish State. Were I to say this aloud I would be greeted by universal laughter. But perhaps five years hence, in any case, certainly fifty years hence, everyone will perceive it." The establishment of the State of Israel in 1948 marked the realization of Herzl's vision.

Fellow delegates: As one of those who called this Congress into being I have been granted the privilege of welcoming you. This I shall do briefly, for if we wish to serve the cause we should economize the valuable moments of the Congress. There is much to be accomplished within the space of three days. We want to lay the foundations of the edifice which is one day to house the Jewish people. The task is so great that we may treat of it in none but the simplest terms. So far as we can now foresee, a summary of the present status of the Jewish question will be submitted within the coming three days. The tremendous bulk of material on hand is being classified by the chairmen of our committees.

We shall hear reports of the Jewish situation in the various countries. You all know, even if only in a vague way, that with few exceptions the situation is not cheering. Were it otherwise we should probably not have convened. The unity of our destiny has suffered a long interruption, although the scattered fragments of the Jewish people have everywhere endured similar vicissitudes. It is only in our days that the marvels of communication have brought about mutual understanding and union between isolated groups. And in these times, so progressive in most respects, we know ourselves to be surrounded by the old, old hatred. Anti-Semitism—you know it, alas, too well!—is the up-to-date designation of the movement. The first impression which it made upon the Jews of today was one of astonishment, which gave way to pain and resentment. Perhaps our enemies are quite unaware how deeply they wounded the sensibilities of just those of us who were possibly not the primary objects of their attack. That very part of Jewry which is modern and cultured, which has outgrown the Ghetto and lost the habit of petty trading, was pierced to the heart. We can assert it calmly, without laying ourselves open to the suspicion of wanting to appeal to the sentimental pity of our opponents. We have faced the situation squarely.

Since time immemorial the world has been misinformed about us. The sentiment of solidarity with which we have been reproached so frequently and so acrimoniously was in process of disintegration at the very time we were being attacked by anti-Semitism. And anti-Semitism served to strengthen it anew. We returned home, as it were. For Zionism is a return to the Jewish fold even before it becomes a return to the Jewish land. We, the children who have returned, find much to redress under the ancestral roof, for some of our brothers have sunk deep into misery. We are made welcome in the ancient house, for it is universally known that we are not actuated by an arrogant desire to undermine that which should be revered. This will be clearly demonstrated by the Zionist platform.

Zionism has already brought about something remarkable, heretofore regarded as impossible: a close union between the ultramodern and the ultraconservative elements of Jewry. The fact that this has come to pass without undignified concessions on the part of either side, without intellectual sacrifices, is further proof, if such proof is necessary, of the national entity of the Jews. A union of this kind is possible only on a national basis.

Doubtless there will be discussions on the subject of an organization the need for which is recognized by all. Organization is an evidence of the reasonableness of a movement. But there is one point which should be clearly and energetically emphasized in order to advance the solution of the Jewish question. We Zionists desire not an international league but international discussion. Needless to say this distinction is of the first importance in our eyes. It is this distinction which justifies the convening of our Congress. There will be no question of intrigues, secret interventions, and devious methods in our ranks, but only of unhampered utterances under the constant and complete check of public opinion. One of the first results of our movement, even now to be perceived in its larger outlines, will be the transformation of the Jewish question into a question of Zion.

A popular movement of such vast dimensions will necessarily be attacked from many sides. Therefore the Congress will concern itself with the spiritual means to be employed for reviving and fostering the national consciousness of the Jews. Here, too, we must struggle against misconceptions. We have not the least intention of yielding a jot of the culture we have acquired. On the contrary, we are aiming toward a broader culture, such as an increase of knowledge brings with it. As a matter of fact, the Jews have always been more active mentally than physically.

It was because the practical forerunners of Zionism realized this that they inaugurated agricultural work for the Jews. We shall never be able, nor shall we desire, to speak of these attempts at colonization in Palestine and in Argentina otherwise than with genuine gratitude. But they spoke the first, not the last word of the Zionist movement. For the Zionist movement must be greater in scope if it is to be at all. A people can be helped only by its own efforts, and if it cannot help itself it is beyond succor. But we Zionists want to rouse the people to self-help. No premature, unwholesome hopes should be awakened in this direction. This is another reason why public procedure, as it is planned by our Congress, is so essential.

Those who give the matter careful consideration must surely admit that Zionism cannot gain its ends otherwise than through an unequivocal understanding with the political units involved. It is generally known that the difficulties of obtaining colonization rights were not created by Zionism in its present form. One wonders what motives actuate the narrators of these fables. The confidence of the government with which we want to negotiate regarding the settlement of Jewish masses on a large scale can be gained by plain language and upright dealing. The advantages which an entire people is able to offer in return for benefits received are so considerable that the negotiations are vested with sufficient importance a priori. It would be an idle beginning to engage in lengthy discussions today regarding the legal form which the agreement will finally assume. But one thing is to be adhered to inviolably: the agreement must be based on rights, and not on toleration. Indeed we have had enough experience of toleration and of "protection" which could be withdrawn at any time.

Consequently the only reasonable course of action which our movement can pursue is to work for publicly legalized guarantees. The results of colonization as it has been carried on hitherto were quite satisfactory within its limitations. It confirmed the much disputed fitness of the Jews for agricultural work. It established this proof for all time, as the legal phrase has it. But colonization in its present form is not, and cannot be, the solution of the Jewish question. And we must admit unreservedly that it has failed to evoke much sympathy. Why? Because the Jews know how to calculate; in fact, it has been asserted that they calculate too well. Thus, if we assume that there are nine million Jews in the world, and that it would be possible to colonize ten thousand Jews in Palestine every year, the Jewish question would require nine hundred years for its solution. This would seem impracticable.

On the other hand, you know that to count on ten thousand settlers a year under existing circumstances is nothing short of fantastic. The Turkish government would doubtless unearth the old immigration restrictions immediately, and to that we would have little objection. For if anyone thinks that the Jews can steal into the land of their fathers, he is deceiving either himself or others. Nowhere is the coming of Jews so promptly noted as in the historic home of the race, for the very reason that it is the historic home. And it would by no means be to our interest to go there prematurely. The immigration of Jews signifies an unhoped-for accession of strength for the land which is now so poor; in fact, for the whole Ottoman Empire. Besides, His Majesty the Sultan[5] has had excellent experiences with his Jewish subjects, and he has been an indulgent monarch to them in turn. Thus, existing conditions point to a successful outcome, provided the whole matter is intelligently and felicitously treated. The financial help which the Jews can give to Turkey is by no means inconsiderable and would serve to obviate many an internal ill from which the country is now suffering. If the Near East question is partially solved together with the Jewish question, it will surely be of advantage to all civilized peoples. The advent of Jews would bring about an improvement in the situation of the Christians in the Orient.

But it is not solely from this aspect that Zionism may count upon the sympathy of the nations. You know that in some lands the Jewish problem has come to mean calamity for the government. If it sides with the Jews, it is confronted by the ire of the masses; if it sides against the Jews, it may call considerable economic consequences down upon its head because of the peculiar influence of the Jews upon the business affairs of the world. Examples of the latter may be found in Russia. But if the government maintains a neutral attitude, the Jews find themselves unprotected by the established regime and rush into the arms of the revolutionaries. Zionism, or self-help for the Jews, points to a way out of these numerous and extraordinary difficulties. Zionism is simply a peacemaker. And it suffers the usual fate of peacemakers, in being forced to fight more than anyone else. But should the accusation that we are not patriotic figure among the more or less sincere arguments directed against our movement, this equivocal objection carries its own refutation with it. Nowhere can there be a question of an exodus of all the Jews. Those who are able or who wish to be assimilated will remain behind and be absorbed. When once a satisfactory agreement is concluded with the various political units involved and a systematic Jewish migration begins, it will last only so long in each country as that country desires to be rid of its Jews. How will the current be stopped? Simply by the gradual decrease and the final cessation of anti-Semitism. Thus it is that we understand and anticipate the solution of the Jewish problem.

All this has been said time and again by my friends and by myself. We shall spare no pains to repeat it again and again until we are understood. On this solemn occasion, when Jews have come together from so many lands at the age-old summons of nationality, let our profession of faith be solemnly repeated. Should we not be stirred by a premonition of great events when we remember that at this moment the hopes of thousands upon thousands of our people depend upon our assemblage? In the coming hour the news of our deliberations and decisions will fly to distant lands, over the seven seas. Therefore enlightenment and comfort should go forth from this Congress. Let everyone find out what Zionism really is, Zionism, which was rumored to be a sort of millennial marvel—that it is a moral, lawful, humanitarian movement, directed toward the long-yearned-for goal of our people. It was possible and permissible to ignore the spoken or written utterances of individuals within our ranks. Not so with the actions of the Congress. Thus the Congress, which is henceforth to be ruler of its discussions, must govern as a wise ruler.

Finally, the Congress will provide for its own continuance, so that we do not disperse once more ineffectual and ephemeral. Through this Congress we are creating an agency for the Jewish people such as it has not possessed heretofore, an agency of which it has stood in urgent need. Our cause is too great to be left to the ambition or the whim of individuals. It must be elevated to the realm of the impersonal if it is to succeed. And our Congress shall live forever, not only until the redemption from age-long suffering is effected, but afterwards as well. Today we are here in the hospitable limits of this free city—where shall we be next year?

But wherever we shall be, and however distant the accomplishment of our task, let our Congress be earnest and highminded, a source of welfare to the unhappy, of defiance to none, of honor to all Jewry. Let it be worthy of our past, the renown of which, though remote, is eternal!

THE IDEAL OF LABOR

A. D. GORDON

In 1904 the forty-eight-year-old East-European socialist Aaron David Gordon arrived in Palestine, intent upon realizing there his ideal of recreating the Jewish nation through renewed contact with the soil and with nature, through physical labor and community living. He rejected urban technological civilization's utilitarian approach to work, nature, society, and fellow man; believed the return to nature and the ethical reorientation of interpersonal relationships to be the basis of an ideal humanity; and wished the Jewish people reborn in the land of Israel, to become *am-adam*, a people which represents man, a "people-incarnating-humanity," a "nation that is one with humanity, the nation in the image of God." From return to the soil (influence of Tolstoy!) Gordon, "the prophet in overalls," expected a renewal of religious faith, which he defined as a sense of cosmic unity, awareness of the unity of all existence and of man's part in it.

Gordon was the leading spirit in the Zionist-Socialist labor movement *Ha-Poel ha-Tzair* (The Young Worker); an organization of young Jewish pioneers in Poland was named Gordonia in recognition of his leadership. Outstanding among his writings (he permitted himself to write only after a full day's work in the fields) are his *Letters from Palestine.* He died in 1922, in Degania, one of the oldest collective settlements in Palestine. The essay which follows was written in 1911.

The Jewish people has been completely cut off from nature and imprisoned within city walls these two thousand years. We have become accustomed to every form of life, except to a life of labor —of labor done at our own behest and for its own sake. It will require the greatest effort of will for such a people to become normal again. We lack the principal ingredient for national life. We lack the habit of labor—not labor performed out of external compulsion, but labor to which one is attached in a natural and organic way. This kind of labor binds a people to its soil and to its national culture, which in turn is an outgrowth of the people's soil and the people's labor.

Now it is true that every people has many individuals who shun physical labor and try to live off the work of others. But a normal people is like a living organism which performs its various functions naturally, and labor is one of its basic and organic functions. A normal people invariably contains a large majority of individuals for whom labor is second nature. But we Jews are different. We have developed an attitude of looking down on manual labor, so that even those who are engaged in it work out of mere compulsion and always with the hope of eventually escaping to "a better life." We must not deceive ourselves in this regard, nor shut our eyes to our grave deficiencies, not merely as individuals but as a people. The well-known talmudic saying, that when the Jews do God's will their labor is done for them by others,[6] is characteristic of our attitude. This saying is significant. It demonstrates how far this attitude has become an instinctive feeling within us, a second nature.

Who among us thinks about this problem? Who is sensitive to it? We have no labor—and yet we are not aware that anything is missing. We take no notice of it even when we talk of our national rebirth. Labor is not only the force which binds man to the soil and by which possession of the soil is acquired; it is also the basic energy for the creation of a national culture. This is what we do not have—but we are not aware of missing it. We are a people without a country, without a living national language, without a living culture—but that, at least, we know and it pains us, even if only vaguely, and we seek ways and means of doing what must be done. But we seem to think that if we have no labor it does not matter—let Ivan, or John, or Mustapha do the work, while we busy ourselves with producing a culture, with creating national values, and with enthroning absolute justice in the world.

After very prolonged and very stubborn battles, the ideal of culture has finally won a place in our national movement. But what kind of culture is it?

By culture we usually mean what is called in Zionist circles "the rebirth of the spirit," or "a spiritual renaissance." But the spirit which we are trying to revive is not the breath of real life which permeates the whole living organism and draws life from it, but some shadowy and abstract spirit, which can express itself only within the recesses of heart and mind. Judging by the deliberations at the Zionist Congress, culture is entirely a matter of ideas or ideology. Such being the case, culture may mean to some of us [. . .] the religious orthodoxy of Mizrahi,[7] while to others it may signify the outlook of the school of Marx and Engels.

A vital culture, far from being detached from life, embraces it in all its aspects. Culture is whatever life creates for living purposes. Farming, building, and road-making—any work, any craft, any productive activity—is part of culture and is indeed the foundation and the stuff of culture. The procedure, the pattern, the shape, the manner in which things are done—these represent the forms of culture. Whatever people feel and think both at work and at leisure, and the relations arising from these situations, combined with the natural surroundings—all that constitutes the spirit of a people's culture. It sustains the higher expressions of culture in science and art, creeds and ideologies. The things we call culture in the most restricted sense, the higher expressions of culture (which is what is usually meant when culture is discussed in our circles)—this is the butter churned out of culture in general, in its broadest sense. But can butter be produced without milk? Or can a man make butter by using his neighbors' milk and still call the butter all his own?

What are we seeking in Palestine? Is it not that which we can never find elsewhere—the fresh milk of a healthy people's culture? What we are come to create at present is not the culture of the academy, before we have anything else, but a culture of life, of which the culture of the academy is only one element. We seek to create a vital culture out of which the cream of a higher culture can easily be evolved. We intend to create creeds and ideologies, art and poetry, and ethics and religion, all growing out of a healthy life and intimately related to it: we shall therefore have created healthy human relationships and living links that bind the present to the past. What we seek to create here is life—our own life—in our own spirit and in our own way. Let me put it more bluntly: In Palestine we must do with our own hands all the things that make up the sum total of life. We must ourselves do all the work, from the least strenuous, cleanest and most sophisticated, to the dirtiest and most difficult. In our own way, we must feel what a worker feels and think what a worker thinks—then, and only then, shall we have a culture of our own, for then we shall have a life of our own.

It all seems very clear: From now on our principal ideal must be Labor. Through no fault of our own we have been deprived of this element and we must seek a remedy. Labor is our cure. The ideal of Labor must become the pivot of all our aspirations. It is the foundation upon which our national structure is to be erected. Only by making Labor, for its own sake, our national ideal shall we be able to cure ourselves of the plague that has affected us for many generations and mend the rent between ourselves and nature. Labor is a great human ideal. It is the ideal of the future, and a great ideal can be a healing sun. Though the purpose of history is not, to be sure, to act the teacher, still the wise can and must learn from it. We can learn from our condition in the past and in the present, for we must now set the example for the future. We must all work with our hands.

We need a new spirit for our national renaissance. That new spirit must be created here in Palestine and must be nourished by our life in Palestine. It must be vital in all its aspects, and it must be all our own.

What we need is zealots of Labor—zealots in the finest sense of the word.

Any man who devotes his life to this ideal will not need to be told how difficult it is, but he will also know that it is of immense importance.

ON ZIONISM, THE LAND OF ISRAEL AND THE ARABS

ALBERT EINSTEIN

Albert Einstein (1879-1955) was born in Ulm, Germany, and studied physics in Zurich, Switzerland. In 1905 he issued his first important papers. He was a professor at Zurich and Prague and, in 1914, became director of the Kaiser Wilhelm Academy of Science in Berlin. In 1913-1916 he published his general, or extended, theory of relativity; in 1922 he was awarded the Nobel Prize. In 1933 he resigned from his Academy post, renounced his German citizenship, and accepted an appointment as professor of theoretical physics at the Princeton Institute of Advanced Study. In 1950 he promulgated his unified field theory, an effort to formulate a series of universal laws which explain the forces that govern the immense expanse of interstellar space and the minute field within the atom of matter. His equation E equals mc^2 had its fruition in the harnessing of atomic energy. George Bernard Shaw described Einstein as one of the eight "universe builders" in history.

Though an opponent of nationalism and averse to political action, Einstein realized the peculiar position of the Jewish community in Europe and, in 1919, joined the Zionist movement and actively supported the rebuilding of the land of Israel. With Chaim Weizmann, president of the World Zionist Organization, he visited the United States in 1921 in behalf of the Zionist cause. He was a member of the Board of Governors of the Hebrew University in Jerusalem. In 1952 he was asked, but refused, to become Chaim Weizmann's successor as President of the State of Israel. The notes that follow, written in 1929 and 1930, indicate his approach to the Zionist idea.

Zionism has a two-fold basis. It arose on the one hand from the fact of Jewish suffering. It is not my intention to paint here a picture of the Jewish martyrdom throughout the ages, which has arisen from the homelessness of the Jew. Even to-day there is an intensity of Jewish suffering throughout the world of which the public opinion of the civilized West never obtains a comprehensive view. In the whole of Eastern Europe the danger of physical attack against the individual Jew is constantly present. The degrading disabilities of old have been transformed into restrictions of an economic character, while restrictive measures in the educational sphere, such as the "numerus clausus" at the universities, seek to suppress the Jew in the world of intellectual life.

There is, I am sure, no need to stress at this time of day that there is a Jewish problem in the Western world also. How many non-Jews have any insight into the spiritual suffering and distortion, the degradation and moral disintegration engendered by the mere fact of the homelessness of a gifted and sensitive people?

What underlies all these phenomena is the basic fact, which the first Zionists recognized with profound intuition, that the Jewish problem cannot be solved by the assimilation of the individual Jew to his environment. Jewish individuality is too strong to be effaced by such assimilation, and too conscious to be ready for such self-effacement.

It is, of course, clear that it will never be possible to transplant to Palestine anything more than a minority of the Jewish people, but it has for a long time been the deep conviction of enlightened students of the problem, Jews and non-Jews alike, that the establishment of a National Home for the Jewish people in Palestine would raise the status and the dignity of those who would remain in their native countries, and would thereby materially assist in improving the relations between non-Jews and Jews in general.

But Zionism springs from an even deeper motive than Jewish suffering. It is rooted in a Jewish spiritual tradition, whose maintenance and development are for Jews the raison d'être of their continued existence as a community. In the re-establishment of the Jewish nation in the ancient home of the race, where Jewish spiritual values could again be developed in a Jewish atmosphere, the most enlightened representatives of Jewish individuality see the essential preliminary to the regeneration of the race and the setting free of its spiritual creativeness.

It is by these tendencies and aspirations that the Jewish reconstruction in Palestine is informed. Zionism is not a movement inspired by chauvinism or by a *sacro egoismo*. I am convinced that the great majority of the Jews would refuse to support a movement of that kind. Nor does Zionism aspire to divest anyone in Palestine of any rights or possessions he may enjoy. On the contrary, we are convinced that we shall be able to establish a friendly and constructive co-operation with the kindred Arab race which will be a blessing to both sections of the population materially and spiritually. During the whole of the work of Jewish colonization not a single Arab has been dispossessed; every acre of land acquired by the Jews has been bought at a price fixed by buyer and seller.

Indeed, every visitor has testified to the enormous improvement in the economic and sanitary standard of the Arab population resulting from the Jewish colonization. Friendly personal relations between the Jewish settlements and the neighboring Arab villages have been formed throughout the country. Jewish and Arab workers have associated in the trade unions of the Palestine railways, and the standard of living of the Arabs has been raised. Arab scholars can be found working the great library of the Hebrew University, while the study of the Arabic language and civilization forms one of the chief subjects of study at this University. Arab workmen have participated in the evening courses conducted at the Jewish Technical Institute at Haifa. The native population has come to realize in an ever-growing measure the benefits, economic, sanitary and intellectual, which the Jewish work of reconstruction has bestowed on the whole country and all its inhabitants. Indeed, one of the most comforting features in the present crisis has been the reports of personal protection afforded by Arabs to their Jewish fellow-citizens against the attacks of the fanaticized mob.

One who, like myself, has cherished for many years the conviction that the humanity of the future must be built up on an intimate community of the nations, and that aggressive nationalism must be conquered, can see a future for Palestine only on the basis of peaceful co-operation between the two peoples who are at home in the country. For this reason I should have expected that the great Arab people will show a truer appreciation of the need which the Jews feel to re-build their national home in the ancient seat of Judaism; I should have expected that by common effort ways and means would be found to render possible an extensive Jewish settlement in the country.

I am convinced that the devotion of the Jewish people to Palestine will benefit all the inhabitants of the country, not only materially, but also culturally and nationally. I believe that the Arab renaissance in the vast expanse of territory now occupied by the Arabs stands only to gain from Jewish sympathy. I should welcome the creation of an opportunity for absolutely free and frank discussion of these possibilities, for I believe that the two great Semitic peoples, each of which has in its way contributed something of lasting value to the civilization of the West, may have a great future in common, and that instead of facing each other with barren enmity and mutual distrust, they should support each other's national and cultural endeavors, and should seek the possibility of sympathetic co-operation. I think that those who are not actively engaged in politics should above all contribute to the creation of this atmosphere of confidence.

I deplore the tragic events of last August[8] not only because they revealed human nature in its lowest aspects, but also because they have estranged the two peoples and have made it temporarily more difficult for them to approach one another. But come together they must, in spite of all.

THE ZIONIST DECLARATION
OF INDEPENDENCE

The end of World War II and the collapse of the Nazi power brought hope that Great Britain would liberalize her policy of restricting Jewish immigration to Palestine (the White Paper of 1939) and permit the survivors of concentration camps to enter the land. This hope was shattered when the mandatory government refused to change the immigration laws and shipped "illegal" immigrants to reception camps in Cyprus. Palestine's embittered Jewish population adopted a policy of non-cooperation; militant groups engaged in terrorist activities. Following unsuccessful negotiations with both the Arabs and the Jews, Great Britain turned the Palestine issue over to the United Nations. In the summer of 1947 a United Nations commission investigated the situation on the spot; acting on its recommendations, the General Assembly of the United Nations, on November 29, 1947, decided on the formation in Palestine of a Jewish State and an Arab State. The Arabs rose in arms against this decision. The Jews prepared for statehood, which was to commence with the withdrawal of the British on May 14-15, 1948. The import of these developments was expounded in three declarations, the first of which is here reprinted.

On this, the third day of Nisan [April 12, 1948], the General Council of the World Zionist Organization, its highest unit, announced to the civilized peoples of the world, to the representatives of the United Nations and to the Jews scattered throughout the world that it has been decided to set up an organ of supreme authority of our national independence in Palestine.

In pursuance of this purpose, we declare that we refuse to remain a minority dependent on the sufferance of others. The mandate is about to end. On May 15 His Majesty's Government will surrender to the United Nations the trust it received from the League of Nations twenty-seven years ago and which it has failed to fulfill. It departed from the spirit of the mandate and replaced it with the selfish purpose of furthering its Middle East interests.

As a result of this policy, our refugees were refused entry in the hour of their direst need. They were interned instead and condemned to lead a life of danger, humiliation and helplessness while the mandatory treated with our sworn enemies, the friends and allies of the Nazis. And while refusing entry to Jews striving desperately after a last refuge they opened our frontiers to hordes of invaders come to make a mockery of the decision of the United Nations. And now the mandatory is proposing to destroy the very foundation of our existence and leave the country in utter chaos.

To prevent this we have resolved this day that the termination of the mandatory government of Palestine shall in fact mark the end of all foreign domination in this country. With the termination of this mandatory rule, a government of the Jewish State shall come into being.

In this hour we turn to the Arab citizens of the Jewish state and our Arab neighbors. We offer peace and friendship. We desire to build our State in common with the Arabs as equal citizens. Our freedom is their freedom. Their future and ours rest on common endeavor.

Sure in the justice of our cause, we are ready to give our all to its achievement and we call on the Jews of all lands, and especially in Palestine, to close their ranks for the carrying out of this, our sublime task. Assured in our faith, we appeal to all nations to grant us this right to our own salvation, and rest our trust in God, the Lord of Israel.

THE STATE OF ISRAEL
Opening Address at the Kneset

CHAIM WEIZMANN

On May 14, 1948, the establishment of the State of Israel was proclaimed. President Truman was the first statesman to recognize the new state *de facto*; the recognition by the Soviet Union followed three days later. The government set up on the day of proclamation and headed by David Ben–Gurion chose Chaim Weizmann to be President of the new state. From May 15, Israel had to defend itself against the invading armies of the neighboring Arab states of Egypt, Iraq, Saudi Arabia, Trans-Jordan, Syria, and Lebanon. On February 24, 1949, Egypt and Israel signed an armistice agreement; other agreements followed, but peace, urgently desired by Israel, was not attained. A few days before the armistice with Egypt, on February 14, Israel's first parliament was opened in Jerusalem; it adopted the traditional Hebrew name, *Kneset*. On February 17 Weizmann was sworn in as President of Israel; the text of his inaugural address is here reproduced.

Chaim Weizmann (1874-1952) was born in Russia's Pale of Settlement. In 1904 he emigrated to England and became a British citizen. His professional field was biological chemistry, which he taught at the University of Manchester, England, and practiced as Director of the British Admiralty Chemical Laboratories in London. An early advocate of the Zionist idea, he rose to undisputed leadership of the movement. In 1917 he succeeded in obtaining the "Balfour Declaration," which secured a Jewish national home in Palestine. He put his trust in quiet diplomacy and negotiation (of which art he was a master). In 1946, disillusioned by the Palestine policy of the British government, he withdrew from politics and devoted himself to his scientific activities—until called to head the reborn State of Israel. *Trial and Error*, Weizmann's autobiography, appeared in 1949.

It is with a feeling of deep reverence and consecration that I rise to open the Constituent Assembly of the State of Israel—the first *Kneset Israel* [Assembly of Israel] of our time in this eternal city of Jerusalem.

This is a great moment in our history. Let us give thanks and praise to the God of Israel, Who in His mercy granted us the privilege of witnessing the redemption of our people after centuries of affliction and suffering. Today's event issued from the great awakening of national will that aroused our people in the last few generations. The first signs came about seventy years ago.

The best among our people, men whose names were then unknown, arose to lead their generation toward fulfillment of the dream of all generations, toward the return to Zion and the restoration of Jewish nationhood.

Those who strove to realize this dream took two paths. The

first was the way of spiritual revival and the return to the well-spring of Jewish tradition, the renewal of the Hebrew language and literature, the gathering of the scattered forces of our people into one bond, the public proclamation of our historic rights, and the enlisting of help and support from the rulers of nations.

Two gatherings mark decisive steps on this road—the Kattowitz conference[9] and the first Zionist Congress.[10] The first conference led to the creation of the World Zionist Organization workshop, where the vision hammered itself into reality, and to the establishment of the Jewish Agency as the Zionist movement's supreme political organ and the instrument of colonization.

Following this path, we secured the Balfour Declaration,[11] the first external recognition of our right to settle as a nation in the land of our fathers.

The second path, that of practical action, of carrying out things, was the path taken by those who could not wait any longer for the nation to gird up its strength in exile and for others to recognize their rights. They thought to force God's hand, as it were; theirs was the daring to go up to the land to try to hasten the redemption of their people by their own handiwork and by the sweat of their brows and by their life's blood.

These were the first pioneers—the Biluim[12]—and all who followed the flag to carve out the road of return and to lay the stone on which the future would be built. In their footsteps came a new generation of immigrants to settle on the land, until the Yishuv [the community of Israel] was created. Those who took the second path also erected an organizational structure, institutions of self-government, local councils in towns and townships and assemblies of the new Jewish community, the *Asefat ha-Nivharim*[13] and the *Vaad Leumi*,[14] which also has its seat in this building.

It is a good while now since the two paths converged and like two members of one body helped reinforce each other until the great day nine months ago—the fifth of Iyar 5708, 14 May 1948—when we proclaimed independence and the establishment of our state. The union of two friends was now completed.

Then, compassed about as we were with blood, fire and pillars of smoke, with the Arab war waged against us from without and within our own house, with chaos bequeathed us by the mandatory, we were not able to hold elections to lay the permanent foundations of our state. A Provisional Government was set up, comprising a legislature and an executive whose authority was derived from earlier elections. In this Provisional Government two former supreme institutions—the Jewish Agency Executive and the *Vaad Leumi*—joined together and were fused into one.

Today we stand on the threshold of a new era. We leave the dawn light of the provisional authority and enter the full sunshine of ordinary democratic rule. This Assembly was elected by a body of citizens. In the elections the will of the entire people was fully and freely expressed. From the outset we are building on solid foundations—foundations of freedom, equality, collective responsibility and national self-discipline.

It was no longer an isolated band of pioneers who elected this Assembly, but an independent nation dwelling in its own, free country. This nation is being conceived as a gathering in of the exiles, for there is not a Jewish community throughout the world whose members have not a share in the State of Israel.

Every day, to our hearts' joy, tens of thousands of our brethren from countries near and far are entering the gates of the country, which stand wide open to receive them. It is our whole prayer that this gathering of exiles will increase and embrace an ever larger multitude of our people who will strike roots here and work side by side with us in building the State and making our unproductive places fruitful again. We will make this our goal before all else, to devote to it our best powers of thought and action.

Heavy indeed is the responsibility laid on us in this Assembly. What we began nine months ago on the same date, we bring to completion tonight—the restoration of the realm of Israel. If we are using state forms molded by the experience of the enlightened nations of the modern world, we know truly that these forms contain the treasured essence of the heritage of Israel.

In the ancient world, this tiny country of ours raised the standard of spiritual revolt against the rights of tyranny and brute force. The law of Israel and the vision of her prophets sounded a new epic of relations between man and man, a new ordering of human society. The authority of the King of Israel was limited by law and tradition. The prophets of Israel did not fear to utter rebuke and reproof to kings and princes, and with inspired words forged weapons to defend the poor and oppressed, strangers and slaves, and the orphan and the widow.

The very principle of the institution of kingship was hateful to the spiritual leaders of the people. "I will not rule over you nor shall my son rule over you. The Lord shall rule over us," declares the judge to the assembled people.[15] The warnings of the prophet against the dangers of tyranny thunder from on high to the ears of people to our last generation.

In Israel this authority of one man was derived from the noble conception that people are naturally free and are freely accepting the rule that law and just judgment do not need compulsion from above to live as ordered by society. The root of the principle of the constitution of that novel state was the limit set for the authority of the king, and in this sense the ancient Hebrew policy was the mother of constitutional government in the modern age.

And now it has fallen to our generation to cement anew the links of that life of freedom that were snapped by tyranny's force nearly 1,900 years ago. I do not know why it is precisely our generation that has been privileged to bring about what many generations before us longed for in the exiles of darkness. Unless we earned it by all the hardships, weariness, sorrow and tribulation that have been our portion during the past seventy years, when one-third of our nation was annihilated.

We suffered torture and affliction as no other nation in the world and because we are a remnant—and no more than a remnant—double and treble responsibility lies upon us to fill the terrible void in our national life.

It is our people who once gave the whole world the spiritual message fundamental to civilization. The world is watching us now to see which way we choose for ourselves in ordering our lives, and is listening to hear whether a new message will go forth from Zion, and what that message will be. The new message was not born without travail and our creative spirit. The creative force of our nation will soon meet the new, serious challenge. The Assembly is called on to frame the will for the supreme test. Let us strive in search of the basis of human life. Let us build a new bridge between science and the spirit of man.

This day is a great day in our lives. Let us not be overarrogant if we say that this is a great day in the history of the world. In this hour a message of hope and good cheer goes forth from this place in the sacred city to all oppressed people and to all who are struggling for freedom and equality. From this place we send fraternal blessings to our brethren throughout the world and to all states, great and small, that have recognized Israel.

STATEMENTS ON THE ARAB REFUGEE PROBLEM

MARTIN BUBER AND DAVID BEN-GURION

Nowhere in modern Jewish life do religious humanism and political realism clash so clearly as on the issue of the Arab refugee problem, a problem engendered by the Israeli-Arab war of 1948. The *Ihud* Association (founded in 1942), whose aim was Jewish-Arab rapprochement and cooperation, thought it unjust (and politically unwise) to separate the human from the political question. The government of Israel, faced by a persistently hostile attitude on the part of the Arab Governments, could not share *Ihud*'s view; it saw the refugee problem as a convenient political weapon in the hands of the Arabs. On previous occasions, e.g., at a press conference in Jerusalem on September 15, 1959, *Ihud* had already urged that "even before a general peace solution and treaty are arrived at, one should start with practical work on the basis of real cooperation between all parties concerned" and "on the basis of absolute equality." The organization hoped that the mere beginning of Jewish-Arab collaboration on a basic problem would create an atmosphere of mutual understanding and constructiveness.

a) The "Ihud"-Association expresses its deep sorrow at the Prime Minister's statement of October 11, 1961, in which he firmly rejects "the insidious proposal for freedom of choice for the refugees" between returning to Israel and accepting compensations and re-settlement elsewhere.

b) The Prime Minister's stand contradicts not only the repeated resolutions of the General Assembly of the United Nations, but also all the principles that the civilized world has come to accept out of humanitarian considerations as well as the Declaration of Rights of Man, as a result of which a vast number of refugees, among them many Jews, have returned to their former homes.

c) The "Ihud"-Association is not unaware of the numerous difficulties and severe problems, particularly concerning security, which are involved in the solution of the Arab Refugee problem. However we believe that, given a sincere desire on the part of all concerned to have hundreds of thousands of refugees transferred to a productive way of living as peace-loving citizens in the Arab States and in the State of Israel, the means to have these problems peacefully solved will be found.

d) The solution of the Arab Refugee problem can only be brought about by full cooperation of all parties: Israel, the Arab States, the Refugees and the UN. This cooperation should start with the setting up of joint committees of experts who should together discuss projects for rehabilitation of the refugees and methods of carrying them out "in a constructive spirit and with a sense of justice and realism" (Hammarskjold),[16] taking into account the economic, demographic, humanitarian and, particularly, security conditions involved in this operation. It will be their special task to ensure that the choice of the refugees will really be a free one, based on objective information of the conditions prevailing in Israel and in the Arab States.

e) The "Ihud"-Association therefore addresses:

1) Both the State of Israel and the Arab States with an appeal to change their present stands as expressed in repeated declarations and to agree to a solution of the Arab Refugee problem through cooperation and mutual understanding;

2) All the nations of the world with an appeal to extend their help to the parties concerned with all the means at their disposal

for the achievement of an agreed solution of the Arab Refugee problem as a first step towards a real peace in the Middle East.

"IHUD"-ASSOCIATION

PROF. MARTIN BUBER

Jerusalem, October 15, 1961

[Following is the text of Prime Minister Ben-Gurion's statement on the Government's policy on the Arab refugee problem:]

1. The Second World War led to a tremendous movement of refugees from one country to another, totaling almost twenty million persons: from India to Pakistan and from Pakistan to India; from East European countries to Germany and from East Germany to West Germany; from one East European country to another; and it would not occur to anyone to put back the clock and repatriate all the refugees to their pre-war homes.

2. Almost all the Arab refugees from Israel left the country before the establishment of the State, immediately after the publication of the UN-Resolution (on Palestine). The number of refugees leaving after the establishment of the State, was very small.

3. Almost all the Arabs who lived in Israel on the day the State was established are here today, and have been joined by some 30,000 refugees whose return was permitted by the Government of Israel for family or other reasons, and by the inhabitants of the "Triangle" area who were added as a result of the Armistice Agreements.

4. The departure of the Arabs, referred to as refugees, from the areas allocated to the Jewish State began immediately after the passage of the UN Resolution. We have uncontrovertible documentary evidence of the fact that they left the country on the orders of the Arab leaders, headed by the Mufti, on the assumption that the invasion of the Arab armies after the departure of the Mandatory Government forces would destroy the Jewish State, and throw all the Jews, dead or alive, into the sea.

5. Immediately after the establishment of the State, in the midst of the Arab armies' invasion, large scale Jewish immigration began —from the DP camps in Germany; from Cyprus—where the

Mandatory Government had detained the immigrants who had not been prepared to be slaughtered by the Nazis, and, especially from the Arab countries: Iraq, Yemen, Egypt, Libya, Tunisia, Morocco, Syria and Lebanon.

6. The number of the Arabs who, before the UN Resolution, lived in the area allocated to the Jewish State by the UN, and who left it voluntarily or on the orders of their leaders, is not larger than the number of the Jewish refugees from the Arab countries, so that what has occurred is an unplanned, but effective, exchange of populations, and there is no practical possibility or moral justification for putting the clock back.

7. There are also Jewish refugees in the State of Israel from areas of Palestine, which were settled by Jews before and during the Mandatory period: the Old City of Jerusalem, the Etzion bloc of settlements, Neveh Yaakov, Atarot, and so forth.

8. In assessing the property of the Arabs who left Israel, it would be inconceivable not to take into account the property of the Jewish refugees from the Arab countries, and from Palestine itself.

9. If compensation is to be paid—and we are not opposed to compensation if the question as a whole is solved—the Jewish refugees are just as entitled to compensation as the Arab refugees.

10. If an Arab refugee problem still exists, this is entirely a result of the violation of the UN Charter by the Arab rulers and their callous treatment of their own people. Israel did not wait for the Arab rulers to return the property of the Jewish refugees, but, regarding them as human beings and brothers, saw to their absorption, housing, employment, health and to the education of their children. The Arab rulers treated the Arab refugees not as human beings and compatriots but as a weapon with which to strike at Israel. Some of the neighboring Arab countries are under-populated, and have plentiful resources of fertile soil and water, as well as a shortage of manpower, but for the purpose of destroying Israel —with the aid of the refugees as well—they are behaving callously to their own people and treating them as nothing more than a political and military weapon with which to undermine and destroy Israel.

11. Israel categorically rejects the insidious proposal for freedom

of choice for the refugees, for she is convinced that this proposal is designed and calculated only to destroy Israel. There is only one practical and fair solution for the problem of the refugees: to re-settle them among their own people in countries having plenty of good land and water and which are in need of additional manpower.

12. If the Arab rulers comply with the Assembly decision and the principles of the UN Charter and enter into direct talks with Israel for a peace settlement, Israel will give all possible assistance towards the settlement of the refugees among their own people as she has done with her own Jewish refugees from Arab lands under conditions much more difficult than those prevailing in the neighboring countries.

I have not been able to submit this reply to the Cabinet, but I know that it reflects the attitude of the entire Government, although there are various nuances in regard to unimportant details.

TOWARDS A NEW WORLD

DAVID BEN-GURION

Ben-Gurion's name is intimately connected with the creation of the modern State of Israel. It was he who proclaimed the Independence of Israel on May 14, 1948. Born in 1886 in Poland, Ben-Gurion (originally Grün) cofounded the *Poale Zion* (Zionist workers' organization) in Poland in 1903; in 1906 he settled in Palestine, worked in agricultural colonies, continued to participate in the leadership of the *Poale Zion* movement, wrote for and edited a periodical of the labor movement, and, in 1908, cofounded the *Hashomer* (Self-defense) organization. During World War I he was exiled by the Turkish Government of Palestine and went to the United States. Here he helped establish the *Hechalutz* (Pioneers for Palestine) and organized the volunteer movement for the Jewish Legion for Palestine. Returning to Palestine in 1917, he took part in founding the *Histadrut*, general association of Jewish workers in the country, and from 1921 to 1935 served as its secretary general; in 1930 he founded the *Mapai* (Labor) party. From 1935 to

1948 he was chairman of the executive bodies of the Zionist Movement and the Jewish Agency for Palestine. He outlined a plan for the foundation of a Jewish commonwealth in Palestine after the war; this plan (the "Biltmore Program") was adopted by the Zionist leadership in 1942. His efforts were crowned by the United Nations resolution of November 1947, which established a Jewish state in a part of Palestine, and by his appointment to head the new state as prime minister and minister of defense. He created the Israel army that protected the young state against the invasion by its Arab neighbors, and, in 1956, executed the Sinai operation. In 1954-1955 his political activity was interrupted by his retirement to the settlement of Sde Boker in the Negev. He resigned his posts in June 1963.

Ben-Gurion the man of action is also a visionary, taking his inspiration from the Biblical prophets. A political writer and orator, he feels at home among the works of Greek philosophers, Spinoza, and the wise men of the East. A nationalist, he thinks in terms of international cooperation and a free world community. The excerpt that follows is the concluding chapter of his *Israel: Years of Challenge*, 1963.

We Jews in our homeland must ask ourselves: Can Israel assist in the progress and development of Asia and Africa? For Israel it is both a moral and a political issue, and from both aspects there is no doubt that Israel must look upon such aid as a historical mission, as necessary for Israel as it is beneficial to those we help.

From the start of our State, before the tide of independence swept over Africa, our Government deemed it a principal aim of foreign policy to form links with the peoples of Asia and help their development forward as far as it could, within the limits of our modest economic and technical resources. Now that most of Black Africa is self-governing, it needs and seeks that co-operation, ancient Ethiopia no less than infant states, and in some of them, relatively speaking, Israel has done a fair amount.

The growing number of the new countries and the massive assets and trained manpower they demand raise some doubt whether it is within Israel's reach to render a sizable measure of help. She is still, and for years will be, herself in need of aid from world Jewry and support from her friends abroad. No other country has such menacing problems of security. The Jewish people in Israel is still more potentially than actually a nation. Post-state immigrants have not yet merged wholly into the new nationhood, its economy, its Hebrew culture. Our scant resources are not enough for existence and urgent development in Galilee, the south, and the Negev, for the consolidation of new settlements; and swifter strides toward economic independence are our immediate need. What, then, can Israel contribute to the new countries in Asia and Africa and how?

The simple and truthful answer is: By what she does for herself in her own country.

Israel stands at the crossroads of Asia, Africa, and Europe. She emerged in western Asia four thousand years ago, when the Middle East was the cradle and center of civilization; in antiquity she endowed mankind with an immortal faith and literature, and thereafter has rubbed shoulders with many peoples in all continents. In the Middle Ages the Jews were concentrated in Asia Minor and North Africa; in the thirteenth century Jewry in Europe began to expand, by 1880 over 88 per cent of it lived there, and by the outbreak of World War II it had laid foundations for the Jewish State.

More than a million immigrants have settled in new Israel, rather less than half from Europe and America, more than half from Asia and Africa. They spoke a medley of tongues; their cultural standards, their original customs, differed vastly. Of that portion of the Land of Israel which is within the borders of the Jewish State, the greater part is desolate wilderness, partly because of man's misdeeds in foreign, and mainly Arab, conquests, and partly through nature's doing.

In Israel the problems of the modern world—the closing of the economic and cultural gap between the rich and politically conscious and the poor and undeveloped—are being solved on a small scale. Barren soil is being fertilized and output increased, to provide a growing population with comfort. Communities far apart in language and history, in culture and economy, are being made into one uniform nation, enjoying the cultural standard and the way of living of enlightened and advanced countries. Israel is sowing the desert, rooting out diseases endemic among immigrants from backward lands, so that in average life expectancy she is now in the front rank.

She is creating new social patterns, founded on mutual assistance and co-operation, without deprivation or discrimination. She is training an army dedicated not only to protecting her frontiers but to integrating newcomers and conquering the desert. She maintains a stable democratic regime, guaranteeing the maximum degree of civic freedom, providing progressively improving public health and educational services. She fosters the ideal of labor, making the workingman a productive and progressive force in society. She brings up her youth to play everywhere a pioneering role. She applies her energies to science and research, for their own sake and so that their discoveries may benefit health, economic development, security, and reclamation. In all this, her paramount aim is the advancement of man.

All are essential tasks, vital to Israel's future, security, and progress, but by discharging them for her own advantage Israel by indirection helps the new states to the best effect and widest extent: by being a model and example. Only during the past few years has Israel attracted the finest of the young leaders of Asia and Africa, from the Philippines and Japan, Cambodia and Burma, Nepal and India, Nigeria and Ghana, Liberia and Ethiopia, Tanganyika and Kenya, Congo and Chad, Guinea and the Ivory Coast, and many more, to study co-operation and agricultural settlement, military organization, development areas, the labor movement, scientific institutions. They have not come because Israel is powerful and rich, but because the new states regard her as a suitable and instructive specimen of a country that is trying, with no little success, to solve problems that concern old and new in Asia and Africa and also in Latin America. The changes we have produced in the economic, social, and cultural structure of our ingathered people and the landscape and economy of the land are those that most Asian and African nations want. From us, more perhaps than from many others, they can learn how feasible and profitable such changes are, and how to bring them about at home.

The history of our people, our ancient past, our dispersion

among the nations, our participation in the progress of recent centuries (as well as our not inconsiderable contribution to that progress), our settlement in the ancient and impoverished homeland, the inexorable imperative and blessing of destiny—these have compelled us to undertake the arduous and revolutionary tasks of the last three generations. Not by copying what others have done, but by carving our own paths, conscious of our unusual circumstances and the things we must do as a veritable act of creation, have we prepared ourselves to be, in miniature, a living pattern for the new peoples.

To insure that they derive the utmost benefit from that example, we must find room for more of their youth in our institutions of higher learning and special seminars, and facilitate practical training in our agricultural, co-operative, and educational undertakings. At the same time, we shall have to send them as many of our experts and instructors as we can spare, as we have begun to do in Burma, Ghana, Ethiopia, Nigeria, and elsewhere and recently also in Latin America. They must feel that they are performing a pioneer mission—not just a job for hire. This should be manifest in an attitude of humanity and fraternity, with neither arrogance nor self-deprecation, toward the peoples among whom they work, and an all-out effort to pass on the best of our knowledge and experience. Representatives of this type, and to our good fortune we have had them so far, will benefit both those they serve and Israel.

Israel, pre-eminently, needs and longs for closer fraternity and true co-operation between peoples. On her land borders, she is surrounded by hostility. She will be safe so long as her army is strong enough to deter her neighbors, but our heavy expenditure on defense slows down and circumscribes our progress in development and education. The surest way of arriving at peace and co-operation with our neighbors is not by proclaiming and preaching peace to the people of Israel, as certain naïve "peace-lovers" do, but by making the largest possible number of friends in Asia and Africa and elsewhere, who will understand Israel's capacity to assist the progress of developing peoples and convey that understanding to our neighbors. That purpose will not lessen our striving for co-operation and friendship with the peoples of Europe and America, where over 90 per cent of the Diaspora dwells: over five million in the United States, some three million in the Soviet Union, and two million in other parts. For many years those two continents, Europe and America, will still be the centers of the world's culture and science, and to satisfy the requirements of our security we must resort to them. Our relations with Asia and Africa will not loosen our ties with Europe and America but strengthen them. The moral precept in our Torah—"Thou shalt love thy neighbor as thyself" (Leviticus 19:18)—accords with historic needs. The creative pioneering of Israel, which gave ampler substance to the dream of Jewish rebirth and salvation, will spur on new peoples by its example, guide them out of darkness, from penury to affluence, from dearth to plenty, and by enhancing Israel's prestige bring us nearer to peace with those about us. [. . .]

So long as we clearly comprehend the real meaning of the great revolution being enacted before our eyes to bring about not only the liberation of all peoples but a true partnership within the increasingly united family of mankind, moving toward stable world peace, so long as we make our contribution to it to the limit of the creativeness and pioneering that are in us, no transient or localized troubles need check or unnerve us.

Three sublime ideals were put before us by Isaiah, son of Amoz: First—

Fear not, for I am with thee;
I will bring thy seed from the east,
And gather thee from the west;
I will say to the north: "Give up,"
And to the south: "Keep not back,
Bring My sons from far,
And My daughters from the end of the earth (Isaiah 43:5-6).

Second—

I the Lord have called thee in righteousness,
And have taken hold of thy hand,
And kept thee, and set thee for a covenant of the people,
For a light of the nations (Isaiah 42:6).

Third—

And He shall judge between the nations,
And shall decide for many peoples;
And they shall beat their swords into plowshares,
And their spears into pruning-hooks;
Nation shall not lift up sword against nation,
Neither shall they learn war any more (Isaiah 2:4).

Superficially, the three seem disparate, and in a fragmented world, with every region compartmentalized, it is doubtful whether any could have come true. The days of the Messiah are not yet, and the redemption of Jewry and mankind comes slowly. The miracles of science and technology in the first half of this century have cleared the way for a metamorphosis of humanity but entail many hazards. And yet, the footsteps of the Messiah are faintly to be heard even now: never before did our people see a return to Zion in such multitudes as in the early days of Israel's revival, though some millions still await it, many of them immured in exile.

The first signs are visible of the fulfillment of the prophecy, "The root of Jesse, that standeth for an ensign of the people, unto him shall the nation seek" (Isaiah 11:10). Youth from most of Africa and Asia, as well as the greatest European and American scientists, come to resurgent Israel to examine and emulate our methods for the advancement of new nations.

There is a great thirst in the world for true peace and a covenant of amity between the nations, and the more subject peoples are freed, to stand on their own feet and reinforce the United Nations, the stronger will be the pressure more speedily to quench that thirst. It is true that the independence of Asian and African peoples has become a new factor in interbloc tension, but these are "pangs of redemption." In our long journey through history we have known more suffering, more persecution, than any other people, but our faith in our future and in that of mankind has not been shaken, our hopes have not been blighted.

Even the Cold War is but a passing phase. Both the Soviet Union and the United States must obey the laws of change, and these two colossi will not forever face one another in militant challenge. In America the strength of the workers, be they laborers, farmers, or scientists, is rising; in the Soviet Union greater freedom and higher standards of living are sought, and as secondary and higher education expand there and the bonds between scientists everywhere draw tighter, the appetite for individual freedom, of thought, speech, and choice, will surely grow, and liberty will triumph in the end.

Today, when the United Nations is mentioned, the "United" is—not without cause—put in quotation marks. The member states are not yet united, and from time to time the Organization becomes a focus of international controversy. But unity of all nations is a paramount necessity, and unity—without quotation marks—will come *when all the peoples are free, internally and externally.* That it will come, even if it be slow in the coming, history decrees.

Israel must fight for this, for her security and future depend on the unity of nations, on the unity, freedom, and equality of all men.

She is a small country, with a small population, and wields no great military or economic power. In the long run, however, it is spiritual power that decides; in the kingdom of the spirit not quantity counts, but quality. It is not two or three Great Powers that will mold the world and determine its fate, but the historic needs of all the nations. Once the distinction between the ruling and dominant and the poor and backward nations is expunged, dictatorship will not last long, the danger of war will pass, confinement of peoples and populations against their will in totalitarian countries will cease, and the captives of Zion will return to their homeland. And the Jewish people, which throughout its four thousand years of existence has believed in the supremacy of the spirit and in love for the stranger and sojourner, which has shown the tremendous things whereof creative human beings are capable when their steps are guided by a pioneering will and their path lit up by the Messianic vision of national and universal redemption—that people will behold the realization of the ideals of Isaiah, and its contribution to the establishment of the new world will bring it peace, security, and the world's respect, and will also strengthen world peace and human brotherhood.

ISRAEL

KARL SHAPIRO

The distinguished American poet Karl Shapiro (born 1913) served as Consultant in Poetry at the Library of Congress, editor of *Poetry: A Magazine of Verse*, and is at present Professor of English at the University of Nebraska. His publications include seven books of poetry (one of which won the Pulitzer Prize in 1945) and a collection of essays, *In Defense of Ignorance* (1960). "Israel," here reprinted, appeared originally in *The New Yorker* and later in *Poems 1940-1953* (1953).

When I think of the liberation of Palestine,
When my eye conceives the great black English line
Spanning the world news of two thousand years,
My heart leaps forward like a hungry dog,
My heart is thrown back on its tangled chain,
My soul is hangdog in a Western chair.

When I think of the battle for Zion I hear
The drop of chains, the starting forth of feet
And I remain chained in a Western chair.
My blood beats like a bird against a wall,
I feel the weight of prisons in my skull
Falling away; my forebears stare through stone.

When I see the name of Israel high in print
The fences crumble in my flesh; I sink
Deep in a Western chair and rest my soul.
I look the stranger clear to the blue depths
Of his unclouded eye. I say my name
Aloud for the first time unconsciously.

Speak of the tillage of a million heads
No more. Speak of the evil myth no more

Of one who harried Jesus on his way
Saying, Go *faster*. Speak no more
Of the yellow badge, *secta nefaria*.
Speak the name only of the living land.

A CALL TO THE EDUCATED JEW

LOUIS D. BRANDEIS

The Brandeis family came to the United States when the revolution of 1848 failed to realize the hopes of freedom-loving Europeans. The most prominent member of this family was Louis Dembitz Brandeis (1856-1941), known as "the People's Attorney," "enemy of bigness" and of monopolies, fighter for social justice and "a truer democracy," and, from 1916 to 1939, Associate Justice of the Supreme Court. Indifferent to Judaism up to the age of fifty, he became interested in Jewish life by observing it on the lower East Side of New York, and, in 1912, joined the Zionist movement. This association brought him "understanding and happiness"; he saw a people's dream developing into reality.

Brandeis came to his conception of Zionism "from that invincible humanism of his, from his fighting faith in freedom, his certainty beyond all doubt that the propositions of the Declaration of Independence are valid for all the families of mankind. . . . Zionism was one more obligation of the people's attorney dedicated to the security of the 'genius of each man's independence' " (Horace M. Kallen). His contribution to Zionism was the development of a practical economic policy for the upbuilding of Palestine and the foundation of the Palestine Economic Corporation in 1925. In 1931 Brandeis Village (Kfar Brandeis) was founded in Palestine in his honor. The address we are reprinting was delivered at a conference of the Intercollegiate Menorah Association and published in the first issue of the *Menorah Journal*, January, 1915.

While I was in Cleveland a few weeks ago, a young man who has won distinction on the bench told me this incident from his early life. He was born in a little village of Western Russia where the opportunities for schooling were meager. When he was thirteen his parents sent him to the nearest city in search of an education.

There, in Bialystok, were good secondary schools and good high schools; but the Russian law, which limits the percentage of Jewish pupils in any school, barred his admission. The boy's parents lacked the means to pay for private tuition. He had neither relative nor friend in the city. But soon three men were found who volunteered to give him instruction. None of them was a teacher by profession. One was a newspaper man; another was a chemist; the third, as I recall, was a tradesman; all were educated men. And throughout five long years these men took from their leisure the time necessary to give a stranger an education.

The three men of Bialystok realized that education was not a thing of one's own to do with what one pleases, that it was not a personal privilege to be merely enjoyed by the possessor, but a precious treasure transmitted; a sacred trust. Yet the treasure which these three men held and which the boy received in trust was much more than an education. It included that combination of qualities which enabled and impelled these three men to give, and the boy to seek and to acquire an education. These qualities embrace: first, intellectual capacity; second, an appreciation of the value of education; third, indomitable will; fourth, capacity for hard work. It was these qualities which enabled the lad, not only to acquire but to so utilize an education that, coming to America, ignorant of our language and of our institutions he attained in comparatively few years the important office he has so honorably filled.

Whence comes this combination of qualities of mind, body and character? These are qualities with which every one of us is familiar, singly and in combination; which you find in friends and relatives; and which others doubtless discover in you. They are qualities possessed by most Jews who have attained distinction or other success. In combination, they may properly be called Jewish qualities. For they have not come to us by accident; they were developed by three thousand years of civilization, and nearly two thousand years of persecution; developed through our religion and spiritual life; through our traditions; and through the social and political conditions under which our ancestors lived. They are, in short, the product of Jewish life.

Our intellectual capacity was developed by the almost continuous training of the mind throughout twenty-five centuries. The Torah led the "people of the book" to intellectual pursuits at times when most of the Aryan peoples were illiterate. Religion imposed the use of the mind upon the Jews, indirectly as well as directly. It demanded of the Jew not merely the love, but also the understanding of God. This necessarily involved a study of the Law. The conditions under which the Jews were compelled to live during the last two thousand years promoted study in a people among whom there was already considerable intellectual attainment. Throughout the centuries of persecution practically the only life open to the Jew which could give satisfaction was the intellectual and spiritual life. Other fields of activity and of distinction which divert men from intellectual pursuits were closed to Jews. Thus they were protected by their privations from the temptations of material things and worldly ambitions. Driven by circumstances to intellectual pursuits their mental capacity gradually developed. And as men delight in that which they do well, there was an ever-widening appreciation of things intellectual.

Is not the Jews' indomitable will—the power which enables them to resist temptation and, fully utilizing their mental capacity, to overcome obstacles—is not that quality also the result of the conditions under which they lived so long? To live as a Jew during the centuries of persecution was to lead a constant struggle for existence. That struggle was so severe that only the fittest could survive. Survival was not possible except where there was strong will, a will both to live and to live as a Jew. The weaker ones passed either out of Judaism or out of existence.

And finally, the Jewish capacity for hard work is also the product of Jewish life, a life characterized by temperate, moral living continued throughout the ages, and protected by those marvelous sanitary regulations which were enforced through the religious sanctions. Remember, too, that amidst the hardship to which our ancestors were exposed it was only those with endurance who survived.

So let us not imagine that what we call our achievements are wholly or even largely our own. The phrase "self-made man" is most misleading. We have power to mar; but we alone cannot make. The relatively large success achieved by Jews wherever the door of opportunity was opened to them is due, in the main, to this product of Jewish life, to this treasure which we have acquired by inheritance, and which we are in duty bound to transmit unimpaired, if not augmented, to coming generations.

But our inheritance comprises far more than this combination of qualities making for effectiveness. These are but means by which man may earn a living or achieve other success. Our Jewish trust comprises also that which makes the living worthy and success of value. It brings us that body of moral and intellectual perceptions, the point of view and the ideals, which are expressed in the term Jewish spirit; and therein lies our richest inheritance.

Is it not a striking fact that a people coming from Russia, the most autocratic of countries, to America, the most democratic of countries, comes here, not as to a strange land, but as to a home? The ability of the Russian Jew to adjust himself to America's essentially democratic conditions is not to be explained by Jewish adaptability. The explanation lies mainly in the fact that the twentieth century ideals of America have been the ideals of the Jew for more than twenty centuries. We have inherited these ideals of democracy and of social justice as we have the qualities of mind, body and character to which I referred. We have inherited also that fundamental longing for truth on which all science, and so largely the civilization of the twentieth century, rests; although the servility incident to persistent oppression has in some countries obscured its manifestation.

Among the Jews democracy was not an ideal merely. It was a practice, a practice made possible by the existence among them of certain conditions essential to successful democracy, namely:

First: An all-pervading sense of duty in the citizen. Democratic ideals cannot be attained through emphasis merely upon the rights of man. Even a recognition that every right has a correlative duty will not meet the needs of democracy. Duty must be accepted as the dominant conception in life. Such were the conditions in the early days of the colonies and states of New England, when American democracy reached there its fullest expression; for the Puritans were trained in implicit obedience to stern duty by constant study of the prophets.

Second: Relatively high intellectual attainments. Democratic ideals cannot be attained by the mentally undeveloped. In a government where everyone is part sovereign, everyone should be competent, if not to govern, at least to understand the problems of government; and to this end education is an essential. The early New Englanders appreciated fully that education is an essential of potential equality. The founding of their common school system was coincident with founding of the colonies; and even the establishment of institutions for higher education did not lag far behind. Harvard College was founded but six years after the first settlement of Boston.

Third: Submission to leadership as distinguished from authority. Democratic ideals can be attained only where those who govern exercise their power not by alleged divine right or inheritance, but by force of character and intelligence. Such a condition implies the attainment by citizens generally of relatively high moral and intellectual standards; and such a condition actually existed among the Jews. These men who were habitually denied rights, and whose province it has been for centuries "to suffer and to think," learned not only to sympathize with their fellows (which is the essence of a democracy and social justice), but also to accept voluntarily the leadership of those highly endowed, morally and intellectually.

Fourth: A developed community sense. The sense of duty to which I have referred was particularly effective in promoting democratic ideals among the Jews, because of their deep-seated community feeling. To describe the Jew as an individualist is to state a most misleading half-truth. He has to a rare degree merged his individuality and his interests in the community of which he forms a part. This is evidenced among other things by his attitude toward immortality. Nearly every other people has reconciled this world of suffering with the idea of a beneficent Providence by conceiving of immortality for the individual. The individual sufferer bore present ills by regarding this world as merely the preparation for another, in which those living righteously here would find individual reward hereafter. Of all nations, Israel "takes precedence in suffering"; but, despite our national tragedy, the doctrine of individual immortality found relatively slight lodgment among us. As Ahad Ha-Am[1] so beautifully said: "Judaism did not turn heavenward and create in Heaven an eternal habitation of souls. It found 'eternal life' on earth, by strengthening the social feeling in the individual; by making him regard himself not as an isolated being with an existence bounded by birth and death, but as part of a larger whole, as a limb of the social body. This conception shifts the center of gravity of the ego not from the flesh to the spirit, but from the individual to the community; and concurrently with this shifting, the problem of life becomes a problem not of individual, but of social life. I live for the sake of the perpetuation and happiness of the community of which I am a member; I die to make room for new individuals, who will mould the community afresh and not allow it to stagnate and remain forever in one position. When the individual thus values the community as his own life, and strives after its happiness as though it were his individual wellbeing, he finds satisfaction, and no longer feels so keenly the bitterness of his individual existence, because he sees the end for which he lives and suffers." Is not that the very essence of the truly triumphant twentieth-century democracy?

Such is our inheritance; such the estate which we hold in trust. And what are the terms of that trust; what the obligations imposed? The short answer is *noblesse oblige*; and its command is twofold. It imposes duties upon us in respect to our own conduct as individuals; it imposes no less important duties upon us as part of the Jewish community or people. Self-respect demands that each of us lead individually a life worthy of our great inheritance and of the glorious traditions of the people. But this is demanded also by respect for the rights of others. The Jews have not only been ever known as a "peculiar people"; they were and remain a distinctive and minority people. Now it is one of the necessary incidents of a distinctive and minority people that the act of any one is in some degree attributed to the whole group. A single though inconspicuous instance of dishonorable conduct on the part of a Jew in any trade or profession has far-reaching evil effects extending to the many innocent members of the race. Large as this country is, no Jew can behave badly without injuring each of us in the end. [. . .] Since the act of each becomes thus the concern of all, we are perforce our brothers' keepers, exacting even from the lowliest the avoidance of things dishonorable; and we may properly brand the guilty as disloyal to the people.

But from the educated Jew far more should be exacted. In view of our inheritance and our present opportunities, self-respect demands that we live not only honorably but worthily; and worthily implies nobly. The educated descendants of a people which in its infancy cast aside the Golden Calf and put its faith in the invisible God cannot worthily in its maturity worship worldly distinction and things material. [. . .]

And yet, though the Jew make his individual life the loftiest, that alone will not fulfill the obligations of his trust. We are bound not only to use worthily our great inheritance, but to preserve, and if possible, augment it; and then transmit it to coming generations. The fruit of three thousand years of civilization and a hundred generations of suffering may not be sacrificed by us. It will be sacrificed if dissipated. Assimilation is national suicide. And assimilation can be prevented only by preserving national characteristics and life as other peoples, large and small, are preserving and developing their national life. Shall we with our inheritance do less than the Irish, the Serbians, or the Bulgars? And must we not, like them, have a land where the Jewish life may be naturally led, the Jewish language spoken, and the Jewish spirit prevail? Surely we must, and that land is our fathers' land; it is Palestine.

The undying longing for Zion is a fact of deepest significance, a manifestation in the struggle for existence.

The establishment of the legally secured Jewish home is no longer a dream. For more than a generation brave pioneers have been building the foundations of our new-old home. It remains for us to build the super-structure. The ghetto walls are now falling. Jewish life cannot be preserved and developed, assimilation cannot be averted, unless there be reestablished in the fatherland a center from which the Jewish spirit may radiate and give to the Jews scattered throughout the world that inspiration which springs from the memories of a great past and the hope of a great future.

The glorious past can really live only if it becomes the mirror of a glorious future; and to this end the Jewish home in Palestine is essential. We Jews of prosperous America above all need its inspiration.

A LETTER TO HENRY FORD

LOUIS MARSHALL

In 1920 Henry Ford's personal organ, *The Dearborn Independent*, began a series of articles charging the Jews with the most heinous conspiracies against the welfare of America and against humanity; they were allegedly seeking to obtain the control of the world in the interest of what was termed "international Jewry." These articles, designed to arouse suspicion, hatred, and prejudice against Jews, were based on the so-called "Protocols of the Elders of Zion," which, in turn, consisted of plagiarisms from a French political pamphlet directed against Napoleon III, published in Brussels in 1865 by a French lawyer, Maurice Joly, and entitled "Dialogues in Hell between Machiavelli and Montesquieu." The articles from *The Dearborn Independent*, which continued for several years, were reprinted in pamphlet form under the title "The International Jew" and distributed both at home and abroad.

Louis Marshall (1856-1929), eminent New York attorney and dedicated civic leader, became the spokesman for the maligned Jewish community. Finally, in 1927, Henry Ford was compelled to retract his anti-Semitic campaign; he sent an apology to Marshall, with an accompanying letter to Earl J. Davis, former Assistant Attorney General of the United States. Marshall's reply to Ford's apology transcends its contemporary significance.

I am in receipt of your letter to Mr. Earl J. Davis accompanied by your statement regarding the long series of vituperative articles which since May, 1920, has appeared in the Dearborn Independent and which contains the most violent attacks upon the Jews. You now declare that after an examination of those articles you feel shocked and mortified because of the harm which they have done, and you ask our forgiveness.

For twenty centuries we Jews have been accustomed to forgive insults and injuries, persecution and intolerance, hoping that we might behold the day when brotherhood and good-will would be universal. We had fondly hoped that in this blessed republic, with its glorious Constitutions and its just laws, it would be impossible to encounter the hatred and rancor to which our brethren have been and still are subjected in other lands. We could not at first credit the information that the Dearborn Independent had permitted itself to be made the vehicle for disseminating exploded falsehoods and the vilest concoctions of vicious minds, invented by adventurers who had barely found asylum here when they attempted to introduce the exotic growths of anti-Semitism.

Happily such excrescences could not flourish on American soil. Happily the enlightened press of this country treated them with contempt and as unworthy of notice. But we Jews none the less suffered the anguish of tortured memories, the nightmares of a horrible past, and the sorrow that, in spite of the progress of civilization, there were those who stood ready to misunderstand us. What seemed most mysterious was the fact that you whom we had never wronged and whom we had looked upon as a kindly man, should have lent yourself to such a campaign of vilification apparently carried on with your sanction.

The statement which you have sent me gives us assurance of your retraction of the offensive charges, of your proposed change of policies in the conduct of the Dearborn Independent, of your future friendship and good-will, of your desire to make amends, and what is to be expected from any man of honor, you couple these assurances with a request for pardon. So far as my influence can further that end, it will be exerted, simply because there flows in my veins the blood of ancestors who were inured to suffering and nevertheless remained steadfast in their trust in God. Referring to the teachings of the Sermon on the Mount, Israel Zangwill [2] once said that we Jews are after all the only Christians. He might have added that it is because essentially the spirit of forgiveness is a Jewish trait.

It is my sincere hope that never again shall such a recrudescence of ancient superstition manifest itself upon our horizon.

THE AMERICAN JEW IN OUR DAY

WALDO FRANK

The American novelist and critic Waldo Frank (b. 1889) interpreted his country's scene in *Our America* (1919), viewed critically its civilization in *The Rediscovery of America* (1929), and discussed American problems in France, Spain, and, especially, in South America. To him, the basic intellectual issue of our time is the transposition into modern social action of the great religious ideas of the Western world; he notes critically that the democracies have forgotten their roots in our religious heritage and calls for "true and spiritual maturity in modern men and women, so that they may cope with the gigantic forces of modern life." This is the problem he concentrated on in *The Bridegroom Cometh* (1938). In *The Jew In Our Day* (1944), he points to the religious aspect of Jewish culture as the source of Jewish survival and seeks to recall the Jews to the profounder aspects of their prophetic tradition and to its determined re-affirmation, in order to offer the world an example of a people serving not its own self but the community of mankind.

Reinhold Niebuhr, in his introduction to this book, urged "a political solution of the problem of the Jews without reference to the final religious problem," since the lofty and universal principle of faith "cannot also be used as the instrument of survival," and in the final analysis "a nation cannot be a church." Yet, Niebuhr admitted, "the Jews have come closer to accomplishing this impossible task than any other people." The following piece is quoted from Chapter 7 of this work.

1

The Jew is not well in our America. As nowhere else in the world, he has opportunity and strength. He shares the challenge of full membership in a free nation which history now raises to its great hour. The paper assets of the American Jew today are enormous. Equally enormous is the discrepancy between his inherited values —those which have borne him through centuries of travail and creation, and the actual standards by which, both as American and Jew, he lives. If the American Jewish community is called to leadership in Israel, it is a case of "the last shall be first." For its contribution to the spiritual and esthetic life of the American world and of the West is in woeful disproportion to its numbers and material might.

This discrepancy between ideal and act is of course not exclusively Jewish; it is a trait of our schizoid American world, whose major prophets and poets—from Roger Williams through Melville and Whitman to the contemporary—are honored more in the breach than in the observance. This dualism, since the Elizabethans archetypical of Anglo-Saxon culture, gives us a key to the ill health of the American Jew. In his need to conform to American life, he has applied himself too passionately well to surface rules and *mores*, unaware of the split in them from the true values of the country. His adjustment to the conditions of actual life has been too perfect to let him know that these are the conditions of a blinding, gradual death. Like all his fellow Americans, also heirs of a Great Tradition, he has become devotedly addicted to a civilization whose immediate aims exile the very values which have nurtured the people and brought forth its present promise.

One example will make clear what I mean. The most beloved figure in American history is Abraham Lincoln. Measure what we revere in this man of simple humbleness, this sharer in the guilt of all his brothers on both sides of the battle line—measure this man of sorrow, this *conscious* man, with what we cultivate and admire in the actualities of our life. Measure his total strangeness from the ways of a folk—complacent, ignorant, and greedy—which daily adores him. And yet our adoration is reasonable, for it is such traits as Lincoln's that have made us strong. In loving him, we acknowledge what is most real in ourselves, however our present life deny it. The same split is discernible in the mind and heart of the American Jew. While he lives, like his brothers, in a shallow world of the will, of acquisition, of illusive comfort, he preserves his innermost devotion to a life governed by the fear of God. For he knows this to have been the life that has given him health and lucid wit to survive.

There is no valid distance between the Jewish community in America and America as a whole, and this—this lack of distance—

is at the root of the disharmony of the American Jews within their own communal life, within themselves and within their beloved country.

2

The heart of every paradox is an unrecognized axiom. As we study this paradox, let us first observe how it troubles the Jews themselves. One large class of successful Jewish Americans vociferously claims that there is no valid difference between the Jews and their fellow citizens; and why should there be? Let, then, no difference be noted. [. . .] This response reveals for the thousandth time the failure of the average liberal mind to understand the organic nature of human history, without which understanding Jewish history becomes a tedious burden. Community is not identity. The cells of a healthy body have a common rhythm and a common transcendent purpose which does not detract from the peculiarity of their especial functions.

A more sensitive, more nostalgic group admits that there must be found within the harmony of American life some difference to justify the continuance of themselves as Jews and as a community in the American whole. They set about seeking "good" distinctions and methods for cultivating them; always zealous against the major threat that such distinctions be too conspicuous, too real—make for any serious Jewish detachment. These conscientious leaders propose that Israel [3] become a "mere" religious denomination, and that the reform of community life be kept within the safe confines of what they call worship, ceremony, research into Jewish history and enhancement of Jewish "culture." Lacking from their plans is the radical application of the prophetic ethics, preached in the sermons of their pulpits, to immediate political and economic problems. Such application might make a conspicuous change in the Jews' way of living; and conspicuousness is the nightmare of these good men. An effective ethics would be too much of a badge of identity like that worn by Israel in Hitler's Europe.

Look back over Israel's centuries before and after the Diaspora, and the pathos of both these attitudes is clear. Can you imagine a contemporary of Baal Shem,[4] Rashi,[5] Jehuda Halevi,[6] Philo,[7] Ezra,[8] or Jeremiah, engaged in the effort to prove that Jews are essentially undistinguishable from their neighbors; or troubled over the need of stimulating congregational methods to establish and justify such distinctions?

A third honorable group differs from the others in admitting the distinctions the first group denies, and in denying the need of cultivating or justifying the distinctions that the second group favors. "We are a people, a nation," it insists, "with the same right *to be* as any other. This right transcends and is antecedent to whatever cultural contributions we may have made or may make. The Jewish people need not justify its existence any more than the Dutch or the Czech." Logically, this group demands its national home. There is something gratefully simple and concrete about the Zionist's position, and I see no argument against it, provided it be kept clear that it solves no essential problem for the Jews who cannot and do not wish to make Palestine their country. For two thousand years the Jewish people have survived, not in a physical past, but in a vitally *present* way of life, which reached many of its greatest heights thousands of miles from the land of Canaan. This way of life gave them the energy, the intelligence and the devotion to adjust to tragic vicissitudes in Africa, Spain, Europe, Poland, and Russia. The past in Palestine was the formative matrix. But it was the constantly renewed present of the Jews in many lands and ages that made possible and justified their survival. To assume, like the more simple-minded political Zionists, that the Jews' tremendous experience and heritage in the entire West can be equated and written off by the repossession of Palestine, is fantastic.

I see no reason why in a decent world order tomorrow the Jews should not work out, with the Arabs, a political-economic control in the Holy Land, which the Hebrew genius stamped forever with its indelible signature. Such a Zionism would be as remote from present-day nationalisms as must be the autonomy of peoples like the Norwegians and Czechs in a rationally federated Europe. But to focus Israel's creative aspiration primarily upon this territorial form is an intolerable shrinkage; and surely no intelligent Zionist demands it. For a thousand years Hebrew genius deepened to universalism. For two thousand years destiny drove it forth into a hostile world from which its nurturing universalism saved it, and which its universalism nurtured and saved. To lop off this deep dimension from Jewish reality would be to maim the modern Jew. He cannot go back to a phase of consciousness which two millennia have superseded. Even when the homeland is rewon for that nucleus of Israel which wants to live in it and to make it into a new womb for Jewish creation, the justification of Israel for all Israel will continue to be his timeliness as a spiritual people.

Why "justification" at all? One claim of many Jews is that Israel needs no more justification for survival than any other minority people. There are small peoples whose persistence is due to their occupation of a land with which their culture has been merged and on which it continues to live. Their claim to survival is a right to their land, which instinctively they identify with the very nature of their bodies. And there is a race like the Negro whose most obvious distinction among Americans is color. This color is only the outward symbol of a long and profound adjustment to life in another continent, which gave them a history and a culture: a possession which they instinctively seek to preserve and to transmute into American life. What is the distinctive possession of the Jews? Not a land, that most of them have not seen for two millennia. Not a color, which is a symbol of the African's adjustment to the tropic Forest. The Jews' distinction is nothing but their *religious culture:* their peculiar and total way of life which consciously "justifies" them, being their obedience to the mandate to live under God—under a universal law. Since Moses, this way of life has of course deviously changed. But the tradition of justification has not been broken. It is the land, it is the color of this people.

The life force of the Jew has been his striving in a *particular* way for that *universal* human reality which he called of God. His difference from other men has been the precise—although not exclusive—difference of a folk conscious of its universal function, and individually working it out within a common humanity less conscious and less specifically devoted to the universal. The Jew has been peculiar because his awareness was universal; because, day by day, in his most intimate acts, he was willing to live according to a prophetic vision that linked him organically with all mankind. This general statement, of course, would require analysis to synthesize it into the different phases of Jewish history. This I have done in other chapters. Here all I must point out is that once a people has reached this height of maturity it cannot become less without betrayal. The child need not be mature. Once he is a man, he can justify his life only by remaining a man. To revert to childhood would be disease and treason. I refuse a less exacting function for the American Jew than the personal, devoted application of Jewish *maturity* to modern American life.

3

The Jew cannot belong to the United States dynamically as a Jew unless in an essential way he is distinct; and accepts his distinction. This does not mean that the Jews need be the one distinct people; it certainly does not mean that they *alone* can express universal values in a particular way of life—but only that they have *their* way of expressing the universal, a way which is Jewish. This is obvious, and the millions of Jews who have failed to feel this need in relation to other men, throughout history have soon lost their distinction, whether in Egypt, Babylon, Alexandria, or Europe.

But the difference of the Jew from his fellow men may vary in one historical case from another. It may be a radical difference of values from those of his hosts. This will make survival dubious. No social body could long tolerate a deeply alien organism within it. The Jew survived in the Middle Ages of Europe because his differences expressed a common harmony with a depth of value in his Christian fellows. Although the ways of expression differed, there was much in tune between them. Moreover, the Jew performed economic functions not only useful but progressive for the health of the wider social organism. In the modern American world the peculiarity of the Jew must consist in a particular expression of a way of life that is both Jewish and deeply American. His particularity must be in basic harmony with the democratic way that is at once American and Jewish.

This paradox of Jewish survival is of course within the secret of all human individuation. The universal expresses itself ever and only through the particular. By living his Jewish distinctness, by living the prophetic values which have made the Jew a vital factor in Occidental culture, the Jew expresses root ideals of American life. In the sense of organic history, the Jew may be called a beginning, and America an end, of Europe. In the form of organic history, it may be that they must meet, in order to realize each other. By the same law, when the Jew loses his distinctness, when willfully or blindly he merges in the surface civilization of America, he not only denies his own values but alienates himself from the root energy of his country. I suspect that in every crisis of the Diaspora this disease of non-distinction from the host culture has appeared and has carried off all those *inertial* Jews whose presence even in Biblical days inspired the constant reference to the saving Remnant. The disease is classic. Classic, also, is the cure. We must see clearly the constant dynamic of Jewish life and its relation with the health of the world we live in. This clear seeing is organic knowledge, which means organic *living*.

4

The health of America depends on the evolution of its democracy. To say we have attained the democratic goal is as blasphemous as to deny that we have painfully, deviously moved toward it. America is not a democratic nation. But indubitably it is more democratic than when Jefferson fought for universal suffrage, when Lincoln fought chattel slavery, and when Bryan[9] tilted against the corporations which were absorbing, with almost no return, the wealth stolen from an expanding people.

The base of American life has been faith in the democratic destiny of man. This faith was the most revolutionary trait of our revolutionary fathers. Many of them were free thinkers, and indifferent to churches. But their political creed secularized the implicit premise of the Judeo-Christian tradition: that God is the potential, absolute presence in every human life; and that therefore in every human being there is the principle of freedom. Man can be free: *the whole man*. And the inevitable grouping of such

free men will be democracy. The revolutionary fathers were too
naive and sanguine. Like the Christianity which fathered them,
they took the psychological process whereby the person attains
freedom too much for granted; they laid too great stress on the
political process whereby free men might organize, and too little
upon a methodology whereby the nuclear whole man might be
formed to become free.

The failure of the democratic process in the Western world
during the eighteenth and nineteenth centuries, whose final collapse was the story of the first four decades of the twentieth
century, is due to the continued schism between the groups of
democratic believers. On the one hand were the liberal politicalists
and radical economists who ignored the psychological-religious
problem of forming and freeing the whole man; on the other hand
were the religionists and esthetes who ignored the social dimension of the whole man, without whose maturity within a social
organism enacting justice there can be no individual freedom. The
schism still exists. So long as it does, a specialized and profoundly
experienced religious social body like the Jews, whose genius has
been precisely the unification of the two aspects of democracy, remains historically potent. All it will need to survive is to learn how
to function.

5

To summarize thus far: there is a profound split between the great
tradition of American life and the common American way. The
Jew, in his successful adaptation to the common way of America,
has divorced himself from America's Great Tradition and from his
own. He is close to the creative sources of our democratic world,
only insofar as he remains creatively close to the energy of his own
religious culture. Hence the paradox becomes a commonplace: to
the extent that he is true to his Jewishness, and thereby lives
"separately and distinguishably," he is harmonious within America.
And insofar as he loses himself among the surfaces of the American world, he cuts himself off from America's nourishing heart
and from his own.

But this must all be made explicitly clear: how Israel's faith is not alone consonant, but organic with the democratic faith; how the common ways of American life—education, arts, pragmatic values, and religion—threaten this faith even while they appear to serve it; how fascism, anti-Semitism and war are today merely symptoms of the disease deep in the "Democracies" which fight them; and how the American Jew, insofar as he has succumbed to the common American way, betrays both America and himself.

From this picture of seeming despair, will rise integrally the great hope of the American Jew. For the disease of the common American way is the disease of the entire modern world. And therefore precisely because the American Jew is centrally involved in it, unto death, he is in the position to create, from his own crisis, consciousness and cure, an *antitoxin* to serve not alone all Israel but—again—all Western man.

This heroic destiny calls for heroic living. We are witnessing today in Europe the need of Jews to die for their great name. Our hearts are bowed before their victory. But the hard truth is that it is easier to die than to live. The hard truth is that dying and saving from death are not enough. Races and cultures have died, not because all their flesh was massacred, but because the spirit of their survivors compounded with the assassins. If every Jew within the hand of Hitler were to disappear tomorrow, there would still be living in the world more Jews than in the days of the Rabbi Akiba.[10]

A more terribly difficult task than to die is set by this hour upon the American Jew. It is to find a way of life and to live it. If he finds it, the Mystery of Israel may be again repeated: his way of survival may become a way of life for the world.

RE-EXAMINATION

LUDWIG LEWISOHN

Ludwig Lewisohn (1883-1955), who was eight years old when his family emigrated from Berlin to the United States, grew up in an environment of the best intellectual traditions of the West and won early acclaim as a literary critic, essayist, short story writer, and novelist of imaginative power and stylistic excellence. From 1919-1924 he was on the staff of *The Nation*, and from 1948 to his death, professor of comparative literature at Brandeis University. His non-fiction includes *Expression in America* (1933) and *The Permanent Horizon* (1934); best known among his novels are *The Case of Mr. Crump* (1926) and *The Island Within* (1928). The latter work is indicative of the dramatic change in Lewisohn's outlook which occurred a few years earlier, when the American writer, until then only faintly aware of his Jewishness, realized the creative force of the Jewish heritage. Lewisohn discovered his roots: not the official, tame, apologetic, complacent Judaism, but a spiritual challenge which has survived centuries of compromise and misunderstanding. The discovery transformed him into an impassioned advocate of a regeneration of Judaism from within. He fought the fallacies of superficial modernity (in which Jew and Gentile are alike involved): fought for standards and values, for a re-examination of the Hebrew tradition, and for a restoration of the meaningful in classical Judaism.

Lewisohn returned to the sources of Judaism, but he did not shut himself off from the world of Western culture. He grew in stature as a master analyst and literary critic; his ear for classical sound and structure grew keener. He believed that to achieve a measure of universality, a writer must belong to a people and have roots in his own culture. Hence, a Jew cannot become a great American poet unless he is first a great Jewish poet. This thesis he presented in *The American Jew* (1950) and in numerous lectures throughout the country. The essay that follows is the first chapter of *The American Jew*; it was written under the impact of the Jewish catastrophe in Europe and the establishment of the State of Israel.

A deep metaphysical anxiety stirs the Western world. Even so nihilistic a movement as that which is called existentialism bears witness to that anxiety. Keen as the feeling is, it is as yet fruitless. It is still a flight from fear and a desire for reassurance. It has not yet entered the moral world or the world of action; it has not yet entered the world of contrition and expiation. It may still for the day and hour be summed up in the saying of Paul Valéry:[11] "There is science, mortally wounded in its moral ambitions and, as it were, dishonored by the cruelty of its applications." The ground is shaking under the feet of Western man; he is hardly yet poised for flight, nor is he on his knees. His heart is still barren and the sky above him empty.

This metaphysical anxiety is shared by not a few Jews. But in them, whether they know it or not, it takes on a different character for the reason that their subconsciousness is not gnawed by guilt. Upon pagan altars they were the sacrifice; the blood-soaked hands of Christendom are spiritually the remotest thing from them in all the world. They are not driven to such enormities as the celebration annually of a Mass of a Messiah with those hands still twitching away from any lustral waters. They are therefore too often still lured by a withered positivism, by a forgetfulness of the great words of Martin Buber:[12] *Vom zeugenden Geist aus dauern wir* (we endure by virtue of the creative power of the spirit.) Nevertheless, the pervasive metaphysical anxiety of Western man is theirs too. It may, through them, if they will it, assume a redemptive form that will transcend themselves.

Meanwhile, there is another, a specifically Jewish disquietude which casts down many hearts, which rasps the nerves of many. Or else, it is a kind of sudden dismay. And it takes yet a third form, that of a huddling, as though all obstacles were now gone, into the transitory comforts of a pagan world. The years of dread and doom are feigned to be over forever—as has always happened in respect of such days. Their memory is repressed. And this process is the easier in this century because the prophecies from Amos on have been fulfilled. The Third Commonwealth, the *Medinat Yisrael*[13] exists. "They shall build the waste cities, and inhabit them; and they shall plant vineyards and drink the wine thereof; they shall also make gardens and eat the fruit of them" (Amos 9:14). May one not then be at ease in one's alien Zion? Need one be agitated further? But though the disclaiming voices are loud, they do not wholly hush the agitation deep within.

There is a nobler Jewish disquietude than this. It manifests itself in an impassioned concern over the status of religion in Israel; it is deeply troubled by the problem of the relation of American Jewry to the people of the State of Israel; it fears chasm and schism and seeks to build a bridge for which there is yet no foundation on this side of the sea. But the foundation must be built. And since it takes time to build foundations that shall last and since the disquietude is deep and cannot afford time, conferences are called and panel discussions invited and "plans for Jewish living today" are sent out for approval and masses of well-meant and sterile words are proliferated. The disquietude persists. And even so it still shrinks from facing other questions, rightly dear and sacred to innumerable souls. How shall we from now on pray for the *herut*, the freedom of Israel, interpreting it, according to the liturgy, as the freedom to gather our exiles from the four corners of the earth? With what countenance shall we at our Passover *sedarim* say *l'shanah haba'a birushalayim*—unto the next year in Jerusalem? The freedom is won; the gates of the land are open to every Jew in the world. Why not in Jerusalem this year—no—on the instant? Planes fly; ships sail.

But we are imprisoned in a world of contingency. The absolute answer to an absolute command is wholly possible only in the realm of the mind, of the spirit. The centrifugal forces of the post-emancipatory *galut*, the state of exile, splintered the Jewish soul and the vast majority of Jews in America, of adherents of the Zionist movement in America, could not afford to grasp and to transmute into action the realities of the Zionist Revolution. For Zionism was in very truth a radical movement. It went to the root of things. It made radical demands based upon radical conclusions. Although secular in its forms and phrasings, it reaffirmed the antique instinctive conviction of Israel that it was a people in exile, that exile knows only mitigation of evil but never knows the good and that therefore secular means, not excluding the power of the human spirit, were to be used to liberate Israel from exile and return it—as the prophets and sages had promised—to its own land. And Zionism meant the people Israel—the whole people. Its negation of the *galut* as a form of human life was total. We will not even leave our dead behind, Herzl wrote in his diaries.

There will be a ship sailing to *Eretz Yisrael* carrying the bones of our fathers.

If American Jews stopped short of embracing this total concept of the entire Jewish people as a people on the march from home-lessness home, it cannot be denied that an element of self-protection was unconsciously at work. Even before the establishment of the Commonwealth and before the opening of the gates of the land it was evident that it could not house all the world's Jews and that the remnants of Europe and the oppressed of the Arab countries must first be rescued and redeemed. Though the world's Jewish population was reduced from 16,000,000 to a bare 10,000,000, the land still was too narrow. A vigorous and numerous *halutziut*, a pioneering movement in America, will help to sustain Israel technically and physically; it will serve American Jewry spiritually and morally. It can barely touch the question of the continuous corporate existence of the Jews in the United States of America. We shall remain here. For the sake of freedom itself, of our own security, of the security of the State of Israel we must sustain and fortify our position in America. How is that to be done? In what character, *as what*, do we remain? Here, at this point, set in new contradictions and difficulties. Here, at this point, arises the great Jewish disquietude of our day.

One thing is clear to all except the self-stupefied laggards of a perished age: we cannot remain in freedom and dignity on the terms of the old pseudo-liberalistic emancipation. For those terms involved, however tacitly, however equivocally, the *aim* of self-annihilation. It implied that aim externally and internally. Macaulay,[14] a man of good will, a highminded man, pleaded for the civil emancipation of the Jews on these terms: (1831) "They are not so well treated as the dissenting sects of Christians are now treated in England; and on this account, and, we firmly believe, on this account alone, they have a more exclusive spirit. Till we have carried the experiment further, we are not entitled to conclude that they cannot be made Englishmen altogether." In the same year of 1831 Gabriel Riesser,[15] pleading for the civil emancipation of his people in Germany wrote: "The question is none other than a question of religious liberty. . . . We are either Germans or we are homeless." There is no merit in hindsight. But it is infinitely curious to observe that Macaulay and Riesser, both conscious liberals and libertarians, proposed a theory of society which sets as its goal and ideal the highest measure of conformity. Both affirm the unitary or, as we should now say, the monolithic state and the identity of society and state. One was willing to grant and the other to demand religious freedom. But since Macaulay did not understand and Riesser chose to forget the character of the Jewish religion, the addition of one more mere sect to those already tolerated was no great concession.

It is clear that passages of similar purport could be quoted by the hundred. The hope and ideal of the emancipation was—as it is still of lazy liberals and anti-Semites with a troublesome conscience bidding them be philo-Semites—that complete liberation would destroy what was held to be the accidentally or sociologically determined separateness of the Jews. And if, in fact, that separateness had been "accidental" or had been determined by so-called social forces of recent origin, the hope need not have been in vain and Jews might have become undifferentiated Frenchmen, Englishmen, Germans. By the same token anti-Semitism ought gradually to have declined and faded. Neither thing took place. Liberals continued to plead for the Jews and to befriend them on the principles of the emancipation; great masses of Jews strove by means ranging from the not wholly ignoble to forms of violent self-degradation to play the game of ultimate annihilation. Apostasy and inter-marriage did decimate the communities and cultural assimilation cut the last ties with the congregation of Israel. But the masses of Jews survived as Jews and anti-Semitism burned with foul and hitherto unheard-of fury and fever and the world of the emancipation crashed with world-historic guilt, shame, martyrdom, ineffable tragedy, and was burned to ashes in Majdanek, Auschwitz and Treblinka.

These are commonplaces to thoughtful Jews and, it is to be hoped, to a few thoughtful Christians. It may be doubted whether the iron tread of history has ever so gigantically confirmed the analyses and prophecies of a group of men as these decades have confirmed the insights and visions of the early Zionists. Yet when a man like Jean-Paul Sartre writes: "It is not the Jewish character which evokes anti-Semitism but on the contrary, it is the anti-Semite who creates the Jew"; when a gifted American Zionist still says wistfully that, after all, fusion was the American ideal, it is clear that the unbending facts of the historic process must once more be emphasized.

Nor is this all. It is necessary to be utterly clear as to the inner character of the modern emancipation before we can examine the groundwork of our being and destiny upon which the *forms* of our survival must be based from now on. The great and disquieting question: in what guise and under what aspects shall we guide and govern our lives in America and what shall be our relationship to the people of the State of Israel, can be answered only on the ground of many re-examinations of history and experience. The first re-examination must be that of the inner meaning of the emancipatory period—the period, roughly, from Napoleon to Hitler, from 1808 to 1933.

The demand from without and the trend from within were to render the Jew indistinguishable from his fellow-citizen except by religion. Since, however, the historic Jewish religion is a form and discipline of the whole of life, sanctifying and setting apart an entire people from the other peoples by that form which intends a spiritualization of man and nature, an *imitatio Dei*, it could not in its authentic form be even approximated to the practice of other religious groupings. Hence all the practices which constitute *kedushah*, the sanctification of life, were gradually abandoned. A remnant of self-respect dictated the disavowal of the hard realistic motives of this process—the diminution of Judaism to the final point of fusion and disappearance. The age placed handsome rationalizations into the hands of the so-called reformers. In an "enlightened age," it was said, the age of, so to speak, Darwin, Haeckel,[16] Huxley, Buckle,[17] Marx, Wellhausen,[18] Harnack[19]— note the unification of trend within the different intellectual disciplines—a man could not be expected to abide by archaic practices, vestiges of a barbaric age, nor could he exclude himself from that community of all mankind which, under the leadership of science and democracy, was being ever more strictly knit into a unity of freedom and brotherhood.

It is hard in 1950 to describe these rationalizations without irony. For two things have happened. That mechanistic universe of impenetrable matter and economic determinism and the unimpeded action of rigid laws is swept away. No vestige of it remains. Einstein's discovery that energy and matter are interchangeable has received the empiric proof of the fission of the atom. Matter is far more like what was once called mind, and the Kantian analysis of the act and process of human knowing has been validated by the last word of astro-physics. Man creates his universe as he goes along and such theories as that of biological evolution are far more symptomatic of limited philosophical trends in man than they are of the processes that actually take place in an objectified universe. And another thing has happened and was destined to happen. The liberalistic world based upon materialistic determinism has also been destroyed. Monstrous rebellions against the re-emerging ethical and living universe have plunged half of the world into a freezing and intolerable hell of spiritual nothingness and slavery to blood and chains and dread. Man, supposing himself liberated by Darwin and Marx from moral responsibility and spiritual *fact*, set out to destroy the classical civilization of the Weşt. To this rebellion more than one-third of the Jewish people fell victim. The metaphysical anxiety of our immediate day bears witness to a growing awareness of what has taken place.

What does this mean? What is its relevancy? The meaning and the relevancy are that all the Jewish rationalizations of a flight from Judaism during the nineteenth and early twentieth century were based upon ugly and transitory fallacies—the most barren and brutal fallacies that ever darkened the spiritual horizon of man. Shall one laugh or weep when an eminent living Jewish scholar repeats the historically conditioned and hence once forgivable errors of the early reformers by an appeal to a "modern mind," basing itself upon a completely discredited view of the sum of things? In brief, all the intellectual bases of the Judaism of the so-called emancipation have crumbled into dust. That way is no longer a way. No trace of it remains.

Such is one aspect of a re-examination of Jewish life between 1808 and 1933, that is, during the era of the false emancipation, of which the shadows fall upon us still. All its trends, Reform, Bundism[20]—all its refusals and all its universalist affirmations— were based upon fallacies shattered and disgraced by their dreadful consequences. There is another aspect, closely allied, of course, with the first. Whatever Jews did, especially Western Jews, during the period in question, was done *under the pressure of forces outside of the Jewish people*. Organic Jewish history—except among Zionists and the Orthodox—was interrupted. It was the powers at whose mercy we were that demanded, from Napoleon on, the negation of our peoplehood and of the Messianic hope. It was the powers of a world totally outside of us that crushed our pride, our self-affirmation, and robbed us of that residual freedom and self-determination which dwelt, however turbidly, in the pre-emancipatory community. It was a pagan world which with its brutal demands, supported by its stupid and brutal and godless notions, crept into and corrupted the very soul of the Jew, especially of the Westernized Jewish intellectual and created that phenomenon, unparalleled in degradation, which is known, and rightly known, as Jewish self-hatred. The manifestations of that self-hatred are with us still.

A distinction of the highest importance is to be made. The term "negation of the *galut*," of the exile, must not be used without discrimination. The pre-emancipatory *galut*—the *galut* of the Rambam,[21] of Rashi[22] and Meir of Rothenburg,[23] of *both*—to span the ages swiftly—the Baal Shem Tov[24] and the Gaon Elijah of Vilna[25] —that *galut*, despite its constant tragedy, is to be affirmed and reverenced as an integral and precious part of Jewish history. But we were forced and driven from our path and made the objects, totally the objects, of forces outside ourselves with the onset of the so-called emancipation. For the world's peoples wanted us to be emancipated not *as* ourselves but *from* ourselves. The immortal miracle is in the ultimate failure of this monstrous attempt which had on its side all the powers and all the principalities of the world. Yet not all minds were wholly clouded and not all moral strength was lost. There did arise the men of the *Hibbat Zion,* "the love of Zion," group and the towers of orthodoxy, that is, of authentic *self-determined Judaism,* did not crumble in the East nor wholly in the West.

It is the post-emancipatory *galut* that must be negated in its essential character—in all its pseudo-philosophic, in all its psychological and political assumptions—as a first step toward even the most preliminary answering of those questions which represent the metaphysical and moral anxiety of the Jews of America in this day and hour. Where did we stand on the eve of that so-called emancipation? What were the forces at work within the organic community of Israel? Those who today have from time to time urged a neo-Orthodox or a neo-Hasidic movement have not necessarily been obscurantists who would shut the door upon a living development of a living Judaism. The examples already given of the changes that will have to be made in the liturgy as a consequence of the existence of the *Medinat Yisrael* illustrate a *kind* of change, a *kind* of development within the history of a living and acting Jewish people. The rabbis, earlier or later, of yesterday or today, who trembled at the assertion of our separateness in the blessings that precede the reading of the Torah either because Gentiles might not like these historically exact assertions or because these assertions did not harmonize with the "modern" theories of a dozen transitory pseudo-sciences—these rabbis were and are the symbols of that unrivaled intellectual and moral degradation to which the Jewish people were reduced, as a people, during the period of false emancipation.

It is from that intellectual and moral degradation that the Jews of America must liberate themselves as an initial act toward any reconstruction, any reorientation, any laying of any new foundations upon which may be built a not ignoble and a self-sustaining life in America. We must think through afresh the question of our character, destiny, attitudes, techniques of living, of our hopes and of our faith, wholly uninfluenced by the devices and the demands of the so-called emancipation. A new emancipation must be initiated—an emancipation from the sordid fallacies of scientific materialism, from the ominous identification of the state with society, from the cowardice which will not criticize our Gentile environment, as civilized Gentiles do daily, from that inner servility which consents to our being merely the object, never the co-determinants of the historic process in which we are involved. History *is* on the march. The State of Israel exists. The great prophecies of our prophets *have* come true. A portion, at least, of our Western world is awakening from the lethargy of materialistic determinism and moral nihilism. [. . .]

PATTERNS OF SURVIVAL

SALO W. BARON

The third major Jewish historian, following Heinrich Graetz and Simon Dubnov, is Salo W. Baron. In his *A Social and Religious History of the Jews* (three volumes, 1937), he undertook a description and analysis of the historical experience of the Jewish people, using the most advanced and refined tools of the historical discipline. In 1952 a new, revised, and vastly expanded edition of this work started to appear. Baron explores all facets and factors of Jewish history, in an attempt to do justice to the variety of forms Judaism assumed throughout three millennia. The result is an awesome historical synthesis.

The Austrian-born Baron (b. 1895) came to the United States in 1926 and served as Professor of Jewish History at the Jewish Institute of Religion and (since 1930) at Columbia University. He is the author also of *The Jewish Community* (three volumes, 1942), *Modern Nationalism and Religion* (1947) and of many studies in his field, an editor of *Jewish Social Studies*, and participates in the leadership of major Jewish scholarly, cultural, and community organizations.

The excerpt that follows is from the essay "The Modern Age," published in *Great Ages and Ideas of the Jewish People*, edited by Leo W. Schwarz, New York, 1956. It documents the historian's profound concern for the future of the Jewish community.

Problems of Jewish cultural creativity are but part of the larger problem as to whether, and for how long, Jews can survive in America. The negative argument is often presented in a twofold way. On the one hand, believers in the permanence of anti-Semitism predict that sooner or later the Jews of every country *must* be overwhelmed by some major cataclysm. They argue that all through history every Jewish community, however flourishing, was destroyed by such an elemental outbreak and American Jewry cannot hope to escape that fate. On the other hand, those observers who believe in the permanence of American democracy and its egalitarian institutions are convinced that Jews will disappear precisely because they are too well off.

Both these arguments can be supported with plenty of evidence from history. Certainly in the thirteenth century no one could have predicted that a few generations later Spanish and Portuguese Jewry would be eliminated from Iberian soil. So certain of their position in the country were the Aragonese Jews in 1219 that, facing the threat of a discriminatory badge because of the resolution adopted two years earlier by the Fourth Lateran Council, they threatened to leave the country if the king resorted to force. King and Church yielded. Yet within less than two centuries the descendants of these Jews faced a large-scale "holy war" preached against them by anti-Semitic rabble-rousers. By the end of the fifteenth century they were told to leave.

More recently, as late at thirty years ago no one would have predicted that Germany would fall back into barbarism and attempt its savage "final solution of the Jewish question" so soon thereafter. In fact, Jews under the Weimar Republic had suffered so little from social discrimination that when the catastrophe finally struck, it found them totally unprepared mentally. Our Cassandras here say, "Wait for the next depression and you will see in America, too, an outbreak of anti-Semitism of unprecedented ferocity." No student of social sciences will be careless enough to predict that such an upheaval is impossible here. Neither will he predict that it *must* happen here. There are no unbreakable historical laws.

That there is a causal relation between economic depressions and anti-Semitic outbreaks is historically far from proved. There certainly is no evidence that in the past American depressions (1873, 1907, 1921) we had any significant upsurge of anti-Jewish feeling. If during the Great Depression after 1929 anti-Semitism made headway on the American scene, the main cause may have been the world-wide Nazi propaganda. As a matter of record, the anti-Semitic movements reached their height in the United States, not during the low points of the Depression in 1930-32, but rather in the late 1930s, when many ravages of the Depression had already been healed and the American economy was again forging ahead. Of course, despair generated by unemployment and the shattering of family fortunes creates a more receptive audience for agitators of all kinds, including those who preach bigotry and hatred toward any chosen scapegoat. But in general, depressions, like other social revolutions, merely accelerate trends already existing in the body politic.

In short, while it is *possible* that some cataclysmic anti-Jewish upheaval might some day put an end to American Jewry, it does not appear likely. Its occurrence would presuppose such a total revamping of the American social and political system, such a total abandonment of the national heritage and radical deviation from the course of American history, that for the time being at least one can relegate the possibility to the realm of pessimistic nightmares.

American Jewry's disappearance as a result of total assimilation is a more tangible danger. Has not the emancipation era as a whole created a deep crisis in Jewish living? This crisis is, naturally enough, most direct where emancipation is at its fullest. One might even quote the historic precedent of China. Because that country so rarely discriminated against foreigners, including Jews, it proved to be in the long run the most assimilatory power in history. The Jews in China, too, of whom we have definite historic traces since the ninth century and who probably settled there several centuries earlier, on and off formed communities of their own. Yet sooner or later these communities were swallowed up in the mainstream of Chinese culture, leaving behind only the debris of architectural monuments, inscriptions, and books. Even in the twentieth century there was a Chinese Jewish community in Kai-Feng, consisting largely of racial Chinese probably with some admixture of original Jewish blood, but this was only a remnant of a much more flourishing community in that and other localities. Would not the same thing happen to Jews in America?

Here the answer, based upon Western history, is definitely in the negative. One might even paradoxically assert that American Jews—indeed, all Western Jews—could not disappear even if they all wished to do so. Historic experience shows that whenever large masses of Jews were suddenly converted to Christianity or Islam, as was the case of the Marranos, the Italian *Neofiti*, the survivors of the Almohade persecutions in North Africa and Spain, or the Turkish *Dönmeh*, they were not absorbed by society at large, but overtly or clandestinely formed a distinct group for generations thereafter. As late as 1904 the Prime Minister of Spain, Miguel Mauras, was chided in open session of Parliament as a *Chueta*, that is, a member of the Marrano group living on the Balearic Islands as Christians since 1492. In the 1920s a Galician engineer, Samuel Schwartz, discovered in Oporto, Portugal, a group of several thousand people who still had distinct knowledge of Jewish customs and festivals. After the publication of Schwartz's book, *Os Cristãos-Novos em Portugal*, in 1925, the world became keenly aware of the existence of a sizable crypto-Jewish community in Portugal four and a quarter centuries after the so-called Expulsion of 1496. The chances are, therefore, that even if the whole American Jewish community were suddenly to adopt Christianity, the result would only be the emergence of a new group of American Judeo-Christians still presenting all the complexities of the Jewish question but devoid of the feature that makes Jewish life worthwhile, namely, its magnificent heritage. Actually, the majority of American Jews do not wish to be converted and have no thought of disappearing. On the contrary, it is manifest from all that has been said here that the forces of survival in religion, education, and culture are more strongly operative now than they were three or four decades ago. The impact of the State of Israel is also becoming more noticeable as time goes on.

Since neither forcible elimination nor voluntary disappearance seems to be a realistic possibility, the only genuine question is what kind of Jews there will be in America and elsewhere a century hence. No one in his senses will have the temerity to predict the type of Judaism and Jewish community which is likely to emerge from the great turmoil of our present world. Yet one thing may confidently be asserted: If American Jewry turns from quantity to quality, if it builds its communal coexistence less upon the quantitative criteria of financial success, statistically measurable memberships or school attendance, and costly and outwardly impressive buildings and institutions, and devotes more attention to the cultivation of the genuinely creative personality and of the substantive and enduring values in religion and culture, the new type of American Jewry will be a cause of pride and satisfaction. To put it bluntly, if someone were to guarantee that in the next generation American Jews will harbor one hundred truly first-rate scholars; one hundred first-rate writers and artists; one hundred first-rate rabbis; one hundred first-rate communal executives; and one hundred first-rate lay leaders—the total number would not exceed five hundred persons, a negligible and statistically hardly recognizable segment of the Jewish population—one could look forward confidently to American Judaism's reaching new heights of achievement.

Jewish historical-ethical monotheism, expressive of the unity of God, of the universe and mankind, is needed more than ever in our divided world. Perhaps the greatest task now confronting humanity is how to establish the supremacy of the moral order above all other sovereignties, including that of the state. A history-oriented and Messianically driven religion alone can counteract the destructive forces of nature, nowadays magnified by the new man-made means of destruction.

In the service of that religion and with this ideal in mind, the Jewish people still has a tremendous mission to perform. Its destiny has made it not only a world people in the course of its history, but has also placed it in a strategic position for service—service to be sure combined with suffering—in this critical epoch of human history. Destiny willed it that the two largest agglomerations of Jews should be found today in the United States and the Soviet Union, the two world powers whose rivalry or cooperation will fatefully determine the whole course of human evolution. The third-largest group of Jews, which before long may outstrip the second, is located in Israel, at the edge of the turbulent Asiatic-African populations, and has an irresistible drive toward reshaping existing international relations. Before the Jewish people a great book of human and Jewish destiny stands open; in it is mirrored its millennial experience in its progression through many civilizations. If only our present generation and its successors can become fully cognizant of their heritage, if only they will delve ever deeper into the mysteries of their people's past and present, they will not only make certain of that people's creative survival, but also significantly help in charting mankind's path toward its ultimate, let us hope Messianic, goals.

THE AMERICAN COUNCIL FOR JUDAISM

ELMER BERGER

This organization, founded in 1943, "seeks to advance the universal principles of Judaism, free of nationalism, and the national, civic, cultural, and social integration into American institutions of Americans of Jewish faith." In *Judaism or Jewish Nationalism: The Alternative to Zionism* (1957) Rabbi Elmer Berger, Executive Vice President of the Council, defends its position against various charges, e.g., that it accuses Jews of "dual loyalty," or that it encourages assimilation, that it does not understand America is a pluralistic society, and others. Chapter 4, here reprinted, states what the organization stands for.

The American Council for Judaism believes Judaism is a religion and that American Jews are individual citizens of the United States; not members of a separate "Jewish" community marked out by secular interests which are different from the secular interests of their fellow Americans of other faiths. Jews differ from their fellow citizens in the way they voluntarily choose to exercise the common American right of worshiping God in accordance with the dictates of conscience. In secular, national, cultural interests

Jews reveal the same diversity as do their fellow citizens of other faiths.

The relationship of the State of Israel to the United States and therefore to any citizen of the United States is a political, secular, national problem. Zionism is a political-national movement committed to the advancement of Israeli national interests through a mechanism which regards all Jews as sharing certain basic national rights, obligations and attributes with the legal citizens of Israel.

Judaism, the Council believes, neither dictates nor implies any special attitudes toward either the sovereign State of Israel or its extra-territorial movement of Zionism's "Jewish" nationalism. Some Jews are Zionists. Some are indifferent. Some are opposed—just as Americans of other faiths.

The majority of people in Israel are Jews. Anti-Zionist Jews are as interested in, and concerned about, them as private citizens as they are in the citizens of Jewish faith in any other country; or as Americans of any other faith generally are interested in *their* co-religionists in foreign lands.

But for anti-Zionist American Jews the State of Israel is a foreign state precisely as it is for Americans of all other faiths. It is the homeland of only its own citizens. American Jews who reject Zionism do not possess—and do not wish to possess—any national rights or obligations in common with the citizens of Israel. They help—and wish to continue to help—their co-religionists in need in Israel, or anywhere else.

In offering Israelis charitable assistance the American Council for Judaism insists that it be genuine philanthropy provided by a group of private citizens in one country to a group of private citizens in another country. Such assistance must not be confused or mingled with any obligations to the Israeli *state*. The giving of such assistance must be a personal, voluntary, spiritual act. It cannot be a national or political responsibility.

The Council maintains a philanthropy to put this important principle into action. It provides assistance for needy Jews and others in less fortunate circumstances in countries other than Israel or in Israel itself. The Council maintains a program of religious education which creatively emphasizes the universal values of

Judaism with particular expressions and customs adapted to our lives as Americans. The Council publishes textbooks for use in religious schools. It advises and, where solicited, provides direction and guidance for a group of religious schools in which Judaism is taught as a faith free of "Jewish" nationalistic content.

A nation-wide membership organized, in some cities, into active local groups called "chapters" supports this work on the basis of agreement with Council principles and objectives.

The Council rejects the thesis that all people of Jewish faith, by virtue of being Jews, hold a common "Jewish" nationality over and above legal and technical citizenship in the many countries in which they live. This rejection includes the Zionist conception of Israel as the "national state" or "homeland" of all Jews.

On the basis of these principles the Council has established a public record which demonstrates the synthetic nature of the Zionist effort to speak for, or represent, all people of Jewish faith. In the American tradition separating church and state the Council holds that no Jew and no organization or combination of organizations of Jews can represent all American Jews politically, or on any issues in the secular, public domain.

The Council believes that the secular State of Israel is, in no way whatsoever, a fulfillment of Biblical prophecy or a fulfillment of Judaism's universalistic ideals. The Israeli state, therefore, has no relevancy to the religious convictions of Jews. The Israeli State was brought about by a national-political machine representing a minority of American Jews (some 500,000 out of more than 5,000,-000 American Jews by Zionism's own figures), who may subscribe to Zionism's thesis that Jews, as Jews, possess a separate nationality and therefore should have a "Jewish" national state.

The American Council for Judaism is a controversial organization because the very principles upon which it is founded have been the subject of controversy for centuries. Whether Jews—in America—are individual, American citizens worshiping God in the ways of one of America's many religious faiths; or members of a nationality regarding the State of Israel or Palestine as its "homeland" has been a general controversy for a great many years.

There are Jews in America subscribing to each concept. Until the Council was organized in 1943, however, only the Zionist side of the controversy maintained an organized effort which was molding public opinion to accept the "Jewish" nationalist definition of Jews.

The establishment of the Council did not create the controversy. It merely provided an organized, reasoned and responsible voice for an open debate of an issue which Zionism had made public long before 1943.

The Council does not apologize for its controversial role. In American life, Zionism too, is highly controversial. Its recognized influence on foreign policy, its admitted blueprint to create a separate "national consciousness" among American Jews and to establish a so-called "Jewish community" with an "overriding interest in its own welfare" have generated vigorous partisanship among the American people generally.

The Council's program is therefore a public service. It demonstrates to Americans and offers to American Jews a way of life for Jews diametrically opposed to the practices of Zionism's self-segregating and separatist nationalism of Zionism. The Council helps to develop the thinking of anti-Zionists on relevant public issues. It makes viable and meaningful the historic tradition of Judaism as a faith of universal—not national or tribal—values.

This debate is as inevitable and unavoidable today as it was in the days of the Old Testament prophets who first conceived a Judaism elevated above tribal or nationalistic horizons.

"My house shall be called a house of prayer for *all* peoples," said the Prophet Isaiah in the name of God (Isaiah 56:7).

SUFFERANCE IS THE BADGE

ABRAM L. SACHAR

Abram L. Sachar, born in New York in 1899, studied history at Washington University, St. Louis, and Cambridge University, specializing in modern history. After teaching history for several years at the University of Illinois, he joined the B'nai B'rith Hillel Foundations in American Universities which, under his leadership, became a major institution in American-Jewish cultural life. In 1948 he was offered the presidency of Brandeis University, established in that year as American Jewry's contribution to the advancement of higher learning. Owing to his tireless efforts, and especially his vision, Brandeis has become a leading center of humanistic studies, scientific research, and cultivation of the arts.

Sachar wrote *History of the Jews* (1930), which presents the subject from the viewpoint of a firm liberal and democrat, and *Sufferance is the Badge* (1939), a survey of the position occupied by the Jews in "the turbulent, disjointed contemporary world." Throughout the latter he stressed the integral relationship between Jewish and general history and the tie between the destiny of the Jews and the fate of the "democratic dogma." It is a moving story, told with careful attention to historic detail and with an unbounded faith in the continuous fecundity of an ancient people. The conclusion of the book, a credo, is here reprinted.

Here is a credo for survival to serve the Jew who is tied to his people by more than the accident of birth. He must be pledged to the democratic way and be prepared to make every practical sacrifice to strengthen and sustain it; he must militantly fight back against the enemies who use the existence of minority groups as a springboard for their unscrupulous ambitions; he must steep himself in his tradition so that he may understand its survival value.

Yet all of this resolution, however brilliantly buttressed by energy and intelligence, goes for naught unless it is rooted in courage, in optimism, in faith that mankind has the capacity to conquer the forces of darkness. No defences are solid when the heart has gone out of the defenders. It was Gilbert Murray[26] who pointed out that the collapse of Hellenic civilization came, not because of the invasions from without, but because of the loss of morale of the Greeks themselves, their Failure of Nerve.

This calls for no manufactured, Pollyanna buoyancy. History is on the side of the optimists. Civilization has again and again demonstrated its capacity to repel the assaults of the barbarians. Sometimes the outlook has been dark, the myrmidons of evil have apparently extinguished all the lights. But the liberal, critical, rational, tolerant spirit rises again, tempered by adversity, stronger because so severely challenged, more precious because so nearly lost. "Delusion may triumph," Macaulay[27] wrote, "but the triumph of delusion is but for a day."

Jews, above all, have no right to fly in the face of their own history by succumbing to the vapors of despondency. There have been other periods when the whole nation has been trapped between the Red Sea and the Egyptians. Only the names of the persecutors and the detractors have been different. Yesterday they were called Pharaoh and Antiochus, Titus and Hadrian, Torquemada[28] and Capistrano.[29] All of them imagined that the stiff-necked Jews had been finally erased. But most of them are remembered today only because history texts carry the record of their failure. The Jew with perspective knows this, and he remembers the unwearied fortitude of Shylock:

> Still have I borne it with a patient shrug,
> For sufferance is the badge of all our tribe.[30]

The Jew can wait for the return of sanity. He can wait with greater confidence today because the very excesses of anti-Semitism have wakened the world to the dangers of barbarism. The Jewish martyrdom has therefore succeeded in marshalling all the forces of justice and decency to be on guard and to fight a united battle.

It may be sentimental to glory in such a fate. The uprooted communities in Germany and Austria and Czechoslovakia, the starved and beaten communities in Poland and Rumania, find little personal comfort in the suggestion that they are playing a benefactor's role. Yet there is historic satisfaction in the realization that a minority group, which has never given up its cultural and religious uniqueness, its ethical protestantism, has survived, and that in its survival it has served, not only itself, but the cause of civilization. This realization is a pillar of cloud by day and a pillar of fire by night. It strengthens the faith that the Hitlers and the Mussolinis [. . .] are merely men of the moment who have pitted themselves against an enduring people.

WHY I CHOOSE TO BE A JEW

ARTHUR A. COHEN   ˅

Arthur A. Cohen (born in 1928 in New York) "represents the American Jew who becomes consciously Jewish not because of tradition or loyalty, nor because of social pressure, but because of his intellectual development" (Ben Halpern). This development led Cohen to reject a Judaism that readily adjusts to the ways of its environment, thus abandoning its historical role: dedication to the supernatural. From this viewpoint Cohen examined critically the development of modern Judaism (*The Natural and the Supernatural Jew*, 1962). In addition, he wrote a book on Martin Buber (1957), one on *The Myth of the Judeo-Christian Tradition* (1965), and edited *Anatomy of Faith*, by Milton Steinberg. His essays and articles have appeared in *The Christian Century, Commonweal, Commentary*, and other journals. The essay here reprinted was first published in *Harper's Magazine*.

Until the present day, the Jew could not *choose* to be a Jew—history forced him to accept what his birth had already defined.

During the Middle Ages he was expected to live as a Jew. He could escape by surrendering to Islam or Christianity, but he could *not* choose to remain anonymous. In the nineteenth century, with the growth of nationalism, Christianity became the ally of patriotism. The Jews of Europe were compelled to prove that their religion did not compromise their loyalty to King, Emperor, Kaiser, or Tsar. But no matter how desperately they tried to allay suspicion by assimilation or conversion, the fact of their birth returned to plague them. Finally, in the Europe of Nazism and Communism, the Jew could not choose—on any terms—to exist at all.

In the United States today, it is at last possible to choose *not* to remain a Jew. The mass migrations of Jews from Europe have ended and the immigrant generation which was tied to the European pattern of poverty and voluntary segregation is dying off. Their children, the second generation, were as suspicious of the gentile American society in which they grew up as they were condescending toward the ghetto world of their parents. The second generation, however, made the Jewish community economically secure and fought anti-Semitism so effectively that, though still present, it is no longer severe. *Their* children—the third generation of Jews now in its twenties and thirties—are able to choose.

For this generation the old arguments no longer hold. It was once possible to appeal to history to prove that Jewish birth was inescapable, but history is no proof to those who are—as many Jews are—indifferent to its evidence. Loyalty to the Jewish people and pride in the State of Israel are no longer enough to justify the choice to be a Jew. The postwar American Jew no longer needs the securities which European Jewry found in Jewish Socialism, Jewish Nationalism, the revival of Hebrew, and the Zionist Movement. *Fear*—the fear of anti-Semitism—and *hope*—the hope for the restoration of Israel—are no longer effective reasons for holding onto Jewish identity. The fear has waned and the hope has been fulfilled.

The irresistible forces of history no longer *compel* the Jew to choose Judaism. In many cases, moreover, he is choosing to repudiate Judaism or to embrace Christianity. I do not say the numbers are alarming. That they exist at all is, however, symptomatic. It is only the exceptional—those who are searching deeply or are moved profoundly, who ever reject or embrace. The majority tend more often to undramatic indifference—to slide into the routine of maturity without asking questions for which no meaningful answers have been offered.

Given the freedom to choose I have decided to embrace Judaism. I have not done so out of loyalty to the Jewish people or the Jewish state. My choice was religious. I chose to believe in the God of Abraham, Isaac, and Jacob; to acknowledge the law of Moses as the Word of God; to accept the people of Israel as the holy instrument of divine fulfillment; to await the coming of the Messiah and the redemption of history.

Many Jews will find my beliefs unfamiliar or unacceptable—perhaps outrageous. The manner in which I arrived at them is not very interesting in itself, but I think two aspects of my experience are worth noting because they are fairly common: I come from a fundamentally unobservant Jewish home and my first religious inclination was to become a Christian.

My parents are both second-generation American Jews whose own parents were moderately religious, but, newly come to America, lacked either the education or the opportunity, patience, and time to transmit to their children their own understanding of Judaism. My parents went to synagogue to observe the great Jewish holidays—Passover, the New Year, and the Day of Atonement—but worship at home, knowledge of the liturgy, familiarity with Hebrew, concern with religious thought and problems, did not occupy them. Their real concern—and they were not unique—was adjusting to American life, achieving security, and passing to their children and those less fortunate the rewards of their struggle.

It would be ungrateful to deny the accomplishments of my parents' generation. They managed to provide their children with secular education and security. But although the flesh was nourished, the spirit was left unattended. When I had finished high school and was ready to leave for college I took with me little sense of what my religion, or any religion, involved. I knew only that in these matters I would have to fend for myself.

When an American Jew studies at an American university it is difficult for him not to be overwhelmed—as I was at the University of Chicago—by the recognition that Western culture is a Christian culture, that Western values are rooted in the Greek and Christian tradition. He may hear such phrases as "Judaeo-Christian tradition" or "the Hebraic element in Western culture," but he cannot be deluded into thinking that this is more than a casual compliment. The University of Chicago, moreover, insisted that its students study seriously the philosophic sources of Western culture, which, if not outspokenly Christian, were surely non-Jewish. I soon found myself reading the classics of Christian theology and devotion—from St. Augustine and St. Anselm through the sermons of Meister Eckhart.

It was not long before my unreligious background, a growing and intense concern with religious problems, and the ready access to compelling Christian literature all combined to produce a crisis —or at least my parents and I flattered ourselves that this normal intellectual experience was a religious crisis. The possibility of being a Christian was, however, altogether real. I was rushed, not to a psychoanalyst, but to a Rabbi—the late Milton Steinberg, one of the most gifted and profound Jewish thinkers of recent years. Leading me gently, he retraced the path backwards through Christianity to Judaism, revealing the groundwork of Jewish thought and experience which supported what I have come to regard as the scaffolding of Christian "unreason."

It was extremely important to me to return to Judaism through the medium of Christianity—to choose after having first received the impress of Western education and Christian thought. Since it would have been possible to become a Christian—to accept Christian history as my history, to accept the Christian version of Judaism as the grounds of my own repudiation of Judaism, to believe that a Messiah had redeemed *me*—I could only conclude that Judaism was not an unavoidable fate, but a destiny to be chosen freely.

My own conversion and, I suspect, the conversion of many other Jews to Judaism, was effected, therefore, through study, reflection, and thought. What first seized my attention was not the day-to-day religious life of the Jewish community around me, but rather principles, concepts, and values. I had first to examine the pressing theological claims of a seemingly triumphant Christianity, before I could accept the ancient claims of a dispersed, tormented, and suffering Jewry.

This may sound reasonable enough to a gentile, but I must point out that it is an extremely unconventional attitude for a Jew. Historically, Judaism has often looked with disfavor upon theology. And today, despite the fact that traditional emotional ties can no longer be relied upon to bind the third generation to Jewish life, American Jewish leadership has not seen fit to encourage the examination of the theological bases of Jewish faith. In fact, the leading rabbinical seminaries teach little Jewish theology as such, give scant attention to Jewish philosophic literature, and have allowed the apologetic comparison of religious beliefs to become a moribund discipline. Even practical problems involving some theological insight—the nature of marriage, the Jewish attitude toward converts, the life of prayer—are dispatched with stratospheric platitudes, or not discussed at all.

Why this distrust of theology? I suspect that some Jewish leaders fear—perhaps not unjustifiably—that theological scrutiny of what they mean by God, Israel, and Law might reveal that they have no theology at all. Others no doubt fear—again not unjustifiably—that their unbending interpretations of Jewish Law and life might have to be revised and re-thought. Theology often produces a recognition of insufficiency, an awareness that valid doctrine is being held for the wrong reasons and that erroneous doctrine is being used to rationalize right action. But the major Jewish argument against Jewish theology is that it is a Christian pastime—that it may, by insinuation and subtle influence, Christianize Judaism. In this view, Christianity is a religion of faith, dogma, and theology and Judaism is a religion which emphasizes *observance* of God's Law, not speculation about it.

For me this argument is a vast oversimplification. Christianity is not without its own structure of discipline, requirements, and laws —the Roman sacraments and the Lutheran and Anglican liturgy, for example—and this structure does not move with the Holy Spirit as easily as St. Paul might have wished. Judaism, on the other hand, is not tied to the pure act. It has matured through the centuries a massive speculation and mystic tradition which attempts to explain the principles upon which right action are founded. Judaism need not, therefore, regret the renewal of theology. It already has one. It is merely a question of making what is now a minor chord in Jewish tradition sound a more commanding note.

As a "convert" who thinks that theology must come first, what do I believe?

The convert, I must point out, is unavoidably both a thinker and a believer—he thinks patiently and believes suddenly. Yet belief, by itself, cannot evict the demons of doubt and despair. As a believer I can communicate my beliefs, but as a thinker I cannot guarantee that they are certain or will never change. As all things that record the encounter of God and man, beliefs are subject to the conditions of time and history, and the pitiable limitation of our capacity to understand such enormous mysteries. As I shall try to show, however, the four beliefs which I have already set down lie at the center of my faith as a Jew. They depend upon one another; they form a whole; they differ profoundly from the substance of Christian belief.

First, I chose to believe in the God of Abraham, Isaac, and Jacob. This is to affirm the reality of a God who acts in history and addresses man. Although this God may well be the same as the abstract gods formulated by philosophers, he is still more than these—he is the God who commanded Abraham to quit the land of the Chaldeans and who wrestled with Jacob throughout the night.

The philosopher and the believer must differ in their method. The philosopher begins by examining that portion of reality to which reason allows him access. The believer, however, must at some point move beyond the limits which reason has defined. He may rightly contend that reason points beyond itself, that the rational is real, but that much in human life—evil, suffering, guilt, and love—is terrifyingly real without ever being rationally comprehensible.

Reason may thus push a man to belief, and it is inaccurate to speak of the believer as though he had deserted or betrayed reason. Informed belief demands philosophic criticism and refinement. The believer is bound to uphold his faith in things he cannot see or verify; but he is foolish if he does not try to define what that belief is and clarify the unique ways in which it makes reality meaningful for him.

For me then to believe in the Biblical God, the God of the Patriarchs, the smoking mountain, the burning bush, was not to surrender reason, but to go beyond it. More than accepting the literal word of the Bible, it meant believing in the Lord of History —the God who creates and unfolds history, and observes its tragic rifts and displacements—from the Tower of Babel to the Cold War; who, in his disgust, once destroyed the world with flood and

later repented his anger; who, forgoing anger, gave the world counsels of revelation, commencing with the gift of Torah to Moses and
continuing through the inspired writings of the ancient rabbis; and
who finally—through his involvement with the work of creation—
prepares it for redemption.

It may seem difficult—indeed for many years it was—to consider
the Bible, which is the source of this belief, as more than the un-
reliable account of an obscure Semitic tribe. But gradually I came
to discover in it an authentic statement of the grandeur and misery
of man's daily existence—a statement which I could accept only
if I believed in a God who could be addressed as "Lord, Lord."

My second belief is an acknowledgment that *the Law of Moses
is the Word of God*. The Bible tells us that the Word of God
broke out over the six hundred thousand Hebrews who assembled
at the foot of Sinai. That Word was heard by Moses—he who had
been appointed to approach and receive. The Word became human—in its humanity, it undoubtedly suffers from the limitation
of our understanding—but it lost none of its divinity.

The Law is always a paradox: it is both the free Word of God
and the frozen formality of human laws. But the Law of Moses
was vastly different from what we usually understand law to be. It
is true that in the days before the Temple was destroyed by Titus
in 70 A.D. divine law was the enforceable law of the judge and the
court; but later the great rabbis who interpreted it conceived of the
revelation of God to Israel, not as law in its common usage, but as
Torah—teaching.

Torah is a fundamental concept for the Jew. Narrowly conceived, it refers to the Pentateuch—the first five books of the Bible
which are the pristine source of all Jewish tradition. In them are
the laws of the Sabbath and the festivals; the foundations of family
and communal morality; and the essentials of Jewish faith—the
unity of God, the election of Israel, and the definition of its special
mission. But, broadly conceived, Torah refers to *any* teaching
which brings man closer to the true God, who is the God of Israel
and the Lord of History.

Torah has two aspects—the actual way of law and observance
(the *halakhah* as it is called in Hebrew) and the theology of the

rabbis which interprets that way (called the *aggadah*). By means of both, according to Jewish tradition, God proposes to lead *all* of his creation to fulfillment, to perfect its imperfections, to mend the brokenness of his creatures. The Jewish people—the guardian of the *halakhah* and the *aggadah*—has been elected to be pedagogue to all the nations of the world, to become on its behalf "a kingdom of priests and a holy people."

Jews can achieve holiness—the primary objective, I believe, of their religion—neither by prayer nor meditation alone. Judaism values prayer only in conjunction with the act; it praises study only in relation to life.

God does not propose or suggest ways to achieve holiness; he commands them. According to Torah, he lays upon each Jew "the yoke of the commandments." To observe the Sabbath is as much a commandment as is the obligation to daily prayer; the grace which accompanies eating as essential as the study of sacred literature. Although tradition distinguishes between practical and intellectual commandments, it considers both to be equally the expressed will of God. The arbitrary and the reasonable—the dietary laws and the prohibition of homosexuality for example—both proceed from God.

Judaism begins with an explicit fact: the revelation of Torah. Many of its commandments may seem trivial. But it should not be expected that God will leave the trivial to man and concern himself only with the broad, general, and universal. The corruption of man takes place not only in the province of principle, but in the small and petty routine of life. The Torah is therefore exalted and picayune, universal and particular, occupied equally with principle and the details of practice. It tolerates no separation between the holy and the profane—all that is secular must become sacred, all that is profane must be kept open to the transforming power of God.

The exact degree to which Jews should fulfill all the commandments of the Law is one of the most difficult and perplexing dilemmas for modern Jews. Orthodox Jews are in principle obligated to observe all of Jewish Law, Reform Jews have cut observance to a minimum (though there is a movement to increase it), Conservative Jews stand somewhere in between. I will not attempt it in this space, but I believe it is possible to show that the fundamental question is not whether the Jew performs the required acts of observance, but whether he is truly aware of the sacred intention of these acts. One can, for example, recite the blessings over the food one eats and feel nothing of the sanctity of food; on the other hand one can silently acknowledge the holiness of eating, and fulfill the command of God. Both are needed—the blessing and the inner acknowledgment, but the former is surely incomplete without the latter.

The third of my beliefs is, as I have indicated, simply an element of God's revelation in Torah—that *the Jewish people have been chosen as a special instrument of God.*

The Jews did not request the attentions of God. There is significant truth—truth moreover which the rabbis of the Talmud endorse—in the popular couplet: "How odd of God, to choose the Jews." Odd, and unsolicited. The ancient rabbis disclaim particular merit. If anyone possessed merit, they repeat, it was not the generation that fled Egypt and braved the wilderness for forty years, but the generations of the Biblical patriarchs—Abraham, Isaac, and Jacob. They had no organizer such as Moses, nor strength of numbers, nor the miracles of the well, manna, and quail. They made a covenant with God on sheer trust. The generation of Sinai was *compelled* to become the people of God or perish. A God of History grows impatient with delay. The God of Israel was profoundly impatient on Sinai.

This tradition of election should not be confused with racial pride or an attitude of arrogant exclusion toward others. The Jew believes neither that the truth flows in his blood nor that the gentile cannot come to possess it. Judaism is exclusive only in the sense that we affirm we possess important truth which is available to all—everyone can join but only on our terms.

The election of Israel is not a conclusion drawn from history— the survival and endurance of the Jews through twenty centuries of destructive persecution could be no more than blind accident. At best it could be construed as a compliment to the resiliency and stubbornness of the Jewish people. Judaism has insisted, however—not as a declaration after the fact, but as a principle of its very existence—that it is both a holy nation chosen by God to be his own and a suffering nation destined to endure martyrdom for his sake. God announces not only that "Ye shall be holy unto me; for I the Lord am Holy, and have separated you from the people, that ye should be mine" (Leviticus 20:26) but that "You only have I known of all the families of the earth: therefore I will visit upon you all your iniquities" (Amos 3:2).

Israel is thus called not only to be the example to the nations, but, being the example, is tried all the more sorely for its transgressions. To be sure, this is not a doctrine for the uncourageous. No one even slightly familiar with the agonies of Jewish history could claim that the election of Israel has brought with it particular reward and security. It is, however, precisely the fact of Jewish suffering which makes its election and mission all the more pertinent to the modern world. To have believed and survived in spite of history is perhaps the only evidence which Judaism can offer to the accuracy of its conviction that it is called to be a holy community.

In the face of Christendom and the obvious success which its claims have enjoyed, it may seem foolish or presumptuous for Judaism—a small and insignificant community of believers—to assert my fourth belief: that *Jesus is not the Messiah of which the Bible speaks*, that Christianity has conceived but one more imperfect image of the end, and that *a Messiah is yet to come who will redeem history*.

But there are enduring reasons why Jews cannot accept Jesus as the Messiah. Both Christian and Jew begin with the conviction of the imperfection of man. The Christian argues, however, that creation has been so corrupted by man as to be saved only through the mediation of Jesus. The Jew considers creation imperfect but, rather than corrupt, he finds it rich with unfulfilled possibility. The role of man is to bring creation to that point at which the Messiah can come to glorify man by bringing him the praise of God—not to save him from self-destruction, as Christianity would have it.

According to Jewish tradition, Moses died from the kiss of God. It would be fitting to conceive the advent of the Messiah and the Kingdom of God as the bestowal of a kiss.

This does not mean that God congratulates man for his good works but rather that he shares both in the agony of history and in its sanctification. Judaism does not imagine that every day we are getting better and better, and that finally we will reach a point where the Messiah will come. As likely as not, it seems to me, history is coming closer each day to suicide. The mission of Judaism is not to stave off disaster but to enlarge man's awareness of the Divine Presence.

Jews believe, if they are to remain Jews, that the Messiah has not come. They can accept Jesus of Nazareth as little more than a courageous witness to truths to which his own contemporaries in Pharisaic Judaism by and large subscribed. Jesus was, as Martin Buber has suggested, one in the line of "suffering servants" whom God sends forth to instruct the nations. It is to the dogmatizing work of St. Paul that one must ascribe the transformation of "prophet" into "Christ"—and it is therefore St. Paul who severs Jesus from the life of Israel. The rejection of Jesus must now stand to the end of time.

The role of Israel and Judaism, until the advent of the true Messiah, is to outlast the world and its solutions—to examine its complacencies, to deflate its securities, to put its principles to the test of prophetic judgment. This is an aristocratic and painful mission, for though Judaism may address the world and lay claim to it, it does not seek to convert it.

Judaism does not say "The world is not changed—therefore we do not believe in the Messiah." This is only partially true, for the coming of the Messiah will mean more than a reformed world in which the wolf and lamb shall share bread together and war shall cease. This social image of salvation is true as far as it goes, but it does not go far enough. The Messiah is not a handyman or a plumber—his task does not consist in "mending" a world that is temporarily faulty but is essentially perfect. The world is to be transformed—not reformed—by the Messiah.

This transformation will come to pass, Judaism believes, only when the world wishes it so deeply that it cannot abide itself more a single moment. At that moment the Messiah may come. This moment of expectancy has not yet arrived. The rabbis have taught us that I, and all of the House of Israel, prevent him from coming. Of this there is no question, but we cannot avoid concluding that he has not come.

For the Jew who comfortably repeats the rituals of his religion without confronting the principles of faith which they express, and for the Jew who was not aware that Judaism had any principles of faith at all, this personal statement may seem shocking. But I do not think my position or my background are by any means unique. If, as I have argued, the present generation of American Jews is indeed the first generation of Jews in centuries who are free to choose to believe as Jews, then, in my terms at least, my argument is important. Now as never before it will be possible for the Jewish people and the State of Israel to survive, but for Jewish *religion* to perish. For me, and for other believing Jews, it is crucial for mankind that Judaism survive. The mission of Judaism is not completed nor the task of the Jewish people fulfilled. If the Jewish people is an instrument sharpened by God for his own purposes, it must go on serving that purpose, sustaining its burden, and keeping that trust which alone can bring all men to redemption.

THE ISSUE IS SILENCE

JOACHIM PRINZ

The American Jewish Congress, founded (in 1922) to "safeguard the civil, political, economic and religious rights of the Jewish people" and to fight all discrimination, joined with men and women of all races and creeds in the sponsorship of the historic March on Washington on behalf of the American Negro. Among the speakers at Lincoln Memorial, August 28, 1963, was Joachim Prinz, President of the American Jewish Congress. Born (1902) and educated in Germany, Dr. Joachim Prinz served as rabbi in Berlin from 1925 to 1937; during the Nazi period he displayed unusual courage and fearlessly faced the

authorities in protecting his community. He came to the United
States in 1937; since 1939 he has been rabbi in Newark, N. J. In
addition to his rabbinical and organizational activities, he has
been writing books in the field of Jewish history and literature.
Following is the text of his address at the March on Washington.

I speak to you as an American Jew.

As Americans we share the profound concern of millions of people
about the shame and disgrace of inequality and injustice which
make a mockery of the great American idea.

As Jews we bring to this great demonstration, in which thousands
of us proudly participate, a twofold experience—one of the spirit
and one of our history.

In the realm of the spirit, our fathers taught us thousands of years
ago that when God created man, he created him as everybody's
neighbor. Neighbor is not a geographic term. It is a moral concept. It means our collective responsibility for the preservation
of man's dignity and integrity.

From our Jewish historic experience of three and a half thousand
years we say:

Our ancient history began with slavery and the yearning for freedom. During the Middle Ages my people lived for a thousand
years in the ghettos of Europe. Our modern history begins with
a proclamation of emancipation.

It is for these reasons that it is not merely sympathy and compassion for the black people of America that motivates us. It is
above all and beyond all such sympathies and emotions a sense
of complete identification and solidarity born of our own painful
historic experience.

When I was the rabbi of the Jewish community in Berlin under
the Hitler regime, I learned many things. The most important
thing that I learned under those tragic circumstances was that
bigotry and hatred are not the most urgent problem. The most
urgent, the most disgraceful, the most shameful and the most
tragic problem is silence.

A great people which had created a great civilization had become a nation of silent onlookers. They remained silent in the

face of hate, in the face of brutality and in the face of mass murder.

America must not become a nation of onlookers. America must not remain silent. Not merely black America, but all of America. It must speak up and act, from the President down to the humblest of us, and not for the sake of the Negro, not for the sake of the black community but for the sake of the image, the idea and the aspiration of America itself.

Our children, yours and mine in every school across the land, each morning pledge allegiance to the flag of the United States and to the republic for which it stands. They, the children, speak fervently and innocently of this land as the land of "liberty and justice for all."

The time, I believe, has come to work together—for it is not enough to hope together, and it is not enough to pray together —to work together that this children's oath, pronounced every morning from Maine to California, from North to South, may become a glorious, unshakeable reality in a morally renewed and united America.

VII. *Allowing the Heart to Speak*

THE REAWAKENING OF MY RELIGIOUS FEELINGS

HEINRICH HEINE

Heine was born in 1797 in Düsseldorf, Germany, and died in 1856, in Paris. In 1825 he converted to the Lutheran church, an event to which he did not attach deep significance. "A Jew by descent, a German by language, he was a Hellene in his art: a scion of the dream-built Hellas of the German classicists. The Greek god's immortal laughter reverberates through his *Collected Works*—where every picture, even the last 'lonely tear,' is corporal, palpable to the point of caricature, and subjective to the point of self-parody. The soaring emotion of a German, the rigid ethics of a Jew, the sculptured ideal of a 'Hellene' (that artistic and artificial product of Humanism, Enlightenment, and French Revolution) mingle in his writing; they are the components of the wittiest poet of modern world literature since Voltaire and Swift" (Hermann Kesten). The excerpt which follows is taken from Heine's *Confessions*.

The reawakening of my religious feelings I owe to that sacred book; for me it became as much a source of healing as an object of the most devout admiration. It is strange! during my whole life I have been strolling through the various festive halls of philosophy, I have participated in all the orgies of the intellect, I have coquetted with every possible system, without being satisfied, like Messalina[1] after a riotous night; and now, after all this, I suddenly find myself on the same platform as Uncle Tom. That platform is the Bible, and I kneel by the side of my dusky brother-in-faith with the same devotion. [. . .]

Previously I had not much admired the character of Moses, probably because the Hellenic spirit was predominant in me, and I could not pardon the lawgiver of the Jews for his hatred of the plastic arts. I failed to perceive that Moses, notwithstanding his enmity to art, was nevertheless himself a great artist, and possessed the true artistic spirit. Only, this artistic spirit with him, as with his Egyptian countrymen, was applied to the colossal and the imperishable. But, unlike the Egyptians, he did not construct his works of art from bricks and granite; he built human pyramids and carved human obelisks. He took a poor shepherd tribe and from it created a nation which should defy centuries; a great, an immortal, a consecrated race, a God-serving people, who should serve as a model and prototype for all other nations: he created Israel. With greater right than the Roman poet, may that artist, the son of Amram and the midwife Jochebed, boast that he had builded him a monument more enduring than bronze.

I have never spoken with proper reverence either of the artist or his work, the Jews; and for the same reason—namely, my Hellenic temperament, which was opposed to Jewish asceticism. My prejudice in favor of Hellas has declined since then. I see now that the Greeks were only beautiful youths, but that the Jews were always men—strong, unyielding men—not only in the past, but to this very day, in spite of eighteen centuries of persecution and suffering. Since that time I have learned to appreciate them better, and, were not all pride of ancestry a silly inconsistency in a champion of the Revolution and its democratic principles, the writer of these pages would be proud that his ancestors belonged to the noble house of Israel, that he is a descendant of those martyrs who gave the world a God and a morality, and who have fought and suffered on all the battle-fields of thought.

The history of the Middle Ages, and even that of modern times, has seldom enrolled on its records the names of such knights of the Holy Spirit, for they generally fought with closed visors. The deeds of the Jews are just as little known to the world as is their real character. Some think they know the Jews because they can recognize their beards, which is all they have ever revealed of themselves. Now, as during the Middle Ages, they remain a wandering mystery, a mystery that may perhaps be solved on the day which the prophet foretells, when there shall be but one shepherd and one flock, and the righteous who have suffered for the good of humanity shall then receive a glorious reward.

You see that I, who in the past was wont to quote Homer, now quote the Bible, like Uncle Tom. In truth, I owe it much. It again awakened in me the religious feeling; and this new birth of religious emotion suffices for the poet, for he can dispense far more easily than other mortals with positive religious dogmas. He possesses grace, and to his spirit the symbolism of heaven and earth is open; he requires no churchly key. The silliest and most contradictory reports are in circulation about me concerning this. Very pious but not very wise men of Protestant Germany have urgently inquired if, now that I am ill and in a religious frame of mind, I cling with more devotion than heretofore to the Lutheran evangelical faith, which, until now, I have only professed after a lukewarm, official fashion.

No, dear friends, in that respect no change has taken place in me, and if I continue to adhere to the evangelical faith at all, it is because now, as in the past, that faith does not at all inconvenience me. I will frankly avow that when I resided in Berlin, I, like several of my friends, would have preferred to separate myself from the bonds of all denominations, had not the rulers there refused a residence in Prussia, and especially in Berlin, to any who did not profess one of the positive religions recognized by the State. As Henry IV once laughingly said: "Paris is well worth a mass," so I could say, with equal justice, "Berlin is well worth a sermon." Both before and after, I could easily tolerate the very enlightened Christianity which at that time was preached in some of the churches of Berlin. It was a Christianity filtered from all superstition, even from the doctrine of the divinity of Christ, like mock-turtle soup without turtle. At that time, I myself was still a god, and no one of the positive religions had more value for me than another. I could wear any of their uniforms out of courtesy, after the manner of the Russian Emperor, who, when he vouchsafes the King of Prussia the honor to attend a review at Potsdam, appears uniformed as a Prussian officer of the guard.

Now that my physical sufferings, and the reawakening of my religious nature, have effected many changes in me, does the uniform of Lutheranism in some measure express my true sentiments? How far has the formal profession become a reality? I do not propose to give direct answers to these questions, but I shall avail myself of the opportunity to explain the services which, according to my present views, Protestantism has rendered to civilization. From this may be inferred how much more I am now in sympathy with this creed.

At an earlier period, when philosophy possessed for me a paramount interest, I prized Protestantism only for its services in winning freedom of thought, which, after all, is the foundation on which, in later times, Leibnitz, Kant and Hegel could build. Luther, the strong man with the axe, in the very nature of things, had to precede these warriors, to open a path for them. For this service I have honored the Reformation as being the beginning of German philosophy, which justified my polemical defense of Protestantism. Now, in my later and more mature days, when the religious feeling again surges up in me, and the shipwrecked metaphysician clings fast to the Bible—now I chiefly honor Protestantism for its services in the discovery and propagation of the Bible. I say 'discovery,' for the Jews, who had preserved the Bible from the great conflagration of the sacred temple, and all through the Middle Ages carried it about with them like a portable fatherland, kept their treasure carefully concealed in their ghettos. Here came by stealth German scholars, the predecessors and originators of the Reformation, made their way there stealthily, to study the Hebrew language and thus acquired the key to the casket wherein the precious treasure was enclosed. [. . .]

Yes, the world is indebted to the Jews for its God and His word. They rescued the Bible from the bankruptcy of the Roman Empire and preserved the precious volume intact during all the wild tumults of the migration of races, until Protestantism came to seek it, translated it into the language of the land and spread it broadcast over the whole world. This extensive circulation of the Bible has produced the most beneficent fruits, and continues to do so to this very day. The propaganda of the Bible Society has fulfilled a providential mission which will bring forth quite different results from those anticipated by the pious gentlemen of the British Christian Missionary Society. The latter expect to elevate a petty, narrow dogma to supremacy, and to monopolize heaven as they do the sea, making it a British Church domain—and lo, without knowing it, they are demanding the overthrow of all Protestant sects; for, as they all draw their life from the Bible, when the knowledge of the Bible becomes universal, all sectarian distinctions will be obliterated. [. . .]

To the observant thinker it is a wonderful spectacle to view the countries where, since the Reformation, the Bible has been exerting its elevating influence on the inhabitants, and has impressed on them the customs, modes of thought and temperaments which formerly prevailed in Palestine, as portrayed both in the Old and in the New Testament. In the Scandinavian and Anglo-Saxon sections of Europe and America, especially among the Germanic races, and also to a certain extent in Celtic countries, the customs of Palestine have been reproduced in so marked a degree that we seem to be in the midst of the ancient Judean life. [. . .]

The readiness with which these races have adopted the Judaic life, customs, and modes of thought is, perhaps, not entirely attributable to their susceptibility of culture. The cause of this phenomenon is, perhaps, to be sought in the character of the Jewish people, which always had a marked racial affinity with the character of the Germanic, and also to a certain extent with that of the Celtic races. Judea has always seemed to me like a fragment of the Occident misplaced in the Orient. In fact, with its spiritual faith, its severe, chaste, even ascetic customs—in short, with its abstract inner life—this land and its people always offered the most marked contrasts to the population of neighboring countries, who, with their luxuriantly varied and fervent nature of worship, passed their existence in a bacchantic dance of the senses.

At a time when, in the temples of Babylon, Nineveh, Sidon and Tyre, bloody and unchaste rites were celebrated, the description of which, even now, makes our hair stand on end, Israel sat under its fig-trees, piously chanting the praises of the invisible God, and exercised virtue and righteousness. When we think of these surroundings we cannot sufficiently admire the early greatness of Israel. Of Israel's love of liberty, at a time when not only in its immediate vicinity, but also among all the nations of antiquity, even among the philosophical Greeks, the practice of slavery was justified and in full sway—of this I will not speak, for fear of compromising the Bible in the eyes of the powers that be. [. . .]

The Mosaic Law, through the institution of the jubilee year,[2] protests still more decidedly. Moses did not seek to abolish the right of property; on the contrary, it was his wish that every one should possess property, so that no one might be tempted by poverty to become a bondsman and thus acquire slavish propensities. Liberty was always the great emancipator's leading thought, and it breathes and glows in all his statutes concerning pauperism. Slavery itself he bitterly, almost fiercely, hated; but even this barbarous institution he could not entirely destroy. It was rooted so deeply in the customs of that ancient time that he was compelled to confine his efforts to ameliorating by law the condition of the slaves, rendering self-purchase by the bondsman less difficult, and shortening the period of bondage.

But if a slave thus eventually freed by process of law declined to depart from the house of bondage, then, according to the command of Moses, the incorrigibly servile, worthless scamp was to be nailed by the ear to the gate of his master's house, and after being thus publicly exposed in this disgraceful manner, he was condemned to lifelong slavery.[3] Oh, Moses! our teacher, Rabbi Moses! exalted foe of all slavishness! give me hammer and nails that I may nail to the gate of Brandenburg our complacent, long-eared slaves in their liveries of black, red and gold.

JOB'S DUNGHEAP

BERNARD LAZARE

Deep feeling for the great moments in Judaism and a radical social orientation were united in the writer and critic Bernard Lazare (1865-1903). Born in Nimes, South France, Lazare spent his active life in Paris. Throughout his life he fought for liberty and social justice, for the rights of the underprivileged, against anti-Semitism and the accusers of Captain Dreyfus, and against bureaucracy and opportunism and for integrity in all issues of public life. Lazare belonged to the circle of Stephan Mallarmé

and contributed to *Entretiens politiques et littéraires*, organ of
the Symbolists.

Among Lazare's works of Jewish interest are, *L'Antisémitism,
son histoire et ses causes* (1894), *L'affair Dreyfus* (1897), and
Le Nationalism juif (1897). Charles Péguy devoted a moving
essay to him in his *Notre Jeunesse* (1910). And Albert Einstein
wrote concerning him: "Here we have the old tragedy of an
honest, warmhearted man who cannot compromise and thus is
doomed to solitude. I have an understanding for it."

Look at Job upon his dungheap, scraping his boils, delighting in
his sores. Look, Christians, and you princes of the Jews, at the
people and what you have done to it.

The demoralization of a people of the poor and the persecuted,
receiving a dole from its rich and having rebelled only against
persecution from without and not against oppression within. Revolutionaries in the society of others and not in its own. Having a
dumb admiration for its own wealthy men, whose honors are reflected upon the poor. Even today in Jewish papers notice is given
of those privileged ones who achieve honors.

The Jews must free themselves in their quality as a people and
within their own nation.

The Jew is still at that stage of inferiority which allows him to
rejoice in the opulence of his leaders.

The Jew felt external oppression most heavily, and this oppression had leveled social conditions among his people. Once external
oppression ceased, he preserved the same respect for the wealthy
class, even though fraternity had disappeared.

The Jews of today.

Servility toward the rich, and at the same time disrespect. Yet
among the Jews there does not exist an ancient financial aristocracy;
the rich Jews in modern society are not the offspring of wealthy
dynasties. The oldest go back a hundred years. Old bourgeois and
rich families among the Jews—such do not exist. At the beginning
of this century there remained in the spirit of the people scorn for
the gold it had handled, and at the same time a lavishness and a

generosity created by that contempt. Today's rich Jew clings to gold and venerates it like the Christian who has always worshiped it (the conquest of America, the gold-seekers). The Jew lost it the moment he got it, and despised it.

In no people so much as in the Jewish people is there to be found so much servility toward the rich; and yet no people has so castigated them by means of the voices of its prophets or the poets of the Psalms. Centuries of oppression have changed that; spirit and soul have become debased. The stiffnecked tribe has become a tribe of slaves that suffers in silence the misdeeds of the powerful by whom it has through so many long years allowed itself to be led. Nevertheless, an awakening seems to be taking place among the lower middle class, the proletariat, the men without work, the beggars. They understand the disadvantages that can exist in being solidary with people who themselves repel that solidarity. Up until now they had the shadow of a reason for not fighting them: they believed them to be Jews, but now that they have become anti-Semites, what are the Jews waiting for to kick them aside, and even to act directly against them?

The rottenness of the Jewish upper classes.

They are not in their own sphere; they exceed all bounds, and their rottenness becomes more stinking. They do not know how far you can go; they do not preserve the balance of their Christian opposite numbers.

The notion which the Christians have of the Jew is a mystical and not a human notion.

The Jews look upon themselves always in relation to the Christians, never as themselves.

Throughout this whole century the Jews have bestirred themselves to prove to the heads of states the advantage which those politicians and their people would gain in emancipating the Jews. As for the advantage to the Jews of being emancipated—that they have not proved.

From his long enslavement the Jew has retained an extreme distrustfulness. And yet his ever precarious state leads him to show enthusiasm for all those who tell him that they will lead him into the Promised Land.

Let us ceaselessly lay claim on behalf of our unhappy brothers to the rights of man, but let us at the same time show them that assimilation is not the end of their wretchedness, but, on the contrary, the source of new miseries.

I am a Jew and I know nothing about the Jews. Henceforth I am a pariah, and I know not out of what elements to rebuild myself a dignity and a personality. I must learn who I am and why I am hated, and that which I can be.

I shall have the courage to point out the ulcers of my people and to cure them.

I have overcome the pride of being a Jew. I know why I am one, and that binds me to the past of my own people, links me to their present, obliges me to serve them, allows me to cry out for all their rights as men.

The danger which threatens a people in slavery for centuries: the danger of being exclusive.

What could the Jew have done to hold out had he not taken refuge in his pride of race.

Every Jew has his system, his idea of the world, his economic and social theory, his means of solving the problem of Jewish wretchedness, of anti-Semitism. He is a great builder of doctrines, an outrageous idealist (Marx, Lassalle).

The Jewish worker cannot do his material task without thinking, without shaping himself an idea of the world and of society; he reasons falsely, often observes badly; but he systematizes; he is a logician and goes to the very end once he has started.

The Jewish water-carrier has his sociology and his metaphysics.

This people drives you insane or makes you mad with rage. You lose your balance when you study it, for circumstances have brought it about that you can have studied it only theoretically, religiously, mystically.

"Thou hast given us like sheep to be eaten; and hast scattered us among the nations," says the Psalmist (44:12).

"Thou hast sold thy people for nought, and hast not increased thy wealth by their price. Thou hast made us a reproach to our neighbors, a scorn and a derision to them that are round about us. Every day my shame is before my eyes and blushes cover my brows when I hear the voice of the contemner and the railers, when I see the enemy, he who wants to revenge himself upon me. It is for thee that we are daily killed, treated like a herd led to the shambles; we are bedded in dust and our body is stuck fast to the ground" (Psalm 44:13-17, 23, 26).

When the winters are harsh, when torrential rains fall, when the aurora borealis ensanguines the sky, when comets lighten it, when earthquakes stagger the cities, when in some fashion the world is shaken, the frightened old women open wide their eyes and whisper, "The time is come, Messiah will come." Blessed are they for having faith and for finding in their terror the supreme consolation; and how greatly would I wish, when the night of my soul becomes darker and darker, when the dreadful anguish of the beyond twists it and tortures it, to be illumined with a sudden enlightenment; and, trembling at once with joy and with terror, also whisper, "Messiah will come."

When one is "the servant of God," the slave of the Lord, one is not the slave of men, and when some day one no longer believes in God, what does there remain within the liberated man?

A CONFESSION OF MY FAITH

AIMÉ PALLIÈRE

Judaism, though open to all men, does not encourage proselytism. Aimé Pallière (1875-1950), a French Catholic, fascinated by Jewish piety, collective priesthood, and faith in the future, turned to Elijah Benamozegh (1823-1900), rabbi in Livorno, for advice on possible conversion to Judaism. The rabbi made him aware of "Noahism," a Jewish concept of a universal religion of humanity, based on monotheism, a just social order, and morality; he suggested to Pallière membership in this covenant rather than in "Mosaism" with its detailed laws and statutes. "The future of the human race lies in this formula. If you come to convince yourself of it, you will be much more precious to Israel than if you submit to the law of Israel. You will be the instrument of the Providence of God to humanity." Without formally leaving the Church, Pallière became an exponent and teacher of Jewish faith, one of the preachers in a liberal Paris synagogue, and founder of a French Jewish periodical, *Foi et réveil*. Under the Nazi occupation of France, he shared the sorrows of the Jewish group. He told the story of his religious development in *Le sanctuaire inconnu* (*The Unknown Sanctuary*, 1926), of which the passage that follows is the conclusion.

In the heart of the Jewish people the working of the spirit of God, difficult, laborious, but never ending, culminated in the historic phenomenon of prophetism, unique in the religious annals of humanity, the great miracle of the history of Israel, and like unto a glorious flower into which its national genius blossomed. In the prophets the development of religious thought attained its culmination. Adonai, the God of Israel, revealed himself to them as the one God, father of all men. Humanity being then conceived of as a great family, the Jewish faith finally cast aside all national boundaries, or rather, in respecting them, it surmounted them and surpassed them; it no longer knew limitation, either of time or of space; it summarized in the Messianic hope its highest, its most universal aspirations.

But it is not only because of its extent that the Jewish religion takes its place in the first rank of the religious beliefs of humankind, it is because of its essence and its depth. Adonai revealing himself as the God of holiness, it is in the secret conscience that religion henceforth finds its purest and completest expression. All the elements of morality scattered in other cults, find themselves united here as in a sheaf. "Ye shall be holy, for I the Lord your God am Holy" (Leviticus 19:2): this precept, which includes all the others, is at one and the same time for Judaism a religion and a rule of life.

Without denying the value and the influence of other religions, I believe that it is easy to demonstrate that the influence of Israel occupies a place apart in the history of humanity, that between it and other religions there is not only a difference in degree, but a difference in kind. In reasoning thus I do not separate Judaism from its great branches, Christianity and Islam, which have spread over the earth, everywhere carrying the knowledge of the one God, the God of Moses, and of the prophets. These, the theologians of the Synagogue point out to us, are two powerful means that divine Providence has used to carry to the pagan nations the benefits of the Hebraic revelation in order to prepare them for the coming of the Messianic times.

But from the Christian side it will be asked of me: Would the development of divine revelation which is manifested in all phases of Jewish history up to the close of the Biblical canon, not have continued, attaining perfection still unknown to Hebrew writings, in those two powerful branches whose vitality is only explained by the presence in them of the life-giving sap that they received from the old trunk of Israel?

It seems to me that two facts claim our attention; in the first place that all of the divine truths which sustain the soul of Christendom and of Islam are Jewish truths, so much so that not one could be cited that Judaism does not possess and that is not borrowed from it. I concede that some of these truths have been better understood and put to better use by Christianity, than by the Jewish people in its entirety, but that is another question. In the second place, there is no doubt that the two great religions, daughters of Hebraism, have misinterpreted many important Jewish truths, and have appropriated others which they have overlaid by strange additions, constituting alteration but not enrichment.

For example, who can but see that the Day of Atonement and Good Friday proclaim the same truth, a truth that may seem but folly to the human reason in implying that the past can be effaced, that the infinite mercy annihilates sin in the soul that repents, and places within it the germ of a new life that may express itself in acts of justice and of holiness? But if the effect of this doctrine of regeneration and of salvation through the profession of a particular creed and through the acceptance of certain historic or so-called historic facts, be subordinated to the obligatory carrying out of certain rites, is it not evident that the revelation which Hebraism has given to us concerning the relations between the human soul and God its Heavenly Father is thereby altered and narrowed?

Let us not forget that while facing the fact of Judeo-Christianity, there is another fact which we must face: it is the existence of millions of pagans, human creatures having the same right to truth, to light, to divine forgiveness that we have, though they have never heard of the Bible nor of the Gospels. In this difficult situation what is the attitude of those who believe in and who lay claim to the Hebraic revelation, under its Jewish or under its Christian form? True religion must give us an explanation of the status of humanity which will not do violence to our reason, our conscience, or our hearts, and will enable us to believe in the salvation of all men. But the soul secure on the secular rock of Judaism, finds itself at the very centre of a religious synthesis which makes it possible to judge and to understand all the fragments of truth scattered throughout the world. The different religions appear as so many special manifestations, corresponding to the needs of the different races, but grouped around the central Truth, and more or less closely related to one another, according to their distance from, or nearness to it.

The entire human race is thus united in a very real spiritual one-ness even though there seem to be, because of the very nature of things, numerous and necessary differences. This does not deter the believer who lays claim to the prophetic tradition, from hasten-ing, through his prayers, the coming of the day when "God shall be One and His Name One" (Zechariah 14:9). What is this future in regard to the perfect and immutable being, who knows neither change nor time, and whose existence is everlastingly present? It signifies that the one God is really worshipped under many forms, in very different cults, but in the Messianic era, the spiritual world will see unity of worship realized.

Thus the believing Israelite attains through prophetism unto the loftiest divine revelation in the past, and through Messianism, to the greatest religious hope in the future. His faith makes him a citizen of the world, and his hope of the Kingdom of God comforts him in the sorrows and shadows of the present, by making it possible for him to glimpse a complete manifestation of the eternal truth that is yet to come.

But the fact of Christianity is also here, and claims our attention, and I feel constrained to seek an explanation of it. It occupies so important a place in the thoughts of men, it has uplifted and enlightened and strengthened such a multitude of souls for heroic struggles, leading them to the sublimest heights of saintliness; it has revealed itself as a source so prodigiously abundant, of devotion and virtue, of science and art, of poetry and eloquence; it has left its impress on so many races and civilizations, and at the same time has appeared under such a multitude of aspects. It suggests so many problems, gives rise to so much criticism, and troubles so many consciences because of the divisions and the conflicts it has engendered, the fanaticisms it has inspired, the persecutions it has instigated, and the travesties of which it is the endless subject, that in truth the mind is confused in the presence of so formidable an enigma. Christianity rests on a revelation of which Israel was appointed guardian, and it teaches on the other hand, that in the plan of a merciful God, the salvation of the nations can only be founded on the condemnation of the people who are the trustees of this revelation. It cannot be possible that a true religion can be built on so flagrant a contradiction. The least that a Christian who had seriously reflected on these problems could say is, that there must be some unfathomed justice in the age-long protest of Israel.

In the thirteenth century of the Christian era the following event occurred, forming a striking analogy to the Gospel story. A man appeared, possessed of a divine vision, capable of revolutionizing the world, of creating a new religion which might have transformed the occidental world entirely from top to bottom, in taking it back to the pure source whence it sprang. I am speaking of the blessed Francis of Assisi, who before his conversion, feeling himself chosen for a unique destiny, said jestingly to his gay young companions: "You will see that one day I shall be adored by the whole world." When the humble penitent of Assisi came to Rome, to kneel at the feet of the sovereign pontiff, to explain to him his plan for the reformation of morals, and his ideal of the religious life, Innocent III, versed in politics, did not repulse the strange seraphic apparition, a living reproach to the corruption of the Church of those days. He made haste, however, to clip the wings of the Franciscan idea, while he opened his arms to him who brought it. He hastened to strip it of its originality, and of its vigor, by giving it a monastic setting; in a word, according to the Gospel expression, by putting new wine into old bottles. Later the Church enshrined St. Francis of Assisi on its altars, and no one saw that the bull of canonization in reality proclaimed the failure of the Franciscan ideal, smothered in its germ.

What would have happened if the Judaism of the first century had accepted and embraced the Gospel instead of refusing it? We would today have in our two Talmuds, by the side of the words of Hillel the Elder and of so many other pious scholars, the *Amar R. Yeshua ben Yosef Hannotzri*, "words of Rabbi Jesus son of Joseph, the Nazarene," of whom it was said: "Surely this learned man was mistaken in the imminent coming of the Kingdom of Heaven in the form of a cosmic upheaval which would change the world, but what sublime things he did say!" Would Judaism, enriched by this spiritual addition, have conquered the pagan world? Would it the better have disentangled from its authentic traditions, the two aspects of the divine Law, the particularist aspect for Israel alone, and the universalist aspect, for all men? No one can say with certainty; all are free to believe it. But Christianity as it is, would not have been born.

Christianity was born of the opposition of Judaism to the preaching of the Gospel, therefore Christians ought to be infinitely grateful to Israel for not accepting it. As for me, convinced that an infinite wisdom directs the religious evolution of humanity according to a providential plan, I could not regret for an instant, that the pagan world should have adopted and interpreted the Gospel story on its own account, and for its own salvation. I refuse, on the other hand, no less energetically to admit that Judaism was wrong in continuing in its hope of the Messianic advent, instead of believing it to be realized. Jerusalem could not abdicate to Rome, and for humanity which still gropes its way so painfully, this fidelity to the divine compact, leaves open before us all the perspectives of salvation.

To those of my Christian brothers, who may read these pages, I then address this appeal in closing: You who know only the body of Judaism and who, in the words of the philosopher Renouvier,[4] find it unworthy, have you ever sought to discover its soul? The thought alone, that this soul throbbed in the heart of Jesus, ought to inspire you with the desire to learn to know it. Within it there burns a fire strangely able to throw light upon the destinies of Christendom, and to bring to it the solution of many of the questions that you ask yourselves.

To my brother Israelites I would say on the other hand: The Church, this other living enigma, is in the habit of portraying the Synagogue with the sacred scroll in her hand and a bandage over her eyes. There is much of truth in this picture, not in the sense given to it by theology, but in that which reveals to us at the same time Jewish history and the present state of Judaism. You possess treasures you know not of, or that you know not how to use, and not only do you leave your spiritual patrimony unproductive, you close your eyes, at times voluntarily, to the perception of the hand of God in the history of Israel. When will you become the conscious instrument of the work that the God of your fathers willed you should achieve in this world?

Benamozegh in the title of his great work[5] summed up universal history, envisaged from the viewpoint of the divine:

"Mankind cannot rise to the essential principles on which society must rest unless it meet with Israel.

"And Israel cannot fathom the deeps of its own national and religious tradition, unless it meet with mankind."

THE ROAD HOME

NATHAN BIRNBAUM

From free thought to nationalism, orthodoxy, and finally independent piety—such is the dramatic road traveled by Dr. Nathan Birnbaum (1864-1937). The Vienna-born journalist turned early (1883) to Zionism (a term he coined prior to its use by Herzl) but soon (1897) began to oppose its emphasis on politics and the exclusive concentration on the upbuilding of Palestine. Now he advocated Jewish cultural autonomy in the Diaspora, exploration of organic Judaism as it flourished in Eastern Europe, and cultivation of the Yiddish language.

The next step on the road to a more complete Judaism was orthodoxy (1921). While accepting the authority of Jewish law, Birnbaum turned away from Western orthodoxy's lack of spiritual depth. Instead, he envisaged a religious fellowship of "Olim" (the Ascending Ones) dedicated to Torah, sanctification of life, Messianic hope, and work. His program attracted only scant attention and he withdrew from all public activity. An independent thinker and uncompromisingly honest, he could not conform to any one of the existing institutional forms of modern Judaism. Among his writings of the decisive later period are *Gottes Volk* (*God's People*, 1918), *Vom Freigeist zum Gläubigen* (*From a Free Thinker to a Believer*, 1919), *Um die Ewigkeit* (*Concerning Eternity*, 1920), *Im Dienste der Verheissung* (*In the Service of Promise*, 1927).

There was a time, at first, when I used to believe that all those who recognized the Jews as a people, with a claim to an individual life of its own, were full, national Jews—no matter in which soil they had their spiritual roots. At that time I did not think at all about religion. To be sure, I knew that in earlier times religion occupied the foremost place in the life of the Jewish people, and it seemed that even today it still wielded a considerable influence.

But that did not concern me, nor those who thought as I did. After all, we were national Jews—national loyalty, not religious conviction, was to us the criterion of a Jew.

Somewhat later I came to realize that it was not good enough merely to acknowledge allegiance to one nation or another, as one pleased; to belong to it, one had to enter into its life and spirit. Of course this view did not let me treat religion with my former indifference: it was in religion that the Jewish spirit had expressed itself through the ages. Yet I still felt that the Jewish religion had lost its significance for present and future. Why, indeed, need it be considered the only, immortal expression of the Jewish spirit? Could this not come to the surface in other, in all, aspects of social and cultural life?

I could not cling to this view for long. It became clear to me that the history of humanity, of all the nations, all the efforts and achievements of culture, had crystallized and developed around religious, spiritual centers. I gazed with awe and fervor upon the mysterious spiritual forces which direct the paths of man according to set goals. Naturally I applied this discovery also to Jewish history; and recognized that the future of the Jewish people, if there was to be one, could only be inspired by, and built around, its central spiritual core. But I was still too deeply steeped in the spirit of materialism to draw practical consequences from my new wisdom. I knew well enough now that religion could not be explained away as a useful invention of man; and I realized that its teachings on the unity and meaningfulness of historic developments were true. But I did not act upon these teachings, because I did not, at this time, truly believe: I did not know God yet.

Today I do; I have meditated much about the matter and, if necessary, I can defend (not, God forbid, prove) my belief in God and all its implications by all manners of rational arguments. For example, I can note the fact that the plan of a man's life, the development of his spirit, is already determined at the moment of his coming into existence; why, then, should nature and history as a whole be considered to be planless, accidental, without a living spirit to direct them from the first? Actually, if there were only a purely mechanical process of world development, we could not speak of moral laws (as we in fact do); these only make sense if we consider humanity capable of freely realizing given spiritual goals. We may consider the development of our world very much like the unreeling of a string from a spool; more and more of the string appears to us, but all of it had already existed before, although invisible to us—and, in the same way, world development may be conceived as the gradual expression of a prior plan laid down by the Eternal Spirit. Religious faith is challenged by the assertion that world development was not planned, and only appears to express a meaningful plan—yet such an assertion is itself based on a new kind of faith. It can hardly be denied that where there appears a plan there must be a planner, that the immense structure of the world presupposes a world builder. From this idea of God as planning for eternity I can derive the omnipotence, omniscience, justice and mercy of God, without concern for the fashionable arguments of our time.

But these, and other, considerations are not the reason for my faith in God today; and it was not they which led me to it. I did not seek God, as people put it, very nicely but hypocritically; I did not have to find Him. He suddenly announced Himself to me and entered into my consciousness. Without any mediating speculation I recognized Him, in whom the spiritual foundations of all nations are anchored, the Father and First Cause of all that exists, the Prime Planner of all developments, the Prime Builder of our world. For a while false shame did not let me submit to this new discovery. But soon it was overcome by a new and burning shame which has not left me to this day: shame that I should have been for so long among those who do not know of Him; that the wisdom of my ancestors, the greatest there ever was on earth, had so long been dormant within me, and the voice of my people silent so long.

It was then that I rid myself of the last vestiges of my materialistic view of history, and came to recognize the unique nature and life of my people. True enough, I realized, the other nations had men who knew of God even before Jewish influence had reached them. But these men only philosophized about Him as a cold and lofty abstraction; they did not love Him, and were not His messengers. He did not inspire them to rise up before their peoples, to proclaim Him to them, to enter with Him into the world. The nations continued to go their diverse ways; they looked for God in the multiplicity of appearances, in the colorful variety of idols. Only to us, to the speck of dust among the mountains; to us, who since time immemorial, had known God without seeking Him, the first and only ones; to us alone was He more than a philosophical discovery. We entered with Him into the world, to understand its meaning and purpose; we entered with Him into history, to shape it according to His will. We alone organized our little community for Him alone, without looking for power or petty profits. Thus we remained lonely and unrecognized among the heathen nations of ancient times—eccentrics for whom they had no use or understanding. Even later, through the ages, when we met with the nations of the world, we stayed in splendid isolation.

We did indeed give them new religious foundations; our Jewish idea of God entered into the world as a perpetual ferment—so that we can almost speak of a "colonial Judaism" among the nations. But again and again the tough pagan strain inherent in the nations asserted itself by rebelling against our great and unique remaking of the human spirit. Ever more frequently they attacked those religious and social institutions and movements in their midst which had been inspired by Judaism (even though these structures themselves had rebelled and developed away from their Jewish origins). They seemed unable to tolerate their Jewish background and component elements. Particularly since the days of the Renaissance, the attacks multiplied upon the Jewish principle, "God first, and only then the world"; and upon the restraints divinely imposed on man. The ancestral instincts of pagan man strove ever more to break through these restraints, and to attain the so-called "free play of forces" which does not only let a Cain slay an Abel but even, on occasion, allows one Abel to destroy another.

We, however, were like men in a well-protected port, looking out upon a storm-swept sea. With astonished eyes we watched the battle raging abroad because of a little part of our Jewish faith. We remained in our safe haven, alone with our holy mysteries of eternity. God had chosen us—and we Him.

LULLABY FOR MIRIAM

RICHARD BEER-HOFMANN

On Beer-Hofmann see the preface to "The Voice of Jacob." The poem, written in 1897 and dedicated to the poet's daughter, bespeaks a profound feeling for his ancestral faith and a harmonious blend of Jewish and purely human elements. The translation is by Sol Liptzin.

Sleep, my child—sleep now and rest!
See there the sun, how it wanes in the west,
Reddening hills as it breathes its last breath.
You—you know nothing of suns and of death,
Turning your eyes to the glare and the light.
Sleep, there are *so* many suns for your sight,
Sleep, my child,—my child, sleep on!

Sleep, my child—the evening wind blows.
Know we from where it comes? Whither it goes?
Dark are all ways, deep hidden and wild,
Yours and mine too and all others, my child!
Blindly we go, all alone do we go,
None can to none be a mate here below—
Sleep, my child,—my child, sleep on!

Sleep, my child, and heed not my song!
Meaning for me does it carry along,
You hear but echo of wind and of sea,
Words—the whole harvest of life may be!
What I have gained, down my grave it will go,
None can to none be an heir here below—
Sleep, my child,—my child, sleep on!

Asleep, my Miriam?—Miriam, my child,
We are but banks of a river, and wild
Flows through us blood of our past, rushing loud
On to the morrow, unresting and proud.
In us are all,—none, none is alone.
You are their life and their life is your own—
Miriam—my life, my child—sleep on!

ALL IN VAIN

JAKOB WASSERMANN

The novels of Jakob Wassermann (1873-1934) "take their inspiration from Dostoevsky, and are on a theme of salvation through suffering. His characters renounced the world for the mystical ecstasy of abnegation. It was the will to power that he hated more than anything else. Like Tolstoy, Wassermann saw salvation as an individual matter. His heroes are not reformers, but saints, and he found no hope for the world except through those who were willing to renounce it" (Krutch). The celebrated novelist (*The World's Illusion*, 1926, *Caspar Hauser*, 1928, *The Maurizius Case*, 1929, *Etzel Andergast*, 1932) considered himself to be both German and Jew, both in a profound sense. He suffered despair and anguish in the realization that deep down "the Jew" was considered an alien. Emancipation and assimilation had failed to bring about the hoped-for understanding, he felt. He rejected the Zionist attempt to solve this dilemma, ascribing to the Jews the prophetic task of being—individually, not as a community—apostles of the spirit. Basically, his Judaism and Germanism alike were determined by his Europeanism: "I am a European, full to the brim with European destiny, moulded by the European spirit." Wassermann described his experiences and views in *Mein Weg als Deutscher und Jude* (1921; *My Life as German and Jew*, 1933), from which the following expression of disappointment is taken.

With the realization of the hopelessness of all efforts the bitterness in one's breast becomes a mortal agony.

Vain to adjure the nation of poets and thinkers in the name of
its poets and thinkers. Every prejudice one thinks disposed of
breeds a thousand others, as carrion breeds maggots.

Vain to present the right cheek after the left has been struck. It
does not move them to the slightest thoughtfulness, it neither
touches nor disarms them: They strike the right cheek too.

Vain to interject words of reason into their crazy shrieking. They
say: He dares to open his mouth? Gag him.

Vain to act in exemplary fashion. They say: We know nothing,
we have seen nothing, we have heard nothing.

Vain to seek obscurity. They say: The coward! He is creeping
into hiding, driven by his evil conscience.

Vain to go among them and offer them one's hand. They say:
Why does he take such liberties, with his Jewish obtrusiveness?

Vain to keep faith with them, as a comrade-in-arms or a fellow
citizen. They say: He is Proteus, he can assume any shape or
form.

Vain to help them strip off the chains of slavery. They say: No
doubt he found it profitable.

Vain to counteract the poison. They brew fresh venom.

Vain to live for them and die for them. They say: He is a Jew.

BEFORE THE STATUE OF APOLLO

SAUL TCHERNICHOVSKY

Born in a village on the borderland between the Ukraine
and the Crimea, far from the seats of Hebrew learning, Saul
Tchernichovsky (1875-1943) became the poet of boundless
affirmation of life. "He betrayed none of the traits of the Ghetto
Jew, none of the tragic conflicts of the Jewish intellectual. He
saw himself at home everywhere, a true child of nature, a citizen
of the world. The sympathies of the poet are world-wide, his outlook universal. He instinctively broke the traditional barriers set
between Jew and Greek. He recognized none of the forbidding
theories bequeathed to his people by centuries of Ghetto life.
He identified himself with the bold conquerors of Canaan, with

the lusty Baal-worshippers of old. Worship of beauty in whatever form, manly vigor, unconquerable will to do and to accomplish, these are the main characteristics of his poetic personality" (Hillel Bavli). Tchernichovsky was fascinated by the common traits manifested by the pagan Greeks and the early Hebrews; in this spirit he "returned" to the worship of Apollo, the god of light and music. He translated into Hebrew works of Homer, "that great seer of a world of beauty," of Plato, Sophocles, and Anacreon; also, the Babylonian epic, *Gilgamesh*, the Finnish epic, *Kalevala*, Longfellow's *Evangeline* and *Hiawatha*. In his idylls, Tchernichovsky celebrated the life of simple Jews in rural southern Russia. Jewish martyrdom ("Passover of the Dejected," "Baruch of Mayence") and the pioneering spirit of the modern land of Israel (*Re-i Adamah, See Here, Earth*) were the themes of some of his other poems. In 1931, the poet settled in Palestine. The poem here reprinted is one of the best known of Tchernichovsky's; the English version appeared first in *The Menorah Journal* IX, 1923.

To thee I come, O long-abandoned god
Of early moons and unremembered days,
To thee whose reign was in a greener world
Among a race of men divine with youth,
Strong generations of the sons of earth:
To thee, whose right arm broke the bound of heaven
To set on thrones therein thy strongest sons,
Whose proud brows with victorious bays were crowned.
Amongst the gods of old thou wert a god,
Bringing for increase to the mighty earth
A race of demi-gods, instinct with life,
Strange to the children of the house of pain.
A boy-god, passionate and beautiful,
Whose mastery was over the bright sun
And over the dark mysteries of life,
The golden shadow-treasuries of song,
The music of innumerable seas—
A god of joyousness and fresh delight,
Of vigor and the ecstasy of life.

I am the Jew. Dost thou remember me?
Between us there is enmity forever!
Not all the multitudes of ocean's waters,
Storm-linking continent with continent,
Could fill the dark abyss between us yawning.
The heavens and the boundless wilderness
Were short to bridge the wideness set between
My fathers' children and thy worshippers.
And yet behold me! I have wandered far,
By crooked ways, from those that were before me,
And others after me shall know this path.
But amongst those that will return to thee
I was the first to free my soul that groaned
Beneath the agony of generations;
For a day came I would endure no more,
And on that day my spirit burst its chains
And turned again towards the living earth.

The people and its God have aged together!
Passions which strengthlessness had laid to sleep
Start into sudden life again, and break
Their prison of a hundred generations.
The light of God, the light of God is mine!
My blood is clamorous with desire of life.
My limbs, my nerves, my veins, triumphant shout
For life and sunlight.
                                And I come to thee,
And here before thy pedestal I kneel
Because thy symbol is the burning sun.
I kneel to thee, the noble and the true,
Whose strength is in the fullness of the earth,
Whose will is in the fullness of creation,
Whose throne is on the secret founts of being.
I kneel to life, to beauty and to strength,
I kneel to all the passionate desires
Which they, the dead-in-life, the bloodless ones,
The sick, have stifled in the living God,

The God of wonders of the wilderness,
The God of gods, Who took Canaan with storm
Before they bound Him in phylacteries.

CREDO

HARRY FRIEDENWALD

Dr. Harry Friedenwald (1864-1950), member of a prominent Baltimore family, ophthalmologist, medical historian, rare-book collector, was a pioneer in the Zionist movement and president of the Federation of American Zionists from 1904 to 1918. In addition, he played a leading role in many Jewish cultural endeavors in the United States. His Credo is reprinted from *Vision: A Biography of Harry Friedenwald*, by Alexandra Lee Levin.

The study of nature, of the physical world in its infinite grandeur and in its ultimate structure, in its elements and the forces acting in them, in its divisions into inorganic and organic worlds impresses us by the evidence it affords of plan, of order, and of system. Our intelligence compels us to recognize an underlying, an intelligent creative power.

One cannot, however, worship a mere mathematical formula.

In the animal world, which is a part of nature, we find what we term spiritual forces and faculties leading up to consciousness, intelligence, reason and the moral sense—reaching their highest forms in man.

Thus the order and system of nature embraces also spiritual forces and faculties. They, too, can be ascribed only to the same creative force. It is this creative, intelligent and moral force which we worship. The Jews recognized this creative force as God and as Unity.

The concept of the Jews as the Chosen People should not be understood in the passive sense of special election as the object of favoritism, but as an active acceptance by the Jewish People of special duties and obligations. The choice is analogous to the ambition for virtue in the individual defined in Funk and Wagnalls' dictionary as "a worthy eagerness to achieve something great and good." It is an historically based self-dedication which imposes on the Jewish People specially high and onerous responsibilities.

The fact that the Jewish People, in the exercise of this self-dedication, have throughout the centuries shown a high degree of spiritual quality, is a noteworthy example of the spiritual and moral order in the universe.

OF THE JEWISH RELIGION

ALBERT EINSTEIN

On Einstein, see the preface to "On Zionism, the Land of Israel, and the Arabs." Here, a word on the man's views on religion, ethics, and the meaning of life. On God: "I cannot believe that God plays dice with the cosmos." On his religious experience: "I assert that the cosmic religious experience is the strongest and the noblest driving force. . . . My religion consists of a humble admiration of the illimitable superior spirit who reveals himself in the slight details we are able to perceive with our frail and feeble minds. . . . That deeply emotional conviction of the presence of a superior reasoning power, which is revealed in the incomprehensible universe, forms my idea of God. . . ." On the meaning of life: "What is the meaning of human life, or for that matter, of the life of any creature? To know an answer to this question means to be religious. You ask: Does it make any sense, then, to pose this question? I answer: The man who regards his own life and that of his fellow creatures as meaningless is not merely unhappy but hardly fit for life." On character: "It is the moral qualities of its leading personalities that are perhaps of even greater significance for a generation and for the course of history than purely intellectual accomplishments. Even these latter are, to a far greater degree than is commonly credited, dependent on the stature of character." His view on Judaism, as documented by the passage that follows, reflects his humanist attitude.

There is, in my opinion, no Jewish view of life in the philosophic sense. Judaism appears to me to be almost exclusively concerned with the moral attitude in and toward life.

Judaism I believe to be rather the content of the life-approach of the Jewish people than the contents of the laws laid down in the Torah and interpreted in the Talmud. Torah and Talmud are for me only the most weighty evidence of the governing concepts of Jewish life in earlier times.

The essence of the Jewish concept of life seems to me to be the affirmation of life for all creatures. For the life of the individual has meaning only in the service of enhancing and ennobling the life of every living thing. Life is holy; i.e., it is the highest worth on which all other values depend. The sanctification of the life which transcends the individual brings with it reverence for the spiritual, a peculiarly characteristic trait of Jewish tradition.

Judaism is not a faith. The Jewish God is but a negation of superstition and an imaginative result of its elimination. He also represents an attempt to ground morality in fear—a deplorable, discreditable attempt. Yet it seems to me that the powerful moral tradition in the Jewish people has, in great measure, released itself from this fear. Moreover it is clear that "to serve God" is equivalent to serving "every living thing." It is for this that the best among the Jewish people, especially the prophets including Jesus, ceaselessly battled. Thus Judaism is not a transcendental religion. It is concerned only with the tangible experiences of life, and with nothing else. Therefore it seems to me to be questionable whether it may be termed a "religion" in the customary sense of the word, especially since no "creed" is demanded of Jews, but only the sanctification of life in its all-inclusive sense.

There remains, however, something more in the Jewish tradition, so gloriously revealed in certain of the psalms; namely, a kind of drunken joy and surprise at the beauty and incomprehensible sublimity of this world, of which man can attain but a faint intimation. It is the feeling from which genuine research draws its intellectual strength, but which also seems to manifest itself in the song of birds. This appears to me to be the loftiest content of the God-idea.

Is this, then, characteristic of Judaism? And does it exist elsewhere under other names? In pure form it exists nowhere, not even in Judaism where too much literalism obscures the pure doctrine. But, nevertheless, I see in Judaism one of its most vital and pure realizations. This is especially true of its fundamental principle of the sanctification of life.

It is noteworthy that in the commandment to keep the Sabbath holy the animals were also expressly included [6]—so strongly was felt as an ideal the demand for the solidarity of all living things. Far more strongly yet is expressed the demand for the solidarity of all humankind; and it is no accident that the socialistic demands for the most part emanated from Jews.

To how great an extent the consciousness of the sanctity of life is alive in the Jewish people is beautifully illustrated by a remark once made to me by Walter Rathenau:[7] "When a Jew says he takes pleasure in the hunt, he lies." It is impossible to express more simply the consciousness of the sanctity and the unity of all life as it exists in the Jewish people.

WHAT I BELIEVE*

SHOLEM ASCH

The most characteristic aspect of the widely known Yiddish novelist, playwright and essayist Sholem Asch (1880-1957), is his emotional involvement in both the Judaic past and present-day problems in Judaism; he approached both with deep compassion. His *Dos Shtetl* (*The Town*, 1904), depicts Jewish life in Eastern Europe; his *Kiddush Hashem* (*Sanctification of the Name*, 1926) is a story of martyrdom. Influenced by the social novel current in European literature at the beginning of the century, he wrote *Three Cities* (1933), a novel dealing with the Jewish experience in pre- and post-revolutionary Russia; another novel, *Salvation* (1934), depicted hasidic life in Eastern Europe. The subject of his *Song of the Valley* (1939) is the land of Israel. In his later years Asch turned to the period of early Christianity and in an effort to transcend the age-old tension between the two communities of faith and to suggest a better understanding of their common roots, wrote *The Nazarene, The Apostle,* and *Mary.* Many of his writings have been translated

*"What I Believe," © 1941, 1969 Ruth Shaffer, Moses Asch, John Asch and the representative of Nathan Asch.

into English and other languages. The Polish-born Asch emigrated to the United States in 1914; the last years of his life
(1955-1957) he spent in Israel.

(1) It is my deepest belief that just as I have a share in the
God of Israel through my faith in Him, that I stand under His authority and am included in the promise of redemption, so my
Christian brother has his equal share in the God of Israel, stands
equally under the authority and is included equally in the promise
of redemption. For he is a son of Israel equally with me. His faith
has made him a son of Abraham, Isaac, and Jacob. My rights are
his, and I have a share in his religious values as he has a share in
mine.

Basing themselves on this concept of equality, the sons of every
faith must justify themselves in works. Man's ladder to God is a
ladder of works. God must be the ultimate expression of our
relationship to each other on earth.

(2) It is my deepest belief that man has been chosen by God's
grace from among all creatures. Apart from the intelligence, which
nature has given to every creature, and which is included in
nature and limited to the objective and conditioned, man—alone
among creatures—possesses a soul which is a part of the endowment from above. Through his soul man stands in mystic contact
with heaven. By means of his soul man can acquire intellectual
and intuitive powers which are outside the competence of nature,
derive from the highest inspiration of the divinity, and are not
limited to the objective and conditioned. God guides every individual destiny through the inspiration of the soul. This soul-
inspiration is given to each one, and not only to the elect, so that
everyone may, in the exercise of his free will, reach to the higher
reason which is the supreme level of the holy spirit.

Each one of us can follow in the footsteps of Amos, abandon
the flocks, and become a prophet in Israel.[8] In keeping with Jewish doctrine I believe in the democracy of divine election; each
one of us can become even a Moses.

(3) Accepting this point of view, it is further my profoundest conviction that the democratic principle—in the social system not less

than in faith—is God's especial gift to man and resides in the act
of grace which God performed for man in choosing him among
all creatures. The democratic principle is interwoven with faith
and cannot be separated from God. In having been chosen by
God we became the children of God: "For sons are ye of the
Lord God" (Deuteronomy 14:1)—all of us, and not just a few
individuals. Any other relationship as between us and God, or as
between ourselves, would contradict the will of the divinity, and
would be incompatible with all that has been given to the Jews
by Moses and the prophets, and all that has been given to the
Christians by Jesus and the Apostles. The democratic principle is
"all the law fulfilled in one word, even in this: Thou shalt love
thy neighbor as thyself." [9] This is the foundation which, together
with the love toward God, was given through Moses, the prophets,
the Pharisees, Jesus of Nazareth, and the Apostles.

"Love thy neighbor as thyself" does not mean that you must
be mild in your dominion over him; it means that you shall not
have any dominion over him. He is a son of liberty not less than
you, and the relationship between you and him can be built only
on a system which assumed the identity of your rights. This is the
democratic principle.

And as the democratic principle is the will of God in relationship between man and man, it is equally his will in the relationship between man and God. "It is not in the heavens" (Deuteronomy 30:12). The divine law was not given to the angels, but to
us, who are of the earth. It lies before us like an open book. The
measure is in our hand.

Hence I believe profoundly that there is no love of God without love of men. Service to mankind is in my view the higher
service of the divinity. But service to mankind must not be seen
in the throwing of crumbs to the poor; as we are equal in our
faith in God, so we must be equal in our faith in man. We must
work out a world order which shall rest upon equal distribution
of labor and rewards. "The right to happiness" must not remain
an empty gesture in our Declaration of Independence, it must be
incorporated in the administrative duties of the state. It must be
interpreted in the material sense to which men are bound by their

nature: in food and clothing and shelter, in the care for the aged, in our regard for widows, for the sick and the weak. All this must become a cardinal obligation for the state, in its administration. The inner security of our citizens must become the cornerstone of our independence and freedom; it must become a tacit obligation, like external security; not because we regard social injustice as the most potent instrument of the devil—though it is, indeed, exactly that—but because without that tacit obligation our professions of faith are as empty as dicers' oaths.

"Though I speak with the tongues of men and of angels, and have not charity, I am become as sounding brass, or a tinkling cymbal. And though I have the gift of prophecy, and understand all mysteries, and all knowledge; and though I have all faith, so that I could remove mountains, and have not charity, I am nothing. And though I bestow all my goods to feed the poor, and though I give my body to be burned, and have not charity, it profiteth me nothing." [10]

(4) It is further my profoundest belief that we must lead a life in faith; that is, we must become that which we undertook to be —a holy people. We can be a holy people only in a pure, ethical life, a life ruled by laws and commandments. But no laws and commandments, though they have a thousand eyes, and though they seem to control all our acts, can purify and sanctify us if the heart of man does not sanctify his life. The heart of man is a filter for all his acts and thoughts. If the heart is sound, man knows that his highest joy is bound up not with dissoluteness and the free play of uncontrollable passion, but with purity, with modesty, and with restraint.

There is no level of corruption from which man cannot redeem himself, by the exercise of his free will. And whenever he makes an effort at such redemption, he can be certain of help from above. For God's act of creation was not single and unique; it is a continuity of relationship through the individual destiny.

I believe, therefore, that for every individual there is salvation, no matter how low he has sunk. "Have I any pleasure at all that the wicked should die? saith the Lord God; and not that he should return from his ways, and live?" (Ezekiel 8:23). The heart of man is bound with the divinity through the radiations of divinity. To the darkest and most horrible retreats to which men have withdrawn from the divinity, a ray of the divinity penetrates. And for this reason we must never despair of a man, much less of a group which is temporarily lost to the divinity. However deep a group has sunk, we must continue to pray for it, and to help it with our desires and sympathies. And no matter how deeply we feel that we have been wronged by such a group, we must exert ourselves to purify our hearts from bitterness.

We were worms in our physical creation; we have become human in our hunger for the divinity. The drink of God, which was lifted to our lips by the authority, has enabled us to mount the ladder of Jacob which rises from earth to heaven. If we will endure, and continue the upward path, we will attain to the true salvation of a world which stands under the authority of God through a single, universal redeemer.

The renewal of faith in the divine force of our moral values, as our sole hope in the darkness of our night, is what I would wish to submit to a suffering humanity.

It is America, which has been saved from the worst terrors of the night, which has not been corrupted with the cynicism which has been the undoing of Europe; it is America, young and powerful, blossoming in the virginity of faith, which must become the leading spirit among the nations. It is America, the land which has taken me in, among so many other homeless ones, as a child of her own, which I would like to see as a "light to the Gentiles" (Isaiah 49:6), leading the world back out of the night into the authority of the one and only God.

HIS FATHER'S JUDAISM

FRANZ KAFKA

In his autobiographical "Letter to His Father," written in November 1919, Franz Kafka (1883-1924), then thirty-six years old, analyzed the unhappy relations between him and his father that marked his youth. "Basically a kindly and soft-hearted person," as Kafka describes him, this father was "too strong" for him—in his role as father. "There remained nothing but the acceptance of the break which existed in the natural world between the generations and in the supernatural world between the Deity and man. Writing the letter, Kafka seems to have resigned himself to accepting this separation as inevitable and final on both the level of reality and the spiritual level beyond" (Heinz Politzer).

The elder Kafka's Judaism, formal, bereft of depth, indifferent, was an integral part of the world which the son had to reject in order to maintain his integrity. Despite its exaggerations and overdrawn lines the picture is typical; Kafka's predicament has been, in various forms, experienced by many modern Jewish intellectuals. His own Judaism expressed itself—indirectly but most keenly—on the sublime level of theological query. Franz Rosenzweig remarked that he has "never read a book that reminded [him] so much of the Bible as [Kafka's] *The Castle.*"

I found little means of escape from you in Judaism. Here some escape would, in principle, have been thinkable, but more than that, it would have been thinkable that we might both have found each other in Judaism or even that we might have begun from there in harmony. But what sort of Judaism was it I got from you? In the course of the years I have taken roughly three different attitudes to it.

As a child I reproached myself, in accord with you, for not going to the synagogue enough, for not fasting, and so on. I thought that in this way I was doing a wrong not to myself but to you, and I was penetrated by a sense of guilt, which was, of course, always ready to hand.

Later, as a boy, I could not understand how, with the insignificant scrap of Judaism you yourself possessed, you could reproach me for not (if for no more than the sake of piety, as you put it) making an effort to cling to a similar insignificant scrap. It was indeed really, so far as I could see, a mere scrap, a joke, not even a joke. On four days in the year you went to the synagogue, where you were, to say the least of it, closer to the indifferent than to

those who took it seriously, patiently went through the prayers
by way of formality, sometimes amazed me by being able to show
me in the prayer book the passage that was being said at the moment, and for the rest, so long (and this was the main thing) as I
was there in the synagogue I was allowed to hang about wherever
I liked. And so I yawned and dozed through the many hours (I
don't think I was ever again so bored, except later at dancing
lessons) and did my best to enjoy the few little bits of variety
there were, as, for instance, when the Ark of the Covenant was
opened, which always reminded me of the shooting galleries where
a cupboard door would open in the same way whenever one got a
bull's-eye, only with the difference that there something interesting
always came out and here it was always just the same old dolls with
no heads. Incidentally, it was also very frightening for me there,
not only, as goes without saying, because of all the people one
came into close contact with, but also because you once mentioned, by the way, that I too might be called up to read the
Torah. That was something I went in dread of for years. But otherwise I was not fundamentally disturbed in my state of boredom,
unless it was by the *bar mitzvah*, but that meant no more than
some ridiculous learning by heart, in other words, led to nothing
but something like the ridiculous passing of an examination, and
then, so far as you were concerned, by little, not very significant
incidents, as when you were called up to read the Torah and came
well out of the affair, which to my way of feeling was purely social,
or when you stayed on in the synagogue for the prayers for the
dead, and I was sent away, which for a long time, obviously because of being sent away and lacking, as I did, any deeper interest,
aroused in me the more or less unconscious feeling that what was
about to take place was something indecent.—That was how it
was in the synagogue, and at home it was, if possible, even more
poverty-stricken, being confined to the first evening of Passover,
which more and more developed into a farce, with fits of hysterical
laughter, admittedly under the influence of the growing children.
(Why did you have to give way to that influence? Because you
brought it about in the first place.) And so there was the religious

material that was handed on to me, to which may be added at most the outstretched hand pointing to "the sons of the millionaire Fuchs," who were in the synagogue with their father at the high holidays. How one could do anything better with this material than get rid of it as fast as possible was something I could not understand; precisely getting rid of it seemed to me the most effective act of "piety" one could perform.

But later on still I did see it again differently and came to realize why it was possible for you to think that in this respect too I was showing ill will and betraying you. You had really brought some traces of Judaism with you from that ghetto-like little village community; it was not much and it dwindled a little more in town and while you were doing your military service, but still, the impressions and memories of your youth did just about suffice to make some sort of Jewish life, especially since you did not, after all, need much of that kind of help, coming as you did of a vigorous stock and being personally scarcely capable of being shaken by religious scruples if they were not very much mixed up with social scruples. At bottom the faith that ruled your life consisted in your believing in the unconditional rightness of the opinions prevailing in a particular class of Jewish society, and hence actually, since these opinions were part and parcel of your own nature, in believing in yourself. Even in this there was still Judaism enough, but it was too little to be handed on to the child; it all dribbled away while you were passing it on. In part it was youthful memories of your own, of a kind that could not be conveyed to others; in part it was your dreaded personality. It was also impossible to make a child, overacutely observant from sheer nervousness, understand that the few flimsy gestures you performed in the name of Judaism, and with an indifference in keeping with their flimsiness, could have any higher meaning. For you they had their meaning as little souvenirs of earlier times, and that was why you wanted to pass them on to me, but this, since after all even for you they no longer had any value in themselves, was something you could do only by means of persuasion or threats; this could, on the one hand, not be successful and could not, on the other hand, but make you, since you utterly failed to recognize your weak position here, very angry with me on account of my apparent obstinacy.

The whole thing is, of course, not an isolated phenomenon. It was much the same with a large section of this transitional generation of Jews, which had migrated from the still comparatively devout countryside to the towns. The situation arose automatically; only it did, as it happened, bring one more source of acrimony, and a fairly painful one, into our relationship, which was already far from lacking in sources of acrimony. On the other hand, although you ought, on this point too, just like myself, to believe in your own blamelessness, you ought, however, to explain this blamelessness by your personality and the conditions of the time, but not merely by external circumstances, that is, not by saying for instance that you had too much other work and too many other worries to be able to give your mind to such things as well. This is the manner in which you are in the habit of twisting your undoubted innocence into an unjust reproach to others. That can be very easily refuted everywhere and here too. It was not a matter of any sort of instruction you ought to have given your children, but of an exemplary life. Had your Judaism been stronger, then your example would have been compelling too; this goes without saying and is, again, by no means a reproach, but only a refutation of your reproaches. You have recently been reading Franklin's memoirs of his youth. I did, in fact, give you this book to read on purpose, but not, as you ironically commented, because of a little passage on vegetarianism, but because of the relationship between the author and his father, as it is there described, and of the relationship between the author and his son, as it is spontaneously revealed in these memoirs written for that son. I do not wish to dwell here on matters of detail.

I have received a certain retrospective confirmation of this view of your Judaism from your attitude in recent years, when it seemed to you that I was taking more interest in Jewish things. As you have a dislike in advance of every one of my activities and particularly of the nature of my interest, so you have had it here too. But in spite of this general attitude, one would really have expected that here you would make a little exception. It was, after all, Judaism of your Judaism that was here stirring, and thus with it the possibility too of the start of new relations between us. I do not deny that if you had shown interest in them these things might, for that very reason, have become suspect in my eyes. For I do not dream of asserting that I am in this respect in any way better than you. But it never came to putting it to the test. Through my mediation Judaism became abhorrent to you and Jewish writings unreadable; they "nauseated" you.—This may have meant that you were insisting that only that Judaism which you had shown me in my childhood was the right one, and beyond that there was nothing. But that you should insist on that was, after all, scarcely thinkable. But then the "nausea" (apart from the fact that it was directed primarily not against Judaism but against me personally) could only mean that unconsciously you did acknowledge the weakness of your Judaism and of my Jewish upbringing, did not wish to be reminded of it in any way, and reacted to all reminders with frank hatred. Incidentally, your negative high esteem of my new Judaism was much exaggerated; first of all, it bore your curse within it, and secondly, in its development the fundamental relationship to one's fellow men was decisive, in my case that is to say fatal.

WHY I AM A JEW

EDMOND FLEG

In a little book bearing the above title, the French poet and playwright Edmond Fleg (1874-1963) expounded his religious beliefs; he was led to a rediscovery of Judaism by the Dreyfus affair. His writings (including the cycle of poems *Écoute Israël*, 1913 and 1921, *Moïse*, 1928, *Israël et moi*, 1936) dwell upon the spiritual element in Judaism. His *Anthologie juive* (1923) brought the works of classical and modern Judaism to the attention of French intellectuals.

Why I Am a Jew, from which the following excerpt is a quota-

tion, was written in 1927 (*Pourquoi je suis juif*); the English
edition, in a translation by Victor Gollancz, appeared in 1943.
It was dedicated to "my grandson who is not yet born." No
grandson was born to him; both his sons fell in the early days
of World War II. In 1937 Fleg was made an officer of the
Legion of Honor.

See this sublime design, which is revealed at the very beginning
and which, from age to age, is realized. Did the Greeks declare to
the world in advance that they would show it Beauty? The
Romans, that they would show it Law? See this people, paltry and
sinful, announcing what will be its history at the very beginning of
its history; see it choose the mission which chooses it, and walking
with it in the way which it has foretold.

See it, this people of eternal sinners, banished twice and surviving two dispersions; and, as commanded by its prophecies,
bringing back from its first exile the divine unity, and preparing,
by the second, human unity. See it driven over the face of the
earth, always near to dying, and always finding some providential
shelter to save it from death.

See it bearing its truth, and, to keep it pure, suffering it to
spread through the world in the light of the blazing stake. See it,
incarnating in its flesh the two loves that torment it, and, at the
very moment when it gives itself, with them, to all the nations of
the earth, reconstructing, for its own survival still, the home of its
memory and its hope, which is the universal hope.

And tell me if, in this unique history, you do not feel the
eternal presence of a thought and a will which have dictated its
task to this people and have made its accomplishment possible, trying it by suffering, saving it in its trials, and guiding it step by step
from its grievous past to its triumphant future.

For me, my child, who have so long sought the proof of the
existence of God—I have found it in the existence of Israel.

I am a Jew because, born of Israel and having lost her, I have felt
   her live again in me, more living than myself.
I am a Jew because, born of Israel and having regained her, I wish
   her to live after me, more living than in myself.

I am a Jew because the faith of Israel demands of me no abdication of the mind.

I am a Jew because the faith of Israel requires of me all the devotion of my heart.

I am a Jew because in every place where suffering weeps, the Jew weeps.

I am a Jew because at every time when despair cries out, the Jew hopes.

I am a Jew because the word of Israel is the oldest and the newest.

I am a Jew because the promise of Israel is the universal promise.

I am a Jew because, for Israel, the world is not yet completed: men are completing it.

I am a Jew because, for Israel, Man is not created: men are creating him.

I am a Jew because, above the nations and Israel, Israel places Man and his Unity.

I am a Jew because, above Man, image of the divine Unity, Israel places the divine Unity, and its divinity.

THE AIR AND EARTH OF VITEBSK

MARC CHAGALL

In February 1962 Hadassah Medical Center in Jerusalem celebrated the dedication of the stained glass windows created by Marc Chagall for the Center's synagogue. Chagall, a native of Vitebsk, Russia (b. 1887), delivered a speech of which the following are excerpts. Translated from the Yiddish by Mrs. Moshe Eliash.

How is it that the air and earth of Vitebsk, my birthplace, and of thousands of years of exile, find themselves mingled in the air and earth of Jerusalem?

How could I have thought that not only my hands with their colors would direct me in my work, but that the poor hands of my parents and of others and still others, with their mute lips and their closed eyes, who gathered and whispered behind me, would direct me as if they also wished to take part in my life?

I feel, too, as though the tragic and heroic resistance movements, in the ghettos, and your war here in this country, are blended in my flowers and beasts and my fiery colors. [. . .]

The more our age refuses to see the full face of the universe and restricts itself to the sight of a tiny fraction of its skin, the more anxious I become when I consider the universe in its eternal rhythm, and the more I wish to oppose the general current.

Do I speak like this because, with the advance of life, the outlines surrounding us become clearer and the horizon appears in a more tragic glow?

I feel as if colors and lines flow like tears from my eyes, though I do not weep. And do not think that I speak like this from weakness—on the contrary, as I advance in years the more certain I am of what I want, and the more certain I am of what I say.

I know that the path of our life is eternal and short, and while still in my mother's womb I learned to travel this path with love rather than with hate.

These thoughts occurred to me many years ago, when I first stepped on Biblical ground, preparing to create etchings for the Bible. And they emboldened me to bring my modest gift to the Jewish people—to that Jewish people which always dreamed of Biblical love, of friendship and peace among all peoples; to that people which lived here, thousands of years ago, among the other Semitic peoples. And this, which is today called "religious art" I created while bearing in mind the great and ancient creations of the surrounding Semitic peoples.

I have concluded two years of labor, creating these twelve stained glass windows for this synagogue in Jerusalem. My hope is that the synagogue will please you and that it will overflow with harmony even as I have prayed.

I saw the hills of Sodom and the Negev, out of whose defiles appear the shadows of our prophets in their yellow garments, the color of dry bread. I heard their ancient words.

Have they not truly and justly shown in their words how to behave on this earth and by what ideal to live?

I LIVE IN YOU, IN EACH OF YOU

ABRAHAM ISAAC KOOK

On Kook, see the preface to "Faith." The poem manifests the author's faith and his love for Israel, both mystically inter-related ("On the Wings of your love I rise to the love of God"). Translated by Morris Silverman, it is included in the *Sabbath and Festival Prayer Book* of the Rabbinical Assembly of America.

Hearken, O my people!
From the very depths of my soul
I speak unto you;
From the core of life where lies the tie
That binds us one to the other,
With devotion, deep and profound,
I declare unto you
That you, each one of you,
All of you, the whole of you,
Your very souls, your generations,—
Only you are the essence of my life.
I live in you, in each of you, in all of you;
In your life, my life has deeper, truer meaning;
Without you I am as naught.
Hope, aspiration and life's intrinsic worth,—
All this I find only when I am with you.
I am bound up inextricably
With the soul of all of you,
And I love you with infinite love;
I cannot feel otherwise.
All life's loves, small and great,
Are treasured in my love of you,
In my love of all of you,
Each one of you, each individual soul
Is a glowing spark of that torch eternal,
Kindling the light of life for me.
You give meaning to life, to labor,

To learning, to prayer, song and hope;
Through the channel of your being, life pulsates in me;
On the wings of your love I rise to the love of God.
Everything becomes crystal-clear to me, unequivocal,
Like a flame in my heart purifying my thoughts.
With you, O my people, my kin-folk, my mother,
Source of my life,
With you I soar the wide spaces of the world;
In your eternity I have life eternal.
In your glory I am honored, in your sorrow I am grieved,
In your affliction, I suffer anguish,
In your knowledge and understanding,
Behold, I am filled with knowledge and understanding.

ON BEING A JEWISH PERSON

FRANZ ROSENZWEIG

The following excerpt is from an essay (written in January
1920) by which Rosenzweig introduced the concept of an independent house of Jewish studies (*Lehrhaus*). The draft of
Rosenzweig's address at the opening of the *Lehrhaus* is reprinted
elsewhere in the volume ("A New Learning"). On Rosenzweig
see the preface to that chapter.

Books are not now the prime need of the day. But what we need
more than ever, or at least as much as ever, are human beings—
Jewish human beings, to use a catchword that should be cleansed
of the partisan associations still clinging to it.

This term should not be taken in its (ostensibly loose) meaning,
which is actually a very narrow one—it should not be taken in
what I would call the petty-Jewish sense that has been assigned
to it by exclusively political or even exclusively cultural Zionism.
I mean it in a sense that though certainly including Zionism goes
far beyond it. *The Jewish human being*—this does not mean a line
drawn to separate us from other kinds of humanity. No dividing
walls should rise here. A reality that only sheer stubbornness can

deny shows that even within the individual many different spheres can touch or overlap.

Just as Jewishness does not know limitations inside the Jewish individual, so does it not limit that individual himself when he faces the outside world. On the contrary, it makes for his humanity. Strange as it may sound to the obtuse ears of the nationalist, being a Jew is no limiting barrier that cuts the Jew off from someone who is limited by being something else. The Jewish human being finds his limitation not in the Frenchman or German but only in another human being as unlimited as himself: the Christian or heathen. Only against them can he measure himself. Only in them does he find individuals who claim to be and are as all-embracing as himself, above and beyond all divisions of nationality and state, ability and character (for these too divide human beings from one another). His Judaism must, to the Jew, be no less comprehensive, no less all-pervasive, no less universal than Christianity is to the Christian human, or heathenism to the heathen humanist.

But how? Does not this mean the revival of that old song, already played to death a hundred years ago, about Judaism as a "religion," as a "creed," the old expedient of a century that tried to analyze the unity of the Jewish individual tidily into a "religion" for several hundred rabbis and a "creed" for several tens of thousands of respectable citizens? God keep us from putting that old cracked record on again—and was it ever intact? No, what we mean by Judaism, the Jewishness of the Jewish human being, is nothing that can be grasped in a "religious literature" or even in a "religious life." The point is simply that it is no entity, no subject among other subjects, no one sphere of life among other spheres of life; it is not what the century of emancipation with its cultural mania wanted to reduce it to. It is something inside the individual that makes him a Jew, something infinitesimally small yet immeasurably large, his most impenetrable secret, yet evident in every gesture and every word—especially in the most spontaneous of them. The Jewishness I mean is no "literature." It can be grasped through neither the writing nor reading of books. It is only lived—and perhaps not even that. One *is* it.

Notes to "The Dynamics of Emancipation"

INTRODUCTION

1. Hermann Cohen, "Religion und Zionismus," *Jüdische Schriften*, Berlin, 1924, II, p. 323.
2. Edmond Fleg, "The Mission of the Jews," *Second Conference of the World Union for Progressive Judaism*, p. 120.
3. Nathan Rotenstreich, "Judaism in the World of Our Day," *Jews in the Modern World*, ed. by Jacob Fried, New York, 1962, II, p. 562.
4. Alexander Altmann, "Judaism and World Philosophy," *The Jews, Their History, Culture and Religion*, ed. by L. Finkelstein, Philadelphia, 1949, II, p. 662.
5. Salo W. Baron, *A Social and Religious History of the Jews*, New York, 1937, II, pp. 364 f.

I. IN THE PERSPECTIVE OF EMANCIPATION

1. Mr. Moerschel: one of Mendelssohn's critics.
2. Johann Andreas Eisenmenger (1654-1704), German anti-Semitic writer on classical Judaism.
3. Johann Jakob Schudt (1664-1722), Christian orientalist and writer on Jewish folklore.
4. Johannes Buxtorf (1564-1629), Christian Hebraist; his son, Johannes Buxtorf, Jr. (1599-1664), published his father's works and translated Maimonides' *Guide to the Perplexed* and Judah ha-Levi's *Kuzari* into Latin.
5. On Moses Mendelssohn, *see* preface to the chapter "A Definition of Judaism" in this volume.
6. At the beginning of the Second Temple period.
7. Samuel Hirsch (1815-1889), theological writer (*Religionsphilosophie der Juden*, two volumes, 1842) and chief rabbi in Luxemburg (1841-1866), later successor of Rabbi David Einhorn in Philadelphia.
8. Samson Raphael Hirsch (1808-1888), representative of neo-Orthodoxy.
9. Epistle to the Hebrews 10:32-35.
10. Lucien Lévy Bruhl, *Les fonctions mentales dans les sociétés inférieures*, Paris, 1910; *L'âme primitive*, 3rd edition, Paris, 1929.
11. Exodus 4:24-26: "A bloody husband thou art, because of the circumcision."

12. Lévy Bruhl, *Les fonctions mentales, op. cit.*, p. 104.
13. Azriel Carlebach, *Exotische Juden*, Berlin, 1932, p. 117; cf. also p. 244.
14. Paul Ehrlich (1854-1915), German biochemist, discoverer of salvarsan, a cure for syphilis; Nobel Prize winner (1908).
15. Henri Bergson (1859-1941), French philosopher, best known for his *Creative Evolution* and *Duration and Simultaneity*; Nobel Prize winner (1927).
16. The Sassoons: Anglo-Indian family, founded by David ben Sasson (1792-1864); industrialists, philanthropists, and communal leaders.
17. E.g., Genesis 15:13.

II. RETHINKING JEWISH FAITH

1. Refers to Zechariah 14:9.
2. Babli, Baba Batra 12a.
3. Egypt.
4. Babli, Sukkah 53a.
5. Judah ha-Levi (eleventh-twelfth centuries), most famous medieval Hebrew poet and important religious thinker (Spain).
6. Babli, Kiddushin 31a.
7. Midrash Genesis Rabbah I, 5.
8. Refers to Deuteronomy 6:5.
9. Israel Baal Shem Tov (1700-1760), founder of Hasidism.
10. Quotation from a prayer.
11. Nehemiah A. Nobel (1871-1922), rabbi in Frankfurt.
12. Apocrypha, "books outside the Biblical canon." Here applied to all "foreign" literature.
13. "Disciples of the wise"; religious scholars.
14. The *Lehrhaus* courses were divided into three parts: classical, historical, and modern Judaism.
15. *Halakhah*: sections in rabbinic literature dealing with the law.
16. *Haggadah*: extra-legal, ethical, theological, poetic materials.

III. RELIGIOUS MOVEMENTS IN MODERN JUDAISM

1. Moses Maimonides (1135-1204), thinker and legal scholar; author of *Guide to the Perplexed* and *Mishneh Torah*.
2. Joseph Albo (ca. 1380-ca. 1435), religious philosopher (Spain).
3. Divine existence, revelation, and reward and punishment.

4. Philo (first century), philosopher and interpreter of the Bible.
5. *See* H. A. Wolfson, *Philo*, I, Cambridge, Mass., 1947, pp. 146 f.
6. *Contra Apionem* II, 16.
7. *Ibid.*
8. Mishnah Berakhot II, 2.
9. Mishnah Gittin IV, 3.
10. *De Specialibus Legibus* IV, 42.
11. *See* E. R. Goodenough, *The Politics of Philo Judaeus*, New Haven, 1938, pp. 86-90.
12. *De Confusione Linguarum* XXIII.
13. H. A. Wolfson, *Philo*, II, Cambridge, Mass., 1947, pp. 427 f.
14. Samuel Holdheim (1806-1860), rabbi, advocate of extreme reform.
15. An allusion to Malachi 1:11.
16. Traditional interpretation of Leviticus 18:5.
17. Men of the Great Synagogue (or Assembly): According to tradition, a body of sages, established by Ezra in the mid-fifth pre-Christian century, and credited with the founding of post-Biblical Judaism.
18. *See* the preface to the chapter "Conservative Judaism" in the present section of the book.

IV. THE DARK YEARS

1. Day of a violent boycott of Jewish businesses.
2. *See* chapter "The Jewish State" in this volume.
3. From the prayerbook.
4. The reference is to Exodus 3:6. In Jewish tradition, *Elohim* is the name of God denoting the attribute of judgment (while the name YHVH denotes mercy).
5. Babli, Shabbat 88a.
6. Trajan ruled 98-117.
7. Memorbuch: memorial books kept by medieval Jewish communities; they recorded important events and names of distinguished scholars and, especially, persecutions and their victims.
8. Compare *The Forty Days of Musa Dagh*, by Franz Werfel, on the self-defense of the Armenians.
9. An allusion to Samson, Judges 16:30.
10. *Jüdische Rundschau* 1946, No. 6.
11. At this point the author discusses the relative merits of Jewish culture in the Land of Israel and in America.
12. Bogdan Chmielnicki (ca. 1593-1657) led the Cossacks in revolts against Poles and in the persecution of the Polish Jews in 1648-1649.

13. Simon Petlura (or Petlyura) headed the pogroms in the Ukraine in 1919.

14. Heinrich Himmler (1900-1945), Nazi leader; from 1936, chief of the secret police (Gestapo). Captured by the British, he committed suicide.

15. Alfred Rosenberg (1893-1946), from 1941 minister of occupied lands in Eastern Europe, was condemned by the International Military Tribunal at Nuremberg and executed.

16. *See* the text in the present section of the book.

17. Vidkun Quisling, Norwegian politician who collaborated in the German conquest of Norway in 1940.

18. Babli, Erubin 19a.

19. Bertold Brecht (1898-1956), German playwright.

20. Franz Kafka (1883-1924), German-Jewish writer.

21. *See* the preceding chapter in this section of the book.

22. Lord Walter E. Moyne (1880-1944), British Minister Resident in Cairo; he was assassinated by two members of the terrorist Stern Group, in an outrage against the restrictive British policy in Palestine.

23. *See* the chapter "On the Agenda: Death" in this section of the book.

24. Sayings of the Fathers II, 5 (Hillel).

V. ZIONISM AND THE LAND OF ISRAEL

1. Muhammad Ali (1769-1849) was from 1805 to 1848 Viceroy of Egypt, which at the time controlled Palestine.

2. Genesis 12:3.

3. Gotthold Ephraim Lessing (1729-1781), German dramatist; friend of Moses Mendelssohn. *Nathan the Wise* (1779) is a drama on toleration.

4. The reference is to the efforts of Baron Maurice de Hirsch (1831-1896), the financier and railroad builder. He had founded the Jewish Colonization Association (ICA) in 1891, and given it an endowment, to resettle impoverished emigrants from Eastern Europe in North and South America. Its most important single endeavor was in Argentina, where a large tract of land had been purchased for agricultural settlement.

5. Abdul-Hamid II (1842-1918) was Sultan 1876-1909.

6. Babli, Berakhot 35b.

7. A party (founded in 1901) representing religious Zionism within the framework of the Zionist movement.

8. Arabic riots against Jewish settlements in Palestine and massacres of about one hundred and thirty Jews.

9. At the conference at Kattowitz (Poland) in 1884 the *Hoveve Zion*

(Lovers of Zion) groups met to discuss organizational plans and the colonization of Palestine. Its leading figure was Leo Pinsker (*see* preface to "Auto-Emancipation").

10. *See* Theodor Herzl's opening address at the first Zionist Congress in this section of the book.

11. Statement issued (November 2, 1917) by Arthur James Balfour, British Foreign Secretary, to the effect that "the British government favors the establishment in Palestine of a national home for the Jewish people." Other governments approved the declaration; it was incorporated in the British mandate for Palestine in 1922.

12. Bilu: movement of the first Zionist settlers in Palestine in 1882-1883.

13. The *Asefat ha-Nivharim*, "Representative Assembly" of the Jewish community in Palestine under the British mandate first met in 1920.

14. The *Vaad Leumi* (National Council) of thirty-six members was elected to represent the Palestinian Jewish Community.

15. Gideon, one of the judges in the pre-monarchal period of ancient Israel, in response to his contemporaries who proposed to institute kingship (Judges 8:22 f.).

16. Dag Hammarskjold, United Nations Secretary General, 1952-1961; killed in 1961 in a plane crash in central Africa.

VI. THE AMERICAN SCENE

1. Ahad Ha-Am (1856-1927), Hebrew writer of the Jewish national renaissance and of cultural Zionism. His collected essays were published as *Al Parashat Derakhim* (*At the Crossroads*). In English: Leon Simon, *Ahad Ha-Am: A Biography*, Philadelphia, 1960; Hans Kohn, ed., *Nationalism and the Jewish Ethic: Basic Writings of Ahad Ha'am*, New York, 1962.

2. Israel Zangwill (1864-1926), English writer, best known for his *Children of the Ghetto* (1892).

3. I.e., Judaism.

4. Israel Baal Shem Tov (1700-1760), founder of Hasidism.

5. Rashi (Rabbi Shelomo ben Yitzhak), eleventh century classical commentator of Bible and Talmud (France-Germany).

6. Judah ha-Levi (eleventh-twelfth centuries), most famous medieval Hebrew poet and important religious thinker (Spain).

7. Philo (first century), Alexandrian philosopher and interpreter of the Bible.

8. Ezra the Scribe (fifth century B.C.), leader and religious reformer; one of the founders of post-Biblical Judaism.

9. William J. Bryan (1860-1925), American lawyer and political leader.

U.S. Secretary of State (1913-1915). Edited the weekly *Commoner*.
10. Akiba: one of the great teachers of the second century Palestine; died as martyr.
11. Paul Valéry (1871-1945), French poet and philosopher.
12. On M. Buber, *see* preface to the chapter "God and Man" in this volume.
13. State of Israel.
14. Thomas B. Macaulay (1800-1859), English statesman and historian, author of *History of England* (1848-1861).
15. Gabriel Riesser (1806-1863), fighter for emancipation of Jews in Germany; member of the Frankfurt parliament (1848).
16. Ernst Haeckel (1834-1919), German biologist; advocate of organic evolution and a monistic philosophy.
17. Henry Thomas Buckle (1821-1862), English historian.
18. Julius Wellhausen (1844-1918), German Protestant historian of ancient Israel.
19. Adolf von Harnack (1851-1930), German Protestant theologian.
20. Bundism: Jewish Socialist movement in Eastern Europe, founded in 1897; it opposed Zionism and cultivated Yiddish language and literature.
21. Rambam: Moses Maimonides (1135-1204), thinker and legal scholar; author of *Guide to the Perplexed* and *Mishneh Torah*.
22. *See* Note 5.
23. Meir of Rothenburg (1220-1293), rabbinic authority (Germany).
24. *See* Note 4.
25. Elijah of Vilna ("The Vilna Gaon," 1720-1797), rabbinic authority (Eastern Europe).
26. Gilbert Murray (1866-1957), British classical scholar.
27. *See* Note 14.
28. Tomas de Torquemada (ca. 1420-1498), Dominican monk; organized the Inquisition in Spain.
29. John of Capistrano (1386-1456), Franciscan monk and papal inquisitor.
30. *Merchant of Venice*, I, III.

VII. ALLOWING THE HEART TO SPEAK

1. Messalina: wife of Emperor Claudius; notorious in Rome for her profligacy.
2. "Ye shall hallow the fiftieth year, and proclaim liberty unto all the inhabitants thereof; it shall be a jubilee unto you; and ye shall return

every man unto his possession, and ye shall return every man unto his family" (Leviticus 25:10).

3. Exodus 21:6.
4. Charles B. Renouvier (1815-1903), French idealistic philosopher and leader in neocriticism.
5. Elijah Benamozegh, *Israel et l'Humanité. Introduction*, Livorno, 1885. Complete edition, by A. Pallière, Paris, 1914.
6. Exodus 20:10.
7. Walter Rathenau (1867-1922), author of works on politics and humanist philosophy; minister of reconstruction in the Weimar Republic (1921); victim of assassination.
8. An allusion to Amos 7:14 f.
9. Galatians 5:14, with reference to Leviticus 19:18.
10. I Corinthians 13:1-3

Sources and Acknowledgments for "The Dynamics of Emancipation"

THANKS are due to the authors and publishers referred to in the list which follows, for permission to include in this volume material copyrighted in their name.

I

A DEFINITION OF JUDAISM: Moses Mendelssohn, *Jerusalem*, Section II. Translated by Alfred Jospe. *Judaism* XII, 4, Fall 1963, pp. 477 f. Copyright 1963, by the American Jewish Congress and used by Dr. Jospe's and the publisher's permission.

THE JEWISH COMMUNITY AND THE STATE: DOCTRINAL DECISIONS OF THE GRAND SANHEDRIN: A. E. Halphen, ed., *Recueil des lois, décrets, ordonnances . . . concernant des Israélites*, Paris, 1851, pp. 20 f. Tr. by Maurice Samuel in E. Fleg, *The Jewish Anthology*, New York, 1925, pp. 255 f. Copyright 1925, by Harcourt, Brace and Company and used by their permission.

SCHOLARSHIP AND EMANCIPATION: Leopold Zunz, *Die gottesdienstlichen Vorträge der Juden*, Berlin, 1832, introduction. Tr. by Harry Zohn for the present volume.

THE HEBREWS AND THE GREEKS: Heinrich Graetz, *History of the Jews*, Philadelphia, 1895, Vol. V, *Retrospect* (abridged). Copyright 1895, by The Jewish Publication Society.

ISRAEL WITHIN THE ORGANISM OF HUMANITY: Moses Hess, *Rome and Jerusalem*, tr. by M. Waxman, New York, 1918, pp. 105-112. Copyright 1918, by Bloch Publishing Company and used by their permission.

AUTO-EMANCIPATION: Leo Pinsker, *Auto-Emancipation*, tr. by D. S. Blondheim, New York, 1906. By permission of the Zionist Organization of America.

EMANCIPATION: James Darmesteter, from "An Essay on the History of the Jews," in *Selected Essays*, tr. from the French by Helen B. Jastrow, Boston–New York, 1895, pp. 241-276. Copyright 1895, by Houghton, Mifflin and Company.

EMANCIPATION AND JUDAISM: Samson Raphael Hirsch, *Nineteen Letters of Ben Uziel*, tr. by Bernard Drachman, New York, 1942, pp. 159-168. Copyright 1942, by Bloch Publishing Co. and used by their permission.

A SPIRITUAL NATION: Simon Dubnov, from *Jewish History: An Essay in the Philosophy of History*, in *Nationalism and History*, ed. K. S. Pinson, Philadelphia, 1958, pp. 322-324. Copyright © 1958 by The Jewish Publication Society and used by the Society's permission.

WHAT ARE THE JEWS?: Erich Kahler, from "Forms and Features of Anti-Judaism," *Social Research* VI, 1939, pp. 484-488. By permission of Professor Kahler and *Social Research*.

JACOB-ISRAEL AND THE WORLD: Yitzhak Lamdan, from "For the Sun Declined," tr. by Simon Halkin, in Halkin, *Modern Hebrew Literature*, New York, 1950, p. 164. Copyright 1950, by Schocken Books, Inc. and used by their permission.

II

JUDAISM AND MANKIND: Abraham Geiger, *Judaism and Its History*, tr. by Charles Newburgh, New York, 1911, pp. 381 f.

FAITH: Thoughts of A. I. Kook, selected from Jacob B. Agus, *Banner of Jerusalem*, New York, 1946, and Herbert Weiner, "The Teachings of Rav Kook," *Commentary* XVII, 5, 1954. By permission of the authors and of the American Jewish Committee.

THE VOICE OF JACOB: Richard Beer-Hofmann, *Jacob's Dream*, tr. by I. B. Wynn: New York, 1946, pp. 156 f. Copyright 1945, by Richard Beer-Hofmann. By permission of the Beer-Hofmann estate and The Jewish Publication Society.

A MINORITY RELIGION: Leo Baeck, *The Essence of Judaism*, New York, 1948, pp. 272-275. Copyright 1948, by Schocken Books, Inc. and used by their permission.

THOU SHALT: Leo Baeck, from "Why Jews in the World?" *Commentary* III, 6, 1947, pp. 503 f. By permission of the American Jewish Committee.

GOD AND MAN: Martin Buber, "The Two Foci of the Jewish Soul" (abridged). *Israel and the World*, New York, 1948, pp. 30-35, and 38 f. Copyright 1948, by Schocken Books, Inc. and used by their permission.

A NEW LEARNING: from *Franz Rosenzweig: His Life and Thought*, ed. by N. N. Glatzer, New York, 1953, pp. 228-234. Copyright 1953, by Schocken Books, Inc. and used by their permission.

III

A DEMOCRATIC THEOCRACY: Samuel Belkin, *In His Image*, London-New York-Toronto, 1960, introduction. © 1960, by Samuel Belkin. By permission of the author and Abelard-Schuman Limited.

THE NEED FOR REFORM: Samuel Hirsch, *Die Reform im Judenthum*, Berlin, 1844, pp. 67-69; tr. in D. Philipson, *The Reform Movement in Judaism*, New York, 1931, pp. 351 ff. Copyright 1907 and 1931, by The Macmillan Company.

NECESSITY OF CHANGE: Appeal by Berlin Reformers, 1845, quoted in D. Philipson, *op. cit.*, pp. 231-234. *See* the preceding item.

INTELLIGENT RELIGION: Isaac Mayer Wise, quoted in D. Philipson, *op. cit.*, pp. 342 ff. *See* the two preceding items.

CONSERVATIVE JUDAISM: Alexander Kohut, *The Ethics of the Fathers*, New York, 1920, pp. 3, 14-17, 48 (selected).

CREATIVE JUDAISM: Mordecai M. Kaplan, *Judaism as a Civilization*, New York, 1934, Chapter XXXII, abridged. Copyright © 1934, by The Macmillan Company and Copyright © 1957, by the Jewish Reconstructionist Foundation, Inc. By permission of Professor Kaplan.

TOWARDS A KINGDOM OF PRIESTS: Louis Finkelstein, "The Good Life," *United Synagogue Review*, 1955. By permission of Dr. Finkelstein.

IV

WEAR THE YELLOW BADGE WITH PRIDE: Robert Weltsch, in *Jüdische Rundschau*, Berlin, April 4, 1933; tr. by Harry Zohn for the present volume. By permission of Dr. Weltsch.

A PRAYER BEFORE KOL NIDRE, Germany, 1935: Leo Baeck, quoted in *Mitteilungsblatt*, Irgun Olej Merkas Europa, Tel Aviv, May 19, 1961, p. 8; tr. by the editor.

THE MEANING OF THIS HOUR: *Between God and Man: From the Writings of Abraham J. Heschel*, ed. by F. A. Rothschild, New York, 1959, pp. 255-258. Copyright © 1959, by F. A. Rothschild. By permission of Professor Heschel, Dr. Rothschild and Harper & Row, Inc.

THE SLAIN IN THE VALLEY OF DEATH: Judah L. Magnes, *In the Perplexity of the Times*, Jerusalem, 1946, pp. 139 f. By permission of the Magnes Press, Jerusalem.

IF GOD LETS ME LIVE: *Anne Frank: The Diary of a Young Girl*,

V

On Zionism, the Land of Israel, and the Arabs: Albert Einstein, *About Zionism: Speeches and Letters*; ed. by Leon Simon, New York, 1931, pp. 76-81 and 85 ff. Copyright 1931, by The Macmillan Company and used by their permission.

The Zionist Declaration of Independence: Quoted in J. Ben-Jacob, *The Rise of Israel*, New York, 1959, pp. 180 f. Copyright 1949, by Jeremiah Ben-Jacob and used by his permission.

The State of Israel, Opening Address by Chaim Weizman: Quoted in Ben-Jacob, *op. cit.*, pp. 196-199. *See* the preceding item.

Statements on the Arab Refugee Problem, by Martin Buber and David Ben-Gurion: *Ner* XIII, 1-2, 1961, pp. II-IV. By permission of the Ihud Association.

Towards a New World: David Ben-Gurion, *Israel: Years of Challenge*, New York, 1963, pp. 231-240. Copyright © 1963, by Massadah-P.E.C. Press Ltd. By permission of Holt, Rinehart and Winston.

Israel: Karl Shapiro, *Poems 1940-1953*, New York, 1953, p. 87. Copyright 1940 to 1953, by Karl Shapiro. By permission of Professor Shapiro and Random House.

VI

A Call to the Educated Jew: *Brandeis on Zionism: A Collection of Addresses and Statements*, ed. by Solomon Goldman, Washington, D. C., 1942, pp. 59-69. Copyright 1942, by the Zionist Organization of America and used by its permission.

A Letter to Henry Ford: *Louis Marshall, Champion of Liberty: Selected Papers and Addresses*, ed. by Charles Reznikoff, Philadelphia, 1957, I, pp. 379 f. Copyright © 1957, by The American Jewish Committee and The Jewish Publication Society and used by their permission.

The American Jew in Our Day: Waldo Frank, *The Jew in Our Day*, New York, 1944, pp. 141-153. Copyright 1944, by Waldo Frank. By permission of Mr. Frank and of Duell, Sloan and Pearce.

Re-Examination: Ludwig Lewisohn, *The American Jew: Character and Destiny*, New York, 1950, pp. 1-15. Copyright 1950, by Ludwig Lewisohn. By permission of Mrs. Ludwig Lewisohn and Farrar, Straus and Giroux.

Patterns of Survival: Salo W. Baron, from "The Modern Age,"

Great Ages and Ideas of the Jewish People, ed. by Leo W. Schwarz, New York, 1956, pp. 481-484. Copyright 1956, by Random House and used by its permission.

THE AMERICAN COUNCIL FOR JUDAISM: Elmer Berger, *Judaism or Jewish Nationalism: The Alternative to Zionism*, New York, 1957, pp. 28-31. Copyright 1957, by Elmer Berger and used by his permission.

SUFFERANCE IS THE BADGE: Abram L. Sachar, *Sufferance is the Badge*, New York-London, 1939, pp. 578-580. Copyright 1939, by Alfred A. Knopf, Inc. By permission of Dr. Sachar and Alfred A. Knopf.

WHY I CHOOSE TO BE A JEW: Arthur A. Cohen, "Why I Choose to be a Jew," *Harper's Magazine*, April, 1959. Copyright 1959, by Harper & Row, Inc. and used by Mr. Cohen's permission.

THE ISSUE IS SILENCE: Joachim Prinz, broadsheet issued by the American Jewish Congress, 1963. By permission of Dr. Prinz.

VII

THE REAWAKENING OF MY RELIGIOUS FEELINGS: Henrich Heine, Confessions, quoted in *Heinrich Heine: A Biographical Anthology*, ed. by Hugo Bieber, Philadelphia, 1956, pp. 432-437. Copyright © 1956, by The Jewish Publication Society and used by its permission.

JOB'S DUNGHEAP: Barnard Lazare, *Job's Dungheap: Essays on Jewish Nationalism and Social Revolution*, tr. by H. L. Binsse, New York, 1948, pp. 41-47. Copyright 1948, by Schocken Books, Inc. and used by their permission.

A CONFESSION OF MY FAITH: Aimé Pallière, *The Unknown Sanctuary: A Pilgrimage from Rome to Israel*, tr. by Louise W. Wise, New York, 1928, pp. 233-243. Copyright 1928, by Bloch Publishing Co. and used by their permission.

THE ROAD HOME: Nathan Birnbaum, in Confession ("Jewish Pocket Books"), New York, 1946, pp. 12-17. By permission of the Spero Foundation and Agudath Israel of America.

LULLABY FOR MIRIAM: Richard Beer-Hofmann, tr. by Sol Liptzin, *Poet Lore*, Winter, 1941; by permission of Mrs. Miriam B.-H. Lens and Professor Liptzin.

ALL IN VAIN: Jacob Wassermann, *My Life as German and Jew*, tr. by S. N. Brainin, New York, 1933, pp. 226 f. Copyright 1933, by

Jacob Wassermann. By permission of Putnam's and Coward-McCann.

BEFORE THE STATUE OF APOLLO: Saul Tchernichovsky, English version by Maurice Samuel, *The Menorah Journal* IX, 1, 1923, pp. 21 ff.

CREDO: *Vision: A Biography of Harry Friedenwald*, by Alexandra Lee Levin, Philadelphia, 1964, pp. 414 f. Copyright © 1964, by The Jewish Publication Society and used by its permission.

OF THE JEWISH RELIGION: Albert Einstein, *The World as I See It*, New York, 1934, pp. 143-146. Copyright 1934, by Cowici, Friede, Inc. and used by permission of the Estate of Albert Einstein.

WHAT I BELIEVE: Sholem Asch, *What I Believe*, tr. by Maurice Samuel, New York, 1941. Copyright © 1941, 1969 by Ruth Shaffer, Moses Asch, John Asch and the representative of Nathan Asch.

HIS FATHER'S JUDAISM: Franz Kafka, *Dearest Father: Stories and Other Writings*, tr. by E. Kaiser and E. Wilkins, New York, 1954, pp. 171-176. Copyright 1954, by Schocken Books, Inc. and used by their permission.

WHY I AM A JEW: Edmond Fleg, *Why I am a Jew*, tr. by Victor Gollancz, London, 1943. By permission of Victor Gollancz, Ltd.

THE AIR AND EARTH OF VITEBSK: Marc Chagall, quoted in *Hadassah Magazine*, March, 1962. By permission of Hadassah, The Women's Zionist Organization of America, Inc.

I LIVE IN YOU, IN EACH OF YOU: Abraham Isaac Kook, tr. by Morris Silverman for the *Sabbath and Festival Prayer Book*, New York, 1946, pp. 284 ff. Copyright 1946, by the United Synagogue of America and the Rabbinical Assembly of America (distributed by Prayer Book Press, Hartford, Connecticut) and used by their permission.

ON BEING A JEWISH PERSON: Franz Rosenzweig, *Kleinere Schriften*, Berlin, 1937, pp. 79-82 ("Bildung und kein Ende," beginning). Tr. in N N. Glatzer, *Franz Rosenzweig: His Life and Thought*, New York, 1953, pp. 214 ff. Copyright 1953, by Schocken Books, Inc. and used by their permission.

Suggestions for Further Reading

PART ONE: *The Rest Is Commentary*

Good historical introductions to the period as a whole or to major parts of it are Salo W. Baron, *A Social and Religious History of the Jews* ("Ancient Times," Vol. I-II, 2d ed., New York: Columbia University Press, 1952); Robert H. Pfeiffer, *History of New Testament Times* (New York, 1949); and Emil Schürer, *The Jewish People in the Time of Jesus Christ* (New York, 1961).

For information on post-Biblical Apocrypha, see the notes to the English translation of *The Apocrypha and Pseudepigrapha of the Old Testament,* edited by R. H. Charles, 2 vols. (Oxford, 1913); Charles Cutler Torrey, *The Apocryphal Literature* (New Haven, 1945); Bruce M. Metzger, *An Introduction to the Apocrypha* (New York, 1957), and the second part of Pfeiffer's *History of New Testament Times.*

Hellenism and Hellenistic Judaism are discussed in Victor Tcherikover, *Hellenistic Civilization and the Jews* (Philadelphia, 1959); Moses Hadas, *Hellenistic Culture* (New York, 1959); Erwin R. Goodenough, *By Light, Light: The Mystic Gospel of Hellenistic Judaism* (New Haven, 1935); Hans Jonas, *The Gnostic Religion* (Boston: Beacon Press, 1958); Elias Bickerman, *The Maccabees* (New York: Schocken Books, 1947); Harry A. Wolfson, *Philo: Foundations of Religious Philosophy in Judaism, Christianity and Islam,* 2 vols. (Cambridge: Harvard University Press, 1947), a classical study of Philo's position in the history of thought; H. St. J. Thackeray, *Josephus the Man and the Historian* (New York, 1929); N. N. Glatzer, *Jerusalem and Rome: From the Writings of Josephus* (New York, 1960).

The Dead Sea (Qumran) brotherhood is surveyed by Millar Burrows, *The Dead Sea Scrolls* (New York, 1955), and *More Light on the Dead Sea Scrolls* (New York, 1958); Frank Moore

Cross, Jr., *The Ancient Library of Qumran* (New York, 1958); *The Scrolls and the New Testament* (a collection of scholarly essays), edited by Krister Stendahl (New York, 1957); *The Dead Sea Scriptures,* trans. by Theodore H. Gaster (New York, 1956).

On Pharisaism, Talmud and Midrash: George Foot Moore, *Judaism in the First Centuries of the Christian Era,* 3 vols. (Cambridge, Mass., 1927–1930); Solomon Zeitlin, *The Sadducees and the Pharisees* (Philadelphia, 1937); Gerson D. Cohen, "The Talmudic Age," *Great Ages and Ideas of the Jewish People* (New York, 1956); N. N. Glatzer, *Hillel the Elder: The Emergence of Classical Judaism* (Washington, 1959); *The Living Talmud,* ed. by Judah Goldin (New York, 1957).

Supplementary material may be found in Elias Bickerman, *From Ezra to the Last of the Maccabees: Greek Foundations of Post-Biblical Judaism* (New York, 1962); G. R. Driver, *The Judaean Scrolls: The Problem and a Solution* (New York, 1965); Shalom Spiegel, *The Last Trial* (on the legends and lore of the command to Abraham to offer Isaac as a sacrifice), (New York, 1968); Solomon Zeitlin, *The Rise and Fall of the Judaean State,* 2 vols. (Philadelphia, 1962, 1967).

PART TWO: *Faith and Knowledge*

(PB: *available in a paperback edition;* JPS: *The Jewish Publication Society*)

A comprehensive treatment of the history of the period is Salo W. Baron, *A Social and Religious History of the Jews* ("High Middle Ages, 500–1200," Vol. III-VIII, 2d ed., New York: Columbia University Press, 1957–58); briefer presentations are Solomon Grayzel, *A History of the Jews* (Philadelphia, JPS, 1947); and Cecil Roth, *A History of the Jews* (New York: Schocken Books, 1961, PB).

Good regional histories are: James Parkes, *A History of Palestine* (New York: Oxford University Press, 1949); Cecil Roth, *The History of the Jews of Italy* (Philadelphia, JPS, 1946); A. Neuman, *The Jews in Spain* (Philadelphia, JPS, 1948); Yitzhak Baer, *A History of the Jews in Christian Spain,* vol. I (Philadelphia, JPS, 1961); Cecil Roth, *The Jews in the Renaissance* (Philadelphia, JPS, 1959), and *A History of the Marranos* (Philadelphia, JPS, 1959, PB); Albert M. Hyamson, *A History of the Jews in England* (London: Methuen, 1928); and Simon Dubnov, *History of the Jews in Russia and Poland,* vol. I (Philadelphia, JPS, 1916).

The Jewish society and community life is discussed in Salo W. Baron, *The Jewish Community* (Philadelphia, JPS, 1942); Israel Abrahams, *Jewish Life in the Middle Ages* (London: Goldston, 1932); Jacob Katz, *Tradition and Crisis: Jewish Society at the End of the Middle Ages* (New York: The Free Press of Glencoe, 1961); and *Exclusiveness and Tolerance, Studies in Jewish-Gentile Relations in Medieval and Modern Times, Scripta Judaica III* (Oxford University Press, 1961, Schocken Books, 1962, PB).

Trends in Jewish thought are analyzed in Isaac Husik, *A History of Medieval Jewish Philosophy* (Philadelphia, JPS, 1958, PB); Alexander Altmann, "Judaism and World Philosophy," *The Jews: Their History, Culture, and Religion,* ed. L. Finkelstein, II (Philadelphia, JPS, 1949); Gerschom G. Scholem, *Major Trends in Jewish Mysticism* (New York: Schocken Books, 1961, PB); Abraham J. Heschel, "The Mystical Element in Judaism," *The Jews* II, *op. cit.;* A. H. Silver, *A History of Messianic Speculation in Israel* (Boston: Beacon Press, 1960, PB); Jacob B. Agus, *The Evolution of Jewish Thought* (London-New York: Abelard-Schuman, 1959); Shalom Spiegel, "On Medieval Hebrew Poetry," *The Jews* II, *op. cit.;* and various essays in *The Legacy of Israel,* ed. I. Abrahams and Charles Singer (Oxford: Clarendon Press, 1928).

Other collections of source material are Jacob R. Marcus, *The Jew in the Medieval World* (Philadelphia, JPS, 1960, PB); Franz Kobler, *A Treasury of Jewish Letters* (Philadelphia, JPS, 1954); Leo W. Schwarz, *Memoirs of My People* (Philadelphia, JPS, 1945, Schocken Books, 1963, PB); and N. N. Glatzer, *A Jewish Reader: In Time and Eternity* (New York: Schocken Books, 1961, PB).

Supplementary material may be found in Yitzhak Baer, *A History of the Jews in Christian Spain,* vol. II (Philadelphia, 1966); Salo W. Baron, *History and Historians* (Chapters on Maimonides and Azariah de'Rossi), (Philadelphia, 1964); Julius

Guttmann, *Philosophies of Judaism* (Philadelphia, 1964); Joachim Prinz, *Popes from the Ghetto: A View of Medieval Christendom* (New York, 1966); Gershom G. Scholem, *On the Kabbalah and its Symbolism* (New York, 1965).

PART THREE: *The Dynamics of Emancipation*

The general background to the modern period offer Salo W. Baron, *A Social and Religious History of the Jews,* Vol. II (New York, 1937); I. Elbogen, *A Century of Jewish Life* (Philadelphia, 1944); U. Z. Engelman, *The Rise of the Jew in the Western World* (New York, 1944); Jacob Fried, ed., *Jews in the Modern World,* two vols. (New York, 1962); Solomon Grayzel, *A History of the Contemporary Jews* (Philadelphia, 1960, PB); Arthur Ruppin, *The Jews in the Modern World* (London, 1934); Howard M. Sachar, *The Course of Modern Jewish History* (Cleveland, 1958).

On emancipation, assimilation, anti-Semitism, and national revival: Salo W. Baron, "Ghetto and Emancipation," *Menorah Journal* XIV (1928), pp. 515–526; Simon Dubnov, *Nationalism and History,* ed. K. Pinson (Philadelphia, 1958, PB); Paul Goodman, *Moses Montefiore* (Philadelphia, 1925); Hans Kohn, "The Jew Enters Western Culture," *Menorah Journal* XVIII (1930), pp. 291–302; Gustav Mayer, "Early German Socialism and Jewish Emancipation," *Jewish Social Studies* I (1939), pp. 409–422; Moses Mendelssohn, *Jerusalem: A Treatise on Ecclesiastical Authority and Judaism* (London, 1838); M. F. Modder, "The Jew in the English Literature of the Nineteenth Century," *Menorah Journal,* XXIII (1935), pp. 46–56; James Parkes, *Enemy of the People: Anti-Semitism* (New York, 1946); Polly Pinsker, "English Opinion and Jewish Emancipation," *Jewish Social Studies* XIV (1952), pp. 51–94; A. L. Sachar, *Sufferance is the Badge* (New York, 1940); Maurice Samuel, *The Great Hatred* (New York, 1940); Werner Sombart, *The Jews and Modern Capitalism* (London, 1913); Thorstein Veblen, "The Intellectual Pre-eminence of Jews in Modern Europe," *Political Science Quarterly* (March 1919); Hermann Walter, *Moses Mendelssohn* (New York, 1930).

Modern Jewish thought is presented in: Alexander Altmann, "Theology in Twentieth Century German Jewry," *Year Book I,*

Leo Baeck Institute (London, 1956); Samuel Belkin, *In His Image* (London-New York-Toronto, 1960); S. H. Bergman, *Faith and Reason* (New York, 1963, PB); Arthur A. Cohen, *The Natural and the Supernatural Jew* (New York, 1962); Ira Eisenstein and Eugene Kohn, ed., *Mordecai M. Kaplan: An Evaluation* (New York, 1952); Maurice S. Friedman, *Martin Buber: The Life of Dialogue* (Chicago, 1955); N. N. Glatzer, *Franz Rosenzweig, His Life and Thought* (New York, 1961, PB); Hayim Greenberg, *The Inner Eye: Selected Essays* (New York, 1953); Hayim Greenberg, *The Inner Eye*, Volume Two (New York, 1964); Abraham J. Heschel, *God in Search of Men* (New York, 1955); Alfred Jospe, ed., *The Jewish Heritage and the Jewish Student* (Washington, 1959); Leo Jung, ed., *Guardians of Our Heritage* (New York, 1958); Horace M. Kallen, "Of Them Which Say They Are Jews," ed. Judah Pilch (New York, 1954); M. M. Kaplan, *The Purpose and Meaning of Jewish Existence* (Philadelphia, 1964); Simon Noveck, ed., *Contemporary Jewish Thought: A Reader* (Washington, 1963); Simon Noveck, ed., *Great Jewish Thinkers of the Twentieth Century* (Washington, 1963); Leon Roth, *Judaism: A Portrait* (New York, 1961); Max Wiener, *Abraham Geiger and Liberal Judaism* (Philadelphia, 1962).

Religious trends and developments are analyzed in: Jacob B. Agus, *The Meaning of Jewish History, Vol. II* (London-New York-Toronto, 1963); Moshe Davis, *The Emergence of Conservative Judaism* (Philadelphia, 1963); Robert Gordis, *Judaism for the Modern Age* (New York, 1955); Will Herberg, *Protestant, Catholic, Jew* (New York, 1955); Mordecai M. Kaplan, *Judaism as a Civilization* (New York, 1934); David Philipson, *The Reform Movement in Judaism* (New York, 1907; rev. ed., 1931); W. Gunther Plaut, *The Rise of Reform Judaism* (New York, 1963); Marshall Sklare, *Conservative Judaism* (Glencoe, Illinois, 1955).

The holocaust and Jewish resistance under the Nazis is dealt with in: Philip Friedman, *Martyrs and Fighters: An Epic of the Warsaw Ghetto* (New York, 1954); John Hersey, *The Wall* (New York, 1951); Leon Poliakov, *Harvest of Hate* (Philadelphia, 1954); Emmanuel Ringelblum, *Notes from the Warsaw Ghetto*, tr. and ed. by Jacob Sloan (New York, 1958); Leo W. Schwarz, *The Redeemers: A Saga of the Years 1945–1952* (New York, 1953);

Marie Syrkin, *Blessed Is the Match* (New York, 1947); Joseph
Tenenbaum, *Underground: The Story of a People* (New York,
1952).

On Zionism, Hebrew renaissance, the land of Israel and the
state: Alex Bein, *Theodor Herzl: A Biography* (Philadelphia,
1956, PB); Abba Eban, *Voice of Israel* (New York, 1957); J.
Garcia-Granados, *The Birth of Israel* (New York, 1949); Benjamin Halpern, *The Idea of the Jewish State* (Cambridge, Mass.,
1961); Joseph Heller, *The Zionist Idea* (New York, 1949); Arthur
J. Hertzberg, *The Zionist Idea* (New York, 1959); Alfred Jospe
and Daniel Thursz, ed., *Israel as Idea and Reality* (Washington,
n.d.); Abraham Revusky, *Jews in Palestine* (New York, 1935);
Leon Simon, *Ahad Ha'am: A Biography* (Philadelphia, 1960);
Shalom Spiegel, *Hebrew Reborn* (Philadelphia, 1962, PB); Melford E. Spiro, *Kibbutz* (New York, 1963, PB); Chaim Weizman,
Trial and Error: An Autobiography (Philadelphia, 1949).

The American scene is surveyed by: Jacob B. Agus, *Guide-
posts in Modern Judaism* (New York, 1954); Leslie A. Fiedler,
The Jew in the American Novel (New York, 1958, PB); Lee M.
Friedman, *Pilgrims in a New Land* (Philadelphia, 1948); Eli
Ginzberg, *Agenda for American Jews* (New York, 1950); Nathan
Glazer, *American Judaism* (Chicago, 1957); Oscar Handlin, *Ad-
venture in Freedom* (New York, 1954); Oscar Janowsky, ed.,
The American Jew: A Reappraisal (Philadelphia, 1964); Mor-
decai M. Kaplan, *The Future of the American Jew* (New York,
1948); Israel H. Levinthal, *Point of View: An Analysis of Ameri-
can Judaism* (London-New York, 1958); Ludwig Lewisohn, *The
American Jew* (New York, 1950).

Supplementary material may be found in Martin Buber,
On Judaism (New York, 1967); Gerson D. Cohen, ed., *Sefer ha-
Qabbalah: The Book of Tradition* by Abraham ibn Daud (Phil-
adelphia, 1967); Ira Eisenstein, *Varieties of Jewish Belief* (New
York, 1966); Arthur Hertzberg, *The French Enlightenment and
the Jews* (Philadelphia, 1968); Milton Himmelfarb, *The Condi-
tion of Jewish Belief* (New York, 1966); Irving Malin and Irwin
Stark, *Breakthrough: a Treasury of Contemporary American-
Jewish Literature* (Philadelphia, 1963); Mordecai M. Kaplan,
A New Zionism (New York, 1965); Walter Laqueur, *The Road*

to *Jerusalem* (New York, 1968); Michael A. Meyer, *The Origins of the Modern Jew* (Detroit, 1967); Jacob Robinson, *And the Crooked Shall be Made Straight* (a new look at the Eichmann Trial), (Philadelphia, 1965); Nathan Rotenstreich, *Jewish Philosophy in Modern Times* (New York, 1968); Melford E. Spiro, *Children of the Kibbutz* (New York, 1965); Elie Wiesel, *Legends of Our Time* (New York, 1968).

Index

Aaron, priest, 3, 76f., 193, 211, 234
Abba, 296, 420
Abba Saul, 431
Abnimos the weaver, 231
Abot (Fathers), 19
Abrabanel, Isaac, 299
Abrabanel, Judah (Leone Ebreo), 299–303
Abraham, 21, 51, 67, 101, 138, 161, 240ff., 294, 296, 311, 313f., 388f., 395f., 414, 454, 464, 469, 472, 587, 662, 749, 752, 787
Abraham bar Hiyya, 273
Abraham el Constantin, 462
Abraham ibn Ezra, 273, 277, 327
Absalom's Hand, 461
Abulafia, Abraham, 424, 427
Academy for Jewish Research (Berlin), 554, 560
Adam, 115f., 160ff., 173, 206f., 210, 223, 328, 442, 468ff., 479
Adler, Cyrus, 606
Ibn Adret, Solomon, 427
Adultery, 145, 147
Africa, 409, 697–702, 718, 720, 736
Against Apion (Josephus), 18, 138–153
Agrippa I, 123–135
Aha bar Jacob, 242
Ahad Haam, 711
Aibu, 298
Akabia ben Mahalalel, 217
Akiba, 176f., 182, 186, 190, 223, 396, 449, 453, 489, 723
Alami, Solomon, 397
Alatino, Moses, 275
Albo, Joseph, 293, 580
Albright, W. F., 8
Alemanno, Johanan, 299
Alexander the Great, 6, 44, 373, 467
Alexander Jannaeus, 68

Alexandria, Alexandrian, 7, 18, 36, 44, 90f., 123f., 138
Al-fadil, 374
Alfasi, 359
"Alfonsine tablets," 274
Aliens, 146
Alkabetz, Solomon, 437
Allegorical interpretation, 92f., 115f.
Almagest (Ptolemy), 273
Almohades, 397
Alphabet of Rabbi Akiba, 470ff.
Altmann, Alexander, 506
Altneushul (Prague), 269
America, 530, 550, 590, 593f, 600, 606, 619, 632, 634, 636ff., 655f., 661, 665, 675, 683, 696, 699–702, 706–757, 762, 765, 790
American Council for Judaism, 738–741
American Jewish Congress, 755
Ammi, 204, 221
Ammon and Moab, 220
Amos, 223
Anacharsis, 151
Anatoli, Jacob, 273, 274, 405
Anaxagoras, 6, 141, 151
Angels, 302, 312, 331ff., 340, 374, 383, 421, 426, 435, 438, 449, 464, 471, 483–486
Animals, 147, 152, 201f., 209, 215, 222, 240f., 243f., 250, 319, 331, 378, 436, 444, 466
Anthropomorphism, 321f.
Antioch, 9
Antiochus III, 9, 45
Antiochus IV, Epiphanes, 9, 43, 45–48, 59ff., 136
Antipater, son of Jason, 55
Anti-Semitism, discrimination, 505, 516, 534f., 547, 610, 632, 635, 648f., 651, 662f., 665–670, 673f., 677, 713f.,

723, 728f., 733ff., 743ff., 763, 765f.;
religious persecution, 7, 47f., 124–
135, 138, 175–183
Apion, 123, 153
Apocalypse, 62
Apocrypha, Biblical, 7f., 23, 24–72,
136f., 159–175, 191
Apollo, 140
Apollonius, 46
Apollonius Molon, 138, 150–153
Apostasy, conversion, 533, 539, 635,
728, 744
Aquinas, Thomas, 85, 283
Arab states, Arabs, 619, 684–688, 691–
698, 727
Arbaa Turim (Jacob ben Asher),
336f., 359
Ardeshir, 373
Argentina, colonization in, 675
Aristobulus II, 68
Aristotle, Aristotelianism, 14, 273,
274, 275, 282, 301, 305, 308, 318,
321, 372, 374, 388, 398f., 405, 484,
574, 581
Ark of the Covenant, 201
Artaxerxes I, 4
Asceticism, 309f., 378, 435
Asch, Sholem, 786–790
Asenath, daughter of Potiphar, 135
Ashdod, 56
Ashkenazi, Bezalel, 435
Asian countries, 694, 697–702, 720, 734
Assimilation, 506, 532ff., 547, 573,
576f., 635, 666, 668, 677, 683, 712,
734, 766, 779
Athens, Athenians, 141, 150f.
Augustine, 85
Augustus, 129–131
Auschwitz, 639, 643, 654–658, 728
Ausitis (Utz), 101
Averroës, 273, 274, 324, 405

Babylonia, 3, 18, 191, 196, 206, 232f.,
236
Baeck, Leo, 561–567, 612ff.
Baer, Y. F., 6
Bahya ibn Pakuda, 293, 295f., 305–
308
Bakunin, M., 526
Balaam, 240

Balfour Declaration, 688f.
de Balmes, Abraham, 274
Barcelona, Debate at, 327, 475–484
Bar Kokhba, 18, 175, 489
Baron, S. W., 507, 733–738
Baruch, Apocalypse of, 11, 18, 173ff.
Basel, 672, 678
Bauer, Bruno, 526
Beauty, 28, 40, 203
Be-er ha-Golah (Judah Loew ben
Bezalel), 473ff.
Beer-Hofman, R., 559ff, 778f.
Behinat Olam (Yedayah ha-Bedersi),
336
Beliar, Belial, 67, 83
Belkin, S., 580–584
Benamozegh, E., 767, 773
Ben Azzai, 187, 223
Benedictions, 185–188
Ben-Gurion, D., 686, 692–704
Benjamin of Tudela, 459–462
Ben Mishle (Samuel ha-Nagid), 352
Ben Sira, Wisdom of, 8, 23–26
Bereshit Rabbati (Moses ha-Dar-
shan), 467f.
Bergen-Belsen, 622
Berger, Elmer, 738–741
Bergman, S. H., 556
Berlin, 587
Berlin, Isaiah, 526
Beroka of Be Hozae, 216
Beruriah, 202
Beth Zur, 54, 56
Bet Middot (Yehiel ben Yekutiel),
379
Bet Yosef (Joseph Caro), 336
Bialystok, 623, 657
Bible, 536ff., 552, 554, 559, 570, 575,
585, 606, 649, 650, 661, 749–762,
769f., 784, 798
Bible quoted, 511f., 521, 524f., 539,
545f., 566, 569, 575, 586, 592f., 612,
614, 620f., 630, 643f., 648, 690,
701f., 712, 725, 740, 751, 753, 767f.,
770, 788, 790
Biblical personages, 324, 337, 344,
379, 389, 421, 430, 438, 461, 464f.,
466f., 469–472, 479, 482, 486, 489
Bickerman, E., 8
"Biltmore Program," 774–778

Bilu, 689
Birnbaum, Nathan, 774–778
Bismarck, Otto v., 666
al-Bitroji, 274
Books, 348f., 352
Brandeis, L. D., 706–713
Brandeis University, 724, 742
Brit Shalom, 619
Brotherhood of men, 509, 534, 540, 551, 597, 618, 648, 704, 714
Bruno, Giordano, 300
Bryan, W. J., 721
Buber, M., 567–574, 725, 744, 754
Buchenwald, 654, 656
Bundism, 731
Burial, 339ff.
Buxtorf, Johannes, 309, 516

Cabet, Etienne, 526
Caesarea, 129
Cain and Abel, 137
Calabrese, Hayyim Vital, 434, 436, 437
Caleb, 51
Caligula, Gaius, 123f.
Calvin, 408
The Castle (Kafka), 791
Chagall, Marc, 797f.
Charity, 152, 224, 230, 362f., 400f.
Charles VI, 274
Charles of Anjou, 274
Chazars, 308
Children, 27, 29f., 146, 213f., 217, 220f., 229, 232, 351, 394
Chmielnicki massacres, 357, 644
Choice of Pearls (Ibn Gabirol), 277, 372
Chosen people, 525, 551, 559f., 595, 783
Christianity, Christians, 16, 18, 44, 62, 235, 271, 272, 308, 379, 382, 390, 397, 400f., 408, 459, 461, 475–484, 509f., 516, 527, 529, 531, 535ff., 546, 548f., 551, 562, 572f., 591, 600, 634, 639, 651, 668ff., 672, 676, 714, 720–736, 744–749, 753, 760–773, 786ff., 801
Church and state, 509, 600
Circumcision, 47f., 51
Civilization, 536f., 557, 598ff., 616, 639f., 642, 647, 678, 742, 761

Civil rights, *see* Emancipation
Claudius, emperor, 124
Clement IV, Pope, 476
Cohen, Arthur A., 744–755
Cohen, Hermann, 505f.
Columbus, 274
Communism, 648, 655, 744
Community, 73–78, 88f., 91f., 117, 141, 562f., 567, 583, 599ff., 711, 733, 747, 753
Concentration camps, ghettos, 561, 565, 622–623, 634f., 637, 639, 642f., 644, 647, 651, 655–659, 686, 728
Congress of Liberated Jews, 632
Congress of Vienna, 539
Conservative Judaism, 592–607, 751f.
Constantinople, 407, 429, 431f., 459, 464
Cordovero, Moses, 437–440
Council of the Four Lands, 363
Covenant, 49, 51, 60, 74ff., 82f., 85, 161f., 164, 177, 393f., 400
Coventry, 649
Creation, 33, 41, 160, 164, 173, 197f., 204–208, 223, 227, 240f., 243f., 248, 277, 298, 306, 318f., 321ff., 327ff., 411, 415f., 420ff., 434, 439, 456, 469f., 485
Crematoria, 633, 641, 645
Crescas, Hasdai, 293, 324
Cresques, 274
Crete, 141
Crossman, R. H. S., 635
Cyrus, edict of, 3

Dance, 473ff.
Daniel, 51, 137, 159
Daniel, Book of, 10ff., 18
Dante, 484ff.
Darius III, 44
Darmesteter, James, 535–538
Darwin, C. R., 668, 729f.
David, 51, 68ff., 162, 222, 248, 250, 344, 390, 452, 461f., 472, 478, 488f.
Davis, Earl J., 713
Day of Atonement, 176, 182
Day of Judgment, 62f., 73, 180, 225
Days of Awe, 312, 370, 402, 453ff.
Dead Sea (Qumran) Brotherhood, 15f., 18, 73–85, 191; *see also* Essenes

Death, 38, 41, 48, 155, 157, 198, 217f.,
   299, 309, 330f., 337–342, 344, 375,
   427, 436, 442, 456ff., 487f., 557,
   624–632, 634f., 654–658, 711
Decamerone (Boccaccio), 403
Deeds, 226, 248f., 251
Degania, 679
Delphi, oracle of, 140
Demetrius II, king, 57
Democracy, 575, 583, 594, 709f., 715,
   720–723, 730, 787
Diagoras of Melos, 151
Dialoghi d'Amore (Leone Ebreo),
   299–303
Dinah, 101
Discorso (S. Luzzatto), 405–410
"Displaced persons," 631–641, 694f.
Disputations, 475–484
Divine Comedy (Dante), 484
Divine Presence (Shekhinah), 198,
   210, 214, 235ff., 239, 298, 309, 337,
   365ff., 387, 426, 430, 455, 465, 473
Diwan (Immanuel ha-Romi), 484–
   488
Doctrines and Beliefs, Book of (Saa-
   dia), 318–321
Dogma, 581
Dosa, 221
Dostoevsky, F., 778
Dov Baer of Mezrich, 441, 446f., 453
Dreyfus affair, 662, 763, 795
Dubnov, S., 543–546, 733
Duties of the Heart (Bahya ibn Pak-
   uda), 305–308

Early Pious Men (Hasidim), 6, 9, 16,
   101, 191
Eastern Europe, 568, 625, 635, 638,
   656, 662, 664, 677ff., 683, 686, 694,
   702f., 706f., 709, 718, 737, 743, 781,
   786
Education, 601f., 606, 702f., 707, 710
Egypt, Egyptians, 45, 51, 91, 125,
   189, 232, 236, 314, 404, 434f., 459,
   466, 659f., 688
Eichmann trial, 612, 643–653, 656f.
Einstein, A., 550, 642, 650, 682–685,
   730, 764, 784f.
Eisenmenger, J. A., 516
Elam, 236
Eleazar, Maccabee, 48

Eleazar, martyr, 44
Eleazar, rabbi, 296
Eleazar ben Shammua, 178, 182f.
Eleazar ben Simeon, 422
Eleazar of Masada, 154–159
Elect, the, 64ff.
Eliezer ben Hyrcanus, 224f.
Eliezer ben Pedat, 203f., 217f.
Eliezer ben Zadok, 189
Elihu, 101, 107, 111f., 240
Elijah, 51, 216, 225, 237f., 247–252,
   434, 472f., 478f., 490
Elijah of Vilna, 441
Eliphaz, Baldad, Sophar, 107–112,
   240
Emancipation, civil rights, 515ff.,
   534–543, 547, 574, 597, 659, 665f.,
   726–734, 756, 765, 779
Emanuel of Portugal, 274
Engels, F., 680
England, 398, 530, 549, 649, 656,
   659f., 688, 727, 762
Enlightenment, 538, 664, 758
Enoch, Book of, 11, 17, 62–66
En Yaakov, 430
En Zetim, 431
Epictetus, 14
Epistle to Yemen (Maimonides), 279,
   392
Equality, 228, 230, 405, 444
Esau, 101, 116, 161, 220, 232
Eschatology, 62–66, 66f., 68–72, 159–
   168, 168–172, 173ff.
Essenes, 15f., 73, 89, 90, 191
Ethics, morality, 26f., 37f., 76f., 86f.,
   89, 91, 141, 146f., 181, 198, 220,
   222f., 372–377, 378f., 379f., 384–
   387, 441, 492, 562f., 582, 591, 606,
   613, 616, 641f., 681, 710, 737, 784
Europe, Europeanism, 509, 514f.,
   637f., 640f., 646, 668, 700f., 719ff.,
   723, 744f., 779, 790
Eusebius, 90
Eve, 206, 328
Every Good Man Is Free (Philo),
   85–89
Evil, 104, 159–165, 187, 420, 434, 571,
   616, 618
Evil desire, 207, 241, 246f., 445, 471
Exile, 235–239, 276, 391, 406f., 419,

427, 430f., 465, 481, 488, 490, 532,
539–545, 548, 571, 635, 699f., 721,
726, 731
Existentialism, 724
Exodus from Egypt, 161, 188ff., 232,
248, 411, 464f., 478
Ezra, Fourth Book of, 11, 18, 159–
172, 173
Ezra and Nehemiah, books of, 4
Ezra the Scribe, 4f., 8, 12, 159f., 191f.,
198, 218, 518, 718

Family, 27–30, 145f.
al-Farabi, 273, 274
Faraj ben Salim, 274
Far Eastern nations, cultures, 548,
550, 694, 735
Fear of God, 24f., 31, 203, 224, 240ff.
Fellow man, 20, 147, 200f., 206, 214,
217, 223, 228, 230, 234f., 252, 318–
321, 327ff., 396, 439, 443f., 446f.,
454, 492
Festivals, 312, 359ff., 366, 370, 401,
430, 432, 452, 505, 726, 746, 750f.,
769, 791ff.
Ficino, Marsilio, 299
Finkelstein, L., 606f.
Flaccus, 123
Fleg, Edmond, 506, 795ff.
Food, eating, 76f., 94, 96ff., 141, 148,
152, 249f.
Force, violence, 616ff., 620
Ford, Henry, 713f.
Four Kingdoms, 10ff., 159, 223, 232f.,
236f., 246
France, 398, 431, 459, 512ff., 530, 549,
638, 728, 763, 768
Francis of Assisi, 772
Franciscan movement, 419
Frank, Anne, 622f.
Frank, Waldo, 715–723
Frankel, Z., 592
Frankfurt-am-Main, 538, 573, 587
Frederick II, 273, 405
Freedom, 157
Free will, 25f., 173, 211, 319, 321,
323–327, 332, 354, 408
French Revolution, 527, 536, 758
Freud, S., 550, 650
Friedenwald, H., 783f.

Friends, friendship, 26, 229, 244f.,
375, 383, 386

Galante, Abraham and Moses, 430,
437
Galen, 274, 484
Galilee, 464
Galut, *see* Exile
Gamaliel I, 189
Gamaliel II, 186
Ganzfried, Solomon, 374
Garden of Eden, 67, 116f., 160, 207,
240, 245
Gaul, 233
Gazara, 54, 56
Geiger, A., 554ff.
Gentiles, 211, 220, 229f., 232, 236,
239, 249, 405, 410, 431, 468, 470ff.,
481, 485, 490
Germany, 408, 459, 492, 515ff., 530f.,
549, 573, 587f., 619, 635, 637, 639,
643, 694, 728, 734, 743, 760, 762
Gerondi, Jonah, 427
Gersonides (Levi ben Gerson), 274,
324
Ghazali, 388
Ghetto, 550, 574, 638, 664, 673, 712,
756, 761, 798
Gikatila, Joseph, 411, 425
Gilles, Master, 477
God, 24ff., 32ff., 37–42, 64ff., 68–71,
79–81, 81–85, 108–114, 115ff., 118–
122, 140, 143ff., 153, 157, 162–166,
178, 180, 204–213, 218–230, 233ff.,
240–245, 248–252, 280ff., 286–289,
300, 307, 326, 379, 388, 426f., 437f.,
442, 450, 454, 463f., 469, 473f.,
481, 485, 509, 511, 518, 520f., 524,
531, 536, 540, 542, 549f., 556, 560f.,
565–573, 586f., 589, 593, 595, 597,
613ff., 618, 622f., 654, 656f., 688,
708, 712, 714, 716, 719, 721, 737f.,
745, 749f., 752, 755f., 760, 762, 768,
770, 775ff., 783f., 787f., 796, 799;
fear and love of, 426; oneness of,
307, 313f., 374, 395, 417, 464, 475,
483, 492; *see also* Fear of God,
Love of God
Gog and Magog, 490
Gordon, A.D., 677–682

Graetz, H., 518–525, 543, 733
"Grand Sanhedrin," 512ff.
Greece, Greeks, 5f., 9, 44, 85f., 89, 91, 95, 115, 123, 126, 138–141, 148–152, 232f., 407, 459, 520, 523, 525, 530, 581, 697, 746, 758–762, 780–783, 796
Greenberg, U.Z., 552
Grimani, Domenico, 274
Gringauz, Samuel, 631–641
Guide to the Perplexed (Maimonides), 277, 279f., 282f., 321ff., 425

Habakkuk, 223
Hadrian, 396
Haggadah (Homiletics), 19, 199, 215, 578
Halakhah (Law), 18, 184, 199, 215, 224, 578, 580, 582, 584, 750f.
Halpern, Ben, 744
Halutzim, 623
Hameiri, Avigdor, 552
Hammarskjold, D., 693
Hamnuna, 412
Hanan the Hidden, 212
Hananiah, Mishael and Azariah, 51, 137, 177
Hananyah ben Teradyon, 178ff.
Hanina, 204, 229
Hanina ben Hakhinai, 181
Hannover, Nathan, 357
Hanukkah, 43, 53
Ha-Poel ha-Tzair, 679
al-Harizi, Judah, 283
Harnack, A. v., 561, 729
Harvard College, 710
Hasid, Hasidut, 303f., 315, 346, 377f., 492
Hasidim, 9, 50, 69, 193; see also Early Pious Men
Hasidism, 441–458, 571, 732, 786
Hasmoneans, 11, 15, 68, 73, 191, 472
Hausner, Gideon, 643–653, 656
Heathen, Heathenism, 52, 67, 522f., 531, 535ff., 551, 591, 725, 762, 770, 773, 781, 801
Heavenly Voice, 177, 181, 183, 198, 225
Hebrew language, 689, 712, 745f., 761

Hebrew University, 619, 683f.
Hechalutz, 623, 696
Hegel, G.W.F., 518, 585, 761
Heine, H., 650, 758–763
Hell, Purgatory, Gehenna, 333, 385, 408, 413, 471, 484–488
Hellenism, 5–10, 12, 14, 16, 43, 135, 191, 537, 638, 742, 758–762
Herod the Great, 17, 123, 126, 128, 154, 191
Herzl, T., 559, 610, 662–678, 726f., 774
Heschel, A.J., 614–619
Hesed, 18, 191, 213
Hess, Moses, 526–531
Hezekiah, king, 240
High Priest, 55ff., 127, 130, 143, 229
Hillel the Elder, and School of, 13f., 16, 190, 191–198, 562, 583, 772
Hippocrates, 352
Hirsch, S.R., 527, 538–543
Hirsch, Samuel, 527, 584–587
Histadrut, 696
History, 466ff., 469f., 508, 528, 535, 615, 733, 742, 749, 752f.
Hitler, A., 633, 644, 647f., 650, 652, 717, 723, 729, 743
Hiyya, 412
Hiyya bar Abba, 227
Holdheim, S., 585
Holiness, 292, 450, 492; Holy Spirit, 67, 78, 209, 249, 473; Saintliness, 303f.
Holland, 622f.
Homer, 139, 150, 537, 760, 781
Honi the Circle-Drawer, 212
House of Study, 365–371, 429; see also Study of the Law, Torah
Hoveve Zion, 532, 659, 662, 732
Humanity, Humanism, 146f., 212, 538, 640, 662, 664, 685, 692, 701ff., 736, 758, 768f.
Humanitarianism, 527ff., 531, 546, 677
Humility, 26, 28, 74, 88, 209, 229, 248, 252, 312, 346, 378f., 380ff., 385, 390, 403, 436, 438, 446f., 486, 492
Hungary, 64
Hutzpit the interpreter, 180

Idolatry, 119, 123, 187
Idumaea, 54
Iggeret Musar (Alami), 397-403
Ihud, 619, 692ff.
Imitatio Dei, 569, 729
Imitation of God, 209f.
Immanuel ha-Romi, 484
Immortality, 41f., 155, 321, 329ff.
Improvement of Moral Qualities,
   (Ibn Gabirol), 372
Indian, 155
Individual, 583f., 586
Innocent III, 772
Intellect, 306, 331, 377, 444
Intelligences, 301f.
Intermarriage, 635, 666f., 728
Isaac, 67, 137, 314, 339, 389, 454, 464,
   472
Isaac, rabbi, 297, 412
Isaiah, 223
Isaiah ha-Levi Horovitz, 428
Ishmael, 220
Ishmael, rabbi, and School of, 176f.,
   336
Islam, 271, 272, 273, 282, 298, 305,
   308, 318, 324, 349, 374f., 377, 390f.,
   460, 548, 550, 736, 744, 769
Israel, the Baal Shem, 303, 441–446,
   447, 456, 568, 615, 718, 731
Israel, land of, 206f., 219, 221, 269,
   309, 313f., 365, 408, 428f., 436, 446,
   459, 476, 511, 513, 526, 551, 585f.,
   589, 619, 635–638, 641f., 656, 659–
   705, 712, 718, 762; *see also* Jerusalem
Israel, people of, 230–233, 250, 270,
   271, 309, 388, 390, 392, 405–410,
   420, 463, 570, 721, 743, 749, 752,
   758f., 763, 780f., 787
Israel, State of, 595, 600, 659–705,
   673, 683, 686–692, 694f., 697f., 701,
   704f., 724f., 727, 729, 732f., 736,
   738ff., 745, 755, 781, 798
Israel ben Michael (Padua), 368
Italy, 408f., 512f., 638, 736, 743
Itinerary (Benjamin of Tudela),
   459–462

Jabneh, 200, 641
Jacob, 66, 116, 232, 314, 392, 404,
   464, 472

Jacob ben Asher, 336
Jacob Joseph of Polnoy, 441
Jaeger, W., 14
James I of Aragon, 475, 483f.
de Janua, Peter, 475
Jason of Cyrene, 43f.
Jason, high priest, 10
Jefferson, T., 221
Jehoshaphat, Valley of, 461
Jeremiah, 173, 718
Jeremiel, angel, 165
Jericho, 198
Jerusalem, 6, 45f., 48ff., 56f., 62, 69ff.,
   124ff., 131, 137, 154, 157, 162, 189ff.,
   193, 235; destruction of, 17, 21,
   154, 159f., 168–172, 173ff., 175,
   191, 233, 341f., 363, 395, 408, 434,
   459–462, 463ff., 472, 641, 659, 670,
   688, 695, 726, 797
Jesus, 390, 404, 460, 476–479, 481f.,
   651, 655, 753f., 760, 772f., 788
Jewish Agency, 689f.
Jewish people, 530f., 548ff., 597f.,
   752f.; *see also* Israel, people of
The Jewish State (Herzl), 610, 662–
   672
Jewish Theological Seminary, 593f.,
   606, 614
Job, and Book of, 17, 100–114, 239–
   245, 655f., 764
Joel ben Abraham Shemariah, 382
Johanan bar Nappaha, 203, 227, 239,
   242, 244f.
Johanan ben Zakkai, 18, 192, 203,
   213, 226, 239, 241, 381, 641
John, Maccabee, 48
John Hyrcanus, 17
Joly, Maurice, 713
Jonathan, Maccabee, 43, 48, 55f., 154
Jonathan ben Amram, 215
Joppa (Jaffa), 54, 56
Jose, 178
Joseph, 51, 135, 137, 176
Joseph, rabbi, 214
Joseph ibn Wakkar, 274
Josephus, Flavius, 15–18, 73, 86, 138–
   153, 154–159, 581, 583f.
Joshua, 51, 238
Joshua ben Hananiah, 213, 225, 241
Joshua ben Hyrcanus, 241
Joshua ben Levi, 237f., 479

Jost, I. M., 518
Judaeo-Roman war, 17
Judah ben Baba, 178, 181
Judah ben Dama, 181f.
Judah ben Elai, 178, 185, 187
Judah the Galilean, 154
Judah bar Ilai, 431
Judah ha-Levi, 272, 289–292, 308–312, 388, 565, 573f., 718
Judah Loew ben Bezalel, 415, 428, 473ff.
Judah the Maccabee, 10f., 43, 48, 52, 154
Judah ibn Makta, 273
Judah the Pious, 303, 377f., 492
Judah the Prince, 180, 184, 214ff., 221, 355
Judaism and mankind, 512ff., 514–518, 538–543, 545f., 552f., 554ff., 563, 621
Jüdische Rundschau, 608, 651
Jüdisches Lehrhaus (Frankfurt), 573–579, 800
Julia Augusta, 131f.
Justice, 181, 208f., 234, 244

Kabbala denudata (Knorr von Rosenroth), 419
Kabbalah, *see* Mysticism
Kaddish, 337, 341
Kafka, F., 655, 790–795
Kahler, Erich, 547–550
Kalisker, Abraham, 446f.
Kallen, H. M., 706
Kalonymus ben Kalonymus, and Calo Kalonymus, 274
Kant, I., 561, 639, 730, 761
Kaplan, M. M., 594–605
Karaites, 308f.
Kattowitz Conference, 532, 689
Kavvanah, 315
Kesten, H., 758
Kidron, brook of, 461
Kimhi, Joseph, 305
al-Kindi, 274
Kingdom of God, 101, 159, 176, 223, 291, 417, 465ff., 581, 584, 618, 661, 754, 771f.
Kingly Crown (Ibn Gabirol), 286–289
Kitzur Shulhan Arukh, 384

Klausner, J., 173
Kneset Israel, 688
Knowledge, 79f., 82f., 92, 95, 99, 118, 123, 193, 195, 200, 240, 279, 293f., 298, 355, 374
Knowledge of God, 277, 282–286, 295, 309, 313, 329, 331, 424, 442, 491f.
Kohler, K., 101
Kohut, A., 592ff.
Kol Sakhal (Leone Modena), 329ff.
Kook, A. I., 556–559, 799f.
Kuzari (Judah ha-Levi), 272, 290, 308–312, 388–391

Labor, 346, 586, 679–682
Lacedaemonians, 141, 150
Lamdam, Y., 552f.
Lassalle, F., 526, 766
Law, commandments, rites, 5, 13, 19f., 43, 47–53, 55f., 58ff., 73, 82, 87, 98, 118ff., 136f., 138–153, 161, 173, 222, 224, 248f., 275, 278, 284, 293f., 296, 307, 320, 325, 338, 343, 353, 355, 382f., 389f., 413, 420f., 432, 455, 473, 488, 510f., 513f., 523, 550, 557f., 561f., 565ff., 571, 575, 580ff., 585, 587f., 591, 593, 596, 605, 748–751, 774, 789; *see also* Torah, Study of the Law
Lazare, B., 763–767
League of Nations, 686
Learning, 574–579, 602
Legacy to Gaius (Philo), 124–135
Leibnitz, 509, 761
Leibniz, 419
Levi, rabbi, 242
Levy-Bruhl, L., 549
Lewisohn, Ludwig, 723–733
Liber continens (Rhazes), 274
Liber de mundo (al-Haytham), 274
Liberty, 586f., 721f., 763
Lincoln, A., 716, 721, 755
Locke, John, 509
Loewe, Louis, 660
Logos, 36
London, 617, 656
Love of God, of man, 21, 38f., 42, 88, 99, 102, 136, 177, 201, 211, 217, 227, 236, 240ff., 245, 249, 251f., 278, 281f., 285f., 291, 293–304, 306f.,

342, 375, 378, 379, 383, 439f., 454, 490, 492, 557ff., 799f.
Low Countries, 408
Lucan, 409
Lucena, 397
Luria, Isaac, 428, 433, 434–437
Luther, M., 761
Luzzatto, M. H., 293, 297f., 303f., 365–371, 380ff.
Luzzatto, Simone, 405
Lycurgus, 139
Lysimachus, 138

Macaulay, T. B., 727f., 743
Maccabees, Maccabean Rebellion, 10f., 24, 43–57, 396
Maccabees, First and Second Books of, 12, 43–61, 136
Maccabees, Fourth Book of, 7, 12, 136ff.
Magnes, J. L., 619ff.
Maidanek, 657, 728
Maimonides, Moses, 272, 279, 282–286, 293, 313f., 315, 321ff., 323–327, 343–347, 353, 391–395, 395f., 397, 405, 419, 425, 427, 430, 437, 488, 491, 580, 731
Malachi, 3, 5
Mallarmé, S., 764
Malmad ha-Talmidim (Jacob Anatoli), 405
Mantino, Jacob, 274, 354
Manual of Discipline, 73–81, 86
Mapai, 696
Marco Polo, 274
Marcus Agrippa, 127
Marranos, 403, 736
Marriage, intercourse, 316, 362, 386f., 420f.
Marshall, Louis, 713f.
Martini, Raymond, 475
Martyrdom, 12, 18, 58–61, 137f., 148, 154–159, 175–183, 390, 395, 396f., 400, 414, 464, 470, 519, 543, 545f., 617, 619f., 632f., 638f., 642, 683, 728, 743, 753, 759, 781, 786
Marx, Karl, 526, 680, 729f., 766
Masada, 17, 154–159, 396
Masorah, 355
Masud, of Fez, 433
Mattathias of Modin, 43, 48–51

Mauras, Miguel, 736
Media, 232f.
Meir, 178, 202
Meir of Rothenburg, 396
Mekor Hayyim (Ibn Gabirol), 286
Mendel of Kotzk, 447–452
Mendelssohn, Moses, 509–512, 517
Mendes, H. P., 661
Menelaus, high priest, 10
Menorat ha-Maor (al-Nakawa), 414
Mercy, Grace, 21, 41, 81, 174, 177, 191, 205, 208f., 210, 213ff., 228, 230, 245f., 250, 298, 380, 382, 420, 438, 457, 471, 485
Meron, 431
Mesillat Yesharim (M. H. Luzzatto), 303f., 365, 380
Messiah, Messianic Age, Messianism, 62, 66, 68, 70ff., 159, 173, 191, 236–239, 240, 250, 269, 276, 357, 364, 371, 391, 406, 428, 434, 436, 441, 452, 464, 467f., 470–473, 475–484, 488–491, 506, 518, 536, 540, 543, 546, 554, 563, 571, 589, 661, 702f., 731, 737f., 745, 747, 753ff., 767–774
Micah, 223
Middle Ages, 541, 574, 720, 744, 756, 759, 761
Midrash, 19, 135, 160, 173, 191–252, 332, 343f., 355, 358, 414, 430, 448, 465ff., 480
Midrash Yetzirat ha-Velad, 332–335
Minos of Crete, 140
Miracles, 186, 212f., 224f., 323, 481, 489
Mishnah, 6, 19, 184–190, 199, 204, 215, 361, 370, 455
Mishneh Torah (Maimonides), 279f., 324–327, 343–347, 384, 488–491
Mizrahi, 680
Modena, Leone, 329ff.
Modin, 48f., 52
Montefiore, M., 659f.
Moses, 58, 60, 66, 95, 115, 118, 123, 130, 139f., 199, 222, 227f., 237f., 249f., 284f., 294, 306, 311, 314, 324, 330, 344f., 394, 396, 398, 413, 428, 472, 478, 486, 510, 578, 581, 593, 596, 616, 745, 749f., 752, 754, 758f., 763, 769, 787f.
Moses de Leon, 419

Moses ibn Ezra, 298f.
Mother and her seven sons, 44, 58–61, 137
"Mourners of Jerusalem," 462, 464
Mourning, 341f.
Moyne, Lord, 657
Muhammad, 392, 482
Muhammad Ali, 659f.
Murray, Gilbert, 742
Music, 425
Mysteries, 80, 204
Mysticism, 293, 305, 315, 353, 357, 365, 406, 411f., 415, 419–440, 441, 492

Nahmanides, Moses, 327ff., 427, 457f., 469f.
Nahor, 101, 113
Nahum of Gamzu, 440
Najara, Israel, 437
al-Nakawa, Israel ibn, 414
Napoleon I, 512f., 729, 731
Napoleon III, 713
Nathan, rabbi, 188, 225
Nathan the Wise (Lessing), 403, 664
Nationality, Jewish; Nationalism, 513, 526, 529f., 532ff., 543f., 596, 632, 668–672, 682, 685, 687–692, 698, 738ff., 745, 774
Nature, 32ff., 87, 95f., 187
Nazi era, Nazism, Nazi leaders, 561, 608, 619, 622–631, 643–653, 686f.. 695, 734f., 744, 755f., 768
Negro, 648, 719, 755ff.
Nehemiah, 4f.
Nehemiah, rabbi, 178
Neo-Kantianism, 561
Neo-Orthodoxy, 539, 587, 597, 732
Neoplatonism, 279, 286, 299, 305, 419
New Jerusalem, 159, 170f., 173
Nicholas II, Pope, 425
Niebuhr, R., 715
Noah, children of, 220
Noah and the Flood, 161
"Noahism," 767
Nobel, N. A., 574
North Africa, 736
Numenius, son of Antiochus, 55
Nuremberg laws, 648
Nuremberg trials, 646f.

Obadiah, the Proselyte, 395f.
Obadiah ben Abraham, 353
Old age, 227
Olives, Mount of, 461
Omar ben al Khataab, 460
On the Contemplative Life (Philo), 90–99
Oral Law, tradition, 13, 184, 251f., 329f., 343, 455, 473
Order, 208
Ordination, 428
Origen, 85
Orthodoxy, 506, 538, 550f., 575, 580, 592, 634, 731, 751, 774
Ottoman Empire, 676

Padua, 365–371
Paideia, 14
Palestine, see Israel, Land of
Palestine Economic Corporation, 706
Pallière, Aimé, 767–773
Paradise, 301, 333, 420, 463f., 471f., 473ff., 484–488; see also Garden of Eden
Pardes Rimmonium (Cordovero), 437
Parents, 27, 146f., 213f., 218, 402
Paris, 512f., 760, 763, 768
Pascal, 293
Passions, 136
Passover, 184, 188ff.
Patience, 196f.
Patriarchs, 67, 115, 161, 221
Paul, 544f., 748, 754
Paulo (Pablo) Christiani, 475–484
Paulus, H. E. G., 539
Peace, 86, 181, 191, 193, 206, 233ff., 238, 244ff., 251, 364, 380, 382, 447, 490f., 521, 529, 612, 701, 703, 798
Péguy, Charles, 764
de Peñaforte, Raymond, 475f., 483
Persecutions, 391ff., 397f., 400, 403, 532, 608–658, 666, 691, 702, 707f., 714, 724, 752, 759, 765, 771
Persia, Persian empire, 3f., 6, 151f., 407
Peter of Abano, 273
Petulra pogroms, 644
Petronius, 134
Pharisees, 8, 15f., 18, 68, 184, 191, 582, 754, 788

Philipson, D., 591

Philo of Alexandria, 7, 16f., 73, 85–99, 115–135, 581, 584, 718

Phinehas, 36, 50f., 137

Physician, medicine, 30, 337f., 349f., 353f.

Pico della Mirandola, 299

Piety, 99, 136, 138, 141, 143, 153, 193, 209, 233, 310ff.

Pinsker, Leo, 532–535

"Pious men of Germany," 378

Pirke de Rabbi Eliezer, 465ff.

Plato, Platonism, 7, 12, 14, 36, 115, 141, 150, 299, 318, 332, 398, 405

Plato of Tivoli, 273

Pliny the Elder, 73

Poale Zion, 696

Poland, 357–364, 408, 637, 656, 679, 743

Politzer, H., 781

Pompey, 68, 409

Pontius Pilate, 128f.

Portugal, 638, 734, 736

Poverty, the poor, rich and poor, 27, 105, 196, 203, 231, 378, 381, 399, 402, 413, 423ff., 430, 439, 451

Prague, 269

Prayer, worship, 26, 30f., 35, 92, 95, 98f., 185–188, 202, 232, 235, 245ff., 298, 304, 311, 315, 316f., 337–342, 361f., 374, 383, 399, 413f., 429f., 430f., 441, 444f., 450f., 458, 460, 558, 571, 601, 605, 610, 613f., 620, 746, 748, 751, 790f., 799; Prayer Book, 286, 289, 411, 416ff.

Pride, 118, 381, 385, 438, 443f.; *see also* Humility

Priest, priesthood, 66f., 76f., 97, 143, 228f., 236, 344f.

Prinz, Joachim, 755ff.

Progress, 536f.

Prophets, prophecy, 31, 39, 53, 57, 78, 92, 137, 211, 218, 221, 239f., 284, 309f., 314, 323, 394, 400, 472, 490, 521f., 524f., 531, 536, 540, 559, 571, 578, 586, 593, 613, 618, 662, 690f., 697, 710, 715, 717, 720f., 726, 733, 740f., 754, 765, 768–771, 784, 787; false, 83

Proselytes, proselytism, 135, 191, 197, 211, 395f., 541

Protagoras, 151

"Protocols of the Elders of Zion," 713

Proudhon, P. J., 526

Provenzal, David and Abraham, 353f.

Proverbs, 352

Providence, 135, 142, 207, 400, 438

Psalms, 361

Psalms of Solomon, 17, 68–72

Ptolemies, the, 7

Ptolemy VI, Philometor, 45

Pugio Fidei (Raymond Martini), 468

Puritans, 709f.

Pythagoras, 141

Raba, 217, 240

Rabbah bar Hanan, 214

Rabbinical Judaism, 580–584, 588, 591, 593f.

Rashi, 358f., 361, 430, 718, 731

Rathenau, W., 786

Rav, 214, 239, 242f.

Reason, 318, 320, 324, 330f., 353, 355, 389, 398f., 427, 473

Reconstructionism, 595

Redemption, salvation, 218, 235–239, 248, 276, 392, 412, 469, 511, 525, 572f., 594, 598, 602f., 619, 745, 750, 787, 789; *see also* Eschatology

Red Sea, 99, 421f.

Reform, liberalism, 554ff., 575, 584–592, 594, 597, 731, 751

Refugees, 686

Religion, Faith, 278, 279, 284, 313f., 374, 377, 398f., 411f., 414, 443, 446, 489, 509, 511, 531, 535, 549, 554f., 557ff., 562ff., 589, 598, 623, 678, 681, 698, 707, 715, 717, 719, 722f., 725, 745, 749, 775, 790, 796, 801

Remnant, 631–641, 691, 721, 727

Renan, E., 535

Renouvier, C. B., 773

Repentance, 38, 201f., 211, 218, 304, 325, 439, 445f., 452, 453ff., 472

Responsibility, 207

"Restoration," 366f., 443f.

Resurrection, 59, 148, 182, 209, 242

Revelation, 13, 218–225, 282, 318, 393f., 405, 485, 492, 506, 509ff., 521,

523, 557, 564, 666, 689, 695, 750f., 769ff.
Revelation, 160
Revolutions of 1830, 1848, 539, 706
Reward, 295, 331
Riesser, Gabriel, 539, 727f.
Righteousness, righteous, 36, 41, 63f., 223, 241
Robert of Anjou, 274
Rokeah, Eleazar, 303, 378, 492
Rokeah (Eleazar Rokeah), 492
Rome, *also,* Roman empire, 12, 17f., 43, 45, 55, 57, 123–135, 154–159, 159f., 175f., 178–182, 232f., 237, 270, 271, 274, 406, 410, 425, 459, 479, 482, 484, 520, 530, 758–762, 773, 796
Rosenzweig, F., 573–579, 791, 800f.
de Rossi, Azariah, 354
Rotenstreich, Nathan, 506
Rothschild, Edmond de, 659
Rothschild family, 550
Russia, 408, 634, 677, 688

Saadia, 305f., 318–321, 324
Sabbatai Zewi, Sabbatianic Movement, 365, 441, 443f.
Sabbath, 47, 50, 87f., 93f., 122f., 148, 152, 181, 196f., 206, 311f., 352, 360f., 366, 399, 401, 411–418, 420, 430, 435, 470, 483, 586, 605, 748f., 791ff.
Sachar, A. L., 741ff.
Sacrifice, 127, 144f., 162, 190, 213, 234, 313, 415, 449, 464, 488, 570f., 586
Sadducees, 15f., 18, 68, 184, 191, 582
Safed, 428–434, 434–437
Samuel, rabbi, 239
Samuel the Pious, 378
Sanhedrin, 12
Sartre, Jean-Paul, 729
Sarug, Israel, 432
Sassoon family, 550
Satan, 41, 101–106, 135, 137, 242, 444, 468
Schechter, S., 593, 607
Scholar, Scholarship, 345, 347, 353ff., 364, 365–371, 381, 387, 402, 515ff., 582, 588, 606
Schudt, J. J., 516

Schürer, E., 12
Schwartz, Samuel, 736
Science, 278, 284, 305, 318, 531, 536f., 702, 725, 730
"Science of Judaism," 514
Scotus, Michael, 405
Scribe, 31f.
Scythians, 151
Secularism, 506, 572, 598
Sefer ha-Musar (Joseph Caspi), 277
Sefer ha-Ot (Abulafia), 425
Sefer Hasidim (Judah the Pious), 377f.
Seleucids, the, 9f.
Seneca, 13
Sepphoris, 227
Septuagint, 7
Servants, slaves, 26f., 87, 96, 147, 154, 249, 378, 382, 473
Seville, 397, 402
Sex laws, 145, 148
Shaftesbury, 509
Shalom, Sh., 552
Shammai, and School of, 186, 188, 190ff., 195
Shapiro, Karl, 704f.
Shaw, G. B., 682
Shefaram, 178
Shemaiah and Abtalion, 191
Sheol, 63f.
Shevet Yehuda (Ibn Verga, 403f.
Shlonsky, A., 552
Shmelke of Nikolsburg, 453ff.
Shulhan Arukh (Joseph Caro), 336, 384, 437
Sicily, 353
Sickness, 27, 30, 337f.
Silence, 376, 384, 386
Siloam, Waters of, 461
Simeon ben Gamaliel, 357
Simeon ben Yohai, 412, 422, 463
Simeon the Just, 357
Simon, high priest, 34ff.
Simon, son of Judah the Prince, 215
Simon, Maccabee, 43, 48, 52, 54–57
Simon ben Gamliel, 176f.
Simon ben Yohai, 178
Sin, sinner, 28, 39, 63, 67f., 80, 140, 162, 202f., 210f., 246, 288, 384, 438f., 443, 445f., 454f., 456, 468, 487f., 558, 570, 583, 613, 770

Sinai, 4, 14, 118–122, 161, 184, 199f., 218f., 224f., 250f., 290, 311, 391–395, 422, 469, 511, 523f., 593, 619, 662, 750, 752; *see also* Revelation
Sitis (Job's wife), 105, 110
Socialism, 526, 575, 745
Social issues, equality, ethics, 520–524, 529, 756f., 763f., 786, 788f.
"Society for the Dissemination of Culture," 532
"Society of the Friends of Reform," 587
Socrates, Socratic, 13, 150, 309, 372
Solitude, 91f.
Solomon, 40, 172, 237, 460, 462, 466, 472
Solomon ibn Gabirol, 286–289, 372–377
Solomon Shloemel ben Hayyim Meinstrl, 428, 434–437
Solon, 6, 139
Sons of Zadok, 74
Soul, 95, 155, 247, 288, 290, 328, 332–335, 416, 448, 474
Soviet Union, 637, 686, 702f., 737
Spain, *also*, Expulsion from, 233, 299, 397f., 401ff., 403, 407, 409, 419, 427, 431, 434, 459, 630, 638, 734, 736
Sparta, 43, 55, 96
Spinoza, 300, 509, 527, 697
State, 513f., 539, 583, 641, 644, 760
Steinberg, Milton, 744, 747
Stirner, M., 526
Stoa, Stoics, 7, 12ff., 36, 85, 115, 136, 141, 332, 581
Study of the Law, 19f., 73, 97f., 122, 142, 146, 199ff., 203, 214f., 218, 224ff., 232, 250f.
Suffering, 59, 100f., 201, 215, 217, 231f., 236, 463f., 467f., 488, 534, 541f., 544f., 551, 559f., 587, 610–658, 666, 678, 683, 688, 702, 710, 712, 714, 737, 759, 796f.
Sukenik, E. L., 81
Survival, 507, 708, 715, 734–783, 742f., 755
Switzerland, 657, 672
Synagogue, 5, 15, 93, 131, 269, 358, 361, 492f., 431, 453ff.
Synod, 589f.

Taalumot Hokhmah (Samuel Ashkenazi), 434
Tabernacles, feast of, 182
Talmud, 19, 184–190, 191–252, 315, 323, 332, 343f., 355, 358, 414, 430, 443, 457, 473, 476, 478, 480, 516, 554, 559, 577f., 581ff., 585, 606, 619, 658, 679, 752, 772, 785
Tanna debe Eliyahu (Seder Eliyahu), 19, 247–252
Tannaim, 582
Tannenbaum, Mordecai, 623f.
Tarfon, 186, 190
Tchernichovsky, S., 780–783
Teacher, 20, 214, 221, 228f., 343
Teacher of Righteousness, 81
Technical Institute, Haifa, 684
Tela ignea satanea (Wagenseil), 476
Temple in Jerusalem, 34ff., 43, 45ff., 52f., 55, 123–135, 144, 156, 188, 311, 341, 460, 469f., 488f; destruction of, 3, 168–172, 213, 235f., 269, 270, 316, 361, 363, 400, 407, 430, 463ff., 469f., 477, 479f., 585f., 750
Temptation, 37, 42, 51
Ten Commandments, 421
"Ten Martyrs," 175–183
Teshuvah, 556
Testament of Job the Saint, 17, 100–114, 239
Testaments of the Twelve Patriarchs, 17, 66f., 100
Thanksgiving Hymns (Qumran), 81–85
Theocracy, 140, 581, 583
Theology, 580f., 602, 614, 747f.
Therapeutae, 17, 90–99
Ibn Tibbon, Judah, 305, 309, 318, 347–352, 372
Ibn Tibbon, Samuel, 283, 348, 392
Tiberias, 184, 227
Tiberius, emperor, 128ff.
Tiferet Yisrael (Judah Loew ben Bezalel), 415f.
Time, 336
Tolstoy, L., 678, 779
Tomer Deborah (Cordovero), 437
Torah, 4, 9, 19f., 74, 76ff., 92f., 136, 177f., 182, 191–194, 197, 199f., 204, 209, 211, 219ff., 231, 233, 244–248,

250, 306, 322f., 380, 391, 394, 398,
403, 413, 421f., 424, 454, 469, 471,
539ff., 543, 557f., 576, 578, 580, 583,
594, 618, 708, 732, 750ff., 785; study
of, 294f., 297, 343–347, 349, 354f.,
357–361, 386, 428f., 451, 458, 465,
489f.
Tosafot, 358f., 430
Trajan, 620
Treblinka, 634, 643, 728
Tree of Life, Knowledge, 67, 81, 328,
442
Trinity, 483f.
Truman, H. S, 687
Truth, 94, 99, 234
Turkey, 403, 407f., 659, 676, 736
Tzavaat ha-Rivash (Baal Shem Tov),
441

Union of American Hebrew Congre-
gations, 590
Union Prayer Book, 590
United Nations, 686, 693, 695, 697,
703
United Synagogue of America, 606
Universalism, 505, 518, 551, 634,
719ff., 740f., 767f., 772
Universe, 300f., 321f.
Uriel, angel, 163
Usha, 178

Vaad Leumi, 689
Valéry, Paul, 725
Vasco da Gama, 274
Vatican, 656
Venice, 405, 409, 431
Ibn Verga, Solomon, Joseph, and
Judah, 403
de Vidas, Elijah, 412, 437
Virgil, 410
Virtue, 96, 141

Warsaw, 617, 624f., 628, 642, 657
Washington, 656
Wassermann, Jakob, 650, 779f.
Weizmann, Chaim, 683, 687

Weltsch, R., 608–612, 651
West, Westernization, 514, 721f.,
724f., 730, 733, 735
Wiesel, Elie, 654–658
Wilderness, 50, 69, 78, 118ff., 219
Wisdom of Solomon, 7, 36–42
Wise, I. M., 590ff.
Wise man, wisdom, 23ff., 36f., 39f.,
91, 116, 192f., 200, 203, 226f., 229f.,
249
Wolfson, H. A., 7, 85, 584
Woman, wife, 26ff., 93, 95, 132, 145,
195, 216f., 344, 351, 401, 432, 474
World to come, 160, 174f., 176f.,
179f., 193f., 204, 216, 229f., 239,
247, 250, 289, 293, 297, 309, 345f.,
353, 411, 414, 424, 432, 442, 458,
470, 473ff., 481, 484, 488, 490
World Wars, 616f., 634, 646, 650, 686,
694, 696, 698, 796

Yadin, Y., 81
Yannai, 270
Yedayah ha-Bedersi, 336
Yehiel ben Yekutiel, 379
Yekutiel (Padua), 369
Yellow Badge, 608–611, 645, 705
Yemen, 391
Yeshiva University, 580
Yeven Metzulah (Hannover), 357–
364
Yitzhak, 242

Zacuto, Abraham, 274
Zaleucus, 139
Zangwill, I., 714
Zechariah, 3, 207
Zion, Mount Zion, 53, 56, 289, 337,
461, 463ff., 472
Zionism, 506, 526, 532, 608f., 611,
634, 636, 651, 659–706, 718f., 726,
731, 739ff., 745, 774, 779, 783, 800
Zionist Congress, 672–678, 680, 689
Zionist Organization, 683, 686, 689
Zohar, 293, 296f., 365, 368, 370, 411–
414, 419–424, 430, 440, 463ff.
Zunz, Leopold, 514–518